KEYS to EFFECTIVE LEARNING

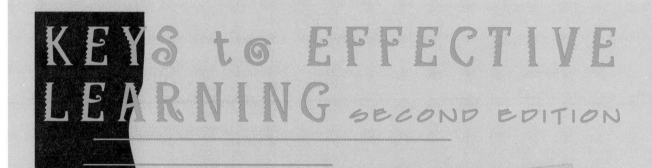

KEYS to EFFECTIVE LEARNING

SECOND EDITION

Carol Carter
Joyce Bishop
Sarah Lyman Kravits

Editorial Consultant:

Richard D. Bucher
Professor of Sociology
Baltimore City Community College

Prentice Hall

Upper Saddle River, New Jersey 07458

Library of Congress Cataloging-in-Publication Data
Carter, Carol.
  Keys to effective learning / Carol J. Carter,
Joyce Bishop, Sarah Lyman Kravits; editorial
consultant, Richard D. Bucher.—2nd ed.
    p. cm.
  Includes bibliographical references (p.) and index.
  ISBN 0-13-012882-1
  1. Study skills. 2. Learning. 3. Cognitive styles.
4. Note-taking. 5. Test-taking skills. I. Bishop, Joyce
(Joyce L.). II. Kravits, Sarah Lyman. III. Bucher,
Richard D., 1949-. IV. Title
LB2395.C27 2000
378.1'0281—dc21   99-39279
                                              CIP

Publisher: *Carol Carter*
Acquisitions editor: *Sande Johnson*
Production editor: *Dee Josephson*
Production liaison: *Barbara Marttine Cappuccio*
Director of manufacturing
 and production: *Bruce Johnson*
Managing editor: *Mary Carnis*
Manufacturing buyer: *Marc Bove*
Formatting / page make-up: *TSI Graphics*
Creative director: *Marianne Frasco*
Interior design: *HRS*
Cover design: *Maria Guglielmo*
Cover illustration: *Sal Alvarez*
Marketing manger: *Jeff McIlroy*
Printer/Binder: *Banta Menasha*

©2000, 1998 by Prentice-Hall, Inc.
Upper Saddle River, New Jersey 07458

Printed in the United States of America
10 9 8 7 6 5 4 3 2 1

ISBN   0-13-012882-1

Prentice-Hall International (UK) Limited, *London*
Prentice-Hall of Australia Pty. Limited, *Sydney*
Prentice-Hall Canada Inc., *Toronto*
Prentice-Hall Hispanoamericana, S.A., *Mexico*
Prentice-Hall of India Private Limited, *New Delhi*
Prentice-Hall of Japan, Inc., *Tokyo*
Prentice-Hall Singapore Pte. Ltd.
Editora Prentice-Hall do Brasil, Ltda., *Rio de Janeiro*

PHOTO CREDITS:

Chapter Opening Photos

Chapter	Source
1	Lois & Bob Schlowsky/Tony Stone Images
2	Sarah Lyman Kravits
3	Tony Perrottet/Omni-Photo Communications, Inc.
4	3M Corporation
5	Phil Schofield/Tony Stone Images
6	Sadayuki Mikami/AP/Wide World Photos
7	Robert Harbison
8	Mark D. Phillips/Photo Researchers, Inc.
9	Jeff Greenberg/Omni-Photo Communications, Inc.
10	Jeff Greenberg/Omni-Photo Communications, Inc.
11	Andy Levin/Photo Researchers, Inc.
12	Chromosohm/Photo Researchers, Inc.
13	Austrian National Tourist Office

Interior Photos

Page	Source
9	Amy Etra/PhotoEdit
21	Deborah Davis/PhotoEdit
45	Robert Brenner/PhotoEdit
54	Tony Freeman/PhotoEdit
85	Robert Harbison
95	Michael Newman/PhotoEdit
121	Robert Harbison
136	Elena Rooraid/PhotoEdit
163	Prentice Hall Canada Library
177	Tomi/PhotoDisc, Inc.
205	Robert Harbison
211	Robert Harbison
241	Walter Hodges/Westlight/Corbis
264	Scott T. Baxter/PhotoDisc, Inc.
283	Robert Harbison
294	Laima E. Druskis/Simon & Schuster/PH College
327	York University
333	Bob Daemmrich/Stock Boston
359	Doug Menuez/PhotoDisc, Inc.
368	Elizabeth Holms/Omni-Photo Communications, Inc.
390	Rick Singer/Simon & Schuster/PH College
407	Esbin/Anderson/Omni-Photo Communications, Inc.
427	Monkmeyer Press
440	Michael Newman/PhotoEdit
464	Myrleen Ferguson/PhotoEdit
470	Robert Brenner/PhotoEdit

Quote Credits

Page	Source
137	Reprinted by permission of Jeremy Tarcher, Inc., a division of The Putnam Publishing Group from the ARTIST'S WAY by Julia Cameron. Copyright © 1992 by Julia Cameron
256	*Simon & Schuster Concise Handbook* by Troyka, © 1990. Reprinted by permission of Prentice-Hall, Inc., Upper Saddle River
282	*Bird by Bird* by Anne Lamott, © 1994, Pantheon Books, a division of Random House, Inc.
295	William Strunk, Jr. and E.B. White. *The Elements of Style*, 3rd Edition. Copyright 1979. All rights reserved. Reprinted by permission from Allyn & Bacon.
300	From *Writing Down the Bones* by Natalie Goldberg, © 1986. Reprinted by arrangement with Shambhala Publications, Inc., 300 Massachusetts Avenue, Boston, MA 02115

Our Mission Statement

Our mission is to help students know and believe in themselves, take advantage of resources and opportunities, set and achieve their goals, learn throughout their lives, discover careers that fulfill and support them, build fruitful and satisfying relationships with others, and experience the challenges and rewards that make life meaningful.

CONTENTS

FOREWORD XIII

PREFACE XV

ACKNOWLEDGMENTS XIX

SUPPLEMENTS XXIII

ABOUT THE AUTHORS XXVII

Part 1 Defining Yourself and Your Goals

CHAPTER 1   Becoming a Lifelong Learner: Opening Doors 3

Thinking It Through   3

Who Is Pursuing an Education Today?   4
The Diverse Student Body   4

How Does Education Promote Success?   5

What Resources Are Available at Your School?   7
People   8
Student Services   9
Organizations   9
Literature   12
Technology   13

Thinking Back, Thinking Ahead   14

How Can You Strive for Success?   15
Get Motivated   16
Make a Commitment   17
Show Initiative   18
Be Responsible   18
Face Your Fears   19

How Can You Build Your Self-esteem?   20
Think Positively   20
Take Action   21
Academic Integrity   22

What Is Your Role in a Diverse World?   23
Diversity Is Real Life   25
Diversity and Teamwork   25
Living Your Role   26

Important Points to Remember   27

CHAPTER 2   Goal Setting and Time Management: Mapping Your Course 41

Thinking It Through   41

What Defines Your Values?   42
Choosing and Evaluating Values   42
How Values Relate to Goals   43

How Do You Set and Achieve Goals?   43
Identifying Your Personal Mission Statement   43
Placing Goals in Time   44
Linking Goals with Values   47
Different Kinds of Goals   47

What Are Your Priorities?   **49**
Thinking Back, Thinking Ahead   *51*

How Can You Manage Your Time?   **53**
Building a Schedule   54
Taking Responsibility for How You
Spend Your Time   57
Being Flexible   59

Why Is Procrastination a Problem?   **60**
Anti-procrastination Strategies   60
Important Points to Remember   *62*

CHAPTER 3   Self-awareness: Knowing
Who You Are and How You
Learn   79

Thinking It Through   *79*

Is There One Best Way to Learn?   **80**

**How Can You Discover Your Learning
Styles?**   **80**
Multiple Intelligences Theory   80
The Reasonable Approach to Learning
Style   83

**What Are the Benefits of Knowing
Your Learning Styles?**   **84**
Study Benefits   84
Classroom Benefits   87
General Benefits   88
Thinking Back, Thinking Ahead   *90*

**How Do You Explore Who You
Are?**   **91**
Self-perception   92
Interests   93
Habits   94
Abilities   95

**How Can You Start Thinking about
Choosing a Major?**   **96**
Exploring Potential Majors   97
Planning Your Curriculum   98
Linking Majors to Career Areas   98
Changing Majors   99
Important Points to Remember   *100*

PART 2   SETTING THE
STAGE FOR LEARNING

CHAPTER 4   Critical and Creative
Thinking: Tapping the Power of Your
Mind   113

Thinking It Through   *113*

What Is Critical Thinking?   **114**
A Critical-Thinking Response to a
Statement   115
The Value of Critical Thinking   116
Learning How Your Mind Works
Through the Thinktrix   117
How Mind Actions Build Thinking
Processes   120

**How Does Critical Thinking Help
You Solve Problems and Make
Decisions?**   **121**
Problem Solving   121
Decision Making   123
Thinking Back, Thinking Ahead   *126*

**How Do You Construct an Effective
Argument?**   **128**

How Do You Establish Truth?   **128**
Distinguishing Fact from
Opinion   129
Challenging Assumptions   130

Why Shift Your Perspective?   **132**

Why Plan Strategically?   **134**

**How Can You Develop Your
Creativity?**   **135**

Characteristics of Creative
People 136
Enhancing Your Creativity 136
Brainstorming Toward a Creative
Answer 137
Creativity and Critical Thinking 137

What Is Media Literacy? 138
Important Points to Remember 140

Seek Understanding 178

How and Why Should You Study with Others? 178
Benefits 178
Strategies for Study Group
Success 180

How Can You "Read" Visual Aids? 181
Understanding Tables 181
Understanding Charts 182
Important Points to Remember 184

CHAPTER 5   Reading and Studying:
Your Keys to Knowledge 155

Thinking It Through 155

What Challenges Does College Reading Present? 156
Working Through Difficult
Texts 156
Managing Distractions 157
Building Comprehension
and Speed 159
Expanding Your Vocabulary 162

Why Define Your Purpose for Reading? 165
Purpose Determines Reading
Strategy 165
Purpose Determines Pace 166
Thinking Back, Thinking Ahead 166

How Can SQ3R Help You Own What You Read? 168
Survey-Question-Read-Recite-Review
(SQ3R) 168
Putting SQ3R to Work 172

How Can You Respond Critically to What You Read? 174
Use SQ3R to "Taste" Reading
Material 174
Ask Questions Based on the Mind
Actions 175
Engage Critical-Thinking
Processes 176
Be Media Literate 177

CHAPTER 6   Listening and Memory:
Taking In and Remembering
Information 199

Thinking It Through 199

How Can You Become a Better Listener? 200
Know the Stages of Listening 202
Manage Listening Challenges 203
Become an Active Listener 205
Thinking Back, Thinking Ahead 208

How Does Memory Work? 209

How Can You Improve Your Memory? 210
Use Specific Memory Strategies 211
Make the Most of Last-Minute
Studying 216
Use Critical Thinking 217

How Can You Use Mnemonic Devices to Boost Memory Power? 217
Create Visual Images
and Associations 219
Create Acronyms 221

How Can Tape Recorders Help You Listen and Remember? 222
Important Points to Remember 224

PART 3 *Targeting Success in School*

Chapter 7   Note Taking and Library Research: Learning from Others   237

Thinking It Through   237

How Does Taking Notes Help You?   238

How Can You Make the Most of Class Notes?   239

Preparing to Take Class Notes   239
What to Do During Class   239
Make Notes a Valuable After-Class Reference   241

What Are Research Notes and How Can You Use Them?   243

What Note-Taking System Should You Use?   244

Taking Notes in Outline Form   245
Using the Cornell Note-Taking System   247
Creating a Think Link   248
Other Visual Note-Taking Strategies   250

How Can You Write Faster When Taking Notes?   250

Thinking Back, Thinking Ahead   252

How Can You Make the Most of Your Library?   254

Start with a Road Map   254
Learn How to Conduct an Information Search   255

How Do You Use a Search Strategy to Conduct Research?   258

Use General Reference Works   258
Search Specialized Reference Works   259
Browse Through Books on Your Subject   260
Use Periodical Indexes to Search for Periodicals   261
Search the Internet   263
Ask the Librarian   263
Use Critical Thinking to Evaluate Every Source   264
Important Points to Remember   265

Chapter 8   Effective Writing: Communicating Your Message   279

Thinking It Through   279

Why Does Good Writing Matter?   280

What Are the Elements of Effective Writing?   281

Writing Purpose   282
Knowing Your Audience   282
Thinking Back, Thinking Ahead   284

What Is the Writing Process?   285

Planning   285
Drafting   292
Revising   297
Editing   301
Important Points to Remember   305

Chapter 9   Test Taking: Showing What You Know   319

Thinking It Through   319

How Can Preparation Help Improve Test Scores?   320

Identify Test Type and Material Covered   320
Choose Study Materials   321
Set a Study Schedule   321
Prepare Through Critical Thinking   321
Take a Pretest   322
Create an Organized Study Plan   322
Prepare Physically   322
Work Through Test Anxiety   322

Studying for a Test When There Are Children Around   326

What General Strategies Can Help You Succeed on Tests?   327
Write Down Key Facts   327
Begin with an Overview of the Exam   327
Read Test Directions   328
Work from Easy to Hard   328
Watch the Clock   328
Master the Art of Intelligent Guessing   328
Follow Directions on Machine-Scored Tests   329
Use Critical Thinking to Avoid Errors   329
Thinking Back, Thinking Ahead   330

How Can You Master Different Types of Test Questions?   332
Multiple Choice Questions   332
True-or-False Questions   334
Essay Questions   335

What Techniques Will Help Improve Performance on Math Tests?   338
How Can You Learn from Test Mistakes?   339
Important Points to Remember   340

PART 4 *A Personal Focus*

CHAPTER 10   Relating to Others: Appreciating Your Diverse World 355

Thinking It Through   355

How Can You Understand and Accept Others?   356
Diversity in Your World   356
The Positive Effects of Diversity   357
Barriers to Understanding   357
Accepting and Dealing with Differences   362
Thinking Back, Thinking Ahead   363

How Can You Express Yourself Effectively?   365
Addressing Communication Issues   365
How Do Your Personal Relationships Define You?   368
Relationship Strategies   368
How Can You Handle Conflict and Criticism?   369
Conflict Strategies   370
Dealing with Criticism and Feedback   370
What Role Do You Play in Groups?   372
Being an Effective Participant   374
Being an Effective Leader   374
Important Points to Remember   376

CHAPTER 11   Personal Wellness: Taking Care of Yourself 387

Thinking It Through   387

How Can You Maintain a Healthy Body?   388
Eating Right   388
Exercising   389
Getting Enough Sleep   391
How Do You Nurture a Healthy Mind?   392
Dealing with Stress   392
Emotional Disorders   395
Thinking Back, Thinking Ahead   398

How Are Alcohol, Tobacco, and Drugs Used and Abused?   400
Alcohol   400
Tobacco   401

Drugs   402
Identifying and Overcoming
Addiction   402

What Should You Consider When Making Sexual Decisions?   407

Sex and Critical Thinking   407
Birth Control   409
Sexually Transmitted Diseases   409
Important Points to Remember   412

PART 5 PREPARING FOR THE FUTURE

CHAPTER 12 Managing Career and Money: Reality Resources   423

Thinking It Through   423

How Can You Plan Your Career?   424

Define a Career Path   424
Map Out Your Strategy   426
Know What Employers Want   427

How Can You Juggle Work and School?   428

Effects of Working While in
School   429
Establishing Your Needs   430
Sources of Job Information   430
Making a Strategic Job Search
Plan   433

What Should You Know about Financial Aid?   434

Student Loans   435
Grants and Scholarships   436
Thinking Back, Thinking Ahead   438

How Can You Create a Budget That Works?   439

The Art of Budgeting   440
A Sample Budget   441
Savings Strategies   442
Managing Credit Cards   443
Important Points to Remember   446

CHAPTER 13 Moving Ahead: Building a Flexible Future   457

Thinking It Through   457

How Can You Live With Change?   458

Accept the Reality of Change   458
Maintain Flexibility   458
Adjust Your Goals   460

What Will Help You Handle Success and Failure?   461

Dealing with Failure   461
Dealing with Success   464
Thinking Back, Thinking Ahead   465

Why Give Back to the Community and the World?   467

Your Imprint on the World   467
Valuing Your Environment   468

Why Is College Just the Beginning of Lifelong Learning?   469

How Can You Live Your Mission?   471

Live with Integrity   471
Roll with the Changes   473
Learn from Role Models   474
Aim for Your Personal Best   474
Important Points to Remember   475

APPENDIX 1 Researching Information and Student Resources on the Internet   A-1

APPENDIX 2 Learning Styles Assessments   A-25

ENDNOTES   E-1

BIBLIOGRAPHY   B-1

INDEX   I-1

FOREWORD

When I was asked to be the student editor for *Keys to Effective Learning*, I jumped at the opportunity to try something I had never done before. As the project progressed, I began to realize the potential of such a publication to help students just like me. Even as I prepare to graduate from Baltimore City Community College, it's not hard for me to recall the frustrations I experienced when first trying to determine what I was going to do with the rest of my life.

When I entered college, I was twenty-one years old and full of energy. My problem was harnessing that energy and focusing it on a goal that would be beneficial in the long run. After trying several different paths and changing my major two or three times, I concluded that many of my interests involved computers and resolving technical problems. That realization, and a lot of hard work, led to my double major in Telecommunications and Computer Electronics and a scholarship to pursue postgraduate education in Computer Information Systems at the University of Baltimore. Thinking back on the whole experience, however, I realize that having a resource like *Keys to Effective Learning* could have saved me lots of valuable time and energy.

More than likely, as you read this book, you are at a crossroads in your life. Many choices will present themselves, and the decisions you make can have a profound effect on the rest of your life. *Keys to Effective Learning* has been carefully designed to provide a foundation of vital skills that are essential in today's ever-changing world. After all, there's a great difference between succeeding and merely surviving, and this book can help you truly succeed.

As you read *Keys to Effective Learning* and take this course, you will find that your results usually reflect your efforts. Therefore, it's in your own best interest that you keep an open mind and play an active role in the pursuit of your goals. Beyond that, keep in mind that success is a journey rather than a destination. Enjoy yourself on the journey!

Michael B. Jackson, Student Editor
Baltimore City Community College graduate

PREFACE

Keys to Effective Learning Owner's Manual: Please Read Before Operating

When you spend money on a coffeemaker, computer, tape deck, or anything else, getting your money's worth means knowing how to operate your purchase so that it delivers what you want (good coffee, perhaps, or internet access, or high-speed dubbing). When you bring the item home, you generally look over the manual or pamphlet that comes with it before you do anything else. The manual describes the parts, how they operate, and what should result if everything is functioning properly. With that in mind, think of this preface as your owner's manual for this book. Reading it might be one of the most helpful actions you take all semester.

As your authors, we have talked to students across the country. We've learned that you are concerned about your future, you want your education to serve a purpose, you are adjusting to constant life changes, and you want honest and direct guidance on how to achieve your goals. We designed the features of *Keys to Effective Learning* based on what you have told us about your needs. Knowing how to use the features in this book — and make the most from your work in this class — will help you maximize the time, effort, and money you are putting into your education.

Following are descriptions of the different pieces of this book and how to use them to your advantage.

The Contents of the Package: What's Included

We chose the topics in this book based on what you need to make the most of your educational experience. You need to *believe in yourself* just to believe that you are worth educating. You need a strong sense of *self, learning style,* and *goals* in order to discover and pursue the best course of study. You need good *study skills* to take in what you learn, retain information, and express your thoughts and opinions. You need to know how to *stay healthy* so that you are in class and awake every time you need to be. You need to *manage your time, money, and relationships* so that you can handle the changes that life hands you. *Keys to Effective Learning* can guide you in all of these areas and more.

The Parts: Useful Features

The features (distinguishing characteristics and sections) of this book are designed to make your life easier by helping you take in and understand the material you read.

Real World Learning. If what you study in this course only helped you read textbooks and pass tests, its usefulness would end at graduation, and you would have to start all over to learn how to deal with the real world. The ideas and strategies you learn that will help you succeed in school are the same ones that will bring you success in your career and in your personal life. Therefore, this book focuses on success strategies as they apply to *school, work,* and *life,* not just the classroom.

Thinking Skills. Being able to remember facts and figures won't do you much good at school or beyond unless you can put that information to work. This book has a chapter on *critical and creative thinking* that will help you explore your mind's seven primary actions – the building blocks to competent thinking. You will also see how to combine those actions in order to perform thinking processes such as problem solving, decision making, and strategic planning. Critical thinking is emphasized in the context of almost every topic throughout the book.

Thinking It Through/Taking Stock. This two-part exercise encourages you to evaluate your progress. At the start of each chapter, the *Thinking It Through* checklist helps you to establish your state of mind. Then, at the beginning of the chapter exercises, *Taking Stock* encourages you to consider how your ideas and opinions may have changed during the course of your reading.

Thinking Back/Thinking Ahead. Occurring in the middle of each chapter, this feature helps you to review and retain what you read. It provides a quick review of what you just read (*Thinking Back*) and a preview of what's to come in the remainder of the chapter (*Thinking Ahead*).

Important Points to Remember. To further solidify what you have read in the chapter, this feature briefly summarizes the information in each of the chapter's major headings.

Skill-Building Exercises. Today's graduates need to be effective thinkers, team players, writers, and strategic planners. The exercises at the end of the chapters will encourage you to develop these valuable career skills and to apply thinking processes to any topic or situation.

> ➤ *Critical Thinking: Applying Learning to Life.* A series of exercises, at the end of every chapter, that encourages you to ask questions and apply critical thinking to your own life.

> ➤ *Teamwork: Combining Forces.* An exercise that gives you a chance to interact and learn in a group setting, building your teamwork and leadership skills in the process.

> ➤ *Writing: Discovery Through Journaling.* A journal writing exercise that provides an opportunity for you to express your thoughts and develop your writing ability.

> ➤ *Career Portfolio: Charting Your Course.* An innovative exercise that enables you to focus on how your work in school contributes to your employability in the workforce, and presents

opportunities for you to compile important work-related information that you will use in your job search and in the workplace itself.

Diversity of Voice. The world is becoming increasingly more diverse in ethnicity, perspective, culture, lifestyle, race, choices, abilities, needs, and more. Every student, instructor, course, and school is unique. One point of view can't possibly apply to everyone. Therefore, many perspectives will emerge from these pages. What you read will speak to your needs, offer ideas, and treat you with respect.

➤ *Windows on the World,* a question-and-answer feature, will appear once per chapter. In it, one person will present a question about an issue in his or her life, and another person who has expertise or has had similar experiences will give advice in response.

➤ *Examples* throughout the text deal with the different situations that different students face – working while in school, parenting, dealing with different financial needs, supporting various lifestyles and schedules, etc.

➤ *Summary words* from languages other than English, one for each chapter, will introduce you to new ideas and invite you to consider how the meaning of each word or phrase might apply to your own life.

Using the Parts: Helpful Hints for Operation

We've worked to make this book as user-friendly as possible. The following features will make your life easier in small but significant ways.

➤ *Perforations.* Each page of this book is perforated so that you can tear out exercises to hand in, should your instructor ask you to do so. You can also tear out sections if you like, perhaps to take with you somewhere or to keep in your date book as a reference.

➤ *Exercises.* The exercises are together at the ends of the chapters, such that if you want to hand them all in you can do so without also removing any of the text. There is a space at the beginning of the exercises for you to write your name.

➤ *Internet Appendix.* This addition at the end of the book is a terrific resource for information about how to use the Internet.

➤ *Definitions.* Selected words are defined in the margins of the text. If you don't know these words, the definitions save you a trip to the dictionary, and if you do know them, the definitions offer a quick and easy refresher.

➤ *Layout and Style.* The book material is divided into parts. Each part has a theme and contains chapters that relate to one another within that theme. Full-color photos, graphics, and cartoons will illustrate key points as well as spice up your reading. Also, at the end of each of the parts, a crossword puzzle offers an entertaining way to review material.

➤ *Long-term usefulness.* Yes, most people sell back some of the textbooks they use. If you take a good look at the material in *Keys to Effective Learning,* however, you may want to keep this book around. We know that you are concerned about the competitiveness of the job market, your future careers, and your quality of life. *Keys to Effective Learning* is a reference that you can return to over and over again as you work toward your goals. Measure the few dollars you would earn back against the worth of having helpful information around when you need it.

Take Action: Read

You are responsible for your education, your growth, your knowledge, and your future. If you know yourself, choose the right paths, and follow them with determination, you will earn the success that you deserve in school, the workplace, and your personal life. The best we can do is offer some great suggestions and strategies and ideas and structures that can help—ultimately, it's up to you to use them. So take whatever fits your particular self with all of its particular situations, needs, and wants, and make it your own. You've made a terrific start by choosing to pursue an education—now take advantage of all it has to give you.

ACKNOWLEDGMENTS

This book has come about through a heroic group effort. We would like to take this opportunity to acknowledge the people who have made it happen. Many thanks to:

> Our student editor, Michael Jackson, for his advice, the foreword, and his writing samples. Mike is a member of Phi Theta Kappa and earned an Associate's Degree in applied sciences, telecommunications, and computer electronics from Baltimore City Community College.

> Student reviewers Sandi Armitage, Marisa Connell, Jennifer Moe, and Alex Toth.

> Our reviewers, for their advice and guidance: Glenda Belote, Florida International University; John Bennett, Jr., University of Connecticut; Ann Bingham-Newman, California State University—LA; Mary Bixby, University of Missouri—Columbia; Barbara Blandford, Education Enhancement Center at Lawrenceville, NJ; Jerry Bouchie, St. Cloud State University; Mona Casady, SW Missouri State University; Janet Cutshall, Sussex County Community College; Valerie DeAngelis, Miami-Dade Community College; Rita Delude, NH Community Technical College; Judy Elsley, Weber State University in Utah; Sue Halter, Delgado Community College in Louisiana; Suzy Hampton, University of Montana; Maureen Hurley, University of Missouri-Kansas City; Karen Iversen, Heald Colleges; Kathryn K. Kelly, St. Cloud State University; Nancy Kosmicke, Mesa State College in Colorado; Frank T. Lyman, Jr., University of Maryland; Barnette Miller Moore, Indian River Community College in Florida; Rebecca Munro, Gonzaga University in Washington; Virginia Phares, DeVry of Atlanta; Brenda Prinzavalli, Beloit College in Wisconsin; Jacqueline Simon, Education Enhancement Center at Lawrenceville, NJ; Carolyn Smith, University of Southern Indiana; Joan Stottlemyer, Carroll College in Montana; Thomas Tyson, SUNY Stony Brook; Rose Wassman, DeAnza College in California; Michelle G. Wolf, Florida Southern College.

➤ The PRE 100 instructors at Baltimore City Community College, Liberty Campus, for their ideas and comments, especially college President Dr. Jim Tschechtelin, Co-ordinator Jim Coleman, and instructors Rita Lenkin Hawkins, Sonia Lynch, Jack Taylor, and Peggy Winfield. Special thanks to Rita for the fear exercise and continual support and feedback. Thanks also to Alice Barr, who puts so much energy into her work with BCCC.

➤ The instructors at DeVry, especially Susan Chin and Carol Ozee, for support and suggestions.

➤ The instructors at Suffolk Community College, and Prentice Hall representative Carol Abolafia, for their helpful comments.

➤ Our editorial consultant Rich Bucher, professor of sociology at Baltimore City Community College, who provided important advice and consultation on diversity.

➤ Dr. Frank T. Lyman for his generous permission to use and adapt his Thinktrix system.

➤ Professor Barbara Soloman for her Learning Styles Inventory.

➤ Marjorie Den, librarian at Connecticut Public Library in Westport, CT, for her assistance with the revised material on library research.

➤ The generous people who contributed stories for Windows on the World: Cherie Andrade, Beverly Andre, Anonymous, Stephen Beck, Laura Brinckerhoff, Edhilvia Campos, Shera Chantel Caviness, Peter Changsak, Rosalia Chavez, Maxine Deverney, Titus Dillard, Jr., Darrin Estepp, Ruth Ham, Jose L. Ivarez, Jr., Hiromi Kodakehara, Angela D. Kvasnica, Raymond Montolvo, Jr., Vernon Nash, Tim Nordberg, Morgan Paar, Richard Pan, Shyama Parikh, the Rev. Eric Gerard Pearman, Jo Anne Roe, Norma Seledon, and Anwar Smith.

➤ Kathleen Cole, Jackie Fitzgerald, Kelley Forrester, Michelle M. Williams, Cynthia Nordberg, and Florence Silverman for their invaluable assistance.

➤ Author Cynthia Leshin for writing the appendix on Internet research.

➤ Our terrific editor, Sande Johnson.

➤ Sue Bierman, currently in faculty development for Prentice Hall, for her innumerable contributions and editorial advice.

➤ Our fabulous production team, especially Barbara Cappuccio, Mary Carnis, Marianne Frasco, Steve Hartner, Marc Bove, and Patrick Walsh.

➤ Our marketing gurus, especially Jeff McIlroy, Kateri Drexler, and Barbara Rosenberg.

- ➤ Frank Mortimer for his work on the website and technology.
- ➤ The Prentice Hall representatives and the management team led by Jerome Grant, who have shown tremendous support for the success of students of all ages.
- ➤ Gary June, President of Education, Career, and Technology, for his support and interest in this discipline.
- ➤ Rit Dojny, Exeecutive Vice President for Higher Education, for his encouragement of student achievement at all levels.
- ➤ Our families and friends, who have encouraged us and put up with our work schedules.
- ➤ We extend a very special thanks to Judy Block, whose research and work on the study skills material, revision of the library material, and editing suggestions on the text as a whole were essential and invaluable.

Finally, for their ideas, opinions, and stories, we would like to thank all of the students and professors with whom we work. Joyce in particular would like to thank the thousands of students who have allowed her, as their professor, the privilege of sharing part of their journey through college. We appreciate that, through reading this book, you give us the opportunity to learn and discover with you—in your classroom, in your home, on the bus, and wherever else learning takes place.

SUPPLEMENTS

SUPPLEMENTS FOR TEACHERS

INSTRUCTOR'S MANUAL

This extensive volume contains approximately 500 pages of materials to help you successfully teach student orientation and student success courses. Organized according to the objectives and lessons of each chapter, the manual includes transparency masters, Test Item File questions, pre- and post-class evaluations, lecture guides, and innovative tips to motivate all kinds of students. *Free to Instructors using the textbook.* (0-13-014370-7)

OVERHEAD TRANSPARENCIES

Full-color acetates that relate directly to the course lecture material and help focus students on key objectives. *Free to Instructors using the textbook.*

POWERPOINT TRANSPARENCIES

These time-saving slides, designed in PowerPoint format and available on 3.5-inch computer disk, will help instructors more easily plan and facilitate each class. *Free to instructors using the textbook.*

STUDENT KEY ADVICE VIDEO

Contains a selection of motivational tips and advice by entering college students, college students in their third and fourth years, and professionals in varying career areas. These tapes are in manageable segments designed so that they can be shown individually or all at once. *Free to adopters of the textbook.* (0-13-233206-X)

ABC NEWS VIDEO LIBRARY

Contains segments that appeared on such award-winning shows as *World News Tonight, Nightline, 20/20,* and *Primetime Live.* These segments are on topics relevant to student success and have been collected into a video library. *Free to adopters of the textbook.* (0-13-746306-5)

FACULTY DEVELOPMENT/SCHOOL IN-SERVICE PROGRAMS

Prentice Hall sponsors a variety of faculty workshops on campuses and in specific cities throughout the year. Workshops can be cross-disciplinary or discipline-specific. Many of our books qualify for special in-services with your faculty on topics that impact effective teaching and learning. Ask your local Prentice Hall representative for details or contact the Denver office at 303/436-0937.

FACULTY DEVELOPMENT TRAINING VIDEO

This library of teaching tips on student success and career development, for first-time instructors as well as those who have taught for years, provides information on how to teach multiple intelligences, critical thinking, and school-to-work transition tips.

PROFESSOR'S ADOPTER PACKAGE

This box contains all instructors' resources listed above, except for the Instructor's Manual. It also contains the New York Times Supplement, Tools for Life Magazine, Student Planner and Student Reflection Journal. All in one place for ease of use, this package is available *free to qualifying adopters*. (013-021595-3)

SUPPLEMENTS AVAILABLE FOR STUDENTS

NCS CAREER TESTING PROGRAM

The Enhanced Version of the Career Assessment Inventory. This test compares occupational interests and personality preferences with individuals in hundreds of careers. Students complete the test, mail it, and receive the test results within seven to ten days. *Available at a discount when packaged with the text.* (0-13-244559-X)

MAJORING IN THE REST OF YOUR LIFE, BY CAROL CARTER

Provides a practical strategy to take students from first-semester freshman year to their first job after graduation. This book offers valuable insights and advice on how to organize, think analytically, set and achieve goals, be innovative and persuasive, improve interpersonal and communication skills, and cope with stress. *Available at a discount when packaged with the text.* (0-13-098351-9)

SEVEN HABITS OF HIGHLY EFFECTIVE PEOPLE, AUDIOCASSETTE, BY STEPHEN R. COVEY

Audiotape program teaches listeners how to achieve success in both business and personal relationships. This approach broadens their way of thinking and leads to greater opportunities and effective problem solving. Available at a discount when packaged with the text. (0-13-098377-2)

THEMES OF THE TIMES, PH NEW YORK TIMES SUPPLEMENTS

These are discipline-specific newspapers geared toward student success and career development. Each is 16 pages in length, and contains articles published in the New York Times within the last year. Free when using the textbook.

The New York Times

WORLD WIDE WEB RESOURCES

Student Success Supersite – http://www.prenhall.com/success. This entire website is devoted to helping students have a positive first-year experience. Its user-friendly features include:

➤ Majors Exploration
➤ Career Advice
➤ Web Links
➤ Tips from Successful Students
➤ Student Bulletin Boards
➤ Faculty Resources

Companion Website – http://www.prenhall.com/success2. This site contains an online study guide referenced directly to the text. For each chapter you will find suggested essay questions, related articles and resources, and more. You can also reach this website by going to the Student Success Supersite and clicking on the picture of the *Keys to Effective Learning* cover.

THE STUDENT PLANNER

Comprised of daily and monthly planners, calendars through the year 2001, an address book, course and class planners, and other organizing materials, the Student Planner is designed to help students organize and manage their time more effectively. *Available free when packaged with the textbook.* (0-13-649120-0)

THE STUDENT JOURNAL

A book that helps students get the most out of the course by encouraging them to keep track of their progress over time. *Available free when packaged with the textbook.* (0-13-672826-X)

ABOUT THE AUTHORS

Carol Carter is Vice President and Director of Student Programs and Faculty Development at Prentice Hall. She has written *Majoring in the Rest of Your Life: Career Secrets for College Students* and *Majoring in High School*. She has also co-authored *Graduating Into the Nineties, The Career Tool Kit, Keys to Career Success, Keys to Study Skills,* and *Keys to Success*. In 1992 Carol and other business people co-founded a nonprofit organization called LifeSkills, Inc., to help high school students explore their goals, their career options, and the real world through part-time employment and internships. LifeSkills is now part of the Tucson Unified School District and is featured in seventeen high schools in Tucson, Arizona.

Joyce Bishop holds a Ph.D. in psychology and has taught for more than twenty years, receiving a number of honors, including Teacher of the Year. For the past four years she has been voted "favorite teacher" by the student body and Honor Society at Golden West College, Huntington Beach, CA., where she has taught since 1986 and is a tenured professor. She is currently working with a federal grant to establish Learning Communities and Workplace Learning in her district, and has developed workshops and trained faculty in cooperative learning, active learning, multiple intelligences, workplace relevancy, learning styles, authentic assessment, team building, and the development of learning communities. She also co-authored *Keys to Success* and *Keys to Study Skills*.

Sarah Lyman Kravits comes from a family of educators and has long cultivated an interest in educational development. She co-authored *The Career Tool Kit, Keys to Success,* and *Keys to Study Skills* and has served as Program Director for LifeSkills, Inc., a nonprofit organization that aims to further the career and personal development of high school students. In that capacity she helped to formulate both curricular and organizational elements of the program, working closely with instructors as well as members of the business community. She has also given faculty workshops in critical thinking, based on the Thinktrix critical thinking system. Sarah holds a B.A. in English and drama from the University of Virginia, where she was a Jefferson Scholar, and an M.F.A. from Catholic University.

OTHER BOOKS BY CAROL CARTER

THE CAREER TOOLKIT
Skills for Success SECOND EDITION

CAROL CARTER & GARY IZUMO
with SARAH LYMAN KRAVITS

Keys to Success
Brief Edition

How to achieve your goals

Carol Carter · Joyce Bishop · Sarah Lyman Kravits

Keys to Success
Second Edition

How to achieve your goals

Carol Carter · Joyce Bishop · Sarah Lyman Kravits

KEYS TO STUDY SKILLS
Opening Doors to Learning

Carol Carter · Joyce Bishop
Mary Bixby · Sarah Lyman Kea

KEYS TO CAREER SUCCESS

**CAROL CARTER
CAROL OZEE · BETH BOLLINGER**

MAJORING IN THE REST OF YOUR LIFE
College and Career secrets for Students

CAROL CARTER · LYNN QUITMAN TROYKA

MAJORING IN HIGH SCHOOL

SURVIVAL TIPS FOR STUDENTS

carol carter

PART 1

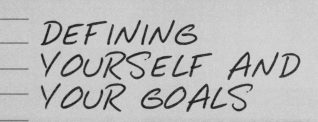

DEFINING YOURSELF AND YOUR GOALS

CHAPTER 1 Becoming a Lifelong Learner: Opening Doors

CHAPTER 2 Goal Setting and Time Management: Mapping Your Course

CHAPTER 3 Self-awareness: Knowing Who You Are and How You Learn

1 BECOMING A LIFELONG LEARNER:
Opening Doors

Thinking It Through

Check those statements that apply to you right now:

❑ I think that the most typical college student is an 18-year-old right out of high school.
❑ Sometimes school feels like a detour that's just keeping me from moving ahead in my life.
❑ When I need help with school or personal issues, I know that there are places I can go but I have no idea how to find them.
❑ One moment I'm determined to succeed, and then I turn around and I've lost all my drive.
❑ I'm not sure how just having self-esteem can get me where I want to go.
❑ I don't really see the point of learning about other cultures; I'm not sure how they concern me.

In this chapter, you will explore answers to the following questions:

➤ Who is pursuing an education today?
➤ How does education promote success?
➤ What resources are available at your school?
➤ How can you strive for success?
➤ How can you build your self-esteem?
➤ What is your role in a diverse world?

Welcome—or welcome back—to your education. Whether you are right out of high school, returning to student life after working for some years, or continuing on a current educational path, you are facing new challenges and changes. Whether you feel excited or worried or both, you have taken an important step. By choosing to pursue the self-improvement, knowledge, and opportunity that an education can provide, you have given yourself a strong vote of confidence.

You are embarking on a new millennium, both as an individual and as a member of the world community. In giving yourself the chance to learn and grow through education, you have the power to create a better world for yourself and others. This book will help you face the challenge by giving you keys—ideas, strategies, and skills— that can lead to success on the three intersecting paths of your existence—college, career, and personal life.

This first chapter will give you an overview of today's educational world and discuss the connection between education and success. You will explore specific success strategies that will help you maximize your educational experience. Finally, you will read about how building your self-esteem and focusing on teamwork can help you achieve your goals and make a difference.

WHO IS PURSUING AN EDUCATION TODAY?

In various forms, learning took place in the ancient civilizations of Rome, Greece, Byzantium, and Islam. Learning institutions became formalized as universities, similar to those of the present day, in medieval Europe as early as the eleventh century. In the early life of the university, students and scholars were men, mostly white, seeking religious and intellectual pursuits. Since that time, universities have evolved, becoming centers for cultural and social inspiration, intellectual growth, and scientific advancements.

Because of federal support and a universal understanding that a formal education should be the right of all people regardless of race, creed, color, age, or gender, schools have become more responsive to many different kinds of students. Although many students still enter college directly after high school, the old standard of finishing a four-year college education at the age of twenty-two is a standard no longer. Some students take longer than four years to finish. Some students return to school later in life. The old rules no longer apply.

The Diverse Student Body

The student population in the United States has changed in significant ways since the 1980s. According to government statistics, developments include growth in the following populations:[1]

> ➤ Students over the age of twenty-five.
> ➤ Students working full-time while in school.
> ➤ Female student population.
> ➤ Students who are also parents.

➤ Minority students.

➤ Students in two-year schools.

➤ Part-time students.

➤ Students taking over four years to get a degree.

The varying needs of an increasingly diverse student body have molded a new educational experience. Whether you have financial restrictions, child-care needs, an unusual work schedule, a particular cultural heritage, or any other situation or need, you are likely to find a program that's right for you.

Education isn't an automatic guarantee of a higher-level, better-paying job. Statistically, however, a better-educated population means better wages and more career fulfillment for workers, which results in a more efficient work force. Businesses, educational institutions, and the general public are becoming aware that education benefits the whole as much as it does the individual. Quality of life can improve when people make the most of their abilities through education.

No school can force you to learn. You are responsible for seeking out opportunities and weaving school into the fabric of your life. Every student's life has its own individual set of challenges, and you may face one or more, such as single parenting, returning to school as an older student, adjusting to cultural diversity, having a physical or learning disability, or working while attending school. Your school can help you work through these and other challenges if you actively seek out solutions and help from available support systems around you. Consider how the hard work of your education might help you build the life you envision.

HOW DOES EDUCATION PROMOTE SUCCESS?

Education—the process of developing and training the mind—should be far more than the accumulation of credit hours. If you take advantage of all education has to offer, you will develop the skills and talents you need to succeed in your career and in life.

How can education help you succeed?

Education gives you tools for lifelong learning. You learn facts while you are in school, but more importantly, you learn how to think. Although some of the facts and figures you learn today may not apply to the world of tomorrow, your ability to think will be useful always, in everything you do.

Education improves your quality of life. Income and employment get a boost from education. The *Digest of Education Statistics 1996* reports that income levels rise as educational levels rise. Figure 1–1 shows average income levels for different levels of educational attainment. Figure 1–2, also from a report in the *Digest,* shows how unemployment rates decrease as educational levels rise.

FIGURE 1-1

MEDIAN ANNUAL EARNINGS OF WORKERS 25 YEARS OLD AND OVER BY HIGHEST-DEGREE ATTAINED AND SEX

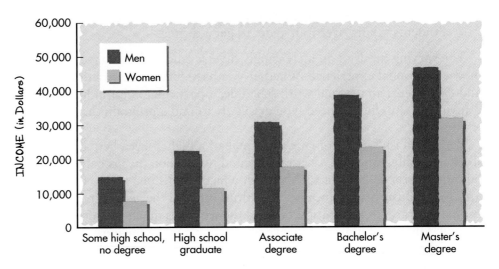

Source: U.S. Department of Commerce, Bureau of the Census, *Current Population Reports,* Series P-60, *Monthly Income of Households, Families, and Persons in the United States:* 1994

FIGURE 1-2

UNEMPLOYMENT RATES OF PERSONS 25 YEARS OLD AND OVER BY HIGHEST LEVEL OF EDUCATION

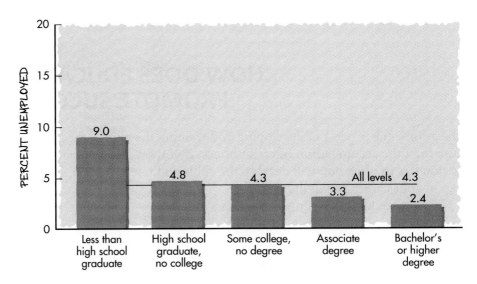

Source: U.S. Department of Labor, Bureau of Labor Statistics, Office of Employment and Unemployment Statistics, unpublished data.

Education expands your self-concept. As you rise to the challenges of education, you will discover that your capacity for knowledge and personal growth is greater than you imagined. As your abilities grow, you become more able to learn and do more in class, on the job, and in your community.

Education enlarges your possibilities. First, through different courses of study, education introduces you to more possible careers and life goals. Second, through the training you receive, it gives you more power to achieve the goals you choose. For example, while taking a writing class, you may learn about journalism careers, which may lead you to take a class in journalistic writing and reporting. Later, you may decide to work on a newspaper and to make journalism your career. In this case an awareness of the path available, combined with an ability to follow it, could change the course of your life.

Education improves your employability and earning potential. Learning additional skills raises your competency so that you can fulfill the requirements of higher-level jobs. In addition, a college degree makes an impression on potential employers and makes you eligible for higher-salaried positions.

Education broadens your worldview. As it introduces you to new ways of learning, doing, being, and thinking, education increases your understanding of diversity and your appreciation of areas that affect and enrich human lives, such as music, art, literature, science, politics, and economics.

Education affects both community involvement and personal health. Education prepares individuals for community activism by helping them understand political, economic, and social conditions and how they affect each individual life. Education also increases health knowledge. The more education you have, the more likely you are to practice healthy habits in your daily life and to make informed decisions.

Education is more than the process of going to school and earning a degree or certificate. Any program, no matter the length or the focus, is an opportunity to improve your mind and skills and to set and strive for goals. Education is also what you make of it. A dedicated, goal-oriented learner will benefit more than a student who doesn't try. If you make the most of your mind, your time, and your educational opportunities, you will realize your potential. Using available resources is part of that process.

WHAT RESOURCES ARE AVAILABLE AT YOUR SCHOOL?

Resources help you make the most of your education. As a student, you are investing money and time. Whether you complete your studies over the course of six months or sixty years, resources can help you get where you want to go. It is up to you to track down the resources that you need—as much as your school wants to help you, people may not always reach out to you directly. Be vocal in requesting services and diligent in finding resources.

On page 10 you will find Table 1–1, a general summary of resources, most or all of which can be found at your school. Most schools offer a student orientation, near the beginning of your first semester, that will explain

Resources, People, organizations, or services that supply help and support for different aspects of college life.

resources and other important information. Even if your school does not, you can orient yourself. Helpful resources include people, student services, organizations, literature (course catalogs and student handbooks), and technology.

People

Your school has an array of people who can help you make the most of your educational experience: instructors, administrative personnel, advisors and counselors, and teaching assistants. Their assistance is provided as part of your educational package. Take the opportunity to get to know them and to let them get to know you. Together you can explore ways in which they can help you achieve your goals.

Instructors

Instructors are more than just sources of information during scheduled class time. They can clarify course material or homework, give advice on course selection in their departments, or pass on educational and career information. Most instructors keep office hours and will tell you the location and times. You are responsible for seeking out your instructor during office hours. If your schedule makes this impossible, let your instructor know, and perhaps you can schedule another time to meet. If your school has an electronic mail (e-mail) system that allows you to send messages by computer, you may be able to communicate with your instructor by using e-mail.

Teaching assistants are people who help an instructor with a course. You may or may not have teaching assistants in your courses. Often they are studying to be instructors themselves. Sometimes they teach the smaller discussion or lab sections that accompany a large group lecture. They can be a great resource for help and advice and are often available if your instructor is too swamped to talk to you.

Administrators

Your school's *administrative personnel* have the responsibility of delivering to you—the student consumer—a first-rate product. That product is the sum total of your education, comprising facilities, instructors, materials, and courses. Although students don't often have regular interaction with administrators, it is the business of the administrative personnel to know how the school is serving you. If you have an issue that you haven't been able to resolve on your own, such as a conflict with an instructor, an inability to get into a class you need, or a school regulation that causes a problem for you, schedule a meeting with your dean or department chair.

Advisors and Counselors

Advisors and counselors can help with both the educational and personal sides of being a student. They provide information, advice, a listening ear, referrals, and other sources of help. Generally, students are assigned academic *advisors* with whom they meet at least once a semester. Your academic advisor will help you with class selection, scheduling, and selecting or designing a **major** when the time comes. Visit your academic advisor more than once a semester if you have questions or want to make changes.

Counselors, although not usually assigned, are available through student services or student health. Don't hesitate to seek a counselor's help if you have something on your mind. Your personal life influences the quality of your work in school. If you put some effort into working through personal problems, you will be more able to do your work well and hand it in on time. Occasionally, an illness or family difficulty may interfere enough with your schoolwork to call for special provisions for the completion of your classes. Most colleges are very willing to assist you during challenging times.

> **Major,**
> An academic subject chosen as a field of specialization, requiring a specific course of study.

Student Services

Basic *services* offered by almost every school include advising and counseling, student health/wellness, career planning and placement, tutoring, and fitness/physical education. Depending on your school, you may also find other services: housing and transportation, adult education services (for adults returning to school), disabled student services, academic centers (writing center, math center, etc., for help with these specific subjects), various support groups, and school publications that help keep you informed.

Often a school will have special services for specific populations. For example, at a school where most of the students commute, there may be a transportation office that helps students locate bus schedules and routes, find parking and sign up for permits, or track down car pools.

Students make inquiries at a job fair at Valley College in Los Angeles, CA.

Organizations

No matter what your needs or interests are, your school probably has an *organization* that would interest you or can help you. Some organizations are sponsored by the school (academic clubs), some are independent but have a branch at the school (government ROTC programs), and some are student-run organizations (Latino Student Association). Some organizations focus on courses of study (Nursing Club), some are primarily social (fraternities and sororities), some are artistic (Chamber Orchestra), and some are geared toward a hobby or activity (Runner's Club). Some you join to help others (Big Brothers or Big Sisters), and some offer help to you (Overeaters Anonymous).

When you consider adding a new activity to your life, weigh its positive effects against the negative ones. Positive effects could be new friends, enjoyable activities, help, a break from schoolwork, stress relief, improved academic performance, increased teamwork and leadership skills, aid to others, and experience that can broaden your horizons. On the negative side there may be a heavy time commitment, dues, inconvenient locations or meeting times, or too much responsibility. Explore any club carefully to see if it makes sense for you.

TABLE 1-1 HOW RESOURCES CAN HELP YOU

RESOURCE	ACADEMIC ASSISTANCE	FINANCIAL ASSISTANCE	JOB/CAREER ASSISTANCE	PERSONAL ASSISTANCE
INSTRUCTORS	Choosing classes, clarifying course material, help on assignments, dealing with study issues		Can tell you about their fields, may be a source of networking contacts	During office hours, are available to talk to you.
ADMINISTRATORS	Academic problems, educational focus, problems with school services		Can be a source of valuable contacts	Can help you sort through personal problems with instructors or other school employees
ACADEMIC ADVISORS	Choosing, changing, or dropping courses; getting over academic hurdles; selecting/changing a major		Can advise you on what job opportunities may go along with your major or academic focus	
PERSONAL COUNSELORS	Can help when personal problems get in the way of academic success	Services may be free or offered on a "sliding scale" depending on what you afford		Help with all kinds of personal problems
FINANCIAL AID OFFICE		Information and counseling on loans, grants, scholarships, financial planning, work-study programs	Information on job opportunities within your school environment (work/study and others)	
ACADEMIC CENTERS	Help with what the center specializes in (reading, writing, math)		Perhaps an opportunity to work at the center	
ORGANIZATIONS AND CLUBS	An academic club, can broaden your knowledge or experience in an area of study; can help you balance school with other enriching activities		Can help you develop skills, build knowledge, and make new contacts that may serve you in your working life	Depending on the club focus, can be an outlet for stress, a source of personal inspiration, a source of important friendships, an opportunity to help others.
FITNESS CENTER(S)		Usually free or low cost to enrolled students		Provides opportunity to build fitness and reduce stress; may have weight room, track, aerobic or dance classes, martial arts, team sports, exercise machines, etc.

TABLE 1-1 HOW RESOURCES CAN HELP YOU (CONTINUED)

RESOURCE	ACADEMIC ASSISTANCE	FINANCIAL ASSISTANCE	JOB/CAREER ASSISTANCE	PERSONAL ASSISTANCE
BULLETIN BOARDS	List academic events, class information, changes and additions to schedules, office hours, academic club meetings	List financial aid seminars, job opportunities, scholarships opportunities	List career forums, job sign-ups, and employment opportunities; offer a place for you to post a message if you are marketing a service	List support group meetings
HOUSING AND TRANSPORTATION OFFICE		Can help find the most financially beneficial travel or housing plan		Can help commuters with parking, bus or train service, and permits; can help with finding on- or off-campus housing
CAREER PLANNING AND PLACEMENT OFFICE		Can help add to your income through job opportunities	Job listings, help with résumés and interviews, possible interview appointments, factual information about the workplace (job trends, salaries, etc.)	
TUTORS	One-on-one help with academic subjects; assistance with specific assignments		If you decide to become a tutor, a chance to find out if teaching and working with people is for you.	
STUDENT HEALTH OFFICE		May provide low-cost or no-cost health care to enrolled students; may offer reduced-cost prescription plan		Wellness care (regular examinations), illness care, hospital, and specialist referrals, and prescriptions
ADULT EDUCATION CENTER	Academic help tailored to the returning adult student	May have specific financial-aid advice	May have job listings or other help with coordinating work and classes	May offer child-care assistance and opportunities to get to know other returning adults
SUPPORT GROUPS AND HOTLINES	If school-related, they offer a chance to hear how others have both stumbled and succeeded in school—and a chance to share your story			Personal help with whatever the hotline or support group specializes in; a chance to talk to someone whose job is to listen.
SCHOOL PUBLICATIONS	Academic news and course changes	News about financial aid opportunities or work/study programs	Job listings, information about the workplace and the job market	Articles and announcements about topics that may help you

To find out about organizations, consult your student handbook, ask friends and instructors, or check the activities office or center if your school has one. Some schools, on registration days, have an area where organizations set up tables and offer information to interested students. Some organizations seek you out, based on your achievements. When you explore any organization, ask what is expected in terms of time, responsibility, and any necessary financial commitment. Talk to students who are currently involved. Finally, if you try an organization and it becomes more than you can handle, bow out gracefully. In the best of all possible worlds, your involvement in organizations will enrich your life, expand your network of acquaintances, boost your time-management skills, and help you achieve goals.

Literature

Two publications can help you find your way through course offerings, department and resource offices, and the campus layout—the college catalog and the student handbook. Most schools provide these materials as a standard part of their enrollment information.

FIGURE 1-3   **COLLEGE CATALOG SEGMENT**

Course Descriptions

ENG 106: Creative Writing (Poetry) (3 credits)

45 lecture hours
Fall
Prerequisite: ENG 101

This course provides practice and constructive criticism in the composition of poetry through class discussion and presentation, individual conferences, and class review of student manuscripts. Readings and analyses of contemporary poets are included.

ENG 107: Creative Writing (Fiction) (3 credits)

45 lecture hours
Spring
Prerequisite: ENG 101

Practice and instruction in the writing of fiction, emphasizing the short story are offered. Class discussions provide analysis, criticism, and helpful information on the writing and marketing of fiction manuscripts.

ENG 112: Medical Writing (3 credits)

45 lecture hours
Fall, Spring - day, eve
Prerequisite: ENG 101

The principles and processes use tion of selected materials typical ical settings are presented. Th the composition of specific clear, straightfoward langu priate to modern medica

ENG 113: Busin

45 lecture hours
Fall, Spring -
Prerequisit

The
tion
ne
t

course emphasizes the composition of spec nical reports in clear, straightfoward lang formats appropiate to modern technica standards.

ENG 175: Writing for Teache

45 lecture hours
Offered by contract for Balti
System teachers

Teachers and othe with a thorough re the kinds of wri the job. Stude exercises a ing and f activiti ing c the I

The *college catalog* lists every department and course available at the school. Each course name will generally have two parts, for example, EN101 or CHEM205. The first part is one or more letters indicating the department and subject matter, and the second part is a number indicating the course level (lower numbers for introductory courses and higher numbers for more advanced ones). The catalog groups courses according to subject matter and lists them from the lowest-level courses to the most advanced, indicating the number of credits earned for each class. See Figure 1–3 for a segment of an actual college catalog from Baltimore City Community College.[2] A course book released prior to each semester will indicate details such as the instructor, the days the course meets, the time of day, the location (building and room), and the maximum number of students who can take the course.

Your college catalog may also give general school policies such as the registration process and withdrawal procedures. It may list the departments to show the range of subjects you may study. It may outline instructional programs, detailing core requirements, as well as requirements for various majors, degrees, and certificates. When you have a question, consult the catalog before you look elsewhere.

Your *student handbook* looks beyond specific courses to the big picture, helping you to navigate student life. In it you will find some or all of the following, and maybe more: information on available housing (for on-campus residents) and on parking and driving (for commuters); overviews of the support offices for students, such as academic advising, counseling, career planning and placement, student health, financial aid, and individual centers for academic subject areas; descriptions of special-interest clubs; and details about library and computer services. It may also list hours, locations, phone numbers, and addresses for offices, clubs, and organizations.

Your student handbook will also describe important policies such as how to add or drop a class, what the grading system means, campus rules, drug and alcohol policies, what kinds of records your school keeps, safety tips, and more. Keep your student handbook where you can find it easily, in your study area at home or someplace safe at school. It can save you a lot of trouble when you need to find information about a resource or service.

Technology

Computers regulate your class schedule and keep a record of your tuition payments. Computer centers on campus provide an opportunity for students to type papers, work on assignments, take tests, log lab results, and send e-mail to instructors and fellow students. You may even have your own personal computer on which you do schoolwork and manage your personal schedule or finances. Here are some tips for exploring how computers can help you in college:

Know what you want from computers. Some people want to know how computers operate and look forward to a career in programming or systems. Others only want to use computers as a tool to achieve a goal—for example, to write articles or to design graphics. Knowing what you want will help you discover how much computer knowledge you need.

Get training. Once you know what you need from computers, give yourself a chance to learn. If you want to focus on programming, look into courses that will earn you a degree in that area. If you will use a computer for other goals, look for software training programs, school-sponsored short courses, or computer learning centers. A typing course can be extremely useful.

Investigate your school's computer system. Each school has its own particular system. Find out what computers are available, when and where you can use them, what software they have, when and how to print your work, and any other policies of your school's computer rooms.

Know what programs you need and what they do. The basics in computer use fall into four general categories: word processing (for papers and other written assignments), **databases** and **spreadsheets** (for organizing and storing large volumes of information and data), the Internet (a worldwide computer network that connects businesses, schools, governments, and people), and e-mail (Internet mail system over which you can send letters, memos, or assignments).

Database,
A collection of data, organized by computer so that one can quickly organize, store, and retrieve it.

Spreadsheet,
A ledger layout, usually found in an accounting program, that allows the user to list and calculate numerical data.

Save, back up, and back up some more. First, save your work onto the hard drive or disk every few minutes; you never know when a power outage might mean that you lose everything you did in the last hour. Second, always back up (copy) your work in a location other than the computer hard drive, such as a 3-inch diskette or a Zip disk. You can never be too safe.

Making the most of your resources is one way to strive for success. The next section offers other strategies for you to consider.

THINKING BACK

1. List and describe four characteristics of today's college students.

   a. _____

   b. _____

   c. _____

   d. _____

2. Name two ways your education can help you succeed in life.

   a. _____

   _____

   b. _____

   _____

3. Briefly discuss how you might use three different resources at your school.

   a. A service: _____

   _____

   b. A person: _____

   _____

   c. An organization: _____

   _____

4. Describe your personal technology needs and how you intend to pursue them.

_____

_____

THINKING AHEAD

1. Name one idea or goal that motivates you to succeed.

_____

2. List three commitments that you have made in the past year.

   a. _____

   b. _____

   c. _____

3. What do you think is your greatest fear about pursuing an education?

_____

_____

4. How would you rate your self-esteem on a scale from 1 to 10? _____

5. Is your school community a diverse population? If so, how?

_____

_____

HOW CAN YOU STRIVE FOR SUCCESS?

Success is a process in motion, not a fixed mark. A successful person is one who is consistently learning, growing, and working toward goals. College provides an opportunity for you to redefine your goals and work hard to achieve them. The former Tom Bradley, son of a Texas sharecropper, became the first African-American mayor of Los Angeles in 1973 and served five successive terms. More than thirty years after Ruth Bader Ginsberg was rejected as a Supreme Court clerk because Justice Felix Frankfurter didn't hire women, she became a Supreme Court justice herself. If you put your energies to the task, you can create any future you envision for yourself.

Striving for success takes effort. It requires motivation, commitment, initiative, responsibility, and a willingness to face your fears. In combination, these strategies will help you to gather and retain what you know as well as to create new knowledge.

Get Motivated

Motivation,

A force that moves a person to action, often inspired by an idea, a fact, an event, or a goal.

Motivation is the energy that fuels your drive to achieve, and a motivator is anything that motivates you. There are at least as many motivators as there are people, and what motivates any given person can change from situation to situation or even from day to day. For example, some potential motivators for attending school could be supporting a family, learning a marketable skill, or improving oneself.

It's human to lose your motivation from time to time. How can you build motivation or renew lost motivation?

➤ Spend time reflecting on why your goal is meaningful to you. Remind yourself of what you wanted.

➤ Make a decision to take one step toward your goal. Sometimes, feeling overwhelmed by a goal immobilizes you. Don't worry about tomorrow. Focus on the step you can take today.

➤ After you take the first step, reward yourself for a job well done. Rewards can be material (a new CD) or they can be more internal (a walk outside or time spent with a friend).

➤ Examine and deal with your obstacles. What's getting in your way? Maybe your health or finances have been troubling you. Decide to put some effort into examining and removing your obstacles, and take steps toward your goal as they become available to you.

➤ Begin or begin again. If you can just get yourself started, you'll feel better as you continue to work toward your goals. A law of physics, Newton's first law of motion, says that things in motion tend to stay in motion and that things at rest tend to stay at rest. Be a thing in motion.

For example, to pass an early-morning writing class that you've already failed once, you decide to implement two strategies. First, you promise yourself that you will go to every class and turn in your work on time. Second, you make a commitment to write daily in a journal. Your motivation: Passing this course is necessary to continue your education, and the writing skills you learn will help you get a good job when you graduate. Moreover, you promise yourself a reward if you get at least a B- in the course.

To reach your goal, you remove obstacles to success. Instead of staying up late and being too tired to go to class, you go to bed earlier and put your alarm clock across the room so that you have to get up to shut it off. If you have trouble following through on your plans, you may want to shift to another strategy, such as trying to schedule afternoon classes to compensate for your sleep habits.

Make a Commitment

How do you focus the energy of motivation? Make a commitment. Commitment means that you do what you say you will do. When you honor a commitment, you prove to yourself and others that your intentions can be trusted. A committed person follows through on a promise.

Commitment doesn't just refer to a personal relationship. You can apply the tasks of commitment—and the rewards—to academic goals, professional relationships, your working life, career goals, and self-improvement. Commitment often stretches over a period of time. You may commit to graduating in three years, to working on your marriage, or to recycling more often. Not only have you made a promise, but also you hold yourself to that promise for as long as the commitment demands.

Commitment requires you to focus your energy on something specific. A decision to "change my life" or "make a million dollars" might intimidate you into staying motionless on the couch. Instead, break any goal into manageable pieces, naming the steps of the process you will use to achieve it.

How do you go about making and keeping a commitment?

> ➤ State your commitment concretely. It's hard to commit to something such as "I'm going to pass this course" because you haven't set yourself clear tasks. Be specific: "I'm going to turn in the weekly essay assignments on time."

> ➤ Get started and note your progress. The long road of a commitment can tire you out. Looking for improvements on the way, no matter how small, can keep you going.

> ➤ Renew your commitment regularly. How many times has your commitment to change faded away in a few weeks—or even a few days? Many people experience fatigue that sets in and clouds their good intentions. You're not a failure if you lose steam; it's normal. Recharge by reflecting on the positive effects of your commitment.

> ➤ Keep track of your commitment. Find ways to remind yourself of your commitments. Keep a list of them in your date book. If they involve events or projects that take place on specific dates, note them on the calendar. Post notes to yourself on your refrigerator, your wall, or your mirror. Talk about your commitments with friends and family. Sometimes, just having someone supporting you and your goals helps you remain more accountable.

For example, you might make this commitment: "I will write in my journal every night before going to sleep." You make journal entries for two weeks, then evaluate what positive effects this daily practice has had on your writing ability. If you were to skip your journal entries for a week, you could renew your commitment by reminding yourself how keeping a journal exercised your writing ability and relieved stress. You might keep track of your commitment by telling a partner or housemate to check on you.

Making and keeping your commitments helps you keep a steady focus on your most important goals. It gives you a sense of accomplishment as you experience gradual growth and progress.

Commitment,
1. A pledge or promise to do something, or
2. Dedication to a long-term course of action

Show Initiative

Initiative,
The power to begin or to follow through energetically with a plan or task; determination.

When you show initiative, you push yourself to take that first difficult step. Initiative helps to get the pursuit of your goals off the ground. It jump-starts your journey and helps to renew motivation along the way. It enables you to respond continually to changes that occur.

Initiative means that you take the first step on your own instead of waiting for people, rules, requirements, or circumstances to drag you along. You show initiative when you go to a counselor for help with a personal problem, talk to a friend about something he or she said that upset you, raise your hand to speak in a classroom, come up with a better way to do a task at work, take a political stand by voting, or start doing fifty abdominal crunches every morning.

Initiative requires you to keep on top of your goals and to listen to your instincts. You may discover that you want to do more than what is expected, which can be positive both at school and in the workplace. Initiative is a spark plug. It ignites the fuel of your motivation and keeps it burning so that you can maintain your commitments.

Be Responsible

Being responsible is all about living up to your obligations, both those that are imposed on you and those that you impose on yourself. It means that you can address situations and challenges that arise in your daily life. Through action, you prove that you are responsible, or "response-able," able to respond. When something needs to be done, a responsible person does the work—as efficiently as possible and to the best of his or her ability.

Responsibility,
The quality of being reliable, trustworthy, and accountable for one's actions.

Responsibility can take enormous effort. Throughout your life you will have moments when you just don't want to respond. In those moments, you need to weigh the positive and negative effects and decide if not responding is worth your while. However, being responsible has definite benefits. For one, you make a crucial impression on others. You earn the trust of your instructors, supervisors, relatives, and friends. When others trust you, they may give you increasing responsibility and opportunities for growth. Trust builds relationships, which in turn feed progress and success.

When you are trusted, you are also respected, and respect brings its own rewards. Supervisors promote employees they respect; instructors give respected students special duties or assignments; friends look to one another for advice and help when they respect each other. Even more important is the self-respect that emerges when you prove that you can live up to your promises. Responsible people are often given power and opportunity because they have shown that they are capable of making the best of both.

For example, when you complete class assignments on time, you demonstrate responsibility. When you correct errors, you demonstrate a commitment to doing well. An instructor who sees these patterns of behavior is more likely to trust and respect you. You don't have to take on the world to show how responsible you can be. Responsibility shows in basic everyday actions: attending class, fulfilling requirements, turning in work on time, being a good friend or parent, and being true to your word.

Face Your Fears

Everyone experiences fear. New experiences are often frightening even as they are exciting. The changes involved in pursuing an education can inspire fear. You may wonder if you can handle the work, if you will make friends, or if you have chosen the right school or program. You may worry that your family and friends may expect too much or may stand in your way. You may also have fears about the future, asking yourself whether you'll be able to apply your education to a job and whether you can earn a living.

Connected with the fear of change is the fear of independence. It's hard to earn and manage money, pay for shelter and food and bills, perhaps care for children or an aging relative, and still find time for rest and relaxation. You should congratulate yourself on choosing to increase your abilities through education. Although some people give in to fear because they feel safer with the familiar—even if it doesn't make them happy—you have taken responsibility for improving your opportunities.

Education presents challenges that demand a willingness to push your limits and face your fears. These five steps will help you face your fears with courage. Through the course of your life you will find yourself taking these steps again and again.

1. Acknowledge your specific fears. The act of naming your fear will begin to diminish it. Be specific. Knowing you fear a course may not inspire you to do anything about it. Focusing in on a fear of an instructor or a particular assignment gives you something to work on.

2. Decide which fears are real and which conceal something deeper. Sometimes one fear hides a larger one. If you fear a test, determine whether you fear the test itself or the fact that if you pass it, you will have to take a tougher class next semester. If you fear the test, take steps to prepare for it. If you fear the next class, you might talk to your instructor about it.

3. Develop a plan of attack. Evaluate what will help you overcome your fear. For example, if you are uneasy about your writing style, develop a realistic picture of your abilities by consulting your instructor, talking to friends in the class, or reading a variety of work by other writers.

4. Move ahead with your plans. Having courage is the key to moving ahead. You may find that the drive to overcome fear forces you to work harder, or you may discover that your fear is so great that you must change your plans. Take the steps you decide will help you most.

5. Talk about your fears with people you trust. Everyone has fears. Often the ideas other people have about gaining control can help you with your own fears. When you share strategies, everybody benefits.

If you acknowledge and evaluate them, fears can provide valuable clues to what blocks your success. They can show you where you need a push or

> "He has not learned the lesson of life who does not every day surmount a fear."
>
> Ralph Waldo Emerson

extra work, and they also can signal a need to make changes or open yourself up to new knowledge. Facing them is one step on the road to healthy self-esteem.

HOW CAN YOU BUILD YOUR SELF-ESTEEM?

Self-esteem—a strong and deeply felt belief that you as a person have value in the world—is part of what leads every successful person to his or her goals. Often, if people believe strongly enough in their value and capabilities, this belief can help to propel them forward. Belief, though, is only half the game. The other half is action and effort that help you feel that you have *earned* that belief. Rick Pitino, a highly successful basketball coach, discusses the necessity of earning self-esteem in his book, *Success Is a Choice*: "Self-esteem is directly linked to deserving success. If you have established a great work ethic and have begun the discipline that is inherent with that, you will automatically begin to feel better about yourself. It's all interrelated. You must deserve victory to feel good about yourself."[3]

Building self-esteem, therefore, involves both thinking positively and taking action. Together, they can generate the belief in yourself that will help you to succeed.

Think Positively

Your attitudes influence your choices and affect how you perceive and relate to others. On the one hand, positive attitude can open your mind to learning experiences and inspire you to take action. On the other hand, a negative attitude can hinder learning and stifle initiative. For example, say you are enrolled in a required course unrelated to your major. If you feel that the course is a waste of time, you probably won't work hard and therefore won't learn much. If, however, you keep an open mind, you might discover that the course teaches you something valuable, introduces you to a friend or instructor who influences your life, or shows you new career possibilities.

One of the ways in which you can create a positive attitude is with **positive self-talk.** When you hear negative thoughts "I'm not very smart" or "I'm not good enough" in your mind, replace them with positive ones "It won't be easy, but I'm smart enough to figure it out" or "I have a lot to offer." You would probably never criticize a good friend in the same way that you sometimes criticize yourself. Try to talk to yourself as if you were talking to someone you care a lot about. The following hints will help you put positive self-talk into action.

Positive self-talk,
Supportive and positive—thinking thoughts and ideas that a person communicates to himself or herself.

Stop negative talk in its tracks and change it to positive talk. If you catch yourself thinking, "I can never write a decent paper," stop and say to yourself, "I can do better than that and next time I will." Then think through how you plan to do it.

● **Pay yourself a compliment.** Be specific: "I have really improved my spelling and proofreading." Some people use word calendars with daily affirmations. These are great reminders of positive self-talk.

Replace words of obligation, which take power from you, with words of personal intent:

I should	*becomes*	I choose to
I have to	*becomes*	I want to
I'll try	*becomes*	I will

Words of intent give you power and control because they imply a personal decision to act. When you say, "I have to be in class by 9:00," you're saying that someone else has power over you and has handed you a required obligation. When you say, "I want to be in class by 9:00 because I don't want to miss anything I need to learn about," you're saying that the choice is yours.

Note your successes. Even when you don't think you are at your best, congratulate yourself on any positive steps. Whether you do well on a paper, get to class on time all week, or have fewer mistakes on this week's paper than last week's, each success helps you believe in yourself. Every step is a step in the right direction, no matter how small. Try keeping a list of your successes in a notebook.

Getting informed by reading the college newspaper.

● It can be very difficult to think positively. If you have a deep-rooted feeling of unworthiness, you may want to see a counselor. Many people have benefited from skilled professional advice.

Take Action

Although thinking positively sets the tone for success, it cannot get you there by itself. You need to give those positive thoughts life and support by taking action. Without action, positive thoughts can become empty statements or even lies.

Consider, for example, a student in a freshman composition class. This student thinks every possible positive thought: "I am a great student. I know how to write well. I can get a B in this class. I will succeed in school." And so on. She even writes her thoughts down on notes and posts them where she can see them. Then, through the semester, this student misses about one-third of the class meetings, turns in some of her papers late, and completely misses a couple of assignments. She doesn't make use of opportunities to work with her study partner. At the end of the course, when she barely passes the class, she wonders how things went so wrong when she had such a positive attitude.

● This student did not succeed because she did not earn her belief in herself through action and effort. You cannot maintain belief unless you give yourself something to believe *in*. By the end of a semester like this, positive thoughts look like lies: "If I can get a B, why did I get a D? If I am such a great student, why did I barely make it through this course?" Eventually, with nothing to support them, the positive thoughts disappear, and with neither positive thoughts nor action, a student will have a hard time achieving any level of success.

Positive thoughts are like seeds. Don't just scatter them on the soil: take action—plant them, water them, and feed them, and they will grow and be fruitful. Here are some ways to get yourself moving:

Make action plans. Be specific about how you plan to take action for any given situation. Figure out exactly what you will do, so that "I am a great student" is backed up by "I will attend every class. I will consult my study partner when I have trouble. I will use peer editing for my papers. I will do the reading the day before each class meeting."

Build your own code of discipline. To provide a framework for the specific actions you plan to take, develop a general plan for yourself to follow, based on what actions are important to your success. Perhaps your top priorities are personal relationships and achievement in school. Construct each day's individual goals and actions so that they help you achieve your larger objectives.

Just do it. It takes a lot of energy to do what you have said you will do. Don't spend energy worrying about how hard it will be, when and how you should do it, what will happen if you do it or don't, and so on. Once you decide on your action, use your energy to just do it. Only then can you reap the benefit.

Acknowledge every step. Even the smallest action is worth your attention because every action reinforces a positive thought. First you believe that you are a great student, then you work hard in class, then you do well on a test, then you believe more emphatically that you are a great student, then you complete a successful group project, then you feel even better about yourself, and so on.

Academic Integrity

**Integrity, **
Adherence to a code of moral values; incorruptibility; honesty.

Integrity is at the heart of your actions as a member of your academic community, as well as of other communities such as your workplace and your family. Having academic integrity means acting with integrity in all aspects of your academic life—classes, assignments, tests, papers, labs, projects, and relations with students and faculty. Academic integrity is part of taking action toward self-esteem.

The fine points of the definition of academic integrity may vary from school to school, but the general principles usually include the following forbidden actions:

➤ Plagiarism (copying the words, ideas, or structure of another person's work and claiming it as your own).

➤ Cheating on tests by referring to materials or using devices that are not authorized by the instructor (e.g., looking at a test that a friend has taken in a section of a course that meets a few hours before your own).

➤ Presenting the work of another person as your own.

➤ Submitting work that you have already submitted elsewhere, in another class or in a previous school.

➤ Getting help with a project on which you are supposed to be working alone.

➤ Altering your academic record without authorization.

➤ Misusing library materials (taking materials without checking them out, keeping materials late, removing materials that are not permitted to be removed, or damaging materials).

➤ Ignoring copyright restrictions on computer software.

➤ Providing unethical aid to another student by allowing your work to be copied, helping a student cheat on a test, aiding a student on an independent project, or selling your work or tests.

Explore your school's specific requirements. Your school's code of honor, or academic integrity policy, should be printed in your student handbook. Read it to be sure you know what is expected of you. As a student enrolled in your school, you have agreed to abide by that policy. You have also agreed to suffer the consequences if you are discovered violating any of your school's policies.

Maintaining an image of academic integrity will certainly help you pass your classes and graduate. But the effects of living with integrity can be life altering and wide ranging, involving far more than a few good grades on tests and papers. Having academic integrity can help you:

➤ Develop a habit of playing fair.

➤ Retain knowledge for later use instead of just long enough for the test.

➤ Interact with others respectfully and with trust.

➤ Build your positive feelings about yourself by acting honorably.

The process of building and maintaining self-esteem isn't easy. It involves many ups and downs, steps forward and slides back, successes and disappointments. Remember that you are in control of your self-esteem, because you alone are ultimately responsible for your thoughts and actions. If you can both believe in yourself and take action that anchors and inspires that belief, you will give yourself the best possible base on which to build a successful life.

WHAT IS YOUR ROLE IN A DIVERSE WORLD?

Diversity isn't just what happens in an international students club, a business that hires people from different backgrounds, or a neighborhood that is home to several cultural groups. Diversity is the mosaic of differences that envelops your communities, your nation, and the world. In addition to races and ethnic groups, diversity occurs in traditions, religions, family

WINDOWS ON THE WORLD: REAL LIFE STUDENT ISSUES

How can I connect to my university community?

Ruth Ham, Dallas Theological Seminary, Dallas, Texas, Christian Education Major

Before I came to Texas, I studied English in my native home of Bangkok, Thailand. Now that I am here I find that the classes I took there, such as English poetry, were interesting but not very practical. The language barrier has made it difficult for me to get to know people.

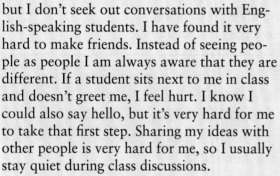

I am ashamed of my English. If someone asks me a direct question I will answer the best I can, but I don't seek out conversations with English-speaking students. I have found it very hard to make friends. Instead of seeing people as people I am always aware that they are different. If a student sits next to me in class and doesn't greet me, I feel hurt. I know I could also say hello, but it's very hard for me to take that first step. Sharing my ideas with other people is very hard for me, so I usually stay quiet during class discussions.

One thing that has helped is joining the international students club. I've met other students who are also struggling with feeling like they belong. We practice our English together. I've also found that my English has improved by writing my thoughts out in English in a journal. It would be nice to find an American friend who has the time to help me with my English. One thing I notice here though is that people seem to always be in a hurry. I want to be more involved at school than just going to class. What else can I do to feel more a part of my school?

Hiromi Kodakehara, University of Nebraska, Omaha, Nebraska

I had to take English for six years in Japan, but I couldn't speak it well at all. When I got to the United States, I was ashamed of my English. In my ESL (English as a Second Language) program in Omaha, not many Americans paid attention to me or to any international students. The only time I spoke English was when I was in class or when I was with my teachers.

One day, I realized: "I am Japanese, and of course I cannot speak English well. Why am I so worried about it? I can talk and act like I am an international student." This helped me to think positively and start reaching out to people. Fortunately, my school has a program called Conversation Partners, to help international students improve their English and a program which registered American families who would take international students in for two weeks. These two programs helped me improve my English and make some good friends. My friends told me that they respected my learning a foreign language. They would say, "Your English is much better than my Japanese."

I am sure your school has international student advisors who can help you find an organization that helps international students. There probably are also nonprofit organizations in your city that want to help foreign students. Through their events and activities, you can make American friends, practice your English, and eventually feel more comfortable talking to Americans. There are, of course, some people who ignore international students, but there are also many friendly Americans who want to be friends but don't know how. You don't have to speak perfect English. You can be proud of taking regular classes with American students, and keeping up with them.

backgrounds, genders, abilities, economic levels, ages, habits, lifestyles, choices, careers, artistic expressions, modes of dress, foods, health conditions, perspectives, opinions, experiences, and more. Diversity touches each of you in a very personal way.

Diversity Is Real Life

You encounter diversity every day through images and information—in newspapers and magazines, on television, and on the radio—that tell you about how different people think and live. People tend to focus on diversity they can see, such as skin color or eye shape, but there are other less visible forms. People who look similar to you may differ from you in important ways. Your fellow student may have a different religion or a hidden disability, for example, or your coworker may have a different sexual orientation. Society is made up of people who transcend labels and have limitless worth.

Diversity has become more important, partly because the world is becoming more interdependent. As people become more aware of other ways of living, they may be more sensitive to differences. The problem is not in the differences but in the way in which people view and treat them. One example is thinking that that it is disrespectful for someone not to look you in the eye during a conversation. In certain cultures, it is considered rude to look people in the eye, especially if that person is in a position of authority.

> "A journey of a thousand miles must begin with a single step."
> Laotzu

Diversity and Teamwork

Think of the path of your accomplishments, and you will find that rarely do you achieve anything using your own efforts alone. Your success at school and at work depends on your ability to cooperate in a team setting—how you communicate, share tasks, and develop a common vision.

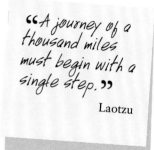

➤ You deal with the challenges of day-to-day life in a family or community team, with the help of parents, siblings, relatives, and/or friends.

➤ You achieve work goals in a work team, with supervisors, co-workers, and/or consultants.

➤ You learn, complete projects, and pass classes as part of an educational team, with instructors, fellow students, tutors, administrators, and/or advisors.

Any team will gain strength from the diversity of its members. In fact, diversity is an asset in a team. Consider a five-person basketball team, made up of a center, a power forward, a small forward, a shooting guard, and a point guard. Each person has a different role and a different style of play, but only by combining their abilities can the players achieve success. The more diverse the team members, the greater the chance that new ideas and solutions will find their way to the table, increasing the chances of solving any problem. As a member of any team, use these three strategies to maximize team success.

1. Open your mind and accept that different team members have valuable roles.
2. Consider the new information and ideas that others offer.
3. Evaluate any idea according to how it improves a situation instead of getting sidetracked by focusing on the person who had the idea. Successful teams use what works, no matter who came up with it.

Living Your Role

It's not always easy to open your mind to differences. However, doing so can benefit both you and others around you. You may consider goals like these as you define your role in the diverse world:

➤ To accept diversity as a fact of life and an asset. The world will only continue to diversify. The more you adapt to and appreciate this diversity, the more enriched your life will be.

➤ To explore differences. Open your mind and learn about what is unfamiliar around you.

➤ To celebrate your own uniqueness, as well as that of others. It's natural to think that your own way is the best way. Expand your horizons by considering your way as one good way and seeking out different and useful ways to which other people can introduce you.

➤ To consider new perspectives. The wide variety of ideas and perspectives brought by people from all different groups and situations creates a wealth of thought from which the world can find solutions to tough and complex problems.

➤ To continue to learn. Education is one of the best ways to become more open-minded about differences. Classes such as sociology and ethics can increase your awareness of the lives and values of people in other cultures. Even though your personal beliefs may be challenged in the process, facing how you feel about others is a positive step toward harmony among people.

Throughout this book you will find references to a diverse mixture of people in different life circumstances. Note especially the Windows on the World feature in every chapter, which highlights people from different backgrounds who are making the effort to learn about themselves and their world. Chapter 10 will go into more detail about communicating across lines of difference and addressing the problems that arise when people have trouble accepting each other's differences. Diversity is not a subject that you study at one point in the semester and then leave behind. It is a theme that touches every part of your life.

In Chinese writing, this character has two meanings: One is "chaos"; the other is "opportunity." The character communicates the belief that every challenging, chaotic, and demanding situation in life also presents an opportunity. By responding to challenges in a positive and active way, you can discover the opportunity that lies within the chaos.

Let this concept reassure you as you begin college. You may feel that you are going through a time of chaos and change. Remember that no matter how difficult the obstacles, you have the ability to persevere. You can create opportunities for yourself to learn, grow, and improve.

IMPORTANT POINTS TO REMEMBER

1. Who is pursuing an education today?

Today's students don't fit any universal mold. They are of all different ages, abilities, cultural backgrounds, and life stages. Many are in school part time while working and/or raising a family. Many attend two-year or night programs, and many are taking longer to complete a degree. These different needs have resulted in a more diversified educational system. Your responsibility is to make your needs clear to your school and to ask for help when you need it.

2. How does education promote success?

Education gives you new knowledge, as well as the tools you need to absorb in that knowledge, retain it, and build on it. It helps you grow and increase your potential, often showing you that you are capable of more than you imagined. It makes you more likely to get involved in community activism, practice personal health habits, and improve your quality of life through better jobs and higher wages. It gives you power to make choices and expands your horizons by preparing you to respond to art, science, politics, and other issues that affect human lives.

3. What resources are available at your school?

Offering resources is part of your school's goal to provide a comprehensive education for each student. People such as instructors, administrators, and advisors can advise and guide you. Services may include advising, health, tutoring, financial aid, and career planning. Various organizations offer opportunities to get involved outside of class. The college catalog describes course offerings, registration and withdrawal procedures, and other important school policies. The student handbook will help you address student life issues including housing, counseling, career planning, and where to find the offices of organizations and services.

4. How can you strive for success?

A successful person is continually growing, learning, and changing. These actions will help you move ahead: getting motivated, showing initiative, making a commitment, being responsible, and facing your fears. Together these actions can help you pursue your goals and adjust to life's constant changes.

5. How can you build your self-esteem?

Self-esteem, or the sense that you have value, can help you achieve your goals. The key is to first believe in yourself and then to take action that helps you feel that you have earned that belief. You can think positively about yourself through different styles of positive self-talk. Then you can fulfill the promise of those positive thoughts through action plans, discipline, and effort. Maintaining academic integrity will also help you maintain self-esteem.

6. What is your role in a diverse world?

Diversity is real life. The modern world exposes you to all kinds of human differences, in gender, race, values and opinions, ethnicity and culture, religion, ability, traditions, ages, and more. Accepting others will help you interact successfully with people in your home, school, and work communities. Successful teamwork in all aspects of your life depends on your ability to value those who are different from you.

Name _____ Date _____

BUILDING SKILLS FOR COLLEGE, CAREER, AND LIFE SUCCESS
CHAPTER 1

TAKING STOCK:
REFINING YOUR THOUGHTS

Look back at the statements you explored at the start of the chapter (see
Thinking It Through on p. 3). Observe whether your attitudes have
changed and what you have learned by studying this chapter.

1. How has the college student body changed in recent years? Name three
   unexpected facts about today's student population.

   _____

   _____

   _____

2. Imagine it's one of those days when you don't know why you're in
   school. Revive your commitment by naming a specific goal of yours and
   two ways that education can help you reach it.

   _____

   _____

   _____

   _____

3. Name three people at your school who can help you sort through personal or school issues.

   _____

   _____

   _____

4. Name one way in which you can recharge your motivation when it falters.

   _____

   _____

   _____

5. List two strategies that can help you when you have trouble believing in yourself—one for thinking positively and one for taking action.

_____

_____

6. Describe how interacting with people who are different from you may affect your life.

_____

_____

_____

7. Find a strategy in this chapter that you like. Discuss how you plan to use it in the next two weeks.

_____

_____

_____

CRITICAL THINKING:
APPLYING LEARNING TO YOUR LIFE

Identify Yourself

Where do you fit in today's student population? Make a brief sketch of yourself in words—describe your particular circumstances, opinions, and needs in a short paragraph. Here are some questions to inspire thought:

➤ How do you describe yourself—your culture, ethnicity, gender, age, lifestyle?

➤ How long are you planning to spend in college?

➤ How would you describe your family?

➤ What is your work situation, if you work?

➤ What is your current living situation?

➤ What do you expect out of your college experience?

➤ What qualities make you special?

_____

_____

_____

_____

_____

_____

Activate Your Self-esteem

Use the two aspects of building your self-esteem to move yourself toward an important school-related goal for this semester. Make your goal as specific as possible, for example, "I want to find a job that allows me to work at night and still have time to study for my day classes."

Your goal: _____

_____

Be positive. What positive thoughts about yourself and your abilities will help you achieve your goal? List them here:

_____

_____

_____

Take action. Get specific about the actions you will take to back up your positive thoughts and achieve your goal. List them here.

_____

_____

_____

_____

_____

The last step is up to you: Just do it.

Facing Your Fears[4]

One valuable solution to any fear is to let go of the need to be perfect (which often prevents people from doing anything at all) and do something. The easiest way to do this is to break the task into manageable units and do one step at a time. First, think of an activity you have been postponing because of fear (fear of success, of failure, of the task, or of perfectionism). Describe it here.

_____

Now list four small activities that would get you closer to working through that fear. If you don't want to start a major project, for example, you could read a book on the subject, brainstorm what you already know about it, or just write one page about it.

1. _____

2. _____

3. _____

4. _____

Commit yourself to one small step that you will take within the next two days. State it here.

_____

List the time you will begin the activity and how much time you will spend doing it.

_____

What reward will you give yourself for having taken that step?

_____

After taking the step, describe how it felt.

_____

Affirm that you have taken that first step and are on the way to success by signing your name here and writing the date. Use the success strategies to make sure you continue on the road toward conquering your fear.

Signature _____ Date _____

TEAMWORK: COMBINING FORCES

Who can help you? Every school is unique and offers its own particular range of opportunities. Investigate your school. Use the resource table as a guide, and explore your student handbook. Make a check mark by the resources that you think will be most helpful to you.

Advisors and counselors	_____	Adult education center	_____
Library/media center	_____	Support groups/hotlines	_____
Instructors	_____	Career/job placement office	_____

Clubs/organizations	_____	Administration	_____
Bulletin boards	_____	Academic centers	_____
Student health center	_____	School publications	_____
Housing and transportation	_____	Tutoring	_____
Wellness/fitness centers	_____	Financial-aid office	_____

Gather in small groups or, if you have a small class, work as one large group together. Each member of each group should choose one or more different resources (make sure no two people within a group explore the same resource). Be sure all resources on the following grid are accounted for. Then, each group member will investigate his or her resources and fill in the information on the grid, answering the questions listed across the top. The two blank spaces at the bottom are for you to use if you find resources not listed here (the grid appears on the next two pages).

After each person has completed his or her investigation, meet again to exchange information and fill in the information on the grid. You now have a resource guide that you can refer to any time. Write here how will use the three resources that you feel will benefit you the most

1. _____

_____

_____

_____

2. _____

_____

_____

3. _____

_____

_____

WRITING: DISCOVERY THROUGH JOURNALING

To record your thoughts, use a separate journal or the lined pages at the end of the chapter.

Academic integrity. What to you are the most important principles of academic integrity? Do you feel that acting with academic integrity will help you or not? How do you feel about your school's academic integrity policy (you can probably find it in your student handbook or course catalog).

RESOURCE	WHO PROVIDES IT?	WHERE CAN YOU FIND IT?	WHEN IS IT AVAILABLE?	HOW CAN IT HELP YOU?	HOW DO YOU ASK FOR IT?	PHONE # OR OTHER KEY DETAILS
Administrative help						
Instructor advice						
Academic advising						
Personal counseling						
Financial aid						
Academic centers						
Organizations and clubs						
Bulletin boards						
Housing and transportation						
Career planning and placement						

RESOURCE	WHO PROVIDES IT?	WHERE CAN YOU FIND IT?	WHEN IS IT AVAILABLE?	HOW CAN IT HELP YOU?	HOW DO YOU ASK FOR IT?	PHONE # OR OTHER KEY DETAILS
Tutoring						
Student health						
Adult education center						
Fitness						
Support groups/ hotlines						
Disabled-student services						
English as a Second Language						

CAREER PORTFOLIO:
CHARTING YOUR COURSE

Setting career goals. Whether you have a current career, have held a few different jobs, or have not yet entered the workplace, college is an ideal time to take stock of your career goals. Even if you won't enter the workplace for a few years, now is not too early to consider what you might like to do after you have finished school. The earlier in your college education that you consider your career goals, the more you can take advantage of college to help prepare you for work, in both job-specific and general ways.

Take some time to think about your working life. Spend a half hour or so brainstorming everything that you wish you could be, do, have, or experience in your career. List your wishes on a blank piece of paper, draw them, depict them with cutouts from magazines, or combine these ideas—whatever you like best.

Here are some wish categories for you to consider, each with a few examples:

Career areas	Teaching elementary school Computer engineering Health-related career
Benefits	Day care Health insurance
Travel	Public transportation commute Opportunities to work on the road
Finances	Primary household income Secondary supplementary income
Family and relationships	Work days so I can spend evenings with family Work nights so I can be a parent during the day
Experiences	Work with people Job that involves travel Work with technology High-energy workplace Work solo from my home
Schedule	Full time Part time Flex time

Now look at your list. You probably have a wide variety of details. To discover how your wishes relate to one another, group them in order of priority. Take three pieces of paper and label them Priority 1, Priority 2,

Priority 3. Write each wish on the piece of paper where it fits, with Priority 1 being the most important, Priority 2 the second most important, and Priority 3 the third.

Look at your priority lists. What do they tell you about what is most important to you? What wishes are you ready to work toward right now? Circle three high-priority wishes that you want to achieve with your entry into a new career.

Name _____ Date _____

Journal Entry

Name _____ Date _____

Journal Entry

2 GOAL SETTING AND TIME MANAGEMENT: Mapping Your Course

Thinking It Through

Check those statements that apply to you right now:

❏ I haven't thought much about exactly what my values are.
❏ I set goals but don't always feel that I achieve them.
❏ I feel that my priorities have changed since I entered college.
❏ I have a date book but I don't use it all that much.
❏ I know it doesn't help me, but I procrastinate.

In this chapter, you will explore answers to the following questions:

➤ What defines your values?
➤ How do you set and achieve goals?
➤ What are your priorities?
➤ How can you manage your time?
➤ Why is procrastination a problem?

People dream of what they want out of life, but not everyone knows how to turn dreams into reality. Often dreams and goals seem far off in time, too difficult, or even completely unreachable. It may seem that you can't see the dream because of all the day-to-day details that get in your way. To make the climb to a place where you can see the big picture, identify the individual steps that you need to take to arrive at your destination. These steps take the format of goals. When you set goals, prioritize, and manage your time effectively, you increase your ability to achieve your dreams.

This chapter explains how taking specific steps toward goals can help you turn your dreams into reality. You will explore how your values relate to your goals. You will see how to create a framework for your life's goals—a personal mission statement—and how to set long-term and short-term goals. You will discover how setting priorities can help you work toward your goals more efficiently. The section on time management will reveal how to translate those goals into daily, weekly, monthly, and yearly steps to give shape and purpose to their achievement. Finally, you will explore the topic of procrastination—how it affects your life and what you can do to minimize the problems it may cause.

WHAT DEFINES YOUR VALUES?

Values,
Principles or qualities that one considers important, right, or good.

Your personal values—for example, family togetherness, a good education, caring for others, and worthwhile employment—are the beliefs that guide your choices for the sum total of all your values is your value system. You demonstrate your particular value system in the priorities you set, how you communicate with others, your family life, your educational and career choices, and even the material things with which you surround yourself.

Choosing and Evaluating Values

Examining the sources of your values—parents, friends, religious beliefs, authority figures, experiences—can help you define those values, trace their origin, and question why you have adopted them. Value sources, however, aren't as important as the process of considering each value carefully to see if it makes sense to you. Some of your current values may have come from television or other media but still ring true. Some may have come from what others have taught you. Some you may have constructed from your own personal experience and opinion.

Each individual value system is unique, even if many values originally come from other sources. Your responsibility is to make sure that your values are your own choice and not the choice of others. Make value choices based on what feels right for you, for your life, and for those involved in your life.

You can be more sure of making choices that are right for you if you try to periodically question and evaluate your values. Ask yourself: Does this value feel right? What effects does it, or might it, have on my life? Am I choosing it to please someone else, or is it truly my choice? Values are a design for life, and you are the one who has to live the life you design.

Life changes and new experiences may bring a change in values. From time to time, try to evaluate the effects that each value has on your life, and see if a shift in values might suit your changing circumstances. For example, the difficulty of a divorce may result in a new value of independence and individuality. After growing up in a homogeneous town, a student who meets other students from unfamiliar backgrounds may come to value living in a diverse community. Your values will grow and develop as you do if you continue to think them through.

How Values Relate to Goals

Understanding your values will help you set goals because any **goal** can help you achieve what you value. If you value spending time with your family, a related goal may be living near your parents. A value of financial independence may generate goals—such as working part time and keeping credit card debt low—that reflect this value. If you value helping others, you might make time for volunteer work.

    Goals enable you to put values into practice. When you set and pursue goals that are based on values, you demonstrate and reinforce values by taking action. The strength of those values, in turn, reinforces your goals. You will experience a stronger drive to achieve if you build goals around what is most important to you.

> **Goal,**
> An end toward which effort is directed; an aim or intention.

HOW DO YOU SET AND ACHIEVE GOALS?

A goal can be something as concrete as buying a health insurance plan or as abstract as working to control your temper. When you set goals and work to achieve them, you engage your intelligence, abilities, time, and energy in order to move ahead. From major life decisions to the tiniest day-to-day activities, setting goals will help you define how you want to live and what you want to achieve.

    Paul Timm, an expert in self-management, feels that focus is a key ingredient in setting and achieving goals: "Focus adds power to our actions. If somebody threw a bucket of water on you, you'd get wet....But if water was shot at you through a high-pressure nozzle, you might get injured. The only difference is focus."[1] Focus your goal-setting energy by defining a personal mission statement, placing your goals in long-term and short-term time frames, evaluating goals in terms of your values, and exploring different types of goals.

Identifying Your Personal Mission Statement

If you choose not to set goals or explore what you want out of life, you may look back on your past with a sense of emptiness. You may not know what you've done or why you did it. However, you can avoid such emptiness by periodically thinking about where you've been and where you want to be.

    One helpful way to determine your general direction is to write a personal mission statement. Dr. Stephen Covey, author of *The Seven Habits of Highly Effective People*, defines a mission statement as a philosophy outlining what you want to be (character), what you want to do (contributions and achievements), and the principles by which you live. Dr.

> "Obstacles are what people see when they take their eyes off the goal."
> New York subway bulletin board

Covey compares the personal mission statement to the Constitution of the United States, a statement of principles that guides the country: "A personal mission statement based on correct principles becomes the same kind of standard for an individual," he says. "It becomes a personal constitution, the basis for making major, life-directing decisions, the basis for making daily decisions in the midst of the circumstances and emotions that affect our lives."[2]

Your personal mission isn't written in stone. It should change as you move from one phase of life to the next—from single person to spouse, from student to working citizen. Stay flexible and reevaluate your personal mission from time to time.

> Here is an example of author Carol Carter's personal mission statement:
>
> My mission is to use my talents and abilities to help people of all ages, stages, backgrounds, and economic levels achieve their human potential through fully developing their minds and their talents. I also aim to balance work with people in my life, understanding that my family and friends are a priority above all else.

A company, like a person, needs to establish standards and principles that guide its many activities. Companies often have mission statements so that each member of the organization clearly understands what to strive for. If a company fails to identify its mission, a million well-intentioned employees might focus their energies in just as many different directions, creating chaos and low productivity.

Here is a mission statement from the company that publishes this text:

> To provide the most innovative resources—books, technology, programs—to help students of all ages and stages achieve their academic and professional goals inside the classroom and out.

You will have an opportunity to write your own personal mission statement at the end of this chapter. Thinking through your personal mission can help you begin to take charge of your life. It can put you in control instead of allowing circumstances and events to control you. If you frame your mission statement carefully so that it truly reflects your goals, it can be your guide in everything you do.

Placing Goals in Time

Everyone has the same 24 hours in a day, but it often doesn't feel like enough. Have you ever had a busy day flash by so quickly that it seems you accomplished nothing? Have you ever felt that way about a longer period of time, like a month or even a year? Your commitments can overwhelm you unless you decide how to use time to plan your steps toward goal achievement.

If developing a personal mission statement establishes the big picture, placing your goals within particular time frames allows you to bring individual areas of that picture into the foreground. Planning your progress step by step will help you maintain your efforts over the extended time period often needed to accomplish a goal. Goals fall into two categories: long term and short term.

Setting Long-term Goals

Establish first the goals that have the largest scope, the long-term goals that you aim to attain over a lengthy period of time, up to a few years or more. As a student, you know what long-term goals are all about. You have set yourself a goal to attend school and earn a degree or certificate. Becoming educated is an admirable goal that often takes years to reach.

Some long-term goals are lifelong, such as a goal to continually learn more about yourself and the world around you. Others have a more definite end, such as a goal to complete a course successfully. To determine your long-term goals, think about what you want out of your professional, educational, and personal life. Here is Carol Carter's long-term goal statement.

> *Carol's Goals:* To accomplish my mission through writing books, giving seminars, and developing programs that create opportunities for students to learn and develop. To create a personal, professional, and family environment that allows me to manifest my abilities and duly tend to each of my responsibilities.

For example, you may establish long-term goals such as these:

➤ I will graduate from school and know that I have learned all that I could, no matter what my GPA is.

➤ I will build my leadership and teamwork skills by forming positive, productive relationships with classmates, instructors, and coworkers.

Competitors strive to complete the New York Marathon

Long-term goals don't have to be lifelong goals. Think about your long-term goals for the coming year. Considering what you want to accomplish in a year's time will give you clarity, focus, and a sense of what needs to take place right away. When Carol thought about her long-term goals for the coming year, she came up with the following:

1. Develop programs to provide internships, scholarships, and other quality initiatives for students.

2. Allow time in my personal life to eat well, run five days a week, and spend quality time with family and friends. Allow time daily for quiet reflection and spiritual devotion.

In the same way that Carol's goals are tailored to her personality and interests, your goals should reflect who you are. Personal missions and goals are as unique as each individual. Continuing the example above, you might adopt these goals for the coming year:

➤ I will earn passing grades in all my classes.

➤ I will join two clubs and make an effort to take a leadership role in one of them.

Setting Short-term Goals

When you divide your long-term goals into smaller, manageable goals that you hope to accomplish within a relatively short time, you are setting short-term goals. Short-term goals narrow your focus, helping you to maintain your progress toward your long-term goals. They are the steps that take you where you want to go. Say you have set the two long-term goals you just read in the previous section. To stay on track toward those goals, you may want to accomplish these short-term goals in the next six months:

➤ I will pass Business Writing I so that I can move on to Business Writing II.

➤ I will attend four of the monthly meetings of the Journalism Club.

These same goals can be broken down into even smaller parts, such as one month.

➤ I will complete five of the ten essays for Business Writing I.

➤ I will write an article for next month's Journalism Club newsletter.

In addition to monthly goals, you may have short-term goals that extend for a week, a day, or even a couple of hours in a given day. Take as an example the article you have planned to write for the next month's Journalism Club newsletter. Such short-term goals may include the following:

➤ Three weeks from now: Final draft ready. Submit it to the editor of the newsletter.

➤ Two weeks from now: Second draft ready. Give it to one more person to review.

➤ One week from now: First draft ready. Ask my writing instructor if he will review it.

➤ By the end of today: Freewrite about the subject of the article, and narrow down to a specific topic.

➤ By 3:00 P.M. today: Brainstorm ideas for the article (more on brainstorming and freewriting in Chapter 8).

As you consider your long-term and short-term goals, notice how all of your goals are linked to one another. As Figure 2–1 shows, your long-term

FIGURE 2-1   **LINKING GOALS TOGETHER**

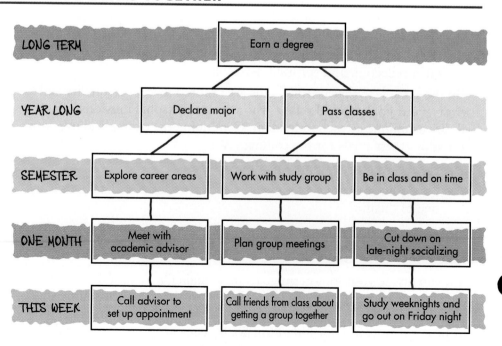

goals establish a context for the short-term goals. In turn, your short-term goals make the long-term goals seem clearer and more reachable. The whole system works to keep you on track.

Linking Goals with Values

If you are not sure how to start formulating your mission, look to your values to guide you. Define your mission and goals according to what is important to you.

If you value physical fitness, your mission statement might emphasize your commitment to staying in shape throughout your life. Your long-term goal might be to run a marathon, and your short-term goals might involve your weekly exercise and eating plan. Similarly, if you value a close family, your personal mission might emphasize family ties and stability. In this case, your long-term goals might involve finding a job that allows for family time. Your short-term goals may focus on helping your son learn a musical instrument or having dinner with your family at least twice a week.

Current and Personal Values Mean Appropriate Goals

When you use your values as a compass for your goals, make sure the compass is pointed in the direction of your real feelings. Watch out for the following two pitfalls.

Setting goals according to other peoples' values.   Friends or family may encourage you to strive for what they think you should value. You may, of course, share their values. If you follow advice that you don't believe in, however, you may have a harder time sticking to your path. For example, someone who attends school primarily because a parent thought it was right may have less motivation than someone who made an independent decision to become a student. Staying in tune with your own values will help you make decisions that are right for you.

Setting goals that reflect values you held in the past.   Life changes can alter your values. The best goals reflect what you believe today. For example, a person who has been through a near-fatal car accident may experience a dramatic increase in how he or she values time with friends and family and a drop in how he or she values material possessions. Someone who survives a serious illness may value healthy living above all else. Keep in touch with your life's changes so your goals can reflect who you are.

Different Kinds of Goals

People have many different goals, involving different parts of life and different values. Since school is currently a focus in your life, examine your educational goals.

Identifying Educational Goals

First, to define a context for your school goals, explore why you have decided to pursue an education. People have many reasons for attending college. You may identify with one or more of the following.

➤ I want to earn a higher salary.

➤ I want to build marketable skills in a particular career area.

➤ My supervisor at work says that a degree will help me move ahead in my career.

➤ Most of my friends were going.

➤ I want to be a student and learn all that I can.

➤ It seems like the only option for me right now.

➤ I am recently divorced and need to find a way to earn money.

➤ Everybody in my family goes to college; it's expected.

➤ I don't feel ready to jump into the working world yet.

➤ I got a scholarship.

➤ My friend loves her job and encouraged me to take courses in the field.

➤ My parent (or a spouse or partner) pushed me to go to college.

➤ I need to increase my skills so I can provide for my kids.

➤ I don't really know.

All of these answers are legitimate, even the last one. Being honest with yourself is crucial if you want to discover who you are and what life paths make sense for you. Whatever your reasons are for being in school, you are at the gateway to a journey of discovery.

It isn't easy to enroll in college, pay tuition, decide what to study, sign up for classes, gather the necessary materials, and actually get yourself to the school and into the classroom. Many people drop out at different places along the way, but somehow your reasons have been compelling enough for you to have arrived at this point. Thinking about why you value your education will help you stick with it.

After considering why you are here, start thinking about your educational goals—what you want out of being here. Consider what is available to you—classes, instructors, class schedule, and available degrees or certificates. Think about your commitment to academic excellence and whether honors and awards are important goals. If you have an idea of the career you want to pursue, consider the degree(s), certificate(s), or test(s) that may be required. Don't forget to ponder what you want out of your time in school in terms of learning, relationships, and personal growth.

Goals in Your Career and Personal Life

Establish your long-term and short-term goals for your other two paths—career and personal life—as well as for your educational path. Remember that all your goals are interconnected. A school goal is often a step toward a career goal and can affect a personal goal.

Career.   Think of your career goals in terms of both *job* and *financial* goals.

➤ First, consider the job you want after you graduate—requirements, job duties, hours, co-workers, salary, transportation, and company size and style. How much responsibility do you want? Do you want to become a manager, a supervisor, an independent contractor, or a business owner?

> ➤ Then, consider financial goals. How much money do you need to pay your bills, live comfortably, and save for the future? Do you need to borrow money for school or a major purchase such as a car? Do you need to reduce your bills? Compare your current financial picture to how you want to live, and set goals that will help you bridge the gap.

Personal life. Consider personal goals in terms of *self*, *family*, and *lifestyle*.

> ➤ First look at yourself—character, personality, health/fitness, and conduct. Do you want to gain confidence and knowledge? Get in shape? Change your social circle? Examine the difference between who you are and who you want to be.
>
> ➤ Then, consider your family goals. Do you want to stay single, marry, be a parent, or increase a family you've already started? Do you want to improve relations with a spouse or other family members? Do you want to live near relatives or far away?
>
> ➤ Finally, consider your ideal lifestyle—where you want to live, in what kind of space, and with whom. How do you want to participate in your community? What do you like to do in your leisure time? Consider goals that allow you to live the way you want to live.

Setting and working toward goals can be frightening and difficult at times. Like learning a new physical task, it takes a lot of practice and repeated efforts. As long as you do all that you can to achieve a goal, you haven't failed, even if you don't achieve it completely or in the time frame you had planned. Even one step in the right direction is an achievement. For example, if you wanted to raise your course grade to a B from a D, and you ended up with a C, you have still accomplished something important.

Achieving goals becomes easier when you are realistic about what is possible. Setting priorities will help you make that distinction.

WHAT ARE YOUR PRIORITIES?

When you set a priority, you identify what's important at any given moment. Prioritizing helps you focus on your most important goals, especially when the important ones are the most difficult. Human nature often leads people to tackle easy goals first and leave the tough ones for later. The risk is that you might never reach for goals that are crucial to your success.

Priority,
An action or intention that takes precedence in time, attention, or position.

To explore your priorities, think about your personal mission and look at your school, career, and personal goals. Do one or two of these paths take priority for you right now? In any path, which goals take priority? Which goals take priority over all?

You are a unique individual, and your priorities are yours alone. What may be top priority to someone else may not mean that much to you, and

WINDOWS ON THE WORLD: REAL LIFE STUDENT ISSUES

How can I stay focused on my school goals?

Rosalia Chavez, University of Arizona, Tuscon, Arizona, Public Administration Major

I married at eighteen and didn't finish high school. My husband became a cocaine addict and grew very possessive of me. After our two sons were born, I decided to get my GED, but he didn't want me to. At this point I knew I had to start making opportunities for myself.

Shortly after I had begun to further my education, my husband overdosed on drugs. His death was very traumatic and difficult to deal with. I am now taking classes full time at

the University of Arizona and I work part time in the Chicano/Hispano student affairs office. I don't feel I'm getting an education just for myself, but for future generations of Hispanic women. There's a view in traditional Hispanic families that women stay home and only the man provides. I would like to empower women by telling them my story and letting them know that they deserve to follow their dreams.

Even though I feel blessed, I have to make daily decisions about priorities, such as, "Do I take this test or stay home with my sick child?" Recently I had to drop a class because my children were sick and I couldn't keep up. My son, who is eleven, has ADHD (attention deficit hyperactivity disorder). He was on medication and under a doctor's care, but when I reapplied for state medical assistance I was denied. Now I can no longer afford his medicine. These situations hinder me as a student because I am so preoccupied.

Can you offer suggestions about how I can keep focused on my school goals?

Norma Seledon, Las Mujeres en Accion, Chicago, Illinois

Your story is not atypical. Your taking control of your life is, however, exemplary. Setting and sticking to your goals is not easy, particularly when you have cultural, societal and even religious factors working against. While women are often strong and tolerant, we sometimes don't give ourselves credit for our strengths. We need to surround ourselves with individuals and experiences that "feed our souls." Another essential is to main-

tain a balance. With many higher education programs designed for those without families it is challenging to meet the demands of school and family. Your desire to learn and grow not only for yourself but for your family and for the community at large will fuel your efforts.

I recognize some of your challenges. In my senior year I had a newborn, was pregnant, worked, and attended school full time. You must prioritize and pace yourself. It may help to speak to professors about your situation. My daughter was due at the midterm of my last semester, and some professors were flexible with assignments. It can't hurt to try.

As director of an organization whose primary focus is Latina leadership and working with survivors of domestic violence, it is difficult being a mother of two preteens and a preschooler. My son is also diagnosed with ADHD. I demand periodic meeting with a team of school officials so that we may approach my son's education from a team perspective.

With patience and perseverance, you will achieve your current goals and set more for yourself. Continue to develop a support system and to share your story. We must all continue to figure out how to distill the beauty and strength of our culture and traditions and discard those elements that hinder women's development. Felicidades!

TWO STUDENTS COMPARE PRIORITIES FIGURE 2-2

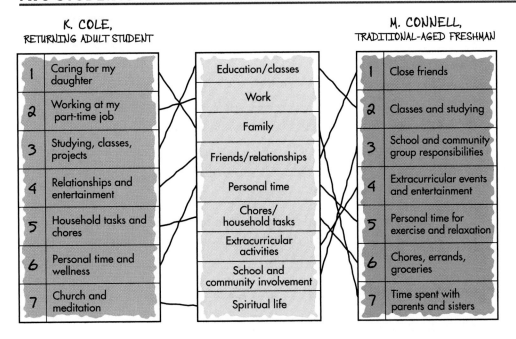

K. COLE,
RETURNING ADULT STUDENT

1. Caring for my daughter
2. Working at my part-time job
3. Studying, classes, projects
4. Relationships and entertainment
5. Household tasks and chores
6. Personal time and wellness
7. Church and meditation

Education/classes
Work
Family
Friends/relationships
Personal time
Chores/household tasks
Extracurricular activities
School and community involvement
Spiritual life

M. CONNELL,
TRADITIONAL-AGED FRESHMAN

1. Close friends
2. Classes and studying
3. School and community group responsibilities
4. Extracurricular events and entertainment
5. Personal time for exercise and relaxation
6. Chores, errands, groceries
7. Time spent with parents and sisters

vice versa. You can see this in Figure 2–2, which compares the priorities of two very different students. Each student's priorities are listed in order, with the first priority at the top and the lowest priority at the bottom.

First and foremost, your priorities should reflect your goals. In addition, they should reflect your relationships with others. For example, if you are a parent, your children's needs will probably be high on the priority list. You may be in school so you can get a better job and give them a better life. If you are in a committed relationship, you may schedule your classes so that you and your partner are home together as often as possible. Even as you consider the needs of others, though, be true to your own goals and priorities so that you can make the most of who you are.

Setting priorities moves you closer to accomplishing specific goals. It also helps you begin planning to achieve your goals within specific time frames. Being able to achieve your goals is directly linked to effective time management.

THINKING BACK

1. How can having a personal mission statement help you define your goals and priorities?

_____

_____

_____

2. Why is it important to have both short-term goals and long-term goals?

_____

_____

_____

_____

3. Name a short-term goal that you hope to accomplish in the next six months, and name a one-month goal that is a step toward the six-month goal.

Six-month goal: _____

_____

One-month goal: _____

_____

4. Name an educational goal, a career goal, and a personal goal of yours.

a. _____

_____

b. _____

_____

c. _____

_____

5. What does it mean to prioritize your goals?

_____

_____

_____

_____

THINKING AHEAD

1. What is your style of time management, and how would you rate yourself as a time manager?

_____

_____

2. What tools do you use that help you manage your time?

_____

_____

3. What kind of situation causes you the most difficulty in managing your time?

_____

_____

4. Do you ever put off things you know you should do? How does this behavior affect your life?

_____

_____

HOW CAN YOU MANAGE YOUR TIME?

Time is one of your most valuable and precious resources. Time doesn't discriminate—everyone has the same twenty-four hours in a day, every day. Your responsibility and your potential for success lie in how you use yours. You cannot change how time passes, but you can spend it wisely by taking steps to achieve your goals. Efficient time management helps you achieve your goals in a steady, step-by-step process.

People have a variety of approaches to time management. Your learning style (see Chapter 3) can help you understand how you use time. For example, students with strong logical-mathematical intelligence tend to organize activities within a framework of time. Because they stay aware of how long it takes them to do something or travel somewhere, they are usually prompt. By contrast, less logical learners with perhaps stronger visual or interpersonal intelligences may neglect such details as how much time they have to complete a task. They can often be late without meaning to be.

Time management, like physical fitness, is a lifelong pursuit. No one can plan a perfect schedule or build a terrific physique and then be "done."

Throughout your life, your ability to manage your time will vary with your stress level, how busy you are, and other factors. Don't expect perfection—just do your best and keep working at it. Time management involves building a schedule, taking responsibility for how you spend your time, and being flexible.

Building a Schedule

Just as a road map helps you travel from place to place, a schedule is a time-and-activity map that helps you get from the beginning of the day (or week or month) to the end as smoothly as possible. Schedules help you gain control of your life in two ways: They allocate segments of time for the fulfillment of your daily, weekly, monthly, and longer-term goals, and they serve as a concrete reminder of tasks, events, due dates, responsibilities, and deadlines. Few moments are more stressful than suddenly realizing you have forgotten to take a test or to be at your job. Scheduling can help you avoid events like these.

Keep a Date Book

A businesswoman writes in her daily planner

Gather the tools of the trade: a pen or pencil and a date book (sometimes called a planner). A date book is indispensable for keeping track of your time. Some of you have date books and may have used them for years. Others may have had no luck with them or have never tried. Even if you don't feel you would benefit from one, give it a try. Paul Timm says, "Most time management experts agree that rule number one in a thoughtful planning process is: Use some form of a planner where you can write things down."

There are two major types of date books. The day-at-a-glance version devotes a page to each day. Although it gives you ample space to write the day's activities, it's harder to see what's ahead. The week-at-a-glance book gives you a view of the week's plans but has less room to write per day. If you write detailed daily plans, you might like the day-at-a-glance version. If you prefer to remind yourself of plans ahead of time, try the book that shows a week's schedule all at once. Some date books contain sections for monthly and yearly goals. You can also create your own sheets for yearly and monthly notations in a notepad section, if your book has one, or on plain paper that you can then insert into the book.

Another option to consider is an electronic planner—a compact mini-computer that can hold a large amount of information. You can use it to schedule your days and weeks, make to-do lists, and create and store an address book. Electronic planners are powerful, convenient, and often fun. However, they certainly cost more than the paper version, and you can lose a lot of important data if something goes wrong with the computer inside. Evaluate your options and decide what works best for you.

Set Weekly and Daily Goals

The most ideal time management starts with the smallest tasks and builds to bigger ones. Setting short-term goals that tie in to your long-term goals has the following benefits:

➤ Increased meaning for your daily activities.

➤ Shaping your path toward the achievement of your long-term goals.

➤ A sense of order and progress.

For college students, as well as working people, the week is often the easiest unit of time to consider at one shot. Weekly goal setting and planning allows you to keep track of day-to-day activities while giving you the larger perspective of what is coming up during the week. Take some time before each week starts to remind yourself of your long-term goals. Keeping long-term goals in mind will help you determine related short-term goals that you can accomplish during the week to come.

Figure 2–3 shows parts of a daily schedule and a weekly schedule.

DAILY AND WEEKLY SCHEDULES
FIGURE 2-3

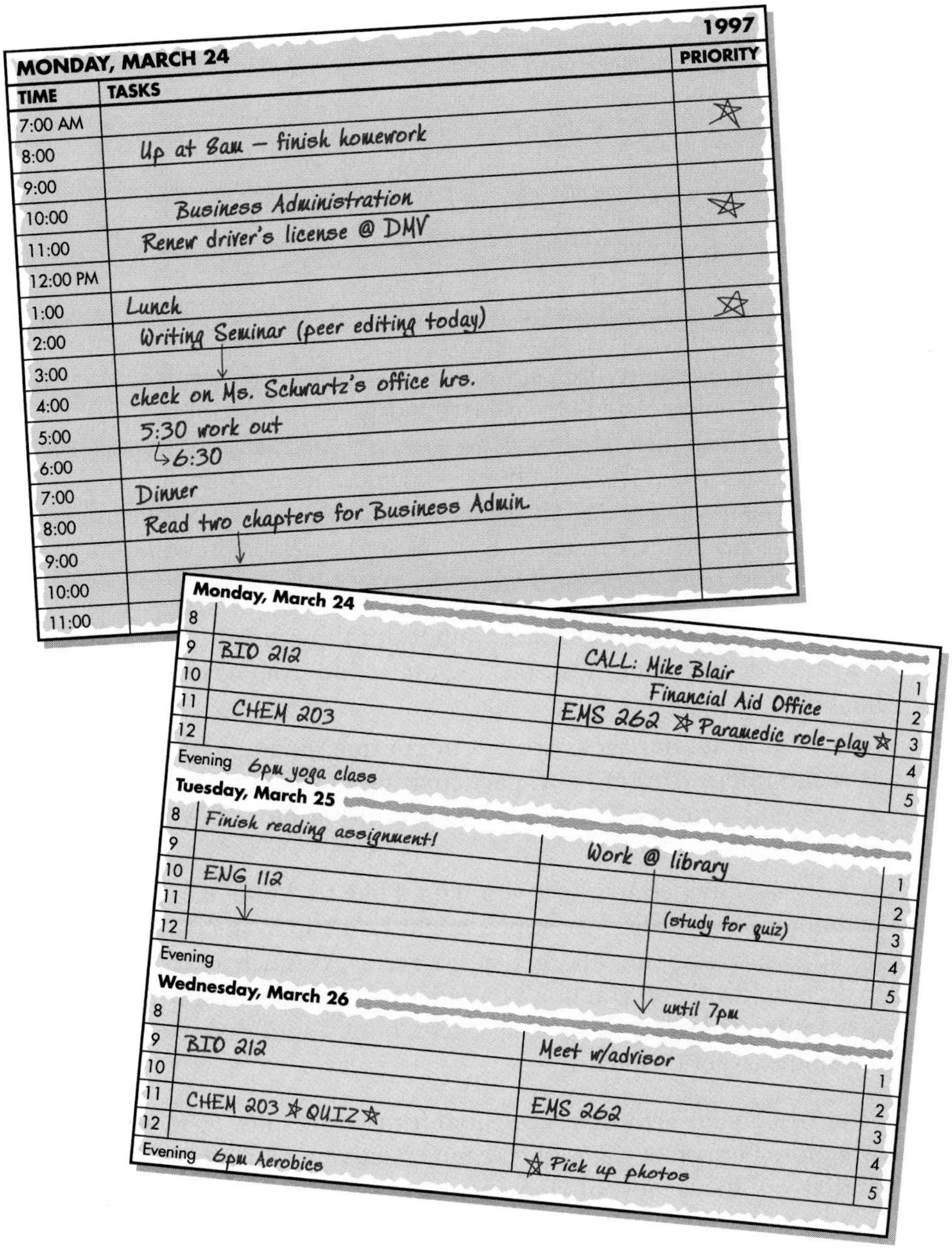

Link Daily and Weekly Goals with Long-term Goals

After you evaluate what you need to accomplish in the coming year, semester, month, week, and day to reach your long-term goals, use your schedule to record those steps. Write down the short-term goals that will enable you to stay on track. Here is how a student might map out two different goals over a year's time.

This year:	Complete enough courses to graduate. Improve my physical fitness.
This semester:	Complete my accounting class with a B average or higher. Lose 10 pounds and exercise regularly.
This month:	Set up study-group schedule to coincide with quizzes. Begin walking and weight lifting.
This week:	Meet with study group; go over material for Friday's quiz. Go for a fitness walk three times; go to weight room twice.
Today:	Go over Chapter 3 in accounting text. Walk for 40 minutes.

Prioritize Goals

Prioritizing enables you to use your date book with maximum efficiency. On any given day, your goals will have varying degrees of importance. Record your goals first, and then label them according to their level of importance, using these categories: Priority 1, Priority 2, and Priority 3. Identify these categories by using any code that makes sense to you. Some people use numbers, as above. Some use letters (A, B, C). Some write activities in different colors according to priority level. Some use symbols (*, +, -).

Priority 1 activities are the most important things in your life. They may include attending class, picking up a child from day care, and paying bills.

Priority 2 activities are part of your routine. Examples include grocery shopping, working out, participating in a school organization, or cleaning. Priority 2 tasks are important but more flexible than priority 1's.

Priority 3 activities are those you would like to do but can reschedule without much sacrifice. Examples might be a trip to the mall, a visit to a friend, a social phone call, or a sports event. As much as you would like to accomplish them, you don't consider them urgent. Many people don't enter priority 3 tasks in their date books until they are sure they have time to get them done.

Prioritizing your activities is essential for two reasons. First, some activities are more important than others, and effective time management requires that you focus most of your energy on priority 1 items. Second,

> "Even if you're on the right track, you'll get run over if you just sit there."
>
> Will Rogers

looking at all your priorities helps you plan when you can get things done. Often, it's not possible to get all your priority 1 activities done early in the day, especially if they involve scheduled classes or meetings. Prioritizing helps you set priority 1 items and then schedule priority 2 and 3 items around them as they fit.

Keep Track of Events

Your date book also enables you to schedule events. Think of events as how they tie in with your long-term goals, just as you would your other tasks. For example, attending a wedding in a few months contributes to your commitment to spending time with your family. Being aware of quiz dates, due dates for assignments, and meeting dates will aid your goals to achieve in school and become involved.

Note events in your date book so that you can be aware of them ahead of time. Write them in daily, weekly, monthly, or even yearly sections, where a quick look will remind you that they are approaching. Writing them down will also help you see where they fit in the context of all your other activities. For example, if you have three big tests and a presentation all in one week, you'll want to take time in the weeks before to prepare for them.

Following are some kinds of events worth noting in your date book:

➤ Due dates for papers, projects, presentations, and tests.

➤ Important meetings, medical appointments, or due dates for bill payments.

➤ Birthdays, anniversaries, social events, holidays, and other special occasions.

➤ Benchmarks for steps toward a goal, such as due dates for sections of a project or a deadline for losing five pounds on your way to twenty.

Taking Responsibility for How You Spend Your Time

When you plan your activities with an eye toward achieving your most important goals, you are taking responsibility for how you live. The following strategies will help you stay in charge of your choices.

Plan your schedule each week. Before each week starts, note events, goals, and priorities. Decide where to fit activities like studying and priority 3 items. For example, if you have a test on Thursday, you can plan study sessions on the preceding days. If you have more free time on Tuesday and Friday than on other days, you can plan workouts or priority 3 activities at those times. Looking at the whole week will help you avoid being surprised by something you had forgotten was coming up.

Make and use to-do lists. Use a to-do list to record the things you want to accomplish. If you generate a daily or weekly to-do list on a separate piece of paper, you can look at all tasks and goals at once. This will help

FIGURE 2-4   A SAMPLE MONTHLY CALENDAR

APRIL
1997

Sunday	Monday	Tuesday	Wednesday	Thursday
		1 *Turn in English paper topic*	2 Dentist 2pm	3
6 Frank's Birthday	7 9am PSYCH TEST WORK	8 6:30pm Meeting @ Student Ctr.	9	
13	(14) ENGLISH PAPER DUE! WORK	15		
20	21			
27				

you consider time frames and priorities. You might want to prioritize your tasks and transfer them to appropriate places in your date book. Some people create daily to-do lists right on their date book pages. You can tailor a to-do list to an important event such as exam week or an especially busy day when you have a family gathering or a presentation to make. This kind of specific to-do list can help you prioritize and accomplish an unusually large task load.

Make thinking about time a priority. Mr. Timm recommends that you devote a minimum of ten to fifteen minutes a day to planning your schedule. Although making a schedule takes time, it can mean hours of saved time later. Say you have two errands to run, both on the other side of town; not planning ahead could result in your driving across town twice in one day. Also, when you take time to write out your schedule, be sure to carry it with you and check it throughout the day. Find a date book size you like—there are books that fit into your briefcase, your bag, or even your pocket.

Post monthly and yearly calendars at home. Keeping a calendar on the wall will help you stay aware of important events. You can purchase one or draw it yourself, month by month, on plain paper. Use a yearly or a monthly version (Figure 2–4 shows part of a monthly calendar), and keep it where you can refer to it often. If you live with family or friends, make the calendar a group project so that you stay aware of each other's plans. Knowing each other's schedules can also help you avoid problems, such as two people needing the car at the same time.

Down time,
Quiet time set aside for relaxation and low-key activity.

Schedule down time. When you're wiped out from too much activity, you don't have the energy to accomplish as much. A little **down time** will refresh you and improve your attitude. Even half an hour a day will help. Fill the time with whatever relaxes you—having a snack, reading, watching television, playing a game or sport, walking, writing, or just doing nothing. Make down time a priority.

Judgments,
Considered opinions, assessments, or evaluations.

Shake off the judgments of others. A student who feels no one will hire him because of his weight may not search for jobs. A student who feels her instructor is prejudiced against her might not study for that instructor's course. Instead of letting **judgments** like these rob you of your control of your time, choose actions that improve your circumstances. If you lose a job, for example, spend an hour a day investigating other job opportunities. If you have trouble with an instructor, address the problem with that instructor directly and try to make the most of your time in the course. If that doesn't work, you could drop the course and retake it in summer school while working part time. Try to find an active option that will allow you to be in control.

Being Flexible

No matter how well you plan your time, the changes that life brings can make you feel out of control. One minute you seem to be on track, and the next minute chaos hits—in forms as minor as a room change for a class or as major as a medical emergency. Coping with changes can cause stress. As your stress level rises, your sense of control dwindles.

Although you cannot always choose your circumstances, you may have some control over how you *handle* them. Use the following ideas to cope with changes large and small.

Day-to-Day Changes

Anytime, small changes can result in priority shifts that jumble your schedule. On Monday, a homework assignment due in a week might be priority 2; then if you haven't gotten to it by Saturday, it has become priority 1. Sometimes a class may be canceled, and you will have extra time on your hands. Perhaps your baby-sitter doesn't show up, and you need to figure out how to provide care for your child.

To be prepared to reschedule tasks as priorities change, start with your mind-set. Think of change as part of life and you will be able to more effectively solve the dilemmas that come up. For some changes that occur frequently, you can think through a backup plan ahead of time (such as having a friend on call for emergency child care). For unexpected extra time on your hands, you could keep some work or reading with you. For others, the best you can do is to keep an open mind about possibilities and to remember to call on your resources in a pinch. Your problem-solving skills (see Chapter 4) will help you build your ability to adjust to whatever changes come your way.

Life Changes

Sometimes changes are more serious than a class schedule shift. Your car breaks down; your relationship falls apart; you fail a class; you or a close family member develops a medical problem; you get laid off at work. Such changes call for more extensive problem solving. They also require an ability to look at the big picture. Whereas a class change affects your schedule for a day, a medical problem may affect your schedule for much longer.

When life hands you a major curve ball, first remember that you still have some choices about how to handle the situation. Then sit down and figure them out, ideally with people who can help you think everything through. Explore all of your options before making a decision (again, the problem-solving and decision-making skills in Chapter 4 will serve you well here). Finally, make full use of your school resources. Your academic advi-

> "The right time is any time that one is still so lucky to have. Live!"
>
> Henry James

sor, counselor, dean, financial aid advisor, and/or instructors may have ideas and assistance to offer you—but they can only help if you let them know what you need.

No matter how well you schedule your time, you will have moments when it's hard to stay in control. Knowing how to identify and avoid procrastination will help you get back on track.

WHY IS PROCRASTINATION A PROBLEM?

Procrastination,
The act of putting off a task until another time.

Procrastination occurs when you postpone tasks. People procrastinate for different reasons. Having trouble with goal setting is one reason. People may project goals too far into the future, set unrealistic goals that are too frustrating to reach, or have no goals at all. People also procrastinate because they don't believe in their ability to complete a task or don't believe in themselves in general. Procrastination is human, and not every instance of procrastination means trouble. If it is taken to the extreme, however, procrastination can develop into a habit that will dominate a person's behavior and cause problems at school, on the job, and at home.

Jane B. Burka and Lenora M. Yuen, authors of *Procrastination: Why You Do It and What To Do About It*, say that habitual procrastinators are often perfectionists who create problems by using their ability to achieve as the only measure of their self-worth: "The performance becomes the only measure of the person; nothing else is taken into account. An outstanding performance means an outstanding person; a mediocre performance means a mediocre person....As long as you procrastinate, you never have to confront the real limits of your ability, whatever those limits are."[3] For the procrastinator, the fear of failure prevents taking the risk that could bring success.

Anti-procrastination Strategies

Following are some ways to fight your tendencies to procrastinate.

Weigh the benefits (to you and others) of completing the task versus the effects of procrastinating. What rewards lie ahead if you get it done? What will be the effects if you continue to put it off? Which situation has better effects? Chances are you will benefit more in the long term from facing the task head-on.

Set reasonable goals. Plan your goals carefully, allowing enough time to complete them. Unreasonable goals can be so intimidating that you do nothing at all. "Pay off the credit-card bill next month" could throw you. However, "Pay off the credit-card bill in ten months" might inspire you to take action.

Break the task into smaller parts. Look at the task in terms of its parts. How can you approach it step by step? If you can concentrate on achieving one small goal at a time, the task may become less of a burden. In addition, setting concrete time limits for each task may help you feel more in control.

Get started whether or not you "feel like it." Going from doing nothing to doing something is often the hardest part of avoiding procrastination. The motivation techniques from Chapter 1 might help you take the first step. Once you start, you may find it easier to continue.

Ask for help with tasks and projects at school, work, and home. You don't always have to go it alone. For example, if you have put off an assignment, ask your instructor for guidance. If you avoid a project because you dislike the employee with whom you have to work, talk to your supervisor about adjusting tasks or personnel. If you need accommodations because of a disability, don't assume that others know about it. Once you identify what's holding you up, see who can help you face the task.

Don't expect perfection. No one is perfect. Most people learn by starting at the beginning and wading through plenty of mistakes and confusion. It's better to try your best than to do nothing at all.

Procrastination is natural, but it can cause you problems if you let it get the best of you. When it does happen, take some time to think about the causes. What is it about this situation that frightens you or puts you off? Answering that question can help you address what causes lie underneath the procrastination. These causes might indicate a deeper issue that you can address.

In Hebrew, the word *chai* means "life," representing all aspects of life—spiritual, emotional, family, educational, and career. Individual Hebrew characters have number values. Because the characters in the word *chai* add up to eighteen, the number eighteen has come to be associated with good luck. The word *chai* is often worn as a good-luck charm. As you plan your goals, think about your view of luck. Many people feel that a person can create his or her own luck by pursuing goals persistently and staying open to possibilities and opportunities. Canadian novelist Robertson Davies once said, "What we call luck is the inner man externalized. We make things happen to us."

Consider that your vision of life may largely determine how you live. You can prepare the way for luck by establishing a personal mission and forging ahead toward your goals. If you believe that the life you want awaits you, you will be able to recognize and make the most of luck when it comes around. *L'Chaim*—to life, and good luck.

IMPORTANT POINTS TO REMEMBER

1. What defines your values?

Values are beliefs and standards, stemming from sources such as parents and friends, that are important to you. Together, they make up your value system, and they guide your life choices. Consider values carefully, questioning and evaluating each to see if it makes sense to you. Make responsible choices, based on what feels right. Because life changes can result in changing values, reassess your values as time goes by. Values can also help you set goals because most goals that are ideal for you will help you achieve what you value. Goals help you put values into practice.

2. How do you set and achieve goals?

A goal is an aim toward which you direct your efforts. Goals can be long term or short term. A personal mission statement helps you define your most important long-term goals and adjust to changing life circumstances. Placing goals within particular time frames—a week, a month, a semester—can help you plan how to pursue them, especially when short-term goals act as steps toward a long-term goal. If you link goals to your values, your goals will reflect what's important to you. Consider your goals in your educational life, your working life, and your personal life. Spend some time evaluating why you are in school and what you want to achieve.

3. What are your priorities?

A priority is an action or intention that takes precedence in time or importance. When you set priorities, you focus your time and energy on what is important to you and leave less important tasks until later. Explore priorities by thinking about your personal mission and what is most important among your goals. Your priorities should reflect your goals, your values, and your relationships with others. Setting priorities helps you to plan to achieve goals within specific time frames.

4. How can you manage your time?

Effective time management will help you achieve your goals. Building a schedule is your main time-management task. This involves using a date book, setting daily and weekly goals, linking those goals to long-term goals, prioritizing, and keeping track of events. When you take responsibility for how you spend your time, you are more able to take steps toward your goals. Taking responsibility means planning each week's schedule, using to-do lists, thinking about your time, posting monthly and yearly calendars, scheduling down time, and avoiding the judgments of others. Flexibility will help you handle the sudden schedule changes that will arise.

5. Why is procrastination a problem?

Procrastination, the habit of putting off tasks, can keep you from achieving your goals. Explore your reasons for procrastinating and take steps to overcome them. Strategies to fight procrastination include asking for help with tasks, weighing the positive and negative effects of procrastination, setting reasonable goals, breaking the task into parts, and avoiding perfectionism.

Name _____   Date _____

BUILDING SKILLS FOR COLLEGE, CAREER, AND LIFE SUCCESS
CHAPTER 2

TAKING STOCK:
REFINING YOUR THOUGHTS

Look back at the statements you explored at the start of the chapter (see Thinking It Through on p. 41). Observe whether your attitudes have changed and what you have learned by studying this chapter.

1. What do you believe are the most dominant sources of your values?

_____

_____

2. How can short-term goal steps help you achieve long-term goals?

_____

_____

3. What are the three levels of priorities? How do you prefer to code them in a date book? Name a priority of yours for this week that corresponds to each level.

_____

_____

4. How can using a date book help you stay focused on your goals? What kind of date book might work best for you?

_____

_____

5. Define procrastination. Give one example of how you have procrastinated recently and the effect it had on your life.

_____

6. Name one goal-setting or time-management strategy that you will try this week. What do you plan to do, and how do you think it will help you?

_____

_____

_____

CRITICAL THINKING:
APPLYING LEARNING TO YOUR LIFE

Your Values

Begin to explore your values by rating the following values on a scale from 1 to 4, 1 being least important to you, and 4 being most important. If you have values that you don't see in the chart, list them in the blank spaces and rate them.

VALUE	RATING	VALUE	RATING
Knowing yourself		Mental health	
Physical health		Fitness/exercise	
Spending time with family		Close friendships	
Helping others		Education	
Being well paid		Being employed	
Being liked by others		Free time/vacations	
Enjoying entertainment		Time to yourself	
Spiritual/religious life		Reading	
Keeping up with news		Staying organized	
Financial stability		Intimate relationship	
Creative/artistic pursuits		Self-improvement	
Lifelong learning		Facing your fears	

Considering your priorities, write your top five values here:

1. _____

2. _____

3. _____

4. _____

5. _____

Short-term Scheduling

Take a close look at your schedule for the coming month, including events, important dates, and steps toward goals. On the calendar layout that follows, fill in the name of the month and appropriate numbers for the days. Then record what you hope to accomplish, including the following:

➤ Due dates for papers, projects, and presentations.

➤ Test dates.

➤ Important meetings, medical appointments, and due dates for bill payments.

➤ Birthdays, anniversaries, and other special occasions.

➤ Steps toward long-term goals.

This kind of chart will help you see the monthly big picture. To stay on target from day to day, check these dates against the entries in your date book and make sure that they are indicated there as well.

Discover How You Spend Your Time

In the chart below, estimate the total time you think you spend per week on each listed activity. Then add the hours. If your number is over 168 (the number of hours in a week), rethink your estimates and recalculate so that the total is equal to or below 168. Then subtract your total from 168. Whatever is left over is your estimate of hours that you spend in unscheduled activities.

ACTIVITY	ESTIMATED TIME SPENT
Class	
Work	
Studying	
Sleeping	
Eating	
Family time/child care	
Commuting/traveling	
Chores and personal business	
Friends and important relationships	
Telephone time	
Leisure/entertainment	
Spiritual life	

168

Minus total _____

Unscheduled time _____

Now spend a week recording exactly how you spend your time. The following chart has blocks showing half-hour increments. As you go through the week, write in what you do each hour, indicating when you started and when you stopped. Don't forget activities that don't feel like "activities," such as sleeping, relaxing, and watching television. Also, be honest—record your actual activities instead of how you want to spend your time or how you think you should have spent your time. There are no wrong answers.

MONDAY		TUESDAY		WEDNESDAY		THURSDAY	
TIME	ACTIVITY	TIME	ACTIVITY	TIME	ACTIVITY	TIME	ACTIVITY
5:00 AM		5:00 AM		5:00 AM		5:00 AM	
5:30 AM		5:30 AM		5:30 AM		5:30 AM	
6:00 AM		6:00 AM		6:00 AM		6:00 AM	
6:30 AM		6:30 AM		6:30 AM		6:30 AM	
7:00 AM		7:00 AM		7:00 AM		7:00 AM	
7:30 AM		7:30 AM		7:30 AM		7:30 AM	
8:00 AM		8:00 AM		8:00 AM		8:00 AM	
8:30 AM		8:30 AM		8:30 AM		8:30 AM	
9:00 AM		9:00 AM		9:00 AM		9:00 AM	
9:30 AM		9:30 AM		9:30 AM		9:30 AM	
10:00 AM		10:00 AM		10:00 AM		10:00 AM	
10:30 AM		10:30 AM		10:30 AM		10:30 AM	
11:00 AM		11:00 AM		11:00 AM		11:00 AM	
11:30 AM		11:30 AM		11:30 AM		11:30 AM	
12:00 PM		12:00 PM		12:00 PM		12:00 PM	
12:30 PM		12:30 PM		12:30 PM		12:30 PM	
1:00 PM		1:00 PM		1:00 PM		1:00 PM	
1:30 PM		1:30 PM		1:30 PM		1:30 PM	
2:00 PM		2:00 PM		2:00 PM		2:00 PM	
2:30 PM		2:30 PM		2:30 PM		2:30 PM	
3:00 PM		3:00 PM		3:00 PM		3:00 PM	
3:30 PM		3:30 PM		3:30 PM		3:30 PM	
4:00 PM		4:00 PM		4:00 PM		4:00 PM	
4:30 PM		4:30 PM		4:30 PM		4:30 PM	
5:00 PM		5:00 PM		5:00 PM		5:00 PM	
5:30 PM		5:30 PM		5:30 PM		5:30 PM	
6:00 PM		6:00 PM		6:00 PM		6:00 PM	
6:30 PM		6:30 PM		6:30 PM		6:30 PM	
7:00 PM		7:00 PM		7:00 PM		7:00 PM	
7:30 PM		7:30 PM		7:30 PM		7:30 PM	
8:00 PM		8:00 PM		8:00 PM		8:00 PM	
8:30 PM		8:30 PM		8:30 PM		8:30 PM	
9:00 PM		9:00 PM		9:00 PM		9:00 PM	
9:30 PM		9:30 PM		9:30 PM		9:30 PM	
10:00 PM		10:00 PM		10:00 PM		10:00 PM	
10:30 PM		10:30 PM		10:30 PM		10:30 PM	
11:00 PM		11:00 PM		11:00 PM		11:00 PM	
11:30 PM		11:30 PM		11:30 PM		11:30 PM	

FRIDAY		SATURDAY		SUNDAY	
TIME	ACTIVITY	TIME	ACTIVITY	TIME	ACTIVITY
5:00 AM		5:00 AM		5:00 AM	
5:30 AM		5:30 AM		5:30 AM	
6:00 AM		6:00 AM		6:00 AM	
6:30 AM		6:30 AM		6:30 AM	
7:00 AM		7:00 AM		7:00 AM	
7:30 AM		7:30 AM		7:30 AM	
8:00 AM		8:00 AM		8:00 AM	
8:30 AM		8:30 AM		8:30 AM	
9:00 AM		9:00 AM		9:00 AM	
9:30 AM		9:30 AM		9:30 AM	
10:00 AM		10:00 AM		10:00 AM	
10:30 AM		10:30 AM		10:30 AM	
11:00 AM		11:00 AM		11:00 AM	
11:30 AM		11:30 AM		11:30 AM	
12:00 PM		12:00 PM		12:00 PM	
12:30 PM		12:30 PM		12:30 PM	
1:00 PM		1:00 PM		1:00 PM	
1:30 PM		1:30 PM		1:30 PM	
2:00 PM		2:00 PM		2:00 PM	
2:30 PM		2:30 PM		2:30 PM	
3:00 PM		3:00 PM		3:00 PM	
3:30 PM		3:30 PM		3:30 PM	
4:00 PM		4:00 PM		4:00 PM	
4:30 PM		4:30 PM		4:30 PM	
5:00 PM		5:00 PM		5:00 PM	
5:30 PM		5:30 PM		5:30 PM	
6:00 PM		6:00 PM		6:00 PM	
6:30 PM		6:30 PM		6:30 PM	
7:00 PM		7:00 PM		7:00 PM	
7:30 PM		7:30 PM		7:30 PM	
8:00 PM		8:00 PM		8:00 PM	
8:30 PM		8:30 PM		8:30 PM	
9:00 PM		9:00 PM		9:00 PM	
9:30 PM		9:30 PM		9:30 PM	
10:00 PM		10:00 PM		10:00 PM	
10:30 PM		10:30 PM		10:30 PM	
11:00 PM		11:00 PM		11:00 PM	
11:30 PM		11:30 PM		11:30 PM	

Now go through the following chart and look at how many hours you actually spent on the activities for which you estimated your hours before. Tally the hours in the boxes in the following table using straight tally marks; round off to half hours and use a short tally mark for a half hour spent. In the third column, total the hours for each activity. Leave the "ideal time in hours" column blank for now.

ACTIVITY	TIME TALLIED OVER ONE-WEEK PERIOD	TOTAL TIME IN HOURS	IDEAL TIME IN HOURS
Example: Class	~~HHt~~ ~~HHt~~ ~~HHt~~ I	16.5	
Class			
Work			
Studying			
Sleeping			
Eating			
Family time/child care			
Commuting/traveling			
Chores and personal business			
Friends and important relationships			
Telephone time			
Leisure/entertainment			
Spiritual life			

Add the totals in the third column to find your GRAND TOTAL: _____

Compare your grand total to your estimated grand total; compare your actual activity hour totals to your estimated activity hour totals. What matches and what doesn't? Describe the most interesting similarities and differences.

_____

_____

What is the one biggest surprise about how you spend your time?

_____

_____

Name one change you would like to make in how you spend your time.

_____

_____

Think about what kinds of changes might help you improve your ability to set and achieve goals. Ask yourself important questions about what you do daily, weekly, and monthly. On what activities do you think you should spend more or less time? Go back to the chart on page 70 and fill in the Ideal Time in Hours column. Consider the difference between actual hours and ideal hours when you think about the changes you want to make in your life.

To-Do Lists

Make a to-do list for what you have to do tomorrow. Include all tasks—priority 1, 2, and 3—and events.

TOMORROW'S DATE _____

1. _____

2. _____

3. _____

4. _____

5. _____

6. _____

7. _____

8. _____

9. _____

10. _____

11. _____

12. _____

● Use a coding system of your choice to indicate priority level of both tasks and events. Use this list to make your schedule for tomorrow in the date book, making a separate list for priority 3 items. At the end of the day, evaluate this system—write below if the list made a difference, and if so, how. If you liked it, use this exercise as a guide for using to-do lists regularly.

_____

_____

_____

_____

Your Procrastination Habits

Name one situation in which you habitually procrastinate.

_____

_____

● _____

_____

What are the effects of your procrastination? Discuss how procrastination may affect the quality of your work, motivation, productivity, ability to be on time, grades, or self-perception.

_____

_____

_____

_____

What you would like to do differently in this situation? How can you achieve what you want?

_____

_____

● _____

_____

TEAMWORK: COMBINING FORCES

Individual priorities. In a group of three or four people, brainstorm long-term goals and have one member of the group write them down. From that list, pick out ten goals that everyone can relate to most. Each group member should then take five minutes alone to evaluate the relative importance of the ten goals and rank them in the order that he or she prefers. Use a 1-to-10 scale, with 1 being the highest priority and 10 the lowest.

Display the rankings of each group member side by side. How many different orders are there? Discuss why each person has a different set of priorities, and be open to different views. What factors in different people's lives have caused them to select particular rankings? If you have time, discuss how priorities have changed for each group member over the course of a year, perhaps by having each person rerank the goals according to his or her needs a year ago.

WRITING: DISCOVERY THROUGH JOURNALING

To record your thoughts, use a separate journal or the lined pages at the end of the chapter.

Personal mission statement. Using the personal mission statement examples in the chapter as a guide, consider what you want out of your life and create your own personal mission statement. You can write it in paragraph form, in a list of long-term goals, or in the form of a think link. Take as much time as you need to be as complete as possible. Write a draft on a separate sheet of paper and take time to revise it before you write the final version here. If you have created a think link rather than a verbal statement, attach it separately.

CAREER PORTFOLIO: CHARTING YOUR COURSE

Career goals and priorities. The most reasonable and reachable career goals are ones that are linked with your school and life goals.

First, name a long-term career goal of yours.

Then imagine that you will begin working toward it. Indicate a series of steps you can take—from short term to long term—that you feel will help you achieve this goal. Write what you hope to accomplish in the next year, the next six months, the next month, the next week, and the next day.

TIME FRAME	CAREER GOAL
One year	
Six months	
One month	
This week	
Today	

Now, explore your job priorities. How do you want your job to benefit you? Note your requirements in each of the following areas.

Salary/wage level _____

Time of day _____

Hours per week (part time vs. full time) _____

Duties _____

Location _____

Flexibility _____

Affiliation with school or financial aid program _____

What kind of job, in the career area for which you listed your goals, might fit all or most of your requirements? List two possibilities here.

1. _____

2. _____

Name _____ Date_____ ●

Journal Entry

Name _____ Date _____

Journal Entry

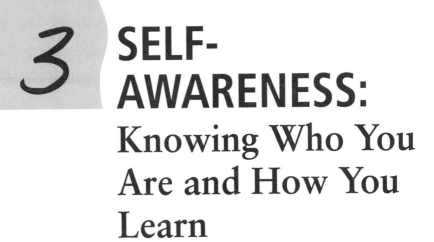

3 SELF-AWARENESS: Knowing Who You Are and How You Learn

Thinking It Through

Check those statements that apply to you right now:

- ❏ I'm not sure what "learning style" means.
- ❏ I feel out of touch in some of my classes.
- ❏ I'm not sure how my learning styles would be linked to the career I choose.
- ❏ I know I have some habits that I'd like to change.
- ❏ I don't know what I want to major in yet.

In this chapter, you will explore answers to the following questions:

- ➤ Is there one best way to learn?
- ➤ How can you discover your learning styles?
- ➤ What are the benefits of knowing your learning styles?
- ➤ How do you explore who you are?
- ➤ How can you start thinking about choosing a major?

Learning is not something you do just in college. Throughout your life, learning can help you keep up with the rapid pace at which technology is changing the world. The Internet allows people to send documents and photographs over phone lines in the blink of an eye. Cameras, cars, stereos, and all kinds of other items have computer chips inside them that control their operation. Medical science has discovered how to isolate the genes that cause certain genetic diseases and characteristics.

Technology is changing so fast that you cannot learn today about everything that will be commonplace five years from now. However, you can learn how to be an effective learner in school and in the workplace so that you can keep pace with changes and continue to grow as a person. In this chapter you will become aware of your learning style by completing an assessment based on the multiple intelligences theory. You will then explore other important elements of self: your self-perception, your preferences, your habits, your abilities, and your limitations.

IS THERE ONE BEST WAY TO LEARN?

Your mind is the most powerful tool you will ever possess. You are accomplished at many skills and can process all kinds of information. However, when you have trouble accomplishing a particular task, you may become convinced that you can't learn how to do anything new. You may feel that those who can do what you can't have the "right" kind of ability. Not only is this perception incorrect, it can also damage your belief in yourself.

Every individual is highly developed in some abilities and underdeveloped in others. Many famously successful people were brilliant in one area but functioned poorly in other areas. Winston Churchill failed the sixth grade. Abraham Lincoln was demoted to a private in the Black Hawk war. Louis Pasteur was a poor student in chemistry. Walt Disney was fired from a job and told he had no good ideas. What some might interpret as a deficiency or disability may be simply a different method of learning.

Learning style,

A particular way in which the mind receives and processes information.

There is no one "best" way to learn. Instead, there are many different learning styles, and different styles are suited to different situations. Each person's **learning style** is unique. Just like personality traits, learning styles are part of people's personal characteristics. Knowing how you learn is one of the first steps in discovering who you are.

HOW CAN YOU DISCOVER YOUR LEARNING STYLES?

Many different assessments give people a method of discovering how they learn. These assessments provide different means of exploring strengths and weaknesses, abilities and limitations. This chapter focuses on one particular assessment. If you want to explore learning styles further, see the two additional assessments in Appendix (2). You can also find information about other assessments, such as the widely used Myers-Briggs Type Indicator (MBTI) or the Keirsey Sorter (a shorter version of the MBTI), through your career or counseling center or even on-line.

After you complete the assessment in this chapter, you will read about strategies that can help you make the most of particular aspects of your style, both in school and beyond. Knowing how you learn will help you to improve your understanding of yourself—how you may function at school, in the workplace, and in your personal life.

Multiple Intelligences Theory

There is a saying, "It is not how smart you are, but how you are smart." In 1983, Howard Gardner, a Harvard University professor, published his theory of multiple intelligences and changed the way people perceive

intelligence and learning. Gardner believes there are at least eight distinct intelligences possessed by all people, and that every person has developed some intelligences more fully than others. Most people have at one time learned something very quickly and comfortably. Most have also had the opposite experience: No matter how hard they tried, something they wanted to learn just would not sink in. According to the multiple intelligences theory, when you find a task or subject easy, you are probably using a more fully developed intelligence; when you have more trouble, you may be using a less developed intelligence.[1]

Following are brief descriptions of the focus of each of the intelligences. Study skills that reinforce each intelligence will be described later in the chapter.

> *Verbal-linguistic intelligence*—ability to communicate through language (listening, reading, writing, speaking)
> *Logical-mathematical intelligence*—ability to understand logical reasoning and problem solving (math, science, patterns, sequences)
> *Bodily-* **kinesthetic** *intelligence*—ability to use the physical body skillfully and to take in knowledge through bodily sensation (coordination, working with hands)
> *Visual-spatial intelligence*—ability to understand spatial relationships and to perceive and create images (visual art, graphic design, charts and maps)
> *Interpersonal intelligence*—ability to relate to others, noticing their moods, motivations, and feelings (social activity, cooperative learning, teamwork)
> *Intrapersonal intelligence*—ability to understand one's own behavior and feelings (self-awareness, independence, time spent alone)
> *Musical intelligence*—ability to comprehend and create meaningful sound (music, sensitivity to sound, understanding patterns)
> Naturalistic intelligence—ability to understand features of the environment (interest in nature, environmental balance, ecosystem, stress relief brought by natural environments)

The multiple intelligences reach beyond helping you understand how you learn. They help you to see how you operate in every arena of life—how you think, how you relate to others, how you understand yourself, and more. Because this chapter focuses on learning styles, however, your collective set of scores will be referred to here as your "learning style." Elsewhere in the text you will find references that illustrate how the intelligences influence other skills and life areas.

Please complete the assessment of your multiple intelligences, called Pathways to Learning. It will help you determine the levels to which your intelligences are developed. Don't be concerned if some of your scores are low. That is true of almost everyone, even your instructors and your authors. In addition, try to answer the questions objectively—look closely at yourself and mark the answers that best indicate who you are, not who you want to be. The more closely you can see who you are today, the more effectively you can set goals for where you want to go from here.

Intelligence,
As defined by H. Gardner, an ability to solve problems or fashion products that are useful in a particular cultural setting or community.

Kinesthetic,
Coming from physical sensation caused by body movements and tensions.

PATHWAYS TO LEARNING[2]

Directions: Rate each statement as follows:

rarely	sometimes	usually	always
1	2	3	4

Write the number of your response (1–4) on the line next to the statement and total each set of six questions.

1. ____ I enjoy physical activities.
2. ____ I am uncomfortable sitting still.
3. ____ I prefer to learn through doing.
4. ____ When sitting I move my leg or hands.
5. ____ I enjoy working with my hands.
6. ____ I like to pace when I'm thinking or studying.

____ **TOTAL for Bodily-Kinesthetic**

7. ____ I use maps easily.
8. ____ I draw pictures/diagrams when explaining ideas.
9. ____ I can assemble items easily from diagrams.
10. ____ I enjoy drawing or photography.
11. ____ I do not like to read long paragraphs.
12. ____ I prefer a drawn map over written directions.

____ **TOTAL for Visual-Spatial**

13. ____ I enjoy telling stories.
14. ____ I like to write.
15. ____ I like to read.
16. ____ I express myself clearly.
17. ____ I am good at negotiating.
18. ____ I like to discuss topics that interest me.

____ **TOTAL for Verbal-Linguistic**

19. ____ I like math in school.
20. ____ I like science.
21. ____ I problem-solve well.
22. ____ I question how things work.
23. ____ I enjoy planning or designing something new.
24. ____ I am able to fix things.

____ **TOTAL for Logical Mathematical**

25. ____ I listen to music.
26. ____ I move my fingers or feet when I hear music.
27. ____ I have good rhythm.
28. ____ I like to sing along with music.
29. ____ People have said I have musical talent.
30. ____ I like to express my ideas through music.

____ **TOTAL for Musical**

31. ____ I like doing a project with other people.
32. ____ People come to me to help settle conflicts.
33. ____ I like to spend time with friends.
34. ____ I am good at understanding people.
35. ____ I am good at making people feel comfortable.
36. ____ I enjoy helping others.

____ **TOTAL for Interpersonal**

37. ____ I need quiet time to think.
38. ____ I think about issues before I want to talk.
39. ____ I am interested in self-improvement.
40. ____ I understand my thoughts and feelings.
41. ____ I know what I want.
42. ____ I prefer to work on projects alone.

____ **TOTAL for Intrapersonal**

43. ____ I enjoy nature whenever possible.
44. ____ I think about having a career involving nature.
45. ____ I enjoy studying plants, animals, or oceans.
46. ____ I avoid being indoors except when I sleep.
47. ____ As a child I played with bugs and leaves.
48. ____ When I feel stressed I want to be out in nature.

____ **TOTAL for Naturalistic**

Below are eight empty bars, corresponding to the eight intelligences. For each intelligence, draw a line at your score and fill in the bar below the line.

Score	Bodily–Kinesthetic	Visual–Spatial	Verbal Linguistic	Logical–Mathematical	Musical	Interpersonal	Intrapersonal	Naturalistic
23								
22								
21								
20								
19								
18								
17								
16								
15								
14								
13								
12								
11								
10								
9								
8								
7								
6								
5								
4								
3								
2								
1								
0								

The Reasonable Approach to Learning Style

No learning style assessment can give you the final word on who you are and what you can and cannot do. It's human to want an easy answer—a one-page printout of the secret to your identity—but this kind of quick fix does not exist. You are a complex person who cannot be summed up by a test or evaluation.

The most reasonable way to approach any learning style assessment is as a reference point rather than as a label. There are no "right" answers, no "best" set of intelligences scores. Instead of boxing yourself into one or more categories, which limits you, approach your learning style assessment as a tool with which you can expand your idea of yourself. Think of it as a new set of eyeglasses for a person with somewhat blurred vision. The glasses will not create new paths and possibilities for you, but they will help you see more clearly the paths and possibilities that already exist. They give you the power to explore and to choose and to move ahead with confidence.

You will continually learn, change, and grow throughout your life. Any evaluation is simply a snapshot, a look at who you are at a given moment. The answers can, and will, change as you change and as circumstances change. They provide an opportunity for you to identify a moment and learn from it by asking questions: Who am I right now? How does this compare to who I want to be?

Use Multiple Intelligences for Understanding

Understanding your multiple intelligences will help you understand your-self. Avoid labeling yourself narrowly by using one intelligence, such as if you were to say, "I'm no good in math." Anyone can learn math; however, some people learn math more efficiently through intelligences other than logical-mathematical. For example, a visual-spatial learner may want to draw diagrams of as much of a math problem as possible.

People are a blend of all the multiple intelligences, in proportions unique to them. Most people are a blend of styles and preferences, with one or two being dominant. When material is very difficult or when you are feeling insecure about learning something new, use your most developed multiple intelligences. When something is easy for you, however, this is an opportunity for you to improve your less developed multiple intelligences. All of your multiple intelligences will continue to develop throughout your lifetime. Learn as much as you can about your preferences and how you can maximize your learning.

In addition, you may change which multiple intelligences you emphasize, depending on the situation. For example, a student might find it easy to take notes in outline style when the instructor lectures in an organized way. However, if another instructor jumps from topic to topic, the student might choose to use the Cornell system or a think link (Chapter 7 goes into detail about note-taking styles).

WHAT ARE THE BENEFITS OF KNOWING YOUR LEARNING STYLES?

Determining your learning style takes work and self-exploration. Understanding your learning style, however, can benefit you in many ways. The following sections will discuss the positive effects of exploring how you learn.

Study Benefits

Most students aim to maximize learning while minimizing frustration and time spent studying. If you know your most and least developed multiple intelligences, you can use techniques that take advantage of your highly developed areas while helping you through your less developed ones. For example, say you perform better in smaller, discussion-based classes. When you have the opportunity, you might choose a course section that is smaller or that is taught by an instructor who prefers group discussion. You might also apply specific strategies to improve your retention in a large-group lecture.

This section describes the techniques that tend to complement the strengths and shortcomings of each intelligence. Remember that you have abilities in all multiple intelligence areas, even though some are dominant. Therefore, you may see useful suggestions under any of the headings. What's important is that you use what works. During this course, try a large number of new study techniques, eventually keeping those you find to be useful.

Bodily-kinesthetic learners like to apply information to the real world. Rather than just reading about something or looking at a visual representation of it, they learn best by taking in information through their own hands-on actions and experiences.

Student-suggested strategies for bodily-kinesthetic learners:

> ➤ Study in a group in which members take turns explaining topics to each other and then discussing them.

➤ Think of practical uses of the course material.

➤ Pace and recite while you learn.

➤ Act out material or design games.

➤ Use flash cards with other people.

➤ Teach the material to someone else.

Visual-spatial learners remember best what they see: diagrams, flowcharts, time lines, films, and demonstration. They may tend to forget spoken words and ideas. Classes generally don't include that much visual information. Note that although words written on paper or shown with an overhead projector are something you see, visual learners learn best from visual cues that don't involve words.

Student-suggested strategies for visual-spatial learners:

➤ Add diagrams to your notes whenever possible. Dates can be drawn on a time line; math functions can be graphed; percentages can be drawn in a pie chart.

➤ Organize your notes so that you can clearly see main points and supporting facts and how things are connected. You will learn more about different styles of note taking in Chapter 7.

➤ Connect related facts in your notes by drawing arrows.

➤ Color-code your notes with differently colored highlighters so that everything relating to a particular topic is the same color.

A student at Renton Technical College connects wires to electronic devices

Verbal-linguistic learners remember much of what they hear and more of what they hear and then say. They benefit from discussion, prefer verbal explanation to visual demonstration, and learn effectively by explaining things to others. Because written words are processed as verbal information, verbal learners learn well through reading. The majority of classes, since they present material through the written word, lecture, or discussion, are geared to verbal learners.

Student-suggested strategies for verbal-linguistic learners:

➤ Talk about what you learn. Work in study groups so that you have an opportunity to explain and discuss what you are learning.

➤ Read the textbook and highlight no more than 10 percent.

➤ Rewrite your notes.

➤ Outline chapters.

➤ Recite information or write scripts and debates.

Logical-mathematical learners retain and understand information better after they have taken time to analyze it carefully. They prefer to organize facts into some kind of system or structure. They also learn information more effectively when it is presented in a structured way.

Student-suggested strategies for logical-mathematical learners:

➤ Organize material logically.

➤ Explain it sequentially to someone.

➤ Develop systems and find patterns within groups of information.

➤ Write outlines and develop charts and graphs.

➤ Write short summaries of the key points of the material.

Musical learners have strong memories for rhymes and can be energized by music. They often have a song running through their minds and find themselves tapping a foot or their fingers when they hear music. They tend to learn information well when it is organized into patterns, similar to musical patterns.

Student-suggested strategies for musical learners:

➤ Create rhymes out of vocabulary words.

➤ Beat out rhythms while studying.

➤ Organize information into structured patterns.

➤ Play instrumental music while studying if it does not distract you, but first determine what type of music most improves your concentration.

➤ Take study breaks and listen to music.

➤ Write a song or rap about your topic, or put new words (containing study information) to a tune you already know.

Interpersonal learners learn effectively when interacting with others. They enjoy and benefit from discussing information with others or explaining to others what they have learned. They often prefer discussion-based classroom environments.

Student-suggested strategies for interpersonal learners:

➤ Study in a group in which members take turns explaining topics to one another and then discuss them.

➤ Whenever possible, choose classes that include extensive use of discussion.

➤ With one or more other students, use flash cards to quiz each other.

➤ Teach the material to someone, or have that person teach it to you.

> "To be what we are, and to become what we are capable of becoming, is the only end of life."
>
> Robert Louis Stevenson

Intrapersonal learners retain and understand information better after they have taken some time to think about it. They benefit from solo reading and studying and tend to process information over time. They may prefer lecture settings or courses that involve independent study and individual research projects.

Student-suggested strategies for intrapersonal learners:

➤ Study in a quiet setting.

➤ When you are reading, stop periodically to think about what you have read.

➤ Reflect on the personal meaning of information. Keep a journal.

➤ Don't just memorize material; think about when it is important and what it relates to, considering the causes and effects involved.

➤ Write short summaries of what the material means to you.

Naturalistic learners feel energized when they are connected to nature. Their career choices and hobbies often reflect their love of nature. They often understand information when it is organized into categories, similar to how plant and animal species are categorized.

Student-suggested strategies for the naturalistic learner:

➤ Study outside whenever practical but only if it is not distracting.

➤ Explore subjects that reflect your love for nature. Learning is much easier when you have a passion for it.

➤ Relate abstract information to something concrete in nature.

➤ Put new information into categories whenever possible.

➤ Take breaks with something you love from nature—a walk, watching your fish, or a nature video. Use nature as a reward for getting other work done.

Classroom Benefits

Knowing your learning style does more than help you adjust to different kinds of material. It can also help you make the most of the teaching styles of your instructors. Your particular learning style may work better with the way some instructors teach and be a mismatch with other instructors. The first step is to understand the various teaching styles you encounter (remember that an instructor's teaching style often reflects his or her learning style). Then the next step is to make adjustments so that you can maximize your learning.

After perhaps two class meetings, you can make a pretty good assessment of any instructor's teaching styles (instructors may exhibit more than one). See Figure 3–1 for some common styles.

After you have an idea of what you're working with, you can assess how well your own styles match up with the teaching styles. If your styles mesh well with an instructor's teaching styles, you're in luck. If not, you have a number of options.

You can bring extra focus to your weaker learning styles. Although it's not easy, working on your weaker points can help you break new ground in your learning. For example, if you're a verbal person in a math- and logic-oriented class, increase your focus and concentration during class so that you get as much as you can from the presentation. Then you can spend extra study time on the material, make a point to ask others from your class to help you, and search for additional supplemental materials and exercises that might reinforce your knowledge.

You can ask your instructor for additional help. For example, if you are a visual person, you might ask your instructor if he or she can recommend

FIGURE 3-1   **TEACHING STYLES**

- **Lecture:** instructor speaks to the class for the entire class period; little or no class interaction

- **Group discussion:** instructor presents material but encourages class discussion throughout

- **Small groups:** instructor presents material and then breaks class into small groups for discussion or project work

- **Visual focus:** instructor uses visual elements such as diagrams, photographs, drawings, or transparencies

- **Verbal focus:** instructor relies primarily on words, either spoken or written on the board or overhead projector

- **Logical presentation:** instructor organizes material in a logical sequence, such as by time or importance

- **Random presentation:** instructor tackles topics in no particular order, jumps around a lot, or digresses

any visuals to look at that would help to illustrate the points made in class. If the class breaks into smaller groups, you might ask the instructor to divide those groups roughly according to learning style, so that the visual students can help each other understand the material.

You can "convert" class material during study time. For example, an interpersonal learner takes a class with an instructor who presents big-picture information in a lecture format. This student might organize study groups and, in those groups, focus on filling in the factual gaps by reading materials assigned for that class. Likewise, a visual student might rewrite notes in different colors to add a visual element—for example, assigning a different color to each main point or topic or using one color for central ideas and another for supporting examples.

Instructors are as individual as students. Taking time to focus on their teaching styles and on how to adjust will help you learn more effectively and avoid frustration. Don't forget to take advantage of your instructor's office hours when you have a learning style issue that is causing you difficulty.

General Benefits

Although schools have traditionally favored verbal-linguistic students, there is no general advantage to one style over another. The only advantage is in discovering your styles through accurate and honest analysis. Following are three general benefits of knowing your learning styles.

1. *You will have a better chance of avoiding problematic situations.* If you don't explore what works best for you, you risk forcing yourself

WINDOWS ON THE WORLD:
REAL LIFE STUDENT ISSUES

How can I make the most of my learning style?

Anwar Smith, Taylor University, Upland, Indiana, Christian Education Major

Recently I took a multiple intelligences assessment. Some of it confirmed what I already knew, but some results were more surprising. I always knew I like to talk things out. I learn best through discussion. I also answered questions that showed I have a high degree of interpersonal intelligence, and I scored well in the verbal-linguistic category.

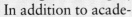

In addition to academics, I play football at Taylor and am managing to keep my GPA up. I'm trying to get all I can out of my education. When I graduate I would like to go back to the inner city of Chicago, where I grew up, and help young people achieve their goals.

I am wondering how my learning style will affect what I want to do with my future. What do you think all this means in regard to my study and work habits?

Rev. Eric Gerard Pearman, M. Div. Ph.D. candidate at the University of Denver, Denver, Colorado

First, I want to commend you on your desire to return to the inner city of Chicago. Your verbal and interpersonal intelligences are well suited for one who feels the "call" to reach out to the needs of youth. Your verbal-linguistic results indicate that you like to talk things out and learn best in group discussion. Find a classmate to talk with about the things you are learning.

Communication is key to solving the problems that affect inner-city children. We need people like yourself who will talk to them and help them help themselves rather than depending on others to help them.

God has brought me from a single-parent home on Chicago's south side through street gang activity and into a doctoral program with a desire to reach out to my old neighborhood. My mother provided the values that helped me make good choices during difficult moments. Participating in gang activity and seeing peers killed during adolescence made me realize that I needed another path in life. Positive influences at the church reinforced the values my mother taught and helped me see that because I lived in "the projects" did not mean that the projects had to live in me.

You obviously have a strong work ethic and deep concern for people. These skills, plus your intelligences, might lead you to consider a seminary education. Seminary can give you an academic challenge and a chance to develop the skills needed for urban ministry. I challenge you to pursue a Ph.D. in the future. Furthering your education will help you provide young people with an appreciation for educational achievement and the benefits that will result from studying and determination.

into career or personal situations that stifle your creativity, development, and happiness. Knowing how you learn and how you relate to the world can help you make smarter choices.

2. *You will be more successful on the job.* Your learning style is essentially your working style. If you know how you learn, you will be able to look for an environment that suits you best and you'll be able to work effectively on work teams. This will prepare you for successful employment in the twenty-first century.

3. *You will be more able to target areas that need improvement.* The more you know about your learning styles, the more you will be able to pinpoint the areas that are more difficult for you. That has two advantages. One, you can begin to work on difficult areas, step by step. Two, when a task requires a skill that is tough for you, you can either take special care with it or suggest someone else whose style may be better suited to it.

Your learning style is one important part of self-knowledge. Next you will explore other important factors that help to define you.

THINKING BACK

1. Name your three most dominant intelligences (based on the Pathways to Learning assessment), and for each one, name a strength of yours associated with that intelligence.

   a. _____

   b. _____

   c. _____

2. What surprised you about your learning style?

   _____

   _____

   _____

3. Name three study strategies that fit your needs based on your multiple intelligences assessment.

   a. _____

   b. _____

   c. _____

THINKING AHEAD

1. Name a situation in which you tend to have a negative opinion of yourself. Why do you think this happens?

   _____

   _____

   _____

2. Name two areas of study/work that interest you. Then, name a major that corresponds to each.

   a. _____

   b. _____

3. Name one habit of yours that you consider "good" and one that you consider "bad," and briefly tell why you would label them this way.

   "Good": _____

   _____

   "Bad": _____

   _____

4. List two of your greatest strengths and two of your limitations.

   Strengths: _____

   _____

   Limitations: _____

   _____

HOW DO YOU EXPLORE WHO YOU ARE?

You are an absolutely unique individual. Although you may share individual characteristics with others, your combination of traits is one of a kind. It could take a lifetime to learn everything there is to know about yourself because you are constantly changing. However, you can start by exploring these facets of yourself: self-perception, interests, habits, and abilities.

Self-perception

Having an accurate image of yourself is difficult. Unfortunately, many people err on the side of negativity. Feeling inadequate from time to time is normal, but a constantly negative self-perception can have destructive effects. Look at people you know who think that they are less intelligent, capable, or attractive than they really are. Observe how that shuts down their confidence and motivation. You do the same to yourself when you perceive yourself negatively.

> **Self-perception,**
> How one views oneself, one's opinion of oneself.

Negative self-perception has effects that lead to a self-fulfilling prophecy, which is something that comes true because you have convinced yourself it will: First you believe that you are incapable of being or doing something, then you neglect to try, and finally you probably don't do or become what you had already decided was impossible.

For example, say you think you can't pass a certain course. Since you feel you don't have a chance, you don't put as much effort into the work for that course. Sure enough, at the end of the semester, you don't pass. The worst part is that you may see your failure as proof of your incapability, instead of realizing that you didn't allow yourself to try. This chain of events can occur in many situations. When it happens in the workplace, people lose jobs. When it happens in personal life, people lose relationships.

Negative self-images may come from one or more different sources. Here are some possibilities:

> ➤ *Critical parents or guardians.* All children hear some criticism. But if you heard repeated negative comments and received little positive reinforcement, you may believe what you heard.
>
> ➤ *Instructors or other authority figures.* As with parents, critical authority figures who focus on the negative may influence your self-perception.
>
> ➤ *Magazines, television, and other media.* The media set a standard for the "right" way to look, to behave, and to work. If you and your life don't seem to match this standard, you may take that as a negative reflection on yourself.
>
> ➤ *Unrealistic expectations.* Many people expect too much of themselves. When they don't live up to these expectations, they are often their own worst critics, labeling efforts as "failures" and playing a constant inner tape of negative self-talk.

Refine your self-image so that it reflects more of your true self. These strategies might help:

> ➤ *Believe in yourself.* If you don't believe in yourself, others may have a harder time believing in you. Work to eliminate negative self-talk. Have faith in your abilities. When you set your goals, stick to them. Know that your mind and will are very powerful.
>
> ➤ *Talk to other people whom you trust.* People who know you well often have a more realistic perception of you than you do of yourself.

➤ *Take personal time.* Stress makes having perspective on your life more difficult. Take time out to clear your mind and think realistically about who you are and who you want to be.

➤ *Look at all of the evidence.* Mistakes can loom large in your mind. Consider what you do well and what you have accomplished as carefully as you consider your stumbles.

Building a positive self-perception is a lifelong challenge. If you maintain a bright but realistic vision of yourself, it will take you far along the road toward achieving your goals.

Interests

Taking some time now to explore your interests will help you later when you select a major and a career. You may be aware of many of your general interests already. For example, you can ask yourself these questions:

➤ What areas of study do I like?

➤ What activities make me happy?

➤ What careers seem interesting to me?

➤ What kind of daily schedule do I like to keep (early riser or night owl)?

➤ What type of home and work environment do I prefer?

Interests play an important role in the workplace. Many people, however, do not take their interests seriously when choosing a career. Some make salary or stability their first priority. Some take the first job that comes along. Some may not realize they can do better. Not considering what you are interested in may lead to an area of study or a job that leaves you unhappy, uninterested, or unfulfilled.

Choosing to consider your interests and happiness takes courage but brings benefits. Think about your life. You spend hours both attending classes and studying outside of class. You will probably spend at least eight hours a day, five or more days a week, up to fifty or more weeks a year as a working contributor to the world. Although your studies and work won't always make you deliriously happy, it is possible to spend your school and work time in a manner that suits you.

Here are three positive effects of focusing on your interests.

1. *You will have more energy.* Think about how you feel when you are looking forward to seeing a special person, participating in a favorite sports activity, or enjoying some entertainment. When you're doing something you like, time seems to pass very quickly. Contrast this with how you feel about disagreeable activities. The difference in your energy level is immense. You will be able to get much more done in a subject or career area that you enjoy.

2. *You will perform better.* When you were in high school, you probably got your best grades in your favorite classes and excelled in your favorite activities. That doesn't change as you get older. You will

usually find the most success in work that you like to do. The more you like something, the harder you work at it—and the harder you work, the more you will improve.

Attitude,
A state of mind or feeling toward something.

3. *You will have a positive attitude.* On the one hand, a positive **attitude** creates a positive environment and might even make up for areas in which you lack ability or experience. On the other hand, even if you perform well, a negative attitude can sour the atmosphere for your co-workers and may ultimately cost you your job. This is especially important when working in a team with others. Because businesses currently emphasize teamwork to such a great extent, your ability to maintain a positive attitude might mean the difference between success and failure.

Habits

A preference for a particular action that you do a certain way, and often on a regular basis or at certain times, is a habit. You might have a habit of showering in the morning, channel surfing with the TV remote control, talking for hours on the phone, or studying late at night. Your habits reveal a lot about you. Some habits you consider to be good habits, and some may be bad habits.

Bad habits earn that title because they can prevent you from reaching important goals. Some bad habits, such as chronic lateness, cause obvious problems. Other habits, such as renting movies three times a week, may not seem bad until you realize that you needed to spend those hours studying. People maintain bad habits because they offer immediate, enjoyable rewards, even if later effects are negative. For example, going out to eat frequently may drain your budget, but at first it seems easier than shopping for food, cooking, and washing dishes.

Good habits are those that have positive effects on your life. You often have to wait longer and work harder to see a reward for good habits, which makes them harder to maintain. If you cut out fattening foods, you wouldn't lose weight in two days. If you reduced your nights out to gain study time, your grades wouldn't improve in a week. When you strive to maintain good habits, trust that the rewards are somewhere down the road. Changing a habit can be a long process.

"*To fall into a habit is to begin to cease to be.*"
Miguel Unamuno

Take time to evaluate your habits. Look at the positive and negative effects of each, and decide which are helpful and which are harmful to you. Here are steps you can take to change a habit that has more negative effects than positive ones.

1. *Be honest about your habits.* Admitting negative or destructive habits can be hard to do. You can't change a habit until you admit that it is a habit.

2. *Recognize the habit as troublesome.* Sometimes the trouble may not seem to come directly from the habit. For example, spending every weekend working on the house may seem important, but you may be overdoing it and ignoring friends and family members.

3. *Decide to change.* You might realize what your bad habits are but do not yet care about their effects on your life. Until you are convinced that you will receive something positive and useful from changing, your efforts will not get you far.

4. *Start today.* Don't put it off until after this week, after the family re-union, or after the semester. Each day lost is a day you haven't had the chance to benefit from a new lifestyle.

5. *Change one habit at a time.* Changing and breaking habits is diffi-cult. Attempting to be perfect overnight will only frustrate you. Try-ing to spend more time with your family, increase studying, and save more money all at once can bring on a fit of deprivation, sending you scurrying back to all your old habits. Easy does it.

6. *Reward yourself appropriately for positive steps taken.* If you earn a good grade, avoid slacking off on your studies the following week. If you've lost weight, avoid celebrating in an ice-cream parlor. Choose a reward that will not encourage you to stray from your target.

7. *Keep it up.* To have the best chance at changing a habit, be consis-tent for at least three weeks. Your brain needs time to become accus-tomed to the new habit. If you go back to the old habit during that time, you may feel like you're starting all over again.

8. *Don't get too discouraged.* Rarely does someone make the decision to change and do so without a setback or two. Being too hard on yourself might cause frustration that tempts you to give up and go back to the habit.

Abilities

Everyone's abilities include both strengths and limitations. Both are part of you. Examining both strengths and limitations is part of establishing the kind of clear vision of yourself that will help you maximize your potential.

Examining blueprints for remodeling a house

Strengths

As you think about your preferences, your particular strengths will come to mind because you often like best the things you can do well. Some strengths seem to be natural—things you learned to do without ever having to work too hard. Others you struggled to develop and continue to work hard to main-tain. Asking yourself these questions may help you define more clearly what your abilities are:

➤ What have I always been able to do well?

➤ What have others often praised about me?

➤ What do I like most about myself, and why?

➤ What is my learning-style profile?

➤ What are my accomplishments—at home, at school, and at work?

As with your preferences, knowing your abilities will help you find a job that makes the most of them. When your job requires you to do work you like, you are more likely to perform to the best of your ability. Keep that in mind as you explore career areas. Assessments and inventories that will help you further assess your abilities may be available at your school's career center or library. Once you know yourself, you will be more able to set appropriate goals.

Limitations

Nobody is perfect, and no one is good at everything. Everyone has limitations. However, that doesn't mean they are any easier to take. Limitations can make you frustrated, stressed, or angry. You may feel as though no one else has the limitations you have or that no one else has as many.

There are three ways to deal with your limitations. The first two—ignoring them or dwelling on them—are the most common. Both are natural, but neither is wise. The third way is to face them and to work to improve them while keeping the strongest focus on your abilities.

Ignoring your limitations can cause you to be unable to accomplish your goals. For example, say you are an active, global learner with a well-developed interpersonal intelligence. You have limitations in logical-mathematical intelligence and in linear thought. Ignoring that fact, you decide that you can make good money in computer programming, and you sign up for math and programming courses. You certainly won't fail automatically. However, if you ignore your limited ability in these courses and don't seek extra help, you may have more than a few stumbles.

Dwelling on your limitations can make you forget you have any strengths at all. This results in negative self-talk and a poor self-perception. Continuing the example, if you were to dwell on your limitations in math, you might very likely stop trying altogether.

Facing limitations and working to improve them is the best response. A healthy understanding of your limitations can help you avoid troublesome situations. In the example, you could face your limitations in math and explore other career areas that use your more well-developed abilities and intelligences. If you decided to stick with computer technology, you could study an area of the field that focuses on management and interpersonal relationships. Or you could continue to aim for a career as a programmer, seeking special help in areas that give you trouble.

HOW CAN YOU START THINKING ABOUT CHOOSING A MAJOR?

Many students come to college knowing what they want to study, but many do not. That's completely normal. College is a perfect time to begin exploring your different interests. In the process, you may discover talents and strengths you never realized you had. For example, taking an environmental class may teach you that you have a passion for finding solutions to pollution problems. You may discover a talent for public speaking and decide to explore on-camera journalism.

Although some of your explorations may take you down paths that don't resonate with your personality and interests, each experience will help to clarify who you really are and what you want to do with your life. Thinking about choosing a major involves exploring potential majors, being open to changing majors, and linking majors to career areas.

Exploring Potential Majors

Here are some steps to help you explore majors that may interest you.

Take a variety of classes. Although you will generally have core requirements to fulfill, use your electives to branch out. Try to take at least one class in each area that sparks your interest.

Don't rule out subject areas that aren't classified as "safe." Friends or parents may have warned you against certain careers, encouraging you to stay with "safe" careers that pay well. Even though financial stability is important, following your dreams is equally important. Choosing between the "safe" path and the path of the heart can be challenging. Only you can decide which is the best for you.

Spend time getting to know yourself, your interests, and your abilities. The more you know about yourself, the more ability you will have to focus on areas that make the most of who you are and what you can do. Pay close attention to which areas inspire you to greater heights and which areas seem to deaden your initiative.

Work closely with your advisor. Begin discussing your major early on with your advisor, even if you don't intend to declare a major right away. For any given major, your advisor may be able to tell you about both the corresponding department at your school and the possibilities in related career areas. You may also discuss with your advisor the possibility of a double major (completing the requirements for two different majors) or designing your own major, if your school offers an opportunity to do so.

Take advantage of other resources. Seek opinions from instructors, friends, and family members. Talk to students who have declared majors that interest you. Explore the course materials your college gives you to see what majors your college offers.

Develop your critical-thinking skills. Working toward any major will help you develop your most important skill—knowing how to use your mind. Critical thinking is the most crucial ingredient in any recipe for school and career success. More than anything, your future career and employer will depend on your ability to think clearly, effectively, creatively, and wisely and to contribute to the workplace by truly making a difference.

> *"The greatest discovery of any generation is that human beings can alter their lives by altering their attitudes of mind."*
>
> Albert Schweitzer

Planning Your Curriculum

You won't necessarily want to plan your entire college course load at the beginning of your first semester. You might find, however, some advantages to thinking through your choices ahead of time. Planning ahead can give you a clearer idea of where you are headed so that you feel in control of your choices in college. It can also help you avoid pitfalls, such as not being able to secure a space in a course that you need to complete your major. Often, when students wait until the last minute to register for the following semester, some courses they want have already been filled, and they may have to take courses they would not necessarily have chosen.

Take advantage of the following ideas and strategies when working to plan your college **curriculum**.

Curriculum,
The particular set of courses required for any degree.

Consult your college catalog. You will get the most general idea of your possibilities by exploring everything your college offers. In addition, what is available to you may go beyond your college's doors. Make sure you check into "study abroad" programs (spending a semester or a year at an affiliated college in a different country) or opportunities to take courses at nearby schools that have arrangements with your school.

Look at the majors that interest you. Each major offered by your college has a list of required courses, which you can find in your catalog or get from an academic advisor. The list may also indicate a recommended order in which you should take the courses—certain ones your first year, certain ones your second, and so on. The list will help you to see if you would like what you would be doing over the next few semesters if you choose a particular major.

Branch out. Even if you already have a pretty clear idea of your primary area of study, look into courses in other interesting areas that don't necessarily connect to your major. Enlarging the scope of your knowledge will help to improve your critical thinking, broaden your perspectives, and perhaps introduce you to career possibilities you had never even considered.

Get creative. Do you have a particular idea about what you want to major in but don't see it listed in your college catalog? Don't immediately assume it's impossible. Talk with your academic advisor. Some schools allow certain students to design their own majors, with help and approval from their advisors. In such a case, you and your advisor would come up with a unique list of courses on your own.

Linking Majors to Career Areas

The point of declaring and pursuing a major is to help you reach a significant level of knowledge in one subject, often in preparation for a particular career area. Before you discard a major as not practical enough, consider where it might be able to take you. Thinking through the possibilities may open doors that you never knew existed. Besides finding an exciting path, you may discover something highly marketable and beneficial to humankind as well.

For each major there are many career options that aren't obvious right away. For example, a student working toward a teaching certification doesn't have to teach public school. This student could develop curricula, act as a consultant for businesses, develop an on-line education service, teach overseas for the Peace Corps, or create a public television program. The sky's the limit.

Explore the educational requirements of any career area that interests you. Your choice of major may be more or less crucial, depending on the career area. For example, pursuing a career in medicine almost always requires a major in some area of the biological sciences, whereas aspiring lawyers may have majored in anything from political science to philosophy. Many employers are more interested in your ability to think than in your specific knowledge and therefore may not pay as much attention to your major as they do to your critical-thinking skills. Ask advisors or people in your areas of interest what educational background is necessary or helpful to someone pursuing a career in that area.

Changing Majors

Some people may change their minds several times before finding a major that fits. Although this may add to the time you spend in college, being happy with your decision is important. For example, an education major may begin student teaching only to discover that he really didn't feel comfortable in front of students. Or a student may declare English as a major only to realize that her passion was in religion.

If this happens to you, don't be discouraged. You're certainly not alone. Changing a major is much like changing a job. Skills and experiences from one job will assist you in your next position, and some of the courses from your first major may apply—or even transfer as credits—to your next major. Talk with your academic advisor about any desire to change majors. Sometimes an advisor can speak to department heads in order to get the maximum number of credits transferred to your new major.

Whatever you decide, realize that you do have the right to change your mind. Continual self-discovery is part of the journey. No matter how many detours you make, each interesting class you take along the way helps to point you toward a major that feels like home.

Sabiduría

In Spanish, the term *sabiduría* represents the two sides of learning, knowledge and wisdom. Knowledge—building what you know about how the world works—is the first part. Wisdom—deriving meaning and significance from knowledge and deciding how to use it—is the second. As you continually learn and experience new things, the *sabiduría* you build will help you make knowledgeable and wise choices about how to lead your life.

Think of this concept as you discover more about how you learn and receive knowledge in all aspects of your life—in school, work, and personal situations. As you learn how your unique mind works and how to use it, you can more confidently assert yourself. As you expand your ability to use your mind in different ways, you can create lifelong advantages for yourself.

IMPORTANT POINTS TO REMEMBER

1. Is there one best way to learn?

Your mind is a powerful tool that functions in a unique way. There is no one way to learn that's best for everyone. Each person has a particular learning style that best fits his or her capabilities. Every individual has some highly developed areas and some underdeveloped areas of ability.

2. How can you discover your learning styles?

Many assessments can help draw the picture of your learning profile. Howard Gardner developed the multiple intelligences theory, which says that people have varying degrees of development within eight different intelligences. The *Pathways to Learning* inventory helps to show where you stand in each intelligence. Taking a reasonable approach toward learning styles involves using assessment results as a reference point rather than a label a way to expand your idea of yourself instead of boxing yourself into a category.

3. What are the benefits of knowing your learning styles?

Knowing your learning styles will benefit your school, work, and personal life. For school, you can tailor your study habits, and sometimes your choice of courses, to suit your styles. The best study strategies for you will maximize efficiency and minimize frustration and time spent. In the classroom, knowledge of learning styles will help you improve your retention of information, as well as your interaction with instructors. More general benefits include more ability to avoid choices that create problematic situations, more knowledge of your working style (often leading to more job success), and more ability to target areas that need improvement.

4. How do you explore who you are?

You are a unique individual with a one-of-a-kind combination of traits and characteristics. Since you are always changing, there will always be more to learn about yourself. However, you can get a pretty good idea of who you are by exploring your self-perception, interests, habits, and abilities (strengths and limitations).

5. How can you start thinking about choosing a major?

First, take the time to explore different majors: take a variety of classes, look into areas that interest you, seek help from your resources, and consider your likes and dislikes and strengths and limitations. Planning your curriculum ahead of time (by checking your course catalog and seeing what courses certain majors require) can help you see more clearly where you are headed. Link majors to career areas by looking at where a particular major might lead you in the working world. Finally, be open to changing majors if you declare a major that later doesn't seem to fit.

Name _____   Date _____

BUILDING SKILLS FOR COLLEGE, CAREER, AND LIFE SUCCESS
CHAPTER 3

TAKING STOCK:
REFINING YOUR THOUGHTS

Look back at the statements you explored at the start of the chapter (see Thinking It Through on p. 79). Observe whether your attitudes have changed and what you have learned by studying this chapter.

1. Describe how you would define "learning style" and what it means to your success.

_____

_____

_____

2. Which classes, or kinds of classes, seem easier to you? Which seem harder? How do you think this relates to your learning styles?

_____

_____

_____

_____

3. What aspects of your learning styles and your personality do you think will play important roles in your career choice?

_____

_____

_____

4. List the steps you can take to change a not-so-beneficial habit.

_____

_____

_____

_____

5. What interests of yours might inform your choice of major? If there are any majors that you are considering, write them here.

_____

_____

_____

6. Choose one strategy from this chapter that you intend to use in the next week. What is your plan?

_____

_____

_____

CRITICAL THINKING:
APPLYING LEARNING TO YOUR LIFE

How Do You Learn Best?

Write here your four strongest intelligences.

_____

_____

_____

_____

Describe a positive experience at work or school that you can attribute to these strengths.

_____

_____

_____

Name your four least developed intelligences.

_____

_____

_____

What challenge do you face that may be related to your least developed intelligences?

_____

_____

_____

_____

Making School More Enjoyable

Name a required class that you are not necessarily looking forward to taking this year. How does your learning style relate to how you feel? Name three study techniques from the chapter that may help you get the most out of the class and enjoy it more.

_____

_____

_____

_____

_____

Your Habits

You have the power to change your habits. List three habits that you want to change. Discuss the effects of each and how they keep you from reaching your goals.

HABIT	EFFECTS THAT PREVENT YOU FROM REACHING GOALS
1.	
2.	
3.	

Out of these three, put a star by the habit you want to change first. Write down a step you can take today toward overcoming that habit.

What helpful habit do you want to develop in its place? For example, if your problem habit were a failure to express yourself when you are angry, a replacement habit might be to talk calmly about situations that upset you as soon as they arise. If you have a habit of cramming for tests at the last minute, you could replace it with a regular study schedule that allows you to cover your material bit by bit over a longer period of time.

_____

_____

_____

One way to help yourself abandon your old habit is to think about how your new habit will improve your life. List two benefits of your new habit.

1. _____

2. _____

Give yourself one month to complete your habit shift. Set a specific deadline. Keep track of your progress by indicating on a chart or calendar how well you did each day. If you avoided the old habit, write an X below the day. If you used the new one, write an N. Therefore, a day when you only avoided the old habit will have an X; a day when you did both will have both letters; a day when you did neither will be blank. You can use the chart below or mark your own calendar. Try pairing up with another student to check on each other's progress.

1	2	3	4	5	6	7	8	9	10	11	12	13	14	15	16
17	18	19	20	21	22	23	24	25	26	27	28	29	30	31	

Don't forget to reward yourself for your hard work. Write here what your reward will be when you feel you are on the road to a new and beneficial habit.

_____

_____

_____

Interests, Majors, and Careers

Start by listing activities and subjects you like.

1. _____

2. _____

3. _____

4. _____

5. _____

6. _____

Name three majors that might relate to your interests and help you achieve your career goals.

1. _____

2. _____

3. _____

For each major, name a corresponding career area you may want to explore.

1. _____

2. _____

3. _____

Keep these majors and career areas in mind as you gradually narrow your course choices in the time before you declare a major.

TEAMWORK:
COMBINING FORCES

Ideas about intelligences. Divide into groups according to four of the multiple intelligences—high scorers in bodily-kinesthetic in one group, high scorers in verbal-linguistic in another, high scorers in visual-spatial in a third, and high scorers in logical-mathematical in the fourth. If you have scored the same in more than one of these intelligences, join whatever group is smaller. With your group, brainstorm four lists for your intelligence: the *strengths* of having this intelligence, the *struggles* it brings, the things that cause particular *stress* for your intelligence, and *career* ideas that tend to suit this intelligence.

Strengths	Struggles	Stressors	Careers
1.	1.	1.	1.
2.	2.	2.	2.

And so on.

If there is time, each group can present this information to the entire class to enable everyone to have a better understanding and acceptance of one another's intelligences. You might also brainstorm strategies for dealing with your intelligence's struggles and stressors, and present those ideas to the class as well.

WRITING: DISCOVERY THROUGH JOURNALING

To record your thoughts, use a separate journal or the lined pages at the end of the chapter.

Your learning style. Discuss the insights you have gained through exploring your multiple intelligences. What strengths have come to your attention? What challenges have been clarified? Talk about your game plan for using your strengths and address your challenges both at school and in the real world.

CAREER PORTFOLIO: CHARTING YOUR COURSE

Self-portrait. A self-portrait is an important step in your career exploration because self-knowledge will allow you to make the best choices about what to study and what career to pursue. Use this exercise to synthesize everything you have been exploring about yourself into one comprehensive "self-portrait." You will design your portrait in "think-link" style, using words and visual shapes to describe your self-perception, learning style, attitudes, habits, preferences, and abilities.

A think link is a visual construction of related ideas, similar to a map or web, that represents your thought process. Ideas are written inside geometric shapes, often boxes or circles, and related ideas and facts are attached to those ideas by lines that connect the shapes. You will learn more about think links in the note-taking section in Chapter 7.

Use the style shown in the example in Figure 3–2, or create your own. For example, in this exercise you may want to create a "wheel" of ideas coming off your central shape, entitled "Me." Then, spreading out from each of these ideas (abilities, learning style, etc.) you would draw lines connecting all of the thoughts that go along with that idea. Connected to "Abilities," for example, might be "Singing," "Good memory,"

"Get along with people," and "Math skills." You don't have to use the wheel image. You might want to design a treelike think link, or a line of boxes with connecting thoughts written below the boxes or anything else you like. Let your design reflect who you are, just as does the think link itself.

FIGURE 3-2   **SAMPLE SELF–PORTRAIT THINK LINK**

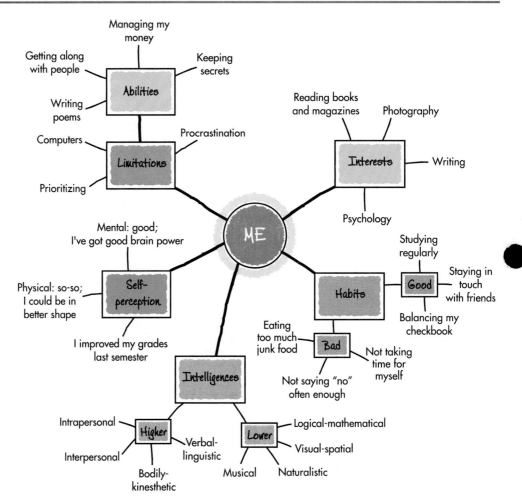

Journal Entry

CROSSWORD REVIEW: PART I
Sharpening Your Skills

ACROSS

3. People who can provide one-on-one help with academic subjects
5. Preferences for actions done in a certain way, often on a regular basis or at particular times
6. A promise or pledge to do something in the future
9. Determination; the power to begin or to follow through with a plan or task
13. Principles, standards, or qualities considered important, right, or good
14. The variety that occurs in every aspect of humanity
15. A subject of academic study in which a student chooses to specialize
16. Adherence to a code of moral values; honesty
17. To put off an action or task until later
18. A time-and-activity map that allocates time for tasks and serves as a reminder

DOWN

1. An end toward which effort is directed; an aim
2. Something that is rated high in importance
4. A method of putting daily tasks down on paper
7. A type of intelligence that focuses on an ability to relate to others and their feelings
8. The ability to solve problems or fashion products that are useful in a community
10. Reliable, trustworthy
11. People, organizations, or services that provide help and support
12. State of mind or feeling toward something

PART 2

SETTING THE STAGE FOR LEARNING

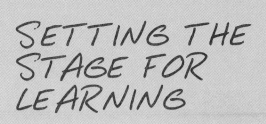

CHAPTER 4 Critical and Creative Thinking: Tapping the Power of Your Mind

CHAPTER 5 Reading and Studying: Your Keys to Knowledge

CHAPTER 6 Listening and Memory: Taking In and Remembering Information

C R E A T E

4 CRITICAL AND CREATIVE THINKING: Tapping the Power of Your Mind

Thinking It Through

Check those statements that apply to you right now:

- ❏ I'm not quite sure what "critical thinking" means.
- ❏ I am usually happy with how I've solved a problem.
- ❏ Plan for next year? I can hardly get past next week.
- ❏ I'm not sure I often take the time to question the validity of my opinions.
- ❏ I think my perspective is generally on target.
- ❏ I consider myself to be a creative person.
- ❏ I trust what I see on television and read in magazines.

In this chapter, you will explore answers to the following questions:

- ➤ What is critical thinking?
- ➤ How does critical thinking help you solve problems and make decisions?
- ➤ How do you construct an effective argument?
- ➤ How do you establish truth?
- ➤ Why shift your perspective?
- ➤ Why plan strategically?
- ➤ How can you develop your creativity?
- ➤ What is media literacy?

Your mind's powers show in everything you do, from the smallest chores (comparing prices of cereals at the grocery store) to the most complex situations (Arthur Fry, shown in the photograph, invented self-adhesive notes). Your mind is able to process, store, and create with the facts and ideas it encounters. Critical and creative thinking are what enable those skills to come alive.

Understanding how your mind works, both its simple actions and more involved thinking processes, is the first step toward critical thinking. When you have that understanding, you can perform the essential critical-thinking task: asking important questions about ideas, information, and media. This chapter will show you both the mind's basic actions and the thinking processes that incorporate them. You will explore what it means to be an open-minded critical and creative thinker, able to ask and understand questions that promote your success in college, career, and life.

WHAT IS CRITICAL THINKING?

Critical thinking is thinking that goes beyond the basic recall of information. The dictionary defines the word *critical* as "indispensable" and "important." Critical thinking is important thinking that involves asking questions. Using critical thinking, you question ideas, create new ideas, turn information into tools to solve problems and make decisions, and take both the long-term and day-to-day view.

A critical thinker asks many kinds of questions about a given piece of information, such as these: *Where did it come from? What could explain it? In what ways is it true or false? How do I feel about it, and why? How is this information similar to or different from what I already know? Is it good or bad? What caused it, and what effects does it have?* Critical thinkers also try to transform information into something they can use. They ask whether information can help them solve a problem, make a decision, learn or create something new, or anticipate the future.

Not thinking critically means not asking questions about information or ideas. A person who does not think critically tends to accept or reject information or ideas without examining them. Table 4–1 compares how a critical thinker and a noncritical thinker might respond to particular situations.

Asking questions (the focus of this table), considering without judgment as many responses as you can, and choosing responses that are as complete and accurate as possible are some of the primary ingredients in critical thinking.

Critical thinking is a skill, and anyone can develop the ability to think critically. One of the most crucial components of this skill is learning information. For instance, part of critical thinking is comparing new information with what you already know. Your prior knowledge makes critical thinking happen by providing a framework within which to evaluate new information. For example, thinking critically about the statement "Shakespeare's character King Richard III is like an early version of Adolf Hitler" is impossible without basic knowledge of World War II and Shakespeare's play *Richard III*.

To examine potential critical-thinking responses in more depth, explore the different questions that a critical thinker may have about one particular statement.

> "We do not live to think, on the contrary, we think in order that we may succeed in surviving."
>
> José Ortega Y Gassett

TABLE 4-1 NOT THINKING CRITICALLY VS. THINKING CRITICALLY

YOUR ROLE	SITUATION	NONQUESTIONING RESPONSE	QUESTIONING RESPONSE
STUDENT	Instructor is lecturing on the causes of the Vietnam war.	You assume everything your instructor says is true.	You consider what the instructor says, write questions about issues you want to clarify, discuss issues with the instructor or classmates.
SPOUSE/PARTNER	Your partner feels he/she does not have enough quality time with you.	You think he/she is wrong and defend yourself.	You ask your partner why he/she thinks this is happening, and together you see how you can improve the situation.
EMPLOYEE	Your supervisor is angry with you about something that happened.	You avoid your supervisor or deny responsibility for the incident.	You determine what the perception is about you and what you might do about it; you talk with your supervisor about it.
NEIGHBOR	People who differ from you move in next door.	You ignore or avoid them; you think their way of living is weird.	You introduce yourself and offer help if they need it; you respectfully explore what's different about them.
CONSUMER	You want to buy a car.	You decide on a brand new car and don't think through how you can pay for it.	You consider the effects of buying a new car vs. a used car; you evaluate what kind of payment you can handle each month.

A Critical-Thinking Response to a Statement

Consider the following statement of opinion: *"My obstacles are keeping me from succeeding in school. Other people make it through school because they don't have to deal with the obstacles that I have."*

Nonquestioning thinkers may accept an opinion like this as an absolute truth. As a result, on the road to achieving their goals, they may lose motivation to overcome such obstacles. In contrast, critical thinkers would examine the opinion through a series of questions. Here are some examples of questions one student might ask (the type of each question is indicated in parentheses):

"What exactly are my obstacles? Examples of my obstacles are a heavy work schedule, single parenting, being in debt, and returning to school after ten years." (**recall**)

"Are there other cases different from mine? I do have one friend who is going through problems worse than mine, and she's getting by. I also know another guy who doesn't have too much to deal with that I can tell, and he's struggling just like I am." (**difference**)

"Who has problems similar to mine? Well, if I consider my obstacles specifically, my statement might mean that single parents and returning adult students will all have trouble in school. That is not necessarily true. People who have trouble in school may still become successful." (**similarity**)

"What is an example of someone who has had success despite obstacles? What about Oseola McCarty, the cleaning woman who saved money all her life and raised $150,000 to create a scholarship at the University of Southern Mississippi? She didn't have what anyone would call advantages, such as a high-paying job or a college education." (**idea to example**)

"What conclusion can I draw from my questions? From thinking about my friend and about Oseola McCarty, I conclude that people can successfully overcome their obstacles by working hard, focusing on their abilities, and concentrating on their goals." (**example to idea**)

"Why do I think this? Maybe I am scared of returning to school and adjusting to a new environment. Maybe I am afraid to challenge myself, which I haven't done in a long time. Whatever the cause, the effect is that I feel bad about myself and don't work to the best of my abilities, and that can hurt me and maybe even my family, who depends on me." (**cause and effect**)

"How do I evaluate the effects of this statement? I think it's harmful. When we say that obstacles equal difficulty, we can damage our desire to try to overcome them. When we say that successful people don't have obstacles, we might overlook that some very successful people have to deal with hidden disadvantages such as learning disabilities or abusive families." (**evaluation**)

Remember these types of questions. When you explore the seven mind actions later in the chapter, refer to these questions to see how they illustrate the different actions your mind performs.

The Value of Critical Thinking

Critical thinking has many important advantages. Following are some of the positive effects, or benefits, of critical thinking.

You will increase your ability to perform thinking processes that help you reach your goals. Critical thinking is a learned skill, just like shooting a basketball or using a word-processing program on the computer. As with any other skill, the more you use it, the better you become at it. The more you ask questions, the better you think. The better you think, the more effective you will be when completing schoolwork, managing your personal life, and performing your job.

You can produce knowledge, rather than just reproduce it. The interaction of newly learned information with what you already know creates new knowledge. Its usefulness can be judged by your ability to apply it. For instance, it won't mean much for an education student to quote the stages of child development on an exam unless he or she can evaluate children's needs on the job.

You can be a valuable employee. You won't be a failure in the workplace if you follow directions. However, you will be even more valuable if you ask strategic questions—ranging from "Is there a better way to deliver phone messages?" to "How can we increase business?"—about how to make improvements. Employees who think critically will be more likely to make progress in their careers.

You can increase your creativity. Critical thinking means inventing new and different questions to ask, possibilities to explore, and ideas to try. Creativity is essential in producing what is new. Being creative improves your sense of humor and your perspective as you cope with problems.

Your mind has some basic moves, or actions, that it performs to understand relationships among ideas and concepts. Sometimes it uses one action by itself, but most often it uses two or more in combination. These actions are the blocks you will use to build the critical-thinking processes you will explore later in the chapter.

Learning How Your Mind Works Through the Thinktrix

Identify your mind's actions by using a system called the Thinktrix, originally conceived by educators Frank Lyman, Arlene Mindus, and Charlene Lopez[1] and developed by numerous other instructors. Based on their studies of how students think, they named seven basic building blocks of thought. These actions are not new to you, although some of their names may be. They represent the ways in which you think all the time.

Through exploring these actions, you can go beyond just thinking and learn *how* you think. This will help you to take charge of your own thinking. The more you know about how your mind works, the more control you will have over thinking processes such as problem solving and decision making.

Following are explanations of each of the mind actions, including examples. As you read, write your own examples in the blank spaces. An icon, or picture, representing each action will help you visualize and remember them.

Recall. *Facts, sequence, and description.* This is the simplest action. When you **recall,** you name or describe facts, objects, or events or put them into sequence. *Examples*:

> ➤ Naming the steps of a geometry proof, in order
> ➤ Remembering your best friends' phone numbers

Your example: Recall two important school-related events this month.

_____

_____

The icon: A string tied around a finger is a familiar image of recall or remembering.

Similarity. *Analogy, likeness, comparison.* This action examines what is **similar** about one or more things. You might compare situations, ideas, people, stories, events, or objects. *Examples*:

➤ Comparing notes with another student to see what facts and ideas you have both considered important

➤ Analyzing the arguments you've had with your partner this month and seeing how they all seem to be about the same problem

Your example: Tell what is similar about two of your best friends.

_____

_____

The icon: Two alike objects, in this case triangles, indicate similarity.

Difference. *Distinction, contrast.* This action examines what is **different** about one or more situations, ideas, people, stories, events, or objects, contrasting them with one another. *Examples*:

➤ Seeing how two instructors differ—one divides the class into small groups for discussions; the other keeps desks in place and delivers lectures

➤ Contrasting a day when you combine work and school with a day when you attend class only

Your example: Explain how your response to a course you like differs from how you respond to a course you don't like as much.

_____

_____

The icon: Two differing objects, in this case a triangle and a square, indicate difference.

Cause and effect. *Reasons, consequences, prediction.* Using this action, you look at what has **caused** a fact, situation, or event and/or what **effects**, or consequences, come from it. In other words, you examine what led up to something and/or what will follow because of it. *Examples*:

➤ Staying up late at night causes you to oversleep, which has the effect of your being late to class. This causes you to miss some of the material, which has the further effect of your having problems on the test.

➤ When you pay your phone and utility bills on time, you create effects such as a better credit rating, uninterrupted service, and a better relationship with your service providers.

Your example: Name what causes you to like your favorite class and the effects that liking the class has on your attitude and/or your work.

_____

_____

The icon: The water droplets making ripples indicate causes and their resulting effects.

Example to idea. *Generalization, classification, conceptualization.* From one or more **examples** (facts or events), you develop a general **idea** or ideas. Grouping facts or events into patterns may allow you to make a general statement about several of them at once. Classifying a fact or event helps you build knowledge. This mind action moves from the specific to the general. *Examples:*

➤ You have had trouble finding a baby-sitter. A classmate even brought her child to class once. Your brother drops his daughter at day care and doesn't like not seeing her all day. From these examples, you derive the idea that your school needs an on-campus day-care program.

➤ You see a movie and you decide it is mostly about pride.

Your example: Name activities you enjoy: From them, come up with an idea of a class you would like to take.

_____

_____

The icon: The arrow and "Ex" pointing to a light bulb on their right indicate how an example or examples lead to the idea (the light bulb, lit up).

Idea to example. *Categorization, substantiation, proof.* In a reverse of the previous action, you take an **idea** or ideas and think of **examples** (events or facts) that support or prove that idea. This mind action moves from the general to the specific. *Examples:*

➤ For a paper, you start with this thesis statement: "Men are favored over women in the modern workplace." To support that idea, you gather examples: Men make more money on average than women in the same jobs, there are more men in upper management positions than there are women, and so on.

➤ You talk to your instructor about changing your major, giving examples that support your idea, such as the fact that you have worked in the field you want to change to and you have fulfilled some of the requirements for that major already.

Your example: Name an admirable person. Give examples that show how that person is admirable.

_____

_____

The icon: In a reverse of the previous icon, this one starts with the light bulb and has an arrow pointing to "Ex." It indicates that you start with the idea, the lit bulb, and then move to the examples that support it.

Evaluation. *Value, judgment, rating.* Here you **judge** whether something is useful or not useful, important or unimportant, good or bad, or right or wrong by identifying and weighing its positive and negative effects (pros and cons). Be sure to consider the specific situation at hand (a cold drink might be good on the beach in August, not so good in the snowdrifts in January). With the facts you have gathered, you determine the value of something in terms of both predicted effects and your own needs. Cause-and-effect analysis always accompanies evaluation. *Examples:*

➤ For one semester, you schedule classes in the afternoons and spend nights working. You find that you tend to sleep late and lose your only study time. From this harmful effect, you evaluate that this schedule doesn't work for you. You decide to schedule earlier classes next time.

➤ Someone offers you a chance to cheat on a test. You evaluate the potential effects if you are caught. You also evaluate the long-term effects of not actually learning the material and of doing something ethically wrong. You decide that it isn't right or worthwhile to cheat.

Your example: Evaluate your mode of transportation to school.

_____

_____

The icon: A set of scales out of balance indicates how you weigh positive and negative effects to arrive at an evaluation.

You may want to use a *mnemonic device*—a memory tool, as explained in Chapter 6—to remember the seven mind actions. Try recalling them by using the word DECRIES—each letter is the first letter of a mind action. You can also make a sentence of words that each start with a mind action's first letter, such as "Really smart dogs cook eggs in enchiladas" (the first letter of each word stands for a mind action).

How Mind Actions Build Thinking Processes

The seven mind actions are the fundamental building blocks that indicate relationships among ideas and concepts. You will rarely use one at a time in a step-by-step process, as they are presented here. You will usually combine them, overlap them, and repeat them, using different actions for different situations. For example, when a test question asks you to explain prejudice, you might give *examples, different* from one another, that show your *idea* of prejudice (combining difference with example to idea).

When you combine mind actions in working toward a specific goal, you are performing a thinking process. Following are explorations of six of the most important critical-thinking processes: solving problems, making decisions, constructing arguments, establishing truth, shifting perspective, and planning strategically. Each thinking process helps to direct your critical thinking toward the achievement of your goals. Figure 4–3, appearing later in the chapter, shows all of the mind actions and thinking processes together and reminds you that the mind actions form the core of the thinking processes.

HOW DOES CRITICAL THINKING HELP YOU SOLVE PROBLEMS AND MAKE DECISIONS?

Problem solving and decision making are probably the two most crucial and common thinking processes. Each one requires various mind actions. They overlap somewhat because every problem that needs solving requires you to make a decision. However, not every decision requires that you solve a problem (for example, not many people would say that deciding what to order for lunch is a problem). Each process will be considered separately here.

Although both of these processes have multiple steps, you will not always have to work through each step. As you become more comfortable with solving problems and making decisions, your mind will automatically click through the steps. Also, you will become more adept at evaluating which problems and decisions need serious consideration and which can be taken care of more quickly and simply.

Meeting for a workshop at Boston University

Problem Solving

Life constantly presents problems to be solved, ranging from average daily problems (how to manage study time or learn not to misplace your keys) to life-altering situations (how to adjust to a severe injury or design a custody plan during a divorce). Choosing a solution without thinking critically may have negative effects. If you use the steps of the following problem-solving process, however, you have the best chance of finding a favorable solution.

You can apply this problem-solving plan to any problem. Using the following steps will maximize the number of possible solutions you generate and will allow you to explore each one as fully as possible.

1. State the problem clearly. What are the facts? *Recall* the details of the situation. Be sure to name the problem specifically, without focusing on causes or effects. For example, a student might state this as a problem: "I'm getting bad grades on my quizzes." However, that may be an effect of the real underlying problem: "I'm not understanding the material."

2. Analyze the problem. What is happening that you feel needs to change? In other words, what *effects* of the situation concern you? What *causes*

these effects? Are there hidden causes? Look at the causes and effects that surround the problem. Continuing the previous example, if some effects of not understanding include poor grades and disinterest, some causes may include poor study habits, not listening in class, or lack of sleep.

Brainstorming,
The spontaneous, rapid generation of ideas or solutions, undertaken by a group or an individual, often as part of a problem-solving process.

3. Brainstorm possible solutions. **Brainstorming** will help you think of examples of how you solved similar problems, consider what is different about this problem, and come up with new possible solutions (see p. 137 for more about brainstorming). To get to the heart of a problem, you must base possible solutions on the most significant causes instead of putting a bandage on the effects. If the student were to aim for better assignment grades to offset the low quiz grades, that might raise his GPA but wouldn't address the lack of understanding. Looking at his study habits, though, might lead him to seek help from his instructor or a study group.

4. Explore each solution. Why might your solution work or not? Might a solution work partially or in a particular situation? Evaluate ahead of time the pros and cons (positive and negative effects) of each plan. Create a chain of causes and effects in your head, as far into the future as you can, to see where this solution might lead. The student might consider the effects of improved study habits, more sleep, tutoring, or dropping the class.

5. Choose and execute the solution you decide is best. Decide how you will put your solution to work. Then, execute your solution. The student could decide on a combination of improved study habits and tutoring.

6. Evaluate the solution that you acted on, looking at its effects. What are the positive and negative *effects* of what you did? In terms of your needs, was it a useful solution or not? Could the solution use any adjustments to be more useful? Would you do the same again or not? In evaluating, you are collecting data. Evaluating his choice, the student may decide that the effects are good but that his fatigue still causes a problem.

7. Continue to refine the solution. Problem solving is always a process. You may have opportunities to apply the same solution over and over again. Evaluate repeatedly, making changes that you decide make the solution better (i.e., more reflective of the causes of the problem). The student may decide to continue to study more regularly but, after a few weeks of tutoring, could opt to trade in the tutoring time for some extra sleep. He may decide to take what he has learned from the tutor so far and apply it to his increased study efforts.

Using this procedure enables you to solve school, work, and personal problems in a thoughtful, comprehensive way. The think link in Figure 4–1 demonstrates a way to visualize the flow of problem solving. Figure 4–2 shows how one person used this plan to solve a problem. It represents the same plan as Figure 4–1 but gives room to write so that it can be used in the problem-solving process.

PROBLEM–SOLVING PLAN   FIGURE 4-1

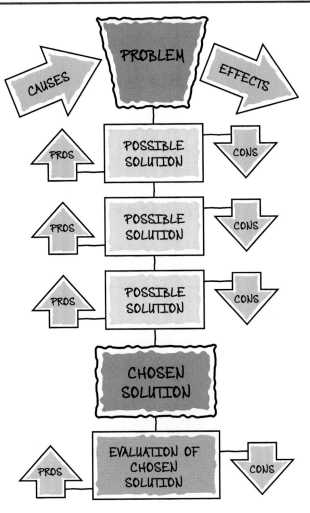

Decision Making

Although every problem-solving process involves making a decision (when you decide which solution to try), not all decisions involve solving problems. Decisions are choices. Making a choice, or decision, requires thinking critically about all of the possible choices and evaluating which will work best for you and for the situation. Decisions large and small come up daily, hourly, even every few minutes. Do you drop a course? Should you stay in a relationship? Can you work part time while in school?

Before you begin the decision-making process, evaluate the level of the decision you are making. Do you have to decide what books to bring to class (usually a minor issue) or whether to quit a good job (often a major life change)? Some decisions are little, day-to-day considerations that you can take care of quickly on your own. Others require thoughtful evaluation, time, and perhaps the input of others you trust. The following is a list of steps for thinking critically through a decision.

1. Decide on a goal. Why is this decision necessary? In other words, what result do you want from this decision, and what is its value? Considering

FIGURE 4-2 **HOW ONE STUDENT WORKED THROUGH A PROBLEM**

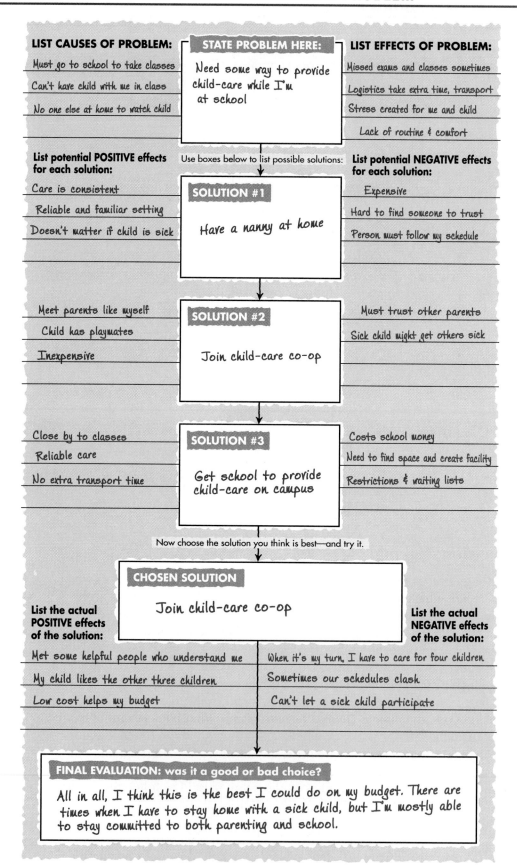

LIST CAUSES OF PROBLEM:

Must go to school to take classes

Can't have child with me in class

No one else at home to watch child

STATE PROBLEM HERE:

Need some way to provide child-care while I'm at school

LIST EFFECTS OF PROBLEM:

Missed exams and classes sometimes

Logistics take extra time, transport

Stress created for me and child

Lack of routine & comfort

Use boxes below to list possible solutions:

List potential POSITIVE effects for each solution:

Care is consistent

Reliable and familiar setting

Doesn't matter if child is sick

SOLUTION #1

Have a nanny at home

List potential NEGATIVE effects for each solution:

Expensive

Hard to find someone to trust

Person must follow my schedule

Meet parents like myself

Child has playmates

Inexpensive

SOLUTION #2

Join child-care co-op

Must trust other parents

Sick child might get others sick

Close by to classes

Reliable care

No extra transport time

SOLUTION #3

Get school to provide child-care on campus

Costs school money

Need to find space and create facility

Restrictions & waiting lists

Now choose the solution you think is best—and try it.

CHOSEN SOLUTION

Join child-care co-op

List the actual POSITIVE effects of the solution:

Met some helpful people who understand me

My child likes the other three children

Low cost helps my budget

List the actual NEGATIVE effects of the solution:

When it's my turn, I have to care for four children

Sometimes our schedules clash

Can't let a sick child participate

FINAL EVALUATION: was it a good or bad choice?

All in all, I think this is the best I could do on my budget. There are times when I have to stay home with a sick child, but I'm mostly able to stay committed to both parenting and school.

Source: Adapted from a heuristic developed by Frank T. Lyman Jr., University of Maryland, 1983.

the *effects* you want can help you formulate your goal. For example, say a student currently attends a small private college. Her goal is to become a physical therapist. The school has a good program, but her father has changed jobs and the family can no longer pay the tuition and fees.

2. Establish needs. *Recall* the needs of everyone (or everything) involved in the decision. The student needs a school with a full physical therapy program; she and her parents need to cut costs; she needs to be able to transfer credits.

3. Name, investigate, and evaluate available options. Brainstorm possible choices, and then look at the facts surrounding each. *Evaluate* the good and bad effects of each possibility. Weigh these effects and judge which is the best course of action. Here are some possibilities that the student in the example might consider:

> ➤ *Continue at the current college.* **Positive effects**: I wouldn't have to adjust to a new place or to new people. I could continue my course work as planned. **Negative effects**: I would have to find a way to finance most of my tuition and costs on my own, whether through loans, grants, or work. I'm not sure I could find time to work as much as I would need to, and I don't think I would qualify for as much aid as I now need.

> ➤ *Transfer to the state college.* **Positive effects**: I could reconnect with people there that I know from high school. Tuition and room costs would be cheaper than at my current school. I could transfer credits. **Negative effects**: I would still have to work some hours or find minimal financial aid. The physical therapy program is small and not very strong.

> ➤ *Transfer to the community college.* **Positive effects**: They have many of the courses I need to continue with the physical therapy curriculum. The school is close by, so I could live at home and avoid paying housing costs. Credits will transfer. The tuition is extremely reasonable. **Negative effects**: I don't know anyone there. I would be less independent. The school doesn't offer a bachelor's degree.

4. Decide on a plan of action and pursue it. Make a choice based on your evaluation, and act on your choice. In this case the student might decide to go to the community college for two years and then transfer back to a four-year school to earn a bachelor's degree in physical therapy. Although she might lose some independence and contact with friends, the positive effects are money saved, opportunity to spend time on studies rather than working to earn tuition, and the availability of classes that match the physical therapy requirements.

5. Evaluate the result. Was it useful? Not useful? Some of both? Weigh the positive and negative effects. If the student decides to transfer, she may find that it can be hard being back at home, although her parents are adjusting to her independence and she is trying to respect their concerns. Fewer social distractions result in her getting more work done. The financial situation is favorable. All things considered, she evaluates that this decision was a good one.

Making important decisions can take time. Think through your decisions thoroughly, considering your own ideas as well as those of others you trust, but don't hesitate to act once you have your plan. You cannot benefit from your decision until you act on it and follow through.

THINKING BACK

1. Looking at these Thinktrix icons, write the name of each mind action.

_____

_____

_____

_____

_____

_____

_____

2. Name one way you used a mind action to think critically this past week.

_____

_____

_____

3. Name the steps in the problem-solving plan.

_____

_____

_____

4. What decision do you have coming up for which you can use the decision-making process?

_____

_____

_____

THINKING AHEAD

1. In your papers or in verbal discussion, do you feel you get your point across effectively? Why or why not?

_____

_____

_____

2. Name an assumption that you have heard someone make. Do you feel it is fact or opinion? Why?

_____

_____

_____

3. Do you think you are a creative person? When do you find you are able to use your creativity?

_____

_____

_____

4. Does a fear of failure ever keep you from trying? If so, when does this happen?

_____

_____

HOW DO YOU CONSTRUCT AN EFFECTIVE ARGUMENT?

In this case, "argument" refers to a persuasive case that you make to prove or disprove a point. You will often encounter situations in which your success depends on your ability to **persuade** someone, either verbally or in writing, to agree with you. You may need to write a paper persuading the reader that a particular historical event changed the world, for example, or you may need to persuade a prospective employer that you are the one for the job.

When you come to crossroads in your life, thinking critically toward a persuasive argument can help you achieve what you want. Put the mind actions to work, using the following steps:

Persuade,

To convince someone through argument or reasoning to adopt a belief, position, or course of action.

Establish the goal—what's at stake. No argument provides an absolute guarantee of achieving a goal, but a persuasive argument will give you your best shot. Ask yourself what you want. For example, imagine that you want a raise and promotion to a new position at work.

Gather examples that support your idea. What will support your request? In this case, you may have consistently gotten good performance reviews and you have ideas for the position you want. These examples argue that your promotion will have positive effects for the company.

Anticipate questions. What will the other person or people ask you to explain? In the example, potential questions may include those: "What have you achieved in your current position?" "What do you know about the position you want to take?" "What new and creative ideas do you have?"

Anticipate points against you. What could someone bring up that argues against what you want? Decide what you will say to defend against opposing points. For example, if your supervisor might say that you can't handle the new position's longer hours, you could look into adjusting your school schedule.

Be flexible. You never know what will happen as you present your argument. You might not even need to push, or it may turn out to be tougher than you thought. By rehearsing your response to questions beforehand, you will be as prepared as possible to handle any twists and turns the conversation may take.

HOW DO YOU ESTABLISH TRUTH?

Investigating the truth and accuracy of information, rather than automatically accepting it as true, is an important critical-thinking process. To seek truth through critical thinking, you question the validity of statements or information. Critical-thinking experts Sylvan Barnet and Hugo Bedau state that when you test for the truth of a statement, you "determine whether what it asserts corresponds with reality; if it does, then it is true, and if it doesn't, then it is false."[2] To determine to what degree a statement "corresponds with reality," ask questions based on the mind actions. The search for truth takes two primary forms: distinguishing fact from opinion and challenging assumptions.

Distinguishing Fact from Opinion

Fact, according to the dictionary, is information presented as objectively real. *Opinion* is defined as a belief, conclusion, or judgment. Whether you are studying for a test or doing research for a paper, being able to distinguish fact from opinion is crucial to your understanding of reading material. Fact and opinion generate different reactions in a reader. If you decide that a statement is opinion, you may focus on deciding whether you agree with that opinion according to how it is supported. If you decide that a statement is fact, your focus moves toward evaluating how that fact is used to support other ideas or opinions.

There is a degree of overlap in fact and opinion. Opinions can be proved to be partially or completely factual after investigation. Statements that seem factual may emerge as opinions if any part of them is proven wrong through questioning. Qualifiers, such as *all, none, never, often, sometimes,* and *many,* will frequently mean the difference between fact and opinion. Absolute qualifiers such as *all* and *none* indicate an opinion more often than a fact, whereas indefinite qualifiers such as *some* and *many* may make a fact out of what seems to be an opinion. For example, "All college students need jobs" is an opinion, whereas "Some college students need jobs" is a fact.

Both facts and opinions require investigation through questioning. To be safe, consider all statements opinions until proven otherwise. Questions you may ask include the following:

> ➤ What facts or examples provide evidence of truth?
> ➤ How does the maker of the statement know this to be true?
> ➤ Is there another fact that disproves this statement or information or shows it to be an opinion?
> ➤ How reliable are the sources of information?
> ➤ What about this statement is similar to or different from other information I consider fact?
> ➤ How could I test the validity of this statement or information?

See Table 4–2 for some more examples of factual statements versus statements of opinion.

Another crucial step in determining the truth is to question the assumptions that you and others hold and which are the underlying force in shaping opinions.

TABLE 4-2 EXAMPLES OF FACTS AND OPINIONS

SUBJECT	FACTUAL STATEMENT	STATEMENT OF OPINION
Animal speed	The cheetah has been clocked at speeds that prove it to be the world's fastest animal.	No animal can ever escape the speed of the cheetah.
Weather	It's raining outside.	This is the worst rainstorm in recent history.
Fats in foods	Meats generally contain more fat than vegetables.	Diners who want to avoid fat should choose a veggie pizza rather than a cheeseburger.

Challenging Assumptions

"If it's more expensive, it's better." "You should study in a library." These statements reveal assumptions—evaluations or generalizations based on observing cause and effect—that can often hide within seemingly truthful statements. An **assumption** can influence choices: You may assume that you should earn a certain degree or own a car. Many people don't question whether their assumptions make sense, nor do they challenge the assumptions of others.

Assumptions come from sources such as parents or relatives, television and other media, friends, and your personal experiences. As much as you think such assumptions work for you, it's just as possible that they can close your mind to opportunities and even cause harm. Think critically to uncover and investigate assumptions. Ask these questions:

1. Is the truth of this statement supported with fact, or does it hide an assumption?
2. In what cases is this assumption true or not true? What examples prove or disprove it?
3. Has making this assumption benefited me or others? Has it hurt me or others? In what ways?
4. If someone taught me this assumption, why? Did that person think it over or just accept it?
5. What harm could be done by always taking this assumption as fact?

For example, here's how you might use these questions to investigate the following statement: "The most productive schedule involves getting started early in the day."

1. This statement hides the following assumption: The morning is when all people feel most energetic and are able to get lots of things done.

> **Assumption,**
> An idea or statement accepted as true without examination or proof.

2. This assumption may be generally true for people who enjoy early morning hours and have a lot of energy during that part of the day. But the assumption may not be true for people who work best in the afternoon or evening hours.

3. Society's basic standard of daytime classes and 8:00 A.M. to 5:00 P.M. working hours supports this assumption. Therefore, the assumption may work for people who have early jobs and classes. It may not work, however, for people who work shifts or who take evening classes.

4. Maybe people who believe this assumption were raised to start their days early. Or perhaps they just go along with what seems to be society's standard. Still, there are plenty of people who operate on a different schedule and yet enjoy successful, productive lives.

5. Taking this assumption as fact could hurt people who don't operate at their peak in the earlier hours. For example, if a "night owl" tries to take early classes, he or she may experience concentration problems that would not necessarily occur later in the day.

THE WHEEL OF THINKING **FIGURE 4-3**

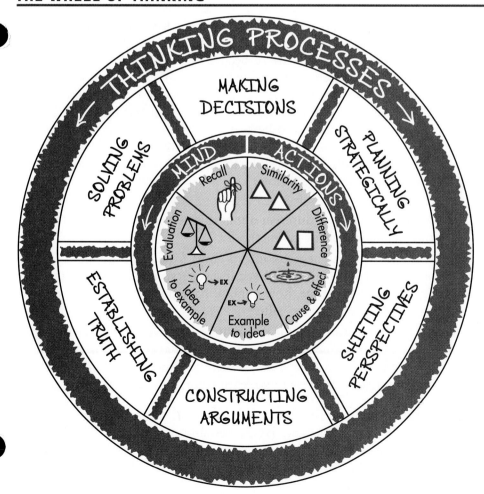

In situations that favor their particular characteristics—later classes and jobs, and career areas that don't require early morning work—such people have just as much potential to succeed as anyone else.

Be careful to question all assumptions, not just those that seem problematic from the start. Form your opinion after investigating the positive and negative effects of any situation.

WHY SHIFT YOUR PERSPECTIVE?

Perspective,
A mental point of view or outlook, based on a cluster of related assumptions, incorporating values, interests, and knowledge.

Seeing the world only from your perspective or point of view, is inflexible, limiting, and frustrating to both you and others. You probably know how hard it can be to relate to someone who cannot understand your situation—an instructor who doesn't like you to leave early on Thursdays for physical therapy, or a friend who can't understand why you would date someone of a different race. Seeing beyond one's own perspective can be difficult, especially when life problems and fatigue take their toll.

However, when you shift your own perspective to consider someone else's, you open the lines of communication and build mutual respect. For example, if you want to add or drop a course and your advisor says it's impossible before listening to everything you have to say, you might not feel much like explaining. But, if your advisor asks to hear your point of view, you may sense that your needs are respected. Feeling respected may encourage you to respond or even to change your mind.

Every time you shift your perspective, you can also learn something new. You may find different and equally valid ways of getting an education, living as a family, or relating to others. Above all else, you may see that each person is entitled to his or her own perspective, no matter how foreign it may be to you. Asking questions like these will help you maintain flexibility and openness in your perspective:

➤ What is similar and different about this person, belief, or method and me, my beliefs or my methods?

➤ What positive and negative effects come from this different way of being, acting, or believing? Even if this perspective seems to have negative effects for me, how might it have positive effects for others—and therefore have value?

➤ What can I learn from this different perspective? Is there anything I could adopt for my own life—something that would help me improve who I am or what I do? Is there anything I wouldn't do myself but that I can still respect and learn from?

Shifting your perspective is at the heart of all successful communication. Being able to shift perspective and communicate more effectively may mean the difference between success and failure in today's diverse world.

WINDOWS ON THE WORLD: REAL LIFE STUDENT ISSUES

How do I solve the problem of getting the classes I want?

Edhilvia Campos, Parkland Community College, Champaign, Illinois, Microbiology Major

Every semester it's a challenge to figure out what classes I will need. I am majoring in microbiology, so I need a lot of science courses, and the ones I want aren't always available. Also, I eventually want to transfer to the University of Illinois. The process for registering and figuring out what will transfer seems complicated.

When I came to the States for college, only a few of my math credits transferred because the math classes I had taken in high school in Venezuela were not acceptable credits for college. My freshman year I took two algebra classes and later found out that they couldn't be applied to my major, which made me feel like I wasted my time. I also don't want to pay for classes that I don't need. Trying to regulate the number of classes you take isn't easy either. One thing I have learned to do is take at least one fun class each semester. Last semester I had to take chemistry and calculus so I decided to take music, too, which was a nice break for me.

I may want to go back to Venezuela during the summers. I've considered taking classes then, but the Venezuelan universities don't really have my major. Once again I'm trying to find out what classes are available that apply to my major. Do you have suggestions for what I can do to make this process more efficient?

Shera Chantel Caviness, University of Memphis, Early Childhood Education—Graduate Major

First and foremost, hang in there. I know that things seem hard now, but it will pay off. Attending college is similar to a "micro" real world. Throughout college, you will have to face problems that must be resolved. I understand that you feel you wasted time and money taking certain classes. But  some classes are not transferable, and extra money has to be utilized to take certain courses before entering a degree program.

To prepare to transfer, get acquainted with an academic counselor at the U. of Illinois (preferably one in your major) to help you. He or she can tell you what will transfer. While at Parkland, find an academic counselor in your field who can guide you toward appropriate courses for that degree. Use the undergraduate catalog to stay informed of the necessary classes for your major.

Get to know the professors in your field because they can help. If some classes are not available for one semester, gather at least eight to ten students to voice their concern about opening a section for that class. The class schedule is done at the beginning of the previous semester, and professors are often unaware of the demand for certain courses because students do not speak up.

If you do plan to return to Venezuela for the summer, only take courses that will apply to your degree or take some classes that are transferable. Check with the counselors before signing up. Always find something valuable in each course you take because this will help you become more well rounded. Remember to think positively, this is only a "micro" real-world experience helping to prepare you for the R-E-A-L world.

WHY PLAN STRATEGICALLY?

If you've ever played a game of chess, participated in a wrestling or martial arts match, or made a detailed plan of how to reach a particular goal, you have had experience with **strategy**. In these situations and many others, you continually have to think about and anticipate what might happen. Often you have to think ahead about how you would respond to several possible occurrences.

Strategy is the plan of action, the method, the "how" behind any goal you want to achieve. Specifically, strategic planning means looking at the next week, month, year, or ten years and exploring the positive and negative effects that your current choices and actions may have in the future. You are planning strategically right now just by being in school. You made a decision that the effort of attending college is a legitimate price to pay for the skills, contacts, and opportunities that will help you in the future.

Being strategic means being versatile, having options, and making choices for how best to accomplish tasks. What are some benefits, or positive effects, of strategic planning?

Strategy is an essential skill at school and at work. A student who wants to do well in a course needs to plan study sessions to complete assignments on time. A lawyer needs to anticipate how to respond to allegations the opposing side may raise in court. Strategic planning creates a vision into the future that allows the planner to anticipate possibilities and, most important, to be prepared for them.

Strategic planning powers your short-term and long-term goal setting. Once you have set goals, plan the steps that will help you achieve them over time. For example, a student who wants to contribute to his tuition might drive a used car and maintain a part-time job. In class, a strategic planner will think critically about the material, knowing that information is most useful later on if it is clearly understood.

Strategic planning helps you keep up with technology. As technology develops, jobs become obsolete. It's possible to spend years in school training for a career area that will be dying by the time you graduate. Strategic planning may lead you to a broader range of courses or a major and career in a growing area, making it more likely that your skills will be in demand when you graduate.

Effective critical thinking is essential to strategic planning. If you aim for a certain goal, what steps will move you toward it? What positive effects do you anticipate these steps will have? What can you learn from similar or different previous experiences in order to take different steps today? Critical thinking runs like a thread through all of your strategic planning.

Here are some tips for becoming a strategic planner:

Develop an appropriate plan. What approach will best achieve your goal? What steps toward your goal will you need to take one year, five years, ten years, or twenty years from now?

Strategy,
A plan of action designed to accomplish a specific goal.

" I have always thought that one man of tolerable abilities may work great changes, and accomplish great affairs among mankind, if he first forms a good plan. "

Benjamin Franklin

Anticipate all possible outcomes of your actions. What positive and negative effects may occur?

Ask the question "how?" How do you achieve your goals? How do you remember what you learn? How do you develop a productive idea at work? How do you distinguish yourself at school and at work?

Experiment with strategies. Try different plans, and evaluate their positive and negative effects to see what works best for you. For example, you might try two different kinds of date books to help you plan your semester, eventually deciding that one works better than the other.

Use human resources. Talk to people who are where you want to be, whether professionally or personally. What caused them to get there? Ask them what they believe are the important steps to take, degrees to have, training to experience, and knowledge to gain.

Be prepared to change. The strategies you are accustomed to may not always be best. If you discover that you need to make a change, take the risk and know that you are on the road to important growth.

In each thinking process, you use your creativity to come up with ideas, examples, causes, effects, and solutions. You have a capacity to be creative, whether you are aware of it or not. Open up your mind and awaken your creativity. It will enhance your critical thinking and make life more enjoyable.

HOW CAN YOU DEVELOP YOUR CREATIVITY?

Everyone is creative. Although the word *creativity* may inspire images of art and music, **creativity** comes in many other forms. It is the power to create, whether the creation is a solution, idea, approach, tangible product, work of art, system, or program. Expand your concept of creativity with these examples of day-to-day creative thinking:

Creativity,
The ability to produce something new through imaginative skill.

➤ Figuring out an alternative plan when your baby-sitter unexpectedly cancels
➤ Planning how to coordinate your work and class schedules
➤ Talking through a problem with an instructor, and finding a way to understand each other
➤ Planning a budget so that you can pay your monthly bills

Creative innovations introduced by all kinds of people continually expand and change the world. Here are some that have had an impact:

➤ Susan B. Anthony and other women fought for and won the right for women to vote.

In art class, a woman paints designs on on stretched cloth

➤ Henry Ford introduced the assembly-line method of automobile construction, making cars cheap enough to be available to the average citizen.

➤ Rosa Parks refused to give up her seat on the bus to a white person, setting off a chain of events that gave rise to the civil rights movement.

➤ Alicia Diaz, director of the Center of Hispanic Policy, Research, and Development, developed corporate partnerships that have become models for small, efficient government.

Even though these particular innovations had wide-ranging effects, the characteristics of these influential innovators can be found in all people who exercise their creative capabilities.

Characteristics of Creative People

Creative people think in fresh new ways that improve the world and increase productivity, consistently responding to change with new ideas. Roger van Oech, an expert on creativity, highlights this kind of flexibility: "I've found that the hallmark of creative people is their mental flexibility," he says. "Like race-car drivers who shift in and out of different gears depending on where they are on the course, creative people are able to shift in and out of different types of thinking depending on the needs of the situation at hand…they're doggedly persistent in striving to reach their goals."[3] Creative people combine ideas and information in ways that form completely new solutions, ideas, processes, uses, or products.

Enhancing Your Creativity

You are naturally creative. One way to spur creative ability is to explore new territory and adjust to change. Although it may feel uncomfortable to try out new ideas or behavior, it can reveal all kinds of possibilities. When you feel yourself resisting, remember that exploring new ideas doesn't mean that what you were doing before was wrong. You are just responding to change with flexibility and creativity.

Following are some ways to enhance your creativity, adapted from material by J. R. Hayes[4] and from material by van Oech.[5]

➤ Spend time in creative settings and with creative people.

➤ Give yourself time to figure out a problem or to evaluate an idea.

➤ Gather as much information and as many ideas as you can when building a creative idea.

➤ Try to generate more than one "right answer" to improve your chances of finding the best one.

➤ Don't always follow strict logic and rules; go off the beaten track.

➤ Be impractical; ask yourself, "What if?"

➤ Let yourself play; creative ideas may surface when your mind is in a play mode.

➤ Don't fear failure.

Brainstorming may combine many of these strategies. Use brainstorming for problem solving, decision making, writing a paper, or whenever you need to free your mind for new possibilities.

Brainstorming Toward a Creative Answer

You are brainstorming when you approach a problem by letting your mind free-associate and come up with as many possible ideas, examples, or solutions as you can, without immediately evaluating them as good or bad. Brainstorming is also referred to as *divergent thinking;* you start with the issue or problem and then let your mind diverge, or go in as many different directions as it wants, in search of ideas or solutions. Here are some guidelines for successful brainstorming:[6]

Don't evaluate or criticize an idea right away. Write down your ideas so that you remember them. Evaluate later, after you have had a chance to think about them. Try to avoid criticizing other people's ideas as well. Students often become stifled when their ideas are evaluated during brainstorming.

Focus on quantity; don't worry about quality until later. Generate as many ideas or examples as you can. The more thoughts you generate, the better the chance that one may be useful. Brainstorming works well in groups. Group members can become inspired by, and make creative use of, one another's ideas.

Consider wild and wacky ideas. Trust yourself to go off the beaten track. Sometimes the craziest ideas end up being the most productive, positive, workable solutions.

Remember, creativity can be developed if you have the desire and patience. Nurture your creativity by being accepting of your own ideas. Your creative expression will become more free with practice.

Creativity and Critical Thinking

Critical thinking and creativity work hand in hand. Critical thinking is inherently creative because it requires you to use given information to come up with ideas or solutions to problems. For example, if you were brainstorming to generate possible causes of fatigue in afternoon classes, you might come up with lack of sleep, too much morning caffeine, or an instructor who doesn't inspire you. Through your consideration of causes and solutions, you have been thinking both creatively and critically.

Creative thinkers and critical thinkers have similar characteristics—both consider new perspectives, ask questions, don't hesitate to question accepted assumptions and traditions, and persist in the search for answers. Only through thinking critically and creatively can you freely question, brainstorm, and evaluate to find the most fitting ideas, solutions, decisions, arguments, and plans.

> "Learning to let yourself create is like learning to walk. Progress, not perfection, is what we should be asking of ourselves."
>
> Julia Cameron

You use critical-thinking mind actions throughout everything you do in school and in your daily life. In this chapter and in some of the other study skills chapters, you will notice mind-action icons placed where they can help you to label your thinking.

WHAT IS MEDIA LITERACY?

Do you believe everything you read, see on television, or hear on the radio? Think about it for a moment. If you trusted every advertisement, you would believe that at least four fast-food restaurants serve "the best burger available." If you agreed with every magazine article, you would know that Elvis passed away years ago and yet still believe that he was shopping for peanut butter last week in Oklahoma. It is impossible to believe it all without becoming completely confused about what is real.

If literacy refers to the ability to read, media literacy can be seen as the ability to read the **media**. *Media literacy*—the ability to respond with critical thinking to the media that you encounter—is essential for a realistic understanding of the information that bombards you daily. It means that instead of accepting anything a newspaper article, magazine advertisement, or TV announcer says is fact, you take time to question the information, using your mind actions and critical-thinking processes.

The people who founded the Center for Media Literacy work to encourage others to think critically about the media. They have put forth what they call the "Five Core Concepts of Media Literacy."[7]

Media,
The agencies of mass communication—television, film, and journalism (magazines and newspapers).

1. *All media are constructions.* Any TV show or advertisement, for example, is not a view of actual life or fact but rather a carefully constructed presentation that is designed to have a particular effect on the viewer—to encourage you to feel a certain emotion, develop a particular opinion, or buy the product advertised. For example, an article that wants the reader to feel good about the president will focus on his strengths rather than his shortcomings.

2. *Media use unique "languages."* The people who produce media carefully choose wording, background music, colors, images, timing, and other factors to produce the effect they want. The next time you go to a movie, listen carefully to the music that plays behind an emotional scene or a high-speed chase.

3. *Different audiences understand the same media message differently.* Individual people understand media in the context of their own unique experiences. For this reason people may often interpret media quite differently. A child who has not experienced violence may be frightened by violent scenes on television, whereas a child who has witnessed or experienced violence may accept such images as normal and acceptable.

4. *Media have commercial interests.* Rather than being driven by the need to tell the truth, media are driven by the intent to sell you

something. Television programs, newspapers, and magazines make sure that the advertisers who support the show or publication get a chance to convey a message to the consumer. Advertising is chosen so that it most appeals to those most likely to be reading or seeing that particular kind of media; for example, ads for toys usually come on during children's programming, and ads for beer and cars dominate the airwaves during major sports events.

5. *Media have embedded values and points of view.* Any media product carries the values of the people who created it. No media is free of someone's opinion of what deserves the most attention. For example, even by choosing the topics on which to write articles, a magazine's editor conveys an opinion that those topics are important. *Runner's World* thinks that how to stay warm on a winter run is important, for example, whereas *Parenting* emphasizes what to do when your child has a fever.

The whole point of media literacy is to approach what you see, hear, and read with thought and consideration. Use your critical-thinking processes to analyze the media and develop an informed opinion.

Ask questions based on the mind actions. Is what you read in an article similar to something you already know to be true? Does a newspaper ad show something that differs from your own experience? Do you evaluate a magazine article as useful or not? Do you agree with the causes or effects that are cited?

Evaluate the truth of the argument. If a TV ad argues that a certain kind of car is the best on the road, evaluate this information in the way that you would any argument. With what facts do they back up their claims? Are the claims opinion? How can you test their validity? Does assuming their claims to be true cause any harm or untruth? From what you know about constructing an argument, what strategies are they using to persuade you to adopt their idea?

Shift your perspective. It is just as important to avoid rejecting the media automatically as it is to avoid accepting them automatically. Any media offering has its own particular perspective, coming from the person or people who created it. Take the time to discover this perspective and then decide if you accept it (even if it may be different from your own). Ask what positive and negative effects adopting this perspective might have on you. For example, if a cigarette ad in a magazine encourages you to adopt the perspective that you should smoke, this may have harmful effects on your health. Or if a newspaper article introduces a new way to get enough calcium in your diet, adopting that perspective might have positive effects.

Becoming a media-literate person will help you become a smart consumer of the media who ultimately is able to be responsible for his or her own actions. Don't let a TV ad or a big, splashy billboard tell you what to do. Take in the message, evaluate it critically, and make your own decision. Media literacy is a key to a responsible, self-powered life.

Κρινειν

The word "critical" is derived from the Greek word *krinein,* which means to separate in order to choose or select. To be a mindful, aware critical thinker, you need to be able to separate, evaluate, and select ideas, facts, and thoughts.

Think of this concept as you apply critical thinking to your reading, writing, and interaction with others. Be aware of the information you take in and of your thoughts, and be selective as you process them. Critical thinking gives you the power to make sense of life by deliberately selecting how to respond to the information, people, and events that you encounter.

IMPORTANT POINTS TO REMEMBER

1. What is critical thinking?

Critical thinking is important thinking with which you question established ideas, create new ideas, and turn information into tools to solve problems and make decisions. The three primary ingredients of critical thinking are asking questions, considering varied responses, and choosing responses that are as complete and accurate as possible. The building blocks of critical thinking are seven mind actions: *recall, similarity, difference, cause and effect, example to idea, idea to example,* and *evaluation.* These mind actions, in various combinations, build the thinking processes that help you achieve your goals. Six of your mind's primary thinking processes are as follows: solving problems, making decisions, constructing an argument, establishing truth, shifting perspective, and planning strategically.

2. How does critical thinking help you solve problems and make decisions?

Although not all decisions are about problems, every problem-solving process involves one or more decisions. Use the steps of the problem-solving process—stating the problem, analyzing the problem, brainstorming solutions, exploring solutions, choosing and executing a solution, and evaluating the solution—to generate solutions and choose one. Decisions are choices that require an evaluation of possibilities. Evaluate a decision by using these steps: Decide on a goal; establish needs; name, investigate, and evaluate available options; decide on a plan of action and pursue it; and evaluate the result.

3. How do you construct an effective argument?

An argument is a position that you take to prove or disprove a point. In your life, you may need to construct an argument when a grade, a job, or a relationship is at stake. The following steps can help you prove your point: Establish your goal, gather examples that support your idea of what you want, anticipate questions and points against your argument, and remain as flexible as possible to handle unexpected twists in the conversation.

4. How can you establish truth?

The search for truth involves distinguishing fact from opinion and challenging assumptions. To evaluate whether a statement is fact or opinion, ask questions that explore the evidence given, the reliability of the source, and how the information compares to other facts that you know. Assumptions—statements or ideas that people accept as true without proof—can shape important life decisions, and sometimes they can be problematic. Challenge your assumptions by asking when they are and aren't true, when they do and don't work, why someone may have made and communicated the assumption, and what harm the assumption can cause.

5. Why shift your perspective?

When you are able to shift your perspective, you open the lines of communication and promote respect. Exploring other perspectives also helps you learn more about what lies outside your experience. Ask questions about how perspectives differ, what positive and negative effects come from different perspectives, how something that seems negative to you may be positive for someone else, and what you can learn from these other points of view.

6. Why plan strategically?

Strategic planning means making long-range plans toward goals, that is, exploring the future effects of today's choices and actions. A strategic plan for the next ten years may have five-year, one-year, six-month, one-month, and one-week steps. To be a strategic planner, you should look for real understanding, anticipate all possible effects of your actions, be driven by asking the question "how?" and develop an appropriate plan using your resources.

7. How can you develop your creativity?

Everyone has the ability to be creative. Actively creative people have such characteristics as flexibility, a willingness to take risks, inquisitiveness, and a broad range of interests. You can enhance your creativity by taking a broad perspective, spending time with creative people, gathering varied input, and letting yourself play. Brainstorming is a creative process that requires you to consider any ideas that come into your head and refrain from evaluating them right away.

8. What is media literacy?

Media literacy is the ability to respond with critical thinking to the media—radio, television, magazines, newspapers, and Internet materials—that you encounter. Thinking critically about the media will bring you to a more complete understanding of the information that comes your way. The five core concepts of media literacy are as follows: Media are constructions; media use specifically chosen "languages;" different audiences understand the same media message differently; media have commercial interests; and media take particular points of view.

Name _____ Date _____

BUILDING SKILLS FOR COLLEGE, CAREER, AND LIFE SUCCESS
CHAPTER 4

TAKING STOCK:
REFINING YOUR THOUGHTS

Look back at the statements you explored at the start of the chapter (see
Thinking It Through on p. 113). Observe whether your attitudes have
changed and how much you learned by studying this chapter.

1. Define critical thinking and give an example.

_____

_____

_____

2. Describe a problem you solved in the past two weeks. What mind actions helped you to solve it?

_____

_____

_____

_____

3. State a goal for which you will plan strategically. What steps will help
you achieve your goal?

_____

_____

_____

4. State an assumption that seems to be true for you. When might it not be
true for someone else?

_____

_____

_____

5. What are some possible harmful effects of not being able to shift your perspective?

_____

_____

_____

6. Name two characteristics of creative people that you feel you have. Describe what happened when you last used your creative powers.

_____

_____

_____

7. What information you recently received from the media did you not believe right away and why?

_____

_____

_____

8. Describe how you will use one of the six thinking processes this week.

_____

_____

_____

 # CRITICAL THINKING:
APPLYING LEARNING TO YOUR LIFE

Make an Important Decision

In this series of exercises you will use the seven mind actions and the decision-making steps. First, write here the decision you need to make. Choose an important decision that needs to be made soon.

_____

_____

_____

Step 1: Name your goal. Be specific: What goal, or desired effects, do you seek from this decision? For example, if your decision is a choice between two jobs, the effects you want might be financial security, convenience, experience, or anything else that is a priority to you. It could also be a combination of these effects.

   Write down the desired effects that together make up your goal. Note priorities by numbering the effects in order of importance.

_____

_____

_____

_____

Step 2: Establish needs. Who and what will be affected by your decision? If you are deciding how to finance your education and you have a family to support, you must take into consideration their financial needs as well as your own when exploring options.

   List here the people, things, or situations that may be affected by your decision and indicate how your decision will affect them.

_____

_____

_____

_____

Step 3: Check out your options. Look at any options you can imagine. Consider options even if they seem impossible or unlikely; you can evaluate them later. Some decisions have only two options (to move to a new apartment or not; to get a new roommate or not); others have a wider selection of choices. For example, if you are a full-time student and the parent of a child, you must coordinate your class schedule with the child's needs. Options could be the following: (1) put the child in day care, (2) ask a relative to care for the child, (3) hire a full-time nanny, or (4) arrange your class schedule so that you can balance the duties with another parent.

   List three possible options for this decision. Then evaluate the potential good and bad effects of each.

Option 1 _____

Positive effects _____

Negative effects _____

Option 2 _____

Positive effects _____

Negative effects _____

Option 3 _____

Positive effects _____

Negative effects _____

Have you or someone else ever made a decision similar to the one you are about to make? What can you learn from that decision that may help you?

_____

_____

_____

Step 4: Make your decision and pursue it to the goal. Taking your entire analysis into account, decide what to do. Write your decision here.

_____

_____

_____

Next is perhaps the most important step: *Act on your decision.*

Step 5: Evaluate the result. After you have acted on your decision, evaluate how everything turned out. Did you achieve the effects you wanted to achieve? What were the effects on you? On others? On the situation? To what extent were they positive, negative, or some of both?

List three effects here. Name each effect, circle Positive or Negative, and explain that evaluation.

Effect _____

        Positive   Negative

Why? _____

Effect _____

        Positive   Negative

Why? _____

Effect _____

        Positive   Negative

Why? _____

Final evaluation: Write one statement in reaction to the decision you made. Indicate whether you feel the decision was useful or not useful, and why. Indicate any adjustments that could have made the effects of your decision more positive.

_____

_____

_____

_____

Brainstorming on the Idea Wheel

Your creative mind can solve problems when you least expect it. Many people report having sudden ideas while exercising, driving, showering, upon waking, or even when dreaming. When the pressure is off, the mind is often more free to roam through uncharted territory and bring back treasures.

To make the most of this mind-float, grab ideas when they surface. If you don't, they roll back into your subconscious as if on a wheel. Since you never know how big the wheel is, you can't be sure when that particular idea will roll to the top again. That's why writers carry notebooks—they need to grab thoughts when they come to the top of the wheel.

Name a problem, large or small, to which you haven't yet found a satisfactory solution. Do a brainstorm without the time limit. Be on the lookout for ideas, causes, effects, solutions, or similar problems coming to the top of your wheel. The minute it happens, grab this book and write your idea next to the problem. Look at your ideas later and see how your creative mind may have pointed you toward some original and workable solutions. You may want to keep a book by your bed to catch ideas that pop up before, during, or after sleep. Use the margins for overflow.

Problem: _____

Ideas: _____

_____

Constructing an Argument about Media Assumptions and Perspectives

Name an assumption that you have seen made in any form of media—television, magazines, and so on. It can be about anything—for example, people, lifestyles, education, differences, money, and relationships. Write it here:

_____

_____

Now you will construct two arguments: one that supports the assumption and one that disputes it. Use your mind actions to ask important questions as you construct your arguments; think of cases or examples that fit and don't fit the assumption, positive and negative effects of believing the assumption, similar and different assumptions, and what experiences might cause the assumption.

Argument supporting _____

_____

_____

_____

Argument disputing _____

_____

_____

_____

Analyze each argument in your mind. Which perspective seems more open-minded? Which works better for situations in your life? Which perspective is closer to yours? Note here which perspective is further from your own and write one thing that you have learned from exploring that side of the argument.

_____

_____

_____

TEAMWORK:
COMBINING FORCES

Group problem solving. As a class, brainstorm a list of problems in your lives. Write the problems on the board or on a large piece of paper attached to an easel. Include any problems you feel comfortable discussing with others. Such problems may involve school, relationships, jobs, discrimination, parenting, housing, procrastination, and others. Divide into groups of two to four, with each group choosing or being assigned one problem to work on. Use the empty problem-solving flowchart to fill in your work.

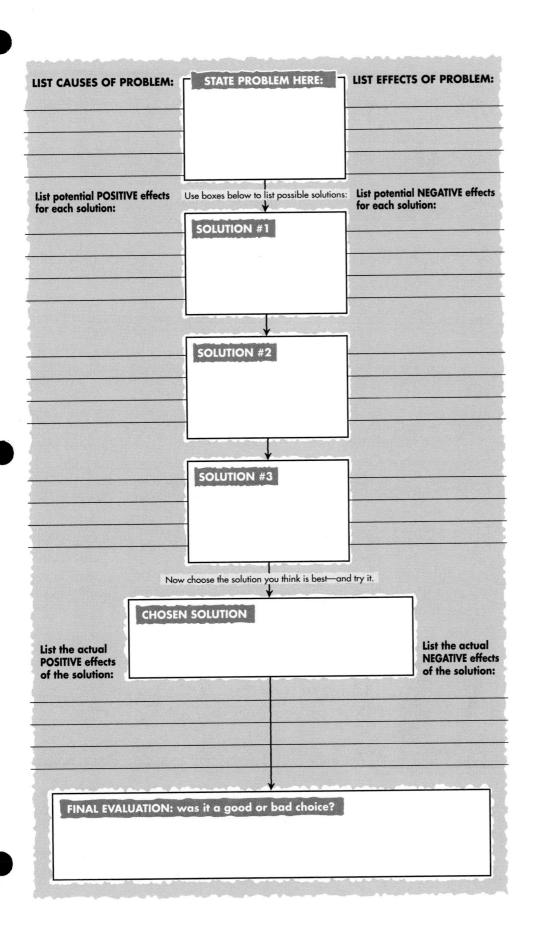

LIST CAUSES OF PROBLEM:

STATE PROBLEM HERE:

LIST EFFECTS OF PROBLEM:

List potential POSITIVE effects for each solution:

Use boxes below to list possible solutions:

List potential NEGATIVE effects for each solution:

SOLUTION #1

SOLUTION #2

SOLUTION #3

Now choose the solution you think is best—and try it.

CHOSEN SOLUTION

List the actual POSITIVE effects of the solution:

List the actual NEGATIVE effects of the solution:

FINAL EVALUATION: was it a good or bad choice?

1. *Identify the problem.* As a group, state your problem specifically, without causes ("I'm not attending all of my classes" is better than "lack of motivation"). Then, look at the causes and effects that surround it. Record the effects that the problem has. List what causes the problem. Remember to look for "hidden" causes (you may perceive that traffic makes you late to school, but getting up too late might be the hidden cause).

2. *Brainstorm possible solutions.* Determine the most likely causes of the problem; from those causes, derive possible solutions. Record all the ideas that group members offer. After ten minutes or so, each group member should choose one possible solution to explore independently.

3. *Explore each solution.* In thinking independently through the assigned solution, each group member should (a) weigh the positive and negative effects, (b) consider similar problems, (c) determine whether the problem requires a different strategy from other problems like it, and (d) describe how the solution affects the causes of the problem. Evaluate your assigned solution. Is it a good one? Will it work?

4. *Choose your top solution(s).* Come together again as a group. Take turns sharing your observations and recommendations, and then take a vote: Which solution is the best? You may have a tie or combine two different solutions. Either way is fine. Different solutions suit different people and situations. Although it's not always possible to reach agreement, try to find the solution that works for most of the group.

5. *Evaluate the solution you decide is best.* When you decide on your top solution or solutions, discuss what would happen if you went through with it. What do you predict would be the positive and negative effects of this solution? Would it turn out to be a truly good solution for everyone?

WRITING: DISCOVERY THROUGH JOURNALING

To record your thoughts, use a separate journal or the lined pages at the end of the chapter.

Strategic planning. Discuss how you set short-term and long-term goals. Do you tend to plan ahead of time? Why or why not? Discuss one long-term goal in terms of what you want in one year, five years, ten years, and twenty years. How do you plan to accomplish this goal? What do you want to achieve?

CAREER PORTFOLIO:
CHARTING YOUR COURSE

Investigate a career area. Choose one career that interests you. Use your critical-thinking processes to think about all aspects of this career strategically. Be an investigator. Find out as many facts as you can and evaluate all opinions based on what you already know.

> What are the different kinds of jobs available in this career?

> What is the condition of the industry—growing, lagging, or holding steady?

> Does this career require you to live in a certain area of the country or world?

> Who can you talk to for more information about this career?

> What are the pros and cons (positive and negative effects) of working in this area?

> What types of people tend to succeed in this career, and what types tend not to do well?

> What are the opinions of those around you about this career?

> What preparation—in school and/or on the job—does this career area require?

Then, write up your findings in a report. Use each question as a separate heading. Keep your research in your portfolio. Write a conclusion about your prospects in this career, based on what you learned in your investigation.

Journal Entry

Name _____ Date _____

Journal Entry

5 READING AND STUDYING: Your Keys to Knowledge

Thinking It Through

❑ I find myself struggling to get through many of my texts.
❑ When I read rapidly, I have trouble understanding or remembering what I read.
❑ When I learn a new vocabulary word, I often don't remember the definition for long.
❑ When I study, I often have to read the same material over and over again to grasp it.
❑ I don't usually study with a group of classmates.
❑ I barely look at tables and charts when I read a text.

In this chapter, you will explore answers to the following questions:

➤ What challenges does college reading present?
➤ Why define your purpose for reading?
➤ How can SQ3R help you own what you read?
➤ How can you respond critically to what you read?
➤ How and why should you study with others?
➤ How can you "read" visual aids?

Your reading background—your past as a reader—may not necessarily prepare you for the new challenges of college reading. Certain reading strategies that worked before may not work so well now. Some high school reading programs promote the misconception that "good readers" are those who can answer the study questions. In high school, you generally had more time to read less material, and there was less necessity for deep-level understanding.

In college, however, you may frequently experience an overload of reading assignments. Furthermore, your reading will often be complex. Even with study guides and other aids, college reading and studying require a step-by-step approach aimed at the construction of meaning and knowledge. The material in this chapter will present techniques that can help you read and study as efficiently as you possibly can, while still having time left over for other things. You will learn how you can overcome barriers to successful reading and why you should have a purpose each time you read. You will explore the SQ3R study technique, see how critical reading can help you maximize your understanding of any text, and learn to understand visual aids.

WHAT CHALLENGES DOES COLLEGE READING PRESENT?

Everyone has reading challenges, such as difficult texts, distractions, a lack of speed and comprehension, and insufficient vocabulary. Following are some ideas about how to meet these challenges. Note that if you have a reading disability, if English is not your primary language, or if you have limited reading skills, you may need additional support. Most colleges provide services for students through a reading center or tutoring program. Take the initiative to seek help if you need it. Many accomplished learners have benefited from help in specific areas.

Working Through Difficult Texts

Although many textbooks are useful teaching tools, some can be poorly written and organized. Students using texts that aren't well written may blame themselves for the difficulty they're experiencing. Because texts are often written to challenge the intellect, even well-written, well-organized texts may be difficult and dense to read.

Generally, the further you advance in your education, the more complex your required reading is likely to be. For example, your sociology professor may assign a chapter on the dynamics of social groups, including those of dyads and triads. When is the last time you heard the terms *dyads* and *triads* in normal conversation? You may feel at times as though you are reading a foreign language as you encounter new concepts, words, and terms. Remember that as you get into your major field of study, you will become accustomed to the vocabulary of your discipline.

Assignments can also be difficult when the required reading is from primary sources rather than from texts. *Primary sources* are original documents rather than another writer's interpretation of the documents. They include the following:

> Historical documents
> Works of literature (novels, poems, and plays)
> Scientific studies, including lab reports and accounts of experiments
> Journal articles

The academic writing found in journal articles and scientific studies is different from other kinds of writing. Some academic writers assume that readers understand sophisticated concepts. They may not define basic terms, provide background information, or supply a wealth of examples to support their ideas. As a result, concepts may be difficult to understand.

Making your way through poorly written or difficult reading material is hard work, which can be accomplished through focus, motivation, commitment, and skill. The following strategies may help.

Approach your reading assignments head-on. Be careful not to prejudge them as impossible or boring before you even start to read.

Accept the fact that some texts may require some extra work and concentration. Set a goal to make your way through the material and to learn it, whatever it takes.

When a primary source discusses difficult concepts that it does not explain, put in extra work to define such concepts on your own. Ask your instructor or other students for help. Consult reference materials in that particular subject area, other class materials, dictionaries, and encyclopedias. For convenience, try creating your own minilibrary at home. Collect reference materials that you use often, such as a dictionary, a thesaurus, a writer's style handbook, and maybe an atlas or computer manual. You may also benefit from owning reference materials in your particular areas of study. "If you find yourself going to the library to look up the same reference again and again, consider purchasing that book for your personal or office library," advises library expert Sherwood Harris.[1]

Look for order and meaning in seemingly chaotic reading materials. The information you find in this chapter on the SQ3R reading technique and on critical reading will help you discover patterns and achieve a greater depth of understanding. Finding order within chaos is an important skill, not just in the mastery of reading, but also in life. This skill can give you power by helping you "read" (think through) work dilemmas, personal problems, and educational situations.

Managing Distractions

With so much happening around you, it's often hard to focus on your reading. Some distractions are external: the telephone or a child who needs attention. Other distractions come from within, as thoughts arise about various topics: a paper due in art history or an Internet site that you want to visit.

Identify the Distraction and Choose a Suitable Action

Pinpoint what's distracting you before you decide what kind of action to take. If the distraction is *external* and *out of your control*, such as construction outside your building or a noisy group in the library, try to move away from it. If the distraction is *external* but *within your control*, such as the television, telephone, or children, take action; for example, turn off the television or let the answering machine answer the phone. Figure 5–1 explores some ways in which parents or other people caring for children may be able to maximize their study efforts.

FIGURE 5-1   **MANAGING CHILDREN WHILE STUDYING**

Managing Children While Studying

Explain what your education entails. Tell them how it will improve both your life and theirs. This applies, of course, to older children who can understand the situation and compare it to their own schooling.

Keep them up to date on your schedule. Let them know when you have a big test or project due and when you are under less pressure, and what they can expect of you in each case.

Keep them active while you study. Give them games, books, or toys to occupy them. If there are special activities that you like to limit, such as watching videos on TV, save them for your study time.

Find help. Ask a relative or friend to watch your children or arrange for a child to visit a friend's house. Consider trading baby sitting hours with another parent, hiring a sitter to come to your home, or using a day care center that is private or school-sponsored.

Offset study time with family time and rewards. Children may let you get your work done if they have something to look forward to, such as a movie night, a trip for ice cream, or something else they like.

Study on the phone. You might be able to have a study session with a fellow student over the phone while your child is sleeping or playing quietly.

Special Notes for Infants

Study at night if your baby goes to sleep early, or in the morning if your baby sleeps late.

Study during nap times if you aren't too tired yourself.

Lay your notes out and recite information to the baby. The baby will appreciate the attention, and you will get work done.

Put baby in a safe and fun place while you study, such as a playpen, motorized swing, or jumping seat.

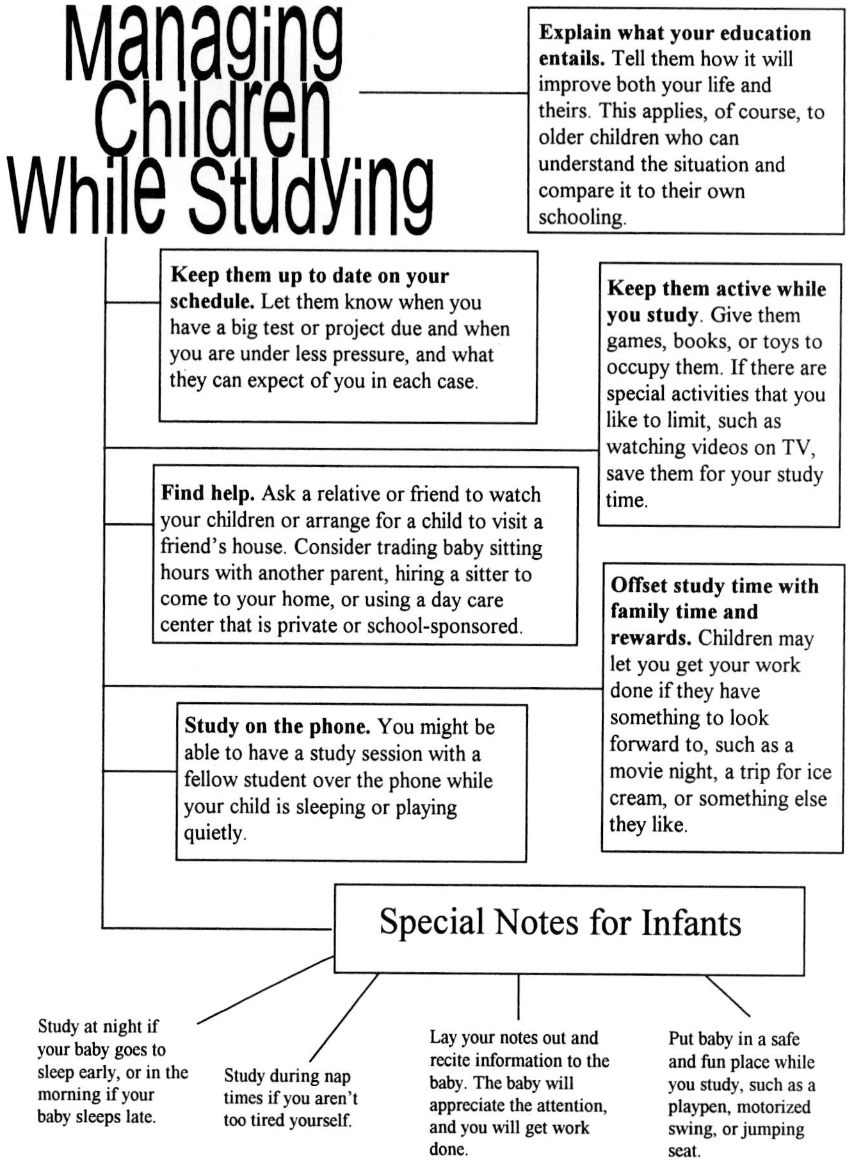

If the distraction is *internal*, different strategies may help you clear your mind. You may want to take a study break and tend to one of the issues that worries you. Physical exercise may relax and refocus you. For some people, studying while listening to music helps to quiet a busy mind. For others, silence may do the trick. If you need silence to read or study and cannot find a truly quiet environment, consider purchasing sound-muffling headphones or even earplugs.

Find the Best Place and Time to Read

Any reader needs focus and discipline to concentrate on the material. Finding a place and time that minimize outside distractions will help you achieve that focus. Here are some suggestions:

Read alone unless you are working with other readers. Family members, friends, or others who are not in a study mode may interrupt your concentration. If you prefer to read alone, establish a relatively interruption-proof place and time, such as an out-of-the-way spot at the library or an after-class hour in an empty classroom. If you study at home and live with other people, you may want to place a "Quiet" sign on the door.

Find a comfortable location. Many students study at a library desk. Others prefer an easy chair at the library or at home, or even the floor. Choose a spot comfortable enough for hours of reading but not so cushy that you fall asleep. Make sure that you have adequate lighting and aren't too hot or too cold.

Choose a regular reading place and time. Choose a spot or two that you like, and return often. Also, choose a time when you feel alert and focused. Some students prefer to read just before or after the class for which the reading is assigned. Eventually, you will associate preferred places and times with focused reading.

If it helps you concentrate, listen to soothing background music. The right music can drown out background noises and relax you. However, the wrong music can make it impossible to concentrate; for some people, silence is better. Experiment to learn what you prefer; if music helps, stick with the type that works better. A personal headset makes listening possible no matter where you are.

Turn off the television. For most people, reading and television don't mix.

Building Comprehension and Speed

Most students lead busy lives, carrying heavy academic loads while perhaps working or even caring for a family. It's difficult to make time to study at all, let alone handle the reading assignments for your different classes. Increasing your reading comprehension and speed will save you valuable time and effort.

Rapid reading won't do you any good if you can't remember the material or answer questions about it. However, reading too slowly can eat up valuable study time and give your mind space to wander. Your goal is to read for maximum speed *and* comprehension. Because greater comprehension is the primary goal and actually promotes faster reading, make comprehension your priority over speed.

Test Your Speed and Comprehension

To make your own reading-speed assessment, time how rapidly you read the following 500-word selection from start to finish without stopping. This excerpt, entitled "Back to School at Middle Age," is adapted from the seventh edition of Grace J. Craig's college text *Human Development*:[2]

Although today's college campuses are filled with 18- to 22-year-olds, they are also filled with older, nontraditional students who are returning to school. Nearly 1.5 million women and more than 700,000 men over the age of 35 are attending college—as 4-year students, in 2-year degree programs, and as graduate students. While there has been a dramatic increase in this segment of the college population, the percentage of typical college students—men and women between the ages of 18 and 22—has actually declined since 1980.

This dramatic demographic shift coincides with the recognition that humans are lifelong learners with cognitive abilities that adapt to life demands. Despite societal stereotypes that the primary period for learning is over after adolescence, we now know that it is during middle age that adults acquire the information and skills they need to meet the changing demands of their jobs. This is as true for bankers as it is for computer scientists, both of whom work in fields that have changed radically in recent years as a result of an explosion in technology.

In large part, middle-aged students are returning to school because they have to. Many are unemployed—the victims of corporate downsizing. Others are moving into the job market after spending time at home as full-time parents. A financial planner who stopped working for 5 years to raise her daughter may need recertification before any firm will hire her. Even adults who worked part-time during their child-rearing years may have to return to school to acquire the knowledge they need to qualify for a full-time job. This is especially true in fields with a high degree of professional obsolescence.

Whatever the reason for their return, studies show that the majority of middle-aged students are conscientious about their work. They attend classes regularly and get better grades, on average, than other segments of the student population.

The decision to return to school involves personal introspection and assessment of one's skills and abilities. The student role is generally different from the other roles middle-aged adults assume, and it requires considerable adaptation. A student is in a subordinate position as a learner. Also, mature adults may find themselves among a large number of students who are considerably younger than they are, and the faculty may also be younger. Initially, the age difference may be a source of discomfort.

Family members must often take on new responsibilities when a middle-aged member assumes the role of college student. A husband may have to do more household chores, while a wife may have to return to work to supplement the family income. In addition, the student may need emotional support. Sometimes this involves awkward role reversals and the disruption of familiar interaction patterns.

With the realization that middle-aged students are here to stay, community colleges and universities are making substantial adjustments to meet their needs. In addition many students receive the training they need at work. Many large corporations run training departments designed to maintain a competent work force.

Source: HUMAN DEVELOPMENT, 7/E by Craig, © 1974. Adapted by permission of Prentice-Hall, Inc., Upper Saddle River, NJ.

Use the following formula to calculate how quickly you read this material:

➤ Note the time it took you in minutes to read the passage. Use decimals for fractions of a minute. That is, if it took you 1 minute and 45 seconds, then write 1.75 minutes.

➤ Divide the number of words in the passage by your reading time.

The number you come up with is your reading speed in words per minute. If you spent 1.75 minutes reading this 500-word selection, you would divide 500 by 1.75 to come up with a reading speed of approximately 286 words per minute.

Now answer the following questions without looking back at the text:

1. How many men and women over the age of 35 are now enrolled in various college programs?

  A. Approximately 1.5 million women and 700,000 men
  B. Five million men and women
  C. Approximately 1.5 million men and 700,000 women

2. How has the enrollment of 18- to 22-year-old college students changed since 1980 in relationship to the total college population?

  A. The percentage of students in this age group has increased.
  B. The percentage of students in this age group has remained the same.
  C. The percentage of students in this age group has decreased.

3. According to the passage, which one of the following reasons does not describe why older adults return to school?

  A. Unemployed adults return to school to acquire new work-related skills.
  B. After spending time at home raising children, many adults are moving into another stage of life, which involves returning to work.
  C. Adults with discretionary income are choosing to invest money in themselves.

4. According to the text, why is the student role different from the other roles middle-aged adults assume?

  A. As learners, students are in a subordinate position, which can be uncomfortable for mature adults.
  B. Adults are not used to studying.
  C. Middle-aged adults often find it difficult to talk to young adults.

Here are the correct answers: 1A, 2C, 3C, 4A. You should have gotten at least three of the four questions correct. In general, your comprehension percentage, as judged by the number of questions like these that you answer correctly, should be above 70 percent. Lower scores mean that you are missing, or forgetting important information.

Methods for Increasing Reading Comprehension

Following are some specific strategies for increasing your understanding of what you read:

Continually build your knowledge through reading and studying. What you already know before you read a passage will greatly influence your ability to understand and remember important ideas. Previous knowledge, including vocabulary, facts, and ideas, gives you a **context** for what you read.

Context,
Written or spoken knowledge that can help illuminate the meaning of a word or passage.

Establish your purpose for reading. When you establish what you want to get out of your reading, you will be able to determine what level of understanding you need to reach and, therefore, on what you need to focus. A detailed discussion of reading purposes follows on pages 165–166.

Remove the barriers of negative self-talk. Instead of telling yourself that you cannot understand, think positively. Tell yourself: *I can learn this material. I am a good reader.*

Think critically. Take advantage of titles, headings, and subheadings that indicate important concepts. Ask yourself questions. Do you understand the sentence, paragraph, or chapter you just read? Are ideas and supporting examples clear to you? Could you clearly explain what you just read to someone else?

Methods for Increasing Reading Speed

The average American adult reads between 150 and 350 words per minute, amd faster readers can be capable of speeds up to 1000.[3] However, the human eye can only move so fast; reading speeds in excess of 350 words per minute involve "skimming" and "scanning" (see p. 168).

➤ Try to read groups of words rather than single words.
➤ Avoid pointing your finger to guide your reading since this will slow your pace.
➤ Try swinging your eyes from side to side as you read a passage, instead of stopping at various points to read individual words.
➤ When reading narrow columns, focus your eyes in the middle of the column and read down the page. With practice, you'll be able to read the entire column width.
➤ Avoid **vocalization** when reading.
➤ Avoid thinking each word to yourself as you read it, a practice known as *subvocalization*. Subvocalization is one of the primary causes of slow reading speed.

Vocalization,
The practice of speaking words and/or moving your lips while reading.

Expanding Your Vocabulary

Lifelong learners consider their vocabulary a work in progress because they never finish learning new words. A strong vocabulary increases reading speed and comprehension; when you understand the words in your reading material, you don't have to stop as often to think about what they mean.

No matter how strong or weak your vocabulary is, you can improve it by using a dictionary, reading and writing words in context, and learning common prefixes and suffixes.

Use a Dictionary

When reading a textbook, the first "dictionary" to search is the glossary. Textbooks often include an end-of-book glossary that explains technical words and concepts. The definitions there are usually limited to the meaning of the term as it is used in the text.

Standard dictionaries provide broader information such as word origin, pronunciation, part of speech, synonyms (words that are similar), antonyms (words with opposite meanings), and multiple meanings. Using a dictionary whenever you read will increase your comprehension. Buy a standard dictionary, keep it nearby, and consult it for help in understanding passages that contain unfamiliar words.

You may not always have time for the following suggestions, but when you can use them, they will help you make the most of your dictionary.

Getting some work done in a quiet corner

Read every meaning of a word, not just the first. Think critically about which meaning suits the context of the word in question, and choose the one that makes the most sense to you.

Substitute a word or phrase from the definition for the word. Use the definition you have chosen. Imagine, for example, that you encounter the following sentence and do not know what the word *indoctrinated* means:

> The cult indoctrinated its members to reject society's values.

In the dictionary, you find several definitions, including *brainwashed* and *instructed*. You decide that the one closest to the correct meaning is *brainwashed*. With this term, the sentence reads as follows:

> The cult brainwashed its members to reject society's values.

Reading and Writing Words in Context

Most people learn words best when they read and use them in written or spoken language. Although a definition tells you what a word means, you may have difficulty remembering that definition if you have no context in which to connect or compare it. Using a word in context after defining it will help to anchor the information so that you can continue to build on it.

Here are some strategies for using context to solidify your learning of new vocabulary words.

Use new words in a sentence or two right away. Do this immediately after reading their definitions, while everything is still fresh in your mind.

Reread the sentence where you originally saw the word. Go over it a few times to make sure you understand how the word is used.

Use the word over the next few days whenever it may apply. Try it while talking to friends, writing letters or notes, or in your own thoughts.

Consider where you may have seen or heard the word before. When you learn a word, going back to sentences you previously didn't "get" may solidify your understanding. For example, most children learn the Pledge of Allegiance by rote without understanding what "allegiance" means. Later, when they learn the definition of "allegiance," the pledge provides a context that helps them better understand the word.

Seek knowledgeable advice. If after looking up a word you still have trouble with its meaning, ask your instructor or a friend if he or she can help you figure it out.

Learn Prefixes and Suffixes

Root,

The central part or basis of a word, around which prefixes and/or suffixes can be added to produce.

Often, if you understand part of a word, you will be able to figure out what the entire word means. Particularly helpful is a working knowledge of common prefixes and suffixes. *Prefixes* are word parts that are added to the beginning of a root, and *suffixes* are added to the end of the root. Table 5–1 contains prefixes and suffixes you may encounter.

Facing the challenges of reading is only the first step. The next important step is to examine why you are reading any given piece of material.

TABLE 5-1   COMMON PREFIXES AND SUFFIXES

PREFIX	PRIMARY MEANING	EXAMPLE
a, ab	from, away	abstain, avert
ad, af, at	to	adhere, affix, attain
con, cor, com	with, together	convene, correlate, compare
di	apart	divert, divorce
il	not	illegal, illegible
ir	not	irresponsible
post	after	postpone, post-partum
sub, sup	under	subordinate, suppose

SUFFIX	PRIMARY MEANING	EXAMPLE
-able	able	recyclable
-arium	place for	aquarium, solarium
-cule	very small	molecule
-ist	one who	pianist
-meter	measure	thermometer
-ness	state of	carelessness
-sis	condition of	hypnosis
-y	inclined to	sleepy

WHY DEFINE YOUR PURPOSE FOR READING?

As with other aspects of your education, asking questions will help you make the most of your efforts. When you define your purpose, you ask yourself *why* you are reading a particular piece of material. One way to do this is by completing this sentence: "In reading this material, I intend to define/learn/answer/achieve...." With a clear purpose in mind, you can decide how much time and effort to expend on various reading assignments. Nearly 375 years ago, Francis Bacon, the great English philosopher, recognized,

> Some books are to be tasted, others to be swallowed, and some few to be chewed and digested; that is, some books are to be read only in parts, others to be read but not curiously; and some few to be read wholly, and with diligence and attention.

Achieving your reading purpose requires adapting to different types of reading materials. Being a flexible reader—adjusting your reading strategies and pace—will help you to adapt successfully.

Purpose Determines Reading Strategy

With purpose comes direction; with direction comes a strategy for reading. Following are five reading purposes, examined briefly. You may have one or more for any "reading event."

Purpose 1: Read for understanding. In college, studying involves reading for the purpose of comprehending the material. The two main components of comprehension are *general ideas* and *specific facts or examples*. These components depend on each other. Facts and examples help to explain or support ideas, and ideas provide a framework that helps the reader to remember facts and examples.

> *General ideas.* General-idea reading is rapid reading that seeks an overview of the material. You search for general ideas by focusing on headings, subheadings, and summary statements.
>
> *Specific facts or examples.* At times, readers may focus on locating specific pieces of information—for example, the stages of intellectual development in young children. Often, a reader may search for examples that support or explain more general ideas—for example, the causes of economic recession. Because you know exactly what you are looking for, you can skim the material quickly.

Purpose 2: Read to evaluate critically. Critical evaluation involves understanding. It means approaching the material with an open mind, examining causes and effects, evaluating ideas, and asking questions that test the writer's argument and search for assumptions. Critical reading brings an understanding of material that goes beyond basic information recall (see pp. 174–178 for more on critical reading).

Purpose 3: Read for practical application. A third purpose for reading is to gather usable information that you can apply toward a specific goal. When you read a computer manual or an instruction sheet for assembling a gas grill, your goal is to learn how to do something. Reading and action usually go hand in hand. Remembering the specifics requires a certain degree of general comprehension.

Purpose 4: Read for pleasure. Some materials you read for entertainment, such as *Sports Illustrated* magazine or the latest John Grisham courtroom thriller. Entertaining reading may also go beyond materials that seem obviously designed to entertain. Whereas some people may read a Jane Austen novel for comprehension, as in a class assignment, others may read her books for pleasure.

Purpose Determines Pace

George M. Usova, senior education specialist and graduate professor at Johns Hopkins University, explains: "Good readers are flexible readers. They read at a variety of rates and adapt them to the reading purpose at hand, the difficulty of the material, and their familiarity with the subject area."[4] For example, you may need to read academic and/or unfamiliar materials more slowly, whereas you will increase your reading speed for journalism, nonfiction and fiction books, magazines, and on-line publications.

So far, this chapter has focused on reading as a deliberate, purposeful process of meaning construction. Recognizing obstacles and defining reading purposes lay the groundwork for effective studying—the process of mastering the concepts and skills contained in your texts.

> "No barrier of the senses shuts me out from the sweet, gracious discourse of my book friends. They talk to me without embarrassment or awkwardness."
>
> Helen Keller

THINKING BACK

1. List four purposes for reading.

   a. _____

   b. _____

   c. _____

   d. _____

2. Name three methods for increasing reading speed.

   a. _____

   b. _____

   c. _____

3. Name three methods for increasing reading comprehension.

a. _____

b. _____

c. _____

4. Explain how using a dictionary can help improve reading comprehension.

_____

_____

_____

THINKING AHEAD

1. Explain the reading strategies that, for you, help you retain information most effectively.

_____

_____

_____

2. If you were to design a study method for yourself, what might that method involve?

_____

_____

_____

3. When tables and charts appear in your textbooks, do they help you? How?

_____

_____

_____

HOW CAN SQ3R HELP YOU OWN WHAT YOU READ?

When you study, you take ownership of the material you read. You learn it well enough to apply it to what you do. For example, by the time students studying to be computer-hardware technicians complete their coursework, they should be able to analyze hardware problems that lead to malfunctions.

Studying also gives you mastery over concepts. For example, a dental hygiene student learns the causes of gum disease, a biology student learns what happens during photosynthesis, and a business student learns about marketing research.

The following technique will help you more effectively understand, learn, study, and remember what you read in your college textbooks.

Survey-Question-Read-Recite-Review (SQ3R)

SQ3R is a technique that will help you grasp ideas quickly, remember more, and review effectively for tests. The symbols S-Q-3-R stand for *survey, question, read, recite,* and *review*—all steps in the studying process. Developed more than fifty-five years ago by Francis Robinson, the technique is still being used today because it works.[5] It is particularly helpful for studying all kinds of textbooks.

Skimming,

Rapid, superficial reading of material to determine central ideas and main elements.

Moving through the stages of SQ3R requires that you know how to skim and scan. Skimming involves rapid reading of chapter elements, including introductions, conclusions, and summaries; the first and last lines of paragraphs; boldface or italicized terms; pictures, charts, and diagrams. The goal of skimming is a quick construction of the main ideas. In contrast, scanning involves the careful search for specific facts and examples. You might use scanning during the review phase of SQ3R, when you need to locate particular information (such as a formula in a chemistry text).

Scanning,

Reading material in an investigative way, searching for specific information.

Survey

The best way to ruin a "whodunit" novel is to flip through the pages to find out how everything turned out. However, when reading textbooks, surveying can help you learn and is encouraged. Surveying refers to the process of previewing, or prereading, a book before you actually study it. Most textbooks include devices that give students an overview of the text as a whole, as well as of the contents of individual chapters. As you look at Figure 5–2, think about how many of these devices you already use.

Question

Your next step is to examine the chapter headings and, on your own paper, write *questions* linked to them. If your reading material has no headings, develop questions as you read. These questions focus your attention and increase your interest, helping you build comprehension and relate new ideas to what you already know. You can take questions from the textbook or

TEXT AND CHAPTER PREVIEWING DEVICES   **FIGURE 5-2**

PREVIEWING DEVICES

- Part openers (if text chapters are divided into sections)
- Chapter titles
- List of objectives
- Chapter outlines
- Opening stories that set the stage for the chapter discussion
- Major and minor chapter headings
- Special learning tools
- Bold and italicized words and phrases
- Internal chapter progress checks
- Notes in the margins
- Tables and figures
- Photo illustrations
- End-of-chapter key terms and concepts
- End-of-chapter review questions, exercises, and problems

- Text preface
- Table of contents
- Chapter summaries

- End-of-text glossary
- Text index
- Text bibliography

At the beginning of the text or chapters   At the end of the text   In the middle, linked to specific chapters

from your lecture notes or come up with them on your own when you survey, based on what ideas you think are most important.

Here is how this technique works. The column on the left contains primary- and secondary-level headings from a section of *Business*, an introductory text by Ricky W. Griffin and Ronald J. Ebert. The column on the right rephrases these headings in question form.

I. THE CONSUMER BUYING PROCESS	I. WHAT IS THE CONSUMER BUYING PROCESS?
A. Problem/Need Recognition	A. Why must consumers first recognize a problem or need before they buy a product?
B. Information Seeking	B. What is information seeking and who answers consumers' questions?
C. Evaluation of Alternatives	C. How do consumers evaluate different products to narrow their choices?
D. Purchase Decision	D. Are purchasing decisions simple or complex?
E. Postpurchase Evaluations	E. What happens after the sale?

There is no "correct" set of questions. Given the same headings, you could create your own particular set of questions. The more useful kinds of questions engage the critical-thinking mind actions and processes found in Chapter 4.

Read

Your questions give you a starting point for *reading,* the first R in SQ3R. Read the material with the purpose of answering each question you raised. Pay special attention to the first and last lines of every paragraph, which should tell you what the paragraph is about. As you read, record key words, phrases, and concepts in your notebook. Some students divide the notebook into two columns, writing questions on the left and answers on the right. This method is called the Cornell note-taking system (see Chapter 7).

If you own the textbook, mark it up in whatever ways you prefer. Your notations will help you to make sense of the material. You may want to write notes in the margins, circle key ideas, or highlight key sections. Some people prefer to underline, although underlining adds more ink to the lines of text and may overwhelm your eye. Although writing in a textbook makes it difficult to sell it back to the bookstore, the increased depth of understanding you can gain is worth the investment.

Selective highlighting may help you pinpoint material to review before an exam, although excessive highlighting may actually interfere with comprehension. Here are some tips on how to strike a balance.

Mark the text after you read the material once through. If you do it on the first reading, you may mark less important passages.

Highlight key terms and concepts. Mark the examples that explain and support important ideas. You might try highlighting ideas in one color and examples in another.

Highlight figures and tables. They are especially important if they summarize text concepts.

Avoid overmarking. A phrase or two is enough in most paragraphs. Set off long passages with brackets rather than marking every line.

Write notes in the margins. Comments like "main point" and "important definition" will help you find key sections later on.

Be careful not to mistake highlighting for learning. You will not learn what you highlight unless you review it carefully. Additional benefits will come from writing highlighted information into your notes.

One critical step in the reading phase is to divide your reading into digestible segments. Pace your reading so that you understand as you go. If you find you are losing the thread of the ideas you are reading, you may want to try smaller segments, or you may need to take a break and come back to it later. Try to avoid reading in mere sets of time—such as, "I'll read for thirty minutes and then quit"—or you may destroy the meaning by stopping in the middle of a key explanation.

Recite

Once you finish reading a topic, stop and answer the questions you raised in the Q stage of SQ3R. You may decide to *recite* each answer aloud, silently speak the answers to yourself, tell the answers to another person as though you were teaching him or her, or write your ideas and answers in brief notes. Writing is often the most effective way to solidify what you have read because writing from memory checks your understanding. Use whatever techniques best suit your learning-style profile (see Chapter 3).

After you finish one section, read the next. Repeat the question-read-recite cycle until you complete the entire chapter. If during this process you find yourself fumbling for thoughts, you may not yet "own" the ideas. Reread the section that's giving you trouble until you master its content. Understanding each section as you go is crucial because the material in one section often forms a foundation for the next.

> *"In books, I could travel anywhere, be anybody, understand worlds long past and imaginary colonies in the future."*
>
> Rita Dove

Review

Review soon after you finish a chapter. Here are some techniques for reviewing:

➤ Skim and reread your notes. Then try summarizing them from memory.

➤ Answer the text's end-of-chapter review, discussion, and application questions.

➤ Quiz yourself, using the questions you raised in the Q stage. If you can't answer one of your own or one of the text's questions, go back and scan the material for answers.

➤ Review and summarize in writing the sections and phrases you have highlighted or bracketed.

➤ Create a chapter outline in standard outline form or think-link form.

➤ Reread the preface, headings, tables, and summary.

➤ Recite important concepts to yourself, or record important information on a cassette tape and play it on your car's tape deck or your portable cassette player.

➤ Make flash cards that have an idea or word on one side and examples, a definition, or other related information on the other. Test yourself.

➤ Think critically: Break ideas down into examples, consider similar or different concepts, recall important terms, evaluate ideas, and explore causes and effects.

➤ Make think links that show how important concepts relate to one another.

If you need help clarifying your reading material, ask your instructor. Pinpoint the material you want to discuss, schedule a meeting with him or her during office hours, and bring a list of questions.

Repeating the review process renews and solidifies your knowledge. That is why it is important to set up regular review sessions, for example, once a week. As you review, remember that refreshing your knowledge is easier and faster than learning it the first time. Reviewing in as many different ways as possible increases the likelihood of retention.

FIGURE 5-3   **USE SQ3R TO BECOME AN ACTIVE READER**

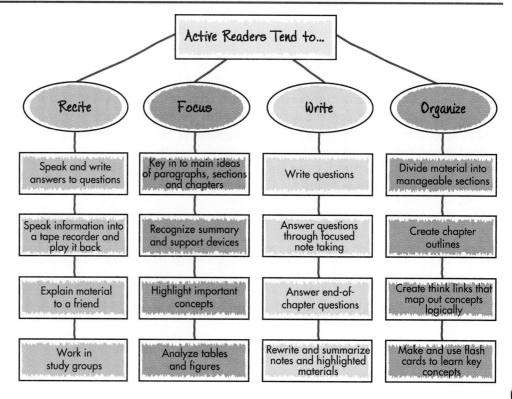

As you can see in Figure 5–3, using SQ3R is part of being an active reader. Active reading involves the specific activities that help you retain what you learn.

Putting SQ3R to Work

The following is an excerpt from *Principles of Microeconomics* by Karl E. Case and Ray C. Fair.[6] Apply the SQ3R technique as you read it. Think through the major points of the passage and use the margins and/or the space provided below to make any notes, comments, or questions.

_____

_____

_____

_____

_____

_____

FIRMS AND HOUSEHOLDS:
THE BASIC DECISION-MAKING UNITS

Throughout this book, we discuss and analyze the behavior of two fundamental decision-making units: firms—the primary producing units in an economy—and households—the consuming units in an economy. Both are made up of people performing different functions and playing different roles. In essence, then, what we are developing is a theory of human behavior.

firm *An organization that transforms resources (inputs) into products (outputs). Firms are the primary producing units in a market economy.*

A **firm** exists when a person or a group of people decides to reproduce a product or products by transforming inputs (that is, resources in the broadest sense) into outputs (the products that are sold in the market). Some firms produce goods; others produce services. Some are large, some are small, and some are in between. But all firms exist to transform resources into things that people want. The Colorado Symphony Orchestra takes labor, land, a building, musically talented people, electricity, and other inputs and combines them to produce concerts. The production process can be extremely complicated. The first flutist in the orchestra, for example, uses training, talent, previous performing experience, a score, an instrument, the conductor's interpretation, and her own feelings about the music to produce just one contribution to an overall performance.

Most firms exist to make a profit for their owners, but some do not. Columbia University, for example, fits the description of a firm: It takes inputs in the form of labor, land, skills, books, and buildings and produces a service that we call education. Although it sells that service for a price, it does not exist to make a profit, but rather to provide education of the highest quality possible.

Still, most firms exist to make a profit. They engage in production because they can sell their product for more than it costs to produce it. The analysis of firm behavior that follows rests on the assumption that *firms make decisions in order to maximize profits.*

entrepreneur *A person who organizes, manages, and assumes the risks of a firm, taking a new idea or a new product and turning it into a successful business.*

An entrepreneur is one who organizes, manages, and assumes the risks of a firm. It is the entrepreneur who takes a new idea or a new product and turns it into a successful business. All firms have implicit in them some element of entrepreneurship. When a new firm is created—whether a proprietorship, a partnership, or a corporation—someone must organize the new firm, arrange financing, hire employees, and take risks. That person is an entrepreneur. Sometimes existing companies introduce new products, and sometimes new firms develop or improve an old idea, but at the root of it all is entrepreneurship, which some see as the core of the free enterprise system.

At the root of the debate about the potential of free enterprise in formerly socialist Eastern Europe is the question of entrepreneurship. Does an entrepreneurial spirit exist in that part of the world? If not, can it be developed? Without it the free enterprise system breaks down.

households *The consuming units in an economy.*

The consuming units in an economy are households. A household may consist of any number of people: a single person living alone, a married couple living with four children, or 15 unrelated people sharing a house. Household decisions are presumably based on the individual tastes and preferences of the consuming unit. The household buys what it wants and can afford. In a large, heterogeneous, and open society such as the United States, wildly different tastes find expression in the marketplace. A six-block walk in any direction on any street in Manhattan or a drive from the Chicago loop south into rural Illinois should be enough to convince anyone that it is difficult to generalize about what people like and do not like.

Even though households have wide-ranging preferences, they also have some things in common. All—even the very rich—have ultimately limited incomes, and all must pay in some way for the things they consume. While households may have some control over their incomes—they can work more or less—they are also constrained by the availability of jobs, current wages, their own abilities, and their accumulated and inherited wealth (or lack thereof).

After reading the excerpt, using SQ3R, answer the following questions. Try not to look back at the material. Instead, examine whether the SQ3R system helped you remember the key points of the passage.

1. What are the two decision-making units called?

   _____

   _____

2. Most firms exist to make a profit. True or false? _____

3. Someone who organizes, manages, and assumes risks is called a(n)

   _____ .

4. A household
   a. is the consuming unit in an economy.
   b. may consist of any number of people.
   c. has ultimately limited incomes.
   d. is constrained by the availability of jobs.
   e. all of the above.

HOW CAN YOU RESPOND CRITICALLY TO WHAT YOU READ?

Textbook features often highlight important ideas and help you determine study questions. As you advance in your education, however, many reading assignments—especially primary sources—will not be so clearly marked. You will need critical-reading skills in order to select important ideas, identify examples that support them, and ask questions about the text without the aid of any special features.

Critical reading enables you to develop a thorough understanding of reading material, through evaluation and analysis. A critical reader is able to discern the main idea of a piece of reading material as well as identify what in that piece is true or useful, such as when using material as a source for an essay. A critical reader can also compare one piece of material to another and evaluate which makes more sense, which proves its thesis more successfully, or which is more useful for the reader's purposes.

Critical reading transcends rote memorization (taking in and regurgitating material). Critical reading is both making meaning of the original text and adding your personal response to it. Engage your critical-thinking processes by using the following suggestions.

Use SQ3R to "Taste" Reading Material

Sylvan Barnet and Hugo Bedau, authors of *Critical Thinking, Reading, and Writing—A Brief Guide to Argument*, suggest that the active reading of SQ3R will help you form an initial idea of what a piece of reading material is all about. Through surveying, skimming for ideas and examples, highlighting and writing comments and questions in the margins, and reviewing, you can develop a basic understanding of its central ideas and contents.[7]

Summarizing, part of the SQ3R review process, is one of the best ways to develop an understanding of a piece of reading material. To construct a **summary**, focus on the central ideas of the piece and the main examples that support them. A summary does not contain any of your own ideas or your evaluation of the material. It simply condenses the material, making it easier to focus on the structure and central ideas of the piece when you go back to read more critically. At that point, you can begin to ask questions, evaluating the piece and introducing your own ideas. Using the mind actions will help.

> **Summary,**
> A concise restatement of the material, in your own words, that covers the main points.

Ask Questions Based on the Mind Actions

The essence of critical reading, as with critical thinking, is asking questions. Instead of simply accepting what you read, seek a more thorough understanding by questioning the material as you go along. Using the mind actions of the Thinktrix to formulate your questions will help you understand the material.

What parts of the material you focus on will depend on your purpose for reading. For example, if you are writing a paper on the causes of World War II, you might look at how certain causes fit your thesis. If you are comparing two pieces of writing that contain opposing arguments, you may focus on picking out their central ideas and evaluating how well the writers use examples to support them.

You can question any of the following components of reading material:

> ➤ The central idea of the entire piece
> ➤ A particular idea or statement
> ➤ The examples that support an idea or statement
> ➤ The proof of a fact
> ➤ The definition of a concept

Following are some ways to critically question reading material, based on the mind actions. Apply them to any component you want to question by substituting the component for the words *it* and *this*.

Similarity:	What does this remind me of, or how is it similar to something else I know?
Difference:	What different conclusions are possible? How is this different from my experience?
Cause and effect:	Why did this happen, or what caused this? What are the effects or consequences of this? What effect does the author want to have, or what is the purpose of this material? What effects support a stated cause?
Example to idea:	How would I classify this, or what is the best idea to fit this example? How would I summarize this, or what are the key ideas? What is the thesis or central idea?
Idea to example:	What evidence supports this, or what examples fit this idea?
Evaluation:	How would I evaluate this? Is it useful, well constructed, or pertinent? Does this example support my thesis or central idea?

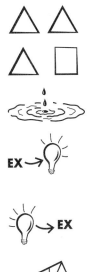

Engage Critical-Thinking Processes

Certain thinking processes from Chapter 4 can help to deepen your analysis and evaluation of what you read. These processes are establishing truth, constructing an argument, and shifting perspective. Within these processes you will ask questions that use the mind actions.

Establishing Truth

With what you know about how to seek truth, you can evaluate any statement in your reading material, identifying it as fact, opinion, or assumption and challenging how it is supported. Evaluate statements, central ideas, or entire pieces of reading material, using such questions as the following:

➤ Is this true? How does the writer know?

➤ How could I test the validity of this?

➤ What assumptions underlie this?

➤ What else do I know that is similar to or different from this?

➤ What information that I already know supports or disproves this?

➤ What examples disprove this as fact or do not fit this assumption?

For example, imagine that a piece of writing states, "The dissolving of the family unit is the main cause of society's ills." You may question the truth of this statement by looking at what facts and examples support it. You may question the writer's sources of information. You may investigate its truth by reading other materials. You could discern that some hidden assumptions underlie this statement, such as an assumed definition of what a family is or of what constitutes "society's ills." You could also find examples that do not fit this assumption, such as successful families that don't fit the definition of "family" used by the writer.

Constructing an Argument

An argument is a main idea and proof given in the form of details. When your reading material contains one or more arguments, you can use what you know about arguments to evaluate whether the writer has constructed his or her argument effectively. Ask questions like the following:

➤ What is the purpose of the writer's argument?

➤ Do I believe this? How is the writer trying to persuade me?

➤ If the author uses cause-and-effect reasoning, does it seem logical?

➤ Do the examples adequately support the central idea of the argument?

➤ What different and perhaps opposing arguments seem just as valid?

➤ If I'm not sure whether I believe this, how could I construct an opposing argument?

Don't rule out the possibility that you may agree wholeheartedly with an argument. However, use critical thinking to make an informed decision, rather than accepting the argument outright.

Shifting Perspective

This critical thinking process will help you understand that many reading materials are written from a particular perspective. For example, if a recording artist and a music censorship advocate were to each write a piece about a controversial song created by that artist, their different perspectives would result in two very different pieces of writing.

A student discusses material at a library table

To analyze perspective, ask questions like the following:

What perspective is guiding this? What are the underlying ideas that influence this material?

Who wrote this and with what intent? For example, promotional materials for a new drug, written by the drug manufacturer, may differ from a doctor's evaluation of the drug.

What does the title of the material tell me about its perspective? For example, a piece entitled "New Therapies for Diabetes" may be more informational, and "What's Wrong with Insulin Injections" may intend to be persuasive.

How does the material's source affect its perspective? For example, an article on health management organizations (HMOs) published in an HMO newsletter may be more favorable and one-sided than one published in the *New York Times*.

Be Media Literate

Everything that you learned about media literacy in Chapter 4 applies to your college reading material. Even seemingly objective textbooks are written by a person or persons who have particular points of view, which may influence the information they include or how they include it. For example, the growing awareness of the multicultural heritage in the United States has prompted revision of many history texts that previously ignored or shortchanged such topics as Native-American history. In all your reading, especially primary sources, remember the following:

➤ Your reading materials are created by people who have particular perspectives.

➤ Authors may use a particular wording or tone to create an effect on a reader.

➤ Different readers may have different interpretations of a piece of reading material, depending on individual perspective and experience.

➤ Uses of media may intend to market a product to you.

➤ Any written material carries the values of the people who created it and is influenced, to varying degrees, by the perspectives and intents of the authors.

As a media-literate reader, you have the ability to stay aware of these realities and to sift through your materials critically so that you gain from them what is most useful to you.

Seek Understanding

The fundamental purpose of all college reading is understanding the material. Reading critically allows you to reach the highest possible level of understanding. Think of your reading process as an archaeological dig. The first step is to excavate a site and uncover the artifacts, which corresponds to your initial survey and reading of the material. As important as the excavation is, the process would be incomplete if you stopped there and just took home a bunch of items covered in dirt. The second half of the process is to investigate each item, evaluate what all of them mean, and derive new knowledge and ideas from what you discover. Critical reading allows you to complete the crucial second half of the process.

Remember that critical reading takes time and focus. Give yourself a chance to be a successful critical reader by finding a time, place, and purpose for your reading. Take advantage of the opportunity to learn from others by working in pairs or groups whenever you can.

HOW AND WHY SHOULD YOU STUDY WITH OTHERS?

Learning doesn't take place in a vacuum. Everything you know and will learn comes from your interaction with the outside world. Often this interaction takes place between you and one or more people. You learn from listening to them, reading what they write, observing them, and trying what they do. In school you listen to instructors and other students, you read materials that people have written, and you model yourself after the behavior and ideas of those whom you most trust and respect.

Learning takes place the same way in your career and personal life. Today's workplace puts the emphasis on work done through team effort. Companies value the ideas, energy, and cooperation that result from a well-coordinated team.

Benefits

If you apply this information to your schoolwork, you will see that studying with one or more other people can enhance your learning in many ways. You will benefit from shared knowledge, solidified knowledge, increased motivation, and increased teamwork ability.

Sharing knowledge. Each student has a unique body of knowledge and individual strengths. Students can learn from each other. To have individual students pass on their knowledge to one another in a study group requires less time and energy than for each of the students to learn all of the material alone.

Solidifying knowledge. Study group members don't just help each other gather knowledge; they also help each other solidify and retain it. When you discuss concepts or teach them to others, you reinforce what you know

How can I cope with my learning disabilities?

Darrin Estepp, Ohio State University, Columbus, Ohio, Undeclared

In elementary school I needed extra help with reading. By high school, I was having a hard time keeping up, and I felt stupid. A test I took showed I had dyslexia. Study assistance helped, but I attended high school for an extra year to improve my record. Then I enrolled in community college and worked part time as a nursing-home cook. I transferred to Ohio State after two years.

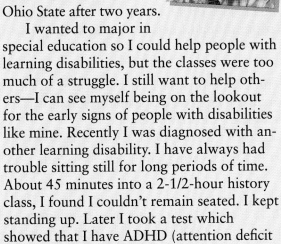

I wanted to major in special education so I could help people with learning disabilities, but the classes were too much of a struggle. I still want to help others—I can see myself being on the lookout for the early signs of people with disabilities like mine. Recently I was diagnosed with another learning disability. I have always had trouble sitting still for long periods of time. About 45 minutes into a 2-1/2-hour history class, I found I couldn't remain seated. I kept standing up. Later I took a test which showed that I have ADHD (attention deficit hyperactivity disorder).

I have trouble with spelling, too. In class, by the time I figure out how to spell a word for my notes I'm far behind. I learn best by hearing, seeing, and doing all at once. If I just hear something it doesn't sink in very well. Not long ago I went to see my learning-disability counselor because it seems no matter how hard I try it's never enough. I keep hanging in there though because I want to prove that I can graduate from a major university. What suggestions do you have for how I can cope with my learning disabilities?

Morgan Paar, Graduate Student, Academy of Art College, San Francisco, California

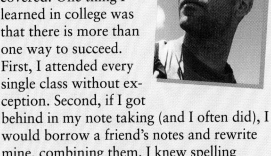

I remember dreading to read out loud to my fourth-grade class. Other students would laugh. Fortunately, this is when my disability was discovered. One thing I learned in college was that there is more than one way to succeed. First, I attended every single class without exception. Second, if I got behind in my note taking (and I often did), I would borrow a friend's notes and rewrite mine, combining them. I knew spelling would get me behind, so in class I would just write away and figure it out when I got home. Third, I made friends with my teachers, and they would help me during their office hours.

One incident showed me anything was possible. A friend worked for a newspaper and asked me to write a story. I laughed—I said I could barely spell my name, never mind write an article. He said, "Come on, computers have spell check." I labored through it, and it appeared as a two-part story in the travel section. I have since had seventeen articles published.

It never gets easy—but one route to success is to do something you love. I write travel stories because I love travel and sharing stories. I am now a filmmaker, and I am studying film in graduate school so I can someday teach it. Darrin, you already know the skills you need to achieve your goals, though maybe they are deep in your subconscious mind. I was twenty-seven years old before I knew what I really wanted to do. Just keep following your passions, never give up, figure out what you need to do to achieve your goals, and know that there is more than one path to your destination. If you love what you do, nothing can stop you.

and strengthen your critical thinking. Part of the benefit comes from simply repeating information aloud and rewriting it on paper, and part comes from how you think through information in your mind before you pass it on to someone else.

Increased motivation. When you study by yourself, you are accountable to yourself alone. In a study group, however, others will see your level of work and preparation, which may increase your motivation.

Increased teamwork ability. The more you understand the dynamics of working with a group and the more experience you have at it, the more you will build your ability to work well with others. This is an invaluable skill for the workplace, and it will contribute to your marketability and promotability.

Strategies for Study Group Success

Not all study groups work the same way. The way you operate your group may depend on the group's personalities, the subject you study, the location of the group, and the size of the group. No matter what your particular group's situation, though, certain general strategies will help.

Choose a leader for each meeting. Rotating the leadership helps all members take ownership of the group. Be flexible. If a leader has to miss class for any reason, choose another leader for that meeting.

Set meeting goals. At the start of each meeting, compile a list of questions you want to address.

Adjust to different personalities. Respect and communicate with members whom you would not necessarily choose as friends. The art of getting along will serve you well in the workplace, where you don't often choose your coworkers.

Share the workload. The most important factor is a willingness to work, not a particular level of knowledge.

Set general goals. Determine what the group wants to accomplish over the course of a semester.

Set a regular meeting schedule. Try every week, every two weeks, or whatever the group can manage.

Create study materials for one another. Give each group member the task of finding a piece of information to compile, photocopy, and review for the other group members.

> *"With one day's reading a man may have the key in his hands."*
> Ezra Pound

Help one another learn. One of the best ways to solidify your knowledge of something is to teach it to someone else. Have group members teach certain pieces of information; make up quizzes for one another; go through flash cards together.

Pool your note-taking resources. Different group members will have different information in their notes because of different interests, missed classes, and different note-taking methods. Compare notes with your group members and fill in any information you don't have. Try other note-taking styles: If you generally use outlines, rewrite your notes in a think link. If you tend to map out ideas in a think link, try recompiling your notes by using the Cornell method (see Chapter 7 for more on note taking).

Visual aids can provide valuable information as you study, whether you are in a group or alone. Explore how to "read" them and make the most of their value as study tools.

HOW CAN YOU "READ" VISUAL AIDS?

Visual aids, including tables and charts, are commonly used in texts and other college materials. They highlight statistical comparisons that show the following:

> *Trends over time* (e.g., the number of televisions per household in 1997 as compared to the number in 1957)
> *Relative rankings* (e.g., the size of the advertising budgets of four major consumer products companies)
> *Distributions* (e.g., students' performance on standardized tests by geographic area)
> *Cycles* (e.g., the regular upward and downward movement of the nation's economy as defined by periods of prosperity and recession)

Tables and charts also summarize concepts that are presented in paragraph form.

Knowing what to look for in visual aids will help you learn to "read" the information they present. The visuals in the following section are from actual textbooks published by Prentice Hall.

Understanding Tables

The two basic types of tables are data tables and word tables. *Data tables* present numerical information—for example, the numbers of students taking a standardized test in fifty states. *Word tables* summarize and consolidate complex information, making it easier to study and evaluate. Look back at Table 1–1 on pages 10–11 for an example of a word table. Table 5–2 is a model of a typical table, including the individual parts and their arrangement on the page.

TABLE 5-2   THE PARTS AND ARRANGEMENTS OF A TABLE

TABLE NO.
TITLE OF TABLE

STUB HEAD	CAPTION		CAPTION	
	SUBCAPTION	SUBCAPTION	SUBCAPTION	SUBCAPTION
STUB	XXXX	XXXX	XXXX	XXXX
STUB	XXXX	XXXX[a]	XXXX	XXXX
STUB	XXXX	XXXX	XXXX	XXXX
STUB	XXXX	XXXX	XXXX	XXXX
STUB	XXXX	XXXX	XXXX	XXXX
TOTAL	XXXX	XXXX	XXXX[b]	XXXX

[a]Footnote
[b]Footnote
Source:

Source: "THE PARTS AND ARRANGEMENTS OF A TABLE" from BUSINESS WRITING, 2E by J. Harold Janis and Howard R. Dresner. Copyright © 1956, 1972 by J. Harold Janis. Reprinted by permission of HarperCollins Publishers, Inc.

The table is arranged in columns and rows and has the following elements:

➤ The *table number* identifies the table and is usually referred to in the text.
➤ The *table title* helps readers focus on the table's message.
➤ *Captions,* also known as column titles, identify the material that falls below them.
➤ *Subcaptions* divide the columns into smaller sections.
➤ The *stubs* refer to the captions running along the horizontal rows. The nature of the stubs is identified by the stub head.
➤ *Footnotes* are used to explain specific details in the table.
➤ The *source* acknowledges where the information comes from.

Understanding Charts

Charts, also known as graphs, present numerical data in visual form to show relationships among the data. Types of charts include pie charts, bar charts, and line charts.

The *pie chart* is the most common and easy-to-understand visual aid. It presents data as wedge-shaped sections of a circle to show the relative size of each item as a percentage of the whole. The pie chart in Figure 5–4 compares the amount of money each of the top five TV network advertisers spends each year to the total spent by all five.

TELEVISION AD EXPENDITURES IN MILLIONS OF DOLLARS

FIGURE 5-4

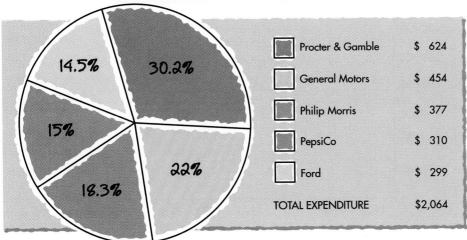

■ Procter & Gamble	$ 624
□ General Motors	$ 454
■ Philip Morris	$ 377
■ PepsiCo	$ 310
□ Ford	$ 299
TOTAL EXPENDITURE	$2,064

Source: Data presented in *Business*, 4th ed., by Ricky W. Griffin and Ronald J. Ebert. Prentice Hall: 1996, p. 526.

Bar charts consist of horizontal bars of varying lengths and show the relative rankings of each bar. While pie charts focus on the size of individual components in relationship to the whole, whereas bar charts demonstrate how items compare with one another. The bar chart in Figure 5–5 shows the number of multinational clients of five major advertising agencies. The information presented from left to right is on the horizontal axis. The information presented from the top to the bottom is on the vertical axis. Here the horizontal axis shows the number of clients, and the vertical shows the agencies' names. Since the values of the horizontal bars are clear, no scale is needed (scales are used to clarify values).

Finally, the lines in *line charts* show continuous trends over time. The horizontal axis shows a span of time, and the vertical axis represents a specific measurement such as dollars or units of various kinds. The line chart in Figure 5–6 shows how the number of men and women earning bachelor's degrees has increased in the past fifty years.

Tables and charts help to make information appealing to the reader. They are valuable study aid that can add to your understanding of what you read.

NUMBER OF MULTINATIONAL CLIENTS OF MAJOR ADVERTISING AGENCIES

FIGURE 5-5

AGENCY	NUMBER of MULTINATIONAL CLIENTS
Grey Advertising	83
McCann-Erickson Worldwide	74
Ogilvy & Mather Worldwide	56
Saatchi & Saatchi Advertising	41
DDB Needham Worldwide	40

Source: Information courtesy of DDB Needham Worldwide.

FIGURE 5-6   **NUMBER OF MEN AND WOMEN EARNING BACHELOR'S DEGREES**

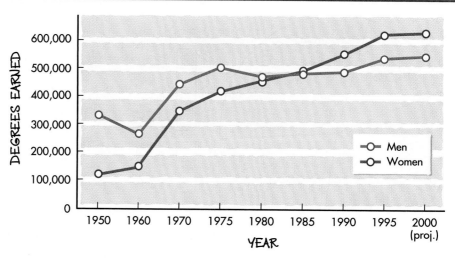

Source: *Psychology*, 2/e by Davis and Palladino © 1997. Reprinted by permission of Prentice Hall, Inc., Upper Saddle River, NJ.

читать

This word may look completely unfamiliar to you, but anyone who can read the Russian language and alphabet will know that it means "read." People who read languages that use different kinds of characters, such as Russian, Japanese, or Greek, learn to process those characters as easily as you process the letters of your native alphabet. Your mind learns to process individually each letter or character you see. This ability enables you to move to the next level of understanding—making sense of the letters or characters when they are grouped to form words, phrases, and sentences.

Think of this concept when you read. Remember that your mind is an incredible tool, processing immeasurable amounts of information so that you can understand the concepts on the page. Give it the best opportunity to succeed by reading as often as you can and by focusing on all of the elements that help you read to the best of your ability.

IMPORTANT POINTS TO REMEMBER

1. What challenges does college reading present?

College students often experience an overload of reading assignments. Conceptually difficult or poorly written texts can present another roadblock. Distractions, the need to build comprehension and speed, and the need to expand vocabulary are three other challenges.

2. Why define your purpose for reading?

Defining your purpose means asking yourself why you are reading a particular piece of material. Having a purpose helps you structure your approach toward reading assignments since different purposes require different levels of time and effort. The four main purposes are comprehension (both general ideas and specific examples), critical evaluation, practical application, and pleasure.

3. How can SQ3R help you own what you read?

SQ3R, the process of surveying, questioning, reading, reciting, and reviewing, encourages active studying. *Surveying* refers to previewing a book before studying it. During the *questioning* phase, you write questions linked to chapter headings. During the *reading* stage, you read the material in order to answer these questions and take notes. During the *reciting* stage, you answer the questions you raised by reciting aloud or silently to yourself, telling another person, or writing them in a notebook. The *review* stage involves skimming and rereading your notes.

4. How can you respond critically to what you read?

Critical-reading skills help you select important ideas, identify supporting examples, and ask questions about any text, developing an understanding of the material through evaluation and analysis. Critical reading involves the use of SQ3R to "taste" the material, asking questions based on the mind actions, and engaging critical-thinking processes (establishing the truth of what you read, evaluating its arguments, and analyzing its perspective). It also means remembering that reading material, like all media, is affected by the perspective and intentions of its authors.

5. How and why should you study with others?

Studying with one or more people can enhance your learning and improve teamwork skills that will serve you well in the workplace. Benefits include shared and solidified knowledge, increased motivation, and increased ability to work with others. Strategies for effective groups study include setting goals, sharing the workload, setting a meeting schedule, and respecting one another.

6. How can you "read" visual aids?

Visual aids, including tables and charts, highlight statistical comparisons and summarize information. Learning to read visual aids depends on understanding their value as learning tools and on learning how tables and charts are constructed and the messages they convey.

Name _____   Date _____

**BUILDING SKILLS FOR COLLEGE, CAREER, AND LIFE SUCCESS
CHAPTER 5**

*TAKING STOCK:
REFINING YOUR THOUGHTS*

Look back at the statements you explored at the start of the chapter (see Thinking It Through on p. 155). Observe whether your attitudes have changed and what you have learned by studying this chapter.

1. Name at least two strategies that will help you get through difficult texts.

_____

_____

2. Name one idea for increasing your reading speed and one idea for increasing your comprehension that you would be likely to use.

_____

_____

3. Name three people at your school who can help you sort through personal or school issues.

_____

_____

4. Describe your reaction to SQ3R. What parts of the strategy do you think will help you most?

_____

_____

_____

5. How might studying with others help you learn?

_____

_____

6. Explain how text tables and charts might help you learn assigned material.

_____

7. Choose one reading or studying strategy you learned in this chapter and explain how you will apply it to your schoolwork during the next week.

_____

_____

_____

? CRITICAL THINKING:
APPLYING LEARNING TO YOUR LIFE

Surveying Your Textbook[8]

Surveying is an important step in SQ3R (survey, question, read, recite, review). Use the following form to conduct this survey on one text you are using this year:

TEXTBOOK SURVEY FORM

1. Textbook name and authors: _____

2. Describe the mission of the book as defined in the preface. ("Mission" is defined by the scope of the book's contents, what it is trying to accomplish, and the readers for whom it is intended.)

_____

_____

_____

3. List three important features that will help you study the material covered in the text. (You will find a list of these features in the preface.)

   a. _____

   b. _____

   c. _____

4. What does the table of contents tell you about the contents and focus of the book? Does the book intend a comprehensive overview of the field or does it focus on a narrow part of the field?

_____

_____

5. Based on your survey, write a short statement about what you expect studying this text will be like.

_____

_____

Surveying Individual Chapters[9]

Conduct the same type of analysis on an individual chapter of the text you just surveyed.

CHAPTER SURVEY FORM

1. Chapter title:_____

    What does the title tell you about the chapter's focus?

_____

2. From the list below, check the study aids contained in the chapter:

    ☐ list of objectives   ☐ tables, charts, and figures

    ☐ chapter outline   ☐ photo illustrations, including captions

    ☐ opening vignette   ☐ end-of-chapter summaries

    ☐ major and minor chapter headings ☐ end-of chapter key terms and concepts

    ☐ bold and italicized words   ☐ end of chapter review questions,
                                          and phrases exercises, and problems
    ☐ internal chapter reviews

    ☐ marginal notes   ☐ other _____

3. Based on your analysis of these elements, which seem likely to help you the most? Why?

_____

_____

_____

_____

4. Identify at least three break points in the chapter that will help you divide it into manageable segments (page number and location on page).

a. _____

b. _____

c. _____

Studying a Text Page

The following page is from the Groups and Organizations chapter in the sixth edition of John J. Macionis's *Sociology*, a Prentice Hall text.[10] Using what you learned in this chapter about study techniques, complete the following questions (you can also mark the page itself).

SOCIAL GROUPS

Virtually everyone moves through life with a sense of belonging; this is the experience of group life. A **social group** refers to *two or more people who identify and interact with one another.* Human beings continually come together to form couples, families, circles of friends, neighborhoods, churches, businesses, clubs, and numerous large organizations. Whatever the form, groups encompass people with shared experiences, loyalties, and interests. In short, while maintaining their individuality, the members of social groups also think of themselves as a special "we."

Groups, Categories, and Crowds

People often use the term "group" imprecisely. We now distinguish the group from the similar concepts of category and crowd.

Category

A *category* refers to people who have some status in common. Women, single fathers, military recruits, homeowners, and Roman Catholics are all examples of categories.

Why are categories not considered groups? Simply because, while the individuals involved are aware that they are not the only ones to hold that particular status, the vast majority are strangers to one another.

Crowd

A *crowd* refers to a temporary cluster of individuals who may or may not interact at all. Students sitting together in a lecture hall do engage one another and share some common identity as college classmates; thus, such a crowd might be called a loosely formed group. By contrast, riders hurtling along on a subway train or bathers enjoying a summer day at the beach pay little attention to one another and amount to an anonymous aggregate of people. In general, then, crowds are too transitory and too impersonal to qualify as social groups.

The right circumstances, however, could turn a crowd into a group. People riding in a subway train that crashes under the city streets generally become keenly aware of their common plight and begin to help each other. Sometimes such extraordinary experiences become the basis for lasting relationships.

Primary and Secondary Groups

Acquaintances commonly greet one another with a smile and the simple phrase "Hi! How are you?" The response is usually a well-scripted "Just fine, thanks. How about you?" This answer, of course, is often more formal than truthful. In most cases, providing a detailed account of how you are *really* doing would prompt the other person to beat a hasty and awkward exit.

Sociologists classify social groups by measuring them against two ideal types based on members' level of genuine personal concern. This variation is the key to distinguishing *primary* from *secondary* groups.

According to Charles Horton Cooley (1864–1929), who is introduced in the box, a **primary group** is *a small social group whose members share personal and enduring relationships.* Bound together by *primary relationships,* individuals in primary groups typically spend a great deal of time together, engage in a wide range of common activities, and feel that they know one another well. Although not without periodic conflict, members of primary groups display sincere concern for each other's welfare. The family is every society's most important primary group.

Cooley characterized these personal and tightly integrated groups as *primary* because they are among the first groups we experience in life. In addition, the family and early play groups also hold primary importance in the socialization process, shaping attitudes, behavior, and social identity.

Source: Sociology, 6/E by John J. Macionis, © 1997. Reprinted by permission of Prentice-Hall, Inc. Upper Saddle River, NJ.

1. Identify the headings on the page and the relationship among them. Which headings are primary-level headings? Which are secondary? Which are tertiary (third-level heads)? Which heading serves as an umbrella for the rest?

_____

_____

2. What do the headings tell you about the content of the page?

_____

_____

_____

_____

_____

_____

_____

_____

_____

_____

3. After reading the chapter headings, write three study questions:

a. _____

b. _____

c. _____

4. Using a marker pen, highlight key phrases and sentences. Write short marginal notes to help you review the material at a later point.

5. After reading this page, list four key concepts that you would need to study:

a. _____

b. _____

c. _____

d. _____

Focusing on Your Purpose for Reading

Read the following paragraphs on kinetic and potential energy and the first law of thermodynamics, taken from *Life on Earth* by Teresa Audesirk and Gerald Audesirk.[11] When you have finished, answer the questions that follow.

Among the fundamental characteristics of all living organisms is the ability to guide chemical reactions within their bodies along certain pathways. The chemical reactions serve many functions, depending on the nature of the organism: to synthesize the molecules that make up the organism's body, to reproduce, to move, even to think. Chemical reactions either require or release **energy**, which can be defined simply as *the capacity to do work*, including synthesizing molecules, moving things around, and generating heat and light. In this chapter we discuss the physical laws that govern energy flow in the universe, how energy flow in turn governs chemical reactions, and how the chemical reactions within living cells are controlled by the molecules of the cell itself. Chapters 7 and 8 focus on photosynthesis, the chief "port of entry" for energy into the biosphere, and glycolysis and cellular respiration, the most important sequences of chemical reactions that release energy.

Energy and the Ability to Do Work

As you learned in Chapter 2, there are two types of energy: **kinetic energy** and **potential energy**. Both types of energy may exist in many different forms. Kinetic energy, or *energy of movement*, includes light (movement of photons), heat (movement of molecules), electricity (movement of electrically charged particles), and movement of large objects. Potential energy, or *stored energy*, includes chemical energy stored in the bonds that hold atoms together in molecules, electrical energy stored in a battery, and positional energy stored in a diver poised to spring (Fig. 4-1). Under the right conditions, kinetic energy can be transformed into potential energy, and vice versa. For example, the diver converted kinetic energy of movement into potential energy of position when she climbed the ladder up to the platform; when she jumps off, the potential energy will be converted back into kinetic energy.

To understand how energy flow governs interactions among pieces of matter, we need to know two things: (1) the quantity of available energy and (2) the usefulness of

the energy. These are the subjects of the laws of thermodynamics, which we will now examine.

The Laws of Thermodynamics Describe the Basic Properties of Energy

All interactions among pieces of matter are governed by the two **laws of thermodynamics**, physical principles that define the basic properties and behavior of energy. The laws of thermodynamics deal with "isolated systems," which are any parts of the universe that cannot exchange either matter or energy with any other parts. Probably no part of the universe is completely isolated from all possible exchange with every other part, but the concept of an isolated system is useful in thinking about energy flow.

The First Law of Thermodynamics States That Energy Can Neither Be Created nor Destroyed

The **first law of thermodynamics** states that within any isolated system, energy can neither be created nor destroyed, although it can be changed in form (for example, from chemical energy to heat energy). In other words, within an isolated system *the total quantity of energy remains constant*. The first law is therefore often **called the law of conservation of energy**. To use a familiar example, let's see how the first law applies to driving your car (Fig. 4-2). We can consider that your car (with a full tank of gas), the road, and the surrounding air roughly constitute an isolated system. When you drive your car, you convert the potential chemical energy of gasoline into kinetic energy of movement and heat energy. The total amount of energy that was in the gasoline before it was burned is the same as the total amount of this kinetic energy and heat.

An important rule of energy conversions is this: Energy always flows "downhill," from places with a high concentration of energy to places with a low concentration of energy. This is the principle behind engines. As we described in Chapter 2, temperature is a measure of how fast molecules move. The burning gasoline in your car's engine consists of molecules moving at extremely high speeds: a high concentration of energy. The cooler air outside the engine consists of molecules moving at much lower speeds: a low concentration of energy. The molecules in the engine hit the piston harder than the air molecules outside the engine do, so the piston moves upward, driving the gears that move the car. Work is done. When the engine is turned off, it cools down as heat is transferred from the warm engine to its cooler surroundings. The molecules on both sides of the piston move at the same speed, so the piston stays still. No work is done.

Source: LIFE ON EARTH by Audesirk/Audesirk, ©1997. Reprinted by permission of Prentice-Hall, Inc., Upper Saddle River, NJ.

1. *Reading for critical evaluation.* Evaluate the material by answering these questions:

a. Were the ideas clearly supported by examples? If you feel one or more were not supported, give an example.

   b. Did the author make any assumptions that weren't examined? If so, name one or more.

   _____

   _____

   c. Do you disagree with any part of the material? If so, which part, and why?

   _____

   _____

2. _Reading for practical application._ Imagine you have to give a presentation on this material the next time the class meets. On a separate sheet of paper, create an outline or think link for the key elements you would discuss.

3. _Reading for comprehension._ Answer the following questions to determine the level of your comprehension.

   a. Name the two types of energy.

   _____

   _____

   b. Which one "stores" energy? _____

   c. Can kinetic energy be turned into potential energy?

   _____

   _____

   d. What term describes the basic properties and behaviors of energy?

   _____

   e. Mark the following statements true (T) or false (F).

      _____ Within any isolated system, energy can be neither created nor destroyed.

      _____ Energy always flows downhill, from high concentration levels to low.

      _____ All interactions among pieces of matter are governed by two laws of thermodynamics.

      _____ Some parts of the universe are isolated from other parts.

Studying Charts and Tables

Following is a series of four pie charts that appear in the "Family" chapter of Macionis's *Sociology* text.[12] Look at the charts and answer the following questions:

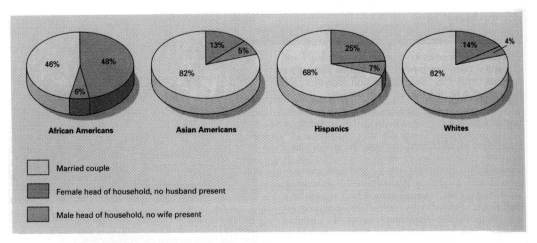

Family Form in the United States, 1993

Source: U.S. Bureau of the Census (1995).

Source: Sociology, 6/E by John J. Macionis, © 1997. Adapted by permission of Prentice-Hall, Inc. Upper Saddle River, NJ.

1. Based on these charts, what specific points is this chapter section likely to cover?

_____

_____

_____

2. What do these charts tell you about the different composition of African American, Asian American, Hispanic, and white families?

_____

_____

_____

3. What does the title tell you about the content of the charts?

_____

_____

4. Name two key concepts that these charts illustrate to you.

_____

_____

Later in Macionis's *Sociology* text the following line chart appears in the "Population and Urbanization" chapter.[13] Analyze the chart and answer the following questions.

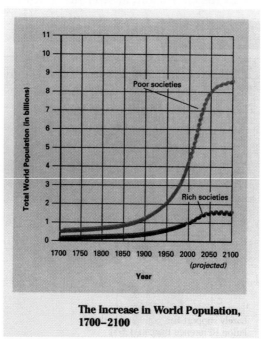

The Increase in World Population, 1700–2100

Source: Sociology, 6/E John Macionis, © 1997. Adapted by permission of Prentice-Hall Inc.,Upper Saddle River. NJ.

1. Based on this chart, what specific points is this chapter section likely to cover?

2. What does the chart tell you about population trends in poor and rich societies?

3. What information is presented on the chart's vertical axis? What information is presented on the horizontal axis?

4. Name a key concept that this chart illustrates to you.

_____

_____

_____

TEAMWORK: COMBINING FORCES

Reading and group discussion. Divide into small groups of three or four. Take a few minutes to preview an article or other short section of reading material assigned to you for this class (other than your textbook). Then, together come up with questions that arose during your preview. Write down your questions. Each person should select one question to focus on while reading (no two people should have the same question). Group members should then read the material on their own, using critical-thinking skills to explore their particular questions as they read, and finally they should write down answers to their questions.

When you answer your question, focus on finding ideas that help to answer the question and examples that support them. Consider other information you know, relevant to your question, that may be similar to or different from the material in the passage. If your questions look for causes or effects, scan for them in the passage. Be sure to make notes as you read.

When you have finished reading critically, gather as a group. Each person should take a turn presenting the question, the response and/or answer that was derived through critical reading, and any other ideas that came up while reading. The group then has an opportunity to present any other ideas to add to the discussion. Continue until each person has had a chance to present what he or she worked on.

WRITING: DISCOVERY THROUGH JOURNALING

To record your thoughts, use a separate journal or the lined page at the end of the chapter.

Reading challenges. What is your most difficult challenge when reading assigned materials? A challenge might be a particular kind of reading material, a reading situation, or the achievement of a certain goal when reading. Considering the tools that this chapter presents, make a plan that addresses this challenge. What techniques might be able to help, and how will you test them? What positive effects do you anticipate they may have on you?

CAREER PORTFOLIO:
CHARTING YOUR COURSE

Reading skills on the job. The society you live and work in revolves around the written word. Although the growth of computer technology may seem to have made technical knowledge more important than reading, the focus on word processing and computer handling of documents has actually increased the need for literate employees. As *The Condition of Education 1996* report states, "In recent years, literacy has been viewed as one of the fundamental tools necessary for successful economic performance in industrialized societies. Literacy is no longer defined merely as a basic threshold of reading ability, but rather as the ability to understand and use printed information in daily activities, at home, at work, and in the community." [14]

On a separate sheet of paper, do the following: For each of the skill areas below, list all of the ways you know in which you use that skill on the job or know you will need to use it in your future career. Then, also for each skill, rate your ability on a scale from 1 to 10, 10 being the highest. Finally, on the same sheet of paper, circle the two skills that you think will be most important for your career.

➤ Ability to define your reading purpose
➤ Reading speed
➤ Reading comprehension
➤ Vocabulary building
➤ Identification and use of text-surveying devices
➤ Evaluating reading material with others
➤ Ability to understand and use visual aids

For the two skills in which you rated yourself lowest, think how you can improve your abilities. Make a problem-solving plan for each area (write it in an outline or use a think link as shown on p. 249).

Journal Entry

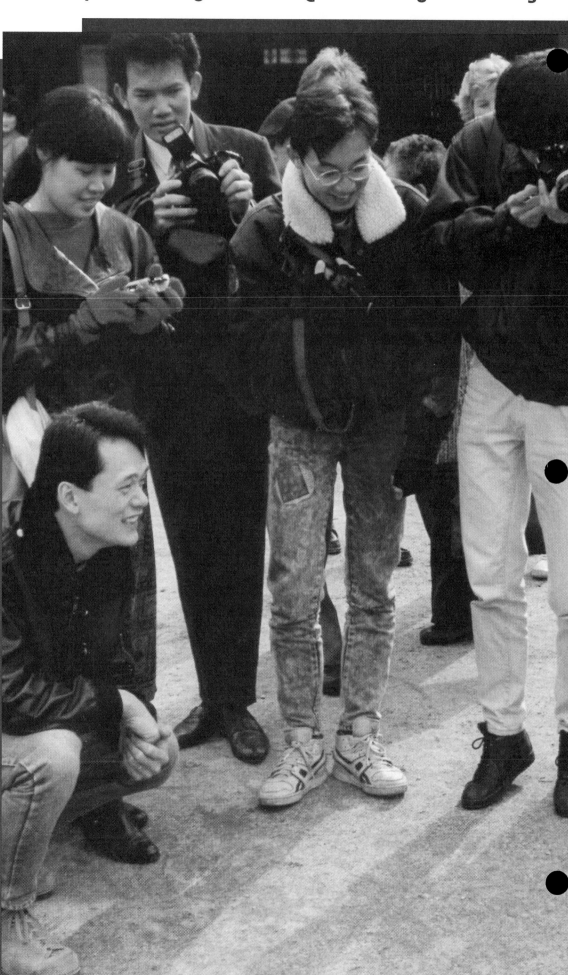

6 LISTENING AND MEMORY: Taking In and Remembering Information

Thinking It Through

Check those statements that apply to you right now:

❑ Although I listen to my instructors, I often do not remember what they say.

❑ When I hear something I don't agree with, I argue with the instructor in my head.

❑ I spend a lot of time memorizing facts for a test, but I forget a lot of material after the test is over.

❑ I use memory games to help me remember important information.

❑ I know that mnemonic devices are supposed to help memory, but I rarely use them.

In this chapter, you will explore answers to the following questions:

➤ How can you become a better listener?
➤ How does memory work?
➤ How can you improve your memory?
➤ How can you use mnemonic devices to boost memory power?
➤ How can tape recorders help you listen and remember?

Although reading probably takes up more time than any other college activity, listening is a close second. You listen in class as instructors discuss key concepts. You listen as members of your study group share ideas. Even when you're just relaxing with friends, you listen to the thoughts and ideas they share with you. With so much time spent listening, learning how to focus your listening is crucial to your success. Compare your listening ability to a camera. Even when you see an image through the viewfinder, you may not be able to tell what it is until you carefully focus the lens.

Even the best listeners can have trouble remembering what they hear and read. If you forget the information on an exam as soon as you finish it, your victory is short term—even if you achieve good grades. Imagine that you're a nursing student: What good is an A on an anatomy exam if you can't remember the location of a particular gland or bone when you meet your first patient? College exposes you daily to facts, opinions, and ideas. If your goal is to remember that information, building knowledge that you can use throughout your life, you need effective memory skills. This chapter will explore specific techniques to boost your ability to take in and remember what you learn.

HOW CAN YOU BECOME A BETTER LISTENER?

Listening,

A process that involves sensing, interpreting, evaluating, and reacting to spoken messages.

The act of hearing isn't quite the same as the act of listening. Whereas *hearing* refers to sensing spoken messages from their source, *listening* involves a complex process of communication. Successful listening results in the speaker's intended message reaching the listener. In school and at home, whereas poor listening results in communication breakdowns and mistakes, skilled listening promotes progress and success. Listening is a teachable—and learnable—skill.

Listening is also one of the most important skills in the workplace. The way in which employees and managers listen to customers and to one another greatly affects their ability to work effectively. If you don't accurately hear what others in your workplace tell you, the quality of your work can be undermined, no matter how much effort you put forth. For example, if an order of "20,000" business cards sounds to you like "2,000," you could have an unhappy customer on your hands. Accurate listening is an important key to workplace success.

To see how complex listening can be, look at Figure 6–1. The left-hand column contains an excerpt from a typical classroom lecture on peer-group influence during adolescence, and the right-hand column records some examples of what an eighteen- or nineteen-year-old student might be thinking while the instructor is speaking. In many ways, the column on the right is more interesting than the one on the left because it reveals the complexity of listening, as well as some of the barriers that block communication.

During the act of listening to a typical classroom lecture, this student doesn't focus consistently on the information presented. Instead, she reacts to specific parts of the message and gets caught up in evaluating and judging what she hears. Internal and external distractions, in the form of hunger and whispering, also affect her concentration.

Although the example in Figure 6–1 isn't real, it represents the kinds of thoughts that can interfere with effective listening. Understanding the listening process and why people may have trouble listening well can help you overcome these barriers.

WHAT THE INSTRUCTOR IS SAYING

WHAT THE STUDENT IS THINKING

A PEER GROUP IS A SOCIAL GROUP MADE UP OF MEMBERS WITH A LOT IN COMMON. DURING ADOLESCENCE, COMMON INTERESTS OFTEN CENTER ON DATING, POPULAR MUSIC, CLOTHING, AND SPORTS.

"PEER GROUPS!" I'VE HEARD THAT TERM BEFORE. I'D BETTER TAKE NOTES; IT'LL PROBABLY BE ON THE TEST.

THE APPEAL OF THE GROUP OFTEN COMES FROM THE FACT THAT ADULTS WOULD NOT APPROVE OF WHAT GROUP MEMBERS ARE DOING. AS A RESULT, ILLEGAL ACTIVITIES—SUCH AS CAR RACING, ALCOHOL ABUSE, AND DRUGS—ARE OFTEN THE MOST POPULAR.

WHAT'S THIS GUY SAYING? THAT MY FRIENDS AND I DO THINGS JUST BECAUSE OUR PARENTS WOULD OBJECT? YEAH, I GUESS I WANT TO BE DIFFERENT, BUT GIMME A BREAK! I DON'T DRINK AND DRIVE. I DON'T DO DRUGS. I DON'T IGNORE MY SCHOOL WORK. ANYWAY, I'D BETTER REMEMBER THE CONNECTION BETWEEN PEER GROUP POPULARITY AND ADULT DISAPPROVAL. WHAT WERE HIS EXACT WORDS? I WISH I REMEMBERED... ON SECOND THOUGHT MAYBE HE HAS A POINT. I KNOW KIDS WHO DO THINGS JUST TO GET A RISE OUT OF THEIR PARENTS.

PEER GROUPS EXERT SUCH A STRONG INFLUENCE DURING ADOLESCENCE BECAUSE THEY GIVE STUDENTS THE OPPORTUNITY TO FORM SOCIAL RELATIONSHIPS THAT ARE SEPARATE AND APART FROM THE ONE THEY HAVE WITH THEIR FAMILIES. THIS IS A TIME OF REBELLION AND BREAKING AWAY: A ROUGH TIME FOR BOTH ADOLESCENTS AND THEIR PARENTS.

IS IT LUNCHTIME YET? I'M REALLY HUNGRY! STOP THINKING OF FOOD AND START LISTENING...BACK TO WORK! YEAH, HE'S RIGHT, SOCIAL RELATIONSHIPS THAT HAVE NOTHING TO DO WITH MY FAMILY ARE IMPORTANT TO ME. I'D BETTER WRITE THIS DOWN.

THE GOOD NEWS FOR PARENTS IS THAT PEER GROUP PRESSURE IS GENERALLY STRONGEST DURING ADOLESCENCE. TEENS ACHIEVE A GREATER BALANCE BETWEEN THE INFLUENCE OF FAMILY AND FRIENDS AS THE YEARS PASS. THIS DOESN'T MAKE IT ANY EASIER FOR PARENTS TRYING TO PERSUADE THEIR SONS AND DAUGHTERS NOT TO DYE THEIR HAIR GREEN OR PIERCE THEIR EYEBROWS, BUT AT LEAST IT TELLS THEM THAT THE REBELLION IS TEMPORARY.

WHY IS HE TALKING DOWN TO US? WHY IS HE REASSURING PARENTS INSTEAD OF FOCUSING ON HOW HARD IT IS FOR TEENS TO DEAL WITH LIFE? HE MUST BE A PARENT HIMSELF... I WISH THOSE GUYS BEHIND ME WOULD STOP TALKING! I CAN'T HEAR THE LECTURE... THERE'S A GENERATION GAP COMING FROM THE FRONT OF THE ROOM THAT'S THE SIZE OF THE GRAND CANYON! WHAT'S WRONG WITH GREEN HAIR AND PIERCED EYEBROWS? HE SOUNDS LIKE HE KNOWS ALL THE ANSWERS AND THAT WE'LL EVENTUALLY SEE THE LIGHT. I'M GOING TO ASK HIM HOW TEENS ARE SUPPOSED TO ACT WHEN THEY BELIEVE THAT THEIR PARENTS' VALUES ARE WRONG. NOW, HOW SHOULD I WORD MY QUESTION...

Know the Stages of Listening

Listening is made up of four stages that build on one another: sensing, interpreting, evaluating, and reacting. These stages take the message from the speaker to the listener and back to the speaker (see Figure 6–2).

During the *sensation* stage (also known as hearing), your ears pick up sound waves and transmit them to the brain. For example, you are sitting in class and hear your instructor say, "The only opportunity to make up last week's test is Tuesday at 5:00 P.M."

In the *interpretation* stage, listeners attach meaning to a message. This involves understanding what is being said and relating the message to what you already know. For example, when you hear this message, you relate it to your knowledge of the test—whether you need to make it up—and what you are doing on Tuesday at 5:00 P.M.

In the *evaluation* stage of listening, you decide how you feel about the message—whether, for example, you like it or agree with it. This involves evaluating the message as it relates to your needs and values. If the message goes against your values or does not fulfill your needs, you may reject it, stop listening, or argue in your mind with the speaker. In this example, if you do need to make up the test but have to work Tuesday at 5:00 P.M., you may evaluate the message as less than satisfactory. As you saw in Figure 6–1, what happens during the evaluation phase can interfere with listening.

The final stage of listening is a *reaction* to the message in the form of direct feedback. In a classroom, direct feedback often comes in the form of questions and comments. Your reaction, in this example, may be to ask the instructor if there is any alternative to that particular test time. If the student in Figure 6–1 actually asks a question, she will give the instructor the opportunity to clarify the lecture or, perhaps, to add information.

FIGURE 6-2   **STAGES OF LISTENING**

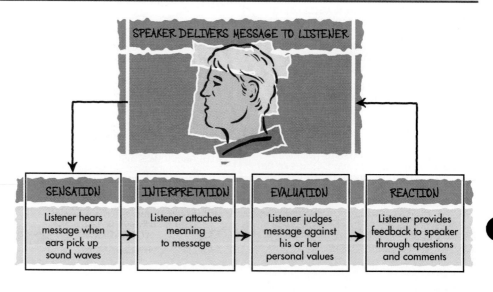

SPEAKER DELIVERS MESSAGE TO LISTENER

SENSATION	INTERPRETATION	EVALUATION	REACTION
Listener hears message when ears pick up sound waves	Listener attaches meaning to message	Listener judges message against his or her personal values	Listener provides feedback to speaker through questions and comments

According to psychologist Beatrice Harris, "People can be trained to listen to content and tone. But learning takes persistence and motivation."[1] Improving your learning skills involves two primary actions: managing listening challenges and becoming an active listener. Although becoming a better listener will help in every class, it is especially important in subjects that are more difficult for you. For example, if your natural strengths are in English and communications, your ability to listen in physics class may make or break your ability to retain information and pass the course.

Manage Listening Challenges

Communication barriers can interfere with listening at every stage. In fact, classic studies have shown that immediately after listening, students are likely to recall only half of what was said. This is partly due to particular listening challenges, such as divided attention and distractions, the tendency to shut out the message, the inclination to rush to judgment, and partial hearing loss or learning disabilities.[2]

To help create a positive listening environment in both your mind and your surroundings, explore how to manage these challenges.

Divided Attention and Distractions

Imagine yourself at a noisy end-of-year party, talking with a friend about plans for the summer, when you hear your name mentioned across the room. Your name was not shouted, and you weren't consciously listening to anything outside your own conversation. However, once you hear your name, you strain to hear more as you now listen with only half an ear to what your friend is saying. Chances are you hear neither person very well.

Situations like this happen all the time and demonstrate the consequences of divided attention. Although you are capable of listening to more than one message at the same time, you may not completely hear or understand any of them. Learning to focus your attention—even as it is being pulled in different directions—is one of your most important listening challenges.

Internal and external distractions often divide your attention. *Internal distractions* include anything from hunger to headache to personal worries. Something the speaker says may also trigger a recollection that may cause your mind to drift. In contrast, *external distractions* include noises (whispering, say, or sirens) and excessive heat or cold. It can be hard to listen in an overheated room that is putting you to sleep.

Your goal is to reduce distractions so that you can focus on what you're hearing. Sitting where you can clearly see and hear will help. When you can clearly see and hear your instructors, you have a much better chance of being able to listen well. You may even be more willing to listen because knowing that instructors can see you may encourage you to receive their messages more actively. To avoid distracting activity, you may want to avoid sitting near or with people who might chat or make noise.

Make sure you are as relaxed and alert as possible. Work to concentrate on class when you're in class and save worrying about personal problems for later. Try not to go to class hungry or thirsty. Dress comfortably. Bring a

> "No one cares to speak to an unwilling listener. An arrow never lodges in a stone; often it recoils upon the sender of it."
>
> St. Jerome

sweater or sweatshirt if you anticipate that the classroom will be too cold. If there's a chance you'll be too warm, wear a removable layer of clothing.

Shutting Out the Message

Instead of paying attention to everything the speaker says, many students fall into the trap of focusing on specific points and shutting out the rest of

the message. If you perceive that a subject is too difficult or uninteresting, you may tune out. Shutting out the message makes it tough to listen well from that point on since the information you miss may be the foundation for what goes on in future classes.

Creating a positive listening environment includes accepting responsibility for listening. Although the instructor is responsible for communicating information to you, he or she cannot force you to listen. You are responsible for taking in the information that comes your way during class.

One important motivation is believing that what your instructors say is valuable. For example, some students might assume that anything not covered in the textbook isn't really important. During class, however, instructors often cover material from outside the textbook and then test on that material. If you work to take in the whole message in class, you will be able to read over your notes later and think critically about what is most important.

The Rush to Judgment

As the student's thoughts in Figure 6–1 show, people may tend to stop listening during the evaluation stage when they hear something they don't like. If you rush to judge what you've heard, your focus turns to your personal reaction rather than the content of the speaker's message. Students who disagree during a lecture often spend a lot of their thinking time figuring out exactly how they want to word a question or comment in response.

Judgments also involve reactions to the speakers themselves. If you do not like your instructors or if you have preconceived notions about their ideas or cultural background, you may decide that their words have little value. Anyone whose words have ever been ignored because of race, ethnic background, gender, or disability understands how prejudice can interfere with listening (see Chapter 10 for more about how prejudice can stifle communication).

Understanding how your emotions and opinions can interfere with listening will help you recognize and control your judgments. Being aware of what you tend to judge will help you avoid putting up a barrier against messages that clash with your opinions or feelings. Consider education as a continuing search for evidence, regardless of whether that evidence supports or negates your point of view.

Partial Hearing Loss and Learning Disabilities

Good listening techniques don't solve every listening problem. Students who have a partial hearing loss have a physical explanation for why listening is difficult. If you have some level of hearing loss, seek out special services that can help you listen in class. You may require special equipment or you might benefit from tutoring. You may be able to arrange to meet with your instructor outside of class to clarify your notes.

Other disabilities, such as attention deficit disorder (ADD) or a problem with processing heard language, can cause difficulties with both focusing on and understanding that which is heard. People with such disabilities have varied ability to compensate for and overcome them. If you have a disability, don't blame yourself for having trouble listening. Your counseling center, student health center, advisor, and instructors should be able to give you particular assistance in meeting your challenges.

A professor at Rensselaer Polytechnic Institute explains a piece of surveying equipment

Become an Active Listener

On the surface, listening seems like a passive activity; you sit back and listen as someone else speaks. Effective listening, however, is really an active process that involves setting a purpose for listening, asking questions, putting listening "spaces" to good use, paying attention to verbal signposts, and knowing what helps and hinders listening.

Set Purposes for Listening

Active listening is only possible if you know (and care) why you are listening. In any situation, establish what you want to achieve through listening, such as greater understanding of the material, staying awake in class, or better note taking. Having a purpose gives you a goal that motivates you to listen.

Ask Questions

Asking questions is not a sign of a lack of intelligence. In fact, a willingness to ask questions shows a desire to learn and is the mark of an active listener and critical thinker. Some questions are *informational*—seeking information—such as any question beginning with the phrase, "I don't understand...." *Clarifying* questions state your understanding of what you have just heard and ask if that understanding is correct. Whereas some clarifying questions focus on a key concept or theme ("So, some learning disorders can be improved with treatment?"), others highlight specific facts ("Is it true that dyslexia can cause people to reverse letters and words?").

Although asking questions and making comments makes you an active participant in the listening process, you might spend so much time thinking about what to ask that you miss some of the message. One way to avoid this is to quickly jot down your questions and come back to them during a discussion period or when you can talk to the instructor alone. When you know that your question is on paper, you may be more able to relax and listen.

Put Listening "Spaces" to Good Use

If you are listening actively, your listening may sometimes seem to outpace the speed of the information coming your way in class. This difference can create small "spaces" of time between segments of spoken information. When this happens, use that time to think about questions and comments, anticipate what the speaker will say next, evaluate the evidence, listen "between the lines" to pick up on unspoken shades of meaning, or summarize key points in your notes. (Chapter 7 will cover effective methods for taking class notes.)

Listening between the lines means paying attention to the way people speak, through body language and tone of voice, rather than just to what is being said. Even though nonverbal cues can sometimes be difficult to read, you can usually assume that when an instructor emphasizes a point by writing it on the blackboard, by speaking more loudly or softly than usual, or by slowing the rate of speech, the message is important. Chapter 7 includes additional information about the cues instructors use to indicate important material, and Chapter 10 discusses nonverbal communication, or body language, in greater detail.

Pay Attention to Verbal Signposts

Verbal signposts,
Spoken words or phrases that call your attention to the information that follows.

You can identify important facts and ideas and predict test questions by paying attention to the speaker's specific choice of words. For example, an idea described as "new and exciting" or "classic" is more likely to be on a test than one described as "interesting." **Verbal signposts** often involve transition words and phrases that help organize information, connect ideas, and indicate what is important and what is not. Let phrases like those in Table 6–1 direct your attention to the material that follows them.

TABLE 6-1 PAYING ATTENTION TO VERBAL SIGNPOSTS

SIGNALS POINTING TO KEY CONCEPTS	SIGNALS OF SUPPORT
There are two reasons for this...	For example,...
Most importantly...	For instance,...
The result is...	Similarly,...

SIGNALS POINTING TO DIFFERENCES	SIGNALS THAT SUMMARIZE
On the contrary...	Finally,...
On the other hand...	Recapping this idea,...
In contrast...	In conclusion,...
However...	As a result,...

Source: Adapted from George M. Usova, *Efficient Study Strategies: Skills for Successful Learning* (Pacific Grove, CA: Brooks/Cole, 1989), p. 69.

Know What Helps and Hinders Listening

Ralph G. Nichols, a pioneer in listening research, wanted to define the characteristics of successful and unsuccessful listeners. To do so, he studied 200 students in the freshman class at the University of Minnesota over a nine-month period. His findings, summarized in Table 6–2, demonstrate that effective listening depends as much on a positive attitude as on specific skills.[3]

Having the habit of effective listening will enable you to acquire knowledge. You also need a good memory, however, so that you can remember what you've heard. A good memory is made up of skills that improve with practice.

TABLE 6-2   WHAT HELPS AND HINDERS LISTENING

LISTENING IS HELPED BY	LISTENING IS HINDERED BY
Making a conscious decision to work at listening; viewing difficult material as a listening challenge	Caring little about the listening process; tuning out difficult material
Fighting distractions through intense concentration	Refusing to listen at the first distraction
Continuing to listen when a subject is difficult or dry, in the hope that one might learn something interesting	Giving up as soon as one loses interest
Withholding judgment until hearing everything	Becoming preoccupied with a response as soon as a speaker makes a controversial statement
Focusing on the speaker's theme by recognizing organizational patterns, transitional language, and summary statements, and details	Getting sidetracked by unimportant details
Adapting note-taking style to the unique style and organization of the the speaker	Always taking notes in outline form, even when a speaker is poorly organized, leading to frustration
Pushing past negative emotional responses and forcing oneself to continue to listen	Letting an initial emotional response shut off continued listening
Using excess thinking time to evaluate summarize, and question what one just heard and anticipating what will come next	Thinking about other things and, as a result, missing much of the message

THINKING BACK

1. List and briefly describe the four stages of listening.

   a. _____

   b. _____

   c. _____

   d. _____

2. Name two internal and two external distractions that may interfere with listening.

   a. _____

   b. _____

   c. _____

   d. _____

3. List four methods for becoming an active listener.

   a. _____

   b. _____

   c. _____

   d. _____

4. Look again at Table 6–2. Which habits, helpful or not so helpful, are part of your listening pattern?

   _____

   _____

   _____

   _____

   _____

   _____

   _____

1. How do you rate your memory? Describe its strengths and weaknesses.

2. List two techniques that you have used to improve your ability to remember.

3. Do you find that it is easier to remember certain types of information than others? Which types are easier for you? If you can think of a reason why, name it.

4. Do you aim to remember information long after your exams are over, or is doing well on tests your primary memory goal? Explain.

HOW DOES MEMORY WORK?

You need an effective memory to use the knowledge you gain throughout your life. Human memory works like a computer. Both have essentially the same purpose: to encode, store, and retrieve information.

During the *encoding stage*, information is changed into usable form. On a computer, this occurs when keyboard entries are transformed into electronic symbols and stored on a disk. In the brain, sensory information becomes impulses that the central nervous system reads and codes.

You are encoding, for example, when you study a list of chemistry formulas.

During the *storage stage,* information is held in memory (the mind's version of a computer hard drive) so it can be used later. In this example, after you complete your studying of the formulas, your mind stores them until you need to use them.

During the *retrieval stage,* memories are recovered from storage by recall, just as a saved computer program is called up by name and used again. In this example, your mind would retrieve the chemistry formulas when you had to take a test or solve a problem.

> "Memory is the stepping-stone to thinking, because without remembering facts, you cannot think, conceptualize, reason, make decisions, create, or contribute."
>
> Harry Lorayne

Memories are stored in three different storage banks. The first, called *sensory memory,* is an exact copy of what you see and hear and lasts for a second or less. Certain information is then selected from sensory memory and moves into *short-term memory,* a temporary information storehouse that lasts no more than ten to twenty seconds. You are consciously aware of material in your short-term memory. Whereas unimportant information is quickly dumped, important information is transferred to *long-term memory*—the mind's more permanent information storehouse.

Suppose your history instructor lists five major causes of the Civil War. As you listen, the incoming information immediately becomes part of sensory memory, and since you are paying attention, it is quickly transferred to short-term memory. Nearby whispering may never get past the stage of sensory memory since your mind selectively pays attention to some things while ignoring others. Realizing that you will probably be tested on this information, you consciously decide that it is important enough to remember. It then becomes part of long-term memory.

Having information in long-term memory does not necessarily mean that you will be able to recall it when needed. Particular techniques can help you improve your recall.

HOW CAN YOU IMPROVE YOUR MEMORY?

Your accounting instructor is giving a test tomorrow on bookkeeping programs. You feel confident because you spent hours last week memorizing the material. Unfortunately, by the time you take the test, you may remember very little—most forgetting occurs within minutes after memorization.

In a classic study conducted in 1885, researcher Herman Ebbinghaus memorized a list of meaningless three-letter words such as CEF and LAZ. He then examined how quickly he forgot them. It happened in a surprisingly short time: Within one hour he had forgotten more than 50 percent of what he had learned; after two days, he knew fewer than 30 percent of the memorized words. Although Ebbinghaus's recall of the nonsense syllables remained fairly stable after that, his experiment shows how fragile memory can be—even when you take the time and expend the energy to memorize information.[4]

If forgetting is so common, why do some people have better memories than others? Some may have an inborn talent for remembering. More often, though, they succeed because they have practiced and mastered techniques for improving recall. Remember that techniques aren't a cure-all for memory difficulties, especially for those with learning disabilities. If you have a disability, the following strategies may help but might not be enough. Seek specific assistance if you consistently have trouble remembering.

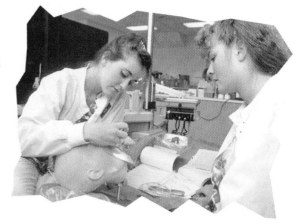

Testing their ability to recall procedures, dental hygiene students practice on the head of a dummy

Use Specific Memory Strategies

As a student, your job is to understand, learn, and remember information—everything from general concepts to specific details. Remembering involves two kinds of memory processes: general remembering and verbatim memorization.

> *General remembering,* the most common type of memory task, involves remembering ideas but not the exact words in which the ideas are expressed.

> *Verbatim memorization* involves learning a mathematical formula, an unfamiliar language, the sequence of operating a machine, and so on.

The following suggestions will help improve your recall in both memory processes.

Develop a Will to Remember

Why can you remember the lyrics to dozens of popular songs but not the functions of the pancreas? Perhaps this is because you want to remember the lyrics, you connect them to a visual image, or you have an emotional tie to them. To achieve the same results at school or on the job, explore for yourself why remembering what you are learning is important.

A simple experiment demonstrates what developing the will to remember can do for you. Think for a moment about the common, ordinary U.S. penny. Although it is easy to remember that Abraham Lincoln's picture is engraved on the penny's head, it is hard to recall anything else. Try it yourself by looking at Figure 6–3 on the next page. Which penny represents the real thing and which are the fakes?[5]

Most people have trouble selecting the correct answer because it was never important for them to focus on the details of the coin's design. Thus, they "forget" because they never created the memory in the first place.

FIGURE 6-3   **CAN YOU RECOGNIZE A REAL PENNY?**

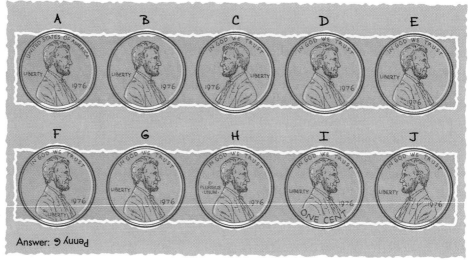

Answer: Penny G

Source: Adopted from R. S. Nickerson and M. J. Adams, "Long-Term Memory for a Common Object," *Cognitive Psychology,* 1979 (11): 287-307. Used with permission of Academic Press, Inc.

Understand What You Memorize

Make sure that everything you want to remember makes sense to you. Something that has meaning is easier to recall than something that is gibberish. This basic principle applies to everything you study—from biology and astronomy to history and English literature. If something you need to memorize makes no sense, consult textbooks, fellow students, or an instructor.

Recite, Rehearse, and Write

When you *recite* material, you repeat it aloud to remember it. Reciting helps you retrieve information as you learn it and is a crucial step in studying (see Chapter 5). Frequently stopping to summarize aloud as you read can maximize your textbook studying. *Rehearsing* is similar to reciting but is done silently. It is the process of mentally repeating, summarizing, and associating information with other information. *Writing* is rehearsing on paper. The act of writing solidifies the information in your memory.

Separate Main Points from Unimportant Details

If you use critical-thinking skills to select and focus on the most important information, you can avoid overloading your memory with extra clutter. To focus on key points, highlight only the most important information in your texts and write notes in the margins about central ideas. When you review your lecture notes, highlight or rewrite the most important information to remember. Figure 6–4 shows how this is done on a section of text that introduces the concept of markets. This excerpt is from the fourth edition of *Marketing: An Introduction*, a Prentice Hall textbook written by professors Philip Kotler and Gary Armstrong.[6]

EFFECTIVE HIGHLIGHTING AND MARGINAL NOTES AID MEMORY

FIGURE 6-4

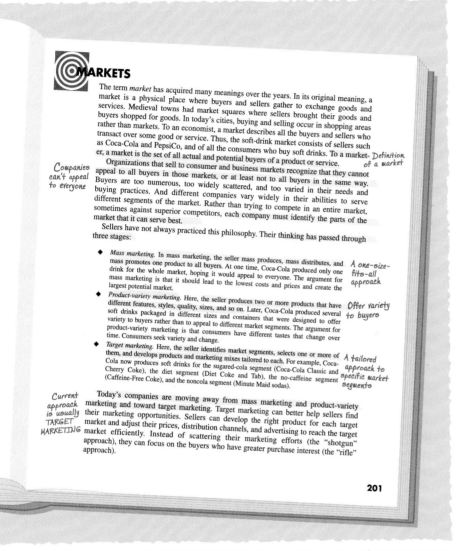

MARKETS

The term *market* has acquired many meanings over the years. In its original meaning, a market is a physical place where buyers and sellers gather to exchange goods and services. Medieval towns had market squares where sellers brought their goods and buyers shopped for goods. In today's cities, buying and selling occur in shopping areas rather than markets. To an economist, a market describes all the buyers and sellers who transact over some good or service. Thus, the soft-drink market consists of sellers such as Coca-Cola and PepsiCo, and of all the consumers who buy soft drinks. To a market- *Definition* er, a market is the set of all actual and potential buyers of a product or service. *of a market*

[*Companies can't appeal to everyone*] Organizations that sell to consumer and business markets recognize that they cannot appeal to all buyers in those markets, or at least not to all buyers in the same way. Buyers are too numerous, too widely scattered, and too varied in their needs and buying practices. And different companies vary widely in their abilities to serve different segments of the market. Rather than trying to compete in an entire market, sometimes against superior competitors, each company must identify the parts of the market that it can serve best.

Sellers have not always practiced this philosophy. Their thinking has passed through three stages:

♦ *Mass marketing.* In mass marketing, the seller mass produces, mass distributes, and mass promotes one product to all buyers. At one time, Coca-Cola produced only one drink for the whole market, hoping it would appeal to everyone. The argument for mass marketing is that it should lead to the lowest costs and prices and create the largest potential market. [*A one-size-fits-all approach*]

♦ *Product-variety marketing.* Here, the seller produces two or more products that have different features, styles, quality, sizes, and so on. Later, Coca-Cola produced several soft drinks packaged in different sizes and containers that were designed to offer variety to buyers rather than to different market segments. The argument for product-variety marketing is that consumers have different tastes that change over time. Consumers seek variety and change. [*Offer variety to buyers*]

♦ *Target marketing.* Here, the seller identifies market segments, selects one or more of them, and develops products and marketing mixes tailored to each. For example, Coca-Cola now produces soft drinks for the sugared-cola segment (Coca-Cola Classic and Cherry Coke), the diet segment (Diet Coke and Tab), the no-caffeine segment (Caffeine-Free Coke), and the noncola segment (Minute Maid sodas). [*A tailored approach to specific market segments*]

[*Current approach is usually TARGET MARKETING*] Today's companies are moving away from mass marketing and product-variety marketing and toward target marketing. Target marketing can better help sellers find their marketing opportunities. Sellers can develop the right product for each target market and adjust their prices, distribution channels, and advertising to reach the target market efficiently. Instead of scattering their marketing efforts (the "shotgun" approach), they can focus on the buyers who have greater purchase interest (the "rifle" approach).

201

Source: Excerpt from MARKETING: AN INTRODUCTION, 4th ed., Philip Kotler and Gary Armstrong, © 1997, p. 201. Reprinted with permission of Prentice-Hall, Inc., Upper Saddle River, NJ.

Study During Short but Frequent Sessions

Research has shown that you can improve your chances of remembering material if you learn it more than once. To get the most out of your study sessions, spread them over time. A pattern of short sessions followed by brief periods of rest is more effective than continual studying with little or no rest. Even though you may feel as though you accomplish a lot by studying for an hour without a break, you'll probably remember more from three 20-minute sessions. With this in mind, try studying during breaks in your schedule. Although studying between classes isn't for everyone, you may find that it can help you remember more of what you study.

Sleep can actually aid memory because it reduces the interference that new memories can create. Since you can't always go to sleep immediately after studying for an exam, try postponing the study of other subjects until your exam is over. When studying for several tests at a time, avoid studying two similar subjects back to back. You'll be less confused when you study history right after biology rather than, for example, chemistry after biology.

Separate Material into Manageable Sections

Generally, when material is short and easy to understand, studying it from start to finish improves recall. With longer material, however, you may benefit from dividing it into logical sections, mastering each section, putting all the sections together, and then testing your memory of all the material. Actors take this approach when learning the lines of a play, and it can work just as well for students.

Practice the Middle

When you are trying to learn something, you usually study some material first, attack other material in the middle of the session, and approach still other topics at the end. The weak link in your recall is likely to be the material you study midway. It pays to give this material special attention in the form of extra practice.

Create Groupings

Grouping,
Forming digestible information segments that are easy to remember.

When items do not have to be remembered in any particular order, the act of **grouping** can help you recall them better. Say, for example, that you have to memorize these five 10-digit numbers:

9806875087   9876535703   7636983561   6724472879   312895312

It may look impossible. If you group the numbers to form telephone numbers, however, the job may become more manageable:

(980) 687-5087   (987) 653-5703   (763) 698-3561   (672) 447-2879
(312) 289-5312

In general, try to keep groups to around ten items or fewer. It's hard to memorize more than that at one time.

Use Visual Aids

Any kind of visual representation of study material can help you remember. Try converting material into a think link or outline. Use any visual that helps you recall it and link it to other information.

Flash cards are a great memory tool. They give you short, repeated review sessions that provide immediate feedback. Make your cards from 3-by-5-inch index cards. Use the front of the card to write a word, idea, or phrase you want to remember. Use the back side for a definition, explanation, and other key facts. Figure 6–5 shows two flash cards used to study for a psychology exam.

FLASH CARDS HELP YOU MEMORIZE IMPORTANT FACTS   **FIGURE 6-5**

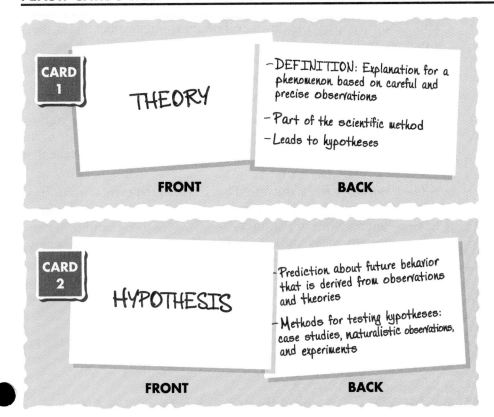

CARD 1

THEORY

—DEFINITION: Explanation for a phenomenon based on careful and precise observations

—Part of the scientific method

—Leads to hypotheses

FRONT   BACK

CARD 2

HYPOTHESIS

—Prediction about future behavior that is derived from observations and theories

—Methods for testing hypotheses: case studies, naturalistic observations, and experiments

FRONT   BACK

Here are some suggestions for making the most of your flash cards:

➤ *Use the cards as a self-test.* Divide them into two piles—the material you know and the material you are learning. You may want to use rubber bands to separate the piles.

➤ *Carry the cards with you and review them frequently.* You'll learn the most if you start using cards early in the course, well ahead of exam time.

➤ *Shuffle the cards and learn the information in various orders.* This will help avoid putting too much focus on some information and not enough on others.

➤ *Test yourself in both directions.* First, look at the terms and provide the definitions or explanations. Then turn the cards over and reverse the process.

Search for Lost Memories by Recreating a Context

People sometimes find themselves in situations in which they want to remember something but can't. One way to recover the lost memory is to try to re-create the context in which the information was learned. What you remember will serve as cues that may help to jog your memory. Creating a memory context involves the following steps:

1. *Place yourself in the situation in which you first encountered the information.* Were you sitting in class or in the library? Were you in your study group? Write down everything you remember about the situation, including what you wore that day, how you felt (happy, annoyed, etc.), and what people said to you about any subject. If you learned the information in class, think about the lecture. What else was covered during the session? Search your notes for clues.

2. *Write down everything you remember about the information you want to recall.* Don't censor any detail, no matter how obvious or insignificant it might seem. Even the smallest detail may be the cue that brings back your lost memory.

3. *Allow yourself to free-associate.* That is, recall the events or information that surrounds the lost memory in the order in which it occurs to you—whether or not that order makes sense. For example, if the information was given during a class lecture, your first memory may be about the instructor's closing remarks. That may trigger a memory of what he or she covered first. Or the flow of memories may start with something that captured your interest during the lecture or something that bothered you.

The memory cues that emerge from these steps just might lead to the information you seek.

Make the Most of Last-Minute Studying

Last-minute studying, or *cramming*, often results in information going into your head and popping right back out shortly after. Study conditions, however, aren't always ideal. Sometimes a busy week may leave you only a few hours to prepare for a big exam. Nearly every student crams sometime during college. If you have a tight schedule, use these hints to make the most of your study time:

➤ *Go through your flash cards,* if you have them, one last time.

➤ *Resist going through your notes or textbook page by page.* Focus on crucial concepts: Don't worry about the rest.

➤ *Create a last-minute study sheet with hard-to-remember material.* On a single sheet of paper, write down key facts, definitions, formulas, and so on. Try to keep the material short and simple. If you prefer visual notes, use think links to map out ideas and their supporting examples (see Chapter 7 for more information about think links).

➤ *Arrive at the exam room a few minutes early.* Study the sheet or your flash cards until you are asked to clear your desk.

➤ *While it is still fresh in your mind, record any helpful information on a piece of scrap paper.* Do this before looking at any test questions. Review this information as needed during the test.

After your exam, evaluate the effects cramming had on your learning. See if you can plan ahead and improve the situation next time.

Use Critical Thinking

Your knowledge of the critical-thinking mind actions can help you remember information. Many of the mind actions use the principle of *association*—considering new information in relation to information you already know. The more you can associate a piece of new information with your current knowledge, the more likely you are to remember it.

Imagine that you have to remember information about a specific historical event—for example, the signing of the Treaty of Versailles, the agreement that ended World War II. You might put the mind actions to work in the following ways:

➤ *Recall* everything that you know about the topic.

➤ Think about how this event is *similar* to other events in history, recent or long ago.

➤ Consider what is *different* and unique about this treaty in comparison to other treaties.

➤ Explore the *causes* that led up to this event, and look at the event's *effects*.

➤ From the general *idea* of treaties that ended wars, explore other *examples* of such treaties.

➤ Think about *examples* of what happened during the treaty signing, and from those examples come up with *ideas* about the tone of the event.

➤ Looking at the facts of the event, *evaluate* how successful you think the treaty was.

Working through every mind action might take time; you don't always have to use every one in every memory situation. Choose the ones that will help you most. The more information and ideas you can associate with the new item you're trying to remember, the more successful you will be.

HOW CAN YOU USE MNEMONIC DEVICES TO BOOST MEMORY POWER?

Certain performers entertain their audiences by remembering the names of 100 strangers or flawlessly repeating 30 ten-digit phone numbers. These performers probably have superior memories, but genetics alone can't produce these results. They also rely on memory techniques, known as **mnemonic devices** (pronounced neh MAHN ick), for assistance.

Mnemonic devices work by connecting information you are trying to learn with simpler information or information that is familiar. Instead of learning new facts by rote (repetitive practice), associations give you a hook on which to hang these facts and to retrieve them. Mnemonic devices make information familiar and meaningful through unusual, unforgettable mental associations and visual pictures.

> **Mnemonic devices,** Memory techniques that involve associating new information with simpler information or information you already know.

> *"The true art of memory is the art of attention."*
> Samuel Johnson

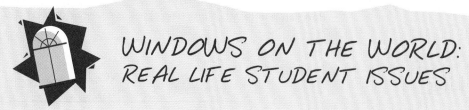
How can I improve my memory?

Shyama Parikh, DePaul University, Chicago, Illinois, Psychology/Prelaw Major

Recently I took a memory test in one of my psychology classes. I discovered that I'm better at remembering a full definition of a word than reading the definition and remembering the word. Most of my classmates had the same results. This surprised all of us; it seems like it would be easier to recall a word than an entire definition, but that was not the case.

Sometimes I find memorization work difficult, even though I know I have the ability. For instance, I know I have the material written down in my notes, down to the exact page, but then on the test, I sometimes can't remember the answers. I find biology especially hard for that reason; there's a lot more memorization because of all the diagrams and classification systems.

I'm aware of mnemonic devices and I try to incorporate those into my study time, but that doesn't always work. I know reading and repetition probably reinforce what I've studied, but I don't always have enough time. I am involved in so many other activities on campus that it's hard to find the time to devote to retaining information for five classes. I think memorization for me is the first step in learning, so I need to learn more effective ways to memorize.

I've just been accepted to law school, and I'm concerned because it seems that law requires learning a lot of technical terms. Can you suggest ways for me to improve my memory?

Stephen Beck, Director, Learn-to-Learn Company, Winston-Salem, North Carolina

A combination of organization, reading comprehension, and reinforcement will help. First, an important point: The definitions exercise you took in your psychology class illustrates how meaning enhances memory. The reason you are more likely to remember a sentence of thirty words than a list of fifteen random words is because the sentence is organized in such a way that it has meaning to you.

When you study, understand how the material is organized. Organization improves recall (that's why mnemonics help when memorizing unrelated items). Because understanding is just as important, though, you need to both organize *and* understand. For instance, if a system of categorizing biology terms makes sense to you, then you are more likely to understand and recall the terms. Mentally placing information in logical categories enhances memory.

Reading comprehension is similar. To enhance your reading comprehension, preview the entire textbook or chapter before reading it. Read the table of contents, chapter titles, sections and subsections. By understanding the organization of the textbook you can more actively make meaningful connections and, therefore, learn the details more efficiently.

The final technique is reinforcement. As you read a text, continually ask yourself whether the information makes sense. If not, try to figure out why you're stuck. How do you know if you have memorized a list? Write it down to find out exactly what you do and do not know. For reinforcement of reading comprehension, pause at good stopping points and try taking notes from memory. This pause and reflect technique is critical for learning new material. Good luck!

Here's an example of the power of mnemonics. Suppose you want to re-member the names of the first six presidents of the United States. You no-tice that the first letters of their last names—Washington, Adams, Jefferson, Madison, Monroe, and Adams—together read W A J M M A. To remem-ber them, first you might add an *e* after the *J* and create a short nonsense word: *wajemma*. Then, to make sure you don't forget the nonsense word, you might picture the six presidents sitting in a row and wearing pajamas. To remember their first names—George, John, Thomas, James, James, and John—you might set the names to the tune of "Happy Birthday" or any musical tune that you know.

There are different kinds of mnemonic devices, including visual images and associations and acronyms. Study how these devices work; then apply them to your own memory challenges.

Create Visual Images and Associations

Visual images are easier to remember than images that rely on words alone. In fact, communication through visual images goes back to the prehistoric era, when people made drawings that still exist on cave walls. It is no acci-dent that the phrase "a picture is worth a thousand words" is so familiar. The best mental images often involve bright colors; three dimensions; action scenes; inanimate objects with human traits; ridiculousness; and humor.

Turning information into mental pictures helps improve memory, espe-cially for visual learners. To remember that the Spanish artist Picasso painted *The Three Women*, you might imagine the women in a circle danc-ing to a Spanish song with a pig and a donkey (pig-asso). Don't reject out-landish images—as long as they help you.

Here is another example: Say you are trying to learn some basic Spanish vocabulary, including the words *carta*, *río*, and *dinero*. Instead of trying to learn these words by rote, you might come up with mental images such as those in Table 6–3.

TABLE 6-3 VISUAL IMAGES AID RECALL

SPANISH VOCABULARY	DEFINITION	MENTAL PICTURE
carta	letter	A person pushing a shopping cart filled with letters into a post office.
río	river	A school of sharks rioting in the river. One of the sharks is pulling a banner inscribed with the word *riot*. A killer shark bites off the *t* in riot as he takes charge of the group. "I'm the king of this river," he says.
dinero	money	A man eating lasagna at a diner. The lasagna is made of layers of money.

FIGURE 6-6 **A MENTAL WALK**

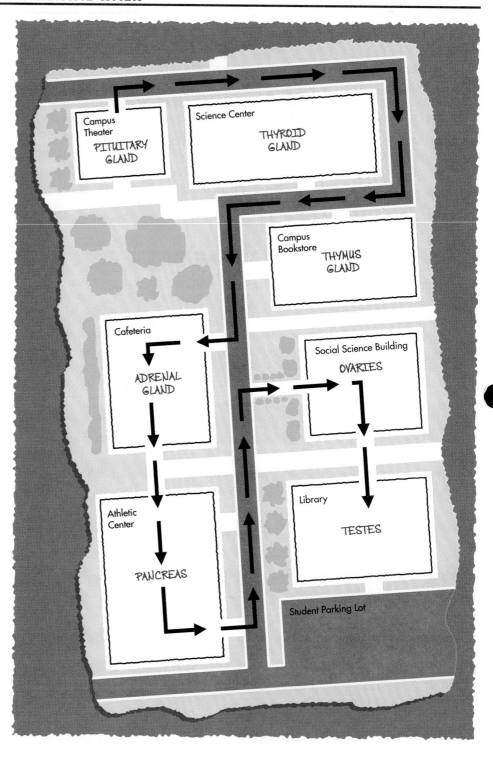

Using Visual Images to Remember Items in a List

Two mental imagery techniques will help you remember items in a list: taking a mental walk in a familiar place and forming an idea chain.

A *mental walk* is a memory strategy in which you imagine that you store new ideas in familiar locations. Think, for example, of the route you take to and from the library. You pass the college theater, the science center, the bookstore, the cafeteria, the athletic center, and the social science building before reaching the library. At each spot along the route, you "place" an idea or concept you want to learn. Say, for example, that in biology you have been assigned the task of remembering the major endocrine glands, starting in the brain and working downward through the body. Using the mental walk technique, here is how you would do this (see Figure 6–6 for a visual representation of this technique):

> At the college theater, you would place the pituitary gland; at the science center, the thyroid gland; at the college bookstore, the thymus gland; at the cafeteria, the adrenal gland; at the athletic center, the pancreas; at the social science building the ovaries (female); and at the library, the testes (male).

An *idea chain* is a memory strategy that involves forming exaggerated mental images of twenty or more items. The first image is connected to the second image, which is connected to the third image, and so on. Imagine, for example, that you want to remember the seven Thinktrix mind actions that appear in the critical-thinking discussion in Chapter 4: recall, similarity, difference, cause and effect, example to idea, idea to example, and evaluation. You can use the visual icons to form an idea chain that goes like this:

The other end of a string tied around your finger ✋ leads to two

pyramids △ △ and ends at a black, square office building next to one

of the pyramids △ ☐ . Inside the building there's a courtyard with a

fountain dripping into a pool 〜💧〜 . On the wall, a painted "ex" and

an arrow direct you to a light bulb EX→💡 , which points to another

"ex" 💡→EX . Lit by the light bulb above, a set of scales weighs mail ⚖️ .

Create Acronyms

Another helpful association method involves the use of the **acronym** . Physics instructors often supply the acronym "Roy G. Biv" to help students remember the colors of the spectrum. Roy G. Biv stands for **r**(ed), **o**(range),

Acronym,
A word formed from the first letters of a series of words, created to help you remember the series.

y(ellow), **g**(reen), **b**(lue), **i**(ndigo), and **v**(iolet). In history, you can remember the Allies during World War II—Britain, America, and Russia—with the acronym BAR.

When you can't create a name like Roy G. Biv, create an acronym from an entire sentence in which the first letter of each word stands for the first letter of the memorized term. When science students want to remember the list of planets in order of their distance from the sun, they learn the sentence: *My very elegant mother just served us nine pickles* (Mercury, Venus, Earth, Mars, Jupiter, Saturn, Uranus, Neptune, and Pluto).

Improving your memory requires energy, time, and work. In school, it also helps to master SQ3R, the textbook study technique that was introduced in Chapter 5. By going through the steps in SQ3R and using the specific memory techniques described in this chapter, you will be able to learn more in less time—and remember what you learn long after exams are over.

HOW CAN TAPE RECORDERS HELP YOU LISTEN AND REMEMBER?

The selective use of a tape recorder can provide helpful backup to your listening and memory skills. It's important, though, not to let tape-recording substitute for active participation. Not all students like to use tape recorders, but if you choose to do so, here are some guidelines and a discussion of potential effects.

Guidelines for Using Tape Recorders

Ask the instructor whether he or she permits tape recorders in class. Some instructors don't mind, whereas others don't allow students to use them.

Use a small, portable tape recorder. Sit near the front for the best possible recording.

Participate actively in class. Take notes just as you would if the tape recorder were not there.

Use tape recorders to make study tapes. Questions on tape can work like audio flash cards. One way to do it is to record study questions, leaving ten to fifteen seconds between questions for you to answer out loud. Recording the correct answer after the pause will give you immediate feedback. For example, part of a recording for a writing class might say, "The three elements of effective writing are…(10–15 seconds) topic, audience, and purpose."

Potential Positive Effects of Using Tape Recorders

➤ You can listen to an important portion of the lecture over and over again.

➤ You can supplement or clarify sections of the lecture that confused you or that you missed.

➤ Tape recordings can provide study materials to listen to when driving or exercising.

➤ Tape recordings can help study groups reconcile conflicting notes.

➤ If you miss class, you might be able to have a friend record the lecture for you.

Potential Negative Effects of Using Tape Recorders

➤ You may tend to listen less in class.

➤ You may take fewer notes, figuring that you will rely on your tape.

➤ It may be time-consuming. When you attend a lecture just to record it and then listen to the entire recording, you have taken twice as much time out of your schedule.

➤ If your tape recorder malfunctions or the recording is hard to hear, you may end up with very little study material, especially if your notes are sparse.

Think critically about whether using a tape recorder is a good idea for you. If you choose to try it, let the tape recorder be an additional resource instead of a replacement for your active participation. Tape-recorded lectures and study tapes are just one study resource among many.

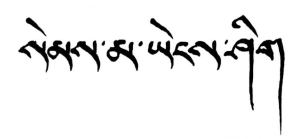

In Sanskrit, the written language of India and other Hindu countries, the characters above read *sem ma yeng chik*, meaning, "do not be distracted." This advice can refer to the focus for a task or job at hand, the concentration required to critically think and talk through a problem, the mental discipline of meditation, or many other situations.

Think of this concept as you strive to improve your listening and memory techniques. Focus on the task, the person, or the idea at hand. Try not to be distracted by other thoughts, other people's notions of what you should be doing, or any negative messages. Be present in the moment to truly hear and remember what is happening around you. Do not be distracted.

IMPORTANT POINTS TO REMEMBER

1. How can you become a better listener?

Listening is a learnable skill that involves the complex process of communication. Listening has four progressive stages: sensing, interpreting, evaluating, and reacting. Part of listening involves managing listening challenges, which include divided attention and distractions, the tendency to shut out all or part of the speaker's message, and the tendency to quickly judge what you hear. You can create a more positive listening environment by working to eliminate distractions, taking responsibility for listening, believing that what your instructors say is valuable, and making sure your emotions and opinions don't interfere with your listening.

Effective listening is also active listening. You will be more involved with what you hear if you set a purpose for listening, ask questions, put "extra" listening time to good use, pay attention to verbal signposts, and know what helps and hinders listening.

2. How does memory work?

Like a computer, the human memory is a system that encodes, stores, and retrieves information. Memories stored in the human brain are placed in three different storage banks: sensory memory, short-term memory, and long-term memory.

3. How can you improve your memory?

Use specific memory strategies such as developing a will to remember; understanding what you memorize; reciting, rehearsing, and writing; focusing on important points while ignoring unimportant details; scheduling short and frequent study sessions with rest in between; separating material into manageable sections; practicing the material you learn in the middle of a study session; grouping material into easy-to-learn segments; using visual aids; and creating a context for lost memories. Knowing how to make the most of last-minute studying and to use critical thinking can also boost your memory power.

4. How can you use mnemonic devices to boost memory power?

Mnemonic devices are memory techniques that associate new information with information you already know. The most effective mnemonics are linked to visual images. You can use visual images to remember items in a list by creating a memory walk or an idea chain. Acronyms, another mnemonic, are words formed from the first letters of words in a series.

5. How can tape recorders help you listen and remember?

Tape recorders can support your listening and memory skills as long as you do not use them as a substitute for active participation. If you tape your lectures, be sure to stay as involved in the class as if the tape recorder weren't there. Use the taped lecture to make study tapes, fill in missed sections of notes, and help clarify confusing points. Make sure that your instructor permits the use of tape recorders before you bring one to class.

Name _____   Date _____

BUILDING SKILLS FOR COLLEGE, CAREER, AND LIFE SUCCESS
CHAPTER 6

TAKING STOCK:
REFINING YOUR THOUGHTS

Look back at the statements you explored at the start of the chapter (see Thinking It Through on p. 199). Observe whether your attitudes have changed and what you have learned by studying this chapter.

1. Give three reasons why it can be difficult to remember what you hear in class.

_____

_____

_____

2. List two things you can do to keep listening when a speaker says something that goes against your personal beliefs.

_____

_____

_____

3. Explain the value—and limitations—of last-minute studying (cramming).

_____

_____

_____

4. Name three strategies that will help you improve your memory.

_____

_____

_____

5. Name two mnemonic devices that will help you remember what you study.

_____

_____

6. Choose one listening or memory strategy you learned in this chapter and explain how you will apply it to your schoolwork during the next week.

_____

_____

? CRITICAL THINKING:
APPLYING LEARNING TO YOUR LIFE

Optimum Listening Conditions

➤ Think of a recent situation (this semester or last semester) in which you have been able to understand and retain most of what you heard in the classroom:

Describe the environment (course title, type of classroom setting, etc.): _____

_____

Describe the instructor's style (lecture, group discussion, question and answer, etc.): _____

_____

Describe your level of preparation for the class: _____

_____

Describe your attitude toward the course:_____

_____

Describe any barriers to listening that you had to overcome in this situation: _____

_____

_____

_____

➤ Now describe a classroom situation you recently experienced where
you feel you didn't retain information well.

Describe the environment (course title, type of classroom setting,
etc.): _____

_____

Describe the instructor's style (lecture, group discussion, question
and answer, etc.): _____

_____

Describe your level of preparation for the class: _____

_____

Describe your attitude toward the course: _____

_____

Describe any barriers to listening that were present in this situation:

_____

_____

➤ Examine the two situations. Based on your descriptions, name three
conditions that seem crucial for you to listen effectively and retain
information.

1. _____

2. _____

3. _____

Describe one way in which you could have improved your listening
and retention in the more difficult situation.

_____

_____

_____

Analyzing Barriers to Listening

Look back at Figure 6–1. Use this figure as a model as you try to record your thoughts in an important listening situation.

Step 1: Borrow an audio teaching tape, a motivation tape, or a taped speech from the library or from a friend.

Step 2: Try to identify the speaker's key points as you listen to the tape.

Step 3: Then take notes in the following manner. Divide a piece of paper into two columns. Title the left column "Speaker's main points," and list words or phrases that summarize the central ideas. Title the right column "Responses/Reactions," and in that column record your thoughts about the speech as they come to your mind. Write down everything you are thinking as you listen.

Step 4: Now listen to the tape again. This time make a particular effort to focus your listening on content rather than on your reactions to the content.

Step 5: Name any factors that affected your ability to hear the speaker's message.

_____

_____

_____

_____

Create a Mnemonic Device

Look back at all the memory principles examined in this chapter. Using what you learned about mnemonic devices, create a mnemonic that allows you to remember these memory principles quickly. You can create a mental picture or an acronym. If you are using a mental picture, describe it here and attach a drawing if you like; if you are using an acronym, write it and then indicate what each letter stands for.

_____

_____

_____

Think of other situations in which you used a mnemonic device to remember something. What was the device? How effective was it in helping you remember the information?

_____

_____

Boost Your Memory

What do you have the most trouble remembering? Is it names, historic dates, scientific formulas, or the actions in a sequence? Write it here.

_____

_____

Now choose three different memory techniques to try. For example, if you have trouble remembering the battles of World War II in order, you could recite and rehearse them, associate each battle with an image, and link the images in a chain. Take three days and try one technique each day. Don't try to memorize the same material every day; choose three "sets" of material that are similar in size and type but have different information (e.g., the time lines of three different battles). Name here the three techniques you use.

1. _____

2. _____

3. _____

After the three days, evaluate. What technique helped the most? How do you plan to apply this technique to other memory challenges?

_____

_____

Create an Idea Chain

Read the following list just once: _radio, stapler, computer, Jackie Joyner Kersee, pen, telephone, Tom Cruise, trombone, index card, orange juice, Maya Lin, Albert Einstein, and barbecued chicken._

Next, try to recall the items in the order in which they appear. How many items did you remember? Most people have trouble remembering more than a few items at the beginning or end of the list.

To improve your recall, create an idea chain that links the first item to the second, the second to the third, and so on. The idea chain should paint an unforgettable picture. Describe your idea chain here:

_____

_____

_____

_____

Wait a day, then use the idea chain to remember the list. How many items stayed with you?

TEAMWORK: COMBINING FORCES

Hone your listening skills. Improve listening through teamwork. Divide into groups of five to nine to play a game called Celebrity. Each group will have two or three teams, each with two or three people (e.g., a group of seven will have two teams of two and one of three). Using small slips of paper, each person must write down the names of five well-known people, one on each slip. The people may be living or dead and can have achieved celebrity status in any field—sports, entertainment, politics, arts and literature, science and medicine, and so on. Each scrap of paper should be folded to conceal the name written on it. Put all of the scraps together in one container. The only other equipment you need is a watch with a second hand.

Within each team of two, there is a giver and a receiver (team members switch roles every time they have a new turn). Teams take turns guessing. While a member of a nonguessing team times the pair for one minute, the giver of the guessing team picks a piece of paper and describes the named celebrity to the receiver without saying any part of the person's name. The giver can use words, sounds, motion, singing, or anything that will help the receiver. (For Jackie Robinson: "Famous baseball player, first black man on a pro team, first name is the same as President Kennedy's wife," etc.) If and when the receiver guesses correctly, the giver keeps that scrap and chooses another, continuing to go through as many names as possible before the minute is up. When time is called, the container of names (minus the names guessed) moves to the next team. (If a name remains unguessed when time is called, that paper has to go back into the container without the giver revealing the name.) When all the names have been guessed, teams count their papers to learn their scores. Everyone then comes together as a class and takes some time to exchange views about the experience.

How did the time limit, teamwork atmosphere, or noise affect your ability to listen? Which names were you more able to guess? Which gave you trouble, and why? Evaluate your skills. Remember that your ability to "think on your feet" in this way is valuable in all kinds of workplace and personal situations.

WRITING: DISCOVERY THROUGH JOURNALING

To record your thoughts, use a separate journal or the lined page at the end of the chapter.

Pushing past your emotions and opinions. Describe your feelings about having to listen to an instructor, supervisor, or other authority with whom you do not agree. How do you react? Do you stop listening? Do you get caught up in an internal argument? Do you try to figure out how you will comment? Brainstorm ideas about what you can do when this kind of situation comes up.

CAREER PORTFOLIO:
CHARTING YOUR PROGRESS

Listening and memory on the job. Any career that you pursue will make use of your listening and memory skills. Whereas memorizing facts for an anatomy test might not seem particularly crucial, for example, a doctor will find that being able to remember where a particular artery is can make the difference in a life-or-death situation.

On a separate sheet of paper, make a list of all of the various listening and memory skills that you can recall from this chapter. Try to write down twelve or more different skills.

Then show your list to three different people who are currently in the work force either part time or full time. Ask them to indicate for you the five skills from your list that they consider to be the most important for workplace success.

When you have completed your three interviews, tally the votes and write your three top skills on another sheet of paper (if you have any tie votes, make the choice yourself of which skill you feel is most important). For each skill, write a brief story about a time when this skill was important to you at work or, if you have not yet been employed, in the classroom.

Journal Entry

CROSSWORD REVIEW: PART II
Sharpening Your Skills

ACROSS

4. Parts of written or spoken material that can throw light on the meaning of a word or passage
5. To repeat, summarize, and associate information with other information, silently in your mind
9. A memory device that involves associating something with information you already know
10. A word formed from the first letters of a series of words, created in order to help you remember the series
12. A graph that shows a continuous trend over time
13. A word part that is added before the central part of a word
14. An idea or statement accepted as true without examination or proof
15. The first stage of listening, when your ears pick up sound waves and transmit them to the brain
17. A system of seven mind actions that represent the ways in which you think
18. Original documents such as works of literature and scientific studies

DOWN

1. A plan of action designed to accomplish a specific goal
2. Rapid reading of various chapter elements, including introductions and summaries
3. Forming digestible information segments that are easy to remember
6. A mind action in which you judge whether something is important or unimportant
7. One of the purposes of reading, involving working to build an understanding of the material
8. A mind action in which you describe facts, objects, or events
11. A mental point of view or outlook, based on a cluster of related assumptions, incorporating values, interests, and knowledge
16. A reading technique for effective textbook reading

PART 3

TARGETING SUCCESS IN SCHOOL

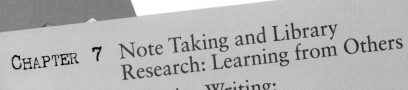

CHAPTER **7** Note Taking and Library Research: Learning from Others

CHAPTER **8** Effective Writing: Communicating Your Message

CHAPTER **9** Test Taking: Showing What You Know

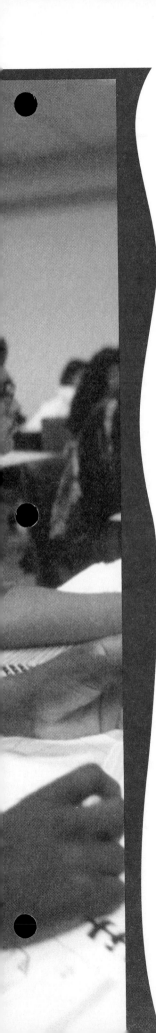

7 NOTE TAKING AND LIBRARY RESEARCH:
Learning from Others

Thinking It Through

Check those statements that apply to you right now:

- ❏ Sometimes I feel as if I don't get much from studying my notes.
- ❏ When I jot down notes on information I find in the library, they rarely help me when I look back at them later.
- ❏ I use one note-taking system for every purpose.
- ❏ No matter how hard I try, I can never write down everything the instructor says.
- ❏ I have never used a computer for library research.
- ❏ When I do library research, I don't normally create a search plan before I start.

In this chapter, you will explore answers to the following questions:

- ➤ How does taking notes help you?
- ➤ How can you make the most of class notes?
- ➤ What are research notes and how can you use them?
- ➤ Which note-taking system should you use?
- ➤ How can you write faster when taking notes?
- ➤ How can you make the most of your library?
- ➤ How do you use a search strategy to conduct research?

Both in school and out, you spend much of your time like a detective in search of knowledge. When you listen to your instructors during class lectures, do independent research, or learn on the job, you are uncovering and gathering information that you may put to use, now or in the future. Note taking and library research can empower you to create new ideas from what you learn. The more knowledge you gather in your "detective work," the more resources you have at your disposal when you soar ahead into new realms of thinking.

The search for knowledge requires varied skills. First, you need to use an effective note-taking system to record what you hear or read.

Second, you need to know how to harness the vast resources of your college library (or libraries). Through informed use of the library, you will be able to access all of these written resources that can help you learn and reach your potential. This chapter will show you note-taking and research skills that can help you make your searches for information successful.

HOW DOES TAKING NOTES HELP YOU?

Note taking isn't always easy to do. You might feel that it prevents you from watching your instructor, that you can't write fast enough, or that you seem to remember enough material even when you don't take notes. The act of note taking, however, involves you in the learning process in many beneficial ways. Weigh whatever you feel are the negative effects of note taking against the potential positive effects. You may see why good note-taking can be a useful habit (see Table 7–1).

Notes help you learn when you are in class, doing research, or studying. Since it is virtually impossible to take notes on everything you hear or read, the act of note taking encourages you to think critically and evaluate what is worth remembering. Asking yourself questions like the following will help you judge what is important enough to write down:

> ➤ Do I need this information?
> ➤ Is the information important to the lecture or reading or is it just an interesting comment?
> ➤ Is the information fact or opinion? If it is opinion, is it worth remembering? (To explore this question, see How Do You Establish Truth? in Chapter 4.)

TABLE 7-1   THE VALUE OF NOTES

✔ Your notes provide written material that helps you study information and prepare for tests.

✔ When you take notes, you become an active, involved listener and learner.

✔ Notes help you think critically and organize ideas.

✔ The information you learn in class may not appear in any text; you will have no way to study it without writing it down.

✔ If it is difficult for you to process information while in class, having notes to read and make sense of later can help you learn.

✔ Note taking allows you to compile information from different research sources and use the information in your writing.

✔ Note taking is a skill that you will use on the job and in your personal life.

Your responses will guide your note taking in class and help you decide what to study before an exam. Similarly, the notes you take while doing research will affect your research efforts. Learn what class notes and research notes are and how to use each to your advantage.

HOW CAN YOU MAKE THE MOST OF CLASS NOTES?

Class notes—the notes you take while listening to an instructor—may contain key terms and definitions (e.g., Marketing research is…), explanations of concepts and processes (what happens during photosynthesis), or narratives of who did what to whom and when (The events that led to the Persian Gulf War are…). If lectures include material that is not in your text or if your instructor talks about specific test questions, your class notes become even more important as a study tool.

Preparing to Take Class Notes

Your class notes have two purposes: First, they should reflect what you heard in class, and second, they should be a resource for studying, writing, or comparing with your text material. Taking good class notes depends on good preparation.

- ➤ Preview the text (or any other assigned reading material) to become familiar with the topic and any new concepts that it introduces. Visual familiarity helps note taking during lectures.

- ➤ Use separate pieces of 8 1/2 -by-11-inch paper for each class. If you use a three-ring binder, punch holes in handouts and insert them immediately following your notes for that day.

- ➤ Find a comfortable seat where you can easily see and hear, and be ready to write as soon as the instructor begins speaking.

- ➤ Choose a note-taking system that helps you handle the instructor's style (you'll be more able to determine this style after a few classes). Whereas one instructor may deliver organized lectures at a normal speaking rate, another may jump from topic to topic or talk very quickly.

- ➤ Set up a support system with two students in each class. That way, when you are absent, you can get the notes you missed (having two "buddies" instead of just one helps you be more sure that at least one person will be in class on any given day).

What to Do During Class

Because no one has time to write down everything he or she hears, the following strategies will help you choose and record what you feel is important, in a format that you can read and understand later. This is not a list of "musts." Rather, it is a source list of ideas to try, as you work to find the note-taking system that works best for you. Keep an open mind and experiment with these strategies until you feel that you have found a successful combination.

Remember that the first step in note taking is to listen actively; you can't write down something that you don't hear. Use the listening strategies in Chapter 6 to make sure you are prepared to take in the information that comes your way during class.

➤ Date and identify each page. When you take several pages of notes during a lecture, add an identifying letter or number to the date on each page: 11/27A, 11/27B, 11/27C, or 11/27—1 of 3, 11/27—2 of 3, 11/27—3 of 3. This will help you keep track of the order of your pages.

➤ Add the specific topic of the lecture at the top of the page. For example:

11/27A—U. S. Immigration Policy After World War II

Since an instructor may revisit a topic days or even weeks after introducing it, this suggestion will help you gather all your notes on the same topic when it is time to study.

➤ If your instructor jumps from topic to topic during a single class, it may help to start a new page for each new topic.

➤ Some students prefer to use only one side of the notepaper because this can make notes easier to read. Others prefer to use both sides, which can be a more economical, paper-saving option. Choose what works best for you.

➤ Record whatever your instructor emphasizes. See Figure 7–1 for more details about how an instructor might call attention to particular information.

FIGURE 7-1 **HOW TO PICK UP ON INSTRUCTOR CUES**

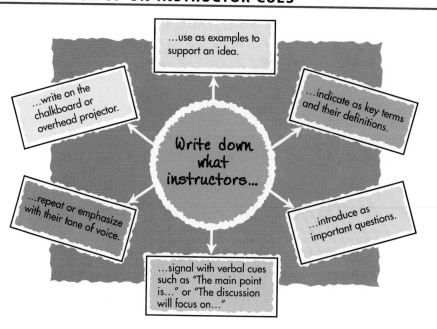

➤ Write down all key terms and definitions. If, for example, your instructor is discussing the stages of mental development in children, as defined by psychologist Jean Piaget, your notes would probably mention such terms as *sensorimotor* and *preoperational*.

➤ Continue to take notes during class discussions and question-and-answer periods. What your fellow students ask about may help you as well.

➤ Write down all questions raised by the instructor; the same questions may appear on a test.

➤ Leave one or more blank spaces between points. This white space will help you review your notes because information will be in self-contained segments. (This suggestion does not apply if you are using a think link.)

➤ Draw pictures and diagrams that help illustrate ideas.

➤ Write quickly but legibly, perhaps using a form of shorthand (see the section on shorthand on pp. 250–252 of this chapter).

Students take notes at Babson College

➤ Indicate material that is especially important with a star, underlining, a highlighter pen, a different color pen, or capital letters.

➤ If you don't understand something, leave space and place a question mark in the margin. Then take advantage of your resources—ask the instructor to explain it after class, discuss it with a classmate, or consult your textbook—and fill in the blank when the idea is clear.

➤ Take notes until the instructor stops speaking. If you stop writing a few minutes before the class is over, you might miss critical information.

➤ Make your notes as legible and organized as possible. You can't learn from notes that you can't read or understand. Remember, you can always rewrite and improve your notes.

➤ Consider that your notes are part but not all of what you need to learn. Using your text to add to your notes after class makes a superior, "deeper and wider" set of information to study.

Make Notes a Valuable After-Class Reference

Class notes are a valuable study tool when you review them regularly. The act of reviewing helps you remember important concepts and links new information to information you already know.

If you can, try to begin your review within a day of the lecture. Read your notes to learn the information, clarify points, write out abbreviations, fill in missing information, and underline or highlight key ideas. You may also want to add headings and subheadings and insert clarifying phrases or sentences. Try to review each week's notes at the end of that week. Think critically about the material in writing, study-group discussions, or quiet reflective thought, using the following questions:

 Can I easily recall the facts I have written?

 What do these ideas mean? What examples support or negate them?

 How do I evaluate these ideas? Why are they important? How fully do I understand them?

 What similar facts or ideas does this information call to mind?

 How does this information differ from what I already know?

 What new ideas can I form from learning this information?

 How do these ideas, facts, and statements relate to one another? Do any of them have cause-and-effect relationships?

Writing a summary of your notes is another important review technique. Summarizing involves critically evaluating which ideas and examples are most important and then rewriting the material in a shortened form, focusing on those important ideas and examples. You may prefer to summarize as you review, although you might also try summarizing your notes from memory after you review them.

Study groups can be a useful way to review notes because group members can benefit from one another's different perspectives and abilities. For example, if you happened to focus well on one particular part of the lecture and lost concentration during another, a fellow student may have been taking good notes on the part you missed. See Chapter 5 for more on effective studying in groups.

Class notes are only one form of note taking. Research notes are another key to school success.

WHAT ARE RESEARCH NOTES AND HOW CAN YOU USE THEM?

Research notes are the notes you take while gathering information to answer a research question. Research notes take two forms: source notes and content notes.

Source notes are the preliminary notes you take as you review available research. They include vital bibliographic information, as well as a short summary and critical evaluation of the work. Write these notes when you consider a book or article interesting enough to look at again. They do not signal that you have actually read something all the way through, only that you plan to review it later on.

Each source note should include the author's full name; the title of the work; the edition (if any); the publisher, year, and city of publication; issue and/or volume number when applicable (such as for a magazine); and the page numbers you consulted. Many students find that index cards work best for source notes. See Figure 7–2 for an example of how you can write source notes on index cards.

The second type of research notes are *content notes*. Unlike brief informational source notes, content notes provide an in-depth look at the source, taken during a thorough reading. Use them to record the information you need to write your draft. Here are some suggestions for taking effective content notes:

> ➤ When a source looks promising, begin reading it and summarizing what you read. Use standard notebook paper that fits into a three-

SAMPLE SOURCE NOTE   **FIGURE 7-2**

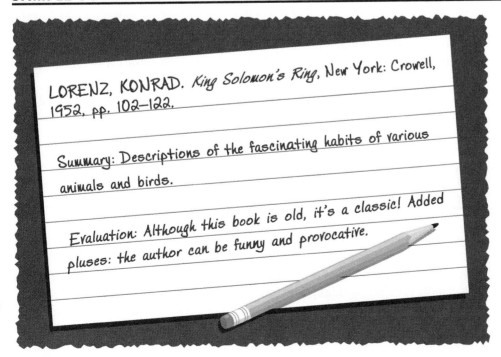

LORENZ, KONRAD. *King Solomon's Ring.* New York: Crowell, 1952, pp. 102–122.

Summary: Descriptions of the fascinating habits of various animals and birds.

Evaluation: Although this book is old, it's a classic! Added pluses: the author can be funny and provocative.

ring binder. This gives you space to write, as well as the flexibility to rearrange the pages into any order that makes sense. (If you prefer using large index cards for content notes, choose 5-by-6-inch or 5-by-8-inch sizes.)

➤ Include bibliographic information and page numbers for every source.

➤ Limit each page to a single source.

➤ If you take notes on more than one subject from a single source, create a separate page for each subject.

➤ If the notes on a source require more than one page, label the pages and number them sequentially. For example, if the source is *Business Week* magazine, your pages might be labeled BW1, BW2, and so on.

➤ Identify the type of note that appears on each page. Evaluate whether it is a summary in your own words, a quotation, or a **paraphrase** .

➤ Write your summary notes in any of the note-taking systems described later in the chapter.

Paraphrase,

A restatement of a written text or passage in another form or other words, often to clarify meaning.

Notations that you make directly on photocopies of sources—marginal notes, highlighting, and underlining—can supplement your content notes. Say, for example, that you are writing a paper on the psychological development of adolescent girls. During your research, you photocopy an article by Dr. Carol Gilligan, an expert in the field. On the photocopy, you highlight important information and make marginal notes that detail your immediate reactions to some key points. Then you take content notes on the article. When it is time to write your paper, you have two different and helpful resources to consult.

Try to divide your time as equally as possible between photocopy notes and content notes. If you use photocopies as your primary reference without making any of your own content notes, you may have more work to do when you begin writing because you will need to spend time putting the source material in your own words. Writing paraphrases and summaries in content notes ahead of time will save you some work later in the process.

Whether you are taking notes in class or while doing research, there are different note-taking systems from which you can choose.

WHAT NOTE-TAKING SYSTEM SHOULD YOU USE?

You will benefit most from the system that feels most comfortable to you and makes the most sense for the type of content covered in any given course. For example, you might take notes in a different style for a history class than for a foreign language class. As you consider each system, remember your intelligences from Chapter 3. Everyone has a different learning and working style, so don't wedge yourself into a system that doesn't

THE STRUCTURE OF AN OUTLINE

FIGURE 7-3

FORMAL OUTLINE	INFORMAL OUTLINE
TOPIC	TOPIC
I. First Main Idea	First Main Idea
A. Major supporting fact	—Major supporting fact
B. Major supporting fact	—Major supporting fact
1. First reason or example	—First reason or example
2. Second reason or example	—Second reason or example
a. First supporting fact	—First supporting fact
b. Second supporting fact	—Second supporting fact
II. Second Main Idea	Second Main Idea
A. Major supporting fact	—Major supporting fact
1. First reason or example	—First reason or example
2. Second reason or example	—Second reason or example
B. Major supporting fact	—Major supporting fact

work for you. The most common note-taking systems include outlines, the Cornell system, and think links.

Taking Notes in Outline Form

When a reading assignment or lecture seems well organized, you may choose to take notes in outline form. When you use an outline, you construct a line-by-line representation, with certain phrases set off by varying indentations, showing how ideas relate to one another and are supported by facts and examples.

Formal Versus Informal Outlines

Formal outlines indicate ideas and examples with Roman numerals, capital and lowercase letters, and numbers. The rules of formal outlines require at least two headings on the same level. That is, if you have a IIA, you must also have a IIB. Similarly, if you have a IIIA1, you must also have a IIIA2. In contrast, informal outlines show the same relationships but replace the formality with a system of consistent indenting and dashes. Figure 7–3

> "Consistency is important. If you use the same system of indicating importance, such as indenting, spacing, or underlining on each page of your notes, your mind will perceive the key information with a minimum of effort."
>
> William H. Armstrong and M. Willard Lampe II

FIGURE 7-4   **SAMPLE FORMAL OUTLINE**

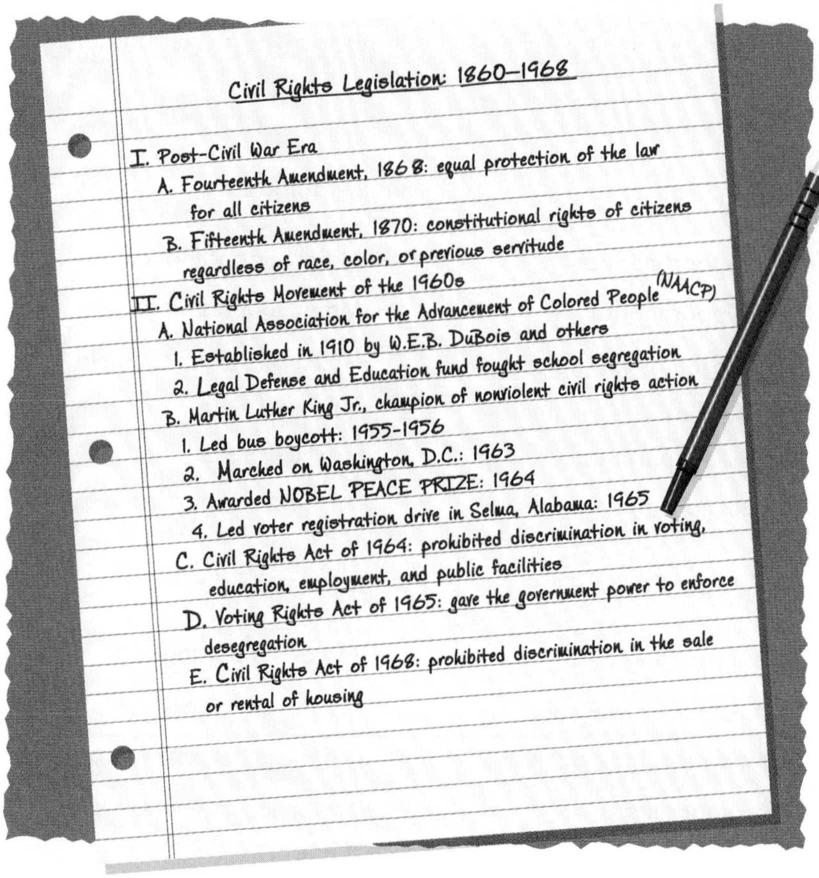

Civil Rights Legislation: 1860–1968

I. Post-Civil War Era
  A. Fourteenth Amendment, 1868: equal protection of the law
    for all citizens
  B. Fifteenth Amendment, 1870: constitutional rights of citizens
    regardless of race, color, or previous servitude
II. Civil Rights Movement of the 1960s
  A. National Association for the Advancement of Colored People (NAACP)
    1. Established in 1910 by W.E.B. DuBois and others
    2. Legal Defense and Education fund fought school segregation
  B. Martin Luther King Jr., champion of nonviolent civil rights action
    1. Led bus boycott: 1955-1956
    2. Marched on Washington, D.C.: 1963
    3. Awarded NOBEL PEACE PRIZE: 1964
    4. Led voter registration drive in Selma, Alabama: 1965
  C. Civil Rights Act of 1964: prohibited discrimination in voting,
    education, employment, and public facilities
  D. Voting Rights Act of 1965: gave the government power to enforce
    desegregation
  E. Civil Rights Act of 1968: prohibited discrimination in the sale
  or rental of housing

shows the difference between the two outline forms. Because making a formal outline can take time, many students find that using informal outlines is better for in-class note taking. Figure 7–4 shows how a student has used the structure of a formal outline to write notes on the topic of civil-rights legislation.

When you use an outline to write class notes, you may have trouble when an instructor rambles or jumps from point to point. The best advice in this case is to abandon the outline structure for the time being. Focus instead on taking down whatever information you can and on drawing connections among key topics. After class, try to restructure your notes and, if possible, rewrite them in outline form.

Guided Notes

From time to time, an instructor may give you a guide, usually in the form of an outline, to help you take notes in the class. This outline may be on the board, on an overhead projector, or on a page that you receive at the beginning of the class.

Although guided notes help you follow the lecture and organize your thoughts during class, they do not replace your own notes. Because they are more of a basic outline of topics than a comprehensive coverage of information, they require that you fill in what they do not cover in detail. If your mind wanders because you think that the guided notes are all you need, you may miss important information.

When you receive guided notes on paper, write directly on the paper if there is room. If not, use a separate sheet and write on it the outline categories that the guided notes suggest. If the guided notes are on the board or overhead, copy them, leaving plenty of space in between for your own notes.

Using the Cornell Note-Taking System

The Cornell note-taking system, also known as the T-note system, was developed more than 45 years ago by Walter Pauk at Cornell University and is now in use throughout the world.[1] The system is successful because it is simple—and because it works. It consists of three sections on ordinary notepaper:

➤ *Section 1,* the largest section, is on the right. Record your notes here in informal outline form.

➤ *Section 2,* to the left of your notes, is the *cue column.* Leave it blank while you read or listen; then fill it in later as you review. You might fill it with comments that highlight main ideas, clarify meaning, suggest examples, or link ideas and examples. You can even draw diagrams.

➤ *Section 3,* at the bottom of the page, is known as the *summary area.* Here you use a sentence or two to summarize the notes on the page. Use this section during the review process to reinforce concepts and provide an overview of what the notes say.

When you use the Cornell system, create the note-taking structure before class begins. Picture an upside-down letter T as you follow these directions, and use Figure 7–5 as your guide.

➤ Start with a sheet of standard loose-leaf paper. Label it with the date and title of the lecture.

➤ To create the *cue column,* draw a vertical line about 2 1/2 inches from the left side of the paper. End the line about 2 inches from the bottom of the sheet.

➤ To create the *summary area,* start at the point where the vertical line ends (about 2 inches from the bottom of the page) and draw a horizontal line that spans the entire paper.

Figure 7–5, on the next page, shows how a student used the Cornell system to take notes in a business course.

FIGURE 7-5   **NOTES TAKEN WITH THE CORNELL SYSTEM**

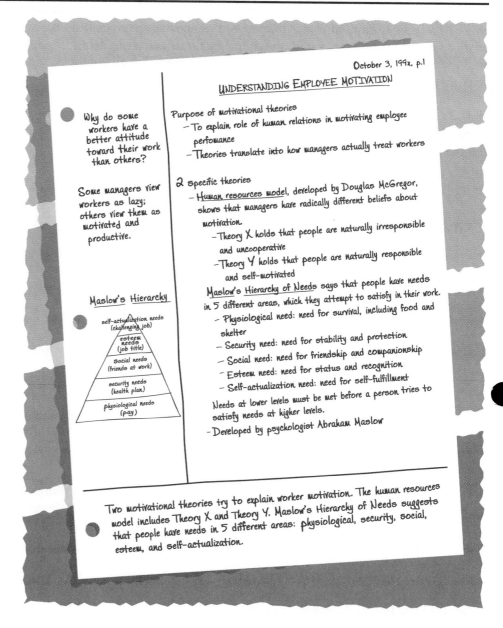

October 3, 199x, p.1

UNDERSTANDING EMPLOYEE MOTIVATION

Why do some workers have a better attitude toward their work than others?

Some managers view workers as lazy; others view them as motivated and productive.

Maslow's Hierarchy

self-actualization needs (challenging job)
esteem needs (job title)
social needs (friends at work)
security needs (health plan)
physiological needs (pay)

Purpose of motivational theories
 — To explain role of human relations in motivating employee performance
 — Theories translate into how managers actually treat workers

2 specific theories
 — Human resources model, developed by Douglas McGregor, shows that managers have radically different beliefs about motivation
   — Theory X holds that people are naturally irresponsible and uncooperative
   — Theory Y holds that people are naturally responsible and self-motivated
Maslow's Hierarchy of Needs says that people have needs in 5 different areas, which they attempt to satisfy in their work.
   — Physiological need: need for survival, including food and shelter
   — Security need: need for stability and protection
   — Social need: need for friendship and companionship
   — Esteem need: need for status and recognition
   — Self-actualization need: need for self-fulfillment
Needs at lower levels must be met before a person tries to satisfy needs at higher levels.
 — Developed by psychologist Abraham Maslow

Two motivational theories try to explain worker motivation. The human resources model includes Theory X and Theory Y. Maslow's Hierarchy of Needs suggests that people have needs in 5 different areas: physiological, security, social, esteem, and self-actualization.

Creating a Think Link

A *think link,* also known as a mind map, is a visual form of note taking. When you draw a think link, you diagram ideas by using shapes and lines that link ideas and supporting details and examples. The visual design makes the connections easy to see, and the use of shapes and pictures extends the material beyond just words. Many learners respond well to the power of   visualization . You can use think links to brainstorm ideas for paper topics as well.

One way to create a think link is to start by circling your topic in the middle of a sheet of paper. Next, draw a line from the circled topic and write the name of one major idea at the end of the line. Circle that idea

Visualization,

The interpretation of verbal ideas through the use of mental visual images.

SAMPLE THINK LINK

FIGURE 7-6

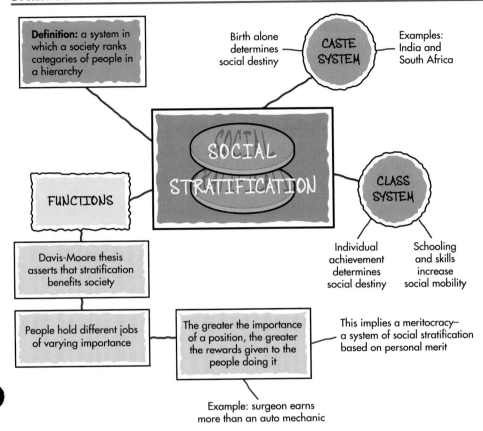

THE JELLYFISH THINK LINK

FIGURE 7-7

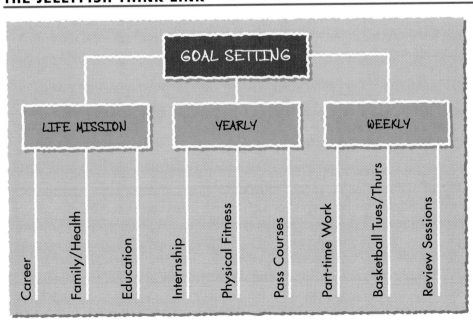

also. Then jot down specific facts related to the idea, linking them to the idea with lines. Continue the process, connecting thoughts to one another by using circles, lines, and words. Figure 7–6 shows a think link on social stratification (a sociology concept) that follows this particular structure.

You can design any kind of think link that feels comfortable to you. Different examples include stair steps, showing connected ideas that build toward a conclusion or a tree shape with roots as causes and branches as effects. Figure 7–7 shows a type of think link sometimes referred to as a "jellyfish."

A think link may be difficult to construct in class, especially if your instructor talks quickly. In this case, use another note-taking system during class. Then make a think link as part of the review process.

Other Visual Note-Taking Strategies

Several other note-taking strategies will help you organize your information and are especially useful to visual learners. These strategies may be too involved to complete quickly during class, so you may want to use them when taking notes on a text chapter or when rewriting your notes for review.

Time lines. A time line can help you organize information—such as dates of French Revolution events or eras of different psychology practices—into chronological order. Draw a vertical or horizontal line on the page and connect each item to the line, in order, noting the dates.

Tables. You will notice tables throughout this text that show information through vertical or horizontal columns. Use tables to arrange information according to particular categories.

Hierarchy,
A graded or ranked series.

Hierarchy charts. Charts showing the **hierarchy** of information can help you understand that information in terms of how each piece fits into the hierarchy. A hierarchy chart could show levels of government, for example, or levels of scientific classification of animals and plants.

Once you choose a note-taking system, your success will depend on how well you use it. Personal shorthand will help you make the most of whatever system you choose.

HOW CAN YOU WRITE FASTER WHEN TAKING NOTES?

Shorthand,
A system of rapid handwriting that employs symbols to represent words, phrases, and letters.

When taking notes, many students feel that they can't keep up with the instructor. Using some personal **shorthand** (not standard secretarial shorthand) can help you push your pen faster. Personal shorthand uses abbreviations and shortened words in addition to replacing words or parts of words with symbols. Because you are the only intended reader, you can misspell and abbreviate words in ways that only you understand.

The only danger with shorthand is that you might forget what your writing means. To avoid this problem, review your shorthand notes while your abbreviations and symbols are fresh in your mind. If there is any confusion, spell out words as you review.

Here are some suggestions that will help you master this important skill:

1. Use the following standard abbreviations in place of complete words:

w/	with	c⨍	compare, in comparison to
w/o	without	⨍⨍	following
→	means; resulting in	Q	question
←	as a result of	p.	page
↑	increasing	*	most importantly
↓	decreasing	<	less than
∴	therefore	>	more than
∵	because	=	equals
≈	approximately	%	percent
+ OR &	and	Δ	change
—	minus; negative	2	to; two; too
NO. OR #	number	VS	versus; against
i.e.	that is,	eg	for example
etc.	and so forth	c/o	care of
ng	no good	lb	pound

2. Shorten words by removing vowels from the middle of words:

prps = purpose
lwyr = lawyer
Crvtte = Corvette (as on a vanity license plate for a car)
cmptr = computer

3. Substitute word beginnings for entire words:

assoc = associate; association
info = information
subj = subject
chem = chemical; chemistry
min = minimum
max = maximum

4. Form plurals by adding *s* to shortened words:

prblms = problems
drctrys = directories
prntrs = printers

5. Make up your own symbols and use them consistently:

b/4 = before
4tn = fortune
2thake = toothache

6. Learn to rely on key phrases instead of complete sentences: For example, write "German—nouns capitalized" instead of "In the German language, all nouns are capitalized."

7. Use standard or informal abbreviations for proper nouns such as places, people, companies, scientific substances, events, and so on.

D.C.	=	Washington, D.C.
It.	=	Italy
FMC	=	Ford Motor Company
H20	=	water
Moz.	=	Wolfgang Amadeus Mozart
WWII	=	World War II

8. If you know you are going to repeat a particular word or phrase often throughout the course of a class period, write it out once at the beginning of the class and then establish an abbreviation that you will use through the rest of your notes. For example, if you are taking notes on the rise and fall of Argentina's former first lady Eva Peron, you might start out by writing "Eva Peron (EP)" and then use "EP" throughout the rest of the class period.

One important reason for taking notes is to record information you gather during library research. Research involves a systematic search for information.

THINKING BACK

1. List three ways in which note taking will help you succeed in college.

a. _____

b. _____

c. _____

2. Identify two steps for each stage of class note taking (before, during, and after class).

Before class: _____

_____

_____

During class: _____

_____

_____

After class: _____

_____

_____

3. Explain the differences between source notes and content notes.

_____

_____

_____

_____

4. Look back at the different note-taking systems discussed in this chapter. Consider one particular course you are currently taking. Which system are you likely to use in that class, and why?

_____

_____

_____

_____

_____

5. Rewrite, and shorten, the following paragraph, using shorthand symbols:

   When you start a new writing project, you face many decisions even before you sit at a keyboard or pick up a pen. What is the most efficient way to sort out all you need to think about? Start by focusing separately on groups of decisions about topic, purpose, audience, and the specific writing situation. Then try to fit the groups together, adjusting them to create a whole.[2]

_____

_____

_____

_____

THINKING AHEAD

1. How do you think you will use research in the career you plan to enter? If you currently work, how do you use research on the job right now?

2. What specific search tools do you expect to find in your school's main library?

3. How have you used computers to explore the resources of your library? Why do you think library computers have changed the research process?

HOW CAN YOU MAKE THE MOST OF YOUR LIBRARY?

A library is a home for information; consider it the "brain" of your college. Libraries contain a world of information—from every novel Toni Morrison ever wrote to scholarship and financial aid directories to on-line job listings to medical journal articles on breast cancer research. It's all there waiting for you; your job is to find what you need as quickly and efficiently as you can.

Start with a Road Map

Most college libraries are bigger than high school and community libraries. You may feel lost on your first visit, or even a few visits after that. Make your life easier right away by learning how your library is organized. Although every library has a different layout, all libraries have certain areas in common.

Reference area. Here you'll find reference books, including encyclopedias, public- and private-sector directories, dictionaries, almanacs, and atlases. You'll also find librarians and/or other library employees who can help direct you to the information you need. Computer terminals, containing the library's catalog of holdings, as well as online bibliographic and full-text databases, are usually part of the reference area.

Book area. Books—and, in many libraries, magazines and journals in bound or boxed volumes—are stored in the *stacks*. A library with "open stacks" will allow you to search for materials on your own. In a "closed-stack" system, a staff member will retrieve materials for you.

Periodicals area. Here you'll find recent issues of popular and scholarly magazines, journals, and newspapers. Most college libraries collect **periodicals**, ranging from *Time* to *Advertising Age* to the *New England Journal of Medicine*. Since you usually cannot check out unbound periodicals, you may find photocopy machines nearby, where you can copy the pages that you need.

Periodicals,
Magazines, journals, and newspapers that are published on a regular basis throughout the year.

Audio/visual materials areas. Many libraries have specialized areas for video, art and photography, and recorded music collections.

Computer areas. Computer terminals, linked to databases and the Internet, are increasingly found in libraries and may be scattered throughout the building or set off in special areas. You may be able to access these databases and the Internet from the college's computer labs and writing centers, or even from your own computer if you have one.

Microform areas. Most libraries have microform reading areas or rooms. Microforms are materials printed on film, either **microfilm** or **microfiche**, that is read through special viewing machines. Many microform reading machines can print hard copies of stored images and text.

Microfilm,
A reel of film on which printed materials are photographed at greatly reduced size for ease of storage.

To learn about your college library, take a library tour or a training session. You might also ask for a pamphlet that describes the layout, and then take some time for a self-tour. Almost all college libraries offer some kind of orientation on how to use their books, periodicals, databases, and Internet hookups. If your school has a network of libraries, including one or more central libraries and other smaller, specialized libraries, explore each one you intend to use.

Microfiche,
A card or sheet of microfilm that contains a considerable number of pages of printed text and/or photographs in reduced form.

Learn How to Conduct an Information Search

The most successful and time-saving library research involves following a specific *search strategy*—a step-by-step method for finding information that takes you from general to specific sources. Starting with general sources usually works best because they provide an overview of your research topic and can lead you to more specific information and sources. For example, an encyclopedia article on the archaeological discovery of the Dead Sea Scrolls—manuscripts written between 250 B.C. and A.D. 68 that trace the roots of Judaism and Christianity—may mention that one of the most important books on the subject is *Understanding the Dead Sea Scrolls*, edited by Hershel Shanks (New York: Random House, 1992). This book, in turn, will lead you to thirteen experts who wrote text chapters.

Defining your exact topic is critical to the success of your search. Although "the Dead Sea Scrolls" may be too broad for your research paper, possibilities of narrower topics may include the following:

➤ How the Dead Sea Scrolls were discovered by Bedouin shepherds in 1947

➤ The historical origins of the scrolls

➤ The process archaeologists used to reconstruct scroll fragments

Conducting a Keyword Search

A *keyword search*—a search for information through the use of specific words and phrases related to the information—will help you narrow your topic. Use your library's computer database for keyword searches. For example, instead of searching through the broad category *art,* you can use a keyword search to narrow your focus to *French art* or more specifically to *French art in the nineteenth century.*

Keyword searches are relatively easy because they use natural language, rather than specialized classification vocabulary. Table 7–2 includes some tips that will help you use the keyword system.

As you search, keep in mind that

➤ Double quotes around a word or phrase will locate the term exactly as you entered it ("financial aid").

➤ Using upper or lower case will not affect the search (*Scholarships* will find *scholarships*).

➤ Singular terms will find the plural (*scholarship* will find *scholarships*).

> "Seeing research as a quest for an answer makes clear that you cannot know whether you have found something unless you know what it is you are looking for."
>
> Lynn Quitman Troyka

TABLE 7-2   HOW TO PERFORM AN EFFECTIVE KEYWORD SEARCH

IF YOU ARE SEARCHING FOR	DO THIS	EXAMPLE
A word	Type the word normally	aid
A phrase	Type the phrase in its normal word order (use regular word spacing) or surround the phrase with double quotation marks	financial aid or "financial aid"
Two or more keywords without regard to word order	Type the words in any order, surrounding the words with quotation marks (use "and" to separate the words)	"financial aid" and "scholarships"
	Type the words in any order (use "or" to separate the words)	"financial aid" or "scholarships"
Topic A or topic B	Type topic A first and then topic B (use "not" to separate the words)	"financial aid" not "scholarships"

WINDOWS ON THE WORLD:
REAL LIFE STUDENT ISSUES

How can I take more complete notes?

Jose L. Ivarez, Jr., Wright College, Chicago, Illinois, Computer Engineering Major

When I started college two semesters ago, I didn't know how important note-taking was going to be. I now know that it's one of the main ways to learn in class. At the end of my very first college class, I had only one sheet of notes. The other students had filled up several sheets. I felt frustrated that they were flipping through pages while I had only a few sentences written down. I realized then that I didn't know the first thing about how to do this.

I have a couple of note-taking problems. First, I tend to daydream. My mind wanders – then all of a sudden I realize I've missed some important information. A couple of my friends of mine said they do this too. I think students get distracted by thinking about personal problems. I know that's what happens to me sometimes. Also, my attention span drops off after about 15 or 20 minutes, so staying focused for an entire lecture period can be a problem. Finally, I can't keep up with how fast the professor talks. I try to concentrate on what's being said, and I may jot down the first point, but then I miss the next three sentences. I seem to have trouble picking out key ideas. But I keep trying. I figure writing down something is better than nothing.

I'm sure my note-taking skills have improved a little since I first started college, but I still have a long way to go. I have a pretty good memory, so that even if I haven't written something down I still might recall it just from having heard it, but I know my grades would be better if my notes weren't so poor. Can you give me suggestions about how I can take more complete notes?

Angela D. Kvasnica, University of Michigan, Ann Arbor, Michigan, Industrial and Operations Engineering Major

Note taking can get very frustrating, but I've found several ways to help me keep my focus. First, I always try to sit in front. This helps eliminate distractions such as the clock, other student's conversations, and people walking in late. Also, sitting in front will allow you to hear the lecturer more  clearly, and you can make eye contact, which keeps you more involved in what's being said.

A second way to focus is to prepare yourself ahead of time. Skim the text readings before the lecture so you will become familiar with the topic and main ideas. While taking notes, focus on writing down as much information as possible. However, it's not necessary to write down everything word for word. To keep up, use abbreviations and paraphrases, and don't worry about spelling, form or organization. You can always recopy your notes later, and rewriting your notes will help reinforce your learning.

Third, put question marks next to the topics or ideas you didn't understand or left incomplete. Then ask your professor for clarification after class or during office hours. To help you gather more complete information, you might want to try using a hand-held, minicassette recorder. Then you can review the lectures and listen for information you may have missed. One note of caution: Ask your instructor for permission to use a recorder.

Finally, compare notes with another student in class. This way you can help each other fill in the gaps. Most importantly: Don't give up. If you keep at it you will become better and better at taking notes, and eventually you'll develop a system that works for you.

HOW DO YOU USE A SEARCH STRATEGY TO CONDUCT RESEARCH?

Knowing where to look during each phase of your search will help you find information quickly and efficiently. A successful search strategy often starts with general reference works, then moves to more specific reference works, books, periodicals, and electronic sources such as the Internet (see Figure 7–8).

Use General Reference Works

CD-ROM,
A compact disk, containing millions of words and images, that can be read by a computer (CD-ROM stands for "compact disk read-only memory").

Begin your research with *general reference works*. These works cover hundreds—and sometimes thousands—of different topics in a broad, nondetailed way. General reference guides are often available on line or on   CD-ROM.
  Among the works that fall into the general reference category are these:

➤ Encyclopedias such as the multivolume *Encyclopedia Americana* and the single-volume *New Columbia Encyclopedia*

➤ Almanacs such as the *World Almanac and Book of Facts*

➤ Yearbooks such as the *McGraw-Hill Yearbook of Science and Technology* and the *Statistical Abstract of the United States*

➤ Dictionaries such as *Webster's New World College Dictionary*

➤ Biographical reference works such as *American Writers*, the *New York Times Biographical Service*, *Webster's Biographical Dictionary*, and *Who's Who* (Various *Who's Who* editions are published for different geographic regions and fields, including art and music, finance, law, literature, and medicine.)

➤ Bibliographies such as *Books in Print* (especially the *Subject Guide to Books in Print*)

FIGURE 7-8   **LIBRARY SEARCH STRATEGY**

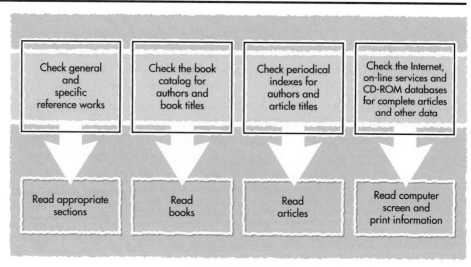

Scan these sources for an overview of your topic. Bibliographies at the end of encyclopedia articles may also lead to other important sources.

Search Specialized Reference Works

After you have an overview of your topic, *specialized reference works* will help you find more specific facts. Specialized reference works include encyclopedias and dictionaries that focus on a narrow field. Although the entries you find in these volumes are short summaries, they focus on critical ideas and on the key words you will need to conduct additional research. Bibliographies that accompany the articles point to the names and works of recognized experts. Examples of specialized reference works, organized by subject, include the following:

Fine arts (including music, art, film, television, and theatre)

➤ *International Cyclopedia of Music and Musicians*
➤ *Oxford Companion to Art*
➤ *International Encyclopedia of Film*
➤ *International Television Almanac*
➤ *The McGraw-Hill Encyclopedia of World Drama*

History

➤ *Dictionary of American Biography*
➤ *Encyclopedia of American History*
➤ *New Cambridge Modern History*

Science and technology

➤ *Encyclopedia of Computer Science and Technology*
➤ *The Encyclopedia of Biological Sciences*
➤ *The McGraw-Hill Encyclopedia of Science and Technology*
➤ *Grzimek's Animal Life Encyclopedia*

Social sciences

➤ *Dictionary of Education*
➤ *Encyclopedia of Psychology*
➤ *International Encyclopedia of the Social Sciences*

Current affairs

➤ *Social Issues Resources Series (SIRS)*
➤ *Great Contemporary Issues Series*
➤ *Facts on File*

Browse Through Books on Your Subject

Use the library catalog to find books and other materials on your topic. The catalog tells you which publications the library owns and where they can be found. Before computers, most library catalogs consisted of endless cards filed in tiny drawers. Today most of these "card catalogs" have been replaced by on-line computer catalogs. When general and specialized reference works lead to a dead end, the catalog may provide a good topic overview.

The library catalog contains a list of every library holding, searchable by author, title, and subject. For example, a library that owns *The Artist's Way: A Spiritual Path to Higher Creativity* by Julia Cameron may list the book in the author catalog under Cameron, Julia, (last name first); in the title catalog, under *Artist's Way* (articles such as *the, a,* and *an* are dropped from the beginnings of titles and subjects); in the subject catalog under "Creative Ability—problems, exercises, etc.," "Self-actualization—psychology," and "Creation—literary, artistic, etc." If you are using a keyword search, you may be able to find this book using "Art" and "Creativity" or "Art" and "Spirituality."

Library Classification Systems

Each catalog listing refers to the library's classification system, which tells you exactly where the publication can be found. Getting to know your library's system will help save time and trouble in your research because you will more quickly know where to go to find what you need. The Dewey decimal and Library of Congress systems are among the most common classification systems.

The Dewey decimal system classifies materials into ten major subject categories (see Figure 7–9) and assigns each library holding a specific *call number.* For example, publications with call numbers between 100 to 199 deal with philosophy. Successive numbers and decimal points divide each major category into subcategories. The more specific the call number, the more targeted your search. For example, a book with a call number of 378 falls into the general social science category and into the subcategory of higher education. Student finances, a narrower topic, uses the call number 378.3.

FIGURE 7-9   **THE DEWEY DECIMAL SYSTEM**

Call Number	Main Classification Category
000–99	General works
100–199	Philosophy
200–299	Religion
300–399	Social sciences
400–499	Languages
500–599	Natural sciences
600–699	Technology and applied sciences
700–799	Fine arts
800–899	Literature
900–999	History and geography

LIBRARY OF CONGRESS SUBJECT CLASSIFICATION SYSTEM   **FIGURE 7-10**

Call Letter	Main Classification Category
A	General Works
B	Philosophy and religion
C	History—Auxiliary sciences
D	History—Topography
E–F	American history—Topography
G	Geography—Anthropology
H	Social sciences
J	Political sciences
K	Law
L	Education
M	Music
N	Fine arts
P	Language—Literature (nonfiction)
Q	Sciences
R	Medicine
S	Agriculture
T	Technology
U	Military science
V	Naval science
Z	Bibliography and library science
P–Z	Literature (fiction)

The Library of Congress System uses a letter-based classification system to divide library holdings according to subject categories (see Figure 7–10). Each category is divided further into specialized subgroups through the addition of letters and numbers.

Become familiar with these classification systems. The more you know about how a library is organized, the more you can focus your research and avoid hours of needless effort.

Use Periodical Indexes to Search for Periodicals

Because of their frequent publication, periodicals are a valuable source of current information. *Journals* are periodicals written for readers with special knowledge and expertise. Whereas *Newsweek* magazine may run a general-interest article on AIDS research, the *Journal of the American Medical Association* may print the original scientific study and direct the article to physicians and scientists. Many libraries display periodicals that are up to a year or two old and convert older copies to microfilm or microfiche. Some libraries also bind recent issues into volumes.

Periodical indexes will lead you to specific articles. One of the most widely used for general information is the *Reader's Guide to Periodical Literature,* available on CD-ROM and in book form. The *Reader's Guide* indexes articles in more than 240 general-interest magazines and newspapers. Many libraries also carry the *Reader's Guide Abstracts,* which include article summaries.

You'll discover other general periodical indexes within the *Infotrac* family of databases (available online or on CD-ROM), including:

➤ *Magazine Index Plus*—an index, summaries, and full text of recent general-interest periodicals

➤ *Health Reference Center*—an index, summaries, and full text of journal articles, reference books and pamphlets on health and medicine

➤ *General BusinessFile*—an index, summaries, and full-text of recent business and trade journals with company information and investment analysts' reports.

Another periodical database family—Ebsco Host—catalogs general and health-related periodicals.

Indexing information is listed in the *Standard Periodical Directory, Ulrich's International Periodicals Directory,* and in *Magazines for Libraries,* edited by Bill Katz. In addition, each database lists the magazines and periodicals it indexes. Because there is no all-inclusive index for technical, medical, and scholarly journal articles, you'll have to search indexes that specialize in such narrow subject areas as history, art, and psychology. Such indexes also include *abstracts* (article summaries), and can be found in electronic or book form. Here are just a few of the indexes you may find in your research:

ABI/Inform	Humanities Index
Applied Science and Technology	Index Medicus
Art Index	Index to Legal Period
BIOSIS Previews	Index to United States Government
Business Periodicals Index	Periodicals
Child Development Abstracts	Modern Language Association
and Bibliography	Bibliography
Education Index	Music Index
ERIC (Educational Resources	PsycINFO
Information Center)	Psychological Abstracts
Film Literature Index	Public Affairs Information Index
General Science Index	Social Science Citation Index
Hispanic American Periodicals Index	Social Science Index
Historical Index	Women Studies Abstracts

You'll also find separate newspaper indexes at your library, in print, microform, CD-ROM, or on line. Some include many different newspapers, whereas others index a single publication:

Chicago Tribune Index	Christian Science Monitor Index
Dow Jones Index	National Newspaper Index
Index to Black Newspapers	Newspaper Abstracts OnDisc
Newsbank	New York Times Index
Wall Street Journal Index	Washington Post Index

Almost no library owns all the publications listed in these and other specialized indexes. However, journals that are not part of your library's collection or that are not available in full-text form on line may be available through an interlibrary loan. *Interlibrary loan* is a process by which you can have your library request materials from another library. You can then use the materials at your library, but you must return them by a specified date. Interlibrary loans can be helpful, but the amount of time you will have to wait for the materials can be unpredictable and may stretch out for weeks.

Search the Internet

In many ways, the Internet is a researcher's dream come true. You'll find sites that teach you how to write a business plan; others that list job openings at major companies; others that provide health, wellness, and nutritional information; and still others that analyze different theories of child development. The special appendix at the end of this book, entitled "Researching Information and Student Resources on the Internet," will help you learn how to find information on the Internet and judge its value in the same way that you evaluate any other material you read.

> *"What sculpture is to a block of marble, education is to an human soul."*
> Joseph Addison

Ask the Librarian

Librarians are information experts who can provide valuable assistance in solving research problems. They can help you locate unfamiliar or hard-to-find sources, navigate computer catalogs and databases, and uncover shortcuts in your research.

Say, for example, you are researching a gun-control bill that is currently before Congress, and you want to contact organizations on both sides of the issue. The librarian may lead you to the *Encyclopedia of Associations*, which lists the National Rifle Association, a progun lobbying organization, and Handgun Control Inc., a gun-control group. By calling or e-mailing these groups or visiting their Web sites, you will get their information on current legislation.

Note that librarians are not the only helpful people in the library. For simplicity's sake, this book will use the word *librarian* to refer to both librarians and other staff members who are trained to help.

Among the specific services librarians provide are the following.

Search services. Here are some tips on getting the best advice:

Be prepared. Know what you're looking for so that you can make a specific request. Instead of asking for information on the American presidency, focus on the topic you expect to write about in your American history paper—for example, how President Franklin D. Roosevelt's physical disability may have affected his leadership during World War II.

Be willing to reach out. Don't feel you have to do it all yourself. Librarians will help you, whether with basic sources or more difficult problems. Asking questions is a sign of willingness to learn, not weakness.

Ask for help when you can't find a specific source—for example, when a specific book is not on the shelf. The librarian may direct you to another source that will work just as well.

A law student explores cases in the law library

Information services. Most libraries answer phone inquiries that can be quickly researched. For example, if you forget to write down the publisher and date of publication of Renee Blank and Sandra Slipp's *Voices of Diversity: Real People Talk about Problems and Solutions in a Workplace Where Everyone Is Not Alike,* call a staff member with the title and author.

Interlibrary loans. If a publication is not available in your library, the librarian can arrange for an interlibrary loan.

Use Critical Thinking to Evaluate Every Source

If all information were equal, then you could trust the accuracy of every book and article, and information from the Internet home page of the National Aeronautics and Space Administration (NASA) would have the same value as information from "Bob's Home Page on Aliens and Extraterrestrials." Since that isn't the case, use critical-thinking skills to evaluate research sources. Here are some critical-thinking questions to ask about every source:

Is the author a recognized expert? A journalist who writes his or her first article on child development may not have the same credibility as an author of three child-development texts.

Does the author write from a particular perspective? An article evaluating liberal democratic policies written by a Republican conservative would almost certainly have a bias.

Is the source recent enough for your purposes? Whereas a history published in 1990 on the U.S. Civil War will probably be accurate in the year 2000, a 1990 analysis of current computer technology will be hopelessly out of date at the turn of the century.

Are the author's sources reliable? Where did the author get the information? Check the bibliography and footnotes not only for the number of sources listed but also for their quality. Find out whether they are reputable, established publications. If the work is based on *primary evidence,* the author's original work or direct observation, does solid proof support the conclusions? If it is based on *secondary evidence,* an analysis of the works of others, are the conclusions supported by evidence?

Have content experts reviewed articles submitted to academic and scientific journals before they were published? Recognized journals have panels of experts who analyze the merits of every article's academic research before accepting the material for publication. For example, the editorial board of the *New England Journal of Medicine,* one of the country's leading medical journals, is made up of physicians who analyze every article's scientific merits and publish only those that meet the highest standards.

As you will see in the Internet research appendix at the end of the text, critical thinking skills are especially important when using the Internet. Accepting information you find there on face value—no matter the source—is often a mistake and may lead to incorrect conclusions.

The library is one of your college's most valuable resources, so take advantage of it. Your library research and critical-thinking skills will give you the ability to collect information, weigh alternatives, and make decisions. These skills will last a lifetime.

Gestalt

The German word *gestalt* refers to a whole that is greater than the sum of its parts. When you can think in terms of *gestalt,* you are able to see both the whole picture and how each individual part contributes to it. To refer to a common phrase, *gestalt* is seeing the whole forest as well as individual trees.

Think of this concept as you consider how note taking and library research can help you build your knowledge and store of information. When you're reading your notes, ask yourself, "Do I truly understand the material, or am I just trying to cram facts into my head?" When you're writing a research paper, ask yourself, "Am I stepping back to see the central idea clearly, so that I can express my thoughts in the best way possible?" As important as the individual facts and examples may be, the *gestalt* is what helps the individual parts of your notes and your research gain a new and important meaning as a whole.

IMPORTANT POINTS TO REMEMBER

1. How does taking notes help you?

Notes help you learn when you are in class, doing research, or studying. The positive effects of taking notes include having written study material, becoming an active and involved listener, and improving a skill that you will use on the job and in your personal life. Note taking also encourages you to think critically and to evaluate what is worth remembering. The notes you take during library research record what you learn from the sources you consult.

2. How can you make the most of class notes?

Class notes may contain critical definitions, explanations of difficult concepts, and narratives of events. Taking comprehensive class notes requires preclass preparation, the skill to report accurately what you hear during class, and a commitment to review the notes after class.

3. How do you use research notes?

Research notes, the notes you take while gathering information to answer a research question, consist of source notes and content notes. Source notes are preliminary notes that you take as you briefly review available research. Content notes are an in-depth, critical look at each source. Index cards work well for either source notes or content notes. Marginal notes and highlighting on photocopied research materials are also helpful.

4. What note-taking system should you use?

You can choose among several note-taking systems for class and research. These include formal or informal outlining, the Cornell system, and think links. Your goal is to find a system you are comfortable using, one that fits the special needs of the situation. For example, the Cornell system or informal outlining may work best during class, whereas think links and formal outlining may be most useful for rewriting your notes during review sessions.

5. How can you write faster when taking notes?

Note taking often requires rapid writing, especially in class. Using a version of personal shorthand, which replaces words with shorter words or symbols, will help you accurately record what the instructor says. To avoid the problem of forgetting what your shorthand means, review your notes while the abbreviations and symbols are fresh in your mind, and spell out words as you review.

6. How can you make the most of your library?

The first step in getting to know this "home for information" is to participate in an orientation or tour. Most libraries will contain one or more reference areas, book areas, a periodicals area, audio/visual materials areas, computer areas, and a microform area. Begin a search strategy by conducting a keyword search, using your library's computer database.

7. How do you use a search strategy to conduct research?

A library search strategy is a step-by-step method, moving from general to specific sources, for finding information. The strategy starts with general reference works and then moves to specialized reference works, the library's book catalog, periodical indexes, and electronic sources including the Internet and CD-ROMs. Conducting a successful search involves being familiar with library classification systems, taking advantage of help from library employees, and using critical thinking to evaluate sources.

Name _____ Date _____

BUILDING SKILLS FOR COLLEGE, CAREER, AND LIFE SUCCESS
CHAPTER 7

TAKING STOCK:
REFINING YOUR THOUGHTS

Look back at the statements you explored at the start of the chapter (see Thinking It Through on p. 237). Observe whether your attitudes have changed and what you have learned by studying this chapter.

1. Name three ways to take better class notes.

_____

_____

_____

2. Explain the kinds of information you plan to include in source notes and content notes.

_____

_____

_____

_____

3. Briefly describe your reactions to the note-taking systems described in this chapter, including outlines, the Cornell system, and think links. What system will help you the most? Why?

_____

_____

_____

_____

4. Name three ways to create your own shorthand. For each, show how you would shorten a word in your own notes.

_____

_____

_____

5. Identify three specific ways in which computers will help you find information at the library.

6. List the stages in the library search strategy.

7. Choose one note-taking or research strategy you learned in this chapter and explain how you will apply it in your schoolwork during the next week.

CRITICAL THINKING:
APPLYING LEARNING TO YOUR LIFE

How Good Are Your Notes?

Look back at two sets of notes that you recently took in two different courses. For each set, evaluate your level of success, using the questions given.

First Set of Notes
Do these notes make sense to you? Why or why not? If they aren't as clear as you'd like them to be, evaluate why that happened (fatigue, distraction, dislike of class material, etc.)

Are these notes complete and accurate? Why or why not?

● Did you feel that you kept up with the lecture? If not, how does that show in the notes?

_____

_____

How do you evaluate your handwriting?

_____

_____

What note-taking system did you use? Did it work for this class or not, and why?

_____

_____

Did you give supporting facts and examples to back up important ideas?

_____

_____

● Do you feel comfortable studying from these notes? Why or why not? If not, what do you need to do to make them more complete?

_____

_____

Second set of notes

Do these notes make sense to you? Why or why not? If they aren't as clear as you'd like them to be, evaluate why that happened (fatigue, distraction, dislike of class material, etc.).

_____

_____

Are these notes complete and accurate? Why or why not?

_____

_____

Did you feel that you kept up with the lecture? If not, how does that show in the notes?

_____

_____

How do you evaluate your handwriting?

_____

_____

What note-taking system did you use? Did it work for this class or not, and why?

_____

_____

Did you give supporting facts and examples to back up important ideas?

_____

_____

Do you feel comfortable studying from these notes? Why or why not? If not, what do you need to do to make them more complete?

_____

_____

Improve Your Notes

Looking at your evaluations of the two sets of notes, generalize about your note-taking skills:

What are your strengths as a note-taker?

_____

_____

_____

What are your note-taking challenges?

_____

_____

_____

Identify two primary goals for improving your note-taking ability.

First goal: _____

_____

● Second goal: _____

_____

Choose the one goal that you feel is most important. List three steps you
will take to attain it.

1. _____

2. _____

3. _____

Make Shorthand Work for You

Look again at the shorthand techniques and symbols discussed in this
chapter. List here any abbreviations you already use.

_____

_____

● _____

Which symbols and abbreviations do you plan to use that are new to you?

_____

_____

State what you can do after class to make sure you understand your shorthand.

_____

_____

Plan one specific class period to make use of as many shorthand
abbreviations as you can. Then evaluate your notes after class.

Do you understand your notes clearly? _____

_____

Which shorthand abbreviations were you most likely to use? _____

_____

● Which shorthand abbreviations do you think were most successful for you? _____

_____

Did any shorthand abbreviations seem to require extra concentration instead of saving you time? If so, which ones?

_____

_____

Follow a Search Strategy

Choose a research topic that interests you—anything from how the Super Bowl has changed sports in America to the communication differences between men and women. Take a trip to the library and use the search strategy described in this chapter to identify the different sources you could use to research your topic. At the library, list three sources in each of the following categories:

TOPIC:

_____

General reference works:

1. _____

2. _____

3. _____

Specialized reference works:

1. _____

2. _____

3. _____

Books found by searching the book catalog:

1. _____

2. _____

3. _____

Periodicals found by searching periodical indexes:

1. _____

2. _____

3. _____

Sources found on the Internet and/or through on-line services:

1. _____

2. _____

3. _____

TEAMWORK:
COMBINING FORCES

Note-taking comparison. This teamwork exercise will show you how your note-taking techniques compare with those of other students. It will also help you analyze what makes one set of notes more useful than another.

➤ Start by choosing a two- to three-page excerpt from your text. The excerpt should contain a lot of "meaty" information, but should have no tables or figures. Don't read the excerpt before you start the exercise.

➤ Form groups of four students. Within each group, one student will play the role of instructor and the other three will be students. Assign different note-taking strategies to each student—one will use outlining, one the Cornell system, and one think links. The "instructor" will read the excerpt as if he or she were delivering a classroom lecture. The "students" will take notes on the material. You will then have three different sets of notes on the same material.

➤ Now come together with all four group participants to review and compare all three versions. Read each version carefully and answer the following questions (use additional paper if necessary):

1. Did all three note-takers record all the important information? If there are differences in the versions, why do you think these differences occurred? (You can ask the note-takers to explain why they chose to include some information and omit information.)

_____

_____

_____

2. How did each student feel about his or her note-taking strategy? Who felt comfortable and who didn't, and why?

_____

_____

3. Evaluate the different sets of notes. For this material and situation, which set of notes is likely to be the most helpful study tool for you?

WRITING: DISCOVERY THROUGH JOURNALING

To record your thoughts, use a separate journal or the lined pages at the end of the chapter.

Research thoughts.

➤ "When I use a library search strategy, I feel like an investigative reporter in search of the facts I need to write a successful story. The more useful sources I find, the better."

➤ "When I use a library search strategy, I feel like I'm overdoing it. I can usually find everything I need in one source, and looking for more information seems like a waste of time."

Which of these statements reflects your attitude toward library research? Describe in more detail how you feel about research. How do you think you might use research skills both in school and on the job? How did reading this chapter affect your attitude toward the usefulness of library research skills?

CAREER PORTFOLIO: CHARTING YOUR COURSE

Research a career. Activate your research skills by doing research on one career that interests you. Put together an informal "research paper" that catalogs all of the basics that you think you would need to know to make a decision on whether to pursue this career past an initial interest.

Use these sources:

➤ General and specific reference works

➤ Periodicals (especially current newspapers, where you can find updated information on the status of your particular career)

➤ The Internet

➤ Any sources found at your school's career center

Include the following topics (as well as any others that seem pertinent to you):

- ➤ Recent growth status of your career (whether opportunities are increasing or decreasing)
- ➤ Strength of this career where you live or want to live
- ➤ Educational requirements (degrees, certificates, and tests)
- ➤ Estimated salaries
- ➤ Potential benefits
- ➤ General duties and skills required
- ➤ Opportunities for advancement
- ➤ Time and location flexibility, if any

Keep this information on hand for when you are ready to start pursuing your career in earnest.

Journal Entry

Name _____ Date _____

Journal Entry

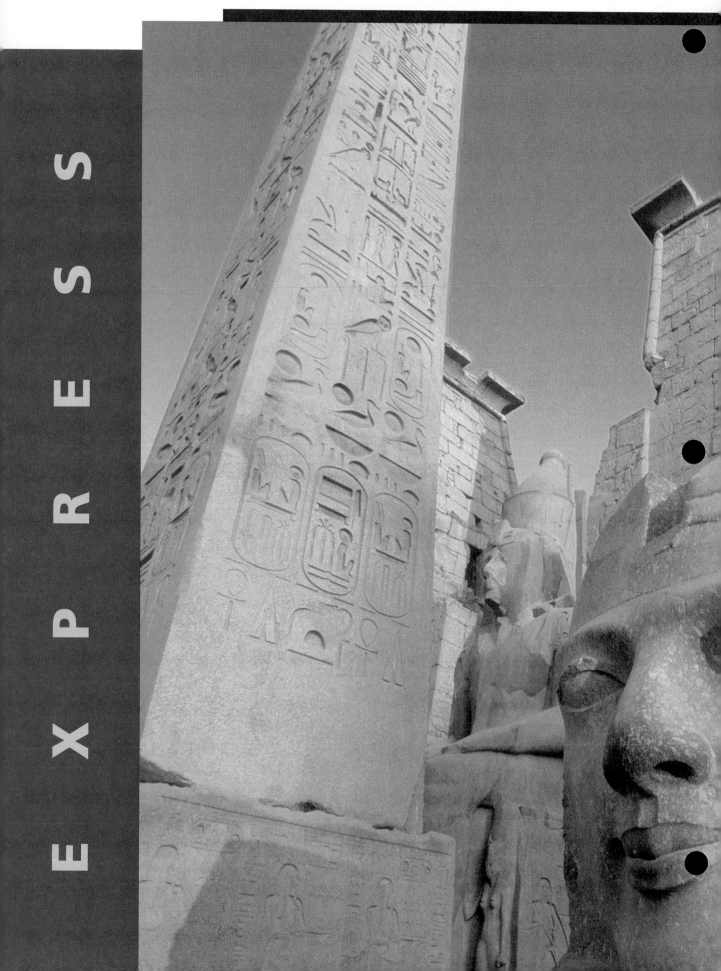

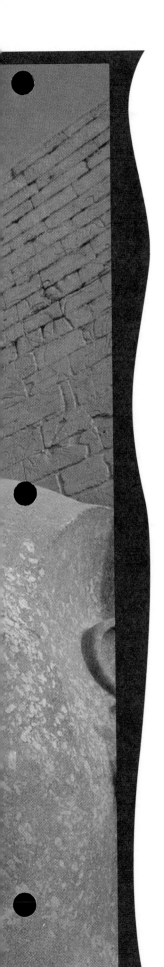

8 EFFECTIVE WRITING: Communicating Your Message

Thinking It Through

Check those statements that apply to you right now:

❑ I'm not sure it matters if I'm not a good writer.
❑ I try to consider the specifics of the assignment before I sit down and write.
❑ When I write, I don't think much about the people who will read my work.
❑ My goal is to be able to write a perfect paper the first time around.
❑ I don't necessarily consider what I already know about a subject before I start my research and writing.
❑ When I revise and edit a paper, I focus mostly on getting my words right.

In this chapter, you will explore answers to the following questions:

➤ Why does good writing matter?
➤ What are the elements of effective writing?
➤ What is the writing process?

Words, joined to form ideas, have enormous power. Far more than a skill needed just for schoolwork, writing is as important today as it has ever been. Instead of disappearing in an age that celebrates computer technology, writing has become the communication tool of choice for people using the Internet, as well as for workers in a wide variety of fields.

People have sought ways to record written forms of communication since ancient times. For the Egyptians, for example, that communication took the form of hieroglyphics. Written communication preserves concepts so that they can reach far beyond one person's circle of acquaintances. Writing allows you to take your ideas out of the realm of thought and give them a form that other people can read and consider.

Whether you are zapping electronic mail across the globe or using a pencil and pad to write a research paper for your history professor, your level of successful communication depends on your ability to express your written ideas completely and well. In this chapter, you will explore the many aspects of learning to be a good writer. Writing is a key to success in school, at work, and in your personal life.

WHY DOES GOOD WRITING MATTER?

In school, almost any course you take will require you to communicate your knowledge and thought processes by writing essays or papers. To express yourself successfully, you need good writing skills. Knowing how to write and communicate ideas is essential outside of school as well, as the following example demonstrates. Imagine that you run a summer internship program at a major TV network. You have two qualified student candidates vying for one internship position. Each student sends you a letter, trying to convince you that he or she is the better person for the job. Parts of each student's response are shown in Figures 8–1 and 8–2.

Which candidate would you choose? The second student's letter is well written, persuasive, logical, and error-free. In contrast, the first student's letter is not thought through clearly and has technical errors. Good writing quality gives the edge to the second student.

As this hypothetical example demonstrates, the ability to write clearly and well can make a huge difference both in school and after graduation because instructors, supervisors, and others judge your thinking ability according to what you write and how you write it. Over the next few years you may write papers, essays, answers to essay test questions, job application letters, résumés, business proposals and reports, memos to coworkers, and letters to customers and suppliers. Good writ-

FIGURE 8-1   **FIRST STUDENT'S WRITING SAMPLE**

> I am a capable student who'se interests are many. I like the news business so much so that I want you to offer me the internship with your company.
>
> My experience will impress you, as I'm sure you will agree I am a reporter for the college news station, and I can be a reporter for you as well. If you let me try. Instructors who know my work like my style. I prefer to think of myself as an individual with a unique style that nothing can match.
>
> I want the summer internship because it will put me at the center of the action. At this point in my education, I deserve the chance to learn from the masters of the business.
>
> I look forward to hearing from you and to the news that I got the internship.

SECOND STUDENT'S WRITING SAMPLE

FIGURE 8-2

From the time I was 8 years old, I was hooked on the news. Instead of watching cartoons on television, I watched Tom Brokaw, Dan Rather, and Peter Jennings. I celebrated the day that CNN started a 24-hour all-news network.

It seemed like a natural step to go into the news business. I started in high school as a reporter, and then I became editor-in-chief of the school paper. As a college freshman, I am majoring in broadcast journalism, and I am also working at the school TV station. Even though I'm starting at the bottom, I believe that there's a learning opportunity around every corner. By the time I take on my first reporting assignment next year, I feel that my knowledge and experience will have grown. I hope it will be enough to make me a competent journalist.

Your internship program will help me learn the news business in an environment I never dreamed of experiencing until later in my career. I look forward to hearing from you and to the possibility of working for your station this summer.

ing skills will help you achieve the goals you set out to accomplish with each writing task.

Good writing depends on and reflects clear thinking. Therefore, a clear thought process is the best preparation for a well-written document, and a well-written document shows the reader a clear thought process. Exposing yourself to the work of other writers helps you learn words, experience concepts, and discover the different ways that a writer can put words together to express ideas. In addition, critical reading generates new ideas you can use in your writing. The processes of reading and writing are interrelated; the skills in one process tend to enhance the skills in the other.

WHAT ARE THE ELEMENTS OF EFFECTIVE WRITING?

Every writing situation is different, depending on three elements. Your goal is to understand each element before you begin to write:

- ➤ *Your purpose*: What do you want to accomplish with this particular piece of writing?
- ➤ *Your topic*: What is the subject about which you will write?
- ➤ *Your audience*: Who will read your writing?

Figure 8–3 shows how these elements depend on one another. As a triangle needs three points to be complete, a piece of writing needs these three

FIGURE 8-3   **THE THREE ELEMENTS OF WRITING**

> **Audience,**
> The reader or readers of any piece of written material.

elements. Consider purpose and   audience   even before you begin to plan. Topic will come into play during the planning stage (the first stage of the writing process).

Writing Purpose

Writing without having set a purpose first is like driving without deciding where you want to go. You'll get somewhere, but chances are it won't be where you needed to be. Therefore, when you write, always decide what you want to accomplish before you start. Although there are many different writing purposes, the two you will most commonly use for school and on the job are to inform and to persuade.

The purpose of *informative writing* is to present and explain ideas. A research paper on how hospitals use donated blood to save lives informs readers without trying to mold opinions. The writer presents facts in an unbiased way, without introducing a particular point of view. Most newspaper articles, except those on the opinion and editorial pages, are examples of informative writing.

Persuasive writing has the purpose of convincing readers that your point of view is correct. Often, persuasive writing seeks to change the mind of the reader. For example, as a member of the college committee on student health, you write a newspaper column asking for blood donations. Through facts, statistics, expert opinions, and examples, you attempt to persuade readers to give blood. Example of persuasive writing include newspaper editorials, business proposals, and books and magazine articles with a point of view.

Other possible writing purposes include *entertaining* the reader and *narrating* (describing an image or event to the reader). Although most of your writing in school will inform or persuade, you may occasionally need to entertain or narrate as well. Sometimes purposes will even overlap—you might write an informative essay that entertains at the same time.

Knowing Your Audience

In almost every case, a writer creates written material so that others can read it. The writer and audience are partners in this process. Knowing who your audience is will help you construct and communicate a message that will be appropriate and meaningful to your readers.

> "*Clear a space for the writing voice. You cannot will this to happen. It is a matter of persistence and faith and hard work. So you might as well just go ahead and get started.*"
>
> Anne Lamott

Key Questions about Your Audience

In school, your primary audience is your instructors. For many assignments, instructors will want you to assume that they are typical readers. Writing for "typical readers" usually means that you should be as complete as possible in your explanations.

At other times you may write papers that intend to address informed instructors or a specific reading audience other than your instructors. In such cases, you may ask yourself some or all of the following questions, depending on which are relevant to your topic:

> - What are my readers' ages, genders, cultural backgrounds, interests, and experiences?

> - What are their roles? Are they instructors, students, employers, or customers?

> - How much do they know about my topic? Are they experts in the field or beginners? Do they have general or specialized knowledge? Do they expect me to use jargon or explain terms?

> - Are they already interested in what I am writing or do I have to convince them that my paper is worth reading?

> - Can I expect my audience to have open or closed minds?

After you answer the questions about your audience, take what you have discovered into consideration as you write. For example, if you are writing a letter to the editor of a computer magazine about Windows 98, the latest computer operating system developed by Microsoft Corporation, you can safely assume that magazine readers know what Windows 98 is and that they understand specialized computer language. Show the same letter to people who have never used a computer and they won't understand much of what they are reading.

Women work on computers at Los Angeles City College

Your Commitment to Your Audience

Your goal is to communicate—to organize your ideas so that readers can follow them. Suppose, for example, you are writing an informative research paper for a nonexpert audience on using on-line services to get a job. One way to accomplish your goal is to first explain what these services are and the kinds of help they offer, then describe each service in greater detail, and finally conclude with how these services will change job hunting in the twenty-first century. Although this is not the only way to approach this topic, it is one option that moves readers from idea to idea in a logical way.

Making your writing the best that it can be involves following the steps of the writing process.

THINKING BACK

1. List the three primary elements that affect every writing situation.

   a. _____

   b. _____

   c. _____

2. List three questions you might ask yourself as you try to picture your readers.

   a. _____

   b. _____

   c. _____

3. As the primary audience for your written work in school, what do instructors expect?

   _____

   _____

   _____

THINKING AHEAD

1. What process do you prefer to follow in the course of writing a paper?

   _____

   _____

2. What planning do you go through before you begin to write?

   _____

   _____

   _____

3. After you finish planning a paper, what do you prefer to do to go from generating ideas to actual writing?

_____

_____

_____

4. List four activities that come to mind when you think about revising and editing.

a. _____

b. _____

c. _____

d. _____

WHAT IS THE WRITING PROCESS?

The writing process provides an opportunity for you to state and refine your thoughts until you have expressed yourself as clearly as possible. Critical thinking plays an important role every step of the way. It is easy to think of the writing process as beginning when you pick up a pen or start keyboarding words into a computer and finishing when you write the last word of your first draft. However, drafting is only one stage of the journey. The four main parts of the process are planning, drafting, revising, and editing.

Planning

Planning gives you a chance to think about what to write and how to write it so that you communicate your message successfully. Planning involves brainstorming for ideas, establishing guidelines, defining and narrowing your topic by using   prewriting strategies , conducting research if necessary, writing a thesis statement, writing a working outline, and completing your research.

Although the steps in preparing to write are listed in sequence, in real life the steps overlap one another as you plan your document. For example, although brainstorming is listed as the first planning step, you may first want to use other prewriting strategies—listed as the second planning step—to learn where your interests lie.

Prewriting strategies, Techniques for generating ideas about a topic and finding out how much you already know before you start your research.

Open Your Mind Through Brainstorming

In many writing situations your instructor will assign a topic. For example, your accounting instructor may ask you to write about the role of ethics in corporate accounting practices. Or your health instructor may ask for a written explanation of the causes of diabetes. In other cases your instructor may assign a broader category and give you the freedom to decide on a topic.

Whether your instructor assigns a specific topic (Amy Tan's novel *The Joy Luck Club*), a partially defined topic (novelist Amy Tan), or a general category within which you make your own choice (Asian-American authors), you should brainstorm to develop more specific ideas about what you want to write. Brainstorming is a creative technique that involves gen-

FIGURE 8-4   **BRAINSTORMING**

Write your ideas in the order they occur to you

* What traditional career planning does: career counseling, help in writing a résumé and cover letter, help in locating actual job openings
* What electronic career counseling adds: help in sending a résumé and cover letter via the Internet within seconds of learning about a job
* Companies post help-wanted notices electronically to broadcast their job openings all over the world
* Wave of the future
* Easy to use
* Traditional career services offer face-to-face meetings
* Counselors and job hunters have electronic "conversations" online
* Job seekers go online to learn about thousands of job listings from all over the world
* History of America Online's Career Center: started with a list of 1,000 jobs a week; two years later there were 10,000 weekly listings

Organize your ideas into categories, associating ideas with sub-ideas and examples

1. What traditional and online career planning offer
   - Career counseling
   - Help in writing a résumé and cover letter
   - Help in locating actual job openings
   - Help in sending a résumé and cover letter via the Internet within seconds of learning about a job

2. Differences between traditional and online career services
   - Face-to-face meetings in traditional services
   - "Conversations" take place electronically in electronic services

3. Posting help-wanted notices electronically
   - Companies instantaneously broadcast news of a job opening all over the world
   - Job seekers learn about tens of thousands of job listings from all over the world
   - It is easy for both parties

4. Future trends
   - Electronic job hunting is the wave of the future
   - America Online's Career Center started with a list of 1,000 jobs a week; two years later there were 10,000 weekly listings

erating ideas about a subject without making judgments (see Chapter 4 for more details).

First, let your mind wander. Write down anything on the assigned subject that come to mind, in no particular order. Then, organize that list into an outline or think link that helps you see the possibilities more clearly. To make the outline or think link, separate list items into general ideas or categories and subideas or examples. Then associate the subideas or examples with the ideas they support or fit.

Figure 8–4 shows an uncensored brainstorming list on the subject of on-line job hunting, made into a list of four logical groupings.[1]

Establish Guidelines

Before narrowing your topic, establish your guidelines by defining the *writing context* and any special requirements of the assignment. The writing context includes the following:

➤ The course for which the paper is written

➤ The deadline—how much time you have to complete the material

➤ Whether the paper will stand alone or be part of a series of related assignments

➤ How long the paper is supposed to be

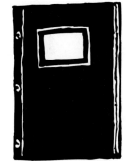

Special requirements refer to any specific requirements for audience or purpose assigned by the instructor. For example, is your assignment a research paper that requires library research? An essay based on readings? A business memo? A letter of complaint?

The writing context and special requirements affect your choice of a final topic. For example, if you had a month and twenty pages to write an informative paper on learning disabilities, you might choose to discuss the symptoms, diagnosis, effects, and treatment of attention deficit disorder. If you were given a week and five pages to write a persuasive essay, you might write about how elementary students with ADD need special training.

Narrow Your Topic Through Prewriting Strategies

When you have established the writing context and requirements and your brainstorming has generated some possibilities, you can begin to narrow your topic. Focus on the subideas and examples from your initial brainstorming session. Because they are relatively specific, they will be more likely to point you toward possible topics.

Choose one or more subideas or examples that you like and explore them by using prewriting strategies such as brainstorming, freewriting, and asking journalists' questions. Prewriting strategies will help you decide which topic you would most like to pursue. They are especially helpful with papers that don't involve research.

FIGURE 8-5 **PART OF A BRAINSTORMING OUTLINE**

Boot camp
- physical conditioning
  ○ swim tests
  ○ intensive training
  ○ ENDLESS push-ups!
- Chief who was our commander
- mental discipline
  ○ military lifestyle
  ○ perfecting our appearance
- self-confidence
  ○ walk like you're in control
  ○ don't blindly accept anything

Brainstorming. The same process you used to generate ideas will also help you narrow your topic further. Generate thoughts about the possibility (or possibilities) you have chosen and write them down. Then, organize them into categories, noticing any patterns that appear. See if any of the subideass or examples seem as if they might make good topics.

Figure 8–5 shows a portion of the prewriting brainstorming outline that the student editor for this book, Michael B. Jackson, constructed from his brainstorming list. The assignment is a five-paragraph essay on a life-changing event. Michael chose to brainstorm the topic of "boot camp," and he organized the ideas he came up with into categories.

Freewriting. Another stream-of-consciousness technique that encourages you to put ideas down on paper as they occur to you is called *freewriting*. When you freewrite, you write whatever comes to mind without censoring your ideas or worrying about grammar, spelling, punctuation, or organization. Freewriting helps you think creatively and gives you an opportunity to begin weaving in information and evidence that you know or have gathered. Freewrite on the subideass or examples you have created to see if you want to pursue any of them. Here is a sample of freewriting from Michael's work:

> Boot camp for the Coast Guard really changed my life. First of all, I really got in shape. We had to get up every morning at 5 A.M., eat breakfast, and go right into training. We had to do endless military-style push-ups—but we later found out that these have a purpose, to prepare us to hit the deck in the event of enemy fire We had a lot of aquatic tests, once we were awakened at 3 A.M. to do one in full uniform! Boot camp also helped me to feel confident about myself and be disciplined. Chief Marzloff was the main person who made that happen. He was tough but there was always a reason. He got angry when I used to nod my head whenever he would speak to me, he said that made it seem like I was blindly accepting whatever he said, which was a weakness. From him I have learned to keep an eye on my body's movements when I communicate. I learned a lot more from him too.

Asking journalists' questions. When journalists begin work on a story, they ask themselves, Who? What? Where? When? Why? and How? You can use these *journalists' questions* to focus your thinking. Ask these questions about any subideas or example to discover what you may want to discuss.

Who?	Who was at boot camp? Who influenced me the most?
What?	What about boot camp changed my life? What did we do?
When?	When in my life did I go to boot camp, and for how long? When did we fulfill our duties?
Where?	Where was camp located? Where did we spend our day-to-day time?
Why?	Why did I decide to go there? Why was it such an important experience?
How?	How did we train in the camp? How were we treated? How did we achieve success?

Prewriting will help you develop a topic broad enough to give you something with which to work but narrow enough to be manageable. See Table 8–1 for an overview of how two different topics can be narrowed from broad ideas to possible topics. Prewriting also helps you see what you know and don't know about a topic. If your assignment requires more than you already know, you may need to do research.

TABLE 8-1   HOW TO DEFINE AND NARROW YOUR WRITING TOPIC

FOCUS ON	EXAMPLE 1	EXAMPLE 2
BROAD TOPIC	Computers	Families
WRITING CONTEXT	Business communication course	Sociology course
PURPOSE	Informative	Informative
AUDIENCE	Instructor and classmates	Instructor
LENGTH	1500 words	1000 words
DEADLINE	2 weeks	1 week
POSSIBLE TOPICS	■ Using on-line services to find work	■ Major changes in the American family since 1970
	■ Using on-line services to conduct business research	■ How shifts in government welfare policies during the early 1990s affected families in poverty

Conduct Research

Much of the writing you do in college will rely on what you already know about a subject, such as when you must write a short essay for freshman composition or for an exam. In these cases, prewriting strategies may generate all the ideas and information you need.

For other writing assignments, however, outside sources are necessary. In such cases, your prewriting exercises help guide your research by identifying areas in which you need more information. Research may take the form of a trip to the library, an interview with an expert, or a connection to an on-line research source. (See Chapter 7 for a detailed description of how to conduct library research.)

Try doing your research in several stages. In the first stage, look for a basic overview that can help you write a thesis statement. Then write an outline or think link that identifies information gaps you still need to fill. Finally, go into more depth in your research, tracking down information that will help you complete your thoughts and take care of the gaps you identified.

Write a Thesis Statement

Your work up to this point prepares you to write a thesis statement, the central message you want to communicate. The thesis statement states your subject and point of view, reflects your writing purpose and audience, and acts as the organizing principle of your paper. A well-written thesis statement summarizes what you want your readers to know and serves as your guide as you write. Here is an example from Michael's paper:

Topic	Coast Guard boot camp
Purpose	To inform and narrate
Audience	Instructor with unknown knowledge about the topic
Thesis statement	Chief Marzloff, our Basic Training Company Commander at the U.S. Coast Guard Basic Training Facility, shaped my life through physical conditioning, developing our self-confidence, and instilling strong mental discipline.

A thesis statement is just as important in a short document, such as a letter, as it is in a long paper. For example, when you write a job application letter, a clear thesis statement will help you tell the recruiter why you deserve the job.

Write a Working Outline and Complete Your Research

The final step in the preparation process involves writing a working outline (in outline or think-link form, whichever you prefer) and completing your research. Use this outline as a loose guide instead of a final structure. As you draft your paper, your ideas and structure may change many times. Only by allowing changes and refinements to occur can you get closer and closer to what you really want to say.

An outline is important for short documents, as well as long ones. It can help to point out holes in your research that a trip to the library can help you fill. (See Chapter 7 for more on outline writing.)

Create a Checklist

Use the checklist in Table 8–2 to make sure your preparation is complete. Under Date Due, create your own writing schedule, giving each task an intended completion date. Work backward from the date the assignment is due and figure out how long it will take to complete each step. Refer to

TABLE 8-2 PREPARATION CHECKLIST

DATE DUE	TASK	IS IT COMPLETE?
	Brainstorm.	
	Define and narrow.	
	Use prewriting strategies.	
	Conduct research if necessary.	
	Write thesis statement.	
	Write working outline.	
	Complete research.	

Chapter 2 for time management skills that will help you schedule your writing process.

For example, if on May 1 you learn that a research paper is due on May 21, you may decide to schedule your work this way:

May 2: Define and narrow.

May 3: Use prewriting strategies.

May 4–5: Conduct research.

May 6: Write thesis statement and working outline.

May 7: Complete research.

May 8–11: Write first draft.

May 12–14: Revise and write second draft.

May 15–17: Revise, edit, and write third (final) draft.

May 18–20: Do final editing and proofreading of final draft.

As you develop your schedule, remember that you'll probably move back and forth between tasks. You might find yourself doing two and even three things on the same day. Stick to the schedule as best you can, while balancing the other demands of your busy life, and check off your accomplishments on the list as you complete them.

Drafting

Some people aim for perfection when they write a first draft. They want to get everything right—from word choice to tone to sentence structure to paragraph organization to spelling, punctuation, and grammar. Try to resist this tendency because it may lead you to shut the door on ideas before you even know they are there.

A *first draft* involves putting your ideas down on paper for the first time—but not the last. You may write many different versions of the assignment until you do one you like. Each version moves you closer to communicating exactly what you want to say in the way you want to say it. It is as if you started with a muddy pond and gradually cleared the mud away until your last version became a clear body of water, showing the rocks and the fish beneath the surface. Think of your first draft as a way of establishing the pond before you start clearing it up.

How you structure the ideas in your paper's body is important, especially for long documents such as research papers and business reports. When you think of drafting, imagine that you are creating a kind of "writing sandwich." The bottom slice of bread is the introduction, the top slice is the conclusion, and the sandwich stuffing is made of central ideas and supporting examples (see Figure 8–6).

The elements of writing a first draft are freewriting, crafting an introduction, organizing the ideas in the body of the paper, formulating a conclusion, and citing sources.

● THE "WRITING SANDWICH"   FIGURE 8-6

Freewriting Your Draft

If the introduction, body, and conclusion are the three parts of the sandwich, freewriting is the process of searching the refrigerator for the ingredients and laying them all on the table. Take everything you have developed in the planning stages and freewrite a very rough draft. Don't censor yourself. For now, don't consciously think about your introduction, conclusion, or structure within the paper's body. Focus on getting your ideas out of the realm of thought and onto the paper, in whatever form they prefer to be at the moment.

When you have the beginnings of a paper in your hands, you can start to shape it into something with a more definite form. First, work on how you want to begin.

Writing an Introduction

The introduction should tell your readers, in broad terms, what the rest of the paper will contain. A thesis statement is essential. Here, for example, is a draft of an introduction for Michael's paper about the Coast Guard. The thesis statement is underlined at the end of the paragraph:

> Chief Marzloff took on the task of shaping the lives and careers of the youngest, newest members of the U.S. Coast Guard. During my eight weeks in training, he was my father, my instructor, my leader, and my worst enemy. He took his job very seriously and demanded that we do the same. <u>The Chief was instrumental in conditioning our bodies, developing our self-confidence, and instilling mental discipline within us.</u>

Hooks,

Elements—including facts, quotes, statistics, questions, stories, or statements—that catch the reader's attention and encourage him or her to want to continue to read.

When you write an introduction, you might try to draw the reader in with an anecdote—a story that is related to the thesis. You can try other **hooks** , including a relevant quotation, dramatic statistics, and questions that encourage critical thinking. Whatever strategy you choose, link it to your thesis statement. In addition, try to state your purpose without referring to its identity as a purpose. For example, in an introductory paragraph, write, "Computer technology is infiltrating every aspect of business" instead of "In this paper, my purpose is to prove that computer technology is infiltrating every aspect of business."

After you have an introduction that seems to set up the purpose of your paper, make sure the body fulfills that purpose.

Creating the Body of a Paper

Evidence,

Proof that informs or persuades, consisting of facts, statistics, examples, and expert opinion.

The body of the paper contains your main points and supporting **evidence** . For evidence to work as a communication tool, it has to be connected clearly and logically with ideas and with other related evidence. Look at the array of ideas and evidence in your draft in its current state. Think about how you might group certain items of evidence with the particular ideas they support. Then, try to find a structure that helps you to organize such evidence groups into a clear pattern. The pattern you choose will determine how you arrange your ideas from beginning to end. Here are some strategies to consider:

Arrange ideas by time. Describe a series of events in the order in which they occurred or in reverse order. This arrangement is commonly used when writing history papers.

Making the most of study time

Arrange ideas according to importance. You can start with the idea that carries the most weight and move to ideas with less value or influence. For instance, in a marketing paper on advertising media, you decide to start with the medium that consumes the most advertising dollars each year and then move to those in which less money is spent. You can also choose to save the best for last by moving from the least important to the most important idea.

Arrange ideas by problem and solution. Start with a specific problem; then discuss one or more suggested solutions. For example, in a paper for your health course, you introduce the problem of alienation and loneliness on campus. Among the solutions you suggest are joining clubs, participating in student government, and seeking professional counseling.

Arrange ideas by location. Here your organizational pattern is determined by geography. If you were writing a sociology paper on out-of-wedlock birthrates in five cities—Los Angeles, Denver, Chicago, Cleveland, and New York—your discussion might move from west to east, along with the cities.

Writing the Conclusion

The conclusion is a statement or paragraph that communicates that your paper is complete. Summarize the information that is in the body of your paper and critically evaluate what is important about it. Try one of the following strategies:

➤ Summarize main points (if material is longer than three pages)

➤ Relate a story, statistic, quote, or question that makes the reader think

➤ Call the reader to action

➤ Look to the future

As you work on your conclusion, try not to introduce new facts or restate what you feel you have proved ("I have successfully proven that violent cartoons are related to increased violence in children.") Let your ideas as they are presented in the body of the paper speak for themselves. Readers should feel that they have reached a natural point of completion.

Crediting Authors and Citing Sources

When you write a paper using any materials other than your own thoughts and recollections, the ideas you gathered in your research become part of your own writing. This does not mean that you can claim these ideas as your own or fail to attribute them to the source. To avoid plagiarism you need to credit authors for their ideas and words.

Writers own their writings just as a computer programmer owns a program that he or she designed or a photographer owns an image that he or she created. A piece of writing and its enclosed ideas are the writer's products, or "intellectual property." Using an idea, phrase, or word-for-word paragraph without crediting its author is the same as using a computer program without buying it or printing a photograph without paying the photographer. It is just as serious as any other theft and may have unfavorable consequences. Most colleges have stiff penalties for plagiarism, as well as for any other cheating offense.

To avoid plagiarism, know the difference between a quotation and a paraphrase. A *quotation* refers to a source's exact words, which are set off from the rest of the text by quotation marks. A *paraphrase* is a restatement of the quotation in your own words, using your own sentence structure. Restatement means to completely rewrite the idea, not just to remove or replace a few words. A paraphrase may not be acceptable if it is too close to the original. Figure 8–7 demonstrates these differences.

Plagiarism often begins by accident when you take research notes. You may forget to include quotation marks around a word-for-word quotation from the source, or you may intend to cite it or paraphrase but never find the time to do so. To avoid forgetting, try writing something like "Quotation from original, rewrite later" next to quoted material and note at that time the specifics of the original document (title, author, source, page number, etc.) so you don't spend hours trying to locate it later.

Even an acceptable paraphrase requires a citation of the source of the ideas within it. Take care to credit any source that you quote, paraphrase, or use as evidence. To credit a source, write a footnote or endnote that de-

Plagiarism,
The act of using someone else's exact words, figures, unique approach, or specific reasoning without giving appropriate credit.

"*Omit needless words. This requires not that the writer make all his sentences short, or that he avoid all detail and treat his subjects only in outline, but that every word tell.*"

William Strunk, Jr.

FIGURE 8-7   **AVOID PLAGIARISM BY LEARNING HOW TO PARAPHRASE²**

QUOTATION

> "The most common assumption that is made by persons who are communicating with one another is…that the other perceives, judges, thinks, and reasons the way he does. Identical twins communicate with ease. Persons from the same culture but with a different education, age, background, and experience often find communication difficult. American managers communicating with managers from other cultures experience greater difficulties in communication than with managers from their own culture."³

UNACCEPTABLE PARAPHRASE

(The underlined words are taken directly from the quoted source.)

> When we communicate, we assume that the person to whom we are speaking <u>perceives, judges, thinks, and reasons the way</u> we do. This is not always the case. Although <u>identical twins communicate with ease, persons from the same culture but with a different education, age, background, and experience often</u> encounter communication problems. Communication problems are common among American managers as they attempt to <u>communicate with managers from other cultures</u>. They experience greater communication problems than when they communicate <u>with managers from their own culture</u>.

ACCEPTABLE PARAPHRASE

> Many people fall into the trap of believing that everyone sees the world exactly as they do and that all people communicate according to the same assumptions. This belief is difficult to support even within our own culture as African Americans, Hispanic Americans, Asian Americans, and others often attempt unsuccessfully to find common ground. When intercultural differences are thrown into the mix, such as when American managers working abroad attempt to communicate with managers from other cultures, clear communication becomes even harder.

scribes it. Use the format preferred by your instructor. Writing handbooks such as the *Modern Language Association* (MLA) *Handbook* contain acceptable formats.

Continue Your Checklist

Create a checklist for your first draft (see Table 8–3). The elements of a first draft do not have to be written in order. In fact, many writers prefer to write the introduction after they complete the body of the paper, so that the introduction will reflect the paper's content and tone. Whatever order you choose, make sure your schedule allows you to get everything done—with enough time left over for revisions.

TABLE 8-3   FIRST DRAFT CHECKLIST

DATE DUE	TASK	IS IT COMPLETE?
	Freewrite a draft.	
	Plan and write the introduction.	
	Organize the body of the paper.	
	Include research evidence in the body.	
	Plan and write the conclusion.	
	Check for plagiarism and rewrite passages to avoid it.	
	Credit your sources.	

Revising

When you revise, you critically evaluate the word choice, paragraph structure, and style of your first draft. Any draft, no matter how good, can always be improved. Be thorough as you add, delete, replace, and reorganize words, sentences, and paragraphs. You may want to print out your draft and then make notes and corrections on the hard copy before you make changes on a typewritten or computer-printed version. Figure 8–8 shows a paragraph from Michael's first draft, with revision comments added.

In addition to revising on your own, some of your classes may include peer review (having students read one another's work and offer suggestions). A peer reviewer can tell you what comes across well and what may be confusing. Having a different perspective on your writing is extremely valuable. Even if you don't have an organized peer-review system, you may want to ask a classmate to review your work as a favor to you.

The elements of revision include being a critical writer, evaluating paragraph structure, and checking for clarity and conciseness.

Being a Critical Writer

Critical thinking is as important in writing as it is in reading. Thinking critically when writing will help you move beyond restating what you have researched and learned. Of course, your knowledge is an important part of your writing. What will make your writing even more important and unique, however, is how you use critical thinking to construct your own new ideas and knowledge from what you have learned.

The key to critical writing is asking the question "So what?" For example, if you were writing a paper on nutrition, you might discuss a variety of good eating habits. Asking "So what?" could lead into a discussion of why these habits are helpful or what positive effects they have. If you were writing a paper on egg imagery in the novel *All the King's Men* by Robert Penn

WINDOWS ON THE WORLD: REAL LIFE STUDENT ISSUES

How can I become more confident about my writing?

Beverly Andre, Triton College, River Grove, Illinois, Continuing Education

The best thing I ever wrote was in the sixth grade. My teacher let us pick a topic, and I chose to write about riding horses because I loved to do it and knew a lot about it. In high school, writing was okay because my English teacher was helpful. On the other hand, writing college papers has been a real challenge. For one thing, I don't think I'm very original when it comes to topic ideas. I also feel I have to come up with college-level vocabulary and mine is not that advanced. If a professor assigns a topic that I know nothing about, I usually don't have as much interest as I do when I'm writing on something I already know about.

One of the reasons I don't like to write is because I don't like looking up information. Knowing how to begin the research gets confusing because there's so much to choose from. Once I do manage to pull the information together, I can't seem to expand on an idea without being redundant. I also have trouble sticking to the point so I go off on all sorts of tangents.

Occasionally I come up with something a professor thinks is interesting. I'm always a little surprised when that happens. The bottom line is that I find it difficult to put my thoughts on paper. Can you help me become a better writer?

Raymond Montolvo, Jr., Writers Program University of Southern California, Los Angeles, California

No matter what your writing goal, in most cases the person you are writing for, your instructor, wants you to improve. Keeping this in mind may help you concentrate on trying to improve your skills instead of worrying about good grades.

I suggest a two-pronged approach to better writing. The first step is to read. Read novels, the newspaper, and nonfiction articles. Reading will help you learn to organize your thoughts, and it increases your vocabulary. If you want to study a specific area, read publications in that area on your own. Create file folders for pieces of writing that you like. For example, make a copy of a business letter that you think is well written, and refer to it when you need to write similar correspondence.

Second, bridge the gap between what you should know and what an instructor can tell you. Ask your instructor what he or she thinks you need to work on. Focus on understanding the assignment and strengthening technical skills. Another tip is to read what you've written, sentence by sentence, and think about how you could say it better.

If you don't know where to begin your research, start with what feels comfortable. If you are at ease with computers, use the Internet. If you prefer libraries, start by asking the reference librarian for assistance. Once you read something that relates to your topic it will refer you to something else.

Finally, don't get frustrated by setbacks. Writing is a process. Set goals you can attain. Instead of sitting down and trying to write a ten-page paper, write a three-page one. Finishing something builds confidence.

SAMPLE REVISION COMMENTS

FIGURE 8-8

military recruits
undergo

Of the changes that ~~happened to us,~~ the physical transformation is

most evident

the ~~biggest. When we arrived at the training facility, it was January, cold~~

TOO much. ↗   *Maybe— upon my January arrival at the*

~~and cloudy. At the time,~~ I was a little thin, but I had been working out

training facility,

and thought that I could physically do anything. Oh boy, was I wrong!

— his trademark
                                                                    ←   *phrase*

The Chief said to us right away: "Get down, maggots!" Upon this

were   *endless*

command, we all to drop to the ground and do military-style push-ups.

∧   ∧

Water survival tactics were also part of the training ~~that we had to complete.~~

unnecessary

Occasionally, my dreams of home were interrupted at 3 a.m. when we

resented

had a surprise aquatic test. Although we ~~didn't feel too happy about~~ this

sub-human treatment at the time, we learned to appreciate how the

conditioning was turning our bodies into fine-tuned machines.

∧
mention how Chief was involved   *say more about this*
                                          (swimming in
                                          uniform incident?)

Warren, you might list all the examples of it that you noticed. Then, asking
"So what?" could lead you to evaluate why that imagery is so strong and
what idea you think those examples convey.

As you revise, ask yourself questions that can help you think through
ideas and examples, come up with your own original insights about the material, and be as complete and clear as possible. Use the mind actions to
guide you. Here are some examples of questions you may ask:

 EX

Are these examples clearly connected to the idea?

Are there any similar concepts or facts I know of that can
add to how I support this?

What else can I recall that can help to support this idea?

In evaluating any event or situation, have I clearly indicated the causes and effects?

 What new idea comes to mind when I think about these examples or facts?

 How do I evaluate any effect, fact, or situation? Is it good or bad, useful or not?

 What different arguments might a reader think of that I should address here?

Finally, critical thinking can help you evaluate the content and form of your paper. As you start your revision, ask yourself the following questions.

➤ Will my audience understand my thesis and how I've supported it?
➤ Does the introduction prepare the reader and capture attention?
➤ Is the body of the paper organized effectively?
➤ Is each idea fully developed, explained, and supported by examples?
➤ Are my ideas connected to one another through logical transitions?
➤ Do I have a clear, concise, simple writing style?
➤ Does the paper fulfill the requirements of the assignment?
➤ Does the conclusion provide a natural ending to the paper?

Evaluating Paragraph Structure

Think of your individual paragraphs as miniversions of your paper, each with an introduction, a body, and a conclusion. Make sure that each paragraph has a *topic sentence* that states the paragraph's main idea (a topic sentence does for a paragraph what a thesis statement does for an entire paper). The rest of the paragraph should support the idea by presenting examples and other evidence. Although some topic sentences may occur just after the first sentence of a paragraph or even at the end, most of them occur at the beginning. An example follows:

> <u>Chief Marzloff played an integral role in the development of our self-confidence.</u> He taught us that anything less than direct eye contact was disrespectful to both him and ourselves. He encouraged us to be confident about our own beliefs and to think about what was said to us before we decided whether to accept it. Furthermore, the Chief reinforced self-confidence through his own example. He walked with his chin up and chest out, like the proud parent of a newborn baby. He always gave the appearance that he had something to do and that he was in complete control.

> "See revision as envisioning again. If there are areas in your work where there is a blur or vagueness, you can simply see the picture again and add the details that will bring your work closer to your mind's picture."
>
> Natalie Goldberg

TABLE 8-4 SHORTEN WORDY EXPRESSIONS

INSTEAD OF	WRITE . . .
in the event that	if
10:20 A.M. in the morning	10:20 A.M.
past experience	experience
this point in time	now
due to the fact that	because
are in the process of	are
call your attention to the fact that	remind you

Examine how your paragraphs flow into one another by evaluating your use of **transitions** . Transitions help readers to move through the text in a natural, logical way. For example, words like *also*, *in addition*, and *next* indicate that another idea is coming. Similarly, *finally, as a result*, and *in conclusion* tell readers a summary is on its way.

Transitions,
Words and phrases that build bridges between ideas, leading the reader from one idea to the next.

Checking for Clarity and Conciseness

Aim to say what you want to say as clearly and concisely as you can. Try to eliminate extra words and phrases. Rewrite wordy phrases in a more straightforward, conversational way. Table 8–4 shows how some phrases can be rewritten.

Some wordy expressions can be eliminated all together. For example, instead of writing,

> In the case of political reform, the new law applies to both the Republican and Democratic parties.

Write,

> The new political reform law applies to Republicans and Democrats.

Editing

In contrast to the critical thinking of revising, *editing* involves correcting technical mistakes in spelling, grammar, punctuation, and style consistency for such elements as abbreviations and capitalizations. Editing comes last, after you are satisfied with your ideas, organization, and style of writing. If you use a computer, you might want to use the grammar-check and spell-check functions to find mistakes. A spell-checker helps, but you still need to check your work on your own. Although a spell-checker won't pick up the mistake in the following sentence, someone who is reading for sense will:

> They are not hear on Tuesdays.

Look also for *sexist language,* which characterizes people according to their gender. Sexist language often involves the male pronoun *he* or *his.* For example, "An executive often spends hours each day going through his electronic mail," implies that executives are always men. A simple change, such as those shown in either of the following sentences, will eliminate the sexist language:

Executives often spend hours each day going through their electronic mail.

or

An executive often spends hours each day going through his or her electronic mail.

Try to be sensitive to words that slight women. *Mail carrier* is preferable to *mailman, student* to *coed.*

Proofreading is the final stage of editing and happens after you have a final version of your paper. Proofreading means reading every word and sentence in the final version to make sure they are accurate. Look for technical mistakes, run-on sentences, and sentence fragments. Look for incorrect word usage and references that aren't clear.

Teamwork can be a big help as you edit and proofread because another pair of eyes may see errors you didn't notice on your own. If possible, have someone look over your work. Ask for feedback on what is clear and what is confusing. Then ask the reader to edit and proofread for errors.

A Final Checklist

You're now ready to complete your revising and editing checklist. All the tasks listed in Table 8–5 should be complete when you submit your final paper.

TABLE 8-5   REVISING AND EDITING CHECKLIST

DATE DUE	TASK	IS IT COMPLETE?
	Check the body of the paper for clear thinking and adequate support of ideas.	
	Finalize introduction and conclusion.	
	Check word spelling and usage.	
	Check grammar.	
	Check paragraph structure.	
	Make sure language is familiar and concise.	
	Check punctuation and capitalization.	
	Check transitions.	
	Eliminate sexist language.	

Your final paper reflects all the hard work you put in during the writing process. Figure 8–9 shows the final version of Michael's paper.

SAMPLE PAPER
FIGURE 8-9

March 19, 1997

Michael B. Jackson

BOYS TO MEN

His stature was one of confidence, often misinterpreted by others as cockiness. His small frame was lean and agile, yet stiff and upright, as though every move were a calculated formula. For the longest eight weeks of my life, he was my father, my instructor, my leader, and my worst enemy. His name is Chief Marzloff, and he had the task of shaping the lives and careers of the youngest, newest members of the U.S. Coast Guard. As our Basic Training Company Commander, he took his job very seriously and demanded that we do the same. Within a limited time span, he conditioned our bodies, developed our self-confidence, and instilled within us a strong mental discipline.

Of the changes that recruits in military basic training undergo, the physical transformation is the most immediately evident. Upon my January arrival at the training facility, I was a little thin, but I had been working out and thought that I could physically do anything. Oh boy, was I wrong! The Chief wasted no time in introducing me to one of his trademark phrases: "Get down, maggots!" Upon this command, we were all to drop to the ground and produce endless counts of military-style push-ups. Later, we found out that exercise prepared us for hitting the deck in the event of enemy fire. Water survival tactics were also part of the training. Occasionally, my dreams of home were interrupted at about 3:00 A.M. when our company was selected for a surprise aquatic test. I recall one such test that required us to swim laps around the perimeter of a pool while in full uniform. I felt like a salmon swimming upstream, fueled only by natural instinct. Although we resented this subhuman treatment at the time, we learned to appreciate how the strict guidance of the Chief was turning our bodies into fine-tuned machines.

Beyond physical ability, Chief Marzloff also played an integral role in the development of our self-confidence. He would often declare in his raspy voice, "Look me in the eyes when you speak to me! Show me that you believe what you're saying!" He taught us that anything less was an expression of disrespect. Furthermore, he appeared to attack a personal habit of my own. It seemed that whenever he would speak to me individually, I would nervously nod my head in response. I was trying to demonstrate that I understood, but to him, I was blindly accepting anything that he said. He would roar, "That is a sign of weakness!" Needless to say, I am now conscious of all bodily motions when communicating with others. The Chief also reinforced self-confidence through his own example. He walked with his square chin up and chest out, like the proud parent of a newborn baby. He always gave the appearance that he had something to do, and that he was in complete control. Collectively, all of the methods that the Chief used were all successful in developing our self-confidence.

Perhaps the Chief's greatest contribution was the mental discipline that he instilled in his recruits. He taught us that physical ability and self-confidence were nothing without the mental discipline required to obtain any worthwhile goal. For us, this discipline began with adapting to the military lifestyle. Our day began promptly at 0500 hours, early enough to awaken the oversleeping roosters. By 0515 hours, we had to have showered, shaved, and perfectly donned our uniforms. At that point, we were marched to the galley for chow, where we learned to take only what is necessary, rather than indulging. Before each meal, the Chief would warn, "Get what you want, but you will eat all that you get!" After making good on his threat a few times, we all got the point. Throughout our stay, the chief repeatedly stressed the significance of self-discipline. He would calmly utter, "Give a little now, get a lot later." I guess that meant different things to all of us. For me, it was a simple phrase that would later become my personal philosophy on life. The Chief went to great lengths to ensure that everyone under his direction possessed the mental discipline required to be successful in boot camp or in any of life's challenges.

Chief Marzloff was a remarkable role model and a positive influence on many lives. I never saw him smile, but it was evident that he genuinely cared a great deal about his job and all the lives that he touched.

This man single-handedly conditioned our bodies, developed our self-confidence, and instilled a strong mental discipline that remains in me to this day. I have not seen the Chief since March 28, 1992, graduation day. Over the years, however, I have incorporated many of his ideals into my life. Above all, he taught us the true meaning of the U.S. Coast Guard slogan, "Semper Peratus" (Always Ready).

Suà

Suà is a Shoshone Indian word, derived from the Uto-Aztecan language, meaning "think." Whereas much of the Native-American tradition in the Americas focuses on oral communication, written languages have allowed Native-American perspectives and ideas to be understood by readers outside the Native-American culture. The writings of Leslie Marmon Silko, J. Scott Momaday, and Sherman Alexis have expressed important insights that all readers can consider.

Think of *suà*, and of how thinking can be communicated to others through writing, every time you begin to write. The power of writing allows you to express your own insights so others can read them and perhaps benefit from knowing them. Explore your thoughts, sharpen your ideas, and remember the incredible power of the written word.

IMPORTANT POINTS TO REMEMBER

 1. Why does good writing matter?

 You will often need to write essays or papers for your courses. Good writing skills are necessary to communicate your knowledge and thought process clearly. Clear, effective writing is also important for your career and in your personal life because others will judge your thinking ability according to what you write and how you write it. A well-written job application letter, for example, can make all the difference.

 2. What are the elements of effective writing?

 The three primary elements are your purpose, your topic, and your audience. Start by defining your purpose for writing: to inform or persuade. Then decide who your readers are and what they know about the topic, so that you can determine how you should write to best suit that audience. Your goal is to write in a complete and organized manner so that your audience can follow your ideas easily. Successful writing communicates your message in a way your readers can understand.

3. What is the writing process?

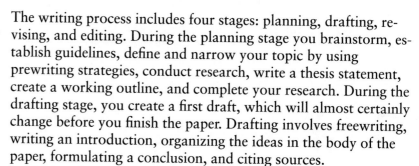

The writing process includes four stages: planning, drafting, revising, and editing. During the planning stage you brainstorm, establish guidelines, define and narrow your topic by using prewriting strategies, conduct research, write a thesis statement, create a working outline, and complete your research. During the drafting stage, you create a first draft, which will almost certainly change before you finish the paper. Drafting involves freewriting, writing an introduction, organizing the ideas in the body of the paper, formulating a conclusion, and citing sources.

During the revision stage you evaluate and improve your first draft by asking critical-thinking questions, evaluating paragraph structure, and aiming for clear and concise language. Finally, you correct errors in spelling, grammar, punctuation, and consistency of usage during the editing stage. Editing involves careful proofreading to make sure the paper is error-free.

Name _____   Date _____

BUILDING SKILLS FOR COLLEGE, CAREER, AND LIFE SUCCESS
CHAPTER 8

TAKING STOCK:
REFINING YOUR THOUGHTS

Look back at the statements you explored at the start of the chapter (see Thinking It Through on p. 279). Observe whether your attitudes have changed and what you have learned by studying this chapter.

1. Name two types of documents that you may write over the next few years. How are they part of getting you where you want to go in life?

_____

_____

_____

2. Explain what you would identify to clarify the writing context of an assignment.

_____

_____

_____

3. Why will knowing your audience help you as a writer?

_____

_____

_____

4. Name the four stages in the writing process and the main purpose of each.

_____

_____

_____

_____

5. Discuss two prewriting strategies and how they can help you plan your research.

6. Name three tasks involved in revising and editing a paper.

7. Choose one writing strategy you learned in this chapter and explain how you will apply it in your schoolwork during the next week.

CRITICAL THINKING:
APPLYING LEARNING TO YOUR LIFE

Audience Analysis

As a reporter for your college newspaper, you have been assigned the job of writing a story about some part of campus life. You submit the following suggestions to your editor-in-chief:

➤ The campus parking lot squeeze: Too many cars and too few spaces
➤ Diversity: how students accept differences and live and work together
➤ Drinking on campus: Is the problem getting better or worse?

Your editor-in-chief asks you the following questions about reader response. Consider that your readers may include students, faculty and administrators, and community members.

1. How would you adjust your writing according to whether readers know or don't know about the subject?

2. Which article idea is likely to have the greatest appeal to all the audiences? Why?

_____

_____

_____

_____

3. For each topic, name the audience (or audiences) that you think would be most interested. If you think one audience would be equally interested in more than one topic, you can name that audience more than once.

Campus parking lot: _____

Student diversity: _____

Drinking on campus: _____

4. If an idea has narrow appeal, should you write about it anyway? Why or why not?

_____

_____

_____

_____

_____

5. How can you make a narrow-interest article interesting to a general audience?

_____

_____

_____

Prewriting

Choose a topic you are interested in and know something about—for example, college sports, handling stress in a stressful world, our culture's emphasis on beauty and youth, or child rearing. Narrow your topic; then use the following prewriting strategies to discover what you already know and what you would need to learn if you had to write an essay about the subject for one of your classes (if necessary, continue this prewriting exercise on a separate sheet of paper).

Brainstorm your ideas:

_____

_____

_____

_____

_____

Freewrite:

_____

_____

_____

_____

_____

Ask journalists' questions:

_____

_____

_____

_____

_____

Writing a Thesis Statement

Write two thesis statements for each of the following topics. The first statement should try to inform the reader, the second should try to persuade. In each case, writing a thesis statement will require that you narrow the topic.

➤ *The rising cost of a college education*
Thesis with an informative purpose: _____

_____

_____

Thesis with a persuasive purpose: _____

_____

➤ *Choosing a major that prepares you for a career*

Thesis with an informative purpose: _____

_____

_____

Thesis with a persuasive purpose: _____

_____

_____

Drafting an Introduction and Conclusion

Imagine that one of the topics you explored in the last few exercises is the basis for a short paper in one of your courses. Use what you learned in the chapter to write an introduction and conclusion (if necessary, continue the exercise on a separate sheet of paper).

Introduction:

_____

_____

_____

_____

_____

_____

Conclusion:

_____

_____

_____

_____

_____

_____

_____

_____

The Art of Paraphrasing

Following is a 204-word quotation from the third edition of *Understanding Psychology* by Charles G. Morris.[4] After reading this quotation, use what you learned in the chapter to paraphrase the ideas:

Several conclusions arise from our investigation of gender diversity. First, although there are some psychological differences between the sexes, they are not as significant as many people suppose. In fact, it is reasonable to say that men and women are much more alike than they are different. Second, the finding that there are some differences between the sexes does not mean that all males or all females are committed to particular ways of behaving. Remember, there are group differences. There is much more variability within a gender than across genders; thus, some males are highly sensitive to nonverbal cues, just as some females are highly aggressive. In short, the existence of some differences between the sexes should not obscure the fact that there are far greater differences within each sex. Finally, psychologists still have much work to do in this area in terms of documenting the diversity between the sexes (i.e., discovering other areas in which males and females behave differently or similarly) and explaining such diversity (i.e., examining the roles of biology and social factors in producing the behaviors). Although gender differences undoubtedly arise from the interaction of both nature and nurture, we are far from certain about the exact contributions of each.

Paraphrase:

_____

_____

_____

_____

_____

_____

TEAMWORK:
COMBINING FORCES

Collaborative Writing. In many jobs, you may be asked to work with other employees to produce written documents, including reports, proposals, procedure manuals, and even important letters and memos. Writing in groups, also known as collaborative writing, involves planning, drafting, revising, and editing.

To see what collaborative writing is like, join three classmates and choose a general topic you are all interested in—for example, "What Colleges Can Do to Help Students Juggle School, Work, and Family" or "Teaching Safe Sex in an Age When Sex Isn't Safe." Now imagine that you and other group members have to write a persuasive paper on some aspect of this topic. Writing the paper involves the following steps:

➤ Each group member should spend an hour in the library to get an overview of the topic so that everyone is able to write about it in general terms.

➤ The group should come together to brainstorm the topic, narrow its focus, and come up with a thesis. Use your research and thesis to write a working outline that specifies what the paper will say and the approach it will take. Divide the writing assignment into parts and assign a part to each group member.

➤ Each group member should draft his or her portion of the paper. Each section should be about two or three paragraphs long.

➤ Photocopy each draft and give a copy to each group member. Working independently, each person should use the suggestions in this chapter to evaluate and revise each section. After the independent revision work is done, come together as a group to hammer out differences and prepare a final, unedited version.

➤ Photocopy this version and distribute it to group members. Have everyone edit the material, looking for mistakes in spelling, grammar, punctuation, and usage. Incorporate the group's changes into a final version you all agree on, and ask every group member to read it. The group's goal is to produce a finished paper that satisfies the thesis and also looks good.

➤ Working alone, each group member should answer the following questions. Finally, compare your responses with those of other group members:

1. What do you see as the advantages and disadvantages of collaborative writing? Is it difficult or easy to write as a team member?

2. What part of the collaborative writing project worked best? Where did you encounter problems?

_____

_____

_____

_____

_____

3. What did you learn from this experience that will make you a more effective collaborative writer on the next project?

_____

_____

_____

_____

_____

WRITING: DISCOVERY THROUGH JOURNALING

To record your thoughts, use a separate journal or the lined page at the end of the chapter.

Affecting words. What piece of powerful writing have you read most recently? Did it make you feel something, think something, and/or do something? If so, why? What can you learn about writing from this piece?

CAREER PORTFOLIO: CHARTING YOUR COURSE

Writing sample: A job interview letter. To secure a job interview, you may have to write a letter describing your background and value to the company. To include in your portfolio, write a one-page, three-paragraph cover letter to a prospective employer. (The letter will accompany your résumé.) Be creative—you may use fictitious names, but select a career and industry that interest you. Use the format shown in the following sample letter.

Firstname Lastname
1234 Your Street
Your, ST 12345

January 1, 2000

Ms. Prospective Employer
Prospective Company
5432 Their Street
Them, ST 54321

Dear Ms. Employer:

On the advice of Mr. X, career center advisor at Y College, I am writing to inquire about the open position of production assistant at KKKK Radio. I read the description of the job and the company as it was listed on the career center board, and I wish to offer myself as a candidate for the position.

I am a senior at Y College and will graduate this spring with a degree in communications. Since my junior year when I declared my major, I have wanted to pursue a career in radio. For the last year I have worked as a production intern at KCOL Radio, the college's station, and have occasionally filled in as a disk jockey on the evening news show. I enjoyed being on the air, but my primary interest is production and programming. My enclosed résumé will tell you more about my background and experience.

I would be pleased to talk with you in person about the position. You can reach me anytime at 555/555-5555 or by e-mail at *xxxx@xx.com*. Thank you for your consideration, and I look forward to meeting you.

Sincerely,

(*sign your name here*)

Firstname Lastname
Enclosure(s) *(use this notation if you have included a résumé or other item with your letter)*

Introductory paragraph: Start with an attention getter—a statement that convinces the employer to read on. For example, name a person the employer knows who told you to write, or refer to something positive about the company that you read in the paper. Identify the position for which you are applying and tell the employer that you are interested in working for the company.

Middle paragraph: Sell your value. Try to convince the employer that hiring you will help the company in some way. Center your "sales effort" on your experience in school and the workplace. If possible, tie your qualifications to the needs of the company. Refer indirectly to your enclosed résumé.

Final paragraph: Close with a call to action. Ask the employer to call you, or tell the employer to expect your call to arrange an interview. Exchange first drafts with a classmate. Read each other's letters and make notes in the margins. Discuss each letter, and make whatever corrections are necessary to produce a well-written, persuasive letter. Create a final draft for your portfolio.

Journal Entry

APPLY

APPLY

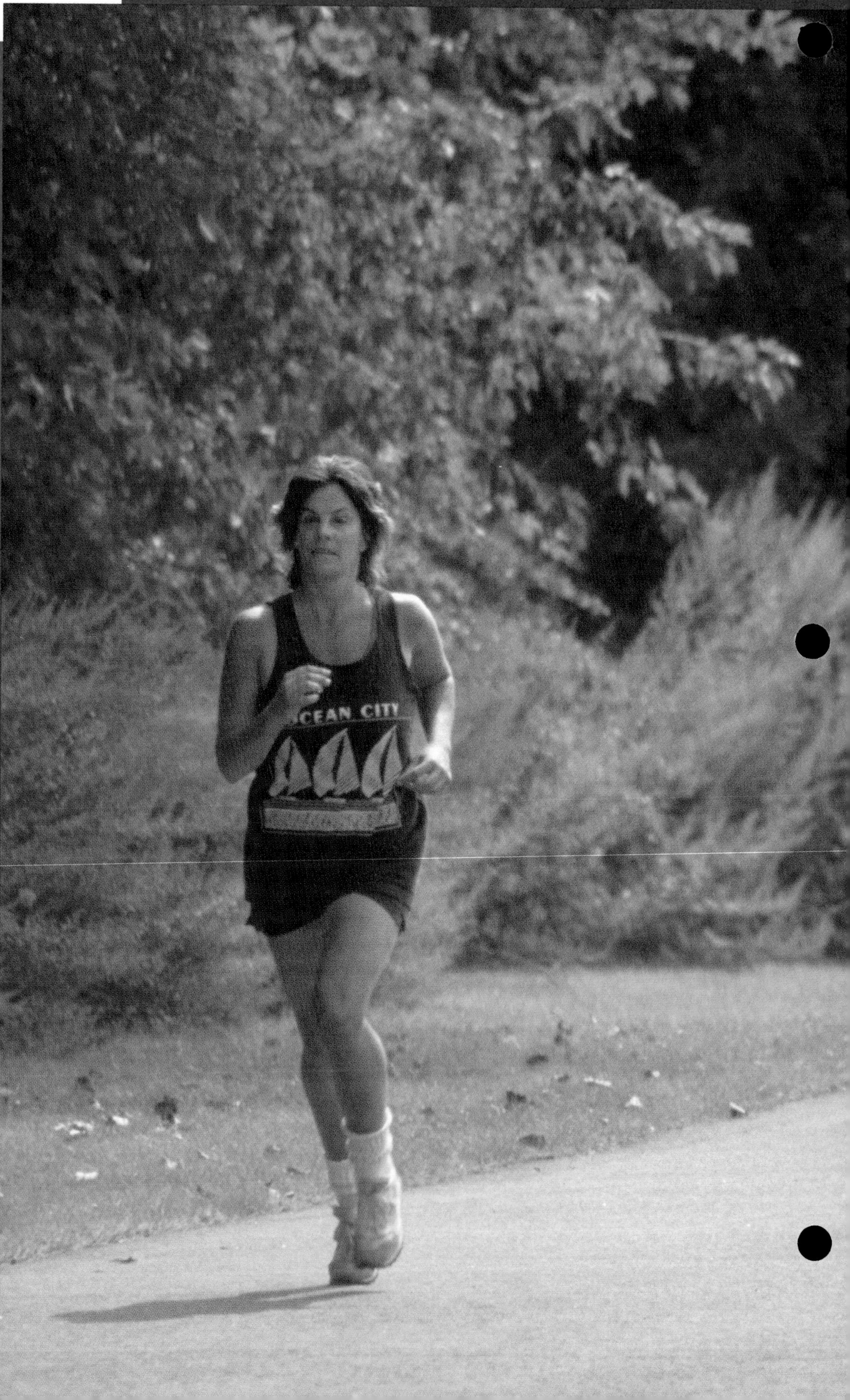

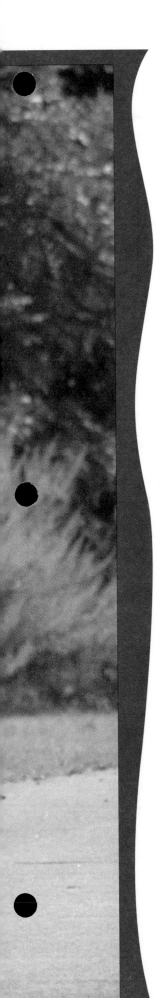

9 TEST TAKING: Showing What You Know

Thinking It Through

Check those statements that apply to you right now:

❑ Before an exam, I don't tend to tailor my studying toward the type of exam it will be; I just do a general review.

❑ I get tense before and during an exam, and the I think tension hurts my test performance.

❑ As soon as the instructor hands out the exam, I begin answering the questions.

❑ I attack all short-answer questions in the same way.

❑ When I answer an essay question, I start writing immediately.

❑ I never look at my answers when I get a test back.

In this chapter, you will explore answers to the following questions:

➤ How can preparation help improve test scores?
➤ What general strategies can help you succeed on tests?
➤ How can you master different types of test questions?
➤ What techniques will help improve performance on math tests?
➤ How can you learn from test mistakes?

For a runner, a race—the equivalent of a test—is a measure of ability at that moment. Doing what the race, or test, measures—running—continues on a regular basis whether or not the test went well. Furthermore, it wouldn't be possible to run a race successfully without a regular schedule of training. Approach any test in a similar way. If you know that you will continue to use the skills that you are being tested on and if you remember that owning the skills is more important than getting a perfect test score, you may be more likely to have a positive attitude toward the test and to retain more of what you learned.

Testing is part of education, even though many students don't look forward to it. See your exams as preparation for life. When you get a job, act as a volunteer, or even work through your family budget, you'll have to apply what you know and put your skills into action—exactly what you do when you take a test.

As you will see in this chapter, test taking involves more than showing up on time with a pencil in hand. It's about preparation, endurance, and strategy. It's also about conquering fears, paying attention to details, and learning from mistakes.

HOW CAN PREPARATION HELP IMPROVE TEST SCORES?

Like a runner who prepares for a marathon by exercising, eating right, taking practice runs, and getting enough sleep, you can take steps to master your exams. The primary step, occupying much of your preparation time, is to study until you know the material that will be on the test (Chapter 5 examines the art of effective studying). Other important steps are the preparation strategies that follow.

Identify Test Type and Material Covered

Before you begin studying, try to determine the type of test and what it will cover:

> ➤ Will it be a short-answer test with true or false and multiple-choice questions, an essay test, or a combination?
> ➤ Will the test cover everything you studied since the semester began, or will it be limited to a narrower topic?
> ➤ Will the test cover only what you learned in class and in the text, or will it also cover outside readings?

Your instructors may answer these questions for you. Even though they may not reveal specific test questions, they might let you know the question format or information covered. Some instructors may even drop hints throughout the semester about possible test questions, either directly ("I might ask a question on this subject on your next exam") or more subtly ("One of my favorite theories is…").

Here are a few other strategies for predicting what may be on a test.

Use SQ3R to identify important ideas and facts. Often, the questions you write and ask yourself when you read assigned materials may be part of the test. Textbook study questions are also good candidates.

Talk to people who took the instructor's course before. Try to find out how difficult the tests are, whether they focus more on assigned readings or class notes, what materials are usually covered, and what types of questions are used. Ask also about instructors' preferences. If you learn that the instructor pays close attention to factual and grammatical accuracy, for example, study accordingly. If he or she has a special appreciation for neatness, writing carefully and cleanly will make an impression.

Examine old tests if instructors make them available in class or on reserve in the library. Old tests help to answer the following questions:

➤ Does the instructor focus on examples and details, general ideas and themes, or a combination?

➤ Can you do well through straight memorization or does the material require critical thinking?

➤ Are the questions straightforward or confusing and sometimes tricky?

➤ Do the tests require the integration of facts from different areas to draw conclusions?

If you can't get copies of old tests and your instructor doesn't give too many details about the test, use clues from the class to predict test questions. After taking the first exam in the course, you will have more information about what to expect in the future.

Choose Study Materials

Once you have identified as much as you can about the subject matter of the test, choose the materials that contain the information you need to study. Save time by making sure that you aren't studying anything you don't need to. Go through your notes, your texts, related primary source materials, and any handouts from your instructor; then, set aside any materials you don't need.

Set a Study Schedule

Use your time-management skills to set a schedule that will help you feel as prepared as you can be. Consider all the relevant factors—the materials you need to study, how many days or weeks until the test date, and how much time you can study each day. If you establish your schedule ahead of time and write it in your date book, you will be much more likely to follow it.

Schedules vary widely according to situation. For example, if you have three days before the test and no other obligations during that time, you might set two 2-hour study sessions during each day. On the other hand, if you have two weeks before a test, classes during the day, and work three nights a week, you might spread out your study sessions over the nights you have off during those two weeks.

Prepare Through Critical Thinking

Using the techniques from Chapter 4, approach your test preparation as an active, critical thinker, working to understand material rather than just to repeat facts. As you study, try to connect ideas to examples, analyze causes and effects, establish truths, and look at issues from different perspectives.

Instructors often look for evidence that you can link seemingly unrelated ideas into logical patterns. As you study, try to explore concepts from different perspectives and connect ideas and examples that on the surface appear to be unrelated. Although you'll probably find answers to these questions in your text or class notes, you may have to work at putting different ideas together. Critical thinking takes work but may promote a greater understanding of the subject and probably a higher grade on the exam.

Critical thinking is especially important for essay tests that ask you to develop and support a thesis. Prepare by identifying three or four potential essay questions and write out your responses.

Take a Pretest

Use questions from your textbook to create your own pretest. Most textbooks, although not all, will include such questions at the ends of chapters. If your course doesn't have an assigned text, develop questions from your notes and from assigned outside readings. Choose questions that are likely to be covered on the test, then answer them under testlike conditions—in quiet, with no books or notes to help you (unless your exam is open-book), and with a clock telling you when to quit. Try to come as close as you can to duplicating the actual test situation.

Create an Organized Study Plan

A checklist, like the one in Figure 9–1, will help you get organized and stay on track as you prepare for each test.

Prepare Physically

When taking a test, you often need to work efficiently under time pressure. If your body is tired or under stress, you might not think as clearly or perform as well as you usually do. If you can, avoid staying up all night. Get some sleep so that you can wake up rested and alert. Remember that adequate sleep can help cement your memories by reducing interference from new memories (see Chapter 6). If you tend to press the snooze button in your sleep, try setting two alarm clocks and placing them across the room from your bed.

Eating right is also important. Sugar-laden snacks will bring up your energy, only to send you crashing back down much too soon. Also, too much caffeine can add to your tension and make it difficult to focus. Eating nothing will leave you drained, but too much food can make you sleepy. The best advice is to eat a light, well-balanced meal before a test. When time is short, grab a quick-energy snack such as a banana, orange juice, or a granola bar.

Work Through Test Anxiety

A certain amount of stress can be a good thing. Your body is alert, and your energy motivates you to do your best. For some students, however, the time before and during an exam can be miserable. Many students have experienced some level of test anxiety at some time during their studies. A bad case of nerves that makes it hard to think or remember, test anxiety can

PRETEST CHECKLIST   **FIGURE 9-1**

Course: _____   Teacher: _____

Date, time, and place of test: _____

Type of test (e.g., Is it a midterm or a minor quiz?): _____

What the instructor has told you about the test, including the types of test questions, the length of the test, and how much the test counts in your final grade: _____

_____

_____

_____

_____

Topics to be covered on the test in order of importance:

1._____

2._____

3._____

4._____

5._____

Study schedule, including materials you plan to study (e.g., texts and class notes) and date you plan to complete each source:

Source   Date of Completion

1._____   _____

2._____   _____

3._____   _____

4._____   _____

5._____   _____

Materials you are expected to bring to the test (e.g., your textbook, a sourcebook, a calculator): _____

_____

Special study arrangements (e.g., plan study-group meetings, ask the instructor for special help, get outside tutoring): _____

_____

_____

Life management issues (e.g., make child-care arrangements, rearrange work hours):_____

_____

_____

Source: Adapted from *Ace Any Test*, 3rd ed., Ron Fry, (Franklin Lakes, NJ: Career Press), 123–124.

also cause physical symptoms such as sweating, nausea, dizziness, headaches, and extreme fatigue. Work through test anxiety by dealing with its two primary aspects: preparation and attitude.

Preparation

Preparation is the basic defense against anxiety. The more confident you feel about your knowledge of the material, the more you'll feel able to perform on test day. In this way, you can consider all of the preparation and study information in this chapter as test anxiety assistance. Also, finding out what to expect on the exam will help you feel more in control. Seek out information about what material will be covered, the question format, the length of the exam, and the points assigned to each question.

Making and following a detailed study plan will help you build the kind of knowledge that can help you fight off anxiety. Divide the plan into a series of small tasks. As you finish each one, you will build your sense of accomplishment, confidence, and control.

Preparation is all about action. Instead of sitting and worrying about the test, put your energy toward concrete, active steps that will help you succeed.

Attitude

Although good preparation will help build your confidence, maintaining a positive *attitude* toward testing is as important as studying. Here are some key ways to maintain an attitude that will help you.

See the test as an opportunity to learn. Sometimes students see a test as an opportunity to fail. Turn this around by focusing on learning. See that a test is an opportunity to show what you have learned, as well as to learn something new about the material and about test taking itself.

See the test as a signpost. It's easy to see a test as a contest to be won or lost. If you pass, or "win" the contest, you might feel no need to retain what you've learned. If you fail, or "lose" the contest, you might feel no need to try again. However, if you see the test as a signpost along the way to a greater goal, you may be more likely to try your best, learn from the experience, and move on.

Give your instructor a positive role. Your instructors don't test you out of a desire to make you miserable. They test you to give you an opportunity to grow and to demonstrate what you have accomplished. They test you so that, in rising to this challenge, you will become better prepared for the challenges that lie ahead, outside of school.

Put the test in perspective. A test is only a small part of your education and an even smaller part of your life. Your test grade does not reflect the kind of person you are or your ability to succeed in life.

Seek study partners who challenge you. Your anxiety may get worse if you study with someone who feels just as anxious and unprepared as you do. Find someone who can inspire you to do your best.

> "A little knowledge that acts is worth infinitely more than much knowledge that is idle."
>
> Kahlil Gibran

Set yourself up for success. Try not to expect failure before you even start. Expect progress of yourself. Take responsibility for creating a setting for success through your preparation and attitude. Know that you are ultimately responsible for the outcome.

Practice relaxation. When you feel test anxiety coming on, take some deep breaths, close your eyes, and visualize positive mental images related to the test, such as getting a good grade and finishing confidently, with time to spare. Do whatever you have to do to ease muscle tension—stretch your neck; tighten and then release your muscles; even take a trip to the restroom to do a couple of forward bends.

Two other important aspects of test anxiety are math anxiety and the specific concerns of the returning adult student.

Coping With Math Anxiety

For many students a special anxiety is associated with taking a math test. As Sheila Tobias, author of *Overcoming Math Anxiety*,[1] explains, math anxiety is linked to the feeling that math is impossible:

> The first thing people remember about failing at math is that it felt like sudden death. Whether it happened while learning word problems in sixth grade, coping with equations in high school, or first confronting calculus and statistics in college, failure was instant and frightening. An idea or a new operation was not just difficult, it was impossible! And instead of asking questions or taking the lesson slowly, assuming that in a month or so they would be able to digest it, people remember the feeling as certain as it was sudden, that they would never go any further in mathematics.

Students who believe they are no good at math probably won't do well on math tests, even if they study. Their attitude creates a huge problem. If you are one of these students, here are some steps you can take to begin thinking about math—and math tests—in a different way.

See the value in learning to use your mind in a mathematical way. Mathematical thinking is another type of critical thinking. It can help you solve the little and big problems in your world, including how to measure the amount of wallpaper you need in a room or how to compare student loan programs.

Think of math as a tool that will help you land a good job. In fields such as engineering and banking, the ability to solve numerical problems is at the heart of the work. In real estate, retail sales, medicine, and publishing, you may use math for such tasks as writing budgets and figuring mortgage rates.

Turn negative self-talk into positive self-talk. Instead of telling yourself that a problem is too hard, tell yourself that if you take small, logical steps, you will succeed. Says Tobias, "If we can talk ourselves into feeling comfortable and secure, we may let in a good idea."[2]

Don't believe that women can't do math. Tobias says that when male students fail a math quiz, they think they didn't work hard enough; but when female students fail, they are three times more likely to feel that they don't have what it takes.[3] Whether you are a man or a woman, work to overcome this stereotype.

Use the people and resources around you. Get to know your math instructor so you're comfortable asking for help. Join a math study group. Have a pep meeting right before a big test. Look for math-anxiety workshops. Seek a tutor who can help you with your skills and build your confidence.

Become comfortable in the world of math. Find a computer program with math games or buy a paperback book with math puzzles. Do percentages and estimates in your head. Have fun with problems and enjoy solving them. Then transfer these feelings to classwork and tests.

Understand math's relationship to your life success. Being at ease with numbers can serve you in day-to-day functions. Percentages can help you compare the financial benefits of different loan programs; adding and subtracting will allow you to balance a checkbook, and fractions will help you compare costs at work. Furthermore, working with numbers helps to develop general thinking skills. The calculation and problem solving involved in math help you develop precision, a focus on detail, and a sense of order.

Test Anxiety and the Returning Adult Student

If you're returning to school after five, ten, or even twenty years, you may wonder if you can compete with younger students or if your mind is still able to learn new material. To counteract these feelings of inadequacy, focus on how your life experiences have given you useful skills. For example, managing work and a family requires strong time-management, planning, and communication skills, which can help you plan your study time, juggle school responsibilities, and interact with students and instructors.

In addition, life experiences give you examples through which you can understand ideas in your courses. For example, your relationships experiences may help you understand psychology concepts, managing your finances may help you understand economics or accounting practices, and work may give you a context for what you learn in a business management course. If you let yourself feel positive about your knowledge and skills, you may improve your ability to achieve your goals.

Studying for a Test When There Are Children Around

Parents who have to juggle child care with study time can find the challenge especially difficult before a test. Here are some suggestions that might help:

Tell your children why this test is important. Discuss the situation in concrete terms that they can understand. For example, a better education and job for you might mean for them a better home, more money to plan outings and vacations, more time to spend as a family, and a happier parent (you).

Explain the time frame. Tell them your study schedule and when the test will occur. Plan a reward after your test—going for ice cream, seeing a movie, or having a picnic.

Keep children active while you study. Stock up on games, books, and videos. If a child is old enough, have him or her invite a friend to play.

Find help. Ask a relative or friend to watch the children during study time, or arrange for your child to visit a friend. Consider trading baby-sitting hours with another parent, hiring a baby-sitter who will come to your home, or enrolling your child in a day-care center.

When you have prepared by using the strategies that work for you, you are ready to take your exam. Now you can focus on methods to help you succeed when the test begins.

WHAT GENERAL STRATEGIES CAN HELP YOU SUCCEED ON TESTS?

Even though every test is different, there are general strategies that will help you handle almost all tests, including short-answer and essay exams.

Write Down Key Facts

Before you even look at the test, write down any key information—including formulas, rules, and definitions—that you studied recently or even just before you entered the test room. Use the back of the question sheet or a piece of scrap paper for your notes (be sure it is clear to your instructor that this scrap paper didn't come into the test room already filled in). Recording this information right at the start will make forgetting less likely.

Begin with an Overview of the Exam

Although exam time is precious, spend a few minutes at the start of the test to get a sense of the kinds of questions you'll be answering, what type of thinking they require, the number of questions in each section, and their point values. Use this information to schedule your time. For example, if a two-hour test is divided into two sections of equal point value—an essay section with four questions and a short-answer section with sixty questions—you can spend an hour on the essays (fifteen minutes per question) and an hour on the short-answer section (one minute per question).

As you make your calculations, think about the level of difficulty of each section. If you think you can handle the short-answer questions in less

An examination at York University in Ontario, Canada

than an hour and that you'll need more time for the essays, rebudget your time in that way.

Read Test Directions

Although it seems obvious, reading test directions carefully can save you trouble. For example, although a history test of 100 true-or-false questions and one essay may look straightforward, the directions may tell you to answer 80 of the 100 questions or that the essay is an optional bonus. If the directions indicate that you are penalized for incorrect answers—meaning that you will lose points instead of simply not gaining points—avoid guessing unless you're fairly certain. These questions may do damage, for example, if you earn two points for every correct answer and lose one point for every incorrect answer.

When you read directions, you may learn that some questions or sections are weighted more heavily than others. For example, the short-answer questions on a test may be worth thirty points, whereas the essays are worth seventy. In this case, it's smart to spend more time on the essays than on the short answers. To stay aware of the specifics of the directions, circle or underline key words and numbers.

Work from Easy to Hard

Begin with the parts or questions that seem easiest to you. One advantage of this strategy is that you will tend to take less time to answer the questions you know well, leaving more time to spend on the questions that may require increased effort and thinking. If you like to work through questions in order, mark difficult questions as you reach them and return to them after you answer the questions you know.

Another advantage of answering easier questions first is that knowing the answers can boost your confidence, helping you to continue to believe in yourself when you work on more difficult sections.

Watch the Clock

Keep track of how much time is left and how you are progressing. You may want to plan your time on a piece of scrap paper, especially if you have one or more essays to write. Wear a watch or bring a small clock with you to the test room. A wall clock may be broken, or there may be no clock at all.

Some students are so concerned about time that they rush through the test and have time left over. In such situations, it's easy to leave early. The best move, however, is to take your time. Stay until the end so that you can refine and check your work; it couldn't hurt, and it might help.

Master the Art of Intelligent Guessing

When you are unsure of an answer on a short-answer test, you can leave it blank or you can guess. In most cases, provided that you are not penalized for incorrect answers, guessing will help you. "Intelligent guessing," writes Steven Frank, an authority on student studying and test taking, "means taking advantage of what you do know in order to try to figure out what you don't. If you guess intelligently, you have a decent shot at getting the answer right."[4]

First, eliminate all the answers you know—or believe—are wrong. Try to narrow your choices to two possible answers; then choose the one you think is more likely to be correct. Strategies for guessing the correct answer in a multiple-choice test will be discussed later in the chapter.

When you check your work at the end of the test, ask yourself whether you would make the same guesses again. Chances are that you will leave your answers alone, but you may notice something that will make you change your mind—a **qualifier** that affects meaning, a remembered fact that will enable you to answer the question without guessing, or a miscalculated step in a math problem.

> **Qualifier,**
> A descriptive word, such as *always*, *never*, or *often*, that changes the meaning of another word or word group.

Follow Directions on Machine-Scored Tests

Machine-scored tests require that you use a special pencil to fill in a small box on a computerized answer sheet. When the computer scans the sheet, it can tell whether you answered the questions correctly.

Taking these tests requires special care. Use the right pencil (usually a number 2) and mark your answer in the correct space. Periodically, check the answer number against the question number to make sure they match. If you mark the answer to question 4 in the space for question 5, not only will you get question 4 wrong, but also your responses for every question that follows will be off by a line. One way to avoid getting off track is to put a small dot next to any number you skip and plan to return to later on.

Neatness counts on these tests because the computer can misread stray pencil marks or partially erased answers. If you mark two answers to a question and only partially erase one, the computer will read both responses and charge you with a wrong answer. Completely fill each answer space and avoid any other pencil marks that could be misinterpreted by the computer.

Use Critical Thinking to Avoid Errors

Critical thinking can help you work through each question thoroughly and avoid errors. Following are some critical-thinking strategies to use during a test.

Recall facts, procedures, rules, and formulas. Base your answers on the information you recall. Think carefully to make sure you recall it accurately.

Think about similarities. If you don't know how to attack a question or problem, consider any similar questions or problems that you have worked on in class or while studying.

Notice differences. Especially with objective questions, items that seem different from that material you have studied may indicate answers you can eliminate.

Think through causes and effects. For a numerical problem, think about how you plan to solve it and see if the answer—the effect of your plan—makes sense. For an essay question that asks you to analyze a condition or situation, consider both what caused it and what effects it has.

Find the best idea to match the example or examples given. For a numerical problem, decide what formula (idea) best applies to the example or examples (the data of the problem). For an essay question, decide what idea applies to, or links, the examples given.

Support ideas with examples. When you put forth an idea in an answer to an essay question, be sure to back up your idea with an adequate number of examples that fit.

Evaluate each test question. In your initial approach to any question, decide what kinds of thinking will best help you solve it. For example, essay questions often require cause-and-effect and idea-to-example thinking, whereas objective questions often benefit from thinking about similarities and differences.

The general strategies you have explored also can help you to address specific types of test questions.

THINKING BACK

1. List three questions you can ask that will help predict test content.

   a. _____

   b. _____

   c. _____

2. Describe two strategies that can help you identify the material covered on a test.

   a. _____

   b. _____

3. Explain three ways you might choose to combat any text anxiety you feel.

   a. _____

   b. _____

   c. _____

4. List the steps to take to get an overview of an exam before you begin answering questions.

    _____

    _____

    _____

    _____

5. Name three ways in which critical thinking can help you avoid common test errors.

    a. _____

    b. _____

    c. _____

THINKING AHEAD

1. Consider how you do on short-answer tests that include multiple-choice and true-or-false questions. What are your favorite kinds of short-answer questions? Which do you tend to make mistakes on, and why do you think this happens?

    _____

    _____

    _____

    _____

2. Describe how you generally handle essay questions. Do you plan your answers by using an outline or think link, or do you write the first thing that comes to your mind?

    _____

    _____

    _____

3. Would you ever consider retaking a test if an improved grade would not count? Why or why not?

_____

_____

_____

HOW CAN YOU MASTER DIFFERENT TYPES OF TEST QUESTIONS?

Objective questions, Short-answer questions that test your ability to recall, compare and contrast.

Although the goal of all test questions is to discover how much you know about a subject, every type of question has a different way of doing so. Answering different types of questions is part science and part art. First, the strategy changes according to whether the question is objective or subjective.

For objective questions , you choose or write a short answer you believe is correct, often making a selection from a limited number of choices. Multiple-choice, fill-in-the-blank, and true-or-false questions fall into this category. Subjective questions demand the same information recall as objective questions, but they also require you to plan, organize, draft, and refine a written response. They may also require more extensive critical thinking and evaluation. All essay questions are subjective. Although some guidelines will help you choose the right answers to both types of questions, part of the skill is learning to "feel" your way to an answer that works.

Subjective questions, Essay questions that require you to express your answer in terms of your own personal knowledge and perspective.

Multiple-Choice Questions

Multiple-choice questions are the most popular type of question on standardized tests. The following strategies can help you answer them.

Carefully read the directions. In the rush to get to work on a question it is easy to read directions too quickly or to skip them. Directions, however, can be tricky. For example, whereas most test items ask for a single correct answer, some give you the option of marking several choices that are correct. For some tests, you might be required to answer only a certain number of the questions.

Read each question thoroughly before looking at the choices. Then try to answer the question. This strategy will reduce the possibility that the choices will confuse you.

Underline key words and phrases in the question. If the question is complicated, try to break it down into small sections that are easy to understand.

"The secret of a leader lies in the tests he has faced over the whole course of his life and the habit of action he develops in meeting those tests."

Gail Sheehy

Pay special attention to words that could throw you off. For example, it is easy to overlook negatives in a question ("Which of the following is not…").

If you don't know the answer, eliminate those answers that you know or suspect are wrong. Your goal is to leave yourself with two possible answers, which would give you a fifty-fifty chance of making the right choice. The following are questions you can ask as you eliminate choices:

- ➤ Is the choice accurate in its own terms? If there's an error in the choice—for example, a term that is incorrectly defined—the answer is wrong.

- ➤ Is the choice relevant? An answer may be accurate, but it may not relate to the essence of the question.

- ➤ Are there any qualifiers? Absolute qualifiers like *always, never, all, none,* or *every* often signal an exception that makes a choice incorrect. For example, the statement that "normal children always begin talking before the age of two" is an untrue statement; whereas most normal children begin talking before age two, some start later. Analysis has shown that choices containing conservative qualifiers (*often, most, rarely,* or *may sometimes be*) are often correct.

- ➤ Do the choices give clues? Does a puzzling word remind you of a word you know? If you don't know a word, does any part of the word—its prefix, suffix, or root—seem familiar? (See Chapter 5 for information on the meanings of common prefixes and suffixes.)

Look for patterns that may lead to the right answer; then make an educated guess. The ideal is to know the material so well that you don't have to guess, but that isn't always possible. Test-taking experts have found patterns in multiple-choice questions that may help you. Here is their advice:

- ➤ Consider the possibility that a choice that is more *general* than the others is the right answer.

- ➤ Consider the possibility that a choice that is *longer* than the others is the right answer.

- ➤ Look for a choice that has a middle value in a range (the range can be from small to large or from old to recent). It is likely to be the right answer.

- ➤ Look for two choices that have similar meanings. One of these answers is probably correct.

- ➤ Look for answers that agree grammatically with the question. For example, a fill-in-the-blank question that has an *a* or *an* before the blank gives you a clue to the correct answer.

Make sure you read every word of every answer. Instructors have been known to include answers that are almost right, except for a single word.

When questions are keyed to a long reading passage, read the questions first. This will help you, when you read the passage, to focus on the information you need to answer the questions.

Here are some examples of the kinds of multiple-choice questions you might encounter in an Introduction to Psychology course[5] (the correct answer follows each question):

---

1. Arnold is at the company party and has had too much to drink. He releases all of his pent-up aggression by yelling at his boss, who promptly fires him. Arnold normally would not have yelled at his boss, but after drinking heavily he yelled because_____.

   a. parties are places where employees are supposed to be able to "loosen up"

   b. alcohol is a stimulant

   c. alcohol makes people less concerned with the negative consequences of their behavior

   d. alcohol inhibits brain centers that control the perception of loudness

   (The correct answer is C.)

2. Which of the following has not been shown to be a probable cause of or influence in the development of alcoholism in our society?
   a. intelligence   c. personality
   b. culture   d. genetic vulnerability

   (The correct answer is A.)

3. Geraldine is a heavy coffee drinker who has become addicted to caffeine. If she completely ceases her intake of caffeine over the next few days, she is likely to experience each of the following EXCEPT_____.
   a. depression   c. insomnia
   b. lethargy   d. headaches

   (The correct answer is C.)

True-or-False Questions

True-or-false questions test your knowledge of facts and concepts. Read them carefully to evaluate what they truly say. If you're stumped, guess (unless you're penalized for wrong answers).

Look for qualifiers in true-or-false questions—such as *all, only,* and *always* (the absolutes that often make a statement false) and *generally, often, usually,* and *sometimes* (the conservatives that often make a statement true)—that can turn a statement that would otherwise be true into one that is false or vice versa. For example, "The grammar rule 'I before E except after C' is always true" is false, whereas "The grammar rule 'I before E except after C' is usually true" is true. The qualifier makes the difference.

Here are some examples of the kinds of true-or-false questions you might encounter in an Introduction to Psychology course. The correct answer follows each question:

Are the following questions true or false?

1. Alcohol use is clearly related to increases in hostility, aggression, violence, and abusive behavior. (True)
2. Marijuana is harmless. (False)
3. Simply expecting a drug to produce an effect is often enough to produce the effect. (True)

Essay Questions

An essay question allows you to express your knowledge and views on a topic in a much more extensive manner than any short-answer question can provide. With the freedom to express your views, though, comes the challenge to both exhibit knowledge and show you have command of how to organize and express that knowledge clearly.

Start by reading the essay questions and deciding which to tackle (if there's a choice). Then focus on what each question is asking, the mind actions you will need to use, and the directions. Read questions carefully and do everything you are asked to do. Some essay questions may contain more than one part.

Watch for certain action verbs that can help you figure out how to think. Table 9–1 explains some words commonly used in essay questions. Underline these words as you read the question, clarify for yourself exactly what they mean, and use them to guide your writing.

Next, budget your time and begin to plan. Create an informal outline or think link to map your ideas and indicate examples you plan to cite in support. Avoid spending too much time on introductions or flowery prose. Start with a thesis statement or idea that states in a basic way what your essay will say (see Chapter 8 for a discussion of thesis statements).

In the first paragraph, introduce the essay's key points. These may be sub-ideas, causes, effects, or even examples. Use simple, clear language in the body of the essay. Carefully establish your ideas and support them with examples, and look back at your outline to make sure you are covering everything. Wrap it up with a conclusion that is short and to the point.

Try to write legibly; if your instructor can't read your ideas, it doesn't matter how good they are. Try printing and skipping every other line if you know your handwriting is problematic. Avoid writing on both sides of the paper since it will make your handwriting even harder to read. You may even want to discuss the problem with the instructor.

Do your best to save time to reread and revise your essay after you finish getting your ideas down on paper. Look for ideas you left out, ideas you didn't support with enough examples, and poorly phrased sentences that might confuse the reader. Check for mistakes in grammar, spelling, punctuation, and

TABLE 9-1 COMMON ACTION VERBS ON ESSAY TESTS

Analyze—Break into parts and discuss each part separately.

Compare—Explain similarities and differences.

Contrast—Distinguish between items being compared by focusing on differences.

Criticize—Evaluate the positive and negative effects of what is being discussed.

Define—State the essential quality or meaning. Give the common idea.

Describe—Visualize and give information that paints a complete picture.

Discuss—Examine in a complete and detailed way, usually by connecting ideas to examples.

Enumerate/List/Identify—Recall and specify items in the form of a list.

Explain—Make the meaning of something clear, often by making analogies or giving examples.

Evaluate—Give your opinion about the value or worth of something, usually by weighing positive and negative effects, and justify your conclusion.

ILLUSTRATE—Supply examples.

Interpret—Explain your personal view of the facts and ideas and how they relate to one another.

OUTLINE—Organize and present the sub-ideas or main examples of an idea.

PROVE—Use evidence and argument to show that something is true, usually by showing cause and effect or giving examples that fit the idea to be proven.

Review—Provide an overview of ideas and establish their merits and features.

State—Explain clearly, simply, and concisely, being sure that each word gives the image you want.

SUMMARIZE—Give the important ideas in brief.

Trace—Present a history of the way something developed, often by showing cause and effect.

usage. No matter what subject you are writing about, having a command of these factors will make your work more complete and impressive.

Here are some examples of essay questions you might encounter in an Introduction to Psychology course. In each case, notice the action verbs from Table 9–1.

1. Summarize the theories and research on the causes and effects of daydreaming. Discuss the possible uses for daydreaming in a healthy individual.
2. Describe the physical and psychological effects of alcohol and the problems associated with its use.
3. Explain what sleep terrors are, what appears to cause them, and who is most likely to suffer from them.

WINDOWS ON THE WORLD: REAL LIFE STUDENT ISSUES

How can I combat test anxiety?

Peter Changsak, Sheldon-Jackson College, Sitka, Alaska

I am a Yu'pik Eskimo from a village on the Yukon River. Before attending college I worked for six years as a clerk at the Native Corporation, a gas station and general store. When the manager passed away the business offered to make me a manager. Even though I knew how to do much of the work, I didn't feel I was ready, so I decided to go to school for more training.

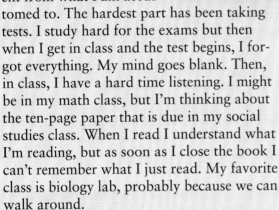

College life is different from what I am accustomed to. The hardest part has been taking tests. I study hard for the exams but then when I get in class and the test begins, I forgot everything. My mind goes blank. Then, in class, I have a hard time listening. I might be in my math class, but I'm thinking about the ten-page paper that is due in my social studies class. When I read I understand what I'm reading, but as soon as I close the book I can't remember what I just read. My favorite class is biology lab, probably because we can walk around.

I love mechanics and construction. When I worked at the Native Corporation we made a new building. I felt like I was a success at work, but I don't feel successful as a student. Sometimes I feel like quitting school altogether, but I also think it can help me have more choices if I stick with it. I'm learning how to be a serious student, but it isn't easy. Can you give suggestions about how I can get over my test anxiety?

Tim Nordberg, Executive Director, Chicago Youth Ministries

In many ways my experience in college was similar to yours. I was raised in a car industry town. I was the first person in my family to go to college, which was intimidating. My first year was hard—I discovered that I read at an eighth-grade level. I hated studying and taking tests. During the spring the college began a building project. I wanted to be outside doing manual work too.

Two factors gave me the endurance to go on. One was seeing my old high school buddies who seemed stuck in the past. A second factor was my desire to fulfill my goals. I thought, "If I fail it won't be because I haven't given it my best."

That summer I took a reading class. School was still not easy that fall, but I was studying to do my best. Classes began to take on a different meaning. I was beginning to learn because I enjoyed the challenge. Today I still love sports and carpentry, but I also love to learn.

Don't fear failure. Just try to do your best. Good test scores will reflect your passion to know what you have studied rather than how good you are at test taking. You are being challenged to survive in new ways, and you are not alone. Ask the student services office to help you. Ask your advisor if they offer a class in study and test-taking tips.

Remember why you came to college—to better equip yourself. As you prepare for classes and tests, spend time reminding yourself what this experience will do for you someday when it is all behind you. Growing in any area of life isn't always fun, and may not seem within reach. But if we give up, we may miss out on a part of us that, in time, would have brought greater rewards.

WHAT TECHNIQUES WILL HELP IMPROVE PERFORMANCE ON MATH TESTS?

Mathematical test problems present a special challenge to some students, especially those who suffer from math anxiety. These strategies may help you overcome any difficulties you might have.

Analyze problems carefully. Make sure that you take all the "givens" into account as you begin your calculations. Focus also on what you want to find or prove.

Write down any formulas, theorems, or definitions that apply to the problem. Do this before you begin your calculations.

Ballpark,
Being approximately proper in numerical range.

Estimate a ballpark solution before you tackle the problem. Then work the problem and check your actual solution against your original estimate. The two answers should be close. If they're not, recheck your work. You may have made a simple calculation error.

Break the calculation into the smallest possible pieces. Go step by step and don't move on to the next step until you are clear about what you've done so far.

Recall how you solved similar problems. Past experience can give you valuable clues to how a particular problem should be handled.

Draw a picture to help you see the problem. This can be a diagram, a chart, a probability tree, a geometric figure, or any other visual image that relates to the problem at hand.

Take your time. Precision demands concentration and focus. Also, if you're using a calculator, one wrong keystroke can mean the difference between a right and wrong answer.

Be neat. When it comes to numbers, a case of mistaken identity can mean the difference between a right and a wrong answer. A 4 that looks like a 9 or a 1 that looks like a 7 can make trouble. Also, if you are writing numbers in columns, be sure that all decimal points are lined up under one another.

Use the opposite operation to check your work. When you come up with an answer, work backward to see if you arrive back at the starting point (which usually indicates that your calculations have been correct). Use subtraction to check your addition; use division to check multiplication; and so on.

Look back at the questions to be sure you did everything that was asked. Did you answer every part of the question? Did you show all the required work? Be as complete as you possibly can.

HOW CAN YOU LEARN FROM TEST MISTAKES?

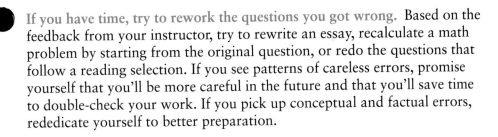

The purpose of a test is to see how much you know, not merely to achieve a grade. Making mistakes, or even failing a test, is human. Rather than ignoring mistakes, examine them and learn from them as you learn from mistakes on the job and in your relationships. Working through your mistakes will help you avoid repeating them again on another test - or outside of school life. The following strategies will help.

Try to identify patterns in your mistakes. Look for the following:

> *Careless errors.* In your rush to complete the exam, did you misread the question or directions, blacken the wrong box on the answer sheet, inadvertently skip a question, or use illegible handwriting?

> *Conceptual or factual errors.* Did you misunderstand a concept or never learn it in the first place? Did you fail to master certain facts? Did you skip part of the assigned text or miss important classes in which ideas were covered?

If you have time, try to rework the questions you got wrong. Based on the feedback from your instructor, try to rewrite an essay, recalculate a math problem by starting from the original question, or redo the questions that follow a reading selection. If you see patterns of careless errors, promise yourself that you'll be more careful in the future and that you'll save time to double-check your work. If you pick up conceptual and factual errors, rededicate yourself to better preparation.

After reviewing your mistakes, fill in your knowledge gaps. If you made mistakes on questions because you didn't know or understand them, develop a plan to comprehensively learn the material. Solidifying your knowledge can help you in exams further down the road, as well as in life situations that involve the subject matter you're studying. You might even consider asking your instructor if you can retake the exam, if you have the time to do so. The score might not count, but you may find that focusing on learning rather than on grades can improve your knowledge and build self-respect.

If you fail a test completely, don't throw it away. First, know that many students have been in your shoes and that you have room to grow and improve. Then try to understand why you failed by reviewing and analyzing your errors. This is especially important for an essay test because whereas most objective questions are fact-based and clearly right or wrong, subjective questions are in large part subject to the opinion of the grader. Respectfully ask the instructor who graded the test for an explanation. You may also want to ask what you could have done to have earned a better grade.

Sine qua non

Although the Latin language is no longer commonly used, it is one of the most dominant ancestors of modern English, and many Latin words and phrases have a place in the English language. The Latin phrase *sine qua non* (pronounced sihn-ay kwa nahn) means, literally, "without which not." Translated into everyday language, a sine qua non is "an absolutely indispensable or essential thing."

Think of true learning as the sine qua non of test taking. When you have worked hard to learn ideas and information, taking it in and using different techniques to review and retain it, you will be more able to take tests successfully, confident that you have the knowledge necessary to answer the required questions. Focus on knowledge so that test taking becomes not an intimidating challenge but an opportunity to show what you know.

IMPORTANT POINTS TO REMEMBER

1. How can preparation help improve test scores?

 Preparation is one key to test success. Strategies that can help improve your approach include identifying test type and coverage; choosing appropriate study materials; setting a study schedule, using critical thinking to prepare for possible questions, taking a pretest, creating an organized study plan, preparing your body by getting enough sleep and eating well, working through test anxiety, and learning to study when you're also taking care of children.

2. What general strategies can help you succeed on tests?

 Although all tests are different, there are methods that will help improve your performance on almost every test. These include writing down key information as soon as the test begins, taking time to skim the exam and get an overview, reading the directions, working from the easiest questions to the hardest, keeping track of time as you work, learning to guess intelligently, knowing how to fill out machine-scored tests, and using critical thinking to avoid errors.

3. How can you master different types of test questions?

 Learning how to approach different types of test questions is important to your success. There are different skills for objective questions, which include multiple-choice and true-or-false questions, and for subjective questions, which include essay questions.

4. What special techniques will help improve your performance on math tests?

Actions you can take to improve your performance on math tests include careful problem analysis; writing down formulas or theorems that apply to problems; breaking calculations into small, easy-to-handle pieces; drawing pictures of problems; recalling how you solved similar problems; and learning to estimate.

5. How can you learn from test mistakes?

The purpose of a test is to see how much you know. Test mistakes can show you where you may need to strengthen your knowledge. When you get your test back, look for careless errors, as well as those that involve concepts and facts. Instead of taking your mistakes as a defeat, treat them as an opportunity to understand what happened and avoid making the same mistake in the future.

Name _____   Date _____

**BUILDING SKILLS FOR COLLEGE, CAREER, AND LIFE SUCCESS
CHAPTER 9**

*TAKING STOCK:
REFINING YOUR THOUGHTS*

Look back at the statements you explored at the start of the chapter (see Thinking It Through on p. 319). Observe whether your attitudes have changed and what you have learned by studying this chapter.

1. List the four exam preparation actions that seem to fit your needs best.

_____

_____

_____

_____

2. What three strategies would you use to fight test or math anxiety?

_____

_____

_____

3. Describe four general test-taking strategies that may help improve your test performance.

_____

_____

_____

_____

4. Give one strategy for each type of question—multiple choice, short answer, and true-or-false.

_____

_____

_____

5. Describe a plan of action for answering essay questions.

_____

_____

_____

_____

6. Describe how you can benefit from reviewing mistakes you make on tests.

_____

_____

_____

7. Name one test-taking strategy you learned in this chapter and explain how you will apply it to your next exam.

_____

_____

_____

CRITICAL THINKING:
APPLYING LEARNING TO YOUR LIFE

Analyze Study Questions

Use a textbook, review book, or study guide for a course you're now taking. Look at the sample study and test questions in the book and complete these exercises:

In the space below, copy down two questions from your materials—perhaps one multiple-choice question and one true-or-false question. For each question, name a strategy or strategies from this chapter that will help you solve it and why.

Question 1: _____

_____

Strategy: _____

_____

Question 2: _____

_____

Strategy: _____

List two essay questions from your materials. For each, describe how a particular strategy or strategies from this chapter will help you answer the question.

Question 1: _____

_____

Strategy: _____

_____

Question 2: _____

_____

Strategy: _____

_____

Look back at Table 9–1, Common Action Verbs on Essay Tests. List the verbs from this table that are found in sample essay questions in your book. Define any verbs from your book that do not appear in the table.

_____

_____

_____

_____

Recognizing and Overcoming Math Anxiety

The following questions will help you learn whether or not you suffer from math anxiety. Answer each question in the space below. If you need more room, use additional paper.

Do you think of yourself as a good or a poor math student? What do you think has influenced your opinion of your mathematical ability?

_____

Are you more likely to freeze on a math test than on any other type of test? Why? Does your performance vary according to how much you study?

_____

_____

_____

When do you use math in real-life situations (such as finances)? How do you feel about it?

_____

_____

_____

When you were younger, do you remember doing well in math, or did you always have problems with the subject? If you can, recall and describe a specific experience that left an impression.

_____

_____

_____

After answering these questions, take a moment to think about the steps you will take to reduce your math anxiety in the future and to improve your test scores. Write down your thoughts:

_____

_____

_____

Test Analysis

When you get back your next test, in any course, take a detailed look at your performance.

1. Write what you think of your test performance and grade. Were you pleased or disappointed? If you made mistakes, were they careless errors or did you lack the facts and concepts?

_____

_____

_____

2. Next, list the test preparation activities that helped you do well on the exam and the activities you wish you had done—and intend to do—for the next exam.

Positive things I did: _____

_____

_____

_____

Positive actions I intend to take next time: _____

_____

_____

_____

3. Finally, list the activities you are not likely to repeat when studying for the next test.

_____

_____

_____

_____

Learning from Your Mistakes

For this exercise, use an exam on which you made one or more mistakes.

Why do you think you answered the question(s) incorrectly?

_____

_____

_____

Did any qualifiers such as *always, sometimes, never, often, occasionally,* or *only* make the question(s) more difficult or confusing? What steps could you have taken to clarify the meaning?

_____

_____

_____

_____

Did you try to guess the correct answer? If so, why do you think you made the wrong choice?

_____

_____

_____

_____

Did you feel rushed? If you had had more time, do you think you would have gotten the right answer(s)? What could you have done to budget your time more effectively?

_____

_____

_____

_____

If an essay question was a problem, what do you think went wrong? What will you do differently the next time you face an essay question on a test?

_____

_____

_____

_____

TEAMWORK: COMBINING FORCES

Study Partners. Choose a study partner in one of your classes. Work together to learn the material for a particular test. Use the checklist on the next page to quiz each other and measure how well you prepare.

Go through the entire checklist before the exam. Help each other overcome areas of weakness, and try to build each other's confidence and test-taking skills. After the exam, meet with your partner to evaluate the checklist. If you like, rewrite it according to your needs, adding new questions that you think should be included or crossing out questions that didn't seem to be necessary. Your improved checklist will help you do even better on the next exam.

_____ I asked the instructor what will be covered on the exam and the format of the test questions.

_____ I tried to learn as much as I could about the kinds of tests the instructor gives by talking to former students and getting copies of old exams.

_____ I used critical thinking to explore difficult concepts that might be on the test.

_____ I took a pretest.

_____ I tried to prepare my body and mind to perform at their best.

_____ I used positive self-talk and other techniques to overcome negative thoughts that might affect my performance.

_____ I have gotten my personal life under control so I can focus on the exam.

_____ I have a plan of action that I will follow when I see the test for the first time. I'll try to get an overview of the test, learn ground rules, schedule my time, and evaluate questions and choices in case I have to guess.

_____ I reviewed strategies for handling multiple-choice, true-or-false, and essay questions and feel comfortable with these.

WRITING: DISCOVERY THROUGH JOURNALING

To record your thoughts, use a separate journal or the lined pages at the end of the chapter.

Tests. Do you experience test anxiety? Describe how tests generally make you feel (you might include an example of a specific test situation and what happened). Identify your specific test-taking fears and write out your plan to overcome fears and self-defeating behaviors.

CAREER PORTFOLIO: CHARTING YOUR COURSE

Test taking and career investigation. Depending on what careers you are considering, you may encounter one or more tests—tests for entry into the field (such as the medical boards), tests on particular equipment (such as a proficiency test on Microsoft Word), or tests that are necessary to move to the next level of employment (such as a technical certification test). This portfolio exercise has two parts. If for any reason no potential career of yours involves tests, complete part two only.

Part one: Choose one career you are thinking about and investigate what tests are involved in entering this particular field. Be sure to look for tests in any of the areas described above. On a separate piece of paper, write down everything you find out about each test involved:

> ➤ What it tests you on
> ➤ When, in the course of pursuing this career, you would need to take the test
> ➤ What preparation is necessary for the test (including coursework)
> ➤ Whether the test will need to be retaken at any time (e.g., airline pilots usually need to be recertified every few years)

Once you have recorded your information, see if there is any possibility of looking at, or even taking, any of the tests you will face if you pursue this particular career. For example, if you will need to be tested on a computer program, your career center or computer center may have the test available. As a practice, look at and/or take any test that you can track down.

Part two: Your school's career center will have one or more "tests" that investigate your interests and abilities and make suggestions about what careers may be suitable for you. Explore the possibilities by taking one or more of these tests at the center. You may end up with results that match what you already want to do—or you may be surprised. Keep an open mind and take time to consider any surprises you encounter. Even if you do not want to follow any of the career areas suggested by the test, think about what the results say about you.

Name _____ Date _____ ●

Journal Entry

Name _____ Date _____

Journal Entry

CROSSWORD REVIEW: PART III
Sharpening Your Skills

ACROSS

5. Preliminary notes, including bibliographic information and a short summary, you take as you review available research
6. A bad case of nerves, occurring in an exam situation, that makes it difficult to think or remember
8. A note-taking system, also called T-note system, that divides a piece of paper into three sections
9. The act of using someone else's exact words, figure, approach, or reasoning without giving credit
11. The third stage of the writing process, involving the evaluation of word choice, paragraph structure, and style
12. A stream-of-consciousness technique that encourages you to put ideas down on paper as they occur to you, without censoring your ideas or worrying about
14. A restatement of a written text or passage in another form or other words, often to clarify meaning
15. A system of organizing notes or thoughts that uses line-by-line phrases set off by varying indentations
16. A descriptive word, such as *always*, *never*, or *often*, that changes the meaning of another word or word group
17. The fourth stage of the writing process, involving the correction of technical mistakes in spelling, grammar, and punctuation
18. A type of library information search that uses natural language

DOWN

1. A type of writing with the purpose of convincing readers to take the readers to take the writer's point of view
2. A notetaking or brainstorming technique that connects examples and ideas through the use of shapes connected by lines
3. A type of test question that offers several selections from which you are to choose the one you think is correct
4. Magazines, journals, and newspapers, which are published on a regular basis
7. A compact disk, containing words and image, that can be read by a computer
10. A type of test question that requires you to express an answer in terms of your knowledge and perspective
13. The reader or readers of any piece of written material

•PART 4

A PERSONAL FOCUS

CHAPTER **10** Relating to Others: Appreciating Your Diverse World

CHAPTER **11** Personal Wellness: Taking Care of Yourself

10 RELATING TO OTHERS: Appreciating Your Diverse World

Thinking It Through

Check those statements that apply to you right now:

❑ When I think of diversity, I think of different races and ethnic groups.
❑ I'm not quite sure why diversity should be important to me.
❑ My personal problems tend to overwhelm me.
❑ I have a difficult time functioning in a group.
❑ I avoid conflict because it makes me uncomfortable.

In this chapter, you will explore answers to the following questions:

➤ How can you understand and accept others?
➤ How can you express yourself effectively?
➤ How do your personal relationships define you?
➤ How can you handle conflict and criticism?
➤ What role do you play in groups?

The greater part of your waking life involves interaction with people—family and friends, peers, fellow students, coworkers, instructors, and many more. When you put energy into your relationships and open the lines of communication, you can receive much in return. Your relationships can also tell you a lot about the world and yourself. Having a strong network of relationships can help you grow and progress toward your goals.

As the world and its communities become more diverse, everyday life will bring you into contact with individuals who differ from you in many ways. This chapter will explore the issues of diversity that can affect the way in which you perceive others and relate to them. You will also explore communication styles, personal relationships, and the roles you can play in groups and on teams. Finally, you will read about various kinds of conflict and criticism, examining how to handle them so that they help you instead of setting you back.

HOW CAN YOU UNDERSTAND AND ACCEPT OTHERS?

Human interaction is an essential element of life. In a diverse world, many people are different from that which you are familiar with and perceive as "normal." Explore diversity in your world, the positive effects of accepting diversity, and how to overcome barriers to understanding. The first requirements for dealing with differences are an open mind and a willingness to learn.

Diversity in Your World

Diversity,
The variety that occurs in every aspect of humanity, involving both visible and invisible characteristics.

For centuries, travel to different countries was seen as part of a complete education. When cultures were so separated, learning about differences was best accomplished through travel. Today, although traveling is still a valuable way to learn, different places and people often come to you. More and more, diversity is part of your community, on your television, on your Internet browser, at your school, in your workplace, and in your family.

You may encounter examples of diversity like these:

> Communities with people from different stages of life
> Coworkers who represent a variety of ethnic origins
> Classmates who speak a number of different languages
> Social situations featuring people from various cultures, religions, and sexual orientations
> Individuals who marry a person or adopt a child from a different racial or religious background
> Diverse restaurants, services, and businesses in the community
> Neighborhoods with immigrants from a variety of class backgrounds
> Different lifestyles, as reflected in the media and popular culture
> People in the workplace who have a variety of disabilities—some more obvious than others

Each person has a choice about how to relate to others—or even whether to relate to them. No one can force you to interact with any other person or to adopt a particular attitude as being "right." Considering two important responsibilities may help you sort through your options:

Your responsibility to yourself lies in being true to yourself, in taking time to think through your reactions to other people. When you evaluate your thoughts, try also to consider their source: Have you heard these ideas from other people or organizations or the media? Do you agree with them? Through critical thinking you can arrive at decisions about which you feel comfortable and confident.

Your responsibility to others lies in treating people with tolerance and respect. No one will like everyone he or she meets, but acknowledging that others deserve respect and have a right to their opinions will build bridges of communication. The more people accept one another, the more all kinds of relationships will be able to thrive.

The Positive Effects of Diversity

More than just "a nice thing to do," accepting diversity has very real benefits to people in all kinds of relationships. Acceptance and respect form the basis for any successful interaction. As more situations bring diverse people into relationships, communication will become more and more dependent on acceptance and mutual understanding.

Consider how positive relationships with diverse people may contribute to success. Relationships among family, friends, and neighbors affect personal life. Relationships among students, instructors, and other school personnel affect student life. Relationships among coworkers, supervisors, and customers and clients affect work life. Understanding and communication in these relationships can bring positive effects such as satisfying relationships, achievement, and progress. Failure to understand and communicate well can have negative effects.

Consider, for example, a situation in which a male Hispanic employee has a female African-American supervisor. On the one hand, if the employee believes negative stereotypes about women or African-American people and resists taking directions from the supervisor, he may lose his job or be viewed as a liability. If the supervisor believes negative stereotypes about men or Hispanic people, she may treat him unfairly and deny the company the benefit of his skills. On the other hand, if both people can respect each another and consider with an open mind any different methods or ideas, their relationship is more likely to become supportive and productive. Both may be more likely to feel comfortable and perform well at work.

Accepting others isn't always easy, and it's common to let perceptions about people block your ability to communicate. Following are some barriers that can hinder your ability to accept and understand others and suggestions for how to overcome them.

Barriers to Understanding

You deserve to feel positive about who you are, where you come from, what you believe, and the others with whom you identify. However, problems arise when people use the power of group identity to put others down or cut themselves off from others. Table 10–1 shows how an open-minded approach can differ from an approach that is characterized by barriers.

Stereotypes, prejudice, discrimination, and fear of differences all can form barriers to communication.

TABLE 10-1   APPROACHES TO DIVERSITY

YOUR ROLE	SITUATION	CLOSED-MINDED APPROACH	OPEN-MINDED APPROACH
Fellow student	For an assignment, you are paired with a student old enough to be your mother.	You assume the student will be closed to the modern world. You think she might preach to you about how to do the assignment.	You get to know the student as an individual. You stay open to what you can learn from her experiences and knowledge.
Friend	You are invited to dinner at a friend's house. When he introduces you to his partner, you realize that he is gay.	You are turned off by the idea of two men in a relationship. You make an excuse to leave early. You avoid your friend after that evening.	You have dinner with the two men and make an effort to get to know more about what their lives are like and who they are individually and as a couple.
Employee	Your new boss is Japanese American, hired from a competing company.	You assume that your new boss is very hard-working, has demanding expectations, and doesn't take time to socialize.	You rein in your assumptions, knowing they are based on stereotypes, and approach your new boss with an open mind.

Stereotypes

An assumption is an idea that you accept without looking for proof (see Chapter 4). A **stereotype** is an assumption about a person or group of people based on one or more characteristics. You may have heard stereotypical assumptions such as these: "Women are too emotional for business"; "Hispanics are Catholic and have tons of kids"; "White people are cold and power-hungry"; "Gay people sleep around"; "Older people can't learn new things." Stereotypes are as common as they are destructive.

> **Stereotype,**
> A standardized mental picture that represents an oversimplified opinion or uncritical judgment.

Why might people stereotype? Here are a few reasons:

People seek patterns and logic. Trying to make sense of a complex world is part of human nature. People often try to find order by using the labels and categories that stereotypes provide.

Stereotyping is quick and easy. Making an assumption about a person from observing an external characteristic is easier than trying to know a person as a unique individual. Labeling a group of people according to a characteristic they seem to have in common takes less time and energy than exploring the differences and unique qualities within the group.

The media encourage stereotyping. The more people see stereotypical images—the unintelligent blonde the funny, overweight person—the easier it is to believe that such stereotypes are universal.

The ease of stereotypes comes at a high price. First and foremost, stereotypes can perpetuate harmful generalizations and falsehoods about others. These false ideas can promote discrimination. For example, if an employer believes that Iranian people cannot speak English well, he or she might not even bother to interview them. Second, stereotypes communicate the message that you don't respect others enough to discover who they really are. This may encourage others to stereotype you in return.

Addressing stereotypes. Recall from the critical-thinking material in Chapter 4 the questions you can ask about an assumption to examine its validity. Apply these questions to stereotypes:

1. In what cases is this stereotype true, if ever? In what cases is it not true?
2. Has stereotyping others benefited me or others? Has it hurt? How?
3. If someone taught me this stereotype, why? Did that person think it over or just accept it?
4. What harm could be done by always accepting this stereotype as true?

Using these steps, think about the stereotypes that you assume are true. When you hear someone else use a stereotype and you know some information that disproves it, volunteer that information. Encourage others to think through stereotypes and to reject them if they don't hold up under examination.

Give others the benefit of the doubt. Thinking beyond stereotypes is an important step toward more open lines of communication.

Hanging out outdoors on campus

Prejudice

Prejudice occurs when people prejudge (make a judgment before they have sufficient knowledge on which to base it). People often form prejudiced opinions on the basis of a particular characteristic—gender, race, sexual orientation, religion, and so on. You may be familiar with the labels for particular prejudices, such as *racism* (prejudice based on race) or *ageism* (prejudice based on age). Any group can be subjected to prejudice, although certain groups have more often been on the receiving end of closed-minded attitudes. Prejudice can lead people to show disrespect toward, harass, and put down others. In some cases, prejudice may lead to unrealistic expectations of others that aren't necessarily negative, such as if someone were to believe that all Jewish people excel in business.

Prejudice can have one or more causes. Some common causes include the following.

People experience the world through the lens of their own particular identity. You grow up in a particular culture and family and learn their attitudes. When you encounter different ideas, you may react by categorizing them. You may also react with **ethnocentrism** .

When people get hurt, they may dislike or blame anyone who seems similar to the person who hurt them. Judging others because of a bad experience is human, especially when a particular characteristic raises strong emotions.

Prejudice,
A preconceived judgment or opinion, formed without just grounds or sufficient knowledge.

Ethnocentrism,
The condition of thinking that one's particular ethnic group is superior to others.

Jealousy and fear of personal failure can lead a person to want to put others down. When people are feeling insecure about their own abilities, they might find it easier to devalue the abilities of others rather than to take risks and try harder themselves.

The many faces of prejudice often show on college campuses. A student may not want to work with students of another race. Campus clubs may tend to limit their membership to a particular group. Religious groups may devalue the beliefs of other religions. Groups that gather because of a common characteristic might be harassed by others. Students may find that instructors judge their abilities and attitudes according to their gender. All of these attitudes block attempts at mutual understanding.

Addressing prejudice. Being critical of people who are different cuts you off from perspectives and people that can enhance the quality of your life. Critical thinking is your key to changing prejudicial attitudes. For example, suppose you find yourself thinking that you don't want to get to know a certain student in your class. Ask yourself: Where did I get this attitude? Am I accepting someone else's judgment? Am I basing my judgments on how this person looks or speaks or behaves? How does having this attitude affect me or others? If you see that your attitude needs to change, have the courage to activate it by considering the person with an open, accepting mind.

Another tactic, and often an extremely difficult one, is to confront people you know when they display a prejudiced attitude. It can be hard to stand up to someone and risk a relationship or, if the person is your employer, even a job. On the other hand, your silence may imply that you agree. Evaluate the situation and decide what choice is more suitable and true to your values.

You have a range of choices when deciding whether to reveal your feelings about someone's behavior. You can decide not to address it at all. You may drop a humorous hint and hope that you make your point. You may make a small comment to test the waters and see how the person reacts. Whatever you do, express your opinion respectfully. Perhaps the other person will take that chance to rethink the attitude; perhaps not. Either way, you have taken an important stand.

Discrimination

Discrimination occurs when people deny others opportunities because of their perceived differences. Prejudice often accompanies discrimination. Discrimination can mean being denied jobs or advancement; equal educational opportunities; equal housing opportunities; services; or access to events, people, rights, privileges, or commodities.

Discrimination occurs in all kinds of situations, revolving around gender, language, race, culture, and other factors. For example, a thirty-two-year-old married woman may not get a job because the interviewer assumes that she will become pregnant. Sheryl McCarthy, an African-American columnist for *New York Newsday*, says in her book *Why Are the Heroes Always White?* "Nothing is quite so basic and clear as having a cab go right past your furiously waving body and pick up the white person next to you."[1] Even so-called majority populations may now experience the power of discrimination. For example, a qualified white man may be passed up for a promotion in favor of a female or minority employee.

Addressing discrimination. United States federal law states that it is unlawful for you to be denied an education, work or the chance to apply for work, housing, or basic rights based on your race, creed, color, age, gender, national or ethnic origin, religion, marital status, potential or actual pregnancy, or potential or actual illness or disability (unless the illness or disability prevents you from performing required tasks and unless accommodations for the disability are not possible). Unfortunately, the law is frequently broken, and incidents go unnoticed. Sometimes people don't report violations, fearing trouble from those they accuse. Other times people aren't aware of their discriminatory attitudes.

> "Minds are like parachutes. They only function when they are open."
>
> Sir James Dewar

First and foremost, be responsible for your own behavior. Never knowingly participate in or encourage discrimination. When you act on prejudicial attitudes by discriminating against someone, the barrier to communication it causes hurts you and anyone else involved. A person who feels denied and shut out may be likely to do the same to you, and may even encourage others to do so.

Second, if you witness a discriminatory act or feel that you have been discriminated against, decide whether you want to approach an authority. You may begin by talking to the person who can most directly affect the situation—an instructor or your supervisor. Don't assume that people know that they have hurt or offended someone. For example, if you have a disability and your school has not accommodated you, speak up. Meet with an advisor to discuss your needs for transport, equipment, or scheduling.

Fear of Differences

It's human instinct to fear the unknown. Many people allow their fears to prevent them from finding out about what's outside their known world. As cozy as that world can be, it also can be limiting, cutting off communication from people who could enrich the world in many different ways.

The fear of differences has many effects. A young person who fears the elderly may avoid visiting a grandparent in a nursing home. Someone in a relationship may fear the commitment of marriage. In each case, the person has denied himself or herself a chance to learn a new perspective, communicate with new individuals, and grow from new experiences.

Addressing fear of differences. Diversity doesn't mean that you have to feel comfortable with everyone or agree with what everyone else believes. The fear of differences, though, can keep you from discovering anything outside your own world. Challenge yourself by exposing yourself to differences. Today's world increasingly presents such opportunities. You can choose a study partner in class who has a different ethnic background. You can expand your knowledge with books or magazines. You can visit a part of town that introduces a culture new to you. Gradually broaden your horizons and consider new ideas.

If you think others are uncomfortable with differences, encourage them to work through their discomfort. Explain the difference so that it doesn't seem so mysterious. Offer to help them learn more in a setting that isn't threatening. Bring to others your message of the positive effects of diversity.

Accepting and Dealing with Differences

Successful interaction with the people around you depends on your ability to accept differences. Ask yourself important questions about what course of action you want to take. Realize that the opinions of family, friends, the media, and any group with which you identify may sometimes lead you into perspectives and actions that you haven't completely thought through. Do your best to sort through outside opinions and make a choice that feels right.

At the forefront of the list of ways to deal with differences is mutual respect. Respect for yourself and others is essential. Admitting that other people's cultures, behaviors, races, religions, appearances, and ideas deserve as much respect as your own promotes communication and learning.

What else can you do to accept and deal with differences?

Avoid judgments based on external characteristics. These include skin color, weight, facial features, or gender.

Cultivate relationships with people of different cultures, races, perspectives, and ages. Find out how other people live and think, and see what you can learn from them.

Educate yourself and others. "We can empower ourselves to end racism through massive education," say Tamara Trotter and Joycelyn Allen in *Talking Justice: 602 Ways to Build and Promote Racial Harmony.*[2] "Take advantage of books and people to teach you about other cultures. Empowerment comes through education." Read about other cultures and people.

Be sensitive to the particular needs of others at school and on the job. Try to put yourself in their place by asking yourself questions about what you would feel and do if you were in a similar situation.

Listen to people whose perspectives clash with or challenge your own. Acknowledge that everyone has a right to his or her opinion, whether or not you agree with it.

Look for common ground—parenting, classes, personal challenges, and interests.

Help other people, no matter how different they may be. Sheryl McCarthy writes about an African American who, in the midst of the 1992 Los Angeles riots, saw a man being beaten and helped him to safety. "When asked why he risked grievous harm to save an Asian man he didn't even know, Williams said, 'Because if I'm not there to help someone else, when the mob comes for me, will there be someone there to save me?'"[3] Continue the cycle of kindness.

Explore your own background, beliefs, and identity. Share what you learn with others.

Cultivate your own personal diversity. Perhaps your father is Native American and Scottish, and your mother is Creole (French, Spanish, and African American). Respect and explore your heritage. Even if you identify with only one group or culture, there are many different sides of you.

Take responsibility for making changes instead of pointing the finger at someone else. Avoid blaming problems in your life on certain groups of people.

Learn from the atrocities of history like slavery and the Holocaust. Cherish the level of freedom you have and seek continual improvement at home and elsewhere in the world.

Teach your children about other cultures. Impress on them the importance of appreciating differences while accepting that all people have equal rights.

Recognize that people everywhere have the same basic needs. Everyone loves, thinks, hurts, hopes, fears, and plans. People are united through their essential humanity.

Expressing your ideas clearly and interpreting what others believe are crucial keys to communicating in a diverse world. Particular strategies can help you communicate effectively with those around you.

THINKING BACK

1. If you were writing a dictionary entry, how would you define the word *diversity*?

   _____

   _____

   _____

2. Name three ways in which diversity has an effect on modern life.

   a. _____

   b. _____

   c. _____

3. What are three diversity-related barriers that can block communication among people?

   a. _____

   b. _____

   c. _____

4. What are some reasons people tend to stereotype?

_____

_____

_____

5. Of the ways a person can accept and deal with differences, what three seem most important to you? Why?

_____

_____

_____

THINKING AHEAD

1. How would you describe yourself as a communicator? How do you prefer to get your message across?

_____

_____

_____

2. What actions do you take to strengthen your personal relationships?

_____

_____

_____

3. How does conflict make you feel? How do you tend to deal with it?

_____

_____

4. In a group situation at school, work, or with friends or family, what role do you tend to play?

_____

_____

_____

HOW CAN YOU EXPRESS YOURSELF EFFECTIVELY?

The only way for people to know one another's needs is to communicate as clearly and directly as possible. Successful communication promotes successful school, work, and personal relationships. Addressing communication issues will help you express yourself effectively.

Addressing Communication Issues

Communication is an exchange between two or more people. The speaker's goal is for the listener (or listeners) to receive the message as the speaker intends. Different people, however, have different styles of communicating. Communication problems may occur when information is not clearly presented or when those who receive information filter it through their own perspectives and interpret it differently. Some of the most common communication issues follow, along with strategies to help you solve them.

Issue: Different styles of communication

Solution: Be aware of the styles of others

It doesn't matter how clear you think you are being if the person you are speaking to can't "translate" your message by understanding your style. Try to take your listener's style into consideration when you communicate. For example, if you are critiquing the essay of a fellow student who tends to focus on detail, saying, "You introduced your central idea at the beginning but then didn't really support it until the fourth paragraph" is far more effective than saying, "Your writing isn't clear."

Conversely, when you are the listener, be aware of the communication style of the person who is speaking to you. As a facet of communication, listening is just as important as speaking. Try to translate the speaker's message into one that makes sense to you. For example, if an employee of yours tends to focus on emotion more than you do, consider his or her messages in that light.

Issue: Communication that goes beyond words

Solution: Become aware of body language

Your actions—gestures, eye movement, facial expression, body positioning and posture, touching behavior, and use of personal space—are the most basic form of communication, called body language. Body language can reinforce or contradict verbal statements. When body language contradicts verbal language, the message conveyed by the body is dominant. Consider, for example, if someone were to ask you how you feel, and you said "Fine" although you don't feel fine at all. In such a case your posture, eye contact, and other body language would convey the real message loud and clear.

To make the most of body language, pay attention to what other people communicate nonverbally. Also, keep an eye on your own body language, and make sure that it reinforces your words and does not confuse anyone to whom you are speaking. Finally, be aware of cultural differences. In the United States, for example, making eye contact is valued, whereas in some other cultures looking an authority figure or superior directly in the eye is considered disrespectful.

Issue: Unclear or incomplete explanation

Solution: Support ideas with examples

When you clarify a general idea with supporting examples that illustrate how it works and what effects it causes, you will help your receiver understand what you mean and therefore have a better chance at holding his or her attention.

For example, if you tell a friend to take a certain class, that person might not take you seriously until you explain why. If you then communicate the positive effects of taking that class (progress toward a major, an excellent instructor, and friendly study sessions), you may get your message across. Work situations benefit from explanation as well. If you assign a task without explanation, you might get a delayed response or find mistakes in your employees' work. If, however, you explain the possible positive effects of the task, you'll have better results.

Issue: Attacking the receiver

Solution: Send "I" messages

When a conflict arises, often the first instinct is to pinpoint what someone else did wrong: "You didn't lock the door!" "You never called last night!" Making an accusation, especially without proof, puts the other person on the defensive and shuts down the lines of communication.

Using "I" messages will help you communicate your own needs rather than focusing on what you think someone else should do differently: "I felt uneasy when I came to work and the door was unlocked." "I became worried about you when I didn't hear from you last night." "I" statements soften the conflict by highlighting the effects that the other person's actions have had on you, rather than the person or the actions themselves. When you focus on your own response and needs, your receiver may feel more free to respond, perhaps offering help and even acknowledging mistakes.

● Issue: Passive or aggressive communication styles

Solution: Become assertive

Among the three major communication styles—aggressive, passive, and assertive—the one that conveys a message in the clearest, most productive way is the   assertive   style. The other two, although commonly used, throw the communication out of balance. Assertive behavior strikes a balance between aggression and passivity. If you can be an assertive communicator, you will be more likely to get your message across while ensuring that others have a chance to speak as well. Table 10–2 compares some characteristics of each kind of communicator.

Assertive, Able to declare and affirm one's own opinions while respecting the rights of others to do the same.

Aggressive communicators focus primarily on their own needs. They can become angry and impatient when those needs are not immediately satisfied. To become more assertive, aggressive communicators might try to take time to think before speaking, avoid ordering people around, use "I" statements, and focus on listening to what the other person has to say.

Passive communicators deny themselves the power that aggressive people grab. They focus almost exclusively on the needs of others instead of on their own needs, experiencing unexpressed frustration and tension. To become more assertive, passive communicators might try to acknowledge anger or hurt more often, speak up when they feel strongly about something, realize that they have a right to make requests, and know that their ideas and feelings are as important as anyone else's.

● Communication is extremely important for building and maintaining personal relationships. Explore the role those relationships play in who you are.

TABLE 10-2   AGGRESSIVE, PASSIVE, AND ASSERTIVE STYLES

AGGRESSIVE	PASSIVE	ASSERTIVE
Loud, heated arguing	Concealing one's own feelings	Expressing feelings without being nasty or overbearing
Physically violent encounters	Denying one's own anger	Acknowledging emotions but staying open to discussion
Blaming, name-calling, and verbal insults	Feeling that one has no right to express anger	Expressing self and giving others the chance to express themselves equally
Walking out of arguments before they are resolved	Avoiding arguments	Using "I" statements to defuse arguments
Being demanding: "Do this"	Being noncommittal: "You don't have to do this unless you really want to"	Asking and giving reasons: "I would appreciate it if you would do this, and here's why…"

HOW DO YOUR PERSONAL RELATIONSHIPS DEFINE YOU?

The relationships you have with friends, family members, and significant others often take center stage. The people with whom you share your life help to define who you are. Since birth, you have acquired knowledge from their verbal and nonverbal language. Those with whom you live, play, study, and work are primary sources of ideas, beliefs, and ways of living.

These influential relationships can affect other areas of your life. On the one hand, you may have experienced conflict that caused you to be unable to sleep, eat, or get any work done. On the other hand, a successful relationship can have positive effects on your life, increasing your success at work or at school.

A couple sit together in the park in autumn

Relationship Strategies

If you can feel good about your personal relationships, other areas of your life will benefit. Here are some strategies for improving your personal relationships.

Make personal relationships a high priority. Nurture the ones you have and be open to new ones. Life is meant to be shared. In some marriage ceremonies, the bride and groom share a cup of wine, symbolizing that the sweetness of life is doubled by tasting it together, and the bitterness is cut in half when shared by two. Any personal relationship can benefit from the experience of this kind of sharing.

Invest time. You devote time to education, work, and the other priorities in your life. Relationships need the same investment. In addition, spending time with people you like can relieve everyday stress and strain. When you make time for others, everyone benefits.

Spend time with people you respect and admire. Life is too short to hang out with people who bring you down, encourage you to participate in activities you don't approve of, or behave in ways that upset you. Develop relationships with people whom you respect, whose choices you admire, and who inspire you to fulfill your potential.

Work through tensions. Negative feelings can multiply when left unspoken. Unexpressed feelings about other issues may cause you to become disproportionately angry over a small issue. Get to the root of the problem. Discuss it, deal with it, and move on.

Refuse to tolerate violence. It isn't easy to face the problem of violence or to leave a violent relationship. People may tolerate violence out of a belief that it will end, a desire to keep their families together, a self-esteem so low that they believe they deserve what they get, or a fear that trying to leave may lead to greater violence. If you find that you are either an aggressor or a victim, do your best to get help.

Show appreciation. If you think of something positive, say it. Thank some- one for a service or express your affection with a smile. A little positive re- inforcement goes a long way toward nurturing a relationship.

If you want a friend, be a friend. If you treat a friend with the kind of loy- alty and support that you appreciate yourself, you are more likely to receive the same in return.

Take risks. It can be frightening to reveal your deepest dreams and frustra- tions, to devote yourself to a friend, or to fall in love. However, giving is what makes a relationship grow. If you take the plunge, you stand to gain the incredible benefits of companionship, which for most people outweigh the risks.

Keep personal problems in their place. Solve personal problems with the people directly involved and no one else. If at all possible, try not to bring your emotions into class or work. Doing so may hurt your performance while doing nothing to help your problem.

If a relationship doesn't work out, find ways to cope. Everyone experiences strain and breakups in intimate relationships, friendships, and family ties. Be kind to yourself and use coping strategies that help you move on. Some people need lots of time alone; others spend time with other friends and family. Some seek counseling. Some people throw their energy into a pro- ject, job, class, or new workout regimen. Some write in a journal or write letters to the person that they never mail. Do what's right for you, and be- lieve that sooner or later you can emerge from the experience stronger and with new perspective.

Now and again, your personal relationships will be in conflict. Follow- ing are ideas for how to deal with conflict and criticism in a productive and positive way.

HOW CAN YOU HANDLE CONFLICT AND CRITICISM?

Conflict and criticism, as unpleasant as they can be, are natural elements in the dynamic of getting along with others. It's normal to want to avoid peo- ple or situations that cause distress. However, if you can face your fears and think about them critically, you can gain valuable insight into human na- ture—your own and that of others. You may be able to make important changes in your life based on what you learn.

Conflict Strategies

Conflicts, both large and small, arise when there is a clash of ideas or interests. You may have small conflicts with a housemate over food left out overnight, a door left unlocked, or a bill that needs paying. On the other end of the spectrum, you might encounter major conflicts with your partner about finances; with an instructor about a failing grade; or with a person who treats you unfairly because of your race, gender, age, or ethnic origin.

Conflict can create anger and frustration, shutting down communication. The two most destructive tendencies are to avoid the conflict altogether (a passive tactic) or to let it escalate into a huge fight (an aggressive tendency). On the one hand, avoidance doesn't make the problem go away; in fact, it will probably worsen. On the other hand, a shouting match gives no one an opportunity or desire to listen.

If calmly and intelligently handled, conflict can shed light on new ideas and help to strengthen bonds between those involved. The primary keys to conflict resolution are calm communication and critical-thinking skills. Think through any conflict using what you know about problem solving.

Identify and analyze the problem. Determine the severity of the problem by looking at its effects on everyone involved. Then, find and analyze its causes.

Brainstorm possible solutions. Consider as many angles as you can, without judgment. Explore what ideas you can come up with from what you or others have done in a similar situation.

Explore each solution. Evaluate the positive and negative effects of each solution. Why might each work, not work, or work partially? What would take into account everyone's needs? What would cause the least stress? Make sure everyone has a chance to express an opinion.

Choose, carry out, and evaluate the solution you decide is best. When you have implemented your choice, evaluate its effects. Decide whether you feel it was a good choice.

One more hint: Use "I" statements. Focus on the effects the problem has had on you rather than focusing on someone who caused it.

Dealing with Criticism and Feedback

Feedback,
Evaluate or corrective information about an action or process.

Constructive,
Promoting improvement or development.

No one gets everything right all the time. People use constructive criticism and **feedback** to communicate what went wrong and to suggest improvements. Consider any criticism carefully. If you always interpret criticism as a threat, you will close yourself off from learning. Even if you eventually decide that you disagree, you can still learn from exploring the possibility. Know that you are strong enough to embrace criticism and become a better person because of it.

Criticism can be either **constructive** or nonconstructive. Criticism is considered constructive when it is offered supportively and contains useful suggestions for improvement. In contrast, nonconstructive criticism focuses on what went wrong, doesn't offer alternatives or help, and is often delivered in a negative or harsh manner. Whereas constructive criticism can promote a sense of hope for improvement in the future, nonconstructive criticism can create tension, bad feelings, and defensiveness.

Any criticism can be offered constructively or nonconstructively. Consider a case in which someone has continually been late to work. A supervisor can offer criticism in either of these ways:

Constructive. The supervisor talks privately with the employee: "I've noticed that you have been late to work a lot. Other people have had to do some of your work. Is there a problem that is keeping you from being on time? Is it something that I or someone else can help you with?"

Nonconstructive. The supervisor watches the employee slip into work late. The supervisor says, in front of other employees, "Nice to see you could make it. If you can't start getting here on time, I might look for someone else who can."

If you can learn to give constructive criticism and deal with whatever criticism comes your way from others, you will improve your relationships and your productivity. When offered constructively and carefully considered, criticism can bring about important changes.

Giving Constructive Criticism

When you offer criticism, use the following steps to communicate clearly and effectively:

1. *Criticize the behavior rather than the person.* Make sure the behavior you intend to criticize is changeable. Chronic lateness can be changed; a physical inability to perform a task cannot.
2. *Define specifically the behavior you want to change.* Try not to drag any side issues into the conversation.
3. *Balance criticism with positive words.* Alternate critical comments with praise in other areas.
4. *Stay calm and be brief.* Avoid threats, ultimatums, or accusations. Use "I" messages. Choose positive, nonthreatening words so the person knows that your intentions are positive.
5. *Explain the effects caused by the behavior that warrants the criticism.* Help the person understand why a change needs to occur, and talk about options in detail. Compare and contrast the effects of the current behavior with the effects of a potential change.
6. *Offer help in changing the behavior.* Lead by example.

Receiving Criticism

When you find yourself on the receiving end of criticism, use these coping techniques:

1. *Listen to the criticism before you speak up.* Resist the desire to defend yourself until you've heard all the details. Decide if the criticism is offered in a constructive or nonconstructive manner.

> "Do not use a hatchet to remove a fly from your friend's forehead."
>
> Chinese proverb

2. *Think the criticism through critically.* Evaluate it carefully. Whereas some criticism may come from a desire to help, other comments may have less honorable origins. People often criticize others out of jealousy, anger, frustration, or displaced feelings. In cases like those, it is best (though not always easy) to let the criticism wash right over you.

3. *If the criticism is nonconstructive, try not to respond right away.* Nonconstructive criticism can inspire anger that might be destructive. Cool down first, and think about the criticism to see if there is anything important hiding under the way in which it was presented. Then, tell the person that you see the value of the criticism, but also communicate how its delivery made you feel.

4. *If it is constructive, ask for suggestions on how to change the criticized behavior.* You could ask, "How would you handle this if you were in my place?"

5. *Before the conversation ends, summarize the criticism and your response to it.* Repeat it back to the person who offered it. Make sure both of you understand the situation in the same way.

6. *If you feel that the criticism is valid, plan a specific strategy for correcting the behavior.* Think over what you might learn from changing your behavior. If you don't agree with the criticism even after the whole conversation, explain your behavior from your point of view.

Remember that the most important feedback you will receive in school is from your instructors, and the most important on-the-job feedback will come from your supervisors, more experienced peers, and occasionally clients. Making a special effort to take in this feedback and consider it carefully will help you learn many important lessons. Furthermore, knowing how to handle conflict and criticism will help you define your role and communicate with others when you work in groups.

WHAT ROLE DO YOU PLAY IN GROUPS?

Group interaction is an important part of your educational, personal, and working life. With a team project at work or a cooperative learning exercise in school, for example, being able to work well together is necessary to accomplish a goal.

The two major roles in the group experience are those of participant and leader. Any group needs both to function successfully. Become aware of the role you tend to play when relating to others. Try different roles to help you decide where you can be most effective. The following strategies (from *Contemporary Business Communication*, by Louis E. Boone, David L. Kurtz, and Judy R. Block) are linked to either participating or leading.[4]

WINDOWS ON THE WORLD: REAL LIFE STUDENT ISSUES

How can I deal with diversity?

Richard Pan, Columbia University, New York City, Engineering Major

I was born in Taiwan and came to the United States when I was twelve. At my high school in Santa Barbara, CA, everyone mingled well. Caucasian kids hung out with Asians and African Americans and we all got along fine. Then when I started college at Columbia University I noticed a difference. The Asian kids hung out only with other Asians, and the Caucasians did the same. I'm used to hanging out with all sorts of people, and I like that. Now I feel this tension. It's as if the Asian kids are thinking, "Why is he bothering to hang out with them?"

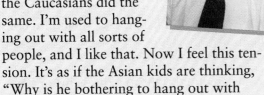

During a summer work program at Harvard I roomed with a Chinese American who advised me to avoid being friends with people from different ethnic groups. Although I don't feel comfortable with his advice, I do think you get judged by both sides when you try to be friends with everybody. Sometimes if I'm with a Caucasian person and other Caucasian people approach us they aren't as friendly, talking only to the other Caucasian kid as if I'm not there. Whenever I've tried to talk to my Asian friends about this problem they respond jokingly, saying something like, "Rich, you're just better at doing that [mingling with other groups] than I am."

Sometimes I feel as if I'm having an identity crisis. I ask myself, "Which side am I on?" I'm not really Asian American because I wasn't born here, but I have become accustomed to America and I like living here. I think overall I've handled the situation pretty well, but I am open to suggestions. Do you have any ideas about how I could do a better job managing this problem?

Jo Anne Roe, Spanish Instructor, Oak Park–River Forest High School

It is wonderful that you have developed the ability to mingle with and enjoy the company of people from diverse backgrounds. This skill will be immensely valuable for your personal and professional future. Your comfort in a multicultural setting reflects self-assurance, maturity, and a clearly defined sense of identity.

The problem which you face—prejudice—does not originate within you, but rather is being imposed upon you. Misunderstanding of, apprehension toward, and nonacceptance of others who are different are facets of an elemental and, sadly, universal flaw in the human psyche. And because it is so painful, it is natural for people to guard themselves against its damage.

Perhaps your Caucasian friends display insensitivity out of fear of being rejected by their peers. Perhaps these same students believe they accept you so completely that not to show that they are aware of your presence is evidence that you are "one of the guys." I imagine that the other Asians are advising you out of sincere concern for you not to be hurt by those with whom they have had negative encounters in the past.

The best advice that I can offer to you is the Golden Rule: Treat other people the way you want them to treat you. In following the wisdom of this refrain, you neither compromise your own outlook on life nor give in to the fears and insecurities of other people, and you maintain human dignity in general. Continue as you are and be patient. Eventually you will begin to see gradual and positive changes in the actions of your friends and family, directly due to the impact you will have made on them through your positive, accepting attitude.

Being an Effective Participant

Some people are happiest when participating in group activities that someone else leads and designs. They don't feel comfortable having the power to set the tone for the group as a whole. They prefer to help things run smoothly by taking on an assigned role in the project and seeing it through. Participators need to remember that they are "part owners" of the process. Each team member has a responsibility for, and a stake in, the outcome. The following strategies will help a participant to be effective.

Participation Strategies

Get involved. If a group decision you don't like is made, and you stayed uninvolved in the decision, you have no one to blame but yourself for not speaking up. Let people know your views. You are as important a team member as anyone else, and your views are likewise valuable.

Be organized. When you participate, stay focused and organized. The more organized your ideas are, the more people will listen, take them into consideration, and be willing to try them.

Be willing to discuss. Everyone has an equal right to express his or her ideas. Even as you enthusiastically present your opinions, be willing to consider those of others.

Keep your word. Do what you say you're going to do. Let people know what you have accomplished. If you bring little or nothing to the process, your team may feel as if you weigh them down.

Focus on ideas, not people. One of the easiest ways to start an argument is for participants to attack people instead of discussing their ideas. Separate the person from the idea, and keep the idea in focus.

Play fairly. Give everyone a chance to participate. Be respectful of other people's ideas. Don't dominate the discussion or try to control or manipulate others.

Being an Effective Leader

Some people prefer to initiate the action, make decisions, and control how things proceed. They have ideas they want to put into practice and enjoy explaining them to others. They are comfortable giving directions to people and guiding group outcomes. Leaders often have a big-picture perspective; it allows them to see how all the different aspects of a group project can come together. In any group the following strategies will help a leader succeed.

Leadership Strategies

Define and limit projects. One of the biggest ways to waste time and energy is to assume that a group will know its purpose and will limit tasks on its own. The leader should define the purpose of the gathering and limit tasks so the group doesn't take on too much.

Map out who will perform which tasks. A group functions best when everyone has a particular contribution to make. You don't often choose whom you work with—in school, at work, or in your family—but you can help different personalities work together by exploring who can do what best. Give people specific responsibilities and trust that they will do their jobs.

Set the agenda. The leader is responsible for establishing and communicating the goal of the project and how it will proceed. Without a plan, it's easy to get off track. Having a written agenda to which group members can refer is helpful. A good leader invites advice from others when determining group direction.

Focus progress. Even when everyone knows the plan, it's still natural to wander off the topic. The leader should try to rein in the discussion when necessary, doing his or her best to keep everyone to the topic at hand. When challenges arise midstream, the leader may need to help the team change direction.

Set the tone. Group members bring different attitudes and mental states to a gathering. Setting a positive tone helps to bring the group together and motivate people to peak performance.

Evaluate results. The leader should determine whether the team is accomplishing its goals. If the team is not moving ahead, the leader needs to make changes and decisions.

If you don't believe that you fit into the traditional definition of a leader, remember that there are other ways to lead that don't involve taking charge of a group. You can lead others by setting an honorable example in your actions, choices, or words. You can lead by putting forth an idea that takes a group in a new direction. You can lead by being the kind of person whom others would like to be.

It takes the equal participation of all group members to achieve a goal. Whatever role works best for you, know that your contribution is essential. You may even play different roles with different groups. You might be a participator at school and a leader in a self-help group. You could enjoy leading a religious group but prefer to take a back seat at work. Find a role that feels comfortable. The happier each group member is, the more effectively the group as a whole will function.

Kente

The African word *kente* means "that which will not tear under any condition." *Kente* cloth is worn by men and women in African countries like Ghana, Ivory Coast, and Togo. There are many brightly colored patterns of *kente*, each beautiful, unique, and special.

Think of how this concept applies to being human. Like the cloth, all people are unique, with brilliant and subdued aspects. Despite any mistreatment or misunderstanding by the people you encounter in your life, you need to remain strong so that you don't tear and give way to disrespectful behavior. This strength can help you to endure, stand up against any injustice, and fight peacefully but relentlessly for the rights of all people.

IMPORTANT POINTS TO REMEMBER

1. How can you understand and accept others?

Your success in school, work, and personal life may depend on how well you can interact with diverse people. Understanding and communication are the keys to interaction. Stereotypes, prejudice, discrimination, and fear of differences can block understanding. Keep an open mind and work to overcome those blocks. If you can accept and promote differences, you will have the greatest chance of broadening your knowledge and relating successfully.

2. How can you express yourself effectively?

Effective communication is one important key to successful relationships. Addressing communication issues—such as different communication styles, body language, unclear explanations, assumptions, and passive or aggressive communication styles—will help.

3. How do your personal relationships define you?

The important people in your life are some of your primary sources of information. As you discover their ideas, beliefs, and ways of doing things, you evaluate that information and decide whether to make it part of who you are. Successful relationships depend on strategies such as investing time, working through tensions, showing appreciation, taking risks, and keeping personal problems in their place. Mentoring relationships can be of special support.

4. How can you handle conflict and criticism?

Conflict and criticism are a natural part of human relationships. Conflicts arise when there is a clash of ideas or interests. Successful conflict resolution requires that you stay assertive, think critically, and use "I" statements. Constructive criticism can help you learn and improve. When giving criticism, avoid accusations and be specific about the behavior you want to criticize. When receiving criticism, listen before you judge and think critically about the criticism. If you agree with it, ask for suggestions of how to change and plan a strategy for doing so.

5. What role do you play in groups?

Individuals play particular roles in groups. The two primary roles are those of leader and participant. Leadership strategies include defining and limiting tasks, setting the agenda and tone, and focusing on progress. Participant strategies include getting involved, being organized, being willing to discuss, and focusing on ideas. The more efficient each group member is, the more effectively the group will function.

Name _____ Date _____

**BUILDING SKILLS FOR COLLEGE, CAREER, AND LIFE SUCCESS
CHAPTER 10**

TAKING STOCK:
REFINING YOUR THOUGHTS

Look back at the statements you explored at the start of the chapter (see Thinking It Through on p. 355). Observe whether your attitudes have changed and what you have learned by studying this chapter.

1. Describe four examples of human diversity other than race or ethnicity.

_____

_____

_____

_____

_____

2. Describe one example of a situation in your life that shows the importance of diversity.

_____

_____

_____

3. What are three ways to improve communication in your relationships?

_____

_____

_____

4. In a group, are you more of a leader or a participant? Name three strategies for success in the role you choose.

_____

_____

_____

5. Discuss a strategy for facing and working through conflict.

_____

_____

_____

6. Name one strategy from this chapter that you think will help you communicate better. State how you plan to put it to use.

_____

_____

_____

CRITICAL THINKING:
APPLYING LEARNING TO YOUR LIFE

Diversity Discovery

Express your own personal diversity. Describe yourself in response to the following questions.

What ethnic background(s) do you have?

_____

_____

Name one or more facts about you that someone wouldn't know from simply looking at you.

_____

_____

Name two values or beliefs that govern how you live, what you pursue, and/or with whom you associate.

_____

_____

What other characteristics or choices define your uniqueness?

_____

_____

Now, join with a partner in your class. Try to choose someone you don't know well. Your goal is to communicate what you have written to your partner, and for your partner to communicate to you in the same way. Talk to each other for ten minutes and take notes on what the other person says. At the end of that period, join together as a class. Each person will describe his or her partner to the class.

What did you learn about your partner that surprised you?

What did you learn that went against any assumptions you may have made about that person based on his or her appearance, background, or behavior?

Has this exercise changed the way you see this person or other people? Why or why not?

The "I"s Have It

In your quest for better communication, rewrite the following sentences so that they are in the less accusatory "I"-message style. Check your answers with other students and/or with your instructor.

1. You blew it completely.

2. Why didn't you tell me the meeting time was changed?

3. You always forget to pick me up.

4. What does it take for you to understand how this machine works?

5. Where did you put the stapler? Did you lose it?

6. You are impossible to understand when you talk like that.

Criticism

Think about any criticism of yourself that you have ignored or rejected.
Choose one item of criticism and write it here.

Now, be honest with yourself. Do you agree with this criticism? Why? How
did the criticism make you feel? How was it delivered?

Based on what you are learning from exploring this criticism, name a
change you plan to make to improve what was criticized or how you react
to criticism.

TEAMWORK:
COMBINING FORCES

Problem solving close to home. Divide into small groups
of two to five. Assign one group member to take notes. Discuss the following questions, one by one:

1. What are the three largest problems my school faces with regard to
   how people get along with and accept others?
2. What could my school do to deal with these three problems?
3. What can each individual student do to deal with these three problems? (Talk about what you specifically feel that you can do.)

When you are finished, gather as a class and hear each group's responses. Observe the variety of problems and solutions. Notice whether more than one group came up with one or more of the same problems. You may want to assign one person in the class to gather all of the responses. That person, together with your instructor, could put these responses into an organized document that you can give to the upper-level administrators at your school.

WRITING: DISCOVERY THROUGH JOURNALING

To record your thoughts, use a separate journal or the lined pages at the end of the chapter.

New perspective.[5] Imagine that you have no choice but to change either your gender or your racial, ethnic, or religious group. Which would you change, and why? What do you anticipate would be the positive and negative effects of the change—in your social life, in your family life, on the job, and at school? How would what you know and experience before the change affect how you would behave after it?

CAREER PORTFOLIO: CHARTING YOUR COURSE

Letters of recommendation. It is important to have letters of recommendation from people who know and respect you. Use them when you apply for jobs, internships, scholarships, or academic programs.

First, create a list of people who have served or could serve as references for you. Brainstorm names from all areas of your human resources:

Instructors	Friends	Present/former employers
Administrators	Family members	Mentors
Counselors	Present/former coworkers	Students

Make a chart that looks like the one that follows (add as many rows as you need). Fill in the information for each reference.

Update the information on this chart as you meet potential references or lose touch with old ones. Keep it on hand for these occasions in which you need a new letter or want to cite a reference on a résumé.

Next, decide which three people you would like to approach to write a letter for you. Choose people who know you well and who have seen you in action, either in school or at work. You will want your references to em-

NAME	ADDRESS	PHONE NUMBER	ASSOCIATION
Jo Trenholm	727 Mercury Way Boston, MA	(617) 555-2808	Current supervisor

phasize your strengths and to discuss qualities like open-mindedness, ability to be a team player, and interpersonal relations. Letters should also contain references to your specific skills, capabilities, and style of working and thinking.

If you have a specific purpose for your letter right now, ask your three references to write letters that suit that purpose. If you don't, keep the information on hand until you do.

When references write letters for you, be sure to thank them right away for their help and to keep them up to date on your activities. Always let a reference know when you have sent a letter out, so that he or she may be prepared to receive a call from the person, company, or program to which you have applied.

Name _____ Date _____

Journal Entry

Name _____ Date _____

Journal Entry

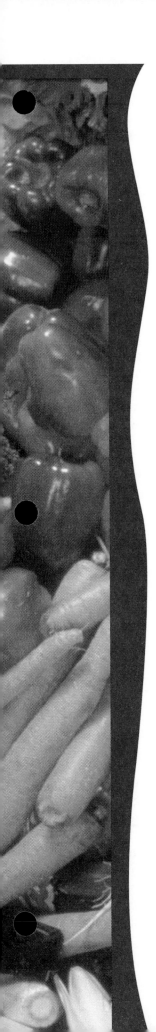

PERSONAL WELLNESS:
Taking Care of Yourself

Thinking It Through

Check those statements that apply to you right now:

☐ I eat a pretty balanced diet.
☐ I'm exhausted a lot of the time.
☐ I have too much stress in my life.
☐ I am in control when it comes to alcohol and drugs.
☐ I don't know much about what it means to be addicted.
☐ I've made sexual decisions in the heat of the moment that I've regretted later.

In this chapter, you will explore answers to the following questions:

➤ How can you maintain a healthy body?
➤ How do you nurture a healthy mind?
➤ How are alcohol, tobacco, and drugs used and abused?
➤ What should you consider when making sexual decisions?

Your mind and body may seem like two independent parts. Consider, though, that your brain is an organ. Just like any other organ, its functioning depends on the health of your body. In this way, an afternoon of in-line skating or a healthy meal can improve your mind. The mind influences the body as well; for example, a positive outlook on life can improve your body's ability to handle stress. Your body and mind are intimately connected and affect one another.

Because of the strong mind-body connection, your physical and mental health affect your ability to succeed in school. It doesn't matter how great your classes are if you aren't physically healthy enough to get to them or mentally healthy enough to focus and learn while you're there. In this chapter you will examine both the physical and mental aspects of wellness, looking at how to maintain your health, as well as how to identify and work through particular health problems that many students face.

HOW CAN YOU MAINTAIN A HEALTHY BODY?

Your daily schedule may leave little time to take good care of yourself. As you complete assignments for class, work at your job, take care of your family, keep up with friends, and/or do chores, you may find yourself feeling stressed. It's important to take time to focus on you. The healthier you are, the more energy you'll have both for yourself and for those who share your life. Eating right, exercising, and getting enough sleep will help you maintain a healthy body.

Eating Right

The food and drink you take in, along with the air you breathe, help build and maintain your body. If you eat well, you are more likely to be strong and healthy. If you take in too much fat, sugar, processed foods, and other nonnutritional substances, your body will operate at reduced power. Learning to make healthier choices about what you eat on a daily basis can lead to more energy, better general health, and an enriched quality of life.

The U.S. Departments of Agriculture and of Health and Human Services have developed a publication called *Dietary Guidelines for Americans*, which lists seven important rules of healthy eating:

1. Eat a variety of foods.
2. Maintain a healthy weight.
3. Choose a diet low in fat and cholesterol.
4. Choose a diet with plenty of vegetables, fruits, and grain products.
5. Use sugars in moderation.
6. Use salt and sodium only in moderation.
7. If you drink alcoholic beverages, do so in moderation.

Maintaining balance and eating in moderation are two guidelines that can help you maintain a healthy diet.

> "To keep the body in good health is a duty. Otherwise we shall not be able to keep our mind strong and clear."
>
> Buddha

Maintaining Balance

If you vary your diet with foods from the different food groups—meats and meat substitutes, dairy, breads and grains, and fruits and vegetables—you are more likely to take in the different nutrients your body needs. Figure 11–1 shows the servings that the U. S. Department of Agriculture recommends. Nutritionists emphasize fruits and vegetables, recommending five servings from that group per day. If that sounds difficult, consider this example: a banana or a glass of juice at breakfast, a salad at lunch (worth two vegetables), an apple for a snack, and green beans with dinner. A good food balance will also help you minimize your intake of fat, which is concentrated mostly in the meat and dairy groups.

FOOD GUIDE PYRAMID **FIGURE 11-1**

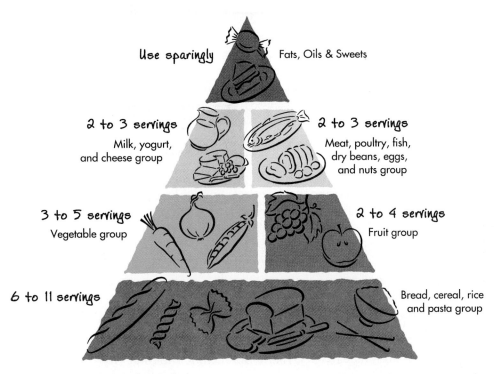

Source: U.S. Government of Agriculture

Eating in Moderation

Your best choice is to practice moderation in everything you eat. College, however, doesn't always make moderation easy. You may be taking snack breaks during late-night study sessions. You may frequent a cafeteria where one price buys all you can eat. You may have fast-food options available at all hours of the day or night. Such opportunities can be hard to resist.

Despite the temptations that may come your way, try to moderate your food intake according to one basic measure: Don't eat more than your body can use. Eating too much of even the healthiest food still means more calories than one body needs. Any extra fuel is stored as fat, whether it comes from rice cakes or ice cream. To avoid packing on extra fat, try to sense your body's messages both for hunger and for fullness. Eat slowly so that you don't miss the "stop" message when it arrives.

Exercising

Good physical fitness increases your energy efficiency. An efficient body system has more energy and more ability to direct it toward problem solving and the fulfillment of goals. A fit body also helps the mind handle stress. During physical activity, the brain releases endorphins, chemical compounds that have a positive and calming effect on the body.

Like a car, your body's physical power can decrease unless you put it to work. Staying in shape requires discipline. For maximum benefit, make regular exercise a way of life. If you haven't been exercising regularly, start slowly. Walking, for example, is one of the most beneficial, most available, and least stressful forms of exercise. If you exercise frequently and are already relatively fit, you may prefer a more intense or longer workout. Always check with a physician before beginning any exercise program, and adjust your program to your physical type and fitness level.

Developing physical fitness and inner calm through yoga

Types of Exercise

The type of exercise you choose depends on such factors as time available, physical limitations, preferences, available facilities, cost, and level of fitness. For example, a person with knee problems may choose to swim or bike, avoiding the demands that running places on the knee joint. Someone who wants to lose fat may take long walks, and someone who wants to gain muscle may work out with weights. You might prefer to play basketball with a team, or you can follow an aerobics tape on your own.

Types of exercise fall into three main categories:

> *Cardiovascular training* is exercise that strengthens your heart muscle and lung capacity. Examples include running, swimming, in-line skating, aerobic dancing, and biking.

> *Strength training* is exercise that strengthens different muscle groups. Examples include using weight machines and free weights or doing push-ups and abdominal crunches.

> *Flexibility training* is exercise that maintains and increases muscle flexibility. Examples include various stretches and forms of yoga.

Some exercises, such as weights or biking, fall primarily into one category. Others combine elements of two or all three, such as astanga yoga, which requires constant movement (cardiovascular), stretching (flexibility), and the support of body weight (strength). For maximum benefit and a comprehensive workout, try alternating your exercise methods through **cross-training** . For example, you could build cardiovascular fitness with brisk walking a few times a week and alternate your walking days with yoga or toning exercises for flexibility and strength. If you lift weights, you could use a stationary bike or stair machine on your off-days for cardiovascular work.

Cross-training,
Alternating types of exercise and combining elements from different types of exercise.

Making Exercise a Priority

Student life, both in school and out, is crammed with responsibilities. You can't always make a nice, neat plan that gets you to the gym three days a week for two hours each time. You also may not have the money for an expensive health club. The following suggestions will help you make exercise a priority, even in the busiest weeks and on the tightest budget. Be sure to check into your school's fitness opportunities—they may be low cost or even included in your tuition.

➤ Walk to classes and meetings on campus.

➤ Take dance, aerobics, martial arts, or yoga classes at a campus fitness center.

➤ Choose the stairs rather than the elevator or escalator.

➤ Purchase exercise tapes for use at home.

➤ Do strenuous chores, if your doctor approves, such as shoveling snow, raking, or mowing.

➤ Play team recreational sports with your school's intramural program or at a local Y club.

➤ Use home exercise equipment such as weights, a treadmill or stair machine, or a mat.

➤ Work out with a friend or family member to combine socializing and exercise, and to help boost your motivation.

Exercise is a key component of a healthy mind and body, as is adequate rest.

Getting Enough Sleep

No one can function well without adequate sleep. During sleep, your body repairs itself while your mind sorts through problems and questions. A lack of sleep, or poor sleep, causes poor concentration and irritability, which can mean a less-than-ideal performance at school and at work. Irritability can also put a strain on personal relationships. Making up for lost sleep with caffeine may raise your anxiety and stress level and leave you more tired than before.

Sleep expert Gregg D. Jacobs, Ph.D., says that different people need different amounts of sleep. "Adults average about seven to seven-and-one-half hours of sleep per night, and many individuals function effectively with four to six hours of sleep."[1] People in their late teens and early twenties may need eight to nine hours. Gauge your needs by evaluating how you feel. If you aren't fatigued or irritable during the day, you may have slept adequately. However, if you are groggy in the morning or doze off at various times, you may be sleep-deprived.

Barriers to a Good Night's Sleep

College students often get inadequate sleep. Worrying about exams, quizzes, or projects coming due may make you restless. Long study sessions may keep you up late, and early classes may get you up early. Assignments pile up and start to seem more important than a good night's sleep. Socializing, eating, and drinking may make it hard to settle down. Noise can be a problem. If you are a parent, your children may disturb your sleep. Some barriers to sleep are within your control, and some are not.

What is out of your control? Barriers such as outside noise and your children's needs require you to do what you can to address the situation and then try to get as much sleep as possible. Try using earplugs or playing relaxing music in your room to counteract outside noise.

What is within your control? Late nights out, food and drink, and your study schedule are often (although not always) within your power to change. Schedule your studying so that it doesn't all pile up at the last minute. Avoid a late dinner the night before a big test. Respectfully ask the people you live with to keep the noise down when you need to rest. Be willing to do the same for them.

Tips for Quality Sleep

Dr. Jacobs recommends the following steps to better sleep.

Reduce consumption of alcohol and caffeine. Caffeine may keep you awake. Alcohol causes you to sleep more lightly, making you feel less rested and refreshed when you awaken.

Exercise regularly. Studies have shown that regular exercise, especially in the late afternoon or early evening, promotes good sleep because it raises body temperature and then allows it to fall.

Complete tasks an hour or more before you sleep. Getting things done some time before you turn in gives you a chance to wind down and calm your brain activity.

Establish a comfortable sleeping environment. Little or no light usually facilitates sleep. Some people like to have quiet, whereas some prefer the calming, steady noise of a fan or air conditioner.

Sleeping well is one of the most important steps to take toward a healthy body and mind. Following are many other important ways to maintain mental health.

HOW DO YOU NURTURE A HEALTHY MIND?

Your success depends on your mental health. Learning some ways to handle stress and preventing or working through emotional disorders are two important steps to a healthy mind.

Dealing with Stress

When you hear the word *stress,* you may think of tension, hardship, problems, anger, and other negative thoughts and emotions. However, stress can have good results, as well as bad. Stress is an effect of life change. It refers not to the change itself but to how you react to the change. For this reason, even positive events can cause stress. Getting married or moving to a bigger and better home can cause as much stress as trouble with an instructor or a problem at work. Reactions vary with individual people. An event that causes one person great anxiety may cause only a mild reaction in another.

Almost any change in your life can create some level of stress. The Holmes-Rahe Social Readjustment Scale, developed by two psychologists, assigns to various life changes a number value indicating the capability of causing stress (a higher number means higher stress). See Table 11–1 for different changes, with their corresponding stress levels. To find your score, add the values of the events that you have experienced in the past year. Scoring over 300 points means that you are at a high risk of illness or injury because of stress. If you score between 150 and 299, your risk is reduced by 30 percent, and if you score under 150, you have only a very small chance of illness or injury.

TABLE 11-1   THE HOLMES–RAHE SCALE TO MEASURE STRESS OF LIFE EVENTS

EVENT	VALUE	EVENT	VALUE
Death of spouse or partner	100	Son or daughter leaving home	29
Divorce	73	Trouble with in-laws	29
Marital separation	65	Outstanding personal achievement	28
Jail term	63	Spouse begins or stops work	26
Personal injury	53	Starting or finishing school	26
Marriage	50	Change in living conditions	25
Fired from work	47	Revision of personal habits	24
Marital reconciliation	45	Trouble with boss	23
Retirement	45	Change in work hours, conditions	20
Changes in family member's health	44	Change in residence	20
Pregnancy	40	Change in schools	20
Sex difficulties	39	Change in recreational habits	19
Addition to family	39	Change in religious activities	19
Business readjustment	39	Change in social activities	18
Change in financial status	38	Mortgage or loan under $10,000	17
Death of a close friend	37	Change in sleeping habits	16
Change to different line of work	36	Change in number of family gatherings	15
Change in number of marital arguments	35	Change in eating habits	15
Mortgage or loan over $10,000	31	Vacation	13
Foreclosure of mortgage or loan	30	Christmas season	12
Change in work responsibilities	29	Minor violation of the law	11

Source: Reprinted with permission from T. H. Holmes and R. H. Rahe, "The Social Readjustment Rating Scale," *Journal of Psychosomatic Research,* 11 (2): 1967. Elsevier Science Inc.

FIGURE 11-2   **YERKES–DODSON LAW**

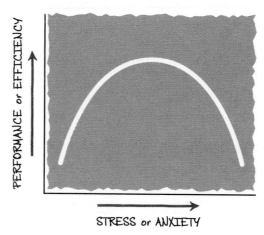

Source: *From Your Maximum Mind* by Herbert Benson, M.D., with William Protor. Copyright ©1987 by Random House, Inc. Reprinted by permission of Times Books, a division of Random House.

Positive Effects of Stress

What you feel in a stressful situation such as the time before a test—increased energy, perhaps, and a heightened awareness that may make you feel on edge—can have positive effects. In fact, moderate levels of stress can actually improve performance and efficiency, whereas too little stress may result in boredom or inactivity, and too much stress may cause an unproductive anxiety level. Figure 11–2, based on research by Drs. Robert M. Yerkes and John D. Dodson, illustrates this concept.[2]

Control over your responses is essential in maintaining a helpful level of stress. You can exercise some level of control by attempting to respond to stressful situations as positively as possible. Perceiving stress as good encourages you to push the boundaries of your abilities. For example, a student who responds positively to the expectations of college instructors might be encouraged to improve study skills and to work on time management in order to have more study time.

Being able to control how you respond will help you deal with the negative effects of stress as well.

Negative Effects of Stress

If you perceive stress as bad, you may pour your energy into unproductive anxiety rather than problem solving. For example, a student who responds negatively to instructors' expectations may become distracted and may skip class or avoid studying. Negative stress may have dangerous physical and psychological effects. Physically, you may experience a change in appetite, more body aches, or increased vulnerability to illnesses. Psychologically, you may be depressed, unable to study or focus in class, unhappy, or anxious. Both kinds of problems may affect your relationships and responsibilities.

Managing Stress

You can activate your sense of positive control in two ways when you are faced with stressful life changes. You may either adjust whatever is causing stress or use stress management techniques to adjust the effect that the change has on you. Start by trying to adjust the cause, before you focus on what you can do about the effect. For example, if increased socializing is causing your grades to slip, consider how you can refocus on your schoolwork and make better decisions about how to manage your time.

If you find that you can adjust the cause, try the following strategies:

Set reasonable, manageable goals. Trying to achieve something that is out of your reach will cause more stress than success.

Break jobs into smaller pieces. Goals will appear more manageable when approached as a series of smaller steps. Perform a smaller task well rather than a larger one not so well.

Avoid procrastination. The longer you wait to do something, the more difficulty you may have doing it. However distasteful the task, it will be much worse when time runs short and the expectations of others hang over your head.

Be thorough. Loose ends can be irritating. Many people find that only when they finish something completely can they enjoy a feeling of accomplishment. Finish the job and move on.

Set boundaries and learn to say no. Don't take responsibility for everyone and everything. Decide what is yours to deal with, then delegate what can be or should be taken care of by someone else.

When a cause lies beyond your control, address its effect on you. For example, if a case of the flu keeps you in bed for a week, you can reduce the negative effects of stress by contacting your instructors or classmates to see what schoolwork you can accomplish while you're sick.

The following are techniques that can help you adjust to the effects of a stressful situation.

Exercise, eat right, and get adequate sleep. Physical health promotes clear thinking.

Do something relaxing. Take breaks regularly: Play music, take a nap, read a book, go for a drive, take a walk, or see a movie. Recreation restores your mind and body.

Change your surroundings. Getting away from situations and locations you associate with stress can lighten the effect it has on you and help you place problems in perspective.

Think critically. Look at the situation and ask yourself questions about how you can improve it. Work through a problem-solving plan. Brainstorm unusual ideas; something just might work.

Positive thinking and taking action can help you control stress. In some cases, however, an emotional disorder may make stress difficult to handle without special treatment.

Emotional Disorders

Everyone encounters the ups and downs of life. Some people have emotional disorders that interfere with their ability to cope. Following are descriptions of disorders that affect people in all walks of life.

Depression

Almost everyone has experienced the sadness or melancholy that life's troubles can cause. However, as many as 10 percent of Americans will experience a major *depression* at some point in their lives, something that is more than temporary blues. A depressive disorder is an illness, not a sign of weakness or a state that can be escaped simply by trying to "snap out of it." This illness requires medical evaluation and is treatable.

A depressive disorder "is a 'whole-body' illness, involving your body, mood, and thoughts."[3] You may feel constantly sad, worried, or anxious. You may lose interest in classes, people, and activities that you normally like. You might be tired all the time, sleep a lot, or have trouble sleeping at all. You could experience a loss of appetite or a desire to eat constantly. You may go to classes and meetings automatically, not participating at all, or you may skip them altogether. You may cry a lot, feel hopeless, and even have thoughts of suicide.

Depression can stem from genetic, psychological, physiological, or environmental causes, or even a combination of different causes. Table 11–2 describes these causes, along with other depression strategies.

TABLE 11-2   IMPORTANT INFORMATION ABOUT DEPRESSION

POSSIBLE CAUSES OF DEPRESSION	HELPFUL STRATEGIES IF YOU FEEL DEPRESSED	SUICIDE WARNING SIGNS
A genetic trait that makes its carrier more likely to suffer depression	Do the best you can and don't have unreasonable expectations of yourself	Statements about hopelessness or worthlessness: "The world would be better off without me"
A chemical imbalance in the brain	Try to be with others rather than alone	Loss of interest in people, things, or activities that the person cares about
Seasonal affective disorder, which occurs when a person becomes depressed in reaction to reduced daylight during autumn and winter	Don't expect your mood to change right away; feeling better will take time.	Preoccupation with suicide or death
Highly stressful situations such as financial trouble, failing a test or class, a death in the family	Try to avoid making major life decisions until your condition improves.	Making arrangements: visiting or calling close friends and relatives, giving things away
Illnesses, injuries, lack of exercise, poor diet	Remember not to blame yourself for your condition.	Sudden sense of happiness or calm. When a person decides to commit suicide, he or she often experiences relief. For this reason others often don't foresee the suicide and may say that the person "seemed to be on an upswing."

Sources: National Institutes of Health Publication No. 94-3561, National Institutes of Health, 1994; and Suicide Awareness\Voices of Education (SA\VE) Web site.

If you recognize yourself anywhere in this discussion of depression, the most important thing to do is to seek help. Start with your school's counseling office or student health program. People at these offices may be able to help or refer you to someone who can. If you know someone else who suffers from depression, see that the person gets immediate medical attention and evaluation, especially if you sense that the person is contemplating suicide. Suicide Awareness\Voices of Education (SA\VE), an organization dedicated to educating the public about suicide prevention, advises you to be understanding and patient with a depressed friend or family member. Don't make too many demands or tell the person that he or she should "get over it."

Clinical depression requires medical treatment. A doctor will help you sort through your symptoms, examine family history, evaluate your situation, and determine the best treatment. Treatments range from therapy to medications to a combination of the two. For some people adequate sleep, a regular exercise program, and a healthier diet may be part of the solution. If you see a doctor and are diagnosed with depression, know that your condition is nothing to be ashamed of, and be proud that you have taken a first step toward recovery.

Eating Disorders

Millions of people develop serious and sometimes life-threatening eating disorders every year. The most common disorders are anorexia nervosa, bulimia, and binge eating.

Anorexia nervosa. Some people develop such a strong desire to be thin that it creates unnatural self-starvation. This condition—*anorexia nervosa*—occurs mainly in young women, although men and older women can also be affected. People with anorexia lose an extreme amount of weight and look painfully thin, although they feel that they are overweight. To reach their unreasonable weight goals they refuse to eat, exercise constantly, use laxatives, and develop obsessive rituals around food.

The causes of anorexia are not fully known. The desire to emulate an "ideal" body type is one factor, and genetics could be involved (eating disorders tend to run in families). Victims of anorexia are often perfectionists, self-critical, and low in self-esteem. Effects of anorexia-induced starvation include loss of menstrual periods in women, impotence in men, damage to organs, heart failure, and even death.

Bulimia. People who binge on excessive amounts of food, usually sweets and fattening foods, and then purge through self-induced vomiting have *bulimia*. They may also use laxatives or exercise obsessively. Bulimia can be hard to notice, because bulimics are often able to maintain a normal appearance. Lee Hoffman of the National Institutes of Mental Health emphasizes, "Because many individuals with bulimia 'binge and purge' in secret and maintain normal or above normal body weight, they can often successfully hide their problem from others for years."[4]

The causes of bulimia, like those of anorexia, can be rooted in a desire to fulfill a body-type ideal or can come from genetically passed-on chemical imbalances. Bulimia patients are often suffering from depression or other psychiatric illnesses. Effects of bulimia include damage to the digestive tract, stomach rupture, and even heart failure because of the loss of important minerals.

Binge eating. Like bulimics, people with *binge-eating disorder* eat large amounts of food and have a hard time stopping. However, they do not purge afterward. Binge eaters are often overweight and feel that they cannot control their eating. As with bulimia, depression and other psychiatric illnesses may be partially responsible for this disorder. Effects are similar to the effects of obesity, such as high blood pressure, increased stress on the body, and high cholesterol.

Eating disorders can go untreated for too long because the sufferer may hide or deny the problem. If you recognize yourself or a friend or relative in these descriptions, know that there are people and resources that can help you. Since eating disorders are a common problem on college campuses, most student health centers and campus counseling centers can provide both medical and psychological help. Treatment can involve any combination of psychotherapy, medical treatments, drug therapy, and even hospitalization or residence in a treatment center.

Food is only one of several possible addictions. Following is an exploration of the use and abuse of other potentially addictive substances.

> " *God grant me the serenity to accept things I cannot change, courage to change things I can, and wisdom to know the difference.* "
>
> Reinhold Niebuhr

THINKING BACK

1. List three strategies that can help you maintain a healthy diet.

    a. _____

    b. _____

    c. _____

2. Name three types of exercise you enjoy.

    a. _____

    b. _____

    c. _____

3. Name three tips for good sleep hygiene that you think would work for you and why.

    a. _____

    b. _____

    c. _____

THINKING BACK

4. Name a situation to which you respond with a high level of stress. What stress management techniques could help, and how would you apply them?

_____

_____

_____

5. Name two emotional disorders that can affect students.

a. _____

b. _____

THINKING AHEAD

1. Do you think that alcohol can be used safely? Explain why or why not.

_____

_____

_____

2. Name two areas of study/work that interest you. Then, name a major that corresponds to each.

_____

_____

_____

3. How has the existence of AIDS and other sexually transmitted diseases affected your current attitude toward sexuality?

_____

_____

HOW ARE ALCOHOL, TOBACCO, AND DRUGS USED AND ABUSED?

Alcohol, tobacco, and drug users are men and women from all socioeconomic levels, racial and cultural groups, and areas of the country. The stereotypical homeless drug or alcohol user actually makes up only a small percentage of substance abusers. Carefully consider the potential positive and negative effects before considering the use of these substances. Although some moderate users are fortunate enough to enjoy long lives, for many others substance abuse can cause financial struggles, emotional traumas, health problems, and even death.

Although the statistics are grim, users may ignore them, preferring to think that substances are fun, help them relax, help them escape problems, or enhance a social occasion. Many people have used a substance, or seen friends use it, and feel that nothing bad had occurred. Such people may feel that tragedies "will never happen to me." However, the fact remains that the use or abuse of alcohol, tobacco, and drugs can cause problems and even destroy lives. Think critically as you read the following sections and take the time to make decisions that are best for you.

Alcohol

Alcohol is a drug as much as it is a beverage. People receive mixed messages about it as they grow up: "Alcohol is fun;" "Alcohol is dangerous;" "Alcohol is for adults only." These conflicting ideas can make drinking appear more glamorous, secretive, and exciting than it really is.

When used in moderation, alcohol may not cause a problem for many people. Many drink only occasionally, and many others choose not to drink at all. The key is to be in control and to ask yourself why you drink. If you drink once in a while at a social gathering or because you like the taste, you are more likely to drink moderately than someone who drinks to escape problems or to fit in with the crowd.

The National Institute on Alcoholic Abuse and Alcoholism (NIAA) offers these statistics about college students and alcohol:[5]

Binge drinking,
Having five or more drinks at one sitting.

> An overwhelming majority of college students—88 percent—have used alcohol.

> **Binge drinking** has the most problematic effects. A 1994 study reports that 40 percent of college students reported binge drinking within two weeks of being surveyed. A total of 31 percent of college women and 52 percent of college men reported binge drinking.

> Students who binge drink are more likely to miss classes, be less able to work, have hangovers, become depressed, engage in unplanned sexual activity, and ignore safer sex practices.

> Greater alcohol use is connected to sexual aggression. Students on campuses reporting high levels of binge drinking experience more incidents of assault and unwanted sexual advances as a result of drinking than do students at campuses with fewer binge drinkers.

➤ Drinking with a group and serving one's own drinks may contribute to greater consumption of alcohol. Both of these situations are common at large gatherings such as fraternity parties.

The bottom line is that heavy drinking causes severe problems. The NIAAA estimates that alcohol contributes to the deaths of 100,000 people every year through alcohol-related illnesses and accidents involving drunk drivers.[6] Heavy drinking can damage the liver, the digestive system, brain cells, and the central nervous system. Indeed, as *The New Wellness Encyclopedia* states, "Chronic, excessive use of alcohol can seriously damage every function and organ of the body."[7] Prolonged use can also cause **addiction**, making it seem impossibly painful for the user to stop drinking.

The self-test on p. 405 will help you determine if your drinking habits may cause problems.

Addiction,
Compulsive physiological need for a habit-forming substance.

Tobacco

College students do their share of smoking. The National Institute on Drug Abuse (NIDA) found that 38.8 percent of college students reported smoking at least once in the year before they were surveyed, and 24.5 percent had smoked once within the month before. Nationally, about 60 million people are habitual smokers.[8] The choice to smoke—often influenced by advertising directed at young people—may soon turn into a harmful addiction.

When people smoke, they inhale nicotine, a highly addictive drug found in all tobacco products. Nicotine's immediate effects may include an increase in blood pressure and heart rate, sweating, and throat irritation. Long-term effects may include high blood pressure, bronchitis, emphysema, stomach ulcers, and heart conditions. Pregnant women who smoke run an increased risk of low birth weight, premature births, or stillbirths.

Inhaling tobacco smoke damages the cells that line the air sacs of the lungs. Smoking has long been thought to cause lung cancer, and in late 1996 researchers found a definitive link. They exposed lung cells to tobacco smoke and saw that the damage to the genes of the cells mirrors the damage seen in lung tumors. Lung cancer causes more deaths in the United States than any other type of cancer. Smoking also increases the risk of mouth, throat, and other cancers.[9]

To quit smoking is extremely difficult and should be attempted gradually. **Withdrawal** symptoms include insomnia, irritability, depression, difficulty in concentration, and tobacco cravings. Some doctors say that it can be harder to quit smoking than it is to kick a heroin habit. Many lifelong smokers will tell you that the best advice is to never start smoking because stopping is so difficult. Even so, if you have smoked regularly, you can quit through motivation and perseverance. Half of all people who have ever smoked have quit. Suggestions for quitting include the following:[10]

Withdrawal,
The discontinuance of the use of a drug, including attendant side effects.

➤ Try the nicotine patch or nicotine gum, and be sure to use them consistently.

➤ Get support and encouragement from a health-care provider, a "quit smoking" program, a support group, and friends and family.

➤ Avoid situations that cause you to want to smoke, such as being around other smokers, drinking alcohol, and highly stressful encounters or events.

➤ Find other ways of lowering your stress level, such as exercise or other activities you enjoy.

➤ Set goals. Set a quit date and tell friends and family. Make and keep medical appointments.

The positive effects of quitting—increased life expectancy, greater lung capacity, and more energy—may inspire any smoker to consider making a lifestyle change. Quitting saves you money as well. Weigh your options and make a responsible choice. To evaluate the level of your potential addiction, you may want to take the self-test on page 405, replacing the words "alcohol" or "drugs" with "cigarettes" or "smoking."

Drugs

According to NIDA, 31.4 percent of college students have used illicit drugs at least once in the year before being surveyed and 16 percent in the month before.[11] Drug users rarely think about the possible effects when choosing to take a drug. However, many of the so-called "rewards" of drug abuse are empty. Drug-using peers may accept you for your drug use and not for who you are. Problems and responsibilities may multiply when you emerge from a high. The pain of withdrawal may not compare to the pain of the damage that long-term drug use can do to your body. Table 11–3 shows the most commonly used drugs and their potential effects.

You are responsible for choosing what you want to introduce into your body. If you think critically about drugs and ask important questions, you can draw your own conclusions. Ask questions like the following: Why do I want to do this? What are the positive and negative effects it might have? If others want me to do it, why? Do I respect the people who want me to do this? How does drug use affect other users I know of? How would my drug use affect the people in my life? The more informed you are, the better able you will be to make choices that help you and avoid choices that harm you.

You can injure your reputation, your student status, or your employment possibilities if you are caught using drugs or if drug use impairs your performance in school or on the job. These days, many companies test both employees and job applicants. One report indicates that alcohol and drug use combined costs employers over $40 billion a year in reduced productivity.[12] Employers don't want to hire a drug user who may have trouble working up to potential. An additional negative effect of drug use is that it violates federal law.

Identifying and Overcoming Addiction

People with addictions have lost their control for any number of reasons, including chemical imbalances in the brain, hereditary tendencies, or stressful life circumstances. When you observe others or yourself and wonder if addiction is a factor, remember that many addicts hide their addictions well. For

TABLE 11-3   HOW DRUGS AFFECT YOU

DRUG CATEGORY	DRUG TYPES	HOW THEY MAKE YOU FEEL	PHYSICAL AFFECTS	DANGER OF PHYSICAL DEPENDENCE	DANGER OF PSYCHOLOGICAL DEPENDENCE
Stimulants	Cocaine, amphetamines	Alert, stimulated, excited	Nervousness, mood swings, stroke or convulsions, psychoses, paranoia, coma at large doses	Relatively strong	Strong
Depressants	Alcohol, Valium-type drugs	Sedated, tired, high	Cirrhosis, impaired blood production; greater risk of cancer, heart attack, and stroke; impaired brain function	Strong	Strong
Opiates	Heroin, codeine, other pain pills	Drowsy, floating, without pain	Infection of organs, inflammation of the heart, hepatitis	Yes, with high dosage	Yes, with high dosage
Cannabinols	Marijuana, hashish	Euphoria, mellowness, little sensation of time	Impairment of judgment and coordination, bronchitis and asthma, lung and throat cancers, anxiety, lack of energy and motivation, reduced ability to produce hormones	Moderate	Relatively strong
Hallucinogens	LSD, mushrooms	Heightened sensual perception, hallucinations, confusion	Impairment of brain function, circulatory problems, agitation and confusion, flashbacks	Insubstantial	Insubstantial
Inhalants	Glue, aerosols	Giddiness, lightheadedness	Damage to brain, heart, liver, and kidneys	Insubstantial	Insubstantial

Source: Adapted from Marc Alan Schuckit, M.D., *Educating Yourself About Alcohol and Drugs: A People's Primer* (New York: Plenum Press, 1995).

every loud, obvious alcohol or drug user, there is someone who abuses substances quietly and secretly, continuing to appear functional and controlled to observers. Women, although they are less likely to be substance abusers, tend to conceal substance problems more carefully than men do.[13]

If you think you may be addicted, look carefully at your situation. Compare the positive and negative effects of your habits and decide if they are worth it. Although others can tell you how they feel and make suggestions, you are the only one who can truly take the initiative to change.

Facing Addiction

Addiction is incredibly hard to face and overcome alone. Because substances often cause physical and chemical changes, quitting often involves a painful withdrawal. Even substances that don't cause chemical changes create psychological dependence, which is difficult to break. Asking for help isn't an admission of failure but a courageous move to reclaim a valuable life. Using the self-test in Figure 11–3, evaluate your behavior to see if you need help.

Working Through Addiction

If you determine that you need to make some changes, there are many resources that can help you along the way. Seek any combination of the following suggestions.

Counseling and medical care. You can find help from school-based, private, government-sponsored, or workplace-sponsored resources. Check with your school's counseling or health center, your personal physician, or a local hospital. If you don't find an appropriate program, a medical professional can refer you to one. Check in the Yellow Pages under "Drug Abuse and Addictions" for services in your area. Some programs are free. Programs that require payment may make allowances for financial limitations, charging you according to what you are able to pay.

Detoxification (detox) centers. If you have a severe addiction, you may need a controlled environment in which to separate yourself completely from the substance you abuse. Some are outpatient facilities that you visit periodically. Other programs provide a twenty-four-hour "home away from home" for you until you have gotten through the critical period of withdrawal. The life changes required by a live-in or drop-in center may require you to withdraw from school for a while.

> *Moderation in all things.*
> Terence

Support groups. You can derive help and comfort from sharing your experiences with others. Alcoholics Anonymous (AA) is the premier support group for alcoholics. Based on a twelve-step recovery program, AA has helped a great number of people over many years. Membership costs little or nothing—members may donate one dollar at meetings if they can afford it. Alcoholics Anonymous has led to many other support groups for addicts such as Overeaters Anonymous and Narcotics Anonymous (NA). Many

FIGURE 11-3   **SUBSTANCE USE AND ABUSE SELF–TEST**

Even one "yes" answer may indicate a need to evaluate your substance use. Answering "yes" to three or more questions indicates that you may benefit from discussing your use with a counselor.

WITHIN THE LAST YEAR:

1. Have you tried to stop drinking or taking drugs but found that you couldn't do so for long?

2. Do you get tired of people telling you they're concerned about your drinking or drug use?

3. Have you felt guilty about your drinking or drug use?

4. Have you felt that you needed a drink or drugs in the morning—as an "eye-opener"—to improve a hangover?

5. Do you drink or use drugs alone?

6. Do you drink or use drugs every day?

7. Have you found yourself regularly thinking or saying, "I need" a drink or any type of drug?

8. Have you lied about or concealed your drinking or drug use?

9. Do you drink or use drugs to escape worries, problems, mistakes, or shyness?

10. Do you find you need increasingly larger amounts of drugs or alcohol to achieve a desired effect?

11. Have you forgotten what happened while drinking or using drugs (had a blackout)?

12. Have you been surprised by how much you were using alcohol or drugs?

13. Have you spent a lot of time, energy, and/or money getting alcohol or drugs?

14. Has your drinking or drug use caused you to neglect friends, your partner, your children, or other family members, or caused other problems at home?

15. Have you gotten into an argument or a fight that was alcohol- or drug-related?

16. Has your drinking or drug use caused you to miss class, fail a test, or ignore schoolwork?

17. Have you rejected planned social events in favor of drinking or using drugs?

18. Have you been choosing to drink or use drugs instead of performing other activities or hobbies you used to enjoy?

19. Has your drinking or drug use affected your efficiency on the job or caused you to fail to show up at work?

20. Have you continued to drink or use drugs despite any physical problems or health risks that your use has caused or made worse?

21. Have you driven a car or performed any other potentially dangerous tasks while under the influence of alcohol or drugs?

22. Have you had a drug- or alcohol-related legal problem or arrest (possession, use, disorderly conduct, driving while intoxicated, etc.)?

Source: Adapted from the Criteria for Substance Dependence and Criteria for Substance Abuse in the *Diagnostic and Statistical Manual of Mental Disorders,* Fourth Edition, published by the American Psychiatric Association, Washington, D.C., and from materials entitled "Are You an Alcoholic?" developed by Johns Hopkins University.

How do I know if I have a substance abuse problem? Where can I go for help?

Anonymous

I'm a freshman at a large university. At first I was afraid of not fitting in because I come from a small town, but I've found some great friends to hang out with. In fact, I'm so busy most of the time, I hardly have time to keep up with my schoolwork. We all share a house near the campus. It's great because it keeps the costs down and I always have plenty of friends around.

Lately, though, it seems like all we do is party. I'm getting kind of worried about how much I'm drinking. I'm sure I can handle it, but I've been waking up with hangovers pretty regularly. I figured out that this last month I didn't go even one day without a drink. I'm feeling like I may have a problem. I just don't want anyone to know.

Laura Brinckerhoff, Program Director, Nonprofit Organization, Graduate of the University of Arizona

I started drinking and using drugs when I was in junior high school. It wasn't until my last year of college, though, that I finally got some help. It's amazing that I lasted so long. Part of my coverup was to give the illusion that everything was fine. If I was in school and doing well, maybe no one would notice that my life was falling apart.

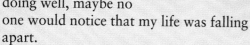

The turning point for me was the realization that I'd die if I continued down the same path. I finally asked for help from my doctor. This was a big step for me because I thought that I was in control. I put my life into his hands and began the journey to recovery. It hasn't been easy though. I've had to let go of unhealthy relationships. I've had to change the way I think about my life. I've had to be humble enough to say, "I need help." But, I'm so glad I did. My life is much more meaningful and rich now.

I believe that most people who are successful at overcoming addictions engage in a regular recovery program. I attend AA [Alcoholics Anonymous] meetings, practice the twelve steps, and lead a spiritually directed life. I don't know of anything that works as well. Another part of staying sober is to serve others who may be struggling with an addiction. That's why I agreed to tell you my story. If you think you're dependent on alcohol or drugs, I recommend you go to an AA meeting right away. By listening to other people's stories, you should be able to tell fairly soon if you have a problem. Try to attend five to ten meetings before you completely make up your mind. Also, if your family or friends have been telling you that you have a problem, then they're probably right. As difficult as it is to hear, listen to them. Their support can help save you a lot of agony. But, regardless of the program you choose, if you're not willing to change the unhealthy patterns in your life or your core beliefs, staying sober will be very difficult. You may end up being a dry drunk—not drinking, but not really happy.

Like me, you may be scared to take the steps to change your life, but it's worth it. I never dreamed that life could be so wonderful and fun. It's the greatest gift God's ever given me.

schools have AA, NA, or other group sessions on campus. A counselor may be able to help you decide what is best for your needs.

When people address their problems directly instead of avoiding them through substance abuse, they can begin to grow and improve. Working through substance-abuse problems can lead to a restoration of both health and self-respect.

WHAT SHOULD YOU CONSIDER WHEN MAKING SEXUAL DECISIONS?

Sexual relationships involve both body and mind on many different levels. Forming your opinions about sexuality takes some thought. In this section, you will explore sexual decision making, birth-control options, and sexually transmitted diseases.

Sex and Critical Thinking

What sexuality means to you and the role it plays in your life are your own private business. However, the physical act of sex goes beyond the private realm. Individual sexual conduct can have consequences such as unexpected pregnancy; the spread of the human immunodeficiency virus (HIV), possibly leading to acquired immune deficiency Syndrome (AIDS) virus; and the transmission of other sexually transmitted diseases (STDs). These consequences affect everyone involved in the sexual act.

Your self-respect depends on making choices that maintain your own health and safety, as well as those of any person with whom you are involved. Think critically about sexual issues, asking important questions and weighing the positive and negative effects of any action before you make a decision. Because it can be difficult to think clearly "in the moment," you may want to do some thinking before situations arise, even though it seems unromantic. You may ask yourself questions such as the following:

Getting to know one another

- ➤ Do I feel ready?
- ➤ Is this the right person, moment, and situation?
- ➤ Do I have what I need to prevent pregnancy and exposure to STDs? If not, what could be the consequences? Can I live with those consequences (pregnancy or disease)? Are they worth it?
- ➤ Does this person truly care for me and not just for what we might be doing?
- ➤ Is this what I really want? Does it fit with my values?
- ➤ Will this enhance our emotional relationship or cause problems later?

Critical thinking can help you consider the effects of sexual activity. One of the possible effects is pregnancy, which birth-control methods are designed to prevent.

TABLE 11-4   METHODS OF BIRTH CONTROL

METHOD	APPROXIMATE EFFECTIVENESS	PREVENTS STDs?	DESCRIPTION
Abstinence	100%	Only if no sexual activity occurs	Just saying "no." No intercourse means no risk of pregnancy. However, alternative modes of sexual activity can still spread STDs.
Condom (male)	94%	Yes, if made of latex	A sheath that fits over the penis and prevents sperm from entering the vagina.
Condom (female)	90%	Yes	A sheath that fits inside the vagina, held in place by two rings, one of which hangs outside. Can be awkward. It is relatively new and may not be widely available.
Diaphragm or cervical cap	85%	No	A bendable rubber cap that fits over the cervix and pelvic bone inside the vagina (the cervical cap is smaller and fits over the cervix only). Both must be fitted initially by a gynecologist and used with a spermicide.
Oral contraceptives (the pill)	97%	No	A dosage of hormones taken daily by a woman, preventing the ovaries from releasing eggs. Side effects can include headaches, weight gain, and increased chances of blood clotting. Various brands and dosages; must be prescribed by a gynecologist.
Spermicidal foams, jellies, inserts	84% if used alone	No	Usually used with diaphragms or condoms to enhance effectiveness, they have an ingredient that kills sperm cells (but not STDs). They stay effective for a limited period of time after insertion.
Intrauterine device (IUD)	94%	No	A small coil of wire inserted into the uterus by a gynecologist (who must also remove it). Prevents fertilized eggs from implanting in the uterine wall. Possible side effects include bleeding.
Norplant	Nearly 100%	No	A series of up to five small tubes implanted by a gynecologist into a woman's upper arm, preventing pregnancy for up to five years. Can be tough to remove. Possible side effects may resemble those of oral contraceptives. Must be removed by a doctor.
Depo-Provera	Nearly 100%	No	An injection that a woman must receive from a doctor every few months. Possible side effects may resemble those of oral contraceptives.
Tubal ligation	Nearly 100%	No	Surgery for women that cuts and ties the fallopian tubes, preventing eggs from traveling to the uterus. Difficult and expensive to reverse. Recommended for those who do not want any more children.
Vasectomy	Nearly 100%	No	Surgery for men that blocks the tube that delivers sperm to the penis. Like tubal ligation, difficult to reverse and only recommended for those who don't want children.
Rhythm method	Variable	No	Abstaining from intercourse during the ovulation segment of the woman's menstrual cycle. Can be difficult to time and may not account for cycle irregularities.
Withdrawal	Variable	No	Pulling the penis out of the vagina before ejaculation. Unreliable, because some sperm can escape in the fluid released prior to ejaculation. Dependent on a controlled partner.

Birth Control

Using birth control is a choice, and it is not for everyone. For some, using any kind of birth control is against their religious beliefs. Others may want to have children. Many sexually active people, however, choose one or more methods of birth control.

In addition to preventing pregnancy, some birth-control methods also protect against sexually transmitted diseases. Table 11–4 describes the most established methods of birth control, with effectiveness percentages and STD prevention based on proper and regular use.

Evaluate the positive and negative effects of each method, for yourself and for your partner. Consider cost, ease of use, convenience, reliability, comfort, and protection against STDs. Communicate with your partner and together make a choice that is comfortable for both of you. If a partner refuses to honor your preference, reevaluate your relationship. A partner who truly cares about you should be concerned about your health and safety. For literature on this subject check your library or bookstore, talk to your doctor, ask a counselor at your student health center, or call a helpful organization. Make informed choices.

Sexually Transmitted Diseases

Sexually transmitted diseases cause health problems from the annoying to the life-threatening. Table 11–5 shows some basic information about common STDs. Each one of these diseases is spread through sexual contact—intercourse or other sexual activity that involves contact with the genitals. All are highly contagious. The only birth-control methods that protect against them are the methods that prevent skin-to-skin contact—the male and female condom (latex or polyurethane only). Most of these STDs can also spread to infants of infected mothers during birth, often causing health problems for the infants. Have a doctor examine any irregularity or discomfort; the sooner you are treated, the less chance you have of suffering permanent damage. Women should have an annual Pap smear to check for diseases or irregularities.

AIDS and HIV

The most serious STD is AIDS, brought on by the spread of the contagious HIV. Not everyone who tests positive for HIV will develop AIDS, but AIDS currently has no cure and results in eventual death. The spread of AIDS has been strong and steady over the last ten years. Figure 11–4 shows some recent statistics on AIDS.

AIDS disarms the body's immune system, making it unable to fight viruses that it normally would kill. HIV can lie undetected in the body for up to ten years before surfacing, and a carrier can spread it during that time. Although AIDS was at first associated with male homosexuals, anyone who is sexually active can contract it. AIDS is growing fastest among heterosexual populations, especially women and children. Medical science continues to develop drugs to combat AIDS and its related illnesses. However, the drugs can cause severe side effects, many have not been thoroughly tested, and none are proven cures.

TABLE 11-5   SEXUALLY TRANSMITTED DISEASES

DISEASE	SYMPTOMS	HEALTH PROBLEMS IF UNTREATED	TREATMENTS
Chlamydia	Discharge, painful urination, swollen or painful joints, change in menstrual periods for women	Can cause pelvic inflammatory disease (PID) in women, which can lead to sterility or ectopic pregnancies; infection; miscarriage or premature birth.	Curable with course of antibiotics; avoid sex until treatment is complete.
Gonorrhea	Discharge, burning while urinating	Can cause PID, swelling of testicles and penis, arthritis, skin problems, infections.	Usually curable with antibiotics; however, certain strains are becoming resistant to medication.
Genital herpes	Blisterlike itchy sores in the genital area, headache, fever, chills	Symptoms may subside and then reoccur, often in response to high stress levels; carriers can transmit the virus even when it is dormant.	No cure; some medications such as Acyclovir reduce and help heal the sores and may shorten recurring outbreaks.
Syphilis	A genital sore lasting one to five weeks, followed by a rash, fatigue, fever, sore throat, headaches, swollen glands	If it lasts over four years, it can cause blindness, destruction of bone, insanity or heart failure; can cause death or deformity of a child born to an infected woman.	Curable with full course of antibiotics.
Human Papilloma Virus (HPV, or genital warts)	Genital itching and irritation, small clusters of warts	Can increase risk of cervical cancer in women; virus may remain in body even when warts are removed and cause recurrences.	Treatable with drugs applied to warts or various kinds of wart removal surgery.
Hepatitis B	Fatigue, poor appetite, vomiting, jaundice, hives	Some carriers will have few symptoms; others may develop chronic liver disease that may lead to other diseases of the liver.	No cure; some will recover, some will not. Bed rest may help ease symptoms.

HIV is transmitted through two types of bodily fluids: fluids associated with sex (semen and vaginal fluids) and blood. People have been known to acquire HIV through sexual relations, by sharing hypodermic needles for drug use, and by receiving tainted blood transfusions. You cannot become infected with the virus unless one of those fluids is involved. Therefore, it is unlikely you would contract HIV from toilet seats, hugging, kissing, or sharing a glass.

The best defense against AIDS is not having sex. The U.S. Department of Health and Human Services reports, "THERE'S ABSOLUTELY NO GUARANTEE EVEN WHEN YOU USE A CONDOM. But most experts believe that the risk of getting AIDS and other sexually transmitted diseases can be greatly reduced if a condom is used properly....Sex with condoms ISN'T totally 'safe sex,'

● **RECENT AIDS STATISTICS**

FIGURE 11-4

In the United States, 548,102 cases of AIDS had been reported to the Centers for Disease Control (CDC) by June of 1996. More than 62 percent of those people have died. AIDS is the leading cause of death in the U. S. for people from the ages of 25 to 44.	Although most AIDS cases are traceable to male-to-male sexual contact or intravenous drug use, heterosexual transmission has increased from 2.5 percent to 16.7 percent of all AIDS cases from 1985 to 1995.
AIDS cases among women increased from 7 to 9 percent of all AIDS cases from 1985 to 1995.	As of June 1996, more than 7000 cases of AIDS in children under 13 had been reported to CDC.

Source: The Centers for Disease Control and Prevention, Atlanta, October 1996.

but it IS 'less risky' sex."[14] Always use a latex condom because natural skin condoms may let the virus pass through. Use K-Y Jelly or a spermicide as a lubricant because petroleum jelly can destroy the latex in condoms and diaphragms. Although some people dislike using condoms, it's a small price for preserving your life.

To be safe, have an HIV test at your doctor's office or at a government-sponsored clinic. Your school's health department may also administer these tests. Recently, home HIV tests have become available over the counter. If you are infected, first inform any recent sexual partners and seek medical assistance. Then contact support organizations in your area or call the National AIDS Hotline at 1-800-342-AIDS.

joie de vivre

The French have a phrase that has become commonly used in the English language as well: *joie de vivre,* which literally means "joy of living." A person with *joie de vivre* is one who finds joy and optimism in many parts of life, who is able to enjoy life's pleasures and find something positive in its struggles. Without experiencing difficult and sometimes painful challenges, people might have a hard time recognizing and experiencing happiness and satisfaction.

Think of this concept as you examine your level of personal wellness. If you focus on what is positive about yourself, that attitude can affect all other areas of your life. Give yourself the gift of self-respect so that you can nourish your body and mind every day, in every situation. Through both stressful obstacles and happy successes, you can find the joy of living.

IMPORTANT POINTS TO REMEMBER

1. How can you maintain a healthy body?

Physical health promotes good mental health and helps you move toward your goals. Maintain a balanced diet and eat in moderation. Get regular exercise, two to five times a week, in a combination of cardiovascular, strength, and flexibility training. Be sure to get adequate sleep because sleep deprivation can disrupt your concentration and affect your skills.

2. How can you nurture a healthy mind?

Mental health involves controlling stress levels and avoiding or treating emotional disorders. Stress is the measure of your reaction to an event or situation and can have positive or negative effects. Control stress by adjusting your life changes or by focusing on effective stress management techniques. Emotional disorders that students may experience include clinical depression and eating disorders. Eating disorders include anorexia nervosa, bulimia, and binge-eating disorder.

3. How are alcohol, tobacco, and drugs used and abused?

The misuse of alcohol, a drug as well as a beverage, contributes to many deaths through drunk driving or alcohol-related illnesses. Smoking damages lung tissue and has recently been proven to cause cancer. Drug use can cause all kinds of physical problems, and users often become physically or psychologically addicted. Facing addiction involves seeking help from medical professionals and groups that support addicts.

4. What should you consider when making sexual decisions?

Sexual decision making requires asking important questions about your wants, needs, and health before you find yourself in a situation involving sex. Become informed about birth control and sexually transmitted diseases and make a careful choice. Sexually active people should be tested for HIV.

Name _____ Date _____

BUILDING SKILLS FOR COLLEGE, CAREER, AND LIFE SUCCESS
CHAPTER 11

TAKING STOCK:
REFINING YOUR THOUGHTS

Look back at the statements you explored at the start of the chapter (see Thinking It Through on p. 387). Observe whether your attitudes have changed and what you have learned by studying this chapter.

1. Define the elements of a balanced diet. Which food group requires special attention?

_____

_____

_____

2. Name three strategies, involving exercise or sleep or both, that can help you become more rested.

_____

_____

_____

3. Discuss what you feel you can do to have a more positive response to a stressful situation.

_____

_____

_____

4. Name two negative effects each of abusing alcohol, tobacco, and drugs.

_____

_____

_____

5. Name five warning signs of addiction.

_____

_____

_____

6. What are some potential effects of making sexual decisions ahead of time?

_____

_____

_____

7. Name one strategy from this chapter that you plan to use in the next month. Describe what you will do and what positive effects you believe it will have on your life.

_____

_____

_____

CRITICAL THINKING:
APPLYING LEARNING TO YOUR LIFE

Health Habits

Examine your habits by keeping track of what you eat, how much you exercise, and how much sleep you get over the course of three fairly normal days. To be as accurate as possible, try not to change your normal habits.

Food. First, on the following chart, tally how many servings you eat each day from the four food groups (meats, dairy, breads and cereals, fruits and vegetables), and also put a tally mark for every time you eat any sweets, caffeine, or high-fat foods. In the last column, indicate when you ate a meal or snack.

Day	Breads	Dairy	Meats	Fruit/ Vegetable	Sweets	Caffeine	High-fat Food	Times
1								
2								
3								

Did you overdo it anywhere? If so, name the category: _____

● Did you not eat enough of any of the four groups? If so, which one(s)?

_____

_____

Evaluate your eating times. Did your eating schedule have positive or negative effects? Describe the effects.

_____

_____

Exercise. Next, log your exercise over the same period. Don't forget to include exercise such as climbing stairs, walking when your ride didn't show up, or cleaning your floors. For each entry, indicate the type of exercise you did and for how long a period of time you exercised (duration).

DAY	TYPE(S) OF EXERCISE	DURATION OF EXERCISE
1		
2		
3		

From this table, evaluate your fitness profile. Are you more or less active than you need to be?

_____

_____

Sleep. During this week, log exactly how many hours you sleep. Indicate exactly when you slept. Include naps and note any waking periods during sleep. Check the appropriate column on days when you felt well rested or run-down.

DAY	MAJOR SLEEP PERIOD	WAKING PERIODS	NAPS	WELL RESTED?	RUN DOWN?
1					
2					
3					

When you felt well rested, what effects did your sleeping pattern have on your day?

_____

_____

When you felt run-down, did a different sleeping pattern that day affect you negatively?

_____

_____

Finally, using your problem-solving skills, come up with a plan to address the changes you would like to make. Illustrate each change—one for food, one for exercise, and one for sleep, if you have changes you want to make in all three areas—using a think link on a separate piece of paper (you may want to use a copy of the problem-solving plan in Chapter 4).

What change in your eating habits would you like to make?

_____

_____

How do you think your exercise program should change (or if you have no program, what do you think you should begin)?

_____

_____

Judging from the information in the table, what change do you need to make to have the ideal sleep schedule for you?

_____

_____

Early Warning Signs of Stress

Step 1. Check any items that you have experienced at least once in the last three months. "Compulsive behaviors" are behaviors that are repeated excessively, such as constant handwashing.

[ ] Indigestion	[ ] Irritability	[ ] Forgetfulness
[ ] Diarrhea/constipation	[ ] Excessive anger	[ ] Poor concentration
[ ] Nausea or vomiting	[ ] Worry	[ ] Distorted perception
[ ] Appetite problems	[ ] Depression	[ ] Compulsive behaviors
[ ] Headaches	[ ] Excessive crying	[ ] Decrease in productivity
[ ] Neck or back pain	[ ] Aggressiveness	[ ] Decrease in creativity
[ ] Allergies	[ ] Isolation	[ ] Living in the past

[ ] Hair loss

[ ] Colds, flu, cold sore

[ ] Teeth grinding

[ ] Problems sleeping

[ ] Fatigue

[ ] Boredom

[ ] Decreased sense of humor

[ ] Critical of self/others

[ ] Decreased motivation

[ ] Decreased self-esteem

[ ] Drinking more

[ ] Smoking more

[ ] Decreased sex drive

[ ] Acting "antsy"

[ ] Accident prone

Step 2. Circle the three items that usually occur as early warning signs of stress for you.

Step 3. From what you know about relieving stress, describe the steps you plan to take when you experience any of the three items you circled.

Note: Discuss any early warning signs with a doctor. Some of the symptoms listed above could also signify a condition that requires medical treatment.

TEAMWORK: COMBINING FORCES

Actively dealing with stress. By yourself, make a list of stressors—whatever events or factors cause you stress. As a class, discuss the stressors you have listed. Choose the five most common. Divide the class into five groups according to who would choose what stressor as his or her most important (redistribute some people if the group sizes are unbalanced). Each group should discuss its assigned stressor, brainstorming solutions and strategies. List your best coping strategies and present it to the class. You may want to make copies of the lists so that every member of the class has five, one for each stressor.

WRITING: DISCOVERY THROUGH JOURNALING

To record your thoughts, use a separate journal or the lined page at the end of the chapter.

Addiction. Describe how you feel about the concept of addiction in any form—to alcohol, drugs, food, a person, or even an unhealthy behavior. How has it touched your life, if at all? How did you deal with it? If you have never faced an addiction or been close to someone who did, describe how you would face it if it ever happened to you.

CAREER PORTFOLIO:
CHARTING YOUR COURSE

Your health record. Just as your health affects your success at school, it affects how you perform on the job. When you apply for many jobs, especially those that require physical activity, you may be asked questions about your health and physical condition. Companies that provide health benefits to their employees may be especially interested in hiring people who take care of their health. You will benefit from (1) being aware of your health status and (2) working to improve any conditions that you have.

On a separate sheet of paper, draw up a "medical record" for yourself. Include the following:

➤ Health insurance plan and policy numbers
➤ Phone numbers of physicians and clinics; phone numbers of other important people to call in a medical emergency
➤ Immunizations: ones you have completed and any you have yet to receive
➤ Surgeries you have had (include reason)
➤ Hospital stays (include reason)
➤ Illnesses and/or diseases
➤ Family health history (parents, grandparents, siblings)
➤ Chronic health problems (arthritis, tendonitis, ulcer, etc.)
➤ Vision and/or hearing statistics, if applicable
➤ Prescriptions used regularly and why
➤ Other

Highlight any conditions you feel you could improve with work or treatment. Choose one and draw up a problem-solving plan for making that improvement a reality.

Look again at the self-test on page 405. Make a copy of the questions and answer them on a separate sheet that you keep with your portfolio. If you feel that your score indicates a problem, write on the sheet what steps you intend to take, and get help.

Consider the positive side of your health as well. Make a list of the areas in which you enjoy very good health. For each, describe briefly how you maintain it.

Keep these lists up to date so you can monitor your health. If you change health plans or apply for a new job, for example, you may need to furnish information about your health record. You'll have many opportunities to refer to this information.

Journal Entry

CROSSWORD REVIEW: PART IV
Sharpening Your Skills

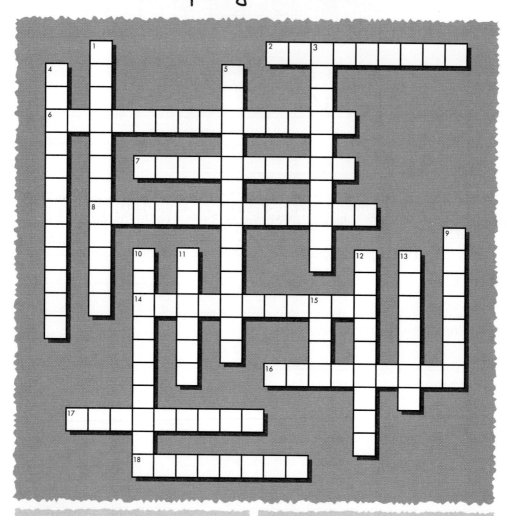

ACROSS

2. A preconceived judgment or opinion, formed without just grounds or sufficient knowledge
6. The denial of jobs, services, or opportunities based on perceived differences
7. A standardized mental picture that represents an oversimplified opinion or uncritical judgment
8. Alternating types of exercise and combining elements from different types of exercise
14. One of the two important roles in group interaction
16. Able to declare and affirm one's own opinions while respecting the rights of others to do the same
17. Compulsive physiological need for a habit-forming substance
18. A highly addictive drug found in all tobacco products

DOWN

1. Criticism offered supportively and containing useful suggestions for improvement
3. Chemical compounds that have a positive and calming effect on the body
4. Types of nonverbal communication, such as gestures and facial expressions
5. Having five or more alcoholic drinks at one sitting
9. A style of communication involving the concealing of one's feelings and the denying of one's own anger
10. A "whole body" illness, involving body, mood, and thoughts, involving extreme sadness
11. A reaction, good or bad, that occurs as an effect of a life change
12. The discontinuance of the use of a drug, including any resulting side effects
13. An eating disorder characterized by bingeing on, and then purging, excessive amounts of food
15. A sexually transmitted disease, caused by HIV, that disarms the body's immune system

PART 5

Preparing for the Future

CHAPTER 12 Managing Career and Money: Reality Resources

CHAPTER 13 Moving Ahead: Building a Flexible Future

P L A N

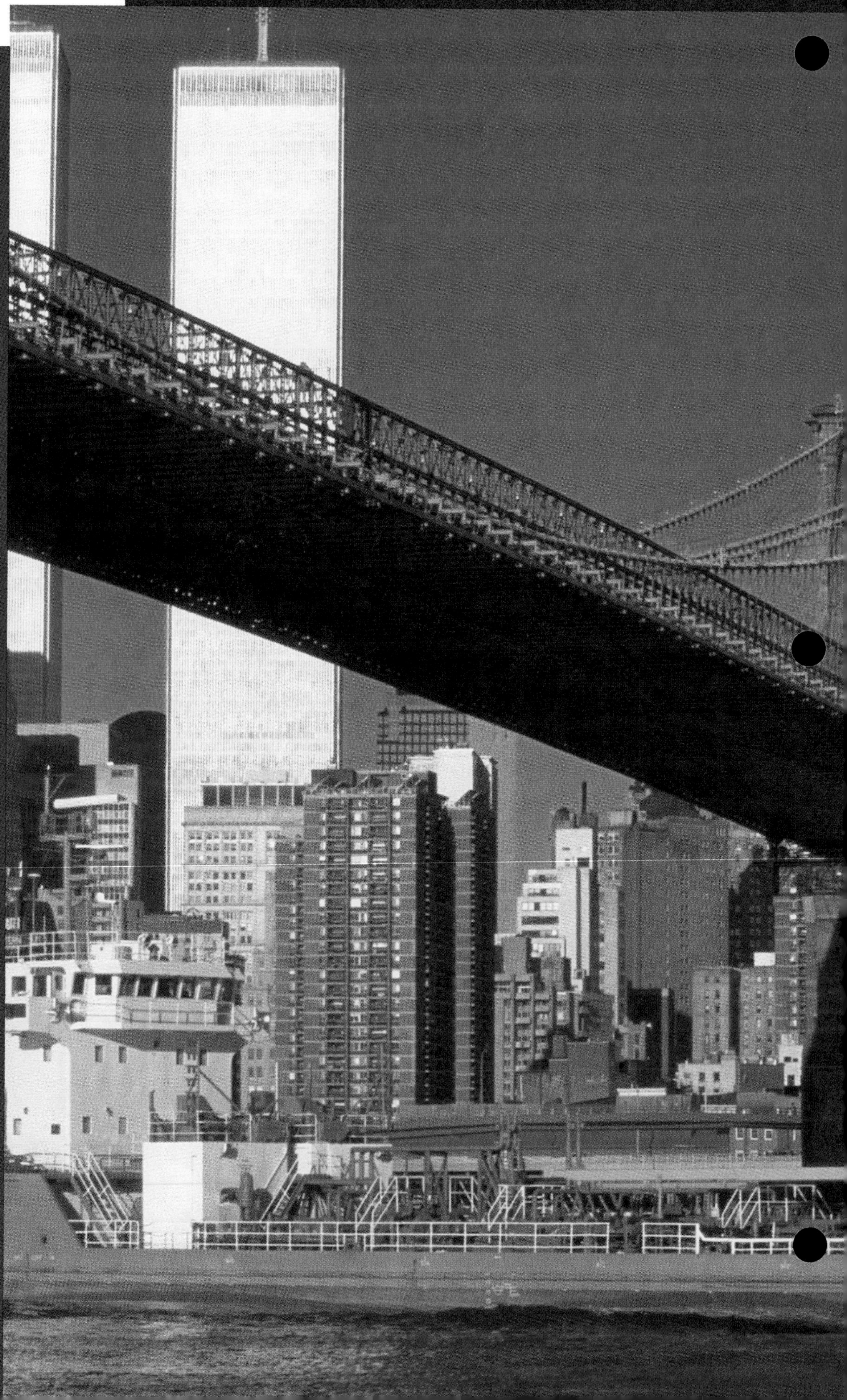

P L A N

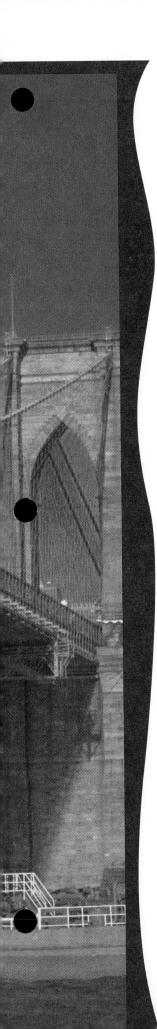

12 MANAGING CAREER AND MONEY:
Reality Resources

Thinking It Through

Check those statements that apply to you right now:

☐ I have no idea what I want to do for a career.
☐ I don't know how to be marketable in the workplace if I don't have experience.
☐ I have a job and it's tough to fit everything in with my classes.
☐ I can't pay for my education on my own.
☐ It's a drag to save money for the future when I need it now.
☐ I've run into trouble with credit cards, but I need them.

In this chapter, you will explore answers to the following questions:

➤ How can you plan your career?
➤ How can you juggle work and school?
➤ What should you know about financial aid?
➤ How can you create a budget that works?

Many people either love their jobs but don't make much money or dislike their jobs but are paid well. Still other people have neither job satisfaction nor a good paycheck to show for their work. The ideal career interests and challenges you *and* pays you enough to live comfortably. Although the changing world brings workplace challenges—caring for children while holding a job, fitting work around a study schedule, keeping on top of the latest work skills—you do have the means to find a career that works for you, whether you want to be an attorney in New York, an archaeologist in northern Africa, or anything else that fits your dreams.

Career exploration, job-hunting strategy, and money management can work together to help you find the ideal career. In this chapter, you will first look at career exploration and how to balance work and school. Then you will explore how to bring in money with financial aid and how to manage the money you have. Managing your resources and investigating career options can help you develop skills and insights that will serve you throughout your life.

HOW CAN YOU PLAN YOUR CAREER?

College is an ideal time to investigate careers, because so many different resources are available to you. You may not have thought too much about it yet. You may have already had a career for years and are looking for a change. You may have been set on a particular career but are now having second thoughts. No matter your starting point, now is the time to make progress.

Even outside this particular chapter, everything you read and work on in this book is geared toward workplace success. As you work on the exercises, you think critically, become a team player, hone writing skills, and develop long-term planning, all of which prepare you to thrive in any career.

Define a Career Path

Aiming for a job in a particular area requires planning the steps that can get you there. Whether these steps take months or years, they help you focus your energies on your goal. Defining a career path involves investigating yourself, exploring potential careers, and building knowledge and experience.

Investigate Yourself

When you explore your learning style in Chapter 3, evaluate your ideal note-taking system in Chapter 7, or look at how you relate to others in Chapter 10, you build self-knowledge. Gather everything that you know about yourself, from this class or any of your other life experiences, and investigate. What do you know or do best? Out of jobs you've had, what did you like and not like to do? How would you describe your personality? And finally, what kinds of careers make the best use of everything you are?

Don't feel as though you should automatically know what you want to do. Most students who have not been in the workplace don't know what career they want to pursue. Students who have been working often return to school to explore other careers that they might prefer. These days, people are changing careers many times in their lives instead of sticking with one choice. This discovery is a lifelong process.

Explore Potential Careers

Career possibilities extend far beyond what you can imagine. Brainstorm about career areas. Ask instructors, relatives, and fellow students about careers that they have or know about. Check your library for books on careers or biographies of people who worked in fields that interest you. Explore careers you discover through newspapers, novels, or nonfiction. If a character in your favorite movie has a job you think you'd like, see what you can find out about it.

Your school's *career center* is an important resource in your investigation. The career center may offer job listings, occupation lists, assessments of skills and personality types, questionnaires that help you pinpoint areas that may suit you, informational material about different careers, and material about various companies. The people who work at the center can help you sort through the material.

TABLE 12-1 CRITICAL-THINKING QUESTIONS FOR CAREER INVESTIGATION

What can I do in this area that I like and/or am good at?	Do I respect the company and/or the industry?
What are the educational requirements (certificates or degrees and courses)?	Do companies in this industry generally accommodate special needs (child care, sick days, flextime, or working at home)?
What skills are necessary?	Do I need to belong to a union?
What wage or salary is normal for an entry-level position, and what benefits can I expect?	Are there opportunities in this industry within a reasonable distance from where I live?
What kinds of personalities are best suited to this kind of work?	What other expectations are there beyond the regular workday (travel, overtime, etc.)?
What are the prospects for moving up to higher-level positions?	Do I prefer a service or manufacturing industry?

Use your critical-thinking skills to broaden your questions beyond just what tasks you perform for any given job. Many other factors will be important to you. Look at Table 12–1 for some of the kinds of questions you might ask as you talk to people or investigate materials.

Build Knowledge and Experience

Having knowledge and experience specific to the career you want to pursue will be valuable on the job hunt. Courses, internships, jobs, and volunteering are four great ways to build both.

Courses. When you narrow your career exploration to a couple of areas that interest you, look through your course catalog and take a course or two in those fields. How you react to these courses will give you important clues to how you feel about the area in general. Be careful to evaluate your experience according to how you feel about the subject matter and not other factors, such as the instructor or the time of day when the class takes place.

Internships. An internship may or may not offer pay. Although this may be a financial drawback, the experience you can gather and contacts you can make may be worth the work. Many internships take place during the summer, but some part-time internships are also available during the school year. Companies that offer internships are looking for people who will work hard in exchange for experience they can't get in the classroom. Internships are one of the best ways to show a prospective employer some real-world experience and initiative.

Internship,
A temporary work program in which a student can gain supervised practical experience in a professional field.

Jobs. No matter how you earn money while you are in college, whether it is in your area of interest or not, you may discover career opportunities that appeal to you. Someone who takes a third-shift legal proofreading job to make extra cash might discover an interest in the law. Someone who answers phones for a newspaper company might be drawn into journalism. Be aware of the possibilities around you.

Volunteering. Offering your services in the community or at your school can introduce you to careers and increase your experience. Some schools have programs that can help you find opportunities to work as an aide on campus or volunteer off campus. Recently, certain schools have even begun listing volunteer activities on student transcripts. Be sure to note volunteer activities on your résumé—many employers seek candidates who have shown commitment through volunteering.

Map Out Your Strategy

After you've gathered enough information to narrow your career goals, plan strategically to achieve them. Make a career time line as shown in Figure 12–1. Mark years and half-year points (and months for the first year), and write in the steps when you think they should happen. Set goals that establish who you will talk to, what courses you will take, what skills you

FIGURE 12-1   **CAREER TIME LINE**

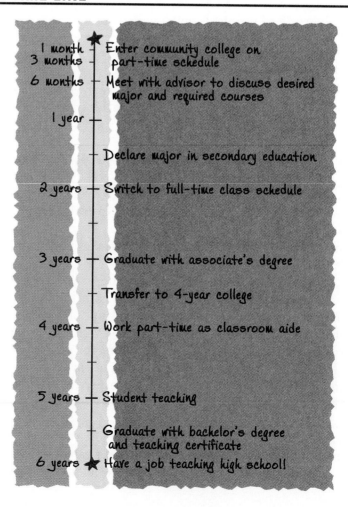

1 month — Enter community college on
3 months — part-time schedule
6 months — Meet with advisor to discuss desired major and required courses

1 year —

— Declare major in secondary education

2 years — Switch to full-time class schedule

3 years — Graduate with associate's degree

— Transfer to 4-year college

4 years — Work part-time as classroom aide

5 years — Student teaching

— Graduate with bachelor's degree and teaching certificate

6 years — Have a job teaching high school!

will work on, what jobs or internships you will investigate, and any other research. Because your path may change, use your time line as a guide.

The road to a truly satisfying career can be long. Although changing careers used to be a risky and rare practice, now people commonly have as many as five careers over the course of their lives, and this number may continue to rise. Seek support as you work toward your goals. Confide in supportive people, talk positively to yourself, and read inspiring books. Two helpful books are *What Color Is Your Parachute?* by Richard Nelson Bolles, and *Zen and the Art of Making a Living: A Practical Guide to Creative Career Design* by Laurence G. Boldt. More are listed in the bibliography.

Know What Employers Want

Certain basic skills will make you an excellent job candidate in any career. Employers look for particular skills and qualities that signify an efficient and effective employee. You can continue to develop these skills as you work in current and future jobs—and you will, if you always strive to improve.

A prospective employee talks with an IBM representative at an employment fair

Communication skills. Being able to listen well and express yourself in writing and speaking is a key to workplace success. Much can be accomplished through efficient, open communication. Being able to adjust to different communication styles is an important factor.

Problem solving. Any job will present problems that need to be solved. An employee who knows how to assess any situation and apply the problem-solving process to it will stand out.

Decision making. Decisions large and small are made in every workplace every day. Knowing how to think through and make decisions will help you in any job.

Teamwork. It is a rare workplace that has only one employee; even then, that person will interact with different kinds of people on the phone or through a computer. The importance of being able to work well with others cannot be overemphasized. If there is a weak link in any team, the whole company suffers.

Intercultural communication. The workplace is becoming increasingly diverse. The more you can work well with people different from yourself and open your mind to their points of view, the more valuable an employee you will be.

Leadership. The ability to influence others in a positive way will earn you respect and keep you in line for promotions. Taking the lead will often command attention.

Creativity. When you can see the big picture as well as the details and can let your mind come up with unexpected new concepts and plans, you will bring valuable suggestions to your workplace.

Commitment. You will encounter many difficult situations at work. The ability to continue to work hard in such situations is extremely important. In addition, if you introduce a new and creative idea, you can gain support for it if you have a strong commitment to it yourself.

Values and integrity. Your personal values and integrity will help guide everything you do. In your actions and decisions, consider what you value and what you believe is right.

Many students need to work and take classes at the same time to fund the education that they hope will move them into better careers. Although you may not necessarily work in a career that interests you, you can hold a job that helps you pay the bills and still make the most of your school time.

HOW CAN YOU JUGGLE WORK AND SCHOOL?

What you are studying today can prepare you to find a job when you graduate that suits your abilities and brings in enough money to support your needs and lifestyle choices. In the meantime, though, you can make work a part of your student life to make money, explore a career, and/or increase your future employability through contacts or résumé building.

FIGURE 12-2 **WORKING STUDENTS**

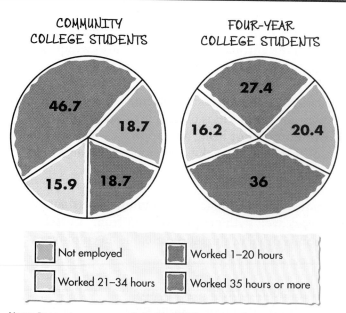

Note: Percentages may not sum to 100 because of rounding.

Source: U.S. Department of Education, National Center for Education Statistics, 1992–93 National Postsecondary Student Aid Study (NPSAS:93), Undergraduate Data Analysis System.

As the cost of education continues to rise, more and more students are working and taking classes at the same time. In the school year 1992–1993, 79 percent of undergraduates worked while in school. Most student workers twenty-three years of age or under held part-time jobs (37.8 percent). Of students over the age of twenty-three, a majority had full-time jobs (nearly 55 percent).[1] Figure 12–2 shows working statistics for both community-college and four-year-college students.

Being an employed student isn't for everyone, although many students don't have a choice. Adding a job to the list of demands on your time and energy may create problems if it sharply reduces study time or family time. However, many people want to work and many need to work to pay for school. Ask yourself important questions about why or why not to work. Weigh the potential positive and negative effects of working. From those answers you can make a choice that you feel benefits you most.

Effects of Working While in School

Working while in school has many different positive and negative effects, depending on the situation. Evaluate any job opportunity by looking at these effects. Following are some that might come into play.

Potential Positive Effects

Money earned. A job can provide crucial income to pay for rent, transportation, food, and important bills. It may even help you put some savings away to create a financial cushion.

General and career-specific experience. Important learning comes from hands-on work. Your education in the field can complement your classroom experience. Even if you don't work in your chosen area, you can improve universal skills such as teamwork and communication.

Being able to keep a job you currently hold. If you leave a job temporarily, your company might not be able to hold your position open until you come back. New mothers who want to take a longer maternity leave than company policy permits may run into this problem. Consider adjusting your responsibilities or hours while still holding your job.

Keeping busy. Work can provide a stimulating break from studying. In fact, working up to fifteen hours a week may actually enhance academic performance because working students often manage their time more efficiently and may gain confidence from their successes in the workplace. Working on campus may help you manage your time and connect to your school experience.

Potential Negative Effects

Time commitment. Whereas nonworking students split their time between academic and personal life, working students must add a third, time-consuming factor. More responsibilities and less time to fulfill them demands more efficient time management. Many schools recommend that students not work more than twenty hours a week while taking a full course load.

Adjusting priorities. The priority level of your job may vary. For a student who depends on the income, work may take priority over study time. Realize that you may have to reduce social activities, exercise at home, cut back on nonacademic activities, or lighten your course load to maintain a job and still study. Your job is important, but earning good grades may be just as crucial.

Shifting gears. Unless your job meshes with your classroom curriculum, it may take some effort to shift gears mentally as you move back and forth between academia and the workplace. Each environment has its own set of people, responsibilities, joys, and problems. Establish mental boundaries that can help you shake off academic stress while at work, and vice versa.

If you consider the positive and negative effects and decide that working will help you, establish what you need in a job.

Establishing Your Needs

Think about what you need before you begin your job hunt. Evaluate any potential job in terms of the factors shown in Table 12–2.

Sources of Job Information

Many different routes can lead to satisfying jobs. Use your school's career planning and placement office, networking skills, classified ads, employment agencies, and on-line services to help you explore.

Your School's Career Planning and Placement Offices

Generally, the career planning and placement office deals with postgraduation job placements, whereas the student employment office, along with the financial aid office, has information about working while in school. At either location you might find workplace information, listings of job opportunities, sign-up sheets for interviews, and contact information for companies. The career office may hold informational sessions on different topics or sponsor career fairs that give you a chance to explore job opportunities.

Many students, because they don't seek job information until they're about to graduate, miss much of what the career office can do. Don't wait until the last minute. Explore your school's career office early in your university life. The people and resources there can help you at every stage of your career and job exploration process.

Networking

Networking,
The exchange of information and/or services among individuals, groups, or institutions.

Networking is one of the most important job-hunting strategies. With each person you get to know, you build your network and tap into someone else's. Imagine a giant think link connecting you to a web of people just a couple of phone calls away. Of course, not everyone with whom you network will be helpful. Keep in contact with as many people as possible in the hope that someone will. You never know who that person might be.

With whom can you network? Friends and family members may know of jobs or other people who can help you. At your school, instructors, ad-

TABLE 12-2   WHAT YOU MAY NEED IN A JOB

NEED	DESCRIPTION
SALARY/WAGE LEVEL	Consider how much money you need to make month by month and yearly. You may need to make a certain amount for the year as a whole, but you may need to earn more of that total amount during the months when you are paying tuition. Consider also the amount that justifies taking the time to work. If a job pays well but takes extra hours that should go toward studying or classes, it might not be worth it. Take time to compare the positive effects with the negative effects of any job's pay structure.
TIME OF DAY	When you can work depends on your school schedule. For example, if you take classes Monday, Tuesday, and Thursday during the day, you could look for a job with weekend or evening hours. If you attend evening classes, a daytime job could work fine.
HOURS PER WEEK (PART TIME VS. FULL TIME)	If you take classes part time, you may choose to work a full-time job. If you are a full time student, it may be best to work part time. Balance your priorities so that you can accomplish your schoolwork and still make the money you need.
DUTIES PERFORMED	If you want hands-on experience in your chosen field, narrow your search to jobs that can provide it. On the other hand, if a regular paycheck is your priority, you might not care as much about what you do. Consider if there is anything you absolutely hate to do. Working somewhere and/or doing something that makes you miserable may not be worth any amount of money.
LOCATION	Weigh the effects of how long it takes to get to a job against what you are getting out of it, and decide whether it is worthwhile. A job at or near your school may give un-paralleled convenience. When you know you can get to work quickly, you can schedule your day more tightly and get more done.
FLEXIBILITY	Even if your classes have regular hours, you might have other projects and meetings at various times. Do you need a job that offers flexibility, allowing you to shift your working time when you have to attend to an academic or family responsibility that takes priority? Choose according to the flexibility you require.
AFFILIATION WITH SCHOOL OR FINANCIAL AID PROGRAM	Some financial aid packages, especially if they involve funds from your school, can require you to take work at the school or a federal organization. In that case you would have to choose among the opportunities offered.
ACCOMMODATION OF SPECIAL NEEDS	If you have a hearing or vision impairment, reduced mobility, children for whom you need day care, or other special needs, you may want to find an employer who can and will accommodate them.

Contact,
A person who serves as a carrier or source of information.

ministrators, or counselors may give you job or **contact** information. People at school employment or career offices can help you locate work. Look to your present and past work experience for more leads. Employers or coworkers may know someone who needs new employees. A former employer might hire you back, if you left on good terms.

The contacts with whom you network aren't just sources of job opportunities. They are people with whom you can develop valuable relationships and from whom you can learn about what they do. Thank your contacts for their help and don't forget them. Networking is a two-way street. Even as you receive help, be ready to extend yourself to others who may need help and advice from you.

Classified Ads

Some of the best job listings are in daily or periodic newspapers. Most papers print help-wanted sections in each issue, organized according to career categories. At the beginning of most help-wanted sections you will find an index that tells you the categories and on what pages they begin in the listings. Individual ads describe the kind of position available and give a telephone number or post office box for you to contact. Some ads include additional information such as job requirements, a contact person, and the salary or wages offered.

You can run your own classified ads in your school or local paper if you have a skill you want to advertise. Many college students make extra cash by doing specific tasks for campus employees or other students, such as typing, editing, cleaning, tutoring, or baby-sitting.

On-line Services

The Internet is growing as a source of job listings. You can access job search databases such as the Career Placement Registry and U.S. Employment Opportunities. Web sites such as CareerPath.com and CareerMosaic list all kinds of positions. Individual associations and companies may also post job listings and descriptions, often as part of their World Wide Web pages. For example, IBM includes job openings on its Web page. Refer to the internet appendix at the end of this book for help on how to find the information you need on the Internet.

Employment Agencies

Employment agencies are organizations that help people find work. Most employment agencies will put you through a screening process that consists of an interview and one or more tests in your area of expertise. For example, someone looking for secretarial work may take a word-processing test and a spelling test, and someone looking for accounting work may take accounting and math tests. If you perform well on the tests and interview, the agency will try to place you in a job.

Most employment agencies specialize in particular careers or skills, such as accounting, medicine, legal, computer operation, graphic arts, child care, and food services. Agencies may place job seekers in either part-time or full-time employment. Many agencies also place people in temporary jobs,

> *"Whatever you think you can do or believe you can do, begin it. Action has magic, grace, and power in it."*
>
> Johann Wolfgang von Goethe

which can work well for students who are available from time to time. Such agencies may have you call in whenever you are free to see if anything is available that day or week.

Making a Strategic Job Search Plan

When you have gathered information on the jobs you want, formulate a plan for pursuing them. Organize your approach according to what you need to do and how much time you have to devote to your search. Do you plan to make three phone calls per day? Will you fill out three job applications a week for a month? Keep a record—on 3-by-5-inch cards, a computer file, or in a notebook—of the following:

➤ People you contact
➤ Companies to which you apply
➤ Jobs you rule out (e.g., jobs that become unavailable or which you find don't suit your needs)
➤ Response from your communications (phone calls to you, interviews, and written communications) and the information on whoever contacted you (names, titles, times, and dates)

Keeping accurate records will enable you to both chart your progress and maintain a clear picture of the process. You never know when information might come in handy again. If you don't get a job now, another one could open up at the same company in a couple of months. In that case, well-kept records would enable you to contact key personnel quickly and efficiently. See Figure 12–3 for a sample file card.

SAMPLE FILE CARD   **FIGURE 12-3**

Job/company: Child-care worker at Morningside Day Care
Contact: Sally Wheeler, Morningside Day Care, 17 Parkside Road,
        Silver Spring, MD 20910
Phone/fax/e-mail: (301) 555-3353 phone, (301) 555-3354 fax, no e-mail
Communication: Saw ad in paper, sent résumé and cover letter on October 7
Response: Call from Sally to set up interview

— Interview on Oct. 15 at 2 p.m., seemed to get a positive response,
   she said she would contact me again by the end of the week

Follow-up: Sent thank-you note on October 16

Your Résumé and Interview

Information on résumés and interviews fills many books. Therefore, your best bet is to consult some that go into more detail, such as *The Resume Kit* by Richard Beatty or *Job Interviews for Dummies* by Joyce Lain Kennedy (don't be insulted by the title; it has lots of terrific information). You'll find additional suggestions in the Bibliography at the end of this book.

Here are a few basic tips to get you started on giving yourself the best possible chance at a job.

Résumé. Your resume should always be typed or printed on a computer. Design your résumé neatly, using an acceptable format (books or your career office can show you some standard formats). Proofread it for errors, and have someone else proofread it as well. Type or print it on a heavier bond paper than is used for ordinary copies. Use white or off-white paper and black ink.

Interview. Pay attention to your appearance. Be clean, neat, and appropriately dressed. Don't forget to choose a nice pair of shoes—people notice. Bring an extra copy of your résumé and any other materials that you want to show the interviewer, even if you have already sent a copy ahead of time. Avoid chewing gum or smoking. Offer a confident handshake. Make eye contact. Show your integrity by speaking honestly about yourself. After the interview is over, no matter what the outcome, send a formal but pleasant thank-you note right away as a follow-up.

Earning the money you need is hard, especially if you work part time so that your job won't interfere with school. Financial aid can take some of the burden off your shoulders. If you can gather one or more loans, grants, or scholarships, they may help make up for what you don't have time to earn.

WHAT SHOULD YOU KNOW ABOUT FINANCIAL AID?

Seeking financial help has become a way of life for many students. Education is an important but often expensive investment. The cost for a year's full-time tuition only (not including room and board) in 1995–1996 ranged from $900 to $15,000, with the national average hovering around $2100 for public institutions and over $11,000 for private ones.[2] Not many people can pay for tuition in full without aid. In fact, according to data compiled in the academic year 1992–1993, over 41 percent of students enrolled received some kind of aid,[3] and that number almost certainly will continue to increase along with rising tuition costs.

Most sources of financial aid don't seek out recipients. Take the initiative to learn how you (or you and your parents, if they currently help to support you) can finance your education. Find the people on campus who can help you with your finances. Do some research to find out what's available, weigh the pros and cons of each option, and decide what would work best for you. Try to apply as early as you can. The types of financial aid available to you are loans, grants, and scholarships.

Student Loans

A loan is given to you by a person, bank, or other lending agency, usually to put toward a specific purchase. You, as the recipient of the loan, must then pay back the amount of the loan, plus interest, in regular payments that stretch over a particular period of time. Interest is the fee you pay for the privilege of using money that belongs to someone else.

Types of Student Loans

The federal government administers or oversees most student loans. To receive aid from any federal program, you must be a citizen or eligible noncitizen and be enrolled in a program of study that the government has determined is eligible. Individual states may differ in their aid programs. Check with your campus financial aid office to learn details about your state and your school in particular.

Following are the main student loan programs to which you can apply if you are eligible. Amounts vary according to individual circumstances. Contact your school or federal student aid office for further information. In most cases, the amount is limited to the cost of your education minus any other financial aid you are receiving. All the information on federal loans and grants comes from the *1999–2000 Student Guide to Financial Aid*, published by the U.S. Department of Education.[4]

Perkins loans. Carrying a low, fixed rate of interest, Perkins loans are available to those with exceptional financial need (need is determined by a government-determined formula that indicates how large a contribution toward your education your family should be able to make). Schools issue these loans from their own allotment of federal education funds. After you graduate, you have a grace period (up to nine months, depending on whether you were a part-time or full-time student) before you have to begin repaying your loan in monthly installments.

Stafford loans. Students enrolled in school at least half-time may apply for a Stafford Loan. Exceptional need is not required. However, students who can prove exceptional need may qualify for a subsidized Stafford Loan, for which the government pays your interest until you begin repayment. There are two types of Stafford Loans. A Direct Stafford Loan comes from government funds, and an FFEL Stafford Loan comes from a bank or credit union participating in the FFEL (Federal Family Education Loan) program. The type available to you depends on your school's financial aid program. You begin to repay a Stafford Loan six months after you graduate, leave school, or drop below half-time enrollment.

PLUS loans. Your parents can apply for a PLUS Loan if they currently claim you as a dependent and if you are enrolled at least half-time. They must also undergo a credit check to be eligible, although the loans are not based on income. If they do not pass the credit check, they may be able to sponsor the loan through a relative or friend who does pass. Interest is variable; the loans are available from either the government or banks and credit unions. Your parents will have to begin repayment sixty days after they receive the last loan payment; there is no grace period.

Grants and Scholarships

Both grants and scholarships require no repayment and therefore give your finances a terrific boost. Grants, funded by the government, are awarded to students who show financial need. Scholarships are awarded to students who show talent or ability in the area specified by the scholarship. They may be financed by government or private organizations, schools, or individuals.

Federal Grant Programs

Pell grants. These grants are need-based. The U.S. Department of Education uses a standard formula to evaluate the financial information you report on your application and determines your eligibility from that score (called an EFC, or Expected Family Contribution). You must also be an undergraduate who has earned no other degrees to be eligible. The Pell Grant serves as a foundation of aid to which you may add other aid sources, and the amount of the grant varies according to the cost of your education and your EFC. Pell Grants require no repayment.

FSEOG (Federal Supplemental Educational Opportunity Grants). Administered by the financial aid administrator at participating schools, FSEOG eligibility depends on need. Whereas the government guarantees that every student eligible for a Pell Grant will receive one, each school receives a limited amount of federal funds for FSEOGs, and once it's gone, it's gone. Schools set their own application deadlines. Apply early. No repayment is required.

Work-study. Although you work in exchange for the aid, work-study is considered a grant. This program is need-based and encourages community service work or work related in some way to your course of study. You will earn at least the federal minimum wage and will be paid by the hour. Jobs can be on campus (usually for your school) or off campus (often with a nonprofit organization or a local, state, or federal public agency). Find out who is in charge of the work-study program on your campus.

Many other important details about federal grants and loans are available in *The 1999–2000 Student Guide to Financial Aid*. You might find this information at your school's financial aid office, or you can request it by mail, phone, or on-line service:

Address:	Federal Student Aid Information Center P.O. Box 84 Washington, D.C. 20044-0084
Phone:	1-800-4-FED-AID (1-800-433-3243) TDD for the hearing-impaired: 1-800-730-8913
Internet address:	www.ed.gov/prog_info/SFA/StudentGuide

Scholarships

Scholarships are given for various abilities and talents. They may reward academic achievement, abilities in sports or the arts, citizenship, or leadership. Certain scholarships are sponsored by federal agencies. If you display exceptional ability and are disabled, female, of an ethnic background classified as a minority (such as African American or Native American), or a child of someone who draws benefits from a state agency (such as a POW, prisoner of war, or MIA, missing in action), you might find scholarship opportunities geared toward you.

All kinds of organizations offer scholarships. You may receive scholarships from individual departments at your school or your school's independent scholarship funds, local organizations such as the Rotary Club, or privately operated aid foundations. Labor unions and companies may offer scholarships for children of their employees. Membership groups such as scouting organizations or the Y might offer scholarships, and religious organizations such as the Knights of Columbus or the Council of Jewish Federations might be another source.

Researching Grants and Scholarships

Most scholarships and grants aren't widely advertised. Ask at your school's financial aid office. Visit your library or bookstore and look in the section on college or financial aid. Guides to funding sources, such as Richard Black's *The Complete Family Guide to College Financial Aid*, catalog thousands of organizations. Check out on-line scholarship search services. Use common sense when applying for aid—fill out the application as neatly as possible and submit it on time or even early. In addition, be wary of scholarship scam artists who ask you to first pay a fee for them to find aid for you.

No matter where your money comes from—financial aid or paychecks from one or more jobs—you can take steps to help it stretch as far as possible. The following section concentrates on budgeting effectively so that you can cover your expenses and still have some left over for savings and fun.

THINKING BACK

1. What four areas help you build the knowledge and experience with which you can define a career path? Of those four, circle the two most important for you.

   _____

   _____

   _____

   _____

2. What are four need categories to consider when job hunting? Circle the category that would take priority for you if you were looking for a job right now.

   _____

   _____

   _____

   _____

3. Name three sources of job-search information and where you can find them.

   _____

   _____

   _____

   _____

4. Name two kinds of federal loans, two kinds of federal grants, and two scholarship sources.

   _____

   _____

   _____

   _____

THINKING AHEAD

1. What is your philosophy about how much money you save and how much you spend?

_____

_____

_____

2. Do you monitor your incoming and outgoing money? If so, how?

_____

_____

_____

3. What kinds of day-to-day strategies help you save money?

_____

_____

_____

4. Do you use credit cards not at all, just enough, or too much? Do you pay on time, or do you fall behind?

_____

_____

_____

HOW CAN YOU CREATE A BUDGET THAT WORKS?

Every time you have some money in your pocket and have to figure out whether it will pay for what you want at that moment, you are **budgeting** your money. It takes some thought and energy to budget efficiently. Consider your resources (money coming in) and expenditures (money flowing out). A smart budget adjusts the money flow for the best possible way to ensure that what comes in will be more than what goes out. Smart budgeting is a worthwhile investment in your future.

Budgeting,
Making a plan for the coordination of resources and expenditures; setting goals with regard to money.

The Art of Budgeting

Budgeting involves following a few basic steps in order: determining how much money you make, determining how much money you spend, subtracting the second number (what you spend) from the first number (what you make), evaluating the result, and basing decisions about how to adjust your spending or earning on that result. Budgeting regularly is easiest. Use a specified time frame, such as a week or a month. Most people budget on a month-by-month basis.

Determine How Much You Make

> *"Put not your trust in money, but put your money in trust."*
>
> Oliver Wendell Holmes

Add up all your money receipts for the month. If you currently have a regular full-time or part-time job, add your pay stubs. If you have received any financial aid, loan funding, or scholarship money, determine how much of that you can allow for each month's income and add it to your total. For example, if you received a $1200 grant for the year, each month would have an income of $100. Be sure, when you are figuring your income, to use the amounts that remain after taxes have been taken out.

Determine How Much You Spend

You may or may not be aware of your spending habits. If you have never before paid much attention to how you spend money, examine your spending patterns. Over a month's time, record expenditures in a small notebook or on a piece of paper on a home bulletin board. You don't have to list everything down to the penny. Just indicate expenditures over five dollars, and count smaller expenditures if they are frequent (such as bus fare). In your list, include an estimate of the following:

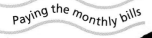
Paying the monthly bills

➤ Rent, mortgage, or school room fees
➤ Tuition or loan payments (divide your annual total by twelve to arrive at a monthly figure)
➤ Books, lab fees, and other educational expenses
➤ Regular bills (heat, gas, electric, phone, car payment, and water)
➤ Credit card or other payments on credit
➤ Food, clothing, toiletries, and household supplies
➤ Child care
➤ Entertainment and related items (eating out, books and publications, and movies)
➤ Health, auto, and home or renters' insurance
➤ Transportation and auto expenses

Subtract what you spend from what you make. Ideally, you will have a positive number. You may end up with a negative number, however, especially if you haven't kept track of your spending. This indicates that you are spending more than you make, which over a long period of time can create debt.

Evaluate the Result

If you have a positive number, decide how to save it if you can. If you have a negative number, ask questions about what is causing the deficit—where you are spending too much or earning too little. Of course, surprise expenses may cause you to spend more than usual in a particular month, such as if you have to pay equipment fees for a course or money to repair your car. However, when a negative number comes up for what seems to be a typical month, you may need to adjust your budget over the long term.

Make Decisions about How to Adjust
Spending or Earning

Looking at what may cause you to overspend, brainstorm possible solutions that address those causes. Solutions can involve either increasing resources or decreasing spending. To deal with spending, prioritize your expenditures and trim the ones you really don't need to make. Do you eat out too much? Can you live without cable, a beeper, or a cellular phone? Cut out unaffordable extras. As for resources, investigate ways to take in more money. Taking a part-time job, hunting down scholarships or grants, or increasing hours at a current job may help.

A Sample Budget

Table 12–3 shows a sample budget of an unmarried student living with two other students. It will give you an idea of how to budget (all expenditures are general estimates, based on averages).

TABLE 12-3   A STUDENT'S SAMPLE BUDGET

Part-time salary: $10 an hour, 20 hours a week. $10 \times 20 = \$200$ a week, $\times 4$ 1/3 weeks (one month) = $866. Student loan from school's financial aid office: $2000 divided by 12 months = $166. Total income per month: $1032.

MONTHLY EXPENDITURES	AMOUNT
Tuition ($6500 per year)	$ 542
Public transportation	$ 90
Phone	$ 40
Food	$ 130
Medical insurance	$ 120
Rent (including utilities)	$ 200
Entertainment/miscellaneous	$ 100
Total spending	**$1222**

$1032 (income) – $1222 (spending) = $–190 ($190 over budget)

To make up the $190 that this student went over budget, he can adjust his spending. He could rent movies or check them out of the library instead of going to the theatre. He could socialize with friends at someone's apartment instead of paying high prices and tips at a bar or restaurant. Instead of buying CDs and tapes, he could borrow them. He could also shop for specials and bargains in the grocery store or go to a warehouse supermarket to stock up on staples at discount prices. He could make his lunch instead of buying it and walk instead of taking public transportation.

Not everyone likes the work involved in keeping a budget. Whereas students with well-developed logical-mathematical intelligences may take to it more easily, less logical learners may resist the structure and detail (see Chapter 3). Visual learners may want to create a budget chart such as the one shown in the example or construct a think link that shows the connections between all the month's expenditures. Use strategies that make budgeting more tangible, such as dumping all of your receipts into a big jar and tallying them at the end of the month. Even if you have to force yourself to do it, you will discover that budgeting can reduce stress and help you take control of your finances and your life.

Savings Strategies

You can save money and still enjoy life. Make your fun less expensive, or save up for a while to splurge on a really special occasion. Here are some suggestions for saving a little bit of money here and there. Small amounts can add up to big savings after a while.

➤ Rent movies or attend bargain matinees.

➤ When safe for the fabric, hand-wash items you ordinarily dry clean.

➤ Check movies, CDs, tapes, and books out of your library.

➤ Make popcorn instead of buying bags of chips.

➤ Walk instead of paying for public transportation.

➤ If you have storage space, buy detergent, paper products, toiletries, and other staples in bulk.

➤ Shop in secondhand stores.

➤ Take advantage of weekly supermarket specials and bring coupons when you shop.

➤ Trade clothing with friends and barter services (plumbing for baby-sitting, for example).

➤ Buy display models of appliances or electronics (stereo equipment, televisions, and VCRs).

➤ Take your lunch instead of buying it.

➤ Find a low-rate long-distance calling plan, use e-mail, or write letters.

> ➤ Save on heat by dressing warmly and using blankets; save on air conditioning by using fans.

> ➤ Have pot luck parties; ask people to bring dinner foods or snacks.

Add your own suggestions here.

_____

_____

_____

You can also maximize savings and minimize spending by using credit cards wisely.

Managing Credit Cards

Most credit comes in the form of a powerful little plastic card. Credit card companies often solicit students on campus or through the mail. When choosing a card, pay attention to the *annual fee* and *interest rates*, the two ways in which a credit card company makes money from you. Some cards have no annual fee; others may charge a flat rate of $10 to $70 per year. Interest rates can be fixed or variable. A variable rate of 12 percent may shoot up to 20 percent when the economy slows down. You might be better off with a mid-range fixed rate that will always stay the same.

Following are some potential effects of using credit.

Positive Effects

Establishing a good credit history. If you use your credit card moderately and pay your bills on time, you will make a positive impression on your creditors . Your *credit history* (the record of your credit use, including positive actions such as paying on time and negative actions such as going over your credit limit) and *credit rating* (your score, based on your history) can make or break your ability to take out a loan or mortgage. How promptly you make loan payments and pay mortgage and utility bills affects your credit rating as well.

Creditors, People to whom debts are owed, usually money.

Emergencies. Few people carry enough cash to handle unexpected expenses. Your credit card can help you in emergencies such as when you need a tow.

Record of purchases. Credit card statements give you a monthly record of purchases made, where they were made, and exactly how much was paid. Using your credit card for purchases that you want to track, such as work expenses, can help you keep records for tax purposes.

WINDOWS ON THE WORLD: REAL LIFE STUDENT ISSUES

How can I handle my credit cards?

Maxine Deverney, Truman College, Chicago, Illinois, Accounting Major

Several years ago my husband and I divorced, and I became a single mother. I was responsible for raising three children on my own, as well as working a full-time job. Four years ago my daughter died at age twenty-one in a car accident. I took custody of her son until he was five. During this traumatic and stressful time was when I began to use credit cards. They make spending so easy. I had four, and I used them to buy school clothes for my own children. Then as they grew older and had children of their own, I helped financially with the grandchildren. I have ten grandchildren.

I have been working steadily for many years. Although I have managed to pay off most of the debt, and I am down to one credit card, I don't want to fall into that trap again. I have worked for four years in financial aid to help students receive grants from their tribes. I am also a secretary. Prior to this I worked as a director for a health clinic at a Chippewa reservation in Michigan. I am of the Potawatomi tribe of Wisconsin. When I graduate from Truman I will have an associates degree in accounting. My goal is to open my own accounting business one day. I would like to do some accounting for small firms and businesses. Can you offer steps I can take to stay debt-free?

Vernon Nash, Business & Housing Development, Chicago, Illinois

I know the challenges of using a credit card to ease the burden while being a working spouse, parent, and student. My challenge was with my son, Anthony, who was shot and had to have his leg amputated. This was devastating to me, my wife, and my other sons. So we used credit cards to get ourselves through as best we could. I suppose it was a way to compensate for the loss we all felt. I quickly found out that the interest and bills were mounting fast.

The problem with credit cards is that after your trying time has come and gone you are faced with a high credit card bill and can feel trapped in a cycle that seems impossible to stop. But it can be done. If you can pay additional money above what the credit card company is asking, you distance yourself from the debt. There are also a few other things you can do to avoid this happening to you again:

1. Determine that you will only buy what you can pay for within thirty days.
2. Pay your credit card bill on time, at least five days before the billing date or payment date, so that you don't rack up more interest payments.
3. Maintain a credit card balance of no more than 7 percent of your annual income.
4. Maintain a one-card limit.

When you graduate and want to start your small business, one of the best places to go for assistance is the Small Business Administration in your area. They can give you information about financing your business. Best of luck to you!

Negative Effects

Credit can be addictive. Credit can be like a drug because the pain of paying is put off until later. If you get hooked, though, you can wind up thousands of dollars in debt. The high interest will enlarge your debt; your credit rating may fall, hurting your eligibility for loans and mortgages; and you may lose your credit cards altogether.

Credit spending can be hard to monitor. Paying by credit can seem so easy that you don't realize how much you are spending. When the bill comes at the end of the month, the total can hit you hard.

You are taking out a high-interest loan. Buying on credit is similar to taking out a loan—you are using money with the promise to pay it back. Loan rates, however, especially on fixed-interest loans, are often much lower than the 11 to 23 percent on credit card debt. Fifteen percent interest per year on a credit card debt that averages $2000 is approximately $300; 5 percent interest per year on a loan in the same amount is $100.

Bad credit ratings can haunt you. Any time you are late with a payment, default on a payment, or in any way misuse your card, a record of that occurrence will be entered into your credit history, lowering your credit rating. If a prospective employer or loan officer discovers a low rating, you will seem less trustworthy and may lose the chance for a job or a loan.

Managing Credit Card Debt

There are ways to manage credit card debt so that it doesn't get worse. Stay in control by having only one or two cards and paying bills regularly and on time. Try to pay in full each month. If you can't, at least pay the minimum. Make as much of a dent in the bill as you can.

If you get into trouble, three steps will help you deal with the situation. First, *admit* that you made a mistake, even though you may be embarrassed. Then, *address* the problem immediately and honestly to minimize the damages. Call the bank or credit card company to talk to someone about the problem. He or she may draw up a payment plan that allows you to pay your debt gradually, in amounts that your budget can manage. Creditors would rather accept small payments than nothing at all.

Finally, *prevent* this problem from happening again. Figure out what got you into trouble and take steps to avoid it in the future if you can. Some financial disasters, such as medical emergencies, may be beyond your control. Overspending on luxuries, however, is something you have the power to avoid. Make a habit of balancing your checkbook. Cut up a credit card or two if you have too many. Don't let a high credit limit tempt you to spend. Pay every month, even if you pay only the minimum. If you work to clean up your act, your credit history will gradually clean up as well.

Sacrifici

In Italy, parents often use the term *sacrifici*, meaning "sacrifices," to refer to tough choices that they make to improve the lives of their children and family members. They may sacrifice a larger home, for example, so they can afford to pay for their children's sports and after-school activities. They give up something in exchange for something else that they have decided is more important to them.

Think of the concept of *sacrifici* as you analyze the sacrifices you can make to get out of debt, reach your savings goals, and prepare for a career that you find satisfying. Many of the short-term sacrifices you are making today will help you do and have what you want in the future. Keep that notion as a light to guide you through the ups and downs of student life.

IMPORTANT POINTS TO REMEMBER

 1. How do you plan your career?

 Begin to define a career path by investigating your abilities and looking at potential careers. Then build knowledge and experience by taking courses, jobs, and internships in areas that interest you. Think critically about what you want out of a career, and construct a strategic plan that will help you achieve your goal. As you follow your plan, prepare yourself to fulfill the expectations that today's employers have.

 2. How can you juggle work and school?

 The rising cost of education has prompted over 40 percent of students to work while in school. Weigh the pros and cons of working to decide if it's right for you. Positive effects may include income, experience, and connections. Negative effects may include the time commitment, adjusting priorities, and shifting gears from school to work. Establish your needs before you begin a job hunt. When you search for a job, take advantage of your school's career planning and placement offices, networking, classified ads, on-line services, and employment agencies.

 3. What should you know about financial aid?

 You can find information about financial aid opportunities through your school's financial aid office, books and pamphlets, and private organizations that may offer scholarships. Different sources of aid include bank and student loans, grants, and scholarships. The federal government sponsors many loans and grants; each one has different requirements.

4. How can you create a budget that works?

Budgeting means setting goals with your money. Consider resources (money in) and needs (money out) when budgeting. The basic steps are determining what you make, determining what you spend, subtracting what you spend from what you make, evaluating the result, and basing a decision about how to adjust spending or earning on that result. Budgeting regularly, such as once a month, works for many people. Managing your credit cards will help you stay on track.

Name _____ Date _____

**BUILDING SKILLS FOR COLLEGE, CAREER, AND LIFE SUCCESS
CHAPTER 12**

*TAKING STOCK:
REFINING YOUR THOUGHTS*

Look back at the statements you explored at the start of the chapter (see Thinking It Through on p. 423). Observe whether your attitudes have changed and what you have learned by studying this chapter.

1. What steps can you take to explore careers that may be right for you?

_____

_____

_____

2. Name four qualities you have that employers look for in job applicants.

_____

_____

_____

3. Name what you believe is the toughest negative effect and the best positive effect of working while in school. Then list two resources that can help you find work.

_____

_____

_____

4. Name the three major sources of financial aid and how you can investigate them.

_____

_____

_____

5. How can you manage your budget so that you can save money over the long term?

_____

_____

_____

_____

6. Name two positive effects and two negative effects of credit card use. How can you get out of trouble if you've missed payments or charged up to your limit?

_____

_____

_____

7. Name one money strategy that you are most likely to use in the next month. Discuss what you will do and what positive effects you think this strategy will have on your life.

_____

_____

_____

_____

❓ CRITICAL THINKING:
APPLYING LEARNING TO YOUR LIFE

Career Possibilities

Take a look at your list of areas of career interest from the Chapter 1 exercises. Write here what you consider your two top choices.

1. _____   2. _____

Investigate one of these. You may want to talk to people in the field, do research at the library, meet with someone at your career planning and placement office, or talk to someone who teaches in the field. Make notes as you investigate. Then, summarize your impressions here. What do you like or dislike? What suits your needs and what would be difficult? Do you plan to keep considering this area or not?

_____

_____

_____

Choose a job possibility in this field and follow up on it by using the following leads. Briefly describe the results of your research from each of the following.

Help-wanted listings in newspapers, magazines, or Internet databases:

_____

_____

_____

Listings of job opportunities and company contact information at your career center, student employment office, or independent employment agency:

_____

_____

_____

Contacts from friends or family members:

_____

_____

_____

Contacts from instructors, administrators, or counselors:

_____

_____

_____

Current or former employers or coworkers:

_____

_____

_____

Your Budget

Part I: Where your money goes. Estimate your current expenses in dollars per month, using the table below. This may require tracking expenses for a month, if you don't keep a record of your spending.

EXPENSE	AMOUNT SPENT
Rent/mortgage or room payment	$
Utilities (electric, heat, gas, water)	$
Food (shopping and eating out)	$
Telephone	$
Tuition	$
Books, lab fees, or other educational expenses	$
Loan payments (education or bank loans)	$
Car expenses (repairs, insurance, monthly payments)	$
Gasoline/public transportation	$
Clothing/personal items	$
Entertainment	$
Child care (caregivers, clothing and supplies, other fees)	$
Medical care/insurance	$
Miscellaneous/unexpected	$
GRAND TOTAL	$

Part II: Where your money comes from. Calculate the money you take in each month. Divide any annual payments by twelve to derive the monthly figure.

INCOME SOURCE	AMOUNT EARNED
Regular work salary/wages (full time or part time)	$
Grants or work-study payments	$
Scholarships	$
Monthly assistance from family members	$
Any independent contracting work	$
Other	$
GRAND TOTAL	$

Now, subtract the grand total of your monthly expenses (Part I) from the grand total of your monthly income (Part II):

My income is $\quad$ \$ _____ per month \$ _____

My expenses are $\quad$ \$ _____ per month -\$ _____

CASH FLOW $\quad$ \$ _____

Choose one:

I have \$+ _____

I have \$– _____

I pretty much break even

Part III: Adjusting your budget. If you have a negative cash flow, you can increase your income, decrease your spending, or do both. Go back to your list of current expenses to determine where you may be able to save. Look also at your list of income sources to determine what you can increase.

My current expenses $\quad$ \$_____ per month

I want to spend $\quad$ \$_____ less per month

My current income $\quad$ \$_____ per month

I want to earn $\quad$ \$_____ more per month

Evaluating your situation, describe here your two most important ideas about how to adjust your budget.

_____

_____

_____

TEAMWORK: COMBINING FORCES

Savings brainstorm. As a class, brainstorm areas that require financial management (such as funding an education, running a household, or putting savings away for the future) and write them on the board. Divide into small groups. Each group should choose one area to discuss (make sure all areas are chosen). In your group, brainstorm strategies that can help with the area you have chosen. Think of savings ideas, ways to control spending, ways to earn more money, and any other methods of relieving financial stress. Agree on a list of possible ideas for your area and share it with the class.

WRITING: DISCOVERY THROUGH JOURNALING

To record your thoughts, use a separate journal or the lined page at the end of the chapter.

Credit cards. Describe how you use credit cards. What do you buy with them? How much do you spend? Do you pay in full each month or run a balance? How does using a credit card make you feel? Discuss any changes you want to make and how they would help you.

CAREER PORTFOLIO: CHARTING YOUR COURSE

Financial and career history. Create for yourself a detailed picture of your finances and work history. First, put your budget exercises, or copies of them, in your portfolio so that you have a record of your spending habits. Then answer these questions on a separate sheet and keep your work on file. Keeping accurate financial records is vital in making intelligent financial decisions. Including your work record will help you maintain an accurate résumé and update it as needed.

In addition, you should always have a copy of important account and credit card numbers separate from your wallet or purse. That way, should you lose your cards, you have records of all of your credit card numbers and can cancel them immediately. *Note:* Do not include any PINs (personal identification numbers) anywhere in your portfolio. For your protection, any record of PINs should be kept separate from credit cards or credit card numbers.

1. What sources make up your financial aid package? List school, federal, and personal loans; scholarship funds; grants; and the amount that you pay out of pocket. Indicate all account numbers; payment plans; and records of payment, including dates and check numbers if applicable.

2. List bank accounts to which you have access, including all names on the accounts, bank names, type of accounts, and account numbers. Include any restrictions on the accounts such as minimum balances or time frames during which you will receive a penalty for removing funds.

3. List any nonacademic loans you are currently repaying, noting the purpose of the loan, repayment schedule, loan payment amounts and

dates of payments made, bank names and loan account numbers, and loan types.

4. List credit cards you use. Include major credit cards (American Express, Visa, MasterCard, Discover, etc.) as well as specific cards such as those for gas stations or department stores. For each card, include the following:

➤ Name on the card
➤ Card number
➤ Expiration date
➤ Date you got the card
➤ Payment style (pay in full, pay minimum each month, etc.)
➤ Problems (late payments, lost cards, card fraud, etc.)
➤ Current balance and date

5. Detail your current job history. List the jobs you have had or currently have. Include the following information for each:

➤ Name of the company or business
➤ Job title
➤ Wages or salary
➤ Job descriptions (your duties and responsibilities)
➤ Dates of your employment
➤ Personal contacts you made and have maintained (possible sources of references)

After you have completed this information, store it in your portfolio. Be sure to update it whenever there are changes.

Journal Entry

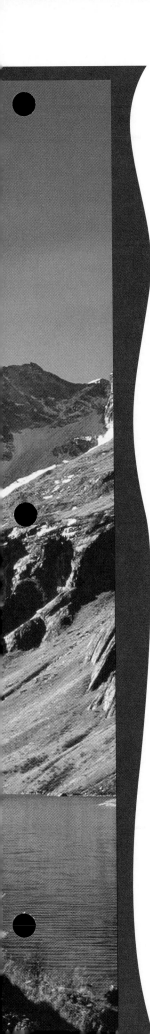

13 MOVING AHEAD:
Building
a Flexible Future

Thinking It Through

Check those statements that apply to you right now:

❑ Every time I think I've got my life under control, something new happens.
❑ I have a hard time shifting gears when I can't achieve my goals.
❑ When I fail or have a setback, I can't keep it in perspective.
❑ I try to find time to help others.
❑ I want to keep learning even after I graduate.
❑ I tend to lose sight of my mission in life.

In this chapter, you will explore answers to the following questions:

➤ How can you live with change?
➤ What will help you handle success and failure?
➤ Why give back to the community and the world?
➤ Why is college just the beginning of lifelong learning?
➤ How can you live your mission?

The end of one path can be the beginning of another. For example, graduation is often referred to as commencement because the end of your student career is the beginning or renewal of your life as a working citizen. As you come to the end of your work in this course, you have built up a wealth of knowledge. Now you have more power to make decisions about what directions you want your studies, your career, and your personal growth to take. As a tree takes food from the ground, sun, and air, you are gathering the resources you need to help you grow.

This chapter will explore how to manage the constant change you will encounter. Developing your flexibility will enable you to adjust goals, make the most of successes, and work through failures. You will consider what is important about giving back to your community and continuing to learn throughout your life. Finally, you will revisit your personal mission, exploring how to revise it as you encounter changes in the future.

HOW CAN YOU LIVE WITH CHANGE?

Even the most carefully constructed plans can be turned upside down by change. In this section, you will explore some ways to make change a manageable part of your life: accepting the reality of change, maintaining flexibility, and adjusting your goals.

Accept the Reality of Change

As Russian-born author Isaac Asimov once said, "It is change, continuing change, inevitable change, that is the dominant factor in society today. No sensible decision can be made any longer without taking into account not only the world as it is, but the world as it will be."[1] Change is a sure thing. Two significant causes of change on a global level are technology and the economy.

Technological Growth

Today's technology has spurred change. Advances in technology come into being daily: Computer companies update programs, new models of cars and machines appear, and scientists discover new possibilities in medicine and other areas. People make changes in the workplace, school, and home to keep up with the new systems and products that technology constantly offers. People and cultures are linked around the world through the Internet and World Wide Web.

The dominance of the media, brought on by technological growth, has increased the likelihood of change. A few hundred years ago, no television or magazines or Internet existed. A village could operate in the same way for years with very little change because there would be little or no contact with anyone from the outside who could introduce new ideas, methods, or plans. Now, the media constantly present people with new ways of doing things. When people can see the possibilities around them, they are more likely to want to discover new horizons.

Economic Instability

Downsize,
To reduce in size; streamline.

The unpredictable economy is the second factor in this age of constant change. Businesses have had to cut costs to survive, which has affected many people's jobs and careers. Some businesses discovered the speed and cost-effectiveness of computers and used them to replace workers. Some businesses have had to **downsize** and have laid off people to save money. Some businesses have merged with others, and people in duplicate jobs were let go. The difficult economy has also had an effect on personal finances. Many people face money problems at home that force them to make changes in how much they work, how they pursue an education, and how they live.

Maintain Flexibility

The fear of change is as inevitable as change itself. When you are comfortable with something, you tend to want it to stay the way it is, whether it is a relationship, a home, or a daily schedule. Change may seem to have negative effects, and consistency positive effects. Think about your life right now. What do you wish would always stay the same? What changes have upset you and thrown you off balance?

You may have encountered any number of changes in your life to date, many of them unexpected. You may have experienced ups and downs in relationships, a change of jobs or schools, a change of residence, or shifts in finances or family life. All of these changes, whether perceived as good or bad, cause a certain level of stress. They also cause a shift in your needs, which may lead to new priorities.

Change Brings Different Needs

Your needs can change from day to day, year to year, and situation to situation. Although you may know about some changes ahead of time, such as when you plan to move in with a partner, others may take you by surprise, such as losing a job. Even the different times of year bring different needs, for example, as a need for extra cash around the holidays or a need for child care when your children are home for the summer.

Some changes that shift your needs occur within a week or even a day. For example, an instructor may inform you that you have a quiz or extra assignment at the end of the week, or your daughter might tell you that she needs you to drive her somewhere that evening. Table 13–1 shows how the effects of certain changes can lead to new priorities.

Flexibility vs. Inflexibility

When change affects your needs, flexibility will help you shift your priorities so that you address those needs. You can react to change with either inflexibility or flexibility, each with its resulting effects.

Inflexibility. Not acknowledging a shift in needs can cause trouble. For example, if you lose your job and continue to spend as much money as you did before, ignoring your need to live more modestly, you can drive yourself into debt and make the situation worse. Or if you continue to spend little time with a partner who has expressed a need for more contact, you may lose the relationship.

Flexibility. Being flexible means acknowledging the change, examining your different needs, and addressing them in any way you can. Discovering what change brings may help you uncover surprising positive effects. For example, a painful breakup can lead you to discover greater capability and independence. In other words, a crisis can spur opportunity, and you may want to adjust your goals in order to pursue it.

Sometimes you may need to resist for a while, until you are ready to face an important change. When you feel ready, being flexible will help you cope with negative effects and benefit from positive effects.

TABLE 13-1   CHANGE PRODUCES NEW PRIORITIES

CHANGE	EFFECTS AND CHANGED NEEDS	NEW PRIORITIES
Lost job	Loss of income; need for others in your household to contribute more income	Job hunting; reduction in your spending; additional training or education to qualify for a different job
New job	Change in daily or weekly schedule; need for increased contribution of household help from others	Time and energy commitment to new job; maintaining confidence, learning new skills
Started school	Fewer hours for work, family, and personal time; responsibility for classwork; need to plan semesters ahead of time	Careful scheduling; making sure you have time to attend class and study adequately; strategic planning of classes and of career goals
Relationship/marriage	Responsibility toward your partner; merging of your schedules and perhaps your finances and belongings	Time and energy commitment to relationship
Breakup/divorce	Change in responsibility for any children; increased responsibility for your own finances; possibly a need to relocate; increased independence	Making time for yourself; gathering support from friends and family; securing your finances; making sure you have your own income
Bought car	Responsibility for monthly payment, and upkeep	Regular income so that you can make payments on time; time and money for upkeep
New baby	Increased parenting responsibility; need money for baby's needs or if you had to stop working; need help with other children	Child care; flexible employment; increased commitment from a partner or other supporter
New cultural environment (from new home, job, or school)	Exposure to unfamiliar people and traditions; tendency to keep to yourself	Learning about the culture with which you are now interacting; openness to new relationships

Adjust Your Goals

Your changing life will often result in the need to adjust goals accordingly. Sometimes goals must change because they weren't appropriate in the first place. Some turn out to be unreachable; some may not pose enough of a challenge; others may be unhealthy for the goal-setter or harmful to others.

Step One: Reevaluate

Before making adjustments in response to change, take time to reevaluate both the goals themselves and your progress toward them.

The goals. First, determine whether your goals still fit the person you have become in the past week or month or year. Circumstances can change quickly. For example, an unexpected pregnancy might cause a female student to rethink her educational goals.

Your progress. If you feel you haven't gotten far, determine whether the goal is out of your range or simply requires more stamina than you had anticipated. As you work toward any goal, you will experience alternating periods of progress and stagnation. Sticking with a tough goal may be the hardest thing you'll ever do, but the payoff may be worth it. You may want to seek the support and perspective of a friend or counselor as you evaluate your progress.

Step Two: Modify

If after your best efforts it becomes clear that a goal is out of reach, *modifying* your goal may bring success. Perhaps the goal doesn't suit you. For example, an active, interpersonal learner might become frustrated while pursuing a detail-oriented, sedentary career such as computer programming.

Based on your reevaluation, you can modify a goal in two ways:

1. *Adjust the existing goal.* To adjust a goal, change one or more aspects that define it—say, the time frame, the due dates, or the specifics of the expectations. For example, a woman with an unexpected pregnancy could adjust her educational due date, taking an extra year or two to complete her course work. She could also adjust the time frame, taking classes at night if she had to care for her child during the day.

2. *Replace it with a different, more compatible goal.* If you find that you just can't handle a particular goal, try to find another that makes more sense for you at this time. For example, a couple who wants to buy a house but just can't afford it can choose to work toward the goal of making improvements to their current living space. Because you and your circumstances never stop changing, your goals should keep up with those changes.

Being open to adjusting your goals will help you manage both failure and success along the way.

> "Risk! Risk anything! Care no more for the opinion of others, for those voices. Do the hardest thing on earth for you. Act for yourself. Face the truth."
>
> Katherine Mansfield

WHAT WILL HELP YOU HANDLE SUCCESS AND FAILURE?

The perfect, trouble-free life is only a myth. The most wonderful, challenging, fulfilling life is full of problems to be solved and difficult decisions to be made. If you want to handle the bumps and bruises without losing your self-esteem, you should prepare to encounter setbacks along with your successes.

Dealing with Failure

Things don't always go the way you want them to go. Sometimes you may come up against obstacles that are difficult to overcome. Sometimes you will let yourself down or disappoint others. You may make mistakes or lose your motivation. All people do, no matter who they are or how smart or accomplished they may be. What is important is how you choose to deal with what goes wrong. If you can arrive at reasonable definitions of failure and success, accept failure as part of being human, and examine failure so that you can learn from it, you will have the confidence to pick yourself up and keep improving.

Measuring Failure and Success

Most people measure failure by comparing where they are to where they believe they should be. Since individual circumstances vary widely, so do definitions of failure. What you consider a failure may seem like a positive step for someone else. Here are some examples:

> Imagine that your native language is Spanish. You have learned to speak English well, but you still have trouble writing it. Making writing mistakes may seem like failure to you, but to a recent immigrant from Nicaragua who knows limited English, your command of the language will seem like a success story.

> If two people apply for internships, one may see failure as receiving some offers but not the favorite one, whereas someone who was turned down may see any offer as a success.

> Having a job that doesn't pay you as much as you want may seem like a failure, but to someone who is having trouble finding any job, your job is a definite success.

Accepting Failure

No one escapes failure, no matter how hard he or she may try (or how successful he or she may be at hiding mistakes). The most successful people and organizations have experienced failures and mistakes. For example, a few years ago America OnLine miscalculated customer use and offered a flat rate per month, resulting in thousands of customers having trouble logging on to the service. You have choices when deciding how to view a failure or mistake. You can pretend it never happened, blame it on someone or something else, blame yourself, or forgive yourself.

Pretending it didn't happen. Avoiding the pain of dealing with a failure can deny you valuable lessons and could even create more serious problems. For example, imagine that a person has unprotected sex with a possibly HIV-infected partner and then denies it ever happened. If that person later discovers that he or she has contracted HIV from the first partner, the deadly virus may have been passed on to any subsequent partners.

Blaming others. Putting the responsibility on someone else stifles opportunities to learn and grow. For example, imagine that an unprepared and inappropriately dressed person interviews for a job and is not hired. If he or she decides that the interviewer is biased, the interviewee won't learn to improve preparation or interview strategies. Evaluate causes carefully and try not to assign blame.

Blaming yourself. Getting angry at yourself for failing, or believing that you should be perfect, can only result in feeling incapable of success and perhaps becoming afraid to try. Negative self-talk can become self-fulfilling.

Forgiving yourself. This is by far the best way to cope. First, although you should always strive for your best, don't expect perfection of yourself or anyone else. Expect that you will do the best that you can with the circumstances of your life. Just getting through another day as a student, employee, and/or parent is an important success. Second, forgive yourself when you fail. Your value as a human being does not diminish when you make a mistake. Forgiving yourself will give you more strength to learn from the experience, move on, and try again.

Once you are able to approach failure and mistakes in a productive way, explore what you can learn from them.

Learning from Failure

Learning from your failures and mistakes involves thinking critically about what happened. The first step is to evaluate what occurred and decide if it was within your control. It could have had nothing to do with you at all. You could have failed to get a job because someone else with equal qualifications was in line for it ahead of you. A family crisis that disrupted your sleep could have affected your studying, resulting in a failing grade on a test. These are unfortunate circumstances, but they are not failures.

On the other hand, something you did or didn't do may have contributed to the failure. If you decide that you have made a mistake, your next steps are to analyze the causes and effects of what happened, make any improvements that you can, and decide how to change your action or approach in the future.

For example, imagine that after a long night of studying, you forgot your part-time work-study commitment the next day.

Analyze causes and effects. *Causes:* Your exhaustion and your concern about your test caused you to forget to check on your work schedule. *Effects:* Because you weren't there, a crucial project wasn't completed. An entire class and instructor who needed the project have been affected by your mistake.

Make any possible improvements on the situation. You could apologize to the instructor and see if there is still a chance to finish up part of the work that day.

Make changes for the future. You could set a goal to note your work schedule regularly in your date book—maybe in a bright color—and to check it more often. You could also arrange your future study schedule so that you will be less exhausted.

Think about the people you consider exceptionally successful. They didn't rise to the top without taking risks and making their share of mistakes. They have built much of their success on their willingness to recognize and learn from their shortfalls. You, too, can benefit from staying open to this kind of active, demanding, hard-won education. Learning involves change and growth. Let what you learn from falling short of your goals inspire new and better ideas.

Think Positively about Failure

When you feel you have failed, how can you boost your outlook?

Stay aware of the fact that you are a capable, valuable person. People often react to failure by becoming convinced that they are incapable and incompetent. Remind yourself of your successes, focus your energy on your best abilities, and know that you have the strength to try again. Realize that your failure isn't a setback as long as you learn from it and rededicate yourself to excellence. The energy you might expend on talking negatively to yourself would be better spent on trying again and moving ahead.

Share your thoughts and disappointment with others. Everybody fails. People refrain from talking about failures out of embarrassment, often feeling as though no one else could have made as big a mistake as they did. When you confide, though, you may be surprised to hear others exchange stories that rival your own. Be careful not to get caught in a destructive cycle of complaining. Instead, focus on the kind of creative energy that can help you find ways to learn from your failures.

Look on the bright side. At worst, you at least have learned a lesson that will help you avoid similar situations in the future. At best, there may be some positive results. If your romance flounders, the extra study time you suddenly have may help you boost your grades. If you fail a class, you may discover that you need to focus on a different subject that suits you better. What you learn from a failure may, in an unexpected way, bring you around to where you want to be.

> *"The word impossible is not in my dictionary."*
> Napoleon

A graduate accepts his diploma

Dealing with Success

Success isn't reserved for the wealthy, famous people you see glamorized in magazines and newspapers. Success isn't money or fame, although it can bring such things. Success is being who you want to be and doing what you want to do. Success is within your reach.

Pay attention to the small things when measuring success. You may not feel successful until you reach an important goal you have set for yourself. However, along the way each step is a success. When you are trying to drop a harmful habit, each time you stay on course is a success. When you are juggling work, school, and personal life, just coping with every new day equals success. If you received a C on a paper and then earned a B on the next one, your advancement is successful.

Remember that success is a process. If you deny yourself the label of success until you reach the top of where you want to be, you will have a much harder time getting there. Just moving ahead toward improvement and growth, however fast or slow the movement, equals success.

Here are some techniques to handle your successes.

First, appreciate yourself. You deserve it. Take time to congratulate yourself for a job well done—whether it be a good grade, an important step in learning a new language, a job offer, a promotion or graduation, or a personal victory over substance abuse. Bask in the glow a bit. Everybody hears about his or her mistakes, but people don't praise themselves (or each other) enough when success occurs. Praise can give you a terrific vote of confidence.

Take that confidence on the road. This victory can lead to others. Based on this success, you may be expected to prove to yourself and others that you are capable of growth, of continuing your successes and building on them. Show yourself and others that the confidence is well founded.

Stay sensitive to others. There could be people around you who may not have been so successful. Remember that you have been in their place and they in yours, and the positions may change many times over in the future. Enjoy what you have, work to build on it and not to take it for granted, and support others as they need it.

Staying sensitive to others is an important goal always, whether you are feeling successful or less than successful. Giving what you can of your time, energy, and resources to the community and the world is part of being aware of what others need. Your contributions can help to bring success to others.

THINKING BACK

1. What are two reasons why today's world is in a state of constant change?

   a. _____

   b. _____

   c. _____

2. Name three ways to manage your life in the face of change.

   a. _____

   b. _____

   c. _____

3. What are four ways in which you can react to a failure or mistake? Circle the one that seems most beneficial. Underline the one you tend toward most often.

a. _____

b. _____

c. _____

d. _____

4. Define success in your own words. What is one way that you might celebrate your success?

_____

_____

THINKING AHEAD

1. How do you feel about volunteering? If you have ever volunteered, briefly describe what you did and your reaction to the experience.

_____

_____

2. In what ways do you feel you will continue to learn after you graduate?

_____

_____

_____

3. Do you predict that your life's mission might change? In what ways?

_____

_____

4. How do you define integrity? What role does integrity play in your life?

_____

_____

_____

WHY GIVE BACK TO THE COMMUNITY AND THE WORLD?

Everyday life is demanding. You can become so caught up in the issues of your own life that you neglect to look outside your immediate needs. However, from time to time you may feel that your mission extends beyond your personal life. You have spent time in this course working to improve yourself. Now that you've come so far, why not extend some of that energy and effort to the world outside? With all that you have to offer, you have the power to make positive differences in the lives of others. Every effort you make, no matter how small, improves the world.

Your Imprint on the World

As difficult as your life can sometimes seem, looking outside yourself can help put everything in perspective. Sometimes you can evaluate your own hardships more reasonably when you look at them in light of what is happening elsewhere. There are many people in the world in need. You have something to give to others. Making a lasting difference in the lives of others is something to be proud of.

Your perspective may change after volunteering at a soup kitchen. Your appreciation of those close to you may increase after you spend time with cancer patients at the local hospice. Your perspective on your living situation may change after you help people improve their housing conditions.

If you could eavesdrop on someone talking about you to another person, how would you like to hear yourself described? What you do for others can have far more impact than you may imagine. Giving one person hope, comfort, or help can improve his or her ability to cope with life's changes. That person in turn may be able to offer help to someone else. As each person makes a contribution, a cycle of positive effects is generated. For example, Betty Ford was helped in her struggle with alcoholism and founded the Betty Ford Center to help others with addiction problems.

How can you make a difference? Many schools and companies are realizing the importance of community involvement and have appointed committees to find and organize volunteering opportunities. Make some kind of volunteering activity a priority on your schedule. Join a group from your company that tutors at a school. Organize a group of students to clean, repair, or entertain at a nursing home or shelter. Look for what's available to you or create opportunities on your own. Table 13–2 lists organizations that provide volunteer opportunities; you might also look into more local efforts or private clearinghouses that set up a number of different smaller projects.

Volunteerism is also getting attention on the national level. The government has made an effort to stress the importance of community service as part of what it means to be a good citizen, and it provides support for that effort through AmeriCorps. AmeriCorps provides financial awards for education in return for community service. If you work for AmeriCorps, you can use the funds you receive to pay current tuition expenses or repay student loans. You may work either before, during, or after your college edu-

TABLE 13-2 ORGANIZATIONS THAT CAN USE YOUR HELP

AIDS-related organizations	American Red Cross	Amnesty International
Audubon Society	Battered women shelters	Big Brothers and Big Sisters
Churches, synagogues, temples, and affiliated organizations such as the YMCA or YWHA	Educational support organizations	Environmental awareness; support organizations such as Greenpeace
Hospitals	Hotlines	Kiwanis, Knights of Columbus, Lions Club, Rotary
Libraries	Meals on Wheels	Nursing homes
Planned Parenthood	School districts	Scouting organizations
Share Our Strength; other food donation organizations	Shelters and organizations supporting the homeless	Sierra Club, World Wildlife Fund

cation. You can find more information on AmeriCorps by contacting this organization:

The Corporation for National and Community Service
1201 New York Avenue, NW
Washington, DC 20525
1-800-942-2677

Sometimes it's hard to find time to volunteer when so many responsibilities compete for your attention. One solution is to combine other activities with volunteer work. Get exercise while cleaning a park; bring the whole family to sing at a nursing home on a weekend afternoon. Whatever you do, your actions will have a ripple effect, creating positive impact for those you help and those they encounter in turn. The strength often found in people who are surviving difficult circumstances can strengthen you as well.

Valuing Your Environment

Your environment is your home. When you value it, you help to maintain a clean, safe, and healthy place to live. What you do every day has an impact on others around you and on the future. One famous slogan says that if you are not part of the solution, you are part of the problem. Every saved bottle, environmentally aware child, and reused bag is part of the solution. Take responsibility for what you can control—your own habits—and develop sound practices that contribute to the health of the environment.

Recycle anything you can. What can be recycled varies with the system set up in your area. You may be able to recycle any combination of plastics, aluminum, glass, newspapers, and magazines. Products that use recycled materials are often more expensive, but if they are within your price range, try to reward the company's dedication by purchasing them.

Trade and reuse items. When your children have grown too old for the crib, baby clothes, and toys, give away whatever is still usable. Give clothing you don't wear to others who can use it. Organizations like the Salvation Army may pick up used items in your neighborhood on certain days or through specific arrangements. Wrap presents in plain newspaper and decorate with markers. Use your imagination—there are many, many items you can reuse, all around you.

Respect the outdoors. Participate in maintaining a healthy environment. Use products that reduce chemical waste. Pick up after yourself. Through volunteering, voicing your opinion, or monetary donations, support the maintenance of parks and the preservation of natural, undeveloped land. Be creative. One young woman planned a cleanup of a local lakeside area as the main group activity for the guests at her birthday party (she joined them, of course). Everyone benefits when each person takes responsibility for maintaining the fragile earth.

Remember that valuing yourself is the base for valuing all other things. Improving the earth is difficult unless you value yourself and think you deserve the best living environment possible. Valuing yourself will also help you understand why you deserve to enjoy the benefits of learning throughout your life.

WHY IS COLLEGE JUST THE BEGINNING OF LIFELONG LEARNING?

Although it may sometimes feel more like a burden, being a student is a golden opportunity. As a student, you are able to focus on learning for a period of time, and your school focuses on you in return, helping you gain access to knowledge, resources, and experiences. Take advantage of the academic atmosphere by developing a habit of seeking out new learning opportunities. That habit will encourage you to continue your learning long after you have graduated, even in the face of the pressures of everyday life.

Learning brings change, and change causes growth. As you change and the world changes, new knowledge and ideas continually emerge. Absorb them so that you can propel yourself into the future. Visualize yourself as a student of life who learns something new every single day.

Here are some lifelong learning strategies that can encourage you to continually ask questions and explore new ideas.

Investigate new interests. When information and events catch your attention, take your interest one step further and find out more. If you are fascinated by politics on television, find out if your school has political clubs you can explore. If a friend of yours starts to take yoga, try a class also. If you really like one portion of a particular class, see if there are other classes that focus on that specific topic. Turn the regretful "I wish I had tried that" into the purposeful "I'm going to do it."

Read books, newspapers, magazines, and other writings. Reading opens a world of new perspectives. See what's on the best-seller list at your bookstore. Ask your friends about books that have changed their lives. Stay on top of current change in your community, your state, your country, and the world by reading newspapers and magazines. A newspaper that has a broad scope, such as the *New York Times* or *Washington Post,* can be an education in itself. Explore religious literature, family letters, and Internet news groups and Web pages. Keep something with you to read in those moments when you have nothing to do.

Spend time with interesting people. When you meet someone new who inspires you and makes you think, keep in touch. Have a potluck dinner party and invite one person or couple from each corner of your life—your family, your work, your school, a club to which you belong, and your neighborhood. Sometimes, meet for reasons beyond just being social. Start a book club, a home-repair group, a play-reading club, a hiking group, or an investing group. Get to know people of different cultures and perspectives. Learn something new from one another.

Continuing education,
Courses that students can take without having to be part of a degree program.

Pursue improvement in your studies and in your career. When at school, take classes outside of your major. After graduation, continue your education both in your field and in the realm of general knowledge. Stay on top of ideas, developments, structural changes, and new technology in your field by seeking out **continuing education** courses. Sign up for career-related seminars. Take single courses at a local college or community learning center. Some companies offer additional on-the-job training or pay for their employees to take courses that will improve their knowledge and skills. If your company doesn't do so, you may want to set a small part of your income aside as a "learning budget."

Nurture a spiritual life. You can find spirituality in many places. You don't have to regularly attend a house of worship to be spiritual, although that may be an important part of your spiritual life. "A spiritual life of some kind is absolutely necessary for psychological 'health,'" says psychologist and author Thomas Moore in his book *The Care of the Soul.* "We live in a time of deep division, in which mind is separated from body and spirituality is at odds with materialism."[2] The words *soul* and *spirituality* hold different meanings for each individual. Decide what they mean to you. Whether you discover them in music, organized re-

Islamic men kneel for prayers in New York City

ligion, friendship, nature, cooking, sports, or anything else, making them a priority in your life will help you find a greater sense of balance and meaning.

Experience what others create. Art is "an adventure of the mind" (Eugene Ionesco, playwright); "a means of knowing the world" (Angela Carter, author); something that "does not reproduce the visible; rather, it makes visible" (Paul Klee, painter); "a lie that makes us realize truth" (Pablo Picasso, painter); a revealer of "our most secret self" (Jean-Luc Godard, filmmaker). Explore all kinds of art and focus on any forms that hold your interest. Seek out whatever moves you—music, visual arts, theatre, photography, dance, domestic arts, performance art, film and television, poetry, prose, and more.

Make your own creations. Bring out the creative artist in you. Take a class in drawing, in woodworking, or in quilting. Learn to play an instrument. Write poems for your favorite people or stories to read to your children. Invent a recipe. Design and build a set of shelves for your home. Create a memoir of your life. You are a creative being. Express yourself, and learn more about yourself, through art.

Lifelong learning is the master key that unlocks every door you will encounter on your journey. If you keep it firmly in your hand, you will discover worlds of knowledge—and a place for yourself within them.

HOW CAN YOU LIVE YOUR MISSION?

As you learn and change, so may your life's mission. Whatever changes occur, your continued learning will give you a greater sense of security in your choices. Recall your mission statement from Chapter 2. Think about how it is changing as you learn and develop. It will continue to reflect your goals, values, and strength if you live with integrity, roll with the changes that come your way, continue to observe the role models in your life, and work to achieve your personal best in all that you do.

Live with Integrity

You've spent a lot of time exploring who you are, how you learn, and what you value. **Integrity** is about being true to that picture you have drawn of yourself while also considering the needs of others. Living with integrity will bring you great personal and professional rewards.

Honesty and sincerity are at the heart of integrity. Many of the decisions you make and act on in your life are based on your underlying sense of what is the right thing to do. Having integrity puts that sense into day-to-day action.

Integrity,
Adherence to a code of moral values; incorruptibility; honesty.

WINDOWS ON THE WORLD: REAL LIFE STUDENT ISSUES

How do I become employable and promotable?

Titus Dillard, Jr., Embry-Riddle Aeronautical University, Daytona Beach, Florida, Aviation/Business Management Major

I transferred from a junior college to Embry-Riddle on a basketball scholarship, without which I probably wouldn't have been able to afford school. I've enjoyed it, but collegiate sports take up a lot of time. We prac-  tice six days a week for 2 1/2 hours a day. Game days, especially away games, require even more time. Coaches tell you to bring books on the road, but there's too many interruptions to really focus on studying. To help pay the bills, I also work ten hours a week as a student assistant for our business academic advisor. It's been a great experience, but again it takes away from my time to study. I'm the first in my family to graduate from college, and my mother is proud of me. But she still has four children at home so I don't like to ask for anything.

Because I haven't been able to focus on academics my grade point average has suffered. I am a senior now so I have very little time to bring it up. There's a naval intelligence program sponsored by the U.S. government that I would like to apply for, but one of the requirements is a GPA of 3.45 or higher. Right now mine is only 2.5.

Last week we had a career exposition at my school and one of the first questions recruiters asked was, "What's your GPA?" I'm thinking about asking my basketball coach for a letter of recommendation to help show that I've been responsible, but I wonder if that will do any good. I want to make a good impression. Do you have any suggestions for how I can become employable and promotable after school?

Cherie Andrade, Hawaii Pacific University, Honolulu, Hawaii, Associate Director of Admissions

It's understandable that you worry about your future. First of all, although you are feeling discouraged about your GPA, try not to dwell on it. I don't think companies look primarily at GPA when considering a candidate. That's only one component of your profile. You have many things going for you. For one, you have an interesting background. Your experiences, such as playing basketball and working part time, have built character and a work ethic. These are important to employers. Remember: Don't judge yourself. Let the people looking at the applications be the judges.

I have three suggestions for your interviews. First, I make an appointment to talk with the director of the Career Services Center on your campus. This person often knows what companies are looking for. Second, if you want to enter the naval intelligence program, you definitely should apply even though one of their qualifications is a high GPA. Career counselors often tell students to apply for what seems farfetched because you might just be exactly what they're looking for. Third, do get a letter of recommendation from your coach, but don't stop there. Try to also get a letter from one of your instructors or the business advisor you work for. Explain to them what you want to accomplish so that they can give you a more focused recommendation.

To land the job or the training you want, you have to step out and take risks. If you pursue your career goals with the same determination and skills you've used to finish four years of college and juggle all your other commitments, I have no doubt you'll find work you love and that you'll continue to develop in your area of expertise.

● The Marks of Integrity

A person of integrity lives by the following principles:

1. *Honest representation of himself or herself and his or her thoughts.* For example, you tell your partner when you are hurt over something that he or she did or didn't do.

2. *Sincerity in word and action.* You do what you say you will do. For example, you tell a coworker that you will finish a project when she has to leave early, and you follow through by completing the work.

3. *Consideration of the needs of others.* When making decisions, you take both your needs and the needs of others into account. You also avoid hurting others for the sake of your personal goals. For example, your sister cares for your elderly father in her home. You spend three nights a week with him so that she can take a course toward her degree.

"And life is what we make it, always has been, always will be."

Grandma Moses

The Benefits of Integrity

● When you act with integrity, you earn trust and respect from yourself and from others. If people can trust you to be honest, to be sincere in what you say and do, and to consider the needs of others, they will be more likely to encourage you, support your goals, and reward your hard work. Integrity is a must for workplace success. To earn promotions, it helps to show that you have integrity in a variety of situations.

Think of situations in which a decision made with integrity has had a positive effect. Have you ever confessed to an instructor that your paper is late without a good excuse, only to find that despite your mistake you have earned the instructor's respect? Have extra efforts in the workplace ever helped you gain a promotion or a raise? Have your kindnesses toward a friend or spouse moved the relationship to a deeper level? When you decide to act with integrity, you can improve your life and the lives of others.

Most important, living with integrity helps you believe in yourself and in your ability to make good choices. A person of integrity isn't a perfect person but one who makes the effort to live according to values and principles, continually striving to learn from mistakes and to improve. Take responsibility for making the right moves, and you will follow your mission with strength and conviction.

Roll with the Changes

● Think again about yourself. How has your idea of where you want to be changed since you first opened this book? How has your self-image changed? What have you learned about your values, your goals, and your styles of communication and learning? Consider how your school, work, and life goals have changed. As you grow and develop, keep adjusting your goals to your changes and discoveries.

Stephen Covey says in *The Seven Habits of Highly Effective People*, "Change—real change—comes from the inside out. It doesn't come from hacking at the leaves of attitude and behavior with quick fix personality ethic techniques. It comes from striking at the root—the fabric of our thought, the fundamental essential **paradigms** which give definition to our character and create the lens through which we see the world."[3]

Examining yourself deeply in that way is a real risk. Most of all, it demands courage and strength of will. Questioning your established beliefs and facing the unknown are much more difficult than staying with things as they are. When you have the courage to face the consequences of trying something unfamiliar, admitting failure, or challenging what you thought you knew, you open yourself to growth and learning opportunities. You can make your way through changes you never anticipated if you make the effort to live your mission—in whatever forms it takes as it changes—each day, each week, each month, and for years to come.

Paradigm,
An especially clear pattern or typical example.

Learn from Role Models

People often derive the highest level of motivation and inspiration from learning how others have struggled through the ups and downs of life and achieved their goals. Somehow, seeing how someone else went through difficult situations can give you hope for your own struggles. The positive effects of being true to oneself become more real when an actual person has earned them.

Learning about the lives of people who have achieved their own version of success can teach you what you can do in your own life. Bessie and Sadie Delany, sisters and accomplished African-American women born in the late 1800s, are two valuable **role models**. They took risks, becoming professionals in dentistry and teaching at a time when women and minorities were often denied both respect and opportunity. They worked hard to fight racial division and prejudice and taught others what they learned. They believed in their intelligence, beauty, and ability to give, and lived without regrets. Says Sadie in their *Book of Everyday Wisdom*, "If there's anything I've learned in all these years, it's that life is too good to waste a day. It's up to you to make it sweet."[4]

Role model,
A person whose behavior in a particular role is imitated by others.

Aim for Your Personal Best

Your personal best is simply the best that you can do, in any situation. It may not be the best you have ever done. It may include mistakes, for nothing significant is ever accomplished without making mistakes and taking risks. It may shift from situation to situation. As long as you aim to do your best, though, you are inviting growth and success.

Aim for your personal best in everything you do. As a lifelong learner, you will always have a new direction in which to grow and a new challenge to face. Seek constant improvement in your personal, educational, and professional life, knowing that you are capable of such improvement. Enjoy the richness of life by living each day to the fullest, developing your talents and potential into the achievement of your most valued goals.

Kaizen is the Japanese word for "continual improvement." Striving for excellence, always finding ways to improve on what already exists, and believing that you can effect change are at the heart of the industrious Japanese spirit. The drive to improve who you are and what you do will help to provide the foundation of a successful future.

Think of this concept as you reflect on yourself, your goals, your life-long education, your career, and your personal pursuits. Create excellence and quality by continually asking yourself, "How can I improve?" Living by *kaizen* will help you to be a respected friend and family member, a productive and valued employee, and a truly contributing member of society. You can change the world.

IMPORTANT POINTS TO REMEMBER

1. How can you cope with change?

Rapid change is a reality of modern life, brought about in large part by advancing technology and a struggling economy. People often resist change because they fear its negative effects. However, being flexible—shifting priorities as change affects your needs—will help you handle change and experience its positive effects. You may need to adjust your goals, either because of life changes or because the first goal wasn't appropriate. First reevaluate your goals and your progress toward them. Then modify your goals by either adjusting or replacing them.

2. What will help you handle success and failure?

A perfect, trouble-free life isn't possible, but that doesn't mean life can't be challenging and wonderful. Accepting failures and successes along the way will help you stay afloat without losing your self-esteem. Deal with failure by defining failure and success, accepting failure as human, and thinking critically about what you can learn from what happened. Deal with success with celebration and confidence, and encourage others to keep working toward their goals.

3. Why give back to the community and the world?

You have the power to make positive differences in the lives of others. One way is by volunteering your time to give others hope, comfort, or help in their time of need. Your school and community have many opportunities for you to donate your time and energy. You can also make a difference by caring for your environment. The earth is everyone's home, and what you do every day affects you, as well as others around you, now and in the future. Recycling and reusing items, as well as respecting the outdoors, will help to preserve the environment for everyone.

4. Why is college just the beginning of lifelong learning?

College is a golden opportunity to focus on learning. However, keeping a focus on learning even after college will help you continue to move ahead both at work and in your personal life. Learning brings change, and change causes growth. Continually taking in new knowledge and ideas will fuel your improvement and progress. Strategies for lifelong learning include investigating new interests, reading, spending time with interesting people, pursuing career improvement, investigating human differences, and exploring your spiritual and artistic sides.

5. How can you live your mission?

Your life's mission is as subject to change as the rest of your life. As goals, personal life, and the world change, your mission must adjust to reflect those developments. Real change comes from having the courage to question your beliefs, face the unknown, and take risks. Find role models who live, or have lived, according to the principles that guide your own life's mission. Accept mistakes and learn from them. Aim for your personal best in everything you do. Live each day to the fullest and take your mission into the future as you work toward your most valued goals.

Name _____ Date _____

BUILDING SKILLS FOR COLLEGE, CAREER, AND LIFE SUCCESS
CHAPTER 13

TAKING STOCK:
REFINING YOUR THOUGHTS

Look back at the statements you explored at the start of the chapter (see
Thinking It Through on p. 457). Observe whether your attitudes have
changed and what you have learned by studying this chapter.

1. Describe a personal event that shows how the changing world has
   affected your life.

_____

_____

_____

_____

2. What can you do when you have to change one of your life goals?

_____

_____

_____

3. Out of all the coping strategies for failure, describe the two that you
   would use and why.

_____

_____

_____

_____

4. Name an opportunity to help others that appeals to you, and explain
   why.

_____

_____

5. Name one way in which you plan to continue to learn throughout your life. What positive effects could this learning have on you?

_____

_____

_____

6. What can you do to maintain a mission that fits you as you change?

_____

_____

7. Name one strategy from this chapter that you will use in the next month. What is your plan?

_____

_____

_____

? CRITICAL THINKING:
APPLYING LEARNING TO YOUR LIFE

Changes in Goals

As changes occur in your life, your goals change and need reevaluation. Think about what may have changed in your school, career, and life goals over the past semester. For each category name an old goal, name the adjusted goal, and briefly discuss why you think the change occurred.

School

Old: _____

New: _____

Why the change? _____

Career

Old: _____

New: _____

Why the change? _____

● *Life*

Old: _____

New: _____

Why the change? _____

Looking at Change, Failure, and Success

Life can go by so fast that you don't take time to evaluate what changes have taken place, what failures you could learn from, and what successes you have experienced. Take a moment now and answer the following questions for yourself.

What are the three biggest changes that have occurred in your life this year?

1. _____

2. _____

3. _____

● Choose one that you feel you handled well. What shifts in priorities or goals did you make?

_____

_____

_____

Choose one that you could have handled better. What happened? What else could you have done?

_____

_____

_____

_____

Now name a personal experience, occurring this year, that you would consider a failure. What happened?

_____

● _____

_____

How did you handle it—did you ignore it, blame it on someone else, or admit and explore it?

_____

_____

_____

What did you learn from experiencing this failure?

_____

_____

_____

Finally, describe a recent success of which you are proudest.

_____

_____

_____

How did this success affect your self-perception?

_____

_____

_____

Lifelong Learning

Review the strategies for lifelong learning in this chapter. Which do you think you can do, or plan to do, in your life now and when you are out of school? Name the three that mean the most to you and briefly discuss the role they play in your life.

_____

_____

_____

_____

_____

_____

TEAMWORK: Combining Forces

Giving back. In your group, research volunteering opportunities in your community. Each group member should choose one possibility to research. Answer questions such as the following: What is the situation or organization? What are its needs? Do any volunteer positions require an application, letters of reference, or background checks? What is the time commitment? Is there any special training involved? Are there any problematic or difficult elements to this experience?

When you have the information, meet again with the group so that each group member knows about each volunteering opportunity. Choose one that you feel you will have the time and ability to try next semester. Suggestions that don't take up too much time include serving in a soup kitchen one night, or driving for Meals on Wheels during a lunch or dinner shift.

WRITING: Discovery Through Journaling

To record your thoughts, use a separate journal or the lined pages at the end of the chapter.

Fifty positive thoughts. Make a list for yourself. The first twenty-five items should be things you like about yourself. You can name anything—things you can do, things you think, things you've accomplished, things you like about your physical self, and so on. The second twenty-five items should be things you'd like to do in your life. These can be of any magnitude—anything from trying Vietnamese food to traveling to the Grand Canyon to keeping your room neat to getting to know someone. They can be things you'd like to do tomorrow or things that you plan to do in twenty years. Be creative. Let everything be possible.

CAREER PORTFOLIO: Charting Your Course

Revised mission statement. Retrieve the mission statement you wrote at the end of Chapter 2. Give yourself a day or so to read it over and think about it. Then revise it according to the changes that have occurred in you. Add new priorities and goals and delete those that are no longer valid. Continue to update your mission statement so that it reflects your growth and development, helping to guide you through the changes that await you in the future.

Journal Entry

Name _____ Date _____

Journal Entry

CROSSWORD REVIEW: PART V
Sharpening Your Skills

ACROSS

2. To reduce in size; streamline
6. The act of working together to accomplish a goal
7. A person whose behavior is imitated by others
12. An ability to shift your priorities in response to life changes
15. A person who serves as a carrier or source of information
16. A particular federally-sponsored loan that comes in two types: "direct" and "FFEL"
17. Monetary awards, requiring no repayment, to students who show financial need
18. Planning for the coordination of resources and expenditures; setting goals with regards to money

DOWN

1. A federal organization that provides financial rewards in exchange for community service work
3. A position, usually unpaid, in which a student can gain supervised practical experience in a particular field
4. The exchange of information and/or services among individuals, groups, or institutions
5. To change or adjust
8. The score you are given based on the record of your credit use
9. The returning and reusing of materials such as plastics, glass, and aluminum
10. People to whom a debt, usually money, is owed
11. Offering your services, without requiring payment, to help those in need
13. An especially clear pattern or typical example
14. A federal, need-based award that acts as a foundation of aid on which you can add other aid sources

Researching Information and Student Resources on the Internet by Cynthia B. Leshin

Searching for information is like a treasure hunt. Unless a researcher has knowledge of all the resources and tools available, then the search for useful information may be a time consuming and frustrating process. In this appendix you will learn about resources on the Internet that will facilitate the search for information of interest to you, your career, and your field of study. Careful thought about the desired knowledge sought, where the best place is to begin to look for that knowledge, and extensive exploring and searching in layers of Web links, usually provides the desired reward—the gold nugget Web site.

The tools that you will learn about and use to conduct and include

> search directories
>> Yahoo
>> Magellan
>> Galaxy
>> Snap
> search engines
>> AltaVista
>> Hot Bot
>> Northern Light
> image surfers
>> Lycos
>> AltaVista
> reference resources.

You will also learn
> how to evaluate information you find on the Internet as to its content validity.

INTERNET RESEARCH TOOLS

The Internet contains many tools that speed the search for information and resources. Research tools called "search directories" and "search engines" are extremely helpful. Other valuable resources include reference resources and search tools for finding images, sounds, and video.

Search Directories

Search directories are essentially descriptive subject indexes of Web sites. They also have keyword searching options. Directories are excellent places to begin your research.

Search Engines

Search engines are different from search directories in that they search World Wide Web sites, Usenet newsgroups, and other Internet resources to find matches to your descriptor keywords. Many search engines also rank the results according to a degree of relevancy. Most search engines provide options for advanced searching to refine your search.

Image Surfers

Search tools are available from search engines such as AltaVista and Lycos to help find images, sounds, video, and photographs.

Reference Resources

Reference resources are collections of Internet sites compiled by individuals or organizations. An example of an excellent reference resource is the Reference Desk with links to online dictionaries, library catalogs, and news resources as well as extensive subject collections.

Basic Guidelines for Becoming a Cybersleuth

Search directories and search engines are marvelous tools to help you find information on the Internet. Search directories are often the best places to begin a search, as they frequently yield more relevant returns on a topic than a search engine, which may produce a high proportion of irrelevant information.

Search engines can be frustrating to use and may not be the best Internet resources to begin with, often supplying thousands of links on your keyword search. Although these search tools have advanced options for refining and limiting a search, researchers may discover that finding the desired information is not easy and that search results frequently offer a high percentage of irrelevant and useless information. For example, using a search engine for a search with the keywords *business management* returned 500,000 occurrences (*hits*) of the words *business* and *management*. Many of the occurrences of these words were in job listings or companies that were advertising their services. This is why search directories are frequently an excellent resource to begin with when starting your research. The search directory may lead you to the goldmine collection of electronic resources you are searching for.

Research Guidelines

When researching information on the Internet, it is essential that you use several search tools. The basic approach to finding information involves the following steps:

1. Begin with a search directory such as
   - Yahoo   http://www.yahoo.com
   - Magellan   http://magellan.mckinley.com
   - Galaxy   http://galaxy.einet.net/galaxy.html
   - Snap   http://www.snap.com

to search for the information under a related topic or category. Explore the links that seem relevant to your topic, and make bookmarks of the ones you would like to investigate further. Look for one site that has a large collection of links on your topic. This is the resource goldmine that you are looking for.

2. Use reference resources to research your topic. This section provides a listing of some excellent resources that can be used to help you find the information you are looking for. The goal is to find one or two Internet sites that have an extensive collection of resources on your topic.

3. Use search engines to further research your topic by determining one or more descriptive words (keywords) for the subject. Enter your keywords into the search dialog box.

4. Determine how specific you want your search to be. Do you want it to be broad or narrow? Use available options to refine or limit your search. Some search engines permit the use of Boolean operators (AND, OR, NOT) that restrict a search. Always check for Advanced Search options or information provided by the search engine on how to refine and limit your search. Some search engines such as Hot Bot have pull-down menus or selections to be checked for limiting your search. You will learn more about advanced searching under the "Search Engine" section.

5. Submit your query.

6. Review your list of hits (a search return based on a keyword).

7. Adjust your search based on the information returned. Did you receive too much information and need to narrow your search? Did you receive too little or no information and need to broaden your keywords?

8. If your return provided too many resources, add additional keywords to limit the search.

9. Use several search directories and search engines for your research. No one search tool will provide a complete resource list.

SEARCH DIRECTORIES

Yahoo

http://www.yahoo.com

Yahoo is one of the most popular search tools on the Internet and is an excellent place to begin your search. Although Yahoo is more accurately described as a search directory, this Web site has an excellent database with search options available. There are two ways to find information using Yahoo: search through the subject directory or use the built-in search engine.

Follow these steps to use Yahoo to search for information:

FIGURE A1-1

Yahoo's home page

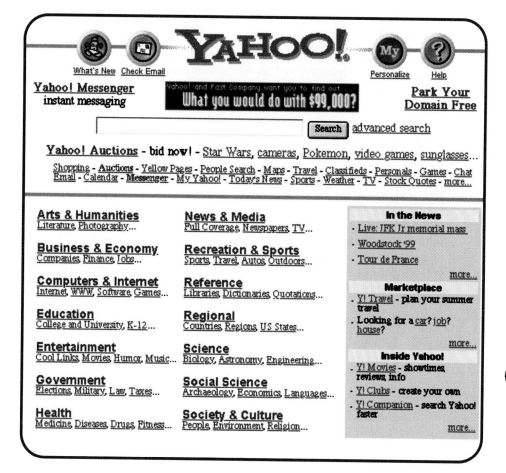

STEP 1

Type in the URL for Yahoo: **http://www.yahoo.com**

NOTE:

If you are using version 4.0 or later of either Netscape Navigator or Internet Explorer you only have to type **yahoo**. The browser enters in the remainder of the URL.

You will be taken to Yahoo's home page.

Notice the broad subject categories as well as links to help find companies (Yellow Pages), people, maps, news, sports, weather, and stock quotes.

STEP 2

Begin by browsing the subject directory. In this example we will do a search for *comets*. Click on a subject category that this topic would fall under. In this case **Science**.

Subject categories under Science

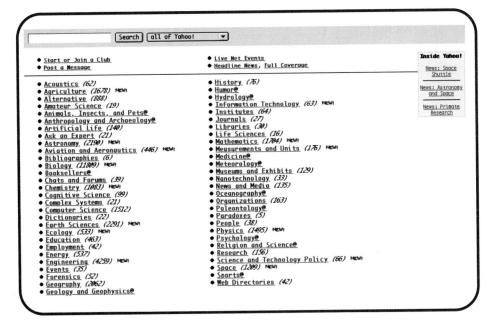

Yahoo's Astronomy directory

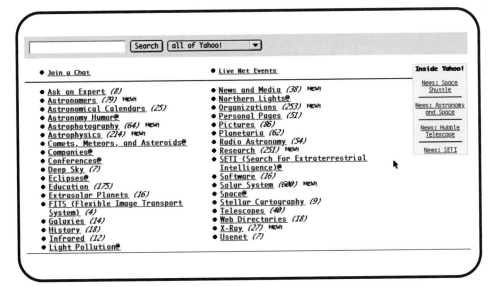

STEP 3

Determine which category would be most appropriate for the topic you are searching for. In this case, we will select **Astronomy**.

Notice the category, **Comets, Meteors, and Asteroids**. Click on that category.

FIGURE A1-4

Subject directory for Comets, Meteors, and Asteroids

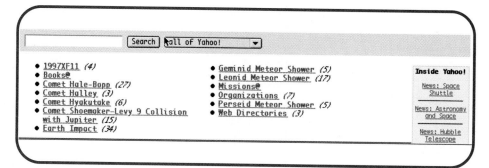

Explore the categories for the information you are searching for.

Finding Resources Using Yahoo's Search Tool

Yahoo has a search engine that can be used to find information in its database.

FIGURE A1-5

Yahoo's dialog box for a keyword search

Enter a descriptive keyword(s) for your subject, one that uniquely identifies or describes what you are looking for. It is often helpful to do a broad search first, though results often present the need to change descriptive keywords or to refine your query.

In this example, we will do a search in the **Society & Culture** category for the **Egypt.**

NOTE

You can do a search that will look for matches throughout Yahoo or you can do a search within a category. In this example our search was restricted to only the Society & Culture category.

Click on the Search button and Yahoo finds matches in its database to the keywords entered.

Yahoo page showing a keyword search for Egypt in the category
Society & Culture

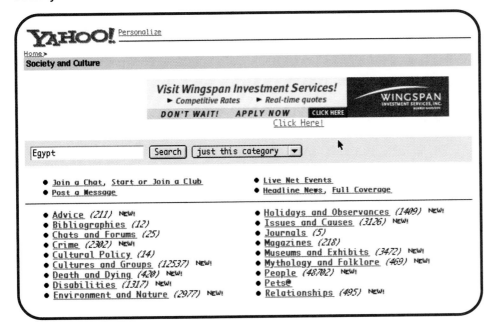

Results of keyword search Egypt in the Society & Culture category

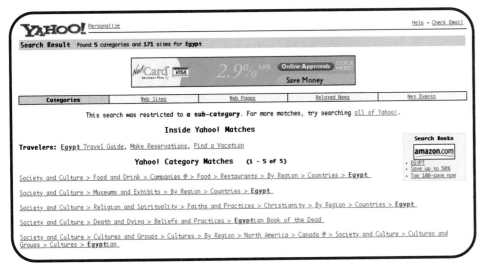

Notice that Yahoo found five additional categories under this broad keyword
search and 246 Internet sites for *Egypt.*

Yahoo Options Limiting a Search

If you are conducting a search using more than one keyword Yahoo's **Options** feature should be used. Search engines work by finding matches to keywords. If more
than one keyword is used then the search engine goes out and finds matches to
both words. As a researcher you must determine the importance of each keyword
and how you want the search engine to use these words in your search.

Click on the **Search Options** link.

Yahoo's home page showing the Options link

You will be taken to this Yahoo page displaying search options for refining and limiting your search. In this example we will do a search for *pyramids of Egypt*. The advanced searching options allows us to indicate how important the keywords are to the search. In this example we tell the search engine to look for both keywords *pyramids AND Egypt*. Note how the search method, **Matches on all words (AND)** has been selected. This option instructs the search engine to look for only matches that have each of the three keywords. Notice the other search options in Figure A1-9 for refining a search.

Yahoo's Option page

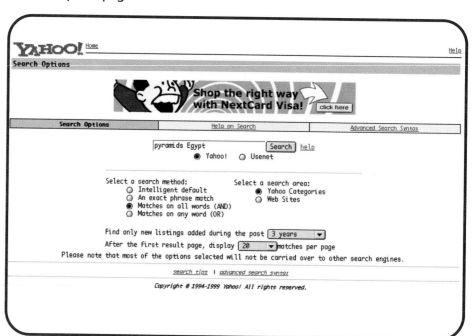

Search results for keywords *pyramids AND Egypt*

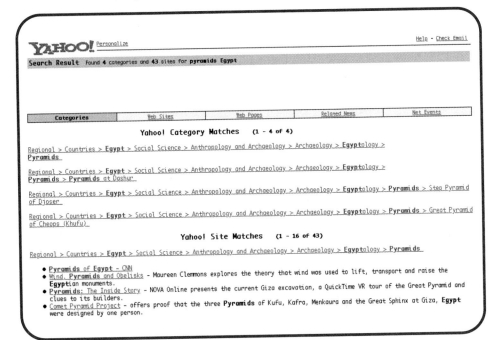

NOTE

A search provides a higher degree of accuracy in matching your keywords when you use Yahoo's Option for refining a search.

Other Search Directories

Explore the subject directories listed below. You will find that their subject categories vary; most have advanced search options for refining your search and as well as built-in search engines for finding keyword matches within their database and the World Wide Web.

➢ Magellan   http://magellan.mckinley.com

➢ Galaxy   http://galaxy.einet.net/galaxy.html

➢ Snap   http://www.snap.com

NOTE

Most search engines also have subject categories to assist with quickly finding information. Yahoo, Magellan, Galaxy, and Snap frequently have categories of information better suited to research.

Magellan

http://magellan.mckinley.com

Magellan is an excellent search directory for quickly finding quality information.

Magellan's home page

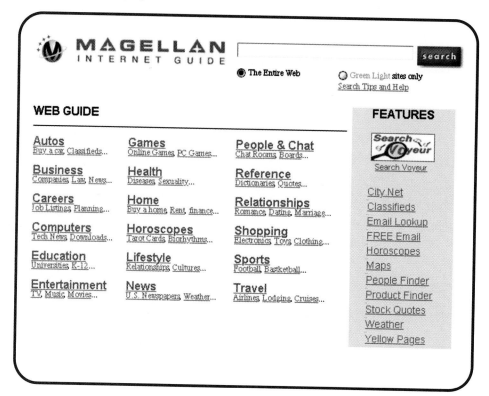

Magellan Internet Guide and the Magellan logo are trademarks of The McKinley Group, Inc., a subsidiary of Excite, Inc., and may be registered in various jurisdictions. Excite screen display copyright 1995-1998 Excite, Inc. Magellan screen display copyright 1998 of The McKinley Group, Inc., a subsidiary of Excite, Inc.

Notice that Magellan has an option that expands your keyword search to the

> entire World Wide Web

> green light sites containing no content intended for mature audiences, or

> reviewed sites that Magellan has chosen for high quality content

Galaxy

http://www.galaxy.com

Galaxy's home page displays a more detailed subject listing.

Click on Galaxy's advanced search option and be taken to a page for search options.

Galaxy's home page directory

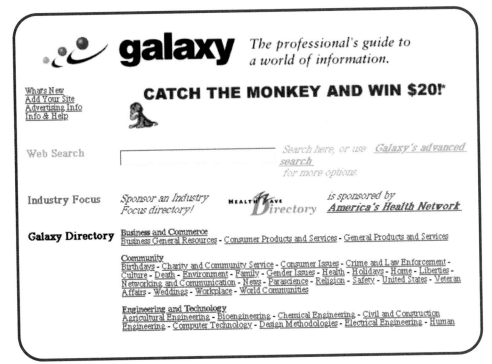

Galaxy's advanced search options

FIGURE A1-14

Snap.com search directory home page

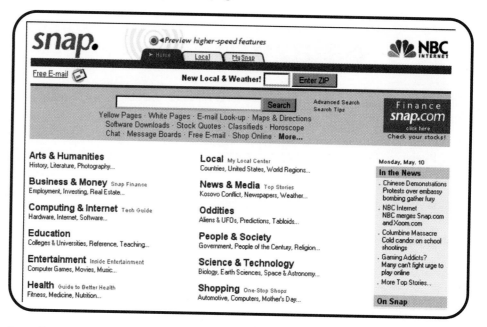

Source Date: May 10, 1999

Snap.com

http://www.snap.com

Snap.com's search directory looks very much like Yahoo's. The comprehensive directory is helpful for quickly finding information.

SEARCH ENGINES

Search engines require a keyword(s) or phrase that is descriptive of the information you are looking for. Begin by listing keywords or phrases on your topic. When you connect to a search engine look for its *Search Tips* or *Advanced Search Options* to help you conduct a more efficient and effective search. Taking this step will save time and help to prevent information overload frustration.

Research Tips for Using Search Engines

Understanding advanced searching options is essential if you are going to quickly find information using search engines. When researching a topic with more than one keyword (i.e., multiple intelligence) use the search engines' advanced capabilities. Most search engines recognize the following conventions for increasing the precision of a search.

Boolean Operators (AND, OR, NOT)

Boolean operators limit and refine keyword searches.

Use **AND** to find documents with both keywords. A search with
multiple AND intelligence
returns documents that contain the word *multiple* and *intelligence*.

Use **OR** to find documents that include any of the search words. A search with

multiple OR intelligence

returns sites that include either the word multiple or intelligence.

Use **NOT** to indicate that a word must *not* appear in the document. A search with

intelligence NOT multiple

Returns results of sites with the word intelligence only.

Quotation Marks

Use quotation marks around a word or phrase to find occurrences of the phrase in quotes.

For example a search with

"Howard Gardner multiple intelligence"

focuses the search on sites that have each of these four keywords.

Quotation marks can also be used with Boolean operators. For example this keyword search with quotes

"multiple intelligence AND frames of mind"

returns documents with the phrase multiple intelligence and frames of mind. Internet sources and discussion of Howard Gardner's book *Frames* of *Mind* will be located using these search refining symbols.

Plus (+) and Minus (-) Sign

The use of the plus (+) sign indicates that the word **must** be present in the document. A minus (-) sign indicates that those words **must not** be present.

A search with

+ comet + Hale-Bopp

returns documents on the Hale-Bopp comet only.

A search with

+comet - Hale-Bopp + Shoemaker-Levy

returns documents with information on Shoemaker Levy comet and **not** Hale-Bopp.

Wildcards

Many search engines support the use of wildcards or truncation symbols in a search. The asterisk (*) is the most commonly used symbol to replace multiple characters.

The search **psych*** produces matches to psychology, psychologist, psychiatrist.

NOTE

Some search engines such as Hot Bot (see Figure A1-17) have these operations built in. Selections are made from a pull-down menu for limiting and refining searches.

Using Search Engines' Advanced Search Options

There are many search engines to help you find information. You will need to use each of them at least several times before you can select the ones that best meet your needs. We will use two search engines, AltaVista and Hot Bot, to research the topic *multiple intelligence*.

AltaVista

http://altavista.digital.com

Digital's AltaVista is an excellent search engine with options for simple and advanced searching. AltaVista's Help states that the standard search tool found on the home page can be used for quickly finding what you are looking for with good results. The advanced search feature is for very specific searches and not for general searching. The advanced search feature is used to find documents within a range of dates or for complex searching using Boolean operators.

In this example we will search for information on *multiple intelligence* using AltaVista's standard search.

FIGURE A1-15

AltaVista home page showing the standard search box

The AltaVista logo and Search Engine Content are copyright and trademarks of Compaq Corporation. Used with permission.

AltaVista suggests using a plus (+) sign in front of words that must be included in the search; a minus (-) is used to exclude words from a search.

FIGURE A1-16

Search results from a standard AltaVista search on *multiple intelligence*

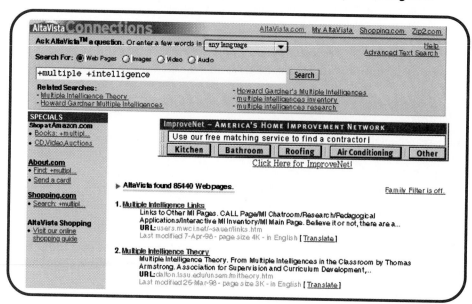

The AltaVista logo and Search Engine Content are copyright and trademarks of Compaq Corporation. Used with permission.

Notice that AltaVista found over 96,710 Web pages matching these keywords as well as books that can be ordered online on the subject.

Hot Bot

http://www.hotbot.com

Hot Bot uses a pulldown menu to refine searches, eliminating the need for Boolean operators, plus and minus signs, and parenthesis.

FIGURE A1-17

Hot Bot search engines showing the pulldown menu option (exact phrase) for refining searches

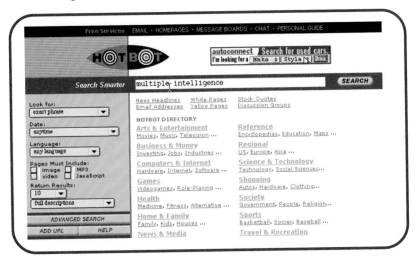

The search for *multiple intelligence* is conducted using Hot Bot. Notice in Figure A1-18 that Hot Bot found 1,170 matches to the keyword phrase *multiple intelligence*. The results also display a link to the 10 most visited multiple intelligence Web sites. This would appear to be a very useful feature of this easy to use search engine.

FIGURE A1-18

Hot Bot search results using an exact phrase match to keyword *multiple intelligence*

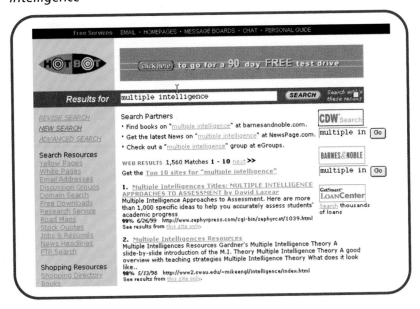

Northern Light

http://www.northernlight.com

Northern Light is a search service that saves time by providing quality information. Search results categorize Internet resources matching keywords in **Custom Search Folders.**

In addition to Internet resources, the Northern Light's **Special Collections** lists articles representing 4,500 journals, reviews, books, magazines, and newswires not readily found on the Web. When choosing a Special Collections item from the results list, a free summary of the article is displayed. If you like the summary and decide to purchase the article you can do so on line by initiating a secured online credit card transaction. Northern Light offers a unique service whereby articles usually only available with a subscription can now be ordered at an affordable price.

A search for *comet* resources will illustrate these two Northern Light search services.

FIGURE A1-19

Home page for Northern Light showing a keyword search for *comet*

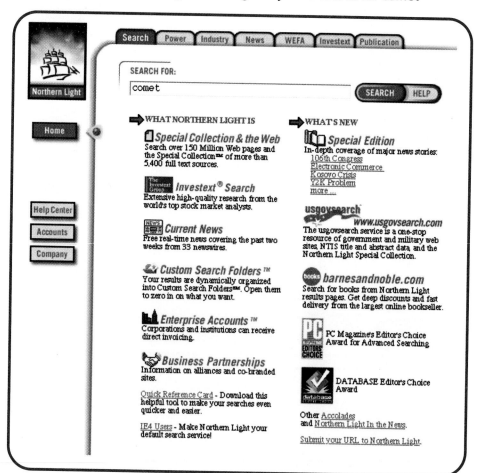

NOTE

Northern Light supports full Boolean capability, the use of plus and minus signs, and parenthesis.

Northern Light's search results for the keyword *comet*

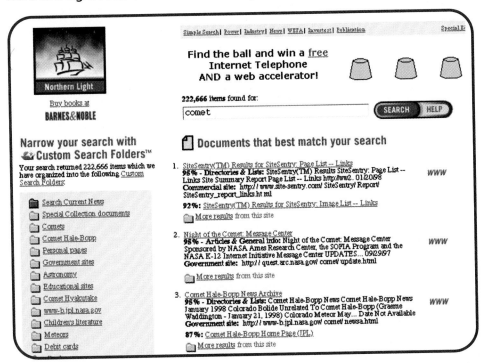

Notice in the left column (Fig. A1-20) the Custom Folders: Comets, Comet Hale-Bopp, **http://www.nao.ac.jp**, Comet Hyakutake, Government sites, Eclipses, Astronomy, and Haley's comet. The Special Collection documents folder is also displayed. Click on this folder for articles on comets from *Astronomy* magazine, *Colliers Encyclopedia*, and *Sky and Telescope* magazine. The full text article is available from Northern Light for a small fee usually ranging from $1.00 to $4.00.

Northern Light's Special Collections folder displaying articles on comets

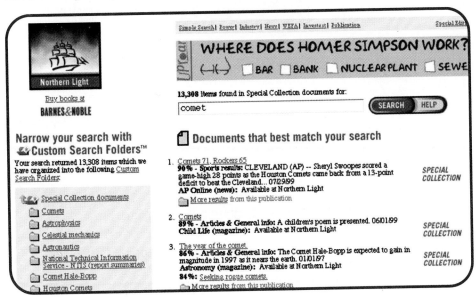

OTHER SEARCH ENGINES

Explore the subject engines listed below to find which best meets your research needs.

- ➤ Excite   http://www.excite.com
- ➤ Infoseek   http://www.infoseek.com
- ➤ Lycos   http://www.lycos.com
- ➤ Web Crawler   http://www.webcrawler.com
- ➤ LookSmart   http://www.looksmart.com

Image Surfers

A few search engines are offering services whereby they search for images. Some even search for video and sound. The two most widely used image surfers are Lycos and AltaVista.

Lycos

http://www.lycos.com

Lycos is one of the older search tools that became one of the first to expanded its services with new search capabilities for finding images and sounds. There are two places to select the pictures search feature (see Figure A1-22): the home page in the left column of search features and by clicking on Search Options under the keyword search box.

FIGURE A1-22

Lycos home page

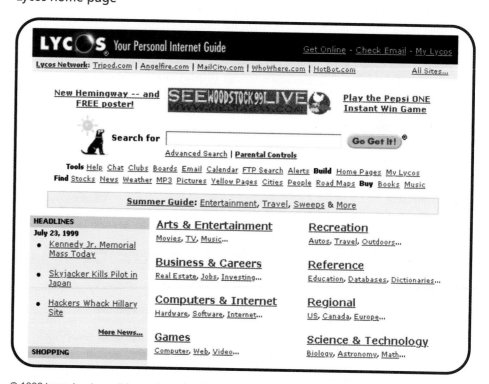

Search options page for selecting pictures

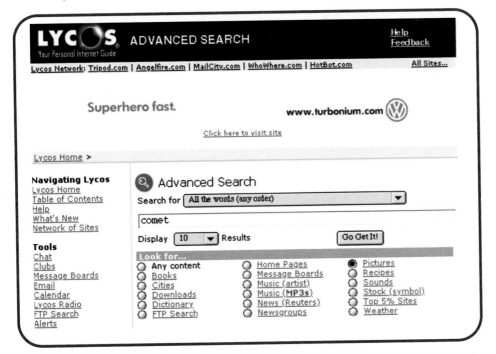

A keyword search is done in Lycos for comet pictures. The following returns are given.

Lycos search returns for comet pictures

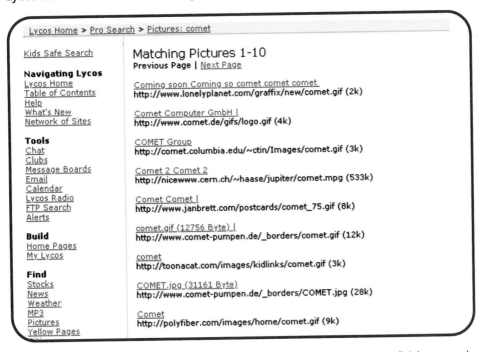

AltaVista Photo Finder
http://www.altavista.digital.com

AltaVista photo finder helps to find color and black and white photographs and art work that match keywords.

FIGURE A1-25

AltaVista search options

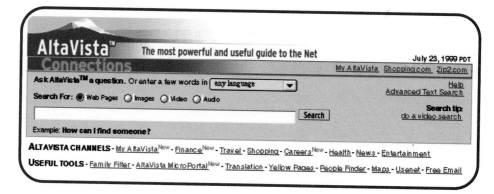

The AltaVista logo and Search Engine Content are copyright and trademarks of Compaq Corporation. Used with permission.

FIGURE A1-26

Click on AV Photo Finder.

AV Photo Finder search box

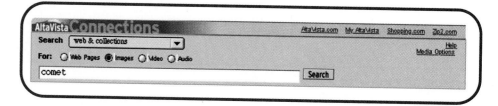

The AltaVista logo and Search Engine Content are copyright and trademarks of Compaq Corporation. Used with permission.

Click on Search and the following color photo resources are displayed. Notice that AltaVista found 2,719 pictures of comets.

FIGURE A1-27

Search results for color photos of comets

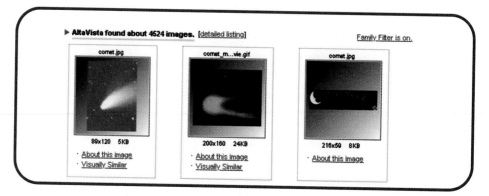

The AltaVista logo and Search Engine Content are copyright and trademarks of Compaq Corporation. Used with permission.

Reference Resources

The Internet is the newest and perhaps largest reference library. This rich source of information is available to Net users. Listed below are a few reference resources that you will find useful.

➤ **Britannica Online**
http://www.eb.com
For a minimal fee you can subscribe to the Britannica Online and Merriam-Webster's Collegiate Dictionary. Some of the encyclopedia text is linked to Internet sites.

➤ **CIA World Fact Book**
http://elo.www.media.mit.edu/people/elo/cia
Published by the Central Intelligence Agency (CIA), The World Fact Book has a subject index for researching facts about countries.

➤ **Encyberpedia**
http://www.encyberpedia.com/ency.htm
The HOTTEST encyclopedia from cyberspace designed to help you find good stuff in the jungle of over two million Web Sites.

➤ **Library of Congress**
http://www.loc.gov
A must visit site of government documents and resources.

➤ **Library Spot**
http://www.libraryspot.com
LibrarySpot is a goldmine of library and reference resources on the Web. Find top dictionaries, encyclopedias, newspapers, maps, geneology tools, and more.

➤ **megaConverter**
http://www.megaconverter.com
MegaConverter.com is an ever-growing set of weights, measures, and units conversion/calculation modules.

➤ **My Virtual Reference Desk**
http://www.refdesk.com/main.html
Links to many excellent reference resources including a link to a subject directory of resources—My Virtual Encyclopedia.

➤ **Noble Citizens of Planet Earth**
http://www.s9.com/biography
This dictionary contains biographical information on more than 18,000 people who have shaped our world from ancient times to the present day. Information contained in the dictionary includes birth and death years, professions, positions held, literary and artistic works, and other achievements.

➤ **OneLook Dictionaries**
http://www.onelook.com
Type in a word and this search tool will look for multiple definitions from a variety of online dictionaries: computer/Internet dictionaries, science, medical, technological, business, sports, religion, acronym, and general.

➤ **Reference Center – The Internet Public Library**
http://www.ipl.org/ref
This virtual library helps to make finding valuable information online easy. Click on a reference shelf and be linked to resources.

➤ **Reference Desk**
http://www-sci.lib.uci.edu/~martindale/Ref.html
This GOLDMINE site has won multiple awards for its SUPERB resource collection. A go to the top of the bookmark list site.

➤ **Reference Indexes**
http://www.lib.lsu.edu/weblio.html
Links to online references such as dictionaries, library catalogs, news-stand, and subject collections.

➤ **Reference Shelf**
http://gort.ucsd.edu/ek/refshelf/refshelf.html
The University of California, San Diego, sponsors this collection of online reference resources.

➤ **Researchpaper.com**
http://www.researchpaper.com/directory.html
This award-winning online research tool offers an archive of thousands of magazines, newspapers, books, and photographs.

➤ **The Virtual Reference Desk**
http://thorplus.lib.purdue.edu/reference/index.html
Purdue University's links to an AWESOME list of valuable online resources.

➤ **US Census Bureau**
http://www.census.gov
An AWESOME resource for data on social, demographic, and economic information.

Evaluating Internet Information

The Internet is analogous to a wilderness frontier that is wild and untamed. With an estimate of 20 to 50 million pages of data created from a variety of sources—individuals, businesses, corporations, nonprofit organizations, schools, special interest groups, or illicit if not illegal sources—it is inherent that not all the information is accurate, unbiased, reputable, scientifically valid, or up-to-date. Unlike scholarly publications, there is no editorial board for most Internet information. It is therefore essential that you understand how to evaluate information you research on the Net.

How strict you are with your evaluation will depend on your purpose. For example, if you are writing a factual report, dissertation, thesis, or paper that others will rely on for accurate content, it will be essential that you are judicious in choosing what information will be reported from the Net.

The first thing you must do when using the Internet for your studies is to determine which resources to use. The following guidelines will assist you with evaluation.

➤ **Information Source.** Where does the information come from—an individual, organization, educational institution, or other source? One way to quickly determine the source of the information is to look at the URL—Net site address. The first address protocol often will give you the source of the information—name of institution and domain. For example, an address such as **http://gort.ucsd.edu** tells the name of the institution—University of California, San Diego—and the *edu* ending indicates an educational institution. An educational institution has a good chance of being a reputable source. Other address endings that are highly likely to be reputable are *gov* for government or *mil* for military. Naturally, you will want to evaluate the information further. Just because the information is from an educational institution, government, or military source does not ensure that the content is factual and reliable.

Check to see if the document resides in an individual's personal Internet account or is part of the organization's official Internet site. This information can often be determined by looking at the URL address pathway.

Is the organization that publishes this document recognized in the field you are studying? Is the organization qualified to be an expert in this topic?

➤ **Authorship.** Closely related to the information source is the reputation of the data and the reliability of its source. Information on an educational institution Web site may be compiled by a student or graduate student who is not as yet an authority on the subject and may enter in written errors or present incorrect data without realizing it. The content may not have been reviewed for accuracy and reliability.

Who is the author? Does the author have credentials to be an expert on the topic? Consider educational background, experience, and other published writings. Have you encountered the author's name in your reading or in bibliographies?

Does the Internet document furnish information on the author such as institutional affiliation, position, experience and credentials? If none of this is provided, is there an email address or a mailing address from which you can request biographical information? Correspond with the author to obtain more information about the source of his or her content.

➤ **Accuracy.** Is the data accurate? Check to see if there is a reference for the information. Does the information come from a published research paper or report, historical document, news publication, or a personal viewpoint? Does the document include a bibliography? Does the author acknowledge related sources?

Although information may be written from a personal view point, don't invalidate it. Bias is to be expected especially if one is a participant in an event. If the writing seems biased, look for inconsistencies or incorrect thinking. Does the author acknowledge that his treatment of the subject is controversial? Are there political or ideological biases? Can you separate fact from opinion? Do any statements seem exaggerated or overly simplified? Has the author omitted any important details? Is the writer qualified to be authoritative?

One example of inaccuracy in Web writing is the use of the words *endangered species* when referring to animals that may in fact be only threatened or vulnerable. Many authors loosely use the words *endangered species*. To cross check this information, a reliable source such as the Convention on International Trade and Endangered Species (CITES) and the International Union for the Conservation of Nature (IUCN) must be used. These international organizations keep the working lists of which species are categorized as either extinct, endangered, threatened, vulnerable, indeterminate, or out of danger.

➤ **Verifiability.** Can the data be verified? Does it appear to be well-researched? Does the author make generalizations without proof or validation? Always be thinking "Show me why or how." In some instances you may need to ask if the data has statistical validity—supported by statistical testing. Watch for errors or omissions.

When numbers or statistical information is reported, it is critical that the data be cross checked with a reliable publication source. For example, some Web factual data contain errors due to carelessness in copying and transposing numbers from a print version to a Web site. Reporting that 17,000 areas of rain forest are destroyed daily when the correct number is 700 acres is an inexcusable error in sloppy copy.

➤ **Consistency of data.** Is the data consistent or does it reflect contradictions with other information on the topic? Are definitions used consistently throughout?

For example, search for reputable Web sites on the rain forest led to the discovery of Public Broadcasting System (PBS) and the Rain Forest Action Network as excellent online references to cross check the consistency of data.

➤ **Quality.** Is the text error free? Is it well organized and grammatically correct? Check for the misspelling of names or carelessness and lack of attention to details in other areas. Information that contains these types of careless errors probably should not be relied on.

Is the tone scholarly, technical, factual, authoritative, or personal?

➤ **Currency.** Is the information current and up-to-date? Does the document include a publication date or a date of copyright? Does it appear to be appropriate and relevant for today? Information that was reported in 1985 is probably not valid today. Look for the most current information unless currency is not an issue.

Bonus guidelines—other important suggestions

➤ Whenever possible, check online information against other sources.
➤ Never use information that you cannot verify.
➤ Question everything that you read. Learn to be critical and skeptical.
➤ Information found on the Internet should complement information from traditional research resources. Never use Internet information as your sole source of knowledge.
➤ "When in doubt, leave it out."

TIP

If you don't know where to find a reliable source to cross check your information go talk with a resource librarian, teacher, or professor. These individuals can be excellent resources for finding publications to verify your data. You can also call a reputable organization.

The information for *"Researching Information and Resources on the Internet"* was taken from chapter IV of **Student Resource Guide to the Internet: Student Success Online** by Cynthia B. Leshin, and published by Prentice Hall. The chapter has additional research resources (subject-oriented collections and virtual libraries) and a comprehensive section on how to reference Internet resources.

APPENDIX 2

Learning Styles Assessments

Because you are a complex individual, there is more than one way to evaluate your learning style and personality traits. Chapter 3 focuses on an evaluation of your multiple intelligences. The purpose of this appendix is to introduce two other assessments that you can use if you have the time and interest to do so. These two assessments, the Learning Styles Inventory and the Personality Spectrum, may give you insights into who you are and how you learn—insights that may reinforce, expand, or even challenge what you already know about yourself.

Learning Styles Inventory

One of the first instruments to measure psychological types, the Myers-Briggs Type Inventory (MBTI), was designed by Katharine Briggs and her daughter, Isabel Briggs Myers. Later David Keirsey and Marilyn Bates combined the sixteen Myers-Briggs types into four temperaments. Barbara Soloman, associate director of the First Year College at North Carolina State University in Raleigh, has developed the following learning styles inventory based on these theories and on her work with thousands of students:

"Students learn in many ways. Mismatches often exist between common learning styles and standard teaching styles. Therefore, students often do poorly and get discouraged. Some students doubt themselves and doubt their ability to succeed in the curriculum of their choice. Some settle for low grades and even leave school. If students understand how they learn most effectively, they can tailor their studying to their own needs."

"Learning effectively" and "tailoring studying to your own needs" means choosing study techniques that help you learn. For example, if a student responds more to visual images than to words, he or she may want to construct notes in a more visual way. Or if a student learns better when talking to people than when studying alone, he or she may want to study primarily in pairs or groups. See Figure A2-1 for information on what styles tend to be dominant among students.

This inventory has four dimensions, within each of which are two opposing styles. At the end of the inventory, you will have two scores in each of the four dimensions. The difference between your two scores in any dimension tells you which of the two styles in that dimension is dominant for you. A few people will score right in between the two styles, indicating that they have fairly equal parts of both styles. Following are brief descriptions of the four dimensions. You will learn more about them in the section on benefits.

FIGURE A2-1   **Percentages of Students with Particular Learning Styles**

Source: Barbara Soloman, North Carolina State University.

Active/Reflective. Active learners learn best by experiencing knowledge through their own actions. Reflective learners understand information best when they have had time to reflect on it on their own.

Factual/Theoretical. Factual learners learn best through specific facts, data, and detailed experimentation. Theoretical learners are more comfortable with big-picture ideas, symbols, and new concepts.

Visual/Verbal. Visual learners remember best what they see: diagrams, flowcharts, time lines, films, and demonstrations. Verbal learners gain the most learning from reading, hearing spoken words, participating in discussions, and explaining things to others.

Linear/Holistic. Linear learners find it easiest to learn material presented step by step in a logical, ordered progression. Holistic learners progress in fits and starts, perhaps feeling lost for a while but eventually seeing the big picture in a clear and creative way.

LEARNING STYLES INVENTORY

Please complete this inventory by circling a or b to indicate your answer to each question. Answer every question and choose only one answer for each question. If both answers seem to apply to you, choose the answer that applies more often.

1. I study best
   a. in a study group.
   b. alone or with a partner.

2. I would rather be considered
   a. realistic.
   b. imaginative.

3. When I recall what I did yesterday, I am most likely to think in terms of
   a. pictures or images.
   b. words or verbal descriptions.

4. I usually think new material is
   a. easier at the beginning and then harder as it becomes more complicated.
   b. often confusing at the beginning but easier as I start to understand what the whole subject is about.

5. When given a new activity to learn, I would rather first
   a. try it out.
   b. think about how I'm going to do it.

6. If I were an instructor, I would rather teach a course
   a. that deals with real-life situations and what to do about them.
   b. that deals with ideas and encourages students to think about them.

7. I prefer to receive new information in the form of
   a. pictures, diagrams, graphs, or maps.
   b. written directions or verbal information.

8. I learn
   a. at a fairly regular pace. If I study hard I'll "get it" and then move on.
   b. in fits and starts. I might be totally confused and then suddenly it all "clicks."

9. I understand something better after
   a. I attempt to do it myself.
   b. I give myself time to think about how it works.

10. I find it easier
    a. to learn facts.
    b. to learn ideas or concepts.

11. In a book with lots of pictures and charts, I am likely to
    a. look over the pictures and charts carefully.
    b. focus on the written text.

12. It's easier for me to memorize facts from
    a. a list.
    b. a whole story or essay with the facts embedded in it.

13. I will more easily remember
    a. something I have done myself.
    b. something I have thought or read about.

14. I am usually
    a. aware of my surroundings. I remember people and places and usually recall where I put things.
    b. unaware of my surroundings. I forget people and places. I frequently misplace things.

15. I like instructors
    a. who put a lot of diagrams on the board.
    b. who spend a lot of time explaining.

16. Once I understand
    a. all the parts, I understand the whole thing.
    b. the whole thing, I see how the parts fit.

17. When I am learning something new, I would rather
    a. talk about it.
    b. think about it.

18. I am good at
    a. being careful about the details of my work.
    b. having creative ideas about how to do my work.

19. I remember best
    a. what I see.
    b. what I hear.

20. When I solve problems that involve some math, I usually
    a. work my way to the solutions one step at a time.
    b. see the solutions but then have to struggle to figure out the steps to get to them.

21. In a lecture class, I would prefer occasional in-class
    a. discussions or group problem-solving sessions.
    b. pauses that give opportunities to think or write about ideas presented in the lecture.

22. On a multiple-choice test, I am more likely to
    a. run out of time.
    b. lose points because of not reading carefully or making careless errors.

23. When I get directions to a new place, I prefer
    a. a map.
    b. written instructions.

24. When I'm thinking about something I've read,
    a. I remember the incidents and try to put them together to figure out the themes.
    b. I know what the themes are after I finish reading and then I have to back up and find the incidents that demonstrate them.

25. When I get a new computer or VCR, I tend to
    a. plug it in and start punching buttons.
    b. read the manual and follow instructions.

26. In reading for pleasure, I prefer
    a. something that teaches me new facts or tells me how to do something.
    b. something that gives me new ideas to think about.

27. When I see a diagram or sketch in class, I am most likely to remember
    a. the picture.
    b. what the instructor said about it.

28. It is more important to me that an instructor
    a. lay out the material in clear, sequential steps.
    b. give me an overall picture and relate the material to other subjects.

SCORING SHEET: Use Table A2-1 to enter your scores.

1. Put 1s in the appropriate boxes in the table (e.g., if you answered **a** to Question 3, put a 1 in the column headed **a** next to the number 3).
2. Total the 1s in the columns and write the totals in the indicated spaces at the base of the columns.

TABLE A2-1 LEARNING STYLES INVENTORY SCORES

ACTV/REFL			FACT/THEO			VISL/VRBL			LINR/HOLS		
Q #	a	b	Q#	a	b	Q#	a	b	Q#	a	b
1			2			3			4		
5			6			7			8		
9			10			11			12		
13			14			15			16		
17			18			19			20		
21			22			23			24		
25			26			27			28		

Write Totals for Each Column in the Spaces Below

3. For each of the four dimensions, circle your two scores on the bar scale and then fill in the bar between the scores. For example, if under "ACTV/REFL" you had 2 **a** and 5 **b** responses, you would fill in the bar between those two scores, as this sample shows:

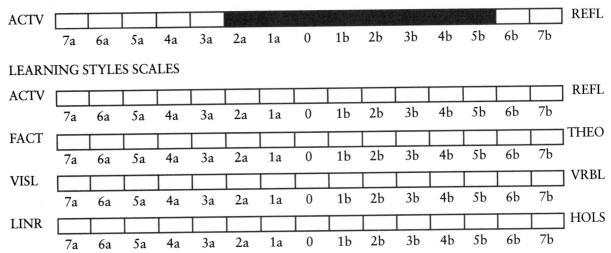

LEARNING STYLES SCALES

If your filled-in bar has the zero close to its center, you are well balanced on the two dimensions of that scale. If your bar is drawn mainly to one side, you have a strong preference for that one dimension and may have difficulty learning in the other dimension.

Personality Spectrum

A system that simplifies learning styles into four personality types has been developed by Joyce Bishop. Her work is based on the Myers-Briggs and Keirsey theories. The personality spectrum will give you a personality perspective on your learning style. Please complete the following assessment.

PERSONALITY SPECTRUM

STEP 1. Rank in order all four responses to each question from <u>**most** like you (4)</u>, to <u>**least** like you (1)</u>. Place a 1, 2, 3, or 4 in each pink box next to the responses.

1. I like instructors who
   - a. tell me exactly what is expected of me.
   - b. make learning active and exciting.
   - c. maintain a safe and supportive classroom.
   - d. challenge me to think at higher levels.

2. I learn best when the material is
   - a. well organized.
   - b. something I can do hands-on.
   - c. about understanding and improving the human condition.
   - d. intellectually challenging.

3. A high priority in my life is to
   - a. keep my commitments.
   - b. experience as much of life as possible.
   - c. make a difference in the lives of others.
   - d. understand how things work.

4. Other people think of me as
   - a. dependable and loyal.
   - b. dynamic and creative.
   - c. caring and honest.
   - d. intelligent and inventive.

5. When I experience stress I would most likely
   - a. do something to help me feel more in control of my life
   - b. do something physical and daring.
   - c. talk with a friend.
   - d. go off by myself.

6. I would probably NOT be close friends with someone who was
   - a. irresponsible.
   - b. unwilling to try new things.
   - c. selfish and unkind to others.
   - d. an illogical thinker.

7. My vacations could be best described as
   - a. traditional.
   - b. adventuresome.
   - c. pleasing to others.
   - d. a new learning experience.

8. One word that best describes me is
   - a. sensible.
   - b. spontaneous.
   - c. giving.
   - d. analytical.

STEP 2. Add up the total points for each column.

TOTAL	TOTAL	TOTAL	TOTAL
Organizer	Adventurer	Giver	Thinker

When you have tallied your scores, plot them on Figure A2—2, the brain diagram, to create a visual representation of your spectrum.

Personality Spectrum –Thinking Preferences & Learning Styles

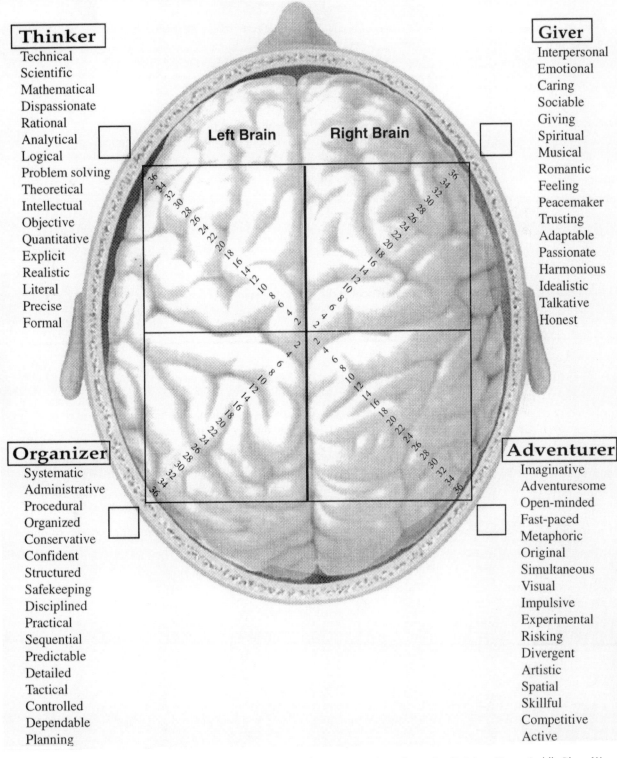

Thinker		**Giver**
Technical		Interpersonal
Scientific		Emotional
Mathematical		Caring
Dispassionate		Sociable
Rational		Giving
Analytical	**Left Brain Right Brain**	Spiritual
Logical		Musical
Problem solving		Romantic
Theoretical		Feeling
Intellectual		Peacemaker
Objective		Trusting
Quantitative		Adaptable
Explicit		Passionate
Realistic		Harmonious
Literal		Idealistic
Precise		Talkative
Formal		Honest

Organizer		**Adventurer**
Systematic		Imaginative
Administrative		Adventuresome
Procedural		Open-minded
Organized		Fast-paced
Conservative		Metaphoric
Confident		Original
Structured		Simultaneous
Safekeeping		Visual
Disciplined		Impulsive
Practical		Experimental
Sequential		Risking
Predictable		Divergent
Detailed		Artistic
Tactical		Spatial
Controlled		Skillful
Dependable		Competitive
Planning		Active

Source: Understanding Psychology 3/E. by Morris, ©1996. Adapted by permission of Prentice-Hall, Inc., Upper Saddle River, NJ.

Your Personality Spectrum assessment can help you maximize your functioning at school and at work. Each personality type has its own abilities, which improve work and school performance; suitable learning techniques; and ways of relating in interpersonal relationships. Table A2—2 explains what suits each type.

TABLE A2-2   PERSONALITY SPECTRUM AT SCHOOL AND WORK

PERSONALITY	STRENGTHS AT WORK AND SCHOOL	INTERPERSONAL RELATIONSHIPS
Organizer	Can efficiently manage heavy work loads Good organizational skills Natural leadership qualities	Loyal Dependable Traditional
Adventurer	Adaptable to most changes Creative and skillful Dynamic and fast-paced	Free Exciting Intense
Giver	Always willing to help others Honest and sincere Good people skills	Giving Romantic Warm
Thinker	Good analytical skills Can develop complex designs Is thorough and exact	Quiet Problem solver Inventive

Benefits of Different Styles

Following is some information about study strategies that correspond to both Learning Styles Inventory and Personality Spectrum dimensions and styles.

Active learners and adventurers like to apply the information to the real world, experience it in their own actions, or discuss or explain to others what they have learned.

Following are student-suggested strategies for active learners:

➤ Study in a group in which members take turns explaining topics to one another and then discussing them.

➤ Think of practical uses of the course material.

➤ Pace and recite while you learn.

➤ Act out material or design games.

➤ Use flash cards with other people.

➤ Teach the material to someone else.

Reflective learners and thinkers retain and understand information better after they have taken time to think about it.

Following are student-suggested strategies for reflective learners:

➤ Study in a quiet setting.

➤ When reading, stop periodically to think about what you have read.

➤ Don't just memorize material; think about why it is important and what it relates to, considering the causes and effects involved.

➤ Write short summaries of what the material means to you.

Factual learners and organizers prefer concrete and specific facts, data, and detailed experimentation. They like to solve problems with standard methods and are patient with details. They don't respond well to surprises and unique complications that upset normal procedure. They are good at memorizing facts.

Following are student-suggested strategies for factual learners:

➤ Ask the instructor how ideas and concepts apply in practice.

➤ Ask for specific examples of the ideas and concepts.

➤ Brainstorm specific examples with classmates or by yourself.

➤ Think about how theories make specific connections with the real world.

Theoretical learners prefer innovation and theories. They are good at grasping new concepts and big-picture ideas. They dislike repetition and fact-based learning. They are comfortable with symbols and abstractions, often connecting them with prior knowledge and experience. Most classes are aimed at theoretical learners.

Following are student-suggested strategies for theoretical learners:

➤ If a class deals primarily with factual information, try to think of concepts, interpretations, or theories that link the facts together.

➤ Because you become impatient with details, you may be prone to careless mistakes on tests. Read directions and entire questions before answering, and be sure to check your work.

➤ Look for systems and patterns that arrange facts in a way that makes sense to you.

➤ Spend time analyzing the material.

Visual learners remember best what they see: diagrams, flowcharts, time lines, films, and demonstrations. They tend to forget spoken words and ideas. Classes generally don't include that much visual information. Note that although words written on paper or shown with an overhead projector are something you see, visual learners learn most easily from visual cues that don't involve words.

Following are student-suggested strategies for visual learners:

➤ Add diagrams to your notes whenever possible. Dates can be drawn on a time line; math functions can be graphed; percentages can be drawn in a pie chart.

➤ Organize your notes so that you can clearly see main points and supporting facts and how things are connected.

➤ Connect related facts in your notes by drawing arrows.

➤ Color-code your notes, using differently colored highlighters, so that everything relating to a particular topic is the same color.

Verbal learners remember much of what they hear and more of what they hear and then say. They benefit from discussion, prefer verbal explanation to visual demonstration, and learn effectively by explaining things to others. Because written words are processed as verbal information, verbal learners learn well through reading.

The majority of classes, since they present material through the written word, lecture, or discussion, are geared to verbal learners.

Following are student-suggested strategies for verbal learners:

➤ Talk about what you learn. Work in study groups so that you have an opportunity to explain and discuss what you are learning.

➤ Read the textbook and highlight no more than 10 percent.

➤ Rewrite your notes.

➤ Outline chapters.

➤ Recite information or write scripts and debates.

Linear learners find it easiest to learn material presented in a logical, ordered progression. They solve problems in a step-by-step manner. They can work with sections of material without yet fully understanding the whole picture. They tend to be stronger when looking at the parts of a whole rather than understanding the whole and then dividing it up into parts. They learn best when taking in material in a progression from easiest to more complex to most difficult. Many courses are taught in a linear fashion.

Following are student-suggested strategies for linear learners:

➤ If you have an instructor who jumps around from topic to topic, spend time outside of class with the instructor or a classmate who can help you fill the gaps in your notes.

➤ If class notes are random, rewrite the material according to whatever logic helps you understand it best.

➤ Outline the material.

Holistic learners learn in fits and starts. They may feel lost for days or weeks, unable to solve even the simplest problems or show the most basic understanding, until they suddenly "get it." They may be discouraged when struggling with material that many other students seem to learn easily. Once they understand, though, they tend to see the big picture to an extent that others may not often achieve. They are often highly creative.

Following are student-suggested strategies for the holistic learner:

➤ Recognize that you are not slow or stupid. Don't lose faith in yourself. You will get it.

➤ Before reading a chapter, preview it by reading all the subheadings, summaries, and any marginal glossary terms. The chapter may also start with an outline and overview of the entire chapter.

➤ Instead of spending a short time on every subject every night, try setting aside evenings for specific subjects and immerse yourself in just one subject at a time.

➤ Try taking difficult subjects in summer school when you are handling fewer courses.

➤ Try to relate subjects to other things you already know. Keep asking yourself how you could apply the material.

ENDNOTES

CHAPTER 1

[1]U.S. Department of Education, National Center for Education Statistics, *Nontraditional Undergraduates: Trends in Enrollment from 1986 to 1992* and *Persistence and Attainment Among 1989–90 Beginning Postsecondary Students,* NCES 97-578 (Washington, DC: U.S. Government Printing Office, 1996), 16–17, 167–168.

[2]*Baltimore City Community College 1996–1998 Catalog* (Baltimore: Baltimore City Community College, Division of Planning and Advancement, 1996), 158.

[3]Rick Pitino, *Success Is a Choice* (New York: Broadway Books, 1997), 40.

[4]Rita Lenken Hawkins, Baltimore City Community College, 1997.

CHAPTER 2

[1]Paul R. Timm, *Successful Self-Management: A Psychologically Sound Approach to Personal Effectiveness* (Los Altos, CA: Crisp Publications, 1987), 22–41.

[2]Stephen Covey, *The Seven Habits of Highly Effective People* (New York: Simon & Schuster, 1989), 70–144, 309–318.

[3]Jane B. Burka and Lenora M. Yuen, *Procrastination* (Reading, MA: Perseus Books 1983), 21–22.

CHAPTER 3

[1]Howard Gardner, *Multiple Intelligences: The Theory in Practice* (New York: HarperCollins, 1993), 5–49.

[2]Joyce Bishop, psychology faculty, Golden West College, Huntington Beach, CA.

CHAPTER 4

[1]Frank T. Lyman, Jr. "Think-Pair-Share, Thinktrix, Thinklinks, and Weird Facts: An Interactive System for Cooperative Thinking," in *Enhancing Thinking Through Cooperative Learning*, ed. Neil Davidson and Toni Worsham (New York: Teachers College Press, 1992), 169–181.

[2]Sylvan Barnet and Hugo Bedau, *Critical Thinking, Reading, and Writing: A Brief Guide to Argument*, 2nd ed. (Boston: Bedford Books, St. Martin's Press, 1996), 43.

[3]Roger von Oech, *A Kick in the Seat of the Pants* (New York: Harper & Row, 1986), 5–21.

[4]J. R. Hayes, *Cognitive Psychology: Thinking and Creating* (Homewood, IL: Dorsey, 1978).

[5]Roger von Oech, *A Whack on the Side of the Head* (New York: Warner Books, 1990), 11–168.

[6]Dennis Coon, *Introduction to Psychology: Exploration and Application*, 6th ed. (St. Paul, MN: West Publishing Company, 1992), 225.

[7]Center for Media Literacy, 1998.

CHAPTER 5

[1]Sherwood Harris, *The New York Public Library Book of How and Where to Look It Up* (Upper Saddle River, NJ: Prentice Hall, 1991), 13.

[2]Grace J. Craig, *Human Development,* 7th ed. (Upper Saddle River, NJ: Prentice Hall, 1996), 568–569.

[3]Steve Moidel, *Speed Reading* (Hauppauge, NY: Barron's Educational Series, 1994), 18.

[4]George M. Usova, *Efficient Study Strategies: Skills for Successful Learning* (Pacific Grove, CA: Brooks/Cole, 1989), 45.

[5]Francis P. Robinson, *Effective Behavior* (New York: Harper & Row, 1941).

[6]Karl E. Case and Ray C. Fair, *Principles of Microeconomics*, 4th ed. (Upper Saddle River, NJ: Prentice Hall, 1996), 73–74.

[7]Sylvan Barnet and Hugo Bedau, *Critical Thinking, Reading, and Writing: A Brief Guide to Argument*, 2nd ed. (Boston: Bedford Books, St. Martin's Press, 1996), 15–21.

[8]Adapted from Robert A. Carman and W. Royce Adams, Jr., *Study Skills: A Student's Guide for Survival*, 2nd ed. (New York: John Wiley, 1984), 131–132.

[9]Ibid., 141.

[10]John J. Macionis, *Sociology,* 6th ed. (Upper Saddle River, NJ: Prentice Hall, 1997), 174.

[11]Teresa Audesirk and Gerald Audesirk, *Life on Earth* (Upper Saddle River, NJ: Prentice Hall, 1997), 55–56.

[12]Macionis, *Sociology*, 468.

[13]Ibid., 564

[14]U.S. Department of Education, National Center for Education Statistics, The *Condition of Education 1996*, NCES 96-304: (Washington, DC: U.S. Government Printing Office, 1996), 84.

CHAPTER 6

[1]Louis E. Boone and David L. Kurtz, *Contemporary Business Communication* (Upper Saddle River, NJ: Prentice Hall, 1994), 39.

[2]Ralph G. Nichols, "Do We Know How to Listen? Practical Helps in a Modern Age," *Speech Teacher*, March 1961, 118–124.

[3]Ibid.

[4]Herman Ebbinghaus, *Memory: A Contribution to Experimental Psychology*, trans. H A. Ruger and C. E. Bussenius (New York: Teachers College, Columbia University, 1885).

[5]Based on an experiment by R. S. Nickerson and M. J. Adams, "Long-term Memory for a Common Object," *Cognitive Psychology*, 1979 (11): 287–307.

[6]Philip Kotler and Gary Armstrong, *Marketing: An Introduction*, 4th ed. (Upper Saddle River, NJ: Prentice Hall, 1997), 201.

CHAPTER 7

[1]Walter Pauk, *How to Study in College*, 5th ed., (Boston: Houghton Mifflin, 1993), 110–114.

[2]Lynn Quitman Troyka, *Quick Access Reference for Writers* (Upper Saddle River, NJ: Simon & Schuster, 1995), 1.

CHAPTER 8

[1]Louis E. Boone, David L. Kurtz, and Judy R. Block, *Contemporary Business Communication*, 2nd ed. (Upper Saddle River, NJ: Prentice Hall, 1997), 508–509.

[2]Analysis based on Lynn Quitman Troyka, *Simon & Schuster Handbook for Writers* (Upper Saddle River, NJ: Prentice Hall, 1996), 530–531.

[3]Philip R. Harris and Robert T. Moran, *Managing Cultural Differences*, 3rd ed. (Houston, TX: Gulf Publishing Company, 1991), 59.

[4]Charles G. Morris, *Understanding Psychology*, 3rd ed. (Upper Saddle River, NJ: Prentice Hall, 1996), 566.

CHAPTER 9

[1]Shelia Tobias, *Overcoming Math Anxiety* (New York: Norton, 1993), 50.

[2]Ibid., 69.

[3]Ibid., 63.

[4]Steven Frank, *The Everything Study Book* (Holbrook, MA: Adams Media, 1996), 208.

[5]Many of the examples of objective questions used in this chapter are from Gary W. Piggrem, Test Item File for Charles G. Morris, *Understanding Psychology*, 3rd ed. (Upper Saddle River, NJ: Prentice Hall, 1996).

CHAPTER 10

[1]Sheryl McCarthy, *Why Are the Heroes Always White?*, (Kansas City, MO: Andrews & McMeel, 1995), 188.

[2]Tamera Trotter and Joycelyn Allen, *Talking Justice: 602 Ways to Building and Promoting Racial Harmony* (Saratoga, CA: R & E Publishers, 1993), 51.

[3]McCarthy, *Why Are the Heroes Always White?* 137.

[4]Louis E. Boone, David L. Kurtz, and Judy R. Block, *Contemporary Business Communication* (Upper Saddle River, NJ: Prentice Hall, 1994), 49–54.

[5]Adapted by Richard Bucher, professor of sociology, Baltimore City Community College, from Paula Rothenberg, William Paterson College of New Jersey.

CHAPTER 11

[1]Herbert Benson and Eileen Stuart, *The Wellness Book* (New York: Simon & Schuster, 1992), 292.

[2]Ibid., 178.

[3]National Institutes of Health Publications No. 94-3561, National Institutes of Health, 1994.

[4]National Institutes of Health Publications No. 94-3477, National Institutes of Health, 1993. Rewritten by Lee Hoffman, Office of Scientific Information, National Institutes of Mental Health.

[5]National Institute of Alcohol Abuse and Alcoholism, No. 29 PH 357, July 1995.

[6]J. McGinnis and W. Foege, "Actual Causes of Death in the United States," *Journal of the American Medical Association*, 270:18 (November 10, 1993), 2208.

[7]Editors of the University of California at Berkeley Wellness Letter, *The New Wellness Encyclopedia* (Boston: Houghton Mifflin, 1995), 72.

[8]"Nicotine Addition," National Institute on Drug Abuse Research Report Series, NIH Publication No. 98-4342, Silver Spring, MD, July 1998.
Web address:
http://www.nida.nih.gov/ResearchReports/Nicotine/nicotine2html#extent

[9]David Stout, "Direct Link Found Between Smoking and Lung Cancer," *New York Times,* October 18, 1996, A1, A19.

[10]"Clinical Practice Guideline on Smoking Cessation," *Agency for Health Care Policy and Research.* Publication No 96-0605, April 1996. A U.S. Government publication (Silver Spring, MD).
Web address: http://www.cdc.gov/tobacco/canquit.htm

[11]*Monitoring the Future*, National Institute on Drug Abuse, National Survey Results on Drug Abuse, Study, 1994.

[12]D. P. Rice et al., *The Economic Costs of Alcohol and Drug Abuse and Mental Illness*, Report Submitted to the Office of Financing and Coverage Policy of the Alcohol, Drug Abuse and Mental Health Administration, U.S. Department of Health and Human Services, 1990, 26.

[13]Kim Painter, "Drinking: Loving and Leaving It," *USA Today*, June 4, 1996, D1.

[14] "Condoms Could Save Your life," U.S. Department of Health and Human Services Publication No. 90-4239.

CHAPTER 12

[1]U.S. Department of Education, National Center for Education Statistics, *Profile of Undergraduates in U.S. Postsecondary Education Institutions*: 1992–93, NCES 96-237 (Washington, DC: U.S. Government Printing Office, 1996), 15.

[2]U.S Department of Education, National Center for Education Statistics, *Digest of Education Statistics 1996.* NCES 96-133 (Washington DC: U.S. Government Printing Office, 1996), 320–321.

[3]Ibid., 324–325.

[4]U.S. Department of Education, *The 1999–2000 Student Guide to Financial Aid.*

CHAPTER 13

[1]Isaac Asimov, "My Own View," in *The Encyclopedia of Science Fiction,* eds. John Clute and Peter Nicholls (New York: St Martin's Press, 1995).

[2]Thomas Moore, *The Care of the Soul* (New York: Harper Perennial, 1992), xi–xx.

[3]Stephen Covey, *The Seven Habits of Highly Effective People* (New York: Simon & Schuster, 1989), 70–144, 309–318.

[4]Sarah Delany and Elizabeth Delany with Amy Hill Hearth, *Book of Everyday Wisdom* (New York: Kodansha International, 1994), 123.

BIBLIOGRAPHY

There is certainly more to know about the subjects we've covered than we can possibly present in a book of reasonable size. Following are some additional resources you may want to consult, many of which have been mentioned in the text. The resources are listed in two sections: books and internet sites. In the section on books, both the subjects and the authors' names are listed in alphabetical order.

Book Resources

AIDS AND OTHER SEXUALLY TRANSMITTED DISEASES

Johnson, Earvin "Magic." *What You Can Do to Avoid AIDS*. New York: Random House, 1996.

Kalichman, Seth C. *Answering Your Questions About AIDS*. Washington, DC: American Psychological Association, 1996.

COLLEGE SUCCESS

Baker, Sunny, and Kim Baker. *College After 30: It's Never Too Late to Get the Degree You Need!* Holbrook, MA: Bob Adams, 1992.

Jeffers, Susan. *Feel the Fear and Do It Anyway*. New York: Fawcett Columbine, 1992.

Shields, Charles J. *Back in School: A Guide for Adult Learners*. Hawthorne, NJ: Career Press, 1994.

Weinberg, Carol. *The Complete Handbook for College Women: Making the Most of Your College Experience*. New York: New York University Press, 1994.

CRITICAL AND CREATIVE THINKING

Bianculli, David. *Teleliteracy: Taking Television Seriously*. New York: Simon & Schuster, 1994.

Cameron, Julia, with Mark Bryan. *The Artist's Way: A Spiritual Path to Higher Creativity*. New York: Putnam's 1995.

deBono, Edward. *Lateral Thinking: Creativity Step by Step*. New York: Perennial Library, 1990.

Noone, Donald J. *Creative Problem Solving*. New York: Barron's, 1998.

Postman, Neil, and Steve Powers. *How to Watch TV News*. New York: Penguin, 1992.

Sark. *Living Juicy: Daily Morsels for Your Creative Soul*. Berkeley, CA: Celestial Arts, 1994.

von Oech, Roger. *A Whack on the Side of the Head*. New York: Warner Books, 1998.

von Oech, Roger. *A Kick in the Seat of the Pants*. New York: Harper & Row, 1986.

COMMUNICATION

Qubein, Nido R. *How to Be a Great Communicator: In Person, on Paper, and at the Podium*. New York: John Wiley, 1996.

Tannen, Deborah. *You Just Don't Understand: Women and Men in Conversation*. New York: Ballantine Books, 1991.

Tannen, Deborah. *Talking from 9 to 5: Women and Men in the Workplace: Language, Sex and Power*. New York: Avon Books, 1995.

DIVERSITY

Bellarosa, James M. *A Problem of Plumbing and Other Stories*. Santa Barbara, CA: J. Daniel, 1989.

Belenky, Mary, Blythe Clinchy, Nancy Goldberger, and Jill Tarule. *Women's Ways of Knowing*. New York: Basic Books, 1997.

Blank, Renee, and Sandra Slipp. *Voices of Diversity: Real People Talk About Problems and Solutions in a Workplace Where Everyone Is Not Alike*. New York: American Management Association, 1994

Cose, Ellis. *The Rage of a Privileged Class*. New York: Harper Perennial, 1995.

Edmunds, R. David, ed. *American Indian Leaders: Studies in Diversity*. Lincoln, NE: University of Nebraska Press, 1980.

Gonzales, Juan L., Jr. *The Lives of Ethnic Americans*, 2nd ed. Dubuque, IA: Kendall/Hunt, 1994.

Hockenberry, John. *Moving Violations*. New York: Hyperion, 1996.

Hull, Gloria, Patricia Bell Scott, and Barbara Smith, eds. *All the Women Are White, All the Blacks Are Men, But Some of Us Are Brave*. Old Westbury, NY: Feminist Press, 1982.

McCarthy, Sheryl. *Why Are the Heroes Always White?* Kansas City, MO: Andrews & McMeel, 1995.

Mandela, Nelson R. *Long Walk to Freedom: The Autobiography of Nelson Mandela*. Boston: Little, Brown, 1995.

Morrison, Toni. *The Bluest Eye*. New York: Plume Books, 1999.

Suskind, Ron. *A Hope in the Unseen: An American Odyssey from the Inner City to the Ivy League*. New York: Broadway Books, 1998.

Takaki, Ronald. *A Different Mirror: A History of Multicultural America*. Boston: Little, Brown, 1994.

Terkel, Studs. *Race: How Blacks and Whites Think and Feel About the American Obsession*. New York: Free Press, 1995.

Trotter, Tamera, and Joycelyn Allen. *Talking Justice: 602 Ways to Build and Promote Racial Harmony*. Saratoga, FL: R & E Publishers, 1993.

West, Cornel. *Race Matters*. New York: Random House, 1994.

Wright, Marguerite A. *I'm Chocolate, You're Vanilla: Raising Healthy Black and Biracial Children in a Race-conscious World*. San Francisco: Jossey-Bass, 1998.

ENGLISH AS A SECOND LANGUAGE

Blosser, Betsy J. *Living in English: Basic Skills for the Adult Learner*. Lincolnwood, IL: National Textbook Co., 1989.

Hornby, A. A., and C. A. Ruse. *Oxford ESL Dictionary for Students of American English*. New York: Oxford University Press, 1991.

FINANCIAL AID

ARCO. *College Scholarships and Financial Aid*, with ARCO's Scholarship Search Software. New York: Simon & Schuster, 1997.

Beckham, Barry, ed. *The Black Student's Guide to Scholarships*, 4th ed. 600 Private Money Sources for Black and Minority Students. Lanham, MD: Madison Books, 1996.

Black, Richard. *The Complete Family Guide to College Financial Aid*. New York: Berkley Publishing Group, 1995.

Cassidy, Daniel J. *The Scholarship Book, 5th ed.: The Complete Guide to Private-Sector Scholarships, Grants, and Loans for Undergraduates*. Upper Saddle River, NJ: Prentice Hall, 1996.

McKee, Cynthia Ruiz, and Phillip C. McKee, Jr. *Cash for College: The Ultimate Guide to College Scholarships*. New York: Hearst Books, 1994.

Oldman, Mark, and Samer Hamadek. *The Princeton Review Student Advantage Guide to America's Top Scholarships*. New York: Random House, 1996.

FITNESS AND NUTRITION

Bailey, Covert, and Ronda Gates. *Smart Eating—Choosing Wisely, Living Lean*. New York: Houghton Mifflin, 1997.

Duyff, Roberta Larson. *The American Dietetic Association's Complete Food and Nutrition Guide*. Minneapolis, MN: Chronimed Publishing, 1998.

Freedman, Miriam, and Janice Hankes. *Yoga at Work: 10-Minute Yoga Workouts for Busy People*. Dorset, Eng.: Element, 1996.

Greene, Bob, and Oprah Winfrey. *Make the Connection: Ten Steps to a Better Body and a Better Life*. New York: Hyperion, 1999.

North, Larry. *Get Fit*. Fort Worth, TX: Summit Group, 1993.

Smith, Kathy. *Walkfit for a Better Body*. New York: Warner Books, 1994.

Smith, Kathy, with Suzanne Schlosberg. *Kathy Smith's Fitness Makeover: A 10-week Guide to Exercise and Nutrition That Will Change Your Life*. New York: Warner Books, 1997.

GENERAL WELLNESS

Benson, Herbert, and Eileen M. Stuart, *The Wellness Book*. New York: Simon & Schuster, 1993.

Editors of the University of California at Berkeley Wellness Letter. *The New Wellness Encyclopedia*. New York: Houghton Mifflin, 1995.

Louden, Jennifer. *The Woman's Comfort Book: A Self-Nurturing Guide for Restoring Balance in Your Life*. San Francisco: Harper San Francisco, 1992.

INSPIRATION

Delany, Sarah, and Elizabeth Delany, with Amy Hill Hearth. *Book of Everyday Wisdom*. New York: Kodansha International, 1994.

Moore, Thomas. *The Care of the Soul*. New York: Harper Perennial, 1992.

LEARNING AND WORKING STYLES

Barger, Nancy J., Linda K. Kirby, and Jean M. Kummerow. *Work Types: Understand Your Work Personality—How It Helps You and Holds You Back, and What You Can Do to Understand It*. New York: Warner Books, 1997.

Gardner, Howard. *Multiple Intelligences: The Theory in Practice*. New York: HarperCollins, 1993.

Goleman, Daniel. *Emotional Intelligence*. New York: Bantam Books, 1997.

Goleman, Daniel. *Working with Emotional Intelligence*. New York: Bantam Books, 1998.

LISTENING

Robbins, Harvey A. *How to Speak and Listen Effectively*. New York: AMACOM, 1992.

MATH

Hart, Lynn, and Deborah Najee-Ullich. *Studying for Mathematics*. New York: HarperCollins, 1997.

Lerner, Marcia. *Math Smart: Essential Math for These Numeric Times*. New York: Villard Books, 1995.

MEMORY

Lorayne, Harry. *Super Memory—Super Student: How to Raise Your Grades in 30 Days*. Boston: Little, Brown, 1990.

MONEY MANAGEMENT

Kelly, Linda. *Two Incomes and Still Broke? It's Not How Much You Make, but How Much You Keep*. New York: Random House, 1998.

Tyson, Eric. *Personal Finances for Dummies*. Foster City, CA: IDG Books, 1996.

Ventura, John. *Beating the Paycheck-to-Paycheck Blues*. Chicago: Dearborn Financial Publishers, 1996.

READING AND STUDYING

Armstrong, William H., and M. Willard Lampe II. *Barron's Pocket Guide to Study Tips: How to Study Effectively and Get Better Grades*. New York: Barron's Educational Series, 1990.

Frank, Steven. *The Everything Study Book*. Holbrook, MA: Adams Media, 1996.

Silver, Theodore *The Princeton Review Study Smart: Hands-on, Nuts and Bolts Techniques for Earning Higher Grades*. New York: Villard Books, 1996.

RÉSUMÉS, INTERVIEWS, JOB SEARCHES, AND CAREERS

Adams, Bob. *The Complete Résumé and Job Search Book for College Students*. Holbrook, MA: Adams Publishing, 1993.

Baldwin, Eleanor. *300 New Ways to Get a Better Job*. Holbrook, MA: Bob Adams, 1991.

Beatty, Richard H. *The Interview Kit*, 3rd ed. New York: John Wiley, 1995.

Beatty, Richard H. *The Resume Kit*, 3rd ed. New York: John Wiley, 1995.

Boldt, Laurence G. *Zen and the Art of Making a Living: A Practical Guide to Creative Career Design*. New York: Arkana, 1993.

Bolles, Richard Nelson. *The 1998 What Color Is Your Parachute?* Berkeley, CA: Ten Speed Press, 1998.

Farr, J. Michael. *The Quick Résumé and Cover Letter Book*. Indianapolis, IN: JIST Works, 1994.

Kennedy, Joyce Lain. *Job Interviews for Dummies*. Foster City, CA: IDG Books, 1996.

Kleiman, Carol. *The 100 Best Jobs for the 1990's and Beyond*. New York: Berkley Books, 1994.

Levering, Robert, and Milton Moskowitz. *The 100 Best Companies to Work for in America*. New York: Plume, 1994.

SELF-IMPROVEMENT

Covey, Stephen. *The Seven Habits of Highly Effective People*. New York: Simon & Schuster, 1990.

STRESS MANAGEMENT

Boenisch, Ed, and C. Michele Haney. *The Stress Owner's Manual: Meaning, Balance, and Health in Your Life*. San Luis Obispo, CA: Impact Publishers, 1996.

McMahon, Susanna. *The Portable Problem Solver: Coping wth Life's Stressors*. New York: Dell, 1996.

Radcliffe, Rebecca Ruggles. *Dance Naked in Your Living Room: Handling Stress and Finding Joy!* Minneapolis, MN: EASE, 1997.

SUBSTANCE ABUSE AND CODEPENDENCY

Beattie, Melody. *Codependent No More: How to Stop Controlling Others and Start Caring for Yourself*. San Francisco: Harper San Francisco, 1996.

Schuckit, Marc Alan. *Educating Yourself about Alcohol and Drugs: A People's Primer*, New York: Plenum Press, 1995. pp. v–viii, 5–143, 368–370.

TEST TAKING

Browning, William G. *Cliffs Memory Power for Exams*. Lincoln, NE: Cliffs Notes, 1990.

Fry, Ron. *"Ace" Any Test*, 3rd ed. Franklin Lakes, NJ: Career Press, 1996.

TIME MANAGEMENT

Burka, Jane B., and Lenora M. Yuen. *Procrastination*. Reading, MA: Perseus Books, 1983.

Fry, Ron. *Managing Your Time*, 2nd ed. Hawthorne, NJ: Career Press, 1994.

Lakein, Alan. *How to Get Control of Your Time and Your Life*. New York: New American Library, 1996.

McGee-Cooper, Ann, with Duane Trammell. *Time Management for Unmanageable People*. New York: Bantam Books, 1994.

Timm, Paul R. *Successful Self-management: A Psychologically Sound Approach to Personal Effectiveness*. Los Altos, CA: Crisp Publications, 1996.

VOLUNTEERING

Digeronimo, Theresa. *A Student's Guide to Volunteering*. Franklin Lakes, NJ: Career Press, 1995.

WRITING

Andersen, Richard. *Powerful Writing Skills*. Hawthorne, NJ: Career Press, 1994.

Cameron, Julia. *The Right to Write: An Invitation Into the Writing Life*. New York: Putnam, 1999.

Delton, Judy. *The 29 Most Common Writing Mistakes (and How to Avoid Them)*. Cincinnati, OH: Writer's Digest Books, 1991.

Friedman, Bonnie. *Writing Past Dark: Envy, Fear, Distractions, and Other Dilemmas in the Writer's Life*. New York: HarperCollins, 1994.

Frueling, Rosemary, and N. B. Oldham. *Write to the Point! Letters, Memos, and Reports That Get Results*. New York: McGraw-Hill, 1992.

Gibaldi, Joseph. *MLA Handbook for Writers of Research Papers*, 4th ed. New York: Modern Language Association of America, 1995.

Goldberg, Natalie. *Writing Down the Bones: Freeing the Writer Within*. Boston: Shambhala, 1986.

Markman, Peter T., and Roberta H., Markman. *10 Steps in Writing the Research Paper*, 5th ed. New York: Barron's Educational Series, 1994.

Staff of the Research and Education Association. *REA's Handbook of English Grammar, Style, and Writing.* Piscataway, NJ: Research and Education Association, 1995.

Strunk, William, Jr., and E. B. White. *The Elements of Style,* 3rd ed. New York: Macmillan, 1995.

Troyka, Lynn Quitman. *Simon & Schuster Handbook for Writers,* 5th ed. Upper Saddle River, NJ: Prentice Hall, 1999.

Internet Resources

The following list of internet sites is just the tip of the iceberg; the World Wide Web contains thousands of sites, many of which may be of interest to you. The immensity of the Web can make it hard to know where to look, however, this list will help you get started. With just a few clicks of the mouse, these sites can put you in touch with the latest information and with people who share your interests. In addition, the following sites will often contain links to other related sites not listed here.

The Internet is changing every day, and sites are often renamed, relocated, or eliminated altogether. Therefore, some of these sites may have changed or may no longer exist when you make your visit. However, if you are interested in the subject, don't give up. Search for additional Internet locations through the search engines and directories described in Appendix 1.

AIDS and Other Sexually Transmitted Diseases

Centers for Disease Control National Prevention Information Network
http://www.cdcnpin.org/

This Federal Centers for Disease Control site includes important information about HIV and AIDS, other sexually transmitted diseases, and tuberculosis.

Stop AIDS Project
http://www.stopaids.org

You'll find valuable information on AIDS prevention (safe-sex guidelines), support, and coping. You'll also find links to other HIV/AIDS-related sites.

College Survival and Student Life

Student Center
http://studentcenter.infomall.org.network.html

An on-line hub for student communication, this site includes discussion forums on music, sports, careers, and other topics. A student home page directory will lead you to students with similar interests.

Student.Com: College Life Online
http://www.student.com/

This on-line "hang-out" includes personal student pages and chat rooms, student writing, Net contests, movie reviews, health information, and more.

t@p Schools and Money
http://www.taponline.com/tap/higher.html

Click on here for the Ultimate College Survival Guide. Included are articles on off-campus living, budgeting, goal setting, overcoming roommate problems, eating cheaply, and much more.

Critical and Creative Thinking

Creativity Web Page
http://www.ozemail.com.au/~caveman/Creative

Click on here for a creative boost, including methods to increase your creativity and techniques for personal growth and self-improvement.

Diversity

Asian-American Resources
http://www.mit.edu:8001/afs/athena.mit.edu/user/i/r/irie/www/aar.html

Here you will find links to clubs, events, and organizations that pertain to Asian-American life, as well as links to related personal home pages.

Britannica Guide to Black History
http://blackhistory.eb.com

Among the features of this site are a time line of black history; sound clips from the speeches of Malcolm X and Martin Luther King, Jr.; and biographies of blacks who achieved greatness.

Diversity Web
http://www.inform.umd.edu:8080/DiversityWeb

Diversity Web has information about diversity initiatives in certain colleges and universities. It shows how those schools are engaging diversity in educational mission, campus climate, curriculum focus, and connections with the larger society.

Latino USA
http://www.latinousa.org

This site of Latino USA, a radio journal of Latino culture, seeks to inform varied audiences about the perspectives of Latinos and about the issues affecting their lives and to improve cross-cultural communication.

English as a Second Language

ELS Language Centers
http://www.els.com

Click on here for information about English as a second language (ESL) courses available nationwide.

The George Washington University ESL Study Hall
http://gwis2.circ.gwu.edu/~gwvcusas/

Maintained by George Washington University, this site will help ESL students improve their reading, writing, vocabulary, grammar, and listening.

Financial Aid

Free Application for Federal Student Aid
http://www.fafsa.ed.gov

This U.S. Department of Education site explains the different types of loans and provides an on-line Free Application for Federal Student Aid (FAFSA) form. Fill it out to see which loans you qualify for.

Sallie Mae
http://www.salliemae.com/

Sallie Mae, which funds four out of ten student loans, developed this site to help students shop for financial aid. You'll be able to search for loans by state, calculate financial eligibility with an on-line calculator, learn answers to frequently asked questions, and benefit from experts' financial aid shopping tips.

The Student Guide: Financial Aid from the U.S. Department of Education
http://www.ed.gov/prog_info/SFA/StudentGuide

Click on this U.S. Department of Education site for detailed information about grants, loans, and work-study programs available through the federal government.

Fitness and Nutrition

FitnessWorld
http://www.fitnessworld.com

This site has information on aerobic and muscular conditioning, flexibility, body composition, equipment selection, exercise programs, and nutritional planning. You'll also find on-line chat forums, a reference library, and advice from personal trainers and exercise scientists.

Food and Nutrition Information Center
http://www.nalusda.gov/fnic

Sponsored by the U.S. Department of Agriculture, this site includes resources on dietary guidelines, nutritional labeling, weight control, food safety, and other topics. You'll also find excellent links to other nutrition-related sites.

Shape Up America!
http://www.shapeup.org/sua

This site provides the latest information on safe weight management, healthy eating, and physical fitness. Click on the Health & Fitness Center to assess your physical activity and determine your body mass index (BMI) at the BMI Center.

General Wellness

Duke University Health Devil Online
http://gilligan.mc.duke.edu/h-devil/

Designed for college students, this site has information on nutrition, drinking, smoking, contraception, pregnancy, sexually transmitted diseases, mental health, and other topics.

Healthwise
http://www.goaskalice.columbia.edu/

Run by Columbia University's Health Education and Wellness program, this site answers students' questions about drugs, nutrition, sex, alcohol, stress, relationships, and fitness and nutrition.

Men's Health Daily
http://www.menshealth.com

Men's health and lifestyle topics are discussed here. Of special interest is a question-and-answer section with answers to common health and fitness questions.

Women's Health Interactive
http://www.womens-health.com

This interactive site encourages women to create a personal health profile and to learn about disease prevention and management. Chat rooms link you to other women and medical specialists.

Inspiration

Wellspring
http://www.wellmedia.com

Here you'll find coverage of meditation, spirituality, and relationships, as well as links to other Web sites that cover personal development and spirituality.

Learning Styles and Learning Disabilities

Children and Adults with Attention Deficit Disorder
http://www.chadd.org

Treatments, classroom tips, and information on the legal rights of people with ADD are all part of this site.

Keirsey Web Site
http://keirsey.com

Here you'll find an on-line version of the Keirsey Temperament Sorter (an adaptation of the Myers-Briggs personality assessment), as well as detailed information about personality types, tips for different types, and links to related sites.

National Attention Deficit Disorder Association
http://www.add.org

You'll find information on the causes of ADD and coping mechanisms for adults and children. You'll also find a list of support groups throughout the United States.

Math

Algebra Online
http://www.algebra-online.com

If you have trouble with math, this site has free private tutoring and interactive tests for different math levels. It also has live chats and a message board.

Professor Freedman's Math Help
http://fc.whyy.org/CCC/alg1/index.html

This site provides information about basic math and algebra and specifically addresses the needs of the community college adult learner. It also provides links for students and teachers to information about learning styles, study skills tips, and ways to reduce math anxiety.

Money Management

Student Advantage
http://www.studentadvantage.com

Click on this site for information on travel, food, and clothing discounts and for a list of the 20,000 stores that honor the Student Advantage discount card. You'll also find campus news and chat rooms. The $20 membership fee hasn't stopped more than 1.5 million students from signing up.

Tripod—Money/Business
http://www.tripod.com/money_business/

This site offers financial and career advice to recent college graduates. You'll even find budget counseling. The general Tripod site (www.tripod.com) provides general "life success" tips on a number of topics.

Reading and Studying

The Perpetual Student
http://www2.web-hyogo.or.jp/~ps/psw/

This site will help you avoid common study mistakes, study efficiently, improve test scores, and stop procrastinating. Students who are returning to school after time away receive special help.

Study Web
http://www.studyweb.com

Click on this site for access to a huge database that is searchable by keyword. The site's Study Buddy contains an encyclopedia, thesaurus, dictionary, calculator, maps, daily news highlights, and other features.

Résumés, Interviews, Job Searches, and Careers

1st Steps in the Hunt: Daily News for Online Job Hunters
http://www.interbiznet.com/hunt/

Here's advice on finding the right job via an on-line job search. Included are a list of the nation's top 100 recruiters, job listings, and other features.

College Grad Job Hunter
http://www.collegegrad.com

Designed for recent grads, this site offers advice on résumé writing and interviewing, as well as a searchable database of entry-level jobs.

Women's Wire
http://www.womenswire.com/work

This site helps women target a career as they juggle work and family responsibilities. You'll also find a chat room and message board, among other features.

Stress Management

Crisis, Grief, & Healing
http://www.webhealing.com/

Run by a clinical social worker, this site is an on-line self-help resource for those who have experienced loss.

Divorce Support Page
http://www.divorcesupport.com/

The stress of divorce can derail your goals. This Web site will help keep you on track during this painful period as it informs you about child custody and support, alimony, and family law issues.

SA/VE
http://www.save.org

With its focus on suicide awareness and education, this site is designed for depressed individuals in need of help, as well as their friends and family.

Substance Abuse and Codependency

National Clearing House for Alcohol and Drug Information
http://www.health.org

This site has a searchable database for substance abuse prevention materials. On-line forums present current news and research.

QuitNet
http://www.quitnet.org

Quitting smoking? Then stop here. Among the resources you'll find are interactive questionnaires, quitting guides, live chat rooms, and information about other smoking-related sites.

Volunteering

Empower Web
http://www.sftoday.com/empower.htm

This site will link you to volunteer organizations, where you can learn about opportunities to do good work.

Writing

Online Writing Lab—Purdue University
http://owl.english.purdue.edu

This site has resources to help solve a variety of writing problems, including basic punctuation and spelling errors and higher-level style questions. "Handouts" target common writing mistakes.

Researchpaper.com
http://www.researchpaper.com

This site will help you plan and write your research paper. You'll find an idea directory and tips on note taking, evaluating sources, and developing a thesis statement.

INDEX

A

Abilities, 95–96
Absolute qualifiers, 129
Academic centers, 10
Academic integrity, 22–23, 33. *See also* Integrity
Acquired immune deficiency syndrome (AIDS)
    explanation of, 409–410
    sexual relations and, 407
    statistics regarding, 411
Acronyms, 221–222
Action, importance of taking, 21–22
Active learners, A–32
Active listening, 205–207
Addiction. *See also* Substance abuse
    explanation of, 401
    identifying and overcoming, 402, 404
    support groups dealing with, 404, 407
Addison, Joseph, 263
Administrators, 8, 10
Adult education centers, 11
Adventurers, A–32
Advisors, 8–10
Aggressive communicators, 367
Alcohol use/abuse. *See also* Addiction; Substance abuse
    binge drinking and, 400
    college students and, 400–401
    sleep problems and, 392
Alcoholics Anonymous (AA), 404, 407
All the King's Men (Warren), 297, 299
Almanacs, 258
AltaVista, A–14

Alta Vista Photo Finder, A–20
AmeriCorps, 467–468
Andrade, Cherie, 472
Andre, Beverly, 298
Anorexia nervosa, 397
Anthony, Susan B., 135
Anxiety
    math, 325–326, 338, 344–345
    test, 322, 324–326, 337
Arguments, 128, 176
Armstrong, Gary, 212, 213
Armstrong, William H., 245
Art, 471
Assertive communicators, 367
Assumptions, 130–132
Attention, divided, 203–204
Attention deficit disorder (ADD), 205
Attention deficit hyperactivity disorder (ADHD), 179
Attitude
    importance of positive, 20–21
    test anxiety and, 324–325
Audesirk, Gerald, 190, 191
Audesirk, Teresa, 190, 191
Audience
    analysis of, 308–309
    explanation of, 282
    writing for, 282–283
Audio/visual materials, 255

B

Bacon, Francis, 165
Ballpark, 338
Bar charts, 183
Barnet, Sylvan, 174
Bates, Marilyn, A–25
Beck, Stephen, 218
Bedau, Hugo, 174
Betty Ford Center, 467

Bibliographies, 258
Binge drinking, 400
Binge eating, 398
Biographical reference works, 258
Birth control methods
    explanation of, 409
    methods of, 408
    sexually transmitted diseases and, 410, 411
Black, Richard, 437
Block, Judy R., 374
Bodily-kinesthetic intelligence, 81–82
Boldt, Laurence G., 427
Bolles, Richard Nelson, 427
Boolean operators, A–12 – A–13
Boone, Louis E., 372
Bradley, Tom, 15
Brainstorming
    function of, 122
    to generate writing ideas, 286–287
    guidelines for, 137
    to narrow writing topics, 288
    recording ideas generated by, 147
    in teams, 150
Briggs, Katharine, A–25
Brinckerhoff, Laura, 406
Budgets/budgeting
    credit card management and, 443, 445
    guidelines for, 440–441
    overview of, 439
    sample, 441–442
    savings strategies for, 442–443
Bulimia, 397
Bulletin boards, 11
Burka, Jane B., 60
Business (Griffin & Ebert), 169

C

Caffeine, 392
Calendars, monthly and yearly, 58
Cameron, Julia, 137, 260
Campos, Edhilvia, 133
Cancer, 401
Cannabinols, 403
Cardiovascular training, 390
Career goals
  charting your, 74–75, 426
  choosing majors and, 96–99
  self-portraits and, 107–108
  setting, 36–37, 48–49
Career Placement Registry, 432
Career planning
  defining career path and,
    424–426
  job searches and, 433–434
  mapping strategy for, 426–427
  overview of, 423
  skill requirements and,
    427–428
Career planning and placement
  offices, 11, 424, 430
CareerMosaic, 432
CareerPath.com, 432
Careers
  exploring potential, 424–425,
    449–450
  health record and, 418
  investigating specific, 151
  job interview letters and,
    314–316
  juggling school and, 428–433
  letters of recommendation and,
    382–383
  researching, 274–275
  testing and, 348–349
The Care of the Soul (Moore), 470
Carter, Carol, 44, 45
Case, Karl E., 172, 173
Catalogs, 12
Cause and effect
  as critical reading question, 175
  as mind action, 118–119
  questions examining, 116
Caviness, Shera Chantel, 133
CD-ROM, 258
Center for Media Literacy, 138
Chai, 61
Change
  accepting, 458, 473–475
  adjusting goals to, 460–461

  dealing with day-to-day, 59–60
  flexibility regarding, 458–459
  life, 59–60
Changsak, Peter, 337
Charts
  exercises in studying, 193–195
  function of, 183–184
  types of, 182–183
Chavez, Rosalia, 50
Cheating, 22, 23
Checklists
  for editing, 302
  to prepare for tests, 322, 323
  for writing, 291–292, 296–297
Childcare
  preparation for tests and,
    326–327
  studying and managing, 158
Cigarettes. *See* Tobacco use
Citations, source, 295–296
Class notes. *See* Notes/note taking
Classified ads, 432
Clubs, 9, 10, 12
Code of honor, 23
College catalogs, 12
College students
  alcohol use and, 400–401
  diversity among, 4–5, 27
  drug use and, 402
  employment and, 428–429
  tobacco use and, 401
Commitment
  to audience, 283
  making and keeping, 17
  in workplace, 428
Communication. *See also* E-mail;
    Nonverbal communica-
    tion
  diversity and issues in,
    365–367, 376
  intercultural, 427
  in workplace, 427
  writing as, 279
Community service, 7, 467–468
*The Complete Family Guide to
    College Financial Aid*
    (Black), 437
Computers
  in libraries, 255
  as resource, 13
  use of, 13–14
Conclusions, written, 294–295
The Condition of Education 1996,
    196

Condoms, 410, 411. *See also* Birth
    control methods
Conflict, 369, 370
Constructive criticism, 370–371
Contacts, 432
*Contemporary Business
    Communication* (Boone,
    Kurtz & Block), 372, 374
Content notes, 243–244
Context
  explanation of, 162
  recreating memory, 215–216
Continuing education, 470
Cornell note-taking system, 170,
    247, 248
Counselors, 8–10
Covey, Stephen, 43–44
Craig, Grace J., 159, 160
Cramming, 216
Creativity
  characteristics of people having,
    136
  critical thinking and, 137–138
  explanation of, 135
  explore your, 471
  methods to enhance, 136–137
  in workplace, 428
Credit cards, 443, 445
Credit history, 443
Credit rating, 443
Creditors, 443
Critical reading
  asking questions during, 175
  critical thinking processes and,
    176–177
  elements of, 174
  exercise in, 190–192
  process of, 178
  use of SQ3R for, 174–175
Critical thinking
  argument construction through,
    128, 141
  creativity and, 137–138,
    141–142
  critical reading and processes
    of, 176–177
  decision making through, 123,
    125–126, 140
  establishing truth through,
    128–132, 141
  to evaluation information
    sources, 264–265
  explanation of, 114, 115, 140
  media literacy and, 138–140, 142

Critical thinking (cont'd)
  memory and, 217
  mind actions to build, 120–121
  overview of, 113
  problem solving through,
    121–124, 140
  responses using, 115–116
  sexual decisions and, 407
  shifting your perspective in,
    132, 141, 177
  strategic planning and,
    134–135, 141
  during testing, 329–330
  Thinktrix and, 117–120
  value of, 116–117
Criticism
  dealing with, 369–371
  giving constructive, 371
  receiving, 371–372
Cross-training, 390
Crossword reviews, 110, 234, 352,
    420, 484
Current affairs reference works,
    259
Curriculum, 98

D

Data, 181
Databases, 13
Date books
  keeping schedules in, 54, 57
  to-do lists in, 58, 73
Davies, Robertson, 61
Decision making
  explanation of, 123
  mind actions to aid in, 144–147
  steps in, 123, 125–126
  through critical thinking, 121
  in workplace, 427
Depressants, 403
Depression, 396–397
Deverney, Maxine, 444
Dewar, Sir James, 361
Dewey decimal system, 260
Diaz, Alicia, 136
Dictionaries, 258
Diet, 322, 388–389
Dietary Guidelines for Americans
    (Department of
    Agriculture), 388
Differences
  as critical reading question, 175
  as mind action, 118

questions examining, 115
Dillard, Titus, Jr., 472
Direct Stafford Loans, 435
Discrimination, 360–361
Distractions
  avoiding, 223
  during listening, 203–204
  during reading, 157–158
Diversity
  accepting and dealing with,
    362–363, 373
  communication and, 365–367,
    427
  discrimination and, 360–361
  elements of, 25
  explanation of, 356
  fear of, 361–362
  goals regarding, 26
  open- and closed-minded
    approaches to, 358
  overview of, 355–357
  positive effects of, 357
  prejudice and, 359–360
  stereotypes and, 357–359
  of student body, 4–5, 27
  teamwork and, 25–26
  understanding of, 7, 28
Divided attention, 203–204
Dodson, John D., 394
Down time, 58
Drafting stage of writing
  checklist during, 296–297
  creating body of paper during,
    294
  crediting authors and citing
    sources during, 295–296
  explanation of, 293
  freewriting during, 293
  writing conclusion during,
    294–295
  writing introduction during,
    293–294
Drug use. *See also* Addiction;
    Substance abuse
  addiction and, 402, 404–407
  affects of, 403
  college students and, 402
Dyslexia, 179

E

Eating disorders, 397–398
Ebbinghaus, Herman, 210–211
Ebert, Ronald J., 169

Ebsco Host, 262
Editing, 301–302
Education
  application of, 30–31
  benefits of, 5, 15–16
  commitment to, 17
  conquering your fears and,
    19–20
  continuing, 470
  important points regarding,
    27–28
  income and, 5, 6
  motivation for, 16
  personal gains through, 6–7
  responsibility and, 18
  success through, 15–16, 27
  taking initiative for, 18
Educational goals, 47–48
E-mail, 8
Emerson, Ralph Waldo, 19
Emotional disorders
  depression and, 396–397
  eating disorders and, 397–398
  overview of, 395
Employment. *See also* Career
    goals; Career planning;
    Careers; Workplace
  college students and, 428–429
  education and, 6, 7
  juggling school and, 429–434
  listening and memory skills
    and, 232
  literacy as requirement for, 196
Employment agencies, 432–433
Employment history, 453–454
Encyclopedia of Associations, 263
Encyclopedias, 258
Environment
  for listening, 204
  for reading, 158, 159
  valuing your, 468–469
Essay questions, 335–336
Estepp, Darrin, 179
Ethnocentrism, 360
Evaluation
  as critical reading question, 175
  as mind action, 120
  questions requiring, 116
Evaluation stage of listening, 202
Evidence, 294
Examples to ideas
  as critical reading question, 175
  as mind action, 119
  questions examining, 116

Exercise
    importance of, 389–390
    as priority, 390–391
    sleep and, 392
    types of, 390
External distractions, 157, 203

F

Facts
    distinguishing opinion from, 129
    examples of, 130
    explanation of, 129
    writing down key, 327
Factual learners, A–33
Failure
    accepting, 462–463
    dealing with, 461–462
    learning from, 463–464
    measuring, 462
    thinking positively about, 464
Fair, Ray C., 172, 173
Family goals, 49. *See also* Goal setting; Goals
Fears
    conquering, 19–20
    facing, 31–32
Federal grants, 436–437
Feedback, 370
FFEL Stafford Loans, 435
Financial aid
    grants and scholarships and, 436–437
    overview of, 434–435
    student loans and, 435–436
Financial aid office, 10
Financial history, 453–454
Fine arts reference works, 259
Fitness centers, 10
Flash cards, 214, 215
Flexibility, 59–60
Flexibility training, 390
Focus, 43
Ford, Betty, 467
Ford, Henry, 136
Formal outlines, 245–246
Frank, Steven, 328–329
Frankfurter, Felix, 16
Franklin, Benjamin, 134
Freewriting, 288, 293
Fry, Arthur, 113
FSEOG (Federal Supplemental Educational Opportunity Grants), 436

G

Galaxy, A–10 – A–11
Gardner, Howard, 80–81
General Business File, 262
General reference works, 258–259
General remembering, 211
Gestalt, 265
Gibran, Kahlil, 324
Gilligan, Carol, 244
Ginsberg, Ruth Bader, 15–16
Givers, A–31
Goal setting
    explanation of, 43
    identifying personal mission statement and, 43–44
    long-term, 45
    personal priorities and, 49, 51
    short-term, 45–47
    time periods and, 44–45, 54–57
Goals
    career, 36–37, 48–49
    for decision making, 123, 125
    educational, 47–48
    explanation of, 43
    overview of, 41–42, 62
    personal, 49
    taking stock of, 64–65
    time management, 54–57
    values and, 43, 47
Goethe, Johann Wolfgang von, 432
Goldberg, Natalie, 300
Griffin, Ricky W., 169
Groupings, as memory strategy, 214
Groups. *See also* Teamwork
    function of, 372, 374
    role of leader and, 374–375
    role of participant and, 374
Guessing, on tests, 328–329
Guided notes, 246–247

H

Hallucinogens, 403
Ham, Ruth, 24
Harris, Beatrice, 203
Hayes, J. R., 136
Health. *See* Wellness
Health records, 418
Health Reference Center, 262
Hearing, 200. *See also* Listening
Hearing loss, 204–205

Hierarchy charts, 250
Highlighting text, 170
History reference works, 259
Holistic learners, A–34
Holmes-Rahe Social Readjustment Scale, 392, 393
Hooks, 294
Hot Bot, A–15
Hotlines, 11
Housing offices, 11
Human Development (Craig), 159, 160
Human immunodeficiency virus (HIV)
    explanation of, 409–410
    sexual relations and, 407
    testing for, 411

I

"I" messages, 366, 370, 380–381
Idea chains, 221, 230
Ideas to examples
    as critical reading question, 175
    as mind action, 119–120
    questions examining, 116
Income, 5–7
Informal outlines, 245–246
Informative writing, 282
Inhalants, 403
Initiative, 18
Instructors
    cues given by, 240
    as resource, 8, 10
Integrity
    benefits of, 473
    elements of, 22–23, 473
    living with, 471
    in workplace, 428
    writing about, 33
Intelligence
    perceptions of, 80–81
    theory of multiple, 80–84
Interlibrary loans, 262
Internal distractions, 158, 203
Internet
    evaluating information available on, A–22 – A–24
    evaluating sources on, 265, A–22 – A–24
    job listings on, 432
    reference resources and, A–21 – A–22
    research guidelines for, A–2 – A–3

Internet (cont'd)
  as research tool, 263, A–1 – A–2
  search directories and, A–3 – A–12
  search engines and, A–12 – A–20
Internships, 425
Interpersonal intelligence, 81, 86
Interpretation stage of listening, 202
Interviews, job, 434
Intrapersonal intelligence
  explanation of, 81
  study strategies and, 86–87
Introductions, written, 293–294
Ivarez, Jose L., Jr., 257

J

Jackson, Michael B., 288
Jacobs, Gregg D., 391, 392
Jellyfish think links, 249, 250
Job interview letters, 314–316
Job interviews, 434
Job Interviews for Dummies (Kennedy), 434
Joie de vivre, 411
Journalists' questions, 289
Journals, 261
Judgments
  rushing to, 204
  shaking off, 58–59

K

Kaizen, 475
Katz, Bill, 262
Keirsey, David, A–25
Keirsey Sorter, 80
Keller, Helen, 166
Kennedy, Joyce Lain, 434
Kente, 376
Keyword searches, 256
Kodakehara, Hiromi, 24
Kotler, Philip, 212, 213
Kurtz, David L., 374
Kvasnica, Angela D., 257
K-Y Jelly, 411

L

Lampe, M. Willard, II, 245
Latin, 340
Leaders/leadership

  role of, 374
  strategies for, 375
  in workplace, 427
Learning, 79–80, 469–471
Learning disabilities
  coping with, 179
  listening skills and, 204–205
  memory strategies and, 211
Learning styles
  classroom benefits of knowing your own, 87–88
  discovering your, 82, 100
  explanation of, 80
  general benefits of knowing your own, 88, 90, 100
  multiple intelligences theory and, 80–81, 83–84 (*See also* Multiple intelligences theory)
  reasonable approach to, 83–84
  study benefits of knowing your own, 84–87
Learning styles assessment
  A-25–A-34
  Learning Styles Inventory method of, A–25 – A–29
  Personality Spectrum method of, A–30 – A–34
Learning Styles Inventory, A–25 – A–29
Leshin, Cynthia B., A–1
Librarians, 263–264
Libraries
  classification systems used by, 260–261
  information searches in, 255–257, 266
  organization and layout of, 254–255, 266
Library of Congress classification systems, 260–261
Library resources. *See also* Research
  general reference works as, 258–259
  holdings in, 260
  librarians as, 263–264
  periodical indexes as, 261–263
  specialized reference works as, 259
Life on Earth (Audesirk & Audesirk), 190, 191
Lifestyle goals, 49. *See also* Goal setting; Goals

Line charts
  exercises in studying, 194–195
  explanation of, 183, 184
Linear learners, A–34
Listening
  active, 205–207
  aids and hindrances to, 207
  analyzing barriers to, 229
  challenges to, 203–205
  complexity of, 201
  elements of, 200, 224
  explanation of, 200
  overview of, 199
  stages of, 202–203
Lists, 221
Literacy, 196
Locke, John, 335
Logical-mathematical intelligence, 81–82
Long-term goals
  explanation of, 45
  linking short-term goals with, 46–47
  for time management, 54–56
Lopez, Charlene, 117
Lung cancer, 401
Lycos, A–18 – A–19
Lyman, Frank, 117

M

Machine-scored tests, 329
Macionis, John J., 189, 193
Magazine Index Plus, 262
Magazines for Libraries, 262
Magellan, A–9 – A–10
Majors
  career areas and, 98–99
  changing, 99
  explanation of, 9
  exploring potential, 97, 101
  planning curriculum and, 98
Mansfield, Katherine, 461
Marketing: An Introduction (Kotler & Armstrong), 212, 213
Math
  anxiety over, 325–326, 338
  improving performance in, 338
  recognizing anxiety over, 344–345
McCarthy, Sheryl, 360–362
McCarty, Oseola, 116

Media
  assumptions and perspectives
    about, 147–148
  explanation of, 138
Media literacy
  benefits of, 139–140
  college reading material and,
    177
  core concepts of, 138–139
  explanation of, 138, 142
Medical records, 418
Memory
  effective listening and, 207
  explanation of, 209–210, 224
  processes of, 211
  research on, 210–211
Memory strategies
  acronyms as, 221–222
  mnemonics as, 217, 219,
    224–225
  tape recorders as, 222–224
  types of, 211–216, 218
  visual images and associations
    as, 219–221
Mental walk, 220, 221
Messages, shutting out, 204
Microfiche, 255
Microfilm, 255
Microform, 255
Mind actions
  critical reading and asking
    questions based on, 175
  decision making through,
    144–147
  function of, 117
  memory and, 217
  thinking processes and,
    120–121
  types of, 117–120
Mindus, Arlene, 117
Mission statements. *See* Personal
    mission statements
Mnemonic devices
  acronyms as, 221–222
  exercise to create, 229
  explanation of, 217, 219
  visual images and associations
    as, 219–221
*Modern Language Association
    Handbook* (Modern
    Language Association),
    295
Moidel, Steve, 162
Montolvo, Raymond, Jr., 298

Moore, Thomas, 470
Motivation, 16, 180
Multiple intelligences theory
  assessment and, 81, 82
  explanation of, 80–81
  learning style and, 80–81,
    83–84 (*See also* Learning
    style)
  teamwork and, 106–107
Multiple-choice questions,
    332–334
Music, during reading, 159
Musical intelligence
  explanation of, 81
  study strategies and, 86
Myers, Isabel Briggs, A–25
Myers-Briggs Type Indicator
    (MBTI), 80
Myers-Briggs Type Inventory
    (MBTI), A–25

N

Narcotics Anonymous (NA), 404,
    407
Nash, Vernon, 444
National Institute on Alcoholic
    Abuse and Alcoholism
    (NIAA), 400, 401
National Institute on Drug Abuse
    (NIDA), 401, 402
Naturalistic intelligence
  explanation of, 81
  study strategies and, 87
Networking, 430–431
*New England Journal of
    Medicine*, 264
Newspaper indexes, 262
Nichols, Ralph G., 207
Nicotine, 401
*1999-2000 Student Guide to
    Financial Aid*
    (Department of
    Education), 435, 437
Nonverbal communication, 206
Nordberg, Tim, 337
Northern Light, A–16 – A–17
Notes/note taking
  benefits of, 238–239, 265
  Cornell system of, 170, 247,
    248
  developing skills in, 257
  outline form of, 245–247
  overview of, 237

  preparation for, 239
  research, 243–244, 266
  strategies for, 239–241
  study groups and, 181
  as study tool, 241–243
  systems of, 245–246
  think link system of, 248–250
  visual strategies of, 250
  writing speed during, 250–252,
    266
  writing summaries of, 242
Nutrition. *See* Diet

O

Objective questions, 332
Opiates, 403
Opinion
  distinguishing fact from, 129
  examples of, 130
  explanation of, 129
  questions to examine, 115–116
Organizations, 9, 10, 12
Organizers, A–33
Ortega Y Gasset, José, 114
Outlines
  formal vs. informal, 245–246
  during planning stage of writ-
    ing, 291
Overcoming Math Anxiety
    (Tobias), 325
Overeaters Anonymous, 404, 407

P

Paar, Morgan, 179
Pan, Richard, 373
Paradigms, 474
Paragraphs, 300–301
Paraphrases
  quotations vs., 295, 296
  of research notes, 244
Paraphrasing, 313
Parikh, Shyama, 218
Parks, Rosa, 136
Participation strategies, 374
Passive communicators, 367
Pathways to Learning, 81, 82
Pauk, Walter, 247
Pearman, Eric Gerard, 89
Pell grants, 436
Perfectionism, 60, 63
Periodicals, 255, 261
Periodicals indexes, 261–263

Perkins loans, 435
Personal goals, 49. *See also* Goal
    setting; Goals
Personal habits, 94–95, 104–105
Personal interests, 93–94
Personal mission statements
    creating your, 74, 481
    identifying your, 43–44
Personality Spectrum, A–20 –
    A–34
Perspective
    explanation of, 132
    shifting your, 132, 141, 177
Persuasive arguments, 128
Persuasive writing, 282
Pie charts
    exercise in studying, 193
    explanation of, 182, 183
Pitino, Rick, 20
Plagiarism
    citing sources to avoid,
        295–296
    explanation of, 22, 23
Planning stage of writing
    brainstorming during, 286–287
    creating checklist during,
        291–292
    explanation of, 285
    guidelines for, 287
    narrowing your topic during,
        287–290
    research during, 290, 291
    writing thesis statement during,
        291–292
    writing working outline during,
        291
PLUS Loans, 436
Positive self-talk, 20–21
Pound, Ezra, 180
Prefixes, 164
Pregnancy, 401
Prejudice, 359–360
Pretests, 322
Prewriting
    exercises in, 309–310
    narrowing writing topic
        through, 287–290
    strategies for, 285
Primary sources, 156–157
Principles of Microeconomics
    (Case & Fair), 172
Priorities
    setting, 49, 51
    setting team, 73–74

time management as, 56–58
Problem solving
    example of, 124
    plan for, 123
    in teams, 148, 150
    through critical thinking,
        121–122
    in workplace, 427
Procrastination
    explanation of, 60
    strategies to avoid, 60–61, 63,
        73
Procrastination: Why You Do It
    and What To Do About It
    (Burka & Yuen), 60
Proofreading, 302

Q

Qualifiers
    explanation of, 129, 329
    in true-or-false questions, 334
Questions
    active listening by asking, 205
    as element of SQ3R, 168–169,
        175
    essay, 335–336
    examining opinions through,
        115–116
    journalists', 289
    objective, 332
    subjective, 332

R

Reaction stage of listening, 202
Reader's Guide Abstracts, 261
Reader's Guide to Periodical
    Literature, 261
Reading
    critical, 174–178, 185
    defining your purpose for,
        165–166, 185
    difficult texts, 156–157
    distractions during, 157–158
    elements of college, 155, 184
    expanding your vocabulary
        during, 162–164
    learning through, 470
    speed and comprehension in,
        159–162, 218
    SQ3R strategy for, 168–175,
        185
    time and place for, 158–159

Recall
    as mind action, 117–118
    questions requiring, 115
    visual images and, 219
Reciting
    to improve memory, 212
    during reading, 170–171
Recycling, 468, 469
Reference areas, library, 254
Reflective learners, A–32 – A–33
Rehearsing, to improve memory,
    212
Relationships, personal, 368–369,
    372
Research. *See also* Internet;
    Libraries; Library
    resources
    assistance from librarians for,
        263–264
    general library reference works
        for, 258–259
    library holdings for, 260
    periodical indexes for, 261–263
    specialized reference works for,
        259
    use of Internet for, A–1 – A–3,
        A–21 – A–24
    use of libraries for, 258–261
    on writing topics, 290
Research notes
    explanation of, 243–244
    plagiarism and, 295
    use of, 266
Resources. *See also* Internet
    benefits of specific, 10–11
    function of, 7–8, 27–28
    organizations as, 9, 12
    people as, 8–9
    to promote teamwork, 32–33
    sample table of, 34–35
    school publications as, 12–13
    student services as, 9
    technology as, 13–14
Responsibility
    importance of taking, 18
    time management as, 57–59
Résumés, 434
    The Resume Kit (Beatty), 434
Reviewing, following reading, 171
Revise stage of writing
    checking for clarity and con-
        ciseness during, 301
    critical thinking during, 297,
        299–300

Revise stage of writing (cont'd)
  evaluating paragraph structure
    during, 300–301
  explanation of, 297
Robinson, Francis, 168
Roe, Jo Anne, 373
Role models, 474
Roots, 164

Sabiduría, 99
Sacrifici, 446
Scanning, 168
Schedules. See also Time manage-
    ment
  activity time estimates and,
    68–72
  date books to keep, 54, 57
  early vs. late class, 131–132
  function of, 54
  setting goals for, 54–55
  study, 321
Scholarships, 437
School publications, 11–13
Schweitzer, Albert, 97
Science and technology reference
    works, 259
Search directories
  explanation of, A–1
  Galaxy, A–10 – A–11
  Magellan, A–9 – A–10
  Snap, A–12
  Yahoo, A–3 – A–9
Search engines
  AltaVista, A–14
  AltaVista Photo Finder, A–20
  Boolean operators and, A–12 –
    A–13
  explanation of, A–12
  Hot Bot, A–15
  Lycos, A–18 – A–19
  Northern Light, A–16 – A–17
  research tips for using, A–12
Seledon, Norma, 50
Self-awareness
  abilities and, 95–96
  habits and, 94–95
  interests and, 93–94
Self-esteem
  activating your, 31
  explanation of, 20
  integrity as element of, 22–23,
    33

keys to building, 28
  positive thinking as element of,
    20–21
  taking action to build, 21–22
Self-perception
  explanation of, 92–93
  sources of negative, 92
  strategies to improve, 92–93
Self-portraits, 107–108
Self-talk, 20–21
Sensation stage of listening, 202
The Seven Habits of Highly
    Effective People (Covey),
    43
Sexual issues
  alcohol and sexual aggression
    and, 400
  birth control and, 408, 409
  critical thinking and, 407
  sexually transmitted diseases
    and, 409–411
Sexually transmitted diseases, 409.
    See also Acquired immune
    deficiency syndrome
    (AIDS); Human immun-
    odeficiency virus (HIV)
Sexually transmitted diseases
    (STDs), 407
Shanks, Hershel, 255–256
Sheehy, Gail, 332
Shorthand, 250–252
Short-term goals
  charting your, 66
  explanation of, 45–46
  linking long-term goals with,
    46–47
  for time management, 54–56
Similarities
  as critical reading question, 175
  as mind action, 118
  questions examining, 116
Skimming, 168
Sleep, 391–392
Smith, Anwar, 89
Smoking. See Tobacco use
Snap, A–12
Social science reference works,
    259
Sociology (Macionis), 189, 193
Soloman, Barbara, A–25
Source notes, 243
Specialized reference works, 259

A Spiritual Path to Higher
    Creativity (Cameron),
    260
Spirituality, 470–471
Spreadsheets, 13
SQ3R technique
  application of, 172–174, 320
  explanation of, 168, 172
  to form initial ideas about
    material, 174–175
  questioning and, 168–169
  reading and, 170
  reciting and, 170–171
  reviewing and, 171
  surveying and, 168
St. Jerome, 203
Stafford loans, 435
Standard Periodical Directory, 262
Stereotypes
  addressing, 359
  effects of, 357
  explanation of, 358–359
Stimulants, 403
Strategic planning, 134–135
Strategy, 134
Strength training, 390
Stress
  changes causing, 59–60, 393
  dealing with, 392–393
  function of, 322
  management of, 394–395
  measurement of, 393
  negative effects of, 394
  positive effects of, 394
  warning signs of, 416–417
Strunk, William, Jr., 295
Student handbooks, 12–13
Student health offices, 11
Student loans, 435–436
Student organizations, 9, 10, 12
Student services, 9
Students. See College students
Study groups
  benefits of, 185
  strategies for, 180–181
Study tapes, 222
Studying. See also Tests
  exercise in, 189–190
  last-minute, 216
  learning style and, 84–87
  memory and, 213–214, 216
  with other individuals, 178,
    180, 185

Suà, 305
Subjective questions, 332
Substance abuse. *See also* Addiction
    addiction and, 402, 404, 407
    alcohol and, 400–401
    detecting problems with, 406
    drugs and, 402, 403
    self-test to evaluate, 405
    tobacco and, 401–402
Subvocalization, 162
Success
    building skills for, 29–30
    dealing with, 464–465
    measuring, 462
    methods of achieving, 28
    through education, 15–16, 27
Success Is a Choice (Pitino), 20
Suffixes, 164
Suicide Awareness/Voices of Education (SA/VE), 397
Summaries, 175, 242
Support groups, 11
Surveying
    exercise in, 187–188
    explanation of, 168

T

Tables
    function of, 183–184
    as note-taking strategy, 250
    types of, 181–182
Tape recorders
    benefits of using, 222–223, 225
    drawbacks of using, 223
    guidelines for using, 222
Teaching assistants, 8
Teaching styles, 87–88
Teamwork. *See also* Groups
    brainstorming and, 452–453
    in collaborative writing, 312–314
    dealing with stress and, 417
    diversity and, 25–26
    diversity issues and, 381–382
    in editing, 302
    to improve listening, 231
    multiple intelligences and, 106–107
    note-taking comparisons and, 273–274
    problem solving as, 148, 150
    resources to promote, 32–33

study groups as, 181
studying for tests as, 347
in workplace, 427
Technology
    as resource, 13–14
    strategic planning to keep up with, 134
Test anxiety
    attitude to combat, 324–325
    coping with, 337
    explanation of, 322
    math, 325–326, 338
    preparation to combat, 324
Test questions
    essay, 335–336
    multiple-choice, 332–334
    true-or-false, 334–335
    types of, 332
Tests. *See also* Studying
    attitude regarding, 324–425
    checklist to prepare for, 322, 323
    childcare and preparation for, 326–327
    critical thinking and, 321–322
    learning from mistakes on, 339, 341
    math, 325–326, 338
    overview of, 319
    physical preparation for, 322
    preparation for, 324, 340
    pretests and, 322
    strategies for, 327–330
    study materials and, 321
    study partners for, 347
    study schedule and, 321
    type of material covered in, 320–321
Textbooks
    features of, 174
    highlighting in, 170
    visual aids in, 181–184
Theoretical learners, A–33
Thesis statements
    exercises in writing, 310–311
    explanation of, 290–291
Think links
    explanation of, 248–250
    self-portrait, 107, 108
Thinkers, A–32 – A–33
Thinktrix
    explanation of, 117
    mind actions of, 117–120, 175
Time lines, 250

Time management. *See also* Schedules
    activity time estimates and, 68–72
    importance of flexibility in, 59–60
    overview of, 55–56, 62–63
    procrastination and, 60–61
    setting goals for, 44–45, 54–57
    taking responsibility for, 57–59
    test taking and, 328
Timm, Paul, 43, 58
T-note system. *See* Cornell note-taking system
Tobacco use, 401–402
Tobias, Sheila, 325
To-do lists
    creating, 72–73
    in date books, 58, 73
    function of, 57–58
Topic sentences, 300
Topics, narrowing, 287–290
Transitions, 301
Transportation office, 9, 11
Troyka, Lynn Quitman, 256
True-or-false questions, 334–335
Truth
    challenging assumptions to seek, 130–132
    critical thinking to seek, 128–129, 176
    distinguishing fact from opinion to seek, 129–130
Tutors, 11

U

Ulrich's International Periodicals Directory, 262
Understanding the Dead Sea Scrolls (Shanks), 255
Unemployment, 6
U.S. Employment Opportunities, 432
Usova, George M., 166

V

Values
    choosing and evaluating, 42–43
    explanation of, 42
    exploring your, 65–66
    linking goals with, 43, 47
    what defines your, 62
    in workplace, 428

van Oech, Roger, 136
Verbal learners, A–26
Verbal signposts, 206
Verbal-linguistic intelligence, 81
Verbatim memorization, 211
Visual aids
    charts as, 182–184
    as memory strategy, 214–215
    in reading material, 181, 185
    tables as, 181–182
Visual images, 219–221
Visual learners, A–33 – A–34
Visualization
    explanation of, 248
    memory and, 219–221
    think links and, 248–250
Visual-spatial intelligence, 81, 82
Vocabulary, 162–164
Vocalization, while reading, 162
Volunteerism, 467–468

Warren, Robert Penn, 297, 299
Wellness
    addiction and, 402, 404–407
    alcohol and, 400–401
    diet and, 322, 388–389

    drugs and, 402, 403
    education and, 7
    emotional disorders and,
        395–398
    exercise and, 389–391
    overview of, 387
    sexual issues and, 407–411
    sleep and, 391–392
    stress and, 392–395 (*See also*
        Stress)
    tobacco and, 401–402
What Color Is Your Parachute?
    (Bolles), 427
*Why Are the Heroes Always
    White?* (McCarthy),
    360–361
Withdrawal, tobacco, 401
Workplace. *See also* Career goals;
        Career planning; Careers;
        Employment
    skills for, 427–428
Work-study programs, 436
Writing
    critical thinking during, 297,
        299–300
    developing confidence in, 298
    elements of effective, 281–283,
        305

    importance of good, 280–281,
        305
    to improve memory, 212
    informative, 282
    persuasive, 282
Writing process
    drafting stage of, 292–297 (*See
        also* Drafting stage of
        writing)
    editing stage of, 301–305
    planning stage of, 285–292 (*See
        also* Planning stage of
        writing)
    revising stage of, 297, 299–301

Yahoo, A–3 – A–9
Yearbooks, 258
Yerkes, Robert M., 394
Yuen, Lenora M., 60

*Zen and the Art of Making a
    Living: A Practical Guide
    to Creative Career Design*
    (Boldt), 427

THINKTRIX MIND ACTIONS

SIMILARITY

Comparing notes with another student to see what facts and ideas you have both considered important

DIFFERENCE

Contrasting a weekday when you work half-day and go to school half-day with a weekday when you attend class and then have the rest of the day to study

CAUSE & EFFECT

When you pay phone and utility bills on time, the effects are a better credit rating, uninterrupted service, and a better relationship with your service providers.

EVALUATION

You have a chance to cheat on a test. After considering the potential effects of not knowing the material after the test and of getting caught, you evaluate that cheating isn't worth it to you.

IDEA to EXAMPLE

Your idea of changing major leads to supporting examples, such as you have already taken classes in the major you want to choose, you have worked in that field, and you don't like your current course of study.

EXAMPLE to IDEA

You have trouble finding a baby-sitter. A classmate has had to bring her child to class. Your brother leaves his daughter at your mom's. From these examples, you derive the idea that your school needs a daycare on campus.

RECALL

Naming the steps of a geometry proof in order, or remembering your friends' phone numbers